SHAKESPEARE SURVEY

ADVISORY BOARD

SHAKESPEARE SURVEY

6 1

Shakespeare, Sound and Screen

EDITED BY

PETER HOLLAND

CAMBRIDGE
UNIVERSITY PRESS

CAMBRIDGE UNIVERSITY PRESS
Cambridge, New York, Melbourne, Madrid, Cape Town, Singapore, São Paulo, Delhi

Cambridge University Press
The Edinburgh Building, Cambridge CB2 8RU, UK

Published in the United States of America by Cambridge University Press, New York

www.cambridge.org
Information on this title: www.cambridge.org/9780521898881

© Cambridge University Press 2008

First published 2008

Printed in the United Kingdom at the University Press, Cambridge

A catalogue record for this publication is available from the British Library

ISBN 978-0-521-89888-1 hardback

EDITOR'S NOTE

Volume 62, on 'Close Encounters with Shakespeare's Text', will be at press by the time this volume appears. The theme of Volume 63 will be 'Shakespeare's English Histories and their Afterlives'.

Submissions should be addressed to the Editor at The Shakespeare Institute, Church Street, Stratford-upon-Avon, Warwickshire CV37 6HP, to arrive at the latest by 1 September 2009 for Volume 63. Pressures on space are heavy and priority is given to articles related to the theme of a particular volume. Please send a copy you do not wish to be returned. Submissions may also be made as attachments to e-mail to pholland@nd.edu. All articles submitted are read by the Editor and at least one member of the Advisory Board, whose indispensable assistance the Editor gratefully acknowledges.

Unless otherwise indicated, Shakespeare quotations and references are keyed to *The Complete Works*, ed. Stanley Wells, Gary Taylor, John Jowett and William Montgomery, 2nd edition (Oxford, 2005).

Review copies should be addressed to the Editor as above. In attempting to survey the ever-increasing bulk of Shakespeare publications our reviewers inevitably have to exercise some selection. We are pleased to receive offprints of articles which help to draw our reviewers' attention to relevant material.

P. D. H.

CONTRIBUTORS

Mark Thornton Burnett, *Queen's University, Belfast*
Catherine Grace Canino, *University of South Carolina Upstate*
Thomas Cartelli, *Muhlenberg College*
Hugh Craig, *University of Newcastle, Australia*
Christy Desmet, *University of Georgia*
Michael Dobson, *Birkbeck, University of London*
Peter Donaldson, *Massachusetts Institute of Technology*
Ian Felce, *University of Cambridge*
Charles R. Forker, *Indiana University, Bloomington*
Russell Jackson, *University of Birmingham*
Michael P. Jensen, *Ashland, Oregon*
John Jowett, *The Shakespeare Institute, University of Birmingham*
Patricia Lennox, *New York University*
Richard Levin, *Stony Brook University*
Jeremy Lopez, *University of Toronto*
Alfredo Michel Modenessi, *Universidad Nacional Autónoma de México*
Anna K. Nardo, *Louisiana State University*
Peter Novak, *University of San Francisco*
Laurie E. Osborne, *Colby College*
Judith Pascoe, *University of Iowa*
Eric Rasmussen, *University of Nevada, Reno*
Simon J. Ryle, *University of Split, Croatia*
Charlotte Scott, *Goldsmiths, University of London*
Lindsey Scott, *University of Chester / University of Liverpool*
James Shaw, *University of Oxford*
Emma Smith, *Hertford College, University of Oxford*
Michael Taylor, *University of New Brunswick*
Olwen Terris, *British Universities Film and Video Council*
Evelyn Tribble, *University of Otago*

CONTENTS

CONTENTS

ILLUSTRATIONS

LIST OF ILLUSTRATIONS

SARAH SIDDONS, THEATRE VOICES AND RECORDED MEMORY

JUDITH PASCOE

Romantic era theatregoers left behind a comet's trail of praise for the dramatic brilliance of Sarah Siddons. The accolades include Hazlitt's hyper-ventilated tribute to 'a being of a superior order [who] had dropped from a higher sphere to awe the world', and Mary Robinson's effusive description of the actress whose '*soul* beam[s] through every veil of fiction . . . making art more lovely than even nature in all its fairest adornments'.[1] I take these testimonials at face value, while privately nursing a grudge against Siddons. When Mary Robinson sought out the actress, Siddons refused to meet her, citing the impossibility of an association which, 'however laudable or innocent, would draw down the malice and reproach of those prudent people who never do ill'.[2] My Sarah Siddons is a bit of a prig, and all Hazlitt's declarations of the power seated on her brow or the passion emanating from her breast never overshadow the cautious woman holding her skirts out of Robinson's path for fear of damaging her own reputation.[3] I began to think about Siddons's voice out of a desire to understand, at a visceral level and as a corrective to my prejudice against her, what made Siddons so great. I think it might be possible, by analysing the acoustic culture of Siddons's vocal performances in key roles, to re-animate a romantic era dramatic repertoire long derided by critics as consisting of mangled versions of Shakespeare's plays and long-forgotten theatrical set-pieces.[4] To 'hear' Siddons's voice – insofar as it is possible to hear the voice of a dead woman – one has to take into account the acoustic transformation of the romantic era theatre, the rise of the elocution movement, and the ways in which the voice was being mediated and 'recorded' in advance of sound recording technology. In his meditation on the sound of David Garrick, Peter Holland notes, 'We have strikingly failed to develop a vocabulary to record in prose (unlike recording on audio cassette) precisely what an actor sounded like.'[5] Still,

---

[1] 'Macbeth' in *Characters of Shakespeare's Plays* in P. P. Howe, ed., *The Complete Works of William Hazlitt*, 21 vols. (London, 1930–4), vol. 4, p. 189; Mary Robinson to John Taylor, 13 October 1794, in A. W. Thibaudeau, ed., *Catalogue of the Collection of Autograph Letters and Historical Documents Formed . . . by A. Morrison*, 6 vols. (1891), vol. 5, p. 287.

[2] Sarah Siddons to John Taylor, 5 August 1793, in Thomas Campbell, *Life of Mrs Siddons*, 2 vols. (1834), vol. 2, p. 182.

[3] William Hazlitt, 'Mrs Siddons' in *A View of the English Stage* in *The Complete Works*, vol. 5, p. 312. The proper Siddons inspires less affection than her more profligate rival Dorothy Jordan, as renowned in comedy as Siddons was in tragedy. Jonathan Bate links Siddons to the rise of a 'defensive middle-class Shakespeare' that resulted from favouring the tragedies over the comedies or romances, *Macbeth* over *Twelfth Night*. Bates concedes 'My argument here has been somewhat pro-Jordan and thus implicitly anti-Siddons', and then goes on to restore a balance by acknowledging the difficulty 'of "reading" the theatre of the era before the advent of audio and video'. Jonathan Bate, 'Shakespeare and the Rival Muses: Siddons versus Jordan' in Robyn Asleson, ed., *Notorious Muse: The Actress in British Art and Culture, 1776–1812* (New Haven, 2003), pp. 100–1.

[4] 'It is not to be denied that the great mass of late eighteenth-century plays make today but dull reading', writes Allardyce Nicoll in *A History of English Drama 1660–1900*, 6 vols. (Cambridge, 1966), vol. 3, p. 1.

[5] Peter Holland, 'Hearing the Dead: The Sound of David Garrrick' in Michael Cordner and Peter Holland, eds., *Players, Playwrights, Playhouses: Investigating Performance, 1660–1800* (Houndmills, Basingstoke, 2007), pp. 248–70.

much can be learned from the failed attempts of romantic era theatre fans to capture Siddons's voice on paper.

Since there are plenty of images of Siddons on stage, we can see Siddons perform, at least in freeze frame, in dozens of paintings and drawings. Henry Fuseli's kinetic oil painting 'Lady Macbeth Seizing the Daggers', provides something close to live-action footage. Static images cannot entirely re-animate the actress who, as Hermione in the statue scene of *The Winter's Tale*, astonished one rapt viewer with a mere sudden movement of her head, but they do give us a sense of what Siddons looked like as she performed. The portrait catalogue appended to the Siddons entry in Philip Highfill's *Biographical Dictionary of Actors, Actresses, et al.* provides an encyclopedia of Siddons iconography, encompassing both grand portraiture and kitsch: Joshua Reynolds's monumental *Sarah Siddons as the Tragic Muse* and Josiah Wedgwood's chess queen.[6] And Robyn Asleson's gorgeous essay anthology, *A Passion for Performance*, makes Siddons portraits readily available to those who cannot travel to London (where portraits by Thomas Lawrence, Thomas Gainsborough and Gilbert Stuart reside), or who are unable to storm the fortress of Bob Jones University (where George Henry Harlow's *Sarah Siddons as Lady Macbeth* hangs in an administrator's office, or so I've been told).[7] It has never been easier to 'see' Siddons perform, although that does not necessarily make it possible to assess her dramatic brilliance.

Siddons's voice, in contrast to her visual presence, is a moving target. The manner in which actors spoke lines changed over the course of her career. Dion Boucicault, in his 1882 *The Art of Acting*, notes the shift in acting styles – and the attendant voice alterations – that occurred at the turn of the nineteenth century.[8] How Siddons sounded to her fans was altered further by romantic era theatre enlargement, which situated more audience members further away from the stage. Siddons's long career also meant that she spoke with a number of different voices – her longstanding fans could compare the voice of a youthful Siddons performing Lady Macbeth to the voice of the middle-aged

actress reprising her most famous role. However, even as the quality of Siddons's voice was altered by the vagaries of changing acting styles, acoustic conditions and physical decline, it maintained a distinctive Siddons-ness that inspired playwrights and enflamed audience members. When Thomas Sedgwick Whalley sent Anna Seward a copy of *The Castle of Montval* in advance of its 1799 staging at Drury Lane, he insisted that she read one part as if it were being spoken by Siddons, 'as written for her manner of speaking, and for her's alone'. Siddons had so imprinted her voice on the aural memories of her fans that Seward could easily comply. She wrote, 'If [Siddons] had any other singularity, except that of being the most perfect speaker that can be heard, she would not be the transcendent actress which she is invariably found in tragedy.'[9]

Siddons's voice is partly recuperable from the written accounts of those who heard her. Her voice was 'clear and good', according to Horace Walpole, but 'deep and dragging' if you trust the report of Frances Burney.[10] Many of those who recall listening to Siddons speak emphasize the size and power of her voice; unlike her brother, who 'had constantly to struggle against a teasing irritation of the

---

[6] Philip H. Highfill, Jr, Kalman A. Burnim and Edward A. Langhans, eds., *A Biographical Dictionary of Actors, Actresses, Musicans, Dancers, Managers and Other Stage Personnel in London, 1660–1800*, 16 vols. (Carbondale, 1991), vol. 14, pp. 37–67.

[7] Robyn Asleson, ed., *A Passion for Performance: Sarah Siddons and Her Portraitists* (Los Angeles, 1999). See also the essays in Asleson's *Notorious Muse*, most of which focus primarily on visual representation. Martin Postle discusses Joshua Reynolds's actress paintings, Frederick Burwick analyses gesture manuals, Shearer West explores body connoisseurship, Heather McPherson analyses political and theatrical caricature, and Joseph Roach attends to Siddons's painted skin.

[8] Dion Boucicault, *The Art of Acting* (1882; New York, 1926), p. 29.

[9] Anna Seward to Revd T. S. Whalley, 7 June 1799, *Letters of Anna Seward: Written Between the Years 1784 and 1807*, 6 vols. (Edinburgh, 1811), vol. 5, pp. 240–1.

[10] Horace Walpole to Lady Ossory, 3 November 1782, *Horace Walpole's Correspondence with the Countess of Upper Ossory*, ed. W. S. Lewis and A. Dayle Wallace, 3 vols. (New Haven, 1965), vol. 2, p. 359. Frances Burney, Journal Letter to Susanna Phillips, 15 August 1787, in Peter Sabor and Lars E. Troide, eds., *Journals and Letters* (London, 2001), p. 251.

lungs', Siddons 'was never balked by deficiency'.[11] According to her biographer James Boaden, Siddons made audiences tremble when, with 'a voice that never broke nor faltered in its climax', she denounced a tyrant in 'striking tones' (186). We can't hope to recreate Siddons's voice by means of written descriptions alone, but by attempting to do so we will learn a great deal about the way in which that voice was cultivated, rehearsed, consumed and memorialized. Walter Ong, who warns against conceiving of oral traditions as if they were nascent versions of a more familiar literary milieu, cautions that literacy 'consumes its own oral antecedents and . . . even destroys their memory', but he goes on to concede that, because it is 'infinitely adaptable . . . [literacy] can restore their memory too'.[12] Siddons spoke lines that had been inscribed on a page, but her delivery transformed these lines into something new and distinctive. Her biographer Thomas Campbell, among others, credited her performances with granting importance to otherwise forgettable works. 'Mrs Siddons's *Margaret of Anjou*', he wrote, 'persuaded half her spectators that Franklin's "Earl of Warwick" was a noble poem'. Campbell went on to write, 'The reading man, who had seen the piece at night adorned by her acting, would, no doubt, next morning, on perusal, find that her performance alone had given splendour to the meteor: but the unreading spectator would probably for ever consider "The Earl of Warwick" a tragedy as good as any of Shakespeare's.'[13]

We can use the texts of Siddons's plays, as well as narrative descriptions of her voice as it spoke the words of those plays, to fashion an imperfect, but still revealing, approximation of her vocal virtuosity, especially if we keep in mind Ong's warning against thinking of a heritage of oral performance as some variant of writing.[14] Siddons's performances left a textual residue in the playscripts on which her acting was based, but it was what her audience members heard – the manner in which she spoke the written lines – that inspired declarations of awe and efforts to preserve her performances. In the pages that follow, I'll discuss one attempt to document Siddons's vocal nuances in writing – the

Scottish law professor George Joseph Bell's notes on what he heard when she played Lady Macbeth – as a means of considering how sound recording came to seem both imperative and perilous. Before turning to Bell's endeavours, however, I will consider briefly the romantic literary fascination with the voice. Romantic poetry in general, and Wordsworth's 'The Solitary Reaper' in particular, dramatizes the anxiety that was generated by the thought of voices being detached from bodies, the signal innovation of sound recording technology.

WILL NO ONE TELL ME WHAT SHE SINGS?

The voice, as we know, fascinated romantic era writers. Siddons's rise to dramatic power roughly corresponded with the full flowering of the Gothic novel, an echo chamber of mysterious sounds and alluring voices. The mysteries of Ann Radcliffe's 1794 *The Mysteries of Udolpho*, for example, consist largely of voices and music transmitted through the air by unknown broadcasters. Romantic poets, too, were fascinated with the voice's potentiality, its authenticity and its possible replication. In his Preface to the *Lyrical Ballads*, Wordsworth laid out his plan to describe incidents in the 'real language of men', and to replicate the voices of ordinary folk who, 'being less under the action of social vanity . . . convey their feelings and notions in simple and unelaborated expressions'.[15] We might also recall the crucial role reading aloud played in romantic poets' writing processes. Wordsworth wrote poems in his head while walking, and he performed the results of these walks for his companions.[16] Shelley's

---

[11] James Boaden, *Memoirs of Mrs Siddons* (Philadelphia, 1893), p. 131; hereafter cited in text.

[12] Walter J. Ong, *Orality and Literacy: The Technologizing of the Word* (1982; repr. New York, 1988), p. 15.

[13] Thomas Campbell, *Life of Mrs Siddons*, vol. 2, p. 5.

[14] Ong compares this habit of thought to thinking of horses as automobiles without wheels. *Orality and Literacy*, p. 12.

[15] Preface to *Lyrical Ballads* (1800) in W. J. B. Owen and Jane Worthington Smyser, eds., *The Prose Works of William Wordsworth*, 3 vols. (Oxford, 1974), vol. 1, pp. 118, 124.

[16] For a discussion of the theatricality of these Wordsworthian performances, see my 'Performing Wordsworth' in *Romantic*

habit of reading everything aloud so infuriated his friend Thomas Hogg that he grabbed a book out of the poet's hands and threw it out the window.[17]

The voice was for romantic poets the marker of something authentic and integral, which explains their fascination with bird song – bird voices are even more innate and mysterious than human ones since they are unmediated by language. Leslie Brisman identifies the two great motivating powers behind the romantic movement as 'the desire to know correctly a state which no longer exists, and the desire to express one's awareness of the fictionality of such a state'.[18] Keats's 'Ode to a Nightingale', Shelley's 'To a Skylark' – the romantic fascination with lost origins gets most fully articulated in poems inspired by bird song. But human voices, too, come to stand in romantic poetry for some fundamental aspect of being, fleeting and irrecuperable. When the narrator of Wordsworth's 'The Solitary Reaper' encounters a woman singing, he creates for her song an imagined lineage and content, but it ultimately eludes him. 'Will no one tell me what she sings?' he cries peevishly, before launching into a final effort to place her song.

Written into 'The Solitary Reaper' is a desire to capture the voice and carry it away, to pin it to the page so that it can be reconsidered at a later date. The poem was composed after Dorothy and William Wordsworth saw reapers working in the Highlands of Scotland, but it was inspired by Wordsworth reading a sentence in Thomas Wilkinson's *Tour in Scotland*. Whether William and Dorothy ever themselves witnessed a solitary reaper is left unclear by Dorothy's note on their travels. She introduces a copy of William's poem by describing the 'small companies of reapers' they had witnessed and goes on to write, 'It is not uncommon in the more lonely parts of the Highlands to see a single person so employed.'[19] Dorothy's observation makes the poem, hazily, the result of multiple possible sightings of single reapers and, more definitely, the result of her brother's reading of Wilkinson's 'beautiful sentence', a sentence William had transcribed in his commonplace book: 'Passed by a Female who was reaping alone, she sung in Erse

as she bended over her sickle, the sweetest human voice I ever heard. Her strains were tenderly melancholy, and felt delicious long after they were heard no more' (*Poetical Works*, 3:444–5).

I rehearse these familiar details of the poem's composition in order to emphasize the several ways in which the girl's voice, as experienced by Wordsworth, was mediated or fictionalized. Wordsworth's poem recalls the voice of a girl heard by Thomas Wilkinson and known to Wordsworth by a line from Wilkinson's as yet unpublished *Tour*, a line that he had read or heard read aloud. Or, perhaps, Wordsworth imagined the girl's voice as a composite of the several possible experiences of reapers to which Dorothy alludes. Either tale of origin makes Wordsworth's repeated emphasis on the singularity of the girl in the first stanza of his poem more striking. She is described as 'single', 'solitary', 'singing by herself' and 'Alone' in the poem's opening lines (*Poetical Works*, 3:77).[20] And the second

---

Theatricality: Gender, Poetry, and Spectatorship (Ithaca, 1997), pp. 184–243.

[17] Hogg writes of Shelley reading Walter Savage Landor's *Gebir*: 'He would read it aloud, or to himself sometimes, with a tiresome pertinacity. One morning, I went to his rooms to tell him something of importance, but he would attend to nothing but *Gebir*. With a young impatience, I snatched the book out of the obstinate fellow's hand, and threw it through the open window into the quadrangle.' Thomas Jefferson Hogg, *The Life of Percy Bysshe Shelley* (St Clair, Michigan, 1970), p. 127. See also David Perkins, 'How the Romantics Recited Poetry', *SEL* 31 (1991), pp. 655–71.

[18] Leslie Brisman, *Romantic Origins* (Ithaca, 1978), [11].

[19] *The Poetical Works of William Wordsworth*, ed. Ernest de Selincourt and Helen Darbishire, 5 vols. (Oxford: Clarendon Press, 1952–9), vol. 3, p. 444; hereafter cited in text as *Poetical Works*.

[20] Peter Manning's essay on 'The Solitary Reaper' takes up Michael Cooke's discussion of Wordsworth's emphasis on the reaper's singularity. Cooke recalls how Frederick Garber uses this emphasis to characterize the reaper's independence and uniqueness, but Cooke asks us to consider the social overtones of her reaping and singing, and to pay more attention to the origin or character of the 'community of response', since 'it is *not* based on a consensus, on a reliable orthodoxy, but rather on spontaneous evocation'. Manning writes, '"Spontaneous evocation" and the notion of an "infallibly efficacious object", however, are really two aspects of the same abstraction: both assume that reactions to experiences

4

stanza further advertises her singularity by emphasizing her voice's distinction from other memorable
voices, those of the nightingale and cuckoo-bird.
By comparing her voice – favourably – to the voices
of these two musical birds, Wordsworth makes the
reaper's voice seem especially singular and alluring.

We should note also the change Wordsworth
works on Wilkinson's inspiring sentence in the
last lines of the poem. Wilkinson claims the tender and melancholy strains of the female singer
'felt delicious long after they were heard no more'.
Wordsworth, by contrast, writes, 'The music in my
heart I bore, / Long after it was heard no more'
(*Poetical Works* 3:77). Wilkinson's line holds out the
hope that the woman's voice could still be experienced in a visceral and satisfying way even after
it was out of hearing range. Wordsworth claims
that he carried the voice away, preserved in his
heart, but the voice seems like a burden, something he 'bore', rather than the sensual experience
Wilkinson describes. Wordsworth's poem stands as
a record of the woman's voice, or the record of
Wilkinson's record, but the narrator's final unsatisfying status as the receptacle of a song that he
can no longer hear even though he claims to carry
it away, suggests that a record is a poor substitute
for the original thrilling experience of hearing the
woman's song.[21] Wayne Koestenbaum describes
early phonograph records as 'tokens of disappearance and comeback', and describes listening to the
opera singer Adelina Patti in an archive after getting to see her shoe: 'I wish I could say I heard
the curtain rise to reveal Patti's voice in its original
splendor. But I still heard the intervening ninety
years, the curtain, the turntable, the hiss of reproduction. It sounded as if Adelina Patti were whispering something I could not understand, or as if
the medium of reproduction itself were whispering
instructions, codes, opacities.'[22]

We might share Koestenbaum's experience
by listening to a cylinder recording of Sarah
Bernhardt intoning lines from Racine's *Phèdre*
(http://tinyurl.com/j6f27). Bernhardt's '*voix d'or*'
(golden voice) thrilled theatre audiences in the
last decades of the nineteenth century, and she
was the first Greatest Actress of All Time to

have her voice preserved by recording technology. But Bernhardt's tremulous declarations, her
high-pitched quavery tones, which we can still hear
(thanks to the Cylinder Preservation and Digitiza-
tion Project at the University of California, Santa
Barbara), cannot convey what Victorian audiences
experienced when they heard her perform. If anything, the sound recording enhances the listener's
acute awareness of temporal distance from the performing woman. Wordsworth's plaintive question
– 'Will no one tell me what she sings?' – documents the narrator's alienation from the language
in which the reaper sings. But it also dramatizes
the plight of a 'listener' who only has access to the
woman's song in the written form of Wilkinson's
sentence, a listener who possesses a record rather
than the original of that song, and who, in making
the secondary recording that is his poem, becomes
overwhelmed by the opacities of recording media.

Wordsworth wrote this poem far in advance of
the sound recording innovations of Thomas Edison, but not so far in advance of Edison's crucial precursors. The first decades of the nineteenth
century represent a turning point in the history
of recording technology since new ways of conceptualizing sensory perception made it possible to
generate the earliest mechanical attempts to transport, amplify and preserve visual or aural experience. Jonathan Crary suggests that a new observer

---

or texts are universal and unmediated.' Peter J. Manning,
'"Will No One Tell Me What She Sings?": "The Solitary
Reaper" and the Contexts of Criticism', *Reading Romantics:
Text and Context* (New York, 1990), p. 254. Following Manning, but in a different direction than the one he pursues, we
might read the poem as a dramatization of mediation, particularly of the newly imagined forms of mediation that would
soon make it possible to store a voice and carry it away.

21 In his reading of the poem as the product of a wartime
England 'divided by momentous questions of foreign policy
and by shifts of economic power that disrupted the traditional
alignment of the classes', Manning draws our attention to the
two-year gap between the Wordsworths' Scots tour and the
writing of the poem, a gap which replicates '[t]he uncrossed
barrier between the speaker and the girl'. '"Will No One
Tell Me What She Sings?"', pp. 266–7, 255.

22 Wayne Koestenbaum, *The Queen's Throat: Opera, Homosexuality, and the Mystery of Desire* (London, 1993), pp. 50, 83.

took shape in Europe during the first decades of the nineteenth century. In advance of the development of photography, optical experience was abstracted and reconstructed by new forms of mass visual culture, such as the stereoscope. These devices, according to Crary, blurred the distinction between internal sensation and external signs, and made it possible to imagine the frozen and transportable image produced by photography.[23]

Crary's postulation of a new observer, one who was newly able to imagine the novel kinds of visual experience that photography unleashed, is matched by sound historians' identification of a new kind of listener who evolved decades in advance of, and served as a necessary precursor to, Edison's efforts to capture sound. John Durham Peters turns our attention to the long tradition of physiological investigation that understood the human nervous system as an extension of media. Peters writes, 'To understand the origins, subsequent trajectory, and larger cultural significance of the recorded voice and assisted hearing, we should look not only to Edison . . . but also to the science of the sense organs that emerged a generation before Edison, and whose greatest representative was Hermann von Helmholtz (1821–94).'[24] As Peters explains, Helmholtz showed that the diverse tone qualities of voices (and of all sounds, for that matter) derive from a combination of fundamental tones and harmonic upper partial tones, evident in the phenomenon of sympathetic vibration or resonance. This understanding made it possible to view all sounds as synthesizable; for Helmholtz, according to Peters, 'sound is sound is sound', and the body organs that produce or perceive these sounds become the equivalent of other types of machine that could carry out the same tasks (184). Peters writes, 'To fathom the voice in the age of its technical reproducibility, one must appreciate the ways that it was already externalized before it was mechanized' (179). Jonathan Sterne points to R. T. H. Laennec's 1816 discovery that a tube of rolled paper applied to the chest of a patient could amplify the sound of the heart as an early instance of 'mediate auscultation' or listening to the body's internal workings through the means of an aid. Sterne argues that this development changes the relationship between a listening doctor and a patient's body, and also lays out the basic tenets of audile technique decades before they would be realized in the form of headphones.[25] In amplifying the beating of the heart, Laennec's paper-tube stethoscope broadcast this sound from the exterior of its owner's chest. By conceptualizing the distinctive qualities of a particular voice as the product of a series of upper partials that could be reproduced by mechanical means, Helmholtz untethered the voice from the body to which it had always been bound.

'Every theory has its historical a priori', writes Friedrich Kittler, who repeatedly reminds us of how technology gets imagined far in advance of the moment when it actually comes to exist.[26] Kittler writes, 'In order for styles and works of art to even appear, epistemological knowledge must first have established the field of their colors and forms.' He goes on to say, '[I]t was Wilhelm and Eduard Weber [who, in 1836, published "Mechanics of the Human Walking Apparatus"], and neither Marey nor Muybridge, neither Edison, nor the Lumière brothers, who programmed the program which goes by the name of film.'[27] Kittler and other media historians continuously cast backward to the span of years we call the romantic period in order to discover the moment when some not-yet-imagined mode of technology makes a preliminary, uncooked, foray into the public sphere. We might read the many romantic

[23] Jonathan Crary, *Techniques of the Observer: On Vision and Modernity in the Nineteenth Century* (Cambridge, MA, 1990), pp. 6, 19.

[24] John Durham Peters, 'Helmholtz, Edison, and Sound History', in Lauren Rabinovitz and Abraham Geil, eds., *Memory Bytes: History, Technology, and Digital Culture* (Durham, 2004), p. 179; hereafter cited in text. See also John M. Picker's lucid explanation of Helmholtz's discoveries in *Victorian Soundscapes* (Oxford, 2003), pp. 84–8.

[25] Jonathan Sterne, *The Audible Past: Cultural Origins of Sound Reproduction* (Durham, 2003), p. 107.

[26] Friedrich A. Kittler, *Gramophone, Film, Typewriter*, trans. Geoffrey Winthrop-Young and Michael Wutz (Stanford, 1999), p. 16.

[27] Friedrich Kittler, 'Man as a Drunken Town-Musician', *Modern Language Notes*, hereafter *MLN* 118 (2003), pp. 639, 648.

works that worry over the ephemerality of the voice as part of a larger culture whose concerns would make sound recording technology conceivable. In this context Wordsworth's 'The Solitary Reaper' becomes a poem that grapples with the more troubling aspects of the newly imaginable means of replicating and transporting the voice. The singing reaper performing for the appreciative audience of first Wilkinson and then Wordsworth was an inadvertent member of a corps of romantic-era performers whose fragile and impermanent voices lent urgency to the task of devising mechanical means of recording sound.

HER VOICE IS SOMEWHAT BROKEN SINCE LAST YEAR

'Pity it is that the momentary beauties flowing from an harmonious elocution cannot, like those of poetry, be their own record!' wrote Colley Cibber, going on to mourn '[t]hat the animated graces of the player can live no longer than the instant breath and motion that presents them; or, at best, can but imperfectly glimmer through the memory or imperfect attestation of a few surviving spectators' (Boaden, *Memoirs*, viii). Cibber, writing in advance of the romantic period, depicts poetry as a Janus-genre encompassing both elocution and inscription, as a self-creating archive.[28] His longing for a means of recording the player's ephemeral graces resonated louder than ever during Siddons's reign. Despite the difficulty of converting a live performance into a textual representation, there was no shortage of efforts, well in advance of sound and visual recording innovations, to preserve Siddons's star turns in print, none more impossibly ambitious than Gilbert Austin's 1806 *Chironomia; or a Treatise on Rhetorical Delivery*. Austin set out to produce a language of symbols 'so simple and so perfect as to render it possible with facility to represent every action of an actor throughout the whole drama, and to record them for posterity, and for repetition and practice'.[29] He used letters to indicate the position of a body part, combining these symbols in elaborate equations to mark tandem motions. The letter 'x', for example, stood for 'extended' and,

combined with a series of other letters, could signal an arm's full range of movement (359). The first letter relayed the position of the hand, the second the elevation of the arm, the third the transverse situation of the arm, and the fourth the motion or force of the gesture (360). By this logic, the notation 'phfd' would indicate 'prone horizontal forward descending' (the motion of one arm), and could be teamed with other strings of letters that indicated the corresponding movements of other body parts (360). The system was so complicated that an actor attempting to follow it would have to take several minutes to achieve one stance in a performance composed of thousands of distinct poses. However misguided the scheme, its ingeniousness suggests the strength of the desire to freeze an actor's performance in time and to render it available for replication.

Austin set out to mark an actor's 'awkward energies, and so bring into the contemplation of posterity the whole identity of the scene' (286). He sought to make it possible for future generations to witness a facsimile of a dead actor's performance. A novice actor, Austin wrote, 'might light his talents at the perpetually burning lamps of the dead, and proceed at once by their guidance towards the highest honors of the drama' (287). The new actor could, in this way, reproduce an old one, so that 'the transitory blaze' of an actor's fame would no longer be 'the subject of just and inevitable regret both to the actor and his historian' (287).

The subject of actors ageing out of their ability to perform at peak effectiveness surfaces repeatedly in romantic era memoirs and diaries. 'One of the

---

28 Cibber's comments might be read alongside recent work on romantic era media history: Celeste Langan's 'Understanding Media in 1805: Audiovisual Hallucination in *The Lay of the Last Minstrel*', *Studies in Romanticism* 40 (2001), pp. 49–70; Peter J. Manning's response to Langan's essay in the same issue, '"The Birthday of Typography": a Response to Celeste Langan', pp. 71–83; and Kevis Goodman's *Georgic Modernity and British Romanticism: Poetry and the Mediation of History* (Cambridge, 2004).

29 Gilbert Austin, *Chironomia; or a Treatise on Rhetorical Delivery* (London, 1806), pp. 274–5. Hereafter cited in text.

most affecting things we know is to see a favourite actor take leave of the stage', wrote William Hazlitt upon the occasion of John Bannister's retirement.[30] Sarah Siddons's inevitable decline inspired the most extensive hand wringing. Writing of Siddons in 1811, Henry Crabb Robinson lamented, 'Her advancing old age is really a cause of pain to me. She is the only actor I ever saw with a conviction that there never was nor ever will be her equal.' On another occasion, after witnessing a diminished Siddons perform in one of her most famous roles – as the heroine of *Venice Preserved* – Robinson wrote, 'Her performance delighted me with a mingled sentiment of pain at the certainty of so soon losing her altogether. Most likely I have seen her Belvidera for the last time.'[31]

Robinson lamented the loss of Siddons's voice most of all. In 1812, after seeing Siddons play Mrs Beverley in *The Gamester*, Robinson commented that although in most respects her acting was not inferior to her former performances, '[h]er Voice appeared to have lost its brilliancy (like a beautiful face through a veil)' (45). After watching her play Queen Katherine in *Henry VIII* for an 1816 Charles Kemble benefit that brought Siddons out of semi-retirement, Robinson wrote, 'Mrs Siddons is not what she was – It was with pain that I perceived the effect of time on the most accomplished of persons – This was more audible to the ear than visible to the eye – There was occasionally an indistinctness in her enunciation and she laboured her delivery most anxiously as if she feared her power of expression was gone' (71). Hazlitt, too, wrote regretfully of witnessing the progress of Siddons's decay: 'Her voice is somewhat broken since last year; her articulation of some words, particularly where the sibillant consonants occur, is defective; and her delivery of the principal passages is unequal, slow, improgressive, and sometimes inaudible.'[32] Siddons's weakened voice foreshadowed its ultimate silencing by death.

George Joseph Bell seems, at first glance, an unlikely recorder of Siddons's fading voice. Born the third son of a Scottish Episcopal clergyman in 1770, he made his notes on Siddons's performances around 1809, by which time he was known as the

author of a treatise on the laws of bankruptcy in Scotland. His Siddons observations (preserved amid the holdings of the Folger Shakespeare Library) are contained in three leather-bound volumes which each have 'Siddons' embossed in gold on the spine. Bell annotated printed plays, using slash marks to indicate the rise or fall of Siddons's voice, and underlining to mark words she spoke with special emphasis. His notes on Siddons in the roles of Lady Macbeth and Queen Katharine were transcribed and published in 1878 by H. C. Fleeming Jenkin (1833–85), an electrical engineer who worked on the development of the telegraph cable. The Jenkin transcripts were reprinted in 1915 by the Dramatic Museum of Columbia University, with an introduction by Brander Matthews.

Bell's status as a recorder of Siddons's vocal nuances, although seemingly removed from his legal endeavours, accords with the combined artistic and scientific propensities of his siblings. Bell's older brother John, a surgeon and anatomist, opened a lecture theatre in Edinburgh and drew the illustrations for his treatise *The Anatomy of the Bones, Muscles, and Joints* (1793–4). George Bell's younger brother Charles, a physiologist and surgeon, attempted to explain the anatomical basis for the artistic representation of emotion in his 1806 *Anatomy of Expression*. All three brothers gave lectures, and so George Bell had a professional interest in the way in which Siddons declaimed her lines.

Bell devoted his most detailed note-taking to Siddons's performance in *Macbeth*, which is understandable given the acclaim she received for that role and the many times she reprised it over the course of her career.[33] Siddons took over the role

---

[30] William Hazlitt, 'On Actors and Acting', *The Round Table, Complete Works*, vol. 4, p. 155.

[31] Henry Crabb Robinson, *The London Theatre 1811–1866*, ed. Eluned Brown (London, 1966), pp. 35, 44; hereafter cited in text.

[32] William Hazlitt, 'Mrs Siddons's Lady Macbeth', *Complete Works*, vol. 18, p. 232.

[33] Mary Jacobus notes that *Macbeth* became particularly charged in the romantic period because of the way in which it mirrored the theatrical and political concerns being enacted in the French Revolution – it became for romantic writers

of Lady Macbeth from the celebrated Hannah Pritchard and made it her own. When John Philip Kemble became acting manager of the Drury Lane theatre, he began regularly performing the role of Macbeth alongside his sister and, in 1794, he opened the newly rebuilt theatre with a spectacular production of *Macbeth* that included rolling thunder, flying witches and a large chorus. When Kemble moved to Covent Garden Theatre in 1803, he staged *Macbeth* seven times during his first season, and the play was also used in 1809 for the opening of that theatre after it was rebuilt. Sarah Siddons played Lady Macbeth nine times during her 1811–12 farewell season, and the role occasionally lured her out of retirement.[34]

One of the reasons why the play provided such a showcase for Siddons's vocal powers is that it takes the female voice as a subject of fascination from its very first scene. *Macbeth* opens with the gathering of witches whose gnomic observations set the course of the events that follow. Their vocal exoticism was highlighted in Kemble's version of the play; cat and toad sounds were conveyed from stage right and stage left in advance of the witches' scripted responses to their unseen animals ('I come, Graymalkin' and 'Paddock calls').[35] (That the ostensibly female witches were played by male actors also drew attention to the oddity of their voices.) Lady Macbeth herself conjures up an animal voice when she anticipates the arrival of the king in Act 1 by saying, 'The raven himself is hoarse, / That croaks the fatal entrance of Duncan.'[36]

Bell begins his commentary on Siddons by describing the first words Lady Macbeth speaks after she reads Macbeth's letter in Act 1, scene 5. He notes that when Siddons spoke the line 'Glamis thou art, and Cawdor, *and shalt be*, / What thou art promised', she did so in 'Exalted prophetic tone, as if the whole future were present to her soul', and he adds that she displayed 'A slight tincture of contempt thruout'.[37] Although Bell does not focus on the way in which Siddons spoke to the exclusion of other performers' speeches – 'Kemble speaks this well', he writes after a line of scene 7 of Act 1 (47) – he dwells most often on the nuances of her voice's volume, speed or

tone. 'Voice changes to assurance and gratulation', he writes of the last line of the speech in which Lady Macbeth advises her husband to compose his face (44). (The speech ends, 'He that's coming / Must be provided for: and you shall put / This night's great business into my dispatch; / Which shall to all our nights and days to come / Give solely sovereign sway and masterdom.') At the opening of Act 3, scene 2, when Siddons spoke the line 'Is Banquo gone from court?', Bell notes that she did so with 'Great dignity and solemnity of voice; nothing of the joy of gratified ambition' (57). A few lines later, Lady Macbeth says, 'Nought's had, all's spent, / Where our desire is got without content: / 'Tis safer to be that which we destroy / Than by destruction dwell in doubtful joy.' In Siddons's delivery, the lines were 'Very mournful' (57).

Bell, in contrast to the author of the *Chironomia*, seems most intent on preserving what it felt like to see and hear Sarah Siddons perform rather than on making it possible for future actors to replicate her performance. He sometimes discusses actors' strategies in terms of specific technique, most notably when he takes Kemble to task for his enactment of the dagger scene. 'There is much stage trick and very cold in this scene of Kemble', he writes, going on to describe the actor as he walks across the stage, starts at the sight of a servant, renews his walk, 'throws up his face, sick, sighs, then a start theatric, and then the dagger' (50). 'Why can't he learn from his sister?' Bell grumbles, then recalls Charles Bell's view that Kemble should have played the scene less stridently. Bell writes, 'Mrs Siddons in reading "Hamlet" showed how

---

'a paradigm of their own unease about the power of the imagination'. '"That Great Stage Where Senators Perform": *Macbeth* and the Politics of Romantic Theatre', *Romanticism, Writing and Sexual Difference* (Oxford, 1989), p. 37.

34 Introduction to *Macbeth* in *John Philip Kemble Promptbooks*, ed. Charles H. Shattuck, 11 vols. (Charlottesville, 1974), vol. 5, pp. i–ii.

35 *Macbeth, John Philip Kemble Promptbooks*, vol. 5, p. 3.

36 *Macbeth, John Philip Kemble Promptbooks*, vol. 5, p. 16.

37 H. C. Fleeming Jenkin, *Mrs Siddons as Lady Macbeth and as Queen Katharine* (New York, 1915), p. 39; hereafter cited in text.

inimitably she could by a mere look, while sitting in a chair, paint to the spectators a horrible shadow in her mind' (50). For Bell, the theatregoers' response to this bit of stage business is of paramount interest; he is more intent on capturing what evoked this response than on suggesting how future actors could replicate a Siddons or Kemble moment. Bell frequently describes not merely how Siddons said something but also how her articulation made him feel. In his annotation of the banquet scene, Bell writes of Siddons, 'Her anxiety makes you creep with apprehension: uncertain how to act. Her emotion keeps you breathless' (62).

Brander Matthews, in his 1915 introduction to Fleeming Jenkin's two essays on Siddons, makes the surprising claim that Bell's efforts at preservation surpassed the productions of the new recording technology. 'In the future', writes Matthews, 'the phonograph may preserve for us the voice of an honored performer; and thus supply material for opinion about the quality of his tones and the justice of his readings.' However, Matthews continues, 'At best, these will be but specimen bricks, and we shall still lack the larger outlines of the performance as a whole.' Matthews believed that there was a 'phenomenal value' in the record that Jenkin preserved of Bell's experience 'while he was actually under the spell of Mrs Siddons' enchantment'.[38] Matthews favours Bell's notes over a phonograph recording because Bell tried to convey what it felt like to hear Siddons perform as well as to describe the quality of her voice as she acted in particular scenes. In calling the phonograph recording a specimen brick, Matthews alludes to the tale of a man who attempted to show what his house looked like by providing one brick. The phonograph record, Matthew feared, removed the voice from its several contexts: from the actors' movements, from the reactions of other actors on stage, and from the audience members' responses. A similar fear suffuses Wordsworth's effort to preserve the voice of the solitary reaper; his poem's many levels of disconnection from the woman's song stoke doubts about the faithfulness and authenticity of the

version of the woman's voice that the poem's narrator attempts to carry away.[39]

Bell's notes stand as one point on a trajectory of efforts to create a written recording of the voice in advance of the moment when a phonograph stylus would 'write' the vibrations of the voice onto a wax cylinder. George Joseph Bell may have been an ancestor of Alexander Bell (1790–1865), a Shakespeare scholar and public reader of Shakespeare's plays, who insisted that his grandson, who became the famous inventor Alexander Graham Bell, memorize great swaths of Shakespeare's plays, including passages from *Macbeth*. Alexander Graham Bell's father, Alexander Melville Bell, devised an alphabet for recording the sounds of all languages and he enlisted his son to serve as his assistant when he gave public lectures on his system of Universal Alphabetics. While the young Bell was out of the room, audience members were encouraged to make strange sounds which Bell senior translated into this system of symbols. When Alexander Graham Bell returned to the hall, he would, on the basis of his father's notations, reproduce a sound that he had never heard. The younger Bell recalled, 'I remember upon one occasion the attempt to follow directions resulted in a curious rasping noise that was utterly unintelligible to me. The audience however, at once responded with loud applause. They recognized it as an imitation of the noise of sawing wood, which had been given by an amateur ventriloquist as a test.'[40] John Peters writes, 'This is the primal scene of the supersession of presence by programming' (190). The graphic representation made it possible to replicate a voice without having ever heard the original. Austin's *Chironomia* had attempted something

---

[38] Brander Matthews, 'Introduction' to H. C. Fleeming Jenkin's *Mrs. Siddons as Lady Macbeth*, p. 20.

[39] Jonathan Sterne argues that it is the very attempt to reproduce sound that introduces the concept of an 'original' or 'authentic' sound: '[T]he original is itself an artifact of the process of reproduction. Without the technology of reproduction, the copies do not exist, but, then, neither would the originals.' Sterne, *The Audible Past*, p. 219.

[40] Alexander Graham Bell, 'Prehistoric Telephone Days', *The National Geographic Magazine* 41 (March 1922), p. 228.

similar – allowing, at least in theory, an actor to replicate the performance of another actor without seeing the original performance. When Matthews saluted Bell's notes as having greater fidelity than a phonograph recording, he communicated his discomfort with a recording medium that could make a voice transportable and a voice's speaker irrelevant. Bell's notes don't allow one to replicate what Siddons did, so one can't leave the woman behind.

SHALL I CALL THEE BIRD, OR BUT A WANDERING VOICE?

Being under the spell of Mrs Siddons's enchantment, in the manner of George Joseph Bell, meant sitting amid a large and noisy theatre audience, rather than listening in comparative solitude to a machine.[41] Wayne Koestenbaum depicts the capturing and immortalizing of vanished women by early phonographic records as a kind of erotic seizure that made possible new venues for listening. He writes, 'Perhaps because the woman's voice was locked into grooves and waves, stolen by the phonographic scientist, the phonograph itself was considered suitable for confined spaces and confined listeners.'[42] Siddons's performing voice was never heard in solitude, not even by herself. According to her biographer, she did not practise her lines aloud as she learned them: 'As to her mode of study, in her apartment it was silent. She conceived there certainly all that she meant to do; but it was only at rehearsal that she knew the effect of voice upon the conception' (Boaden 218).

Siddons died decades before Thomas Edison could have tracked her down in order to record her celebrated voice as part of his effort to 'preserve for future generations the voices as well as the words of our Washingtons, our Lincolns, our Gladstones, etc., and to have them give us their "greatest effort" in every town and hamlet in the country, upon our holidays'.[43] Edison's comment unintentionally conjures the perils of voice recording that were also evoked by Wordsworth's poetry. The voices of Washington, Lincoln and Gladstone, in repeatable and portable format, might be thrust into new and tawdry contexts, valued as entertainment

rather than as vatic pronouncements. Edison avowed utter confidence in the phonograph's ability to replicate the voice faithfully – '[I]t catches and reproduces the voice just as it is', he wrote – and it was crucial to his enterprise that this seem to be the case.[44] Even though the voice could be successfully replicated only under conditions that bore little resemblance to any stage performance, the salesmen of the new technology wanted listeners to believe that the voice emanating from the phonograph (and, later, from its mechanical descendants) was just as 'natural' and 'authentic' as the one they heard uttered in a live performance.[45]

Not accidentally, Edison's agent in England, George Gouraud, took up romantic poetry in advertising the new technology, attributing to the phonograph recording the kind of 'natural' sound Wordsworth celebrated in one of his bird poems. As John Picker notes in his study of Victorian soundscapes, Gouraud suggested that Edison cloak his new technology in romantic terms by quoting a line from Wordsworth's 'To the Cuckoo'.[46] He encouraged Edison to introduce his first transatlantic cylinder with the line, 'Shall I call thee bird, or but a wandering voice?' Gouraud wrote, 'Nothing could be more appropriate than the words, "But a wandering voice", and I have registered them in connection with the word "Phonogram"'.[47] The line

---

[41] Edmund Kean was so infuriated by the sounds of nut cracking emanating from the gallery while he was performing that he gave instructions to his followers to buy up every nut in town. Spurred by the sudden increase in nut demand, local fruiterers increased their stocks. The actor Squire Bancroft recalls, 'Crack! – crack! – crack! was the running fire throughout the succeeding performances, and the rest of Kean's engagement was fulfilled in torment'. *Mr and Mrs Bancroft On and Off the Stage*, 2 vols. (London, 1888), vol. 1, p. 148.

[42] Wayne Koestenbaum, *The Queen's Throat*, p. 49.

[43] Thomas Edison, 'The Phonograph and its Future', *North American Review*, No. 262 (May–June 1878), p. 534.

[44] *The Diary and Sundry Observations of Thomas Alva Edison*, ed. Dagobert D. Runes (New York, 1968), p. 83.

[45] See Jonathan Sterne's discussion of the necessity of studio recording. *The Audible Past*, pp. 225–46.

[46] John Picker, *Victorian Soundscapes*, p. 116.

[47] Quoted in Frank Andrews, *The Edison Phonograph: The British Connection* (London, 1986), pp. xiv–xv.

would help to underscore the fidelity of the recorded sound, its indistinguishability from the voice of its maker. But it also, however inadvertently, highlighted the anxiety evoked by detached voices set free to wander aimlessly through the atmosphere.[48] Even if the recorded voice was an exact replica of the original one, its very detachment created listening possibilities that were, especially in the case of an actor's voice, entirely different from its first aural context.

Wordsworth's poem, like other romantic era poems, uses a bird's voice to ponder the discrepancies between lived and remembered (or imagined) experience. The bird, experienced through its song, is both reassuringly familiar ('The same whom in my schoolboy days / I listened to') and disconcertingly strange ('No bird, but an invisible thing, / A voice, a mystery'). The poem concludes by glorifying the schoolboy's bird, which was 'still a hope, a love; / Still longed for, never seen', by comparison to a present listening experience. Wordsworth writes, 'And I can listen to thee yet; / Can lie upon the plain / And listen, till I do beget / That golden time again.'[49] The poem calls into question the 'original' experience of the cuckoo song since that experience is a creation of a later moment's begetting. And the newly begotten version of the bird pales when placed beside the earlier experience of listening to something that was 'still a hope, a love', perhaps because it had not yet been repeated.

Sarah Siddons died nearly forty years in advance of phonograph recording and by so doing she solidified her reputation as the immortal Siddons. The belief in a fundamental unrecordability that lurks behind Wordworth's poetic treatments of the voice, and which survives in Brander Matthews's unfavourable reference to phonograph recording, helped to fuel the engine of Siddonian myth making. What's to be gained by attempting to exhume Siddons's voice? A series of questions, I hope –

some of passing interest, some with field-altering potential. How did Siddons sound? is just one of these questions, and probably not the most interesting one. Some others: Why was romantic theatre so thrilling? How can we comprehend the cultural productions of writers who had particular dramatic performances ringing in their ears without knowing the lines of popular plays, let alone the sonic combustions set off by a Siddons? What if sound recording innovation was largely fuelled by a romantic nostalgia for lost performances? How can we help our students to hear the features of romantic poetry that impelled Shelley to insist on reading it out loud?[50] These are just a few of the questions that an attention to voice in the romantic period might force us to consider, whether or not we ever find out how Siddons sounded when she performed.

By leaving no impression of her voice on wax, Siddons spared herself future disparagement. No one will ever experience boredom, disappointment or pique while listening to a Siddons CD. No one can ever hit the pause button and abandon Siddons in mid performance. But rather than letting her rest in silent, uncontested triumph, we should try to make her speak again so that we can comprehend the aural fixations of romantic literary culture, as well as the romantic era enthusiasm for plays we no longer know how to hear.

---

[48] John Peters writes, 'Both sound recording and alphabetic writing lifted old limits that held voices in check – distance, dissipation, and discretion. A captured voice forfeits its body, mortality, and authorial control. With the ability to record, amplify, and transmit sound by machines, the voice apparently lost its finitude.' 'Helmholtz, Edison, and Sound History', p. 178.

[49] Wordsworth, 'To the Cuckoo', *The Poetical Works*, vol. 2, pp. 207–8.

[50] But see Susan Wolfson's excellent collection, *'Soundings of Things Done': The Poetry and Poetics of Sound in the Romantic Ear and Era* <www.rc.umd.edu/praxis/soundings/about.html.>

PLAYING WITH SHAKESPEARE'S PLAY: BRANAGH'S *LOVE'S LABOUR'S LOST*

ANNA K. NARDO

With a few notable exceptions, Kenneth Branagh's *Love's Labour's Lost* (2000) has not fared well with academic critics or reviewers in the popular press. Some object to the film on aesthetic grounds. They decry Branagh's decision to cast actors, not trained singers and dancers, in a production whose central conceit is the substitution of song and dance conventions from the heyday of the American movie musical for the rhetorical and poetic fireworks of its sixteenth-century British original. A film whose subtitle is 'a romantic musical comedy' must, they argue, be judged, at least in part, on the quality of its singing and dancing, both of which are amateurish. Others have argued that Branagh appropriates (or misappropriates) the conventions of the American film musical of the 1930s, 1940s and even 1950s indiscriminately despite the film's 1939 setting, and, in any case, these conventions violate the Shakespearian source text. The Hollywood musical requires that the couples' final union be prepared for in the song and dance sequences, but in Shakespeare's radical comedy the women not only refuse to dance during the ill-fated masque of the Muscovites, but in the end postpone any possible union beyond the bounds of the play's action.[1]

Bypassing questions of performance and genre, cultural critics have focused on Branagh's negotiation of his own, as well as Shakespeare's, identity in this unusual hybrid film. Is Branagh the Irish outsider who seeks to appropriate the cultural capital of British high culture, 'Shakespeare', for a contemporary, especially American, popular audience? Or is he the Olivier rival who deliberately sets his film at the moment just before *Henry V* claimed film

as a medium for Shakespeare? Or, recognizing the subordinate position of British high culture to American popular film, has Branagh adopted the Hollywood role assigned to the African-American actor – the minstrel who enacts a caricature of his/her culture in order to make a decent living?[2]

---

[1] For positive (albeit not uncritical) reception of the film, see Derek Elley, 'Branagh's Bold "Labour" of Love', *Daily Variety*, 14 February 2000; A. O. Scott, 'What Say You, My Lords? You'd Rather Charleston?' *The New York Times*, 9 June 2000 (http://movies2.nytimes.com); Neil McDonald, 'Branagh's Labours Lost', *Quadrant*, 46.4 (2002); and Samuel Crowl, *Shakespeare at the Cineplex: The Kenneth Branagh Era* (Athens, 2003), pp. 38–46. For representative examples of negative reviews, see Joseph Cunneen, 'Dancing Fools', *National Catholic Reporter*, 30 June 2000; Stanley Kauffmann, 'Well, Not Completely Lost', *The New Republic*, 10 July 2000; James Bowman, 'All That Jazz', *American Spectator*, July/August 2000. For academic critiques of the film, see Laurie E. Osborne, 'Introduction', *Colby Quarterly* 37 (2001), 1–14, pp. 10–11; Ramona Wray, 'Nostalgia for Navarre: The Melancholic Metacinema of Kenneth Branagh's *Love's Labour's Lost*', *Literature/Film Quarterly*, 30 (2002), 171–8; Gayle Holste, 'Branagh's Labour's Lost: Too Much, Too Little, Too Late', *Literature/Film Quarterly*, 30 (2002), 228–9; Michael D. Friedman, '"I won't dance, don't ask me": Branagh's *Love's Labour's Lost* and the American Film Musical', *Literature/Film Quarterly*, 32 (2004), 134–43; Kelli Marshall, '"It Doth Forget to Do the Thing It Should": Kenneth Branagh, *Love's Labour's Lost*, and (Mis)Interpreting the Musical Genre', *Literature/Film Quarterly*, 33 (2005), 83–91.

[2] Courtney Lehmann, *Shakespeare Remains: Theater into Film, Early Modern to Postmodern* (Ithaca, NY, 2002), pp. 161–89. Katherine Eggert, 'Sure Can Sing and Dance: Minstrelsy, the Star System, and the Post-postcoloniality of Kenneth Branagh's *Love's Labour's Lost* and Trevor Nunn's *Twelfth Night*', in *Shakespeare, the Movie, II: Popularizing the Plays on*

To my mind, the cultural critics have ignored and the aesthetic critics have missed the point of the film's exuberant play. Branagh has chosen a comedy with the thinnest of plots and one-dimensional characters, whose true subject is glittering artifice. *Love's Labour's Lost* exults in the seemingly endless possibilities of language play available in late sixteenth-century England as Anglo-Saxon, Latinate, French and Italian influences collide to generate courtly Euphuism, the inkhorn terms and grammatical precisionism of schoolmen, the rhetorical sophistry of wits at the Inns of Court, and the effusions of Petrarchan sonneteers.[3] While the play luxuriates in the comic possibilities of linguistic slippage, it simultaneously critiques the excesses of wit that can destabilize a society dependent on trust in verbal oaths. In the comedy's final scene, the glitter of linguistic artifice dims and tarnishes before the realities of time and death.

Although the play's dramatization of the instability of language has attracted late twentieth-century academic critics, its arcane linguistic humour would seem to make it wholly inaccessible to a turn-of-the-twenty-first-century film audience. Apparently, translating the word play through comic stage business has produced some recent theatrical successes, but the festive communal energy that can carry the play on stage is not available in film.[4] As all reviewers and critics recognize, Branagh tries to find a correlative to the aristocratic wit of Shakespeare's lords and ladies in the sophistication and grace of Hollywood musicals, especially of the 1930s.[5] But several fault the film because they don't find a direct translation: witty Shakespearian aristocrats = flawless Fred and Ginger performances. The expectations behind this equation lead, in turn, to the two major objections to the film's ruling premise: (1) the conventions of the Hollywood musical jar against the plot and language of the source text, (2) the film indulges in nostalgia for a simpler time.

These critiques rest, however, on a mistaken assumption about what precisely Branagh seeks to translate from play to film. Just as the King, Biron, Dumaine and Longueville are playing at being Petrarchan lovers, so Branagh's lords and ladies are

playing at being Fred and Ginger. Neither Shakespeare's nor Branagh's foursomes duplicate the masterful performances of their idols. Just as Shakespeare's comedy plays with linguistic and theatrical fads and conventions, so Branagh's film plays with the conventions and traditions of the movie musical. Just as *Love's Labour's Lost* is a meta-linguistic, meta-poetic and meta-theatrical comedy, so *Love's Labour's Lost: A Romantic Musical Comedy* is a meta-musical. Thus, my goal is to detail how Branagh has translated Shakespeare's exuberant play with the tropes and traditions of his emerging medium, the English language, into play with the tropes and traditions of the twentieth-century's emerging medium, film.

Love's Labour's Lost has more rhyme than any other Shakespeare play,[6] and almost every scene includes a set-piece of bravura linguistic display: for example, Biron's witty paradoxes that prove true study to be the contemplation of a beloved's face (1.1.54–99), the lords' metamorphosis into Petrarchan sonneteers (4.2.106–19; 4.3.24–39, 57–70), Armado's adieu to valour and his self-abandonment before Cupid's power (1.2.159–76), and Holofernes's alliterative epitaph on the death of the deer (4.2.56–62). In each of these examples, the dialogue that furthers the action pauses

Film, TV, Video, and DVD, ed. Richard Burt and Lynda E. Boose (London, 2003), pp. 72–88.

[3] C. L. Barber, 'The Folly of Wit and Masquerade in *Love's Labour's Lost*', in *Shakespeare's Festive Comedy: A Study of Dramatic Form and its Relation to Social Custom* (Princeton, NJ, 1959), pp. 87–118; Felicia Hardison Londré, '*Love's Labour's Lost* and the Critical Legacy', in her '*Love's Labour's Lost*': *Critical Essays* (New York, 1997), pp. 6–8.

[4] John S. Pendergast, '*Love's Labour's Lost*': *A Guide to the Play* (Westport, CT, 2002), p. 159.

[5] The play has had a number of musical treatments in the past: e.g. a 1919 musical comedy (see Koshi Nakanori, 'The Structure of *Love's Labour's Lost*', in Londré, *Critical Essays*, p. 290) and an opera in 1973, with a libretto by W. H. Auden and Chester Kallman (see Pendergast, *Guide*, pp. 160–2). The protagonist of Thomas Mann's novel *Dr. Faustus* is composing an opera based on the play: Philip French, 'If music be the food of Shakespeare, let's dance . . .', *Observer* (London), 2 April 2000, Review: 9.

[6] Pendergast, *Guide*, p. 6.

and the audience is treated to clever language (that is intensely aware of its own cleverness), poetic language (whose conventionality asks us to question the depth of the lovers' passion) and the comic misuse of language by the pretentious courtier and schoolman.

Branagh's film marks these moments of transition from language that furthers the play's slight plot to language as sheer performance by invoking the central convention of musical comedy: that sudden shift into an alternate reality when characters burst into song and dance while walking down the street. In the play's opening scene as the King and Biron begin to argue in rhymed couplets about 'the end of study' (1.1.55), the music swells and the two debaters launch into George Gershwin's and Desmond Carter's 'I'd Rather Charleston', a competition song and dance that Fred Astaire and his sister Adele exchanged in the 1926 London production of *Lady Be Good*. The King urges Biron to sign the oath to renounce pleasure and devote three years to study by singing, 'In you I never can detect / The slightest signs of intellect . . . You never seem inclined to use your mind . . . Take a lesson from me.' But Biron trips away, crooning, 'I'd rather Charleston.'[7] In this interlude, Branagh comments with allusive play on the lords' project of retreat: in 1939, the time of the action announced in the film's opening newsreel, the Charleston, the dance craze of 'the roaring twenties', was decidedly old-fashioned. Thus, on the eve of the Second World War, the allusion signals Biron's preference for a carefree time about to come to an end. Here Branagh is not simply translating the linguistic artifice of the King's and Biron's rhyming debate into a show tune. He is also playing as self-consciously with musical tradition as Shakespeare plays with the traditional debates about whether the active or the contemplative life will garner more fame (1.1.1–14). Nostalgia is what is being played with; nostalgia is not the mode adopted by the player, Branagh.

Throughout the film, Branagh plays with the musical comedy's characteristic leap to another level of reality. The example most often cited by reviewers is the parallel scene to Biron's initial rejection of the oath, in which the lords, obviously forsworn, beg him to 'prove / Our loving lawful and our faith not torn' (4.3.282–3). Reviewers applaud the seamless segue from Biron's Petrarchan hyperbole ('when love speaks, the voice of all the gods / Make heaven drowsy with the harmony' (4.3.320–1)) to the lovers' levitation to the domed ceiling of their study, painted with astronomical symbols, as they sing, 'Heaven, / I'm in heaven . . . When we're out together dancing / Cheek to cheek.'[8] In Biron's dazzling rhetoric, which substitutes study of their heavenly beloveds for dry academic study, Shakespeare both appropriates and mocks the power of wit. And Longueville admits as much when he begs, 'O, some authority how to proceed, / Some tricks, some quillets how to cheat the devil' (4.3.285–6). Likewise, Branagh both appropriates and mocks the sudden shift into an alternate reality that defines the musical genre.[9] The over-the-top levitation in Branagh's film both translates the lovers' hyperbolic rapture and frames the entire sequence as playing at, by ludicrously exaggerating, not duplicating, such well-known musical numbers as Fred Astaire's dance on the ceiling in *Royal Wedding* (1951).

But Branagh's translation of Shakespeare's self-conscious linguistic play begins even before the oft-noted levitation. Shakespeare, of course, dramatizes the lords' yielding to passion in their shift from witty banter to imitation of Petrarchan sonnet and Ovidian elegy. The excess and conventionality of their conceits – eyebeams that bear Jove's lightening, tears that reflect the beloved's face, and May blossoms that only breezes, not the lover, can caress – signal the lords' self-absorption in a passion as suspect as their original project of retreat from the world. Branagh translates both the

---

7 Desmond Carter, 'I'd Rather Charleston', *International Lyrics Playground*, 2 January 2006, http://lyricsplayground.com.

8 Samuel Crowl, '*Love's Labor's Lost*', *Shakespeare Bulletin*, 18 (2000), 37–8. Debra Tuckett, 'Review of *Love's Labour's Lost*', *Early Modern Literary Studies*, 6 (2000): 6 pars. 2 January 2006, http://purl.oclc.org/emls/06-1/tuckrev.htm. 'Cheek to Cheek', in *The Complete Lyrics of Irving Berlin*, ed. Robert Kimball and Linda Emmet (New York, 2001), p. 303.

9 Rick Altman, *The American Film Musical* (Bloomington, 1987), pp. 58–89.

linguistic elevation from dialogue to love poetry and Shakespeare's mockery of the lords' self-absorption as each, thinking himself unseen, dances into the study singing such lyrics as 'I fell – / And it was swell . . . [I'm your] big and brave and handsome Romeo . . . I've got a crush on you, Sweetie Pie . . . The world will pardon my mush.' These lines from a George and Ira Gershwin tune (composed first for the 1928 Broadway musical *Treasure Girl*, then reused in *Strike Up the Band*) mock the conventions of Tin Pan Alley ballads as thoroughly as Shakespeare mocks Petrarchism.[10] Furthermore, as the lords float around the ceiling, crooning Irving Berlin's 'Cheek to Cheek' and caressing photographs of their ladies, suddenly the film shifts to yet another level of unreality, as a dissolve propels the levitating lords into a fantasy ballet – that staple of the movie musical in which repressed passion is released in dance.[11] To capture the illusions of Shakespeare's gentlemen fancying themselves witty sonneteers, on a par with the quintessential courtier Sir Philip Sidney, Branagh invokes the convention of the dream ballet: suddenly the lords metamorphose into swells dressed in Fred's top hat and tails, and their ladies sweep into the off-limits courtyard in a swirl of Ginger's chiffon. The fact that Kenneth Branagh's and Alicia Silverstone's graceful posing can't hold a candle to Fred and Ginger's brilliant 'Cheek to Cheek' *pas de deux* in *Top Hat* (1935) only emphasizes the fact that we are in the midst of a fantasy – indeed a fantasy (being able to dance like Fred) within a fantasy (being levitated by the power of one's own 'mush').

In one, telling instance, however, this description of Branagh's play with the musical convention of the fantasy ballet doesn't square with the performance. Adrian Lester as Dumaine doesn't merely pose gracefully; he can dance. As the final starry-eyed lover to reveal his passion to his three spying oath-mates, Lester glides into the study dancing on top of tables and elegantly tipping over chairs in a homage to both the athleticism of Gene Kelly, who slides over furniture in 'Moses Supposes' (*Singin' in the Rain*, 1952), and the grace of Fred Astaire, who dances up to and tips over the backs of desk chairs in *Let's Dance* (1950). Even in this convincing imitation of movie musical dancing, however, the film maintains its stance of exuberant play that reprises and revises a past not always worthy of nostalgia.

Shakespeare's comedy, no less than Hollywood's musicals, participates in the racist denigration of blackness pervasive in Western culture. The lords of Navarre and the ladies of France both mock the 'dark' Rosaline. And when Biron defends his lady – 'No face is fair that is not full so black' – the lords reframe his poetic exaggeration as a game much enjoyed by young wits, the paradoxical praise of an ugly woman:

DUMAINE
To look like her are chimney-sweepers black.
LONGUEVILLE
And since her time are colliers counted bright.
KING
And Ethiops of their sweet complexion crack.
(4.3.264–6)

Then, as a prelude to their masque of the Muscovites, they send in 'blackamoors with music' (stage directions). Three-and-a-half centuries later, Hollywood still represented people of colour as musical servants, most notoriously casting Bill 'Bojangles' Robinson, the world-renowned tap dancer, as Shirley Temple's old family retainer in *The Little Colonel* (1935) and *The Littlest Rebel* (1935). One year later in *Swing Time*, Fred Astaire performed his only blackface number, 'Bojangles in Harlem'. Wearing an exaggerated version of Robinson's characteristic check jacket and bowler hat, and dancing with three huge black silhouettes, Fred 'covered' Robinson's famous tap style.[12] The

---

[10] 'I've Got a Crush on You', in *The Complete Lyrics of Ira Gershwin*, ed. Robert Kimball (New York, 1994), pp. 128–9.

[11] Altman, *Film Musical*, pp. 82–5.

[12] Jim Haskins and N. R. Mitgang, *Mr. Bojangles: The Biography of Bill Robinson* (New York, 1988), pp. 224–6, 229–32. In the stage show, *Blackbirds of 1928*, in which Bill Robinson danced, 'The first-act finale . . . featured the magnified shadows of the performers', a stage effect repeated several years later in the first production of *Porgy and Bess*. Robinson and Astaire apparently shared a deep mutual admiration. See Haskins,

racism of these source texts becomes more grist for the mill of Branagh's allusive play. Whereas Biron, Longueville and the King only fantasize that they can dance like Fred, Dumaine actually can – as Lester, the black actor, 'covers' a dance routine by Fred, the white dancer, who 'covered' a dance routine by Bill Robinson, the great black tapper whose brilliance shined through even the demeaning roles Hollywood offered him. Ignoring Branagh's allusive play leads Katherine Eggert to find in Lester's performance only the absence of Fred Astaire.[13] Explicating Branagh's play, however, reveals how he simultaneously retranslates Shakespeare's language of blackness (omitted in the film) and recasts Hollywood's representation of black dancers.

The same kind of play with musical tradition allows Branagh to revise Hollywood's gender stereotypes as well – only this time Shakespeare's language-based theatre counters Hollywood's tendency to display 'dames' to the male gaze.[14] *Love's Labour's Lost* requires a comparatively large number of female roles. Furthermore, the ladies sparkle in every exchange of witty repartee, remaining unmarried and in charge of their land and lives in the end. Branagh preserves Shakespeare's representation of feminine freedom and power by playing competing musical allusions against one another. While the love-sick King spies on the ladies' tent with binoculars (the male gaze *par excellence*), the girls wake up and perform their morning exercises to an Irving Berlin tune that Fred, as a carefree bachelor, sings before he meets and falls for Ginger in *Top Hat*:

> I wake up ev'ry morning with a smile on my face,
> . . .
> No strings and no connections,
> No ties to my affections –
> I'm fancy free
> And free for anything fancy.[15]

Prancing through their 'Bloomer Girl' exercises, the females, not the males as in the source text, dance their commitment to the single life. Nevertheless, they add, 'Bring on the big attraction; / My decks are cleared for action', making it clear that

their intent from the outset has been to enjoy mocking their admirers (cf. 2.1.215–27).

Still bound by his oath, each lord can only gaze longingly at a photo of his unattainable 'proud fair' lodged in the park beyond the lords' cloister. Branagh gives his audience the perspective of the lords' longing gaze by recreating Busby Berkeley aerial shots of the girls' geometric poses and a water ballet of synchronized bathing beauties à la Esther Williams. This montage of the girls' morning routine, although sung to a tune from *Top Hat*, recalls another routine from the eminently forgettable Berkeley musical, *Dames* (1934), which transforms some 50+ chorines – who wake up, brush their teeth, primp and set off for work – into fragmented facets of a kaleidoscope. Whereas, in such Berkeley and Williams routines, ranks of unindividuated Hollywood 'dames' are reduced to geometrical patterns, Branagh alludes to these production numbers in order to translate the delight Shakespeare's high-spirited ladies take in teasing the lords. In full sight of men who sin against their oaths if they welcome the ladies within their gates and sin against courtesy if they don't (2.1.90–110), the giggling girls revel in self-display as they trade in their old-fashioned bloomers for gold lamé swim suits.

Branagh's deliberately anachronistic mixture of periods and styles (e.g. turn-of-the-century Bloomer Girls morph into 1950s Esther Williams bathing beauties) foils any attempt to read the film as a cultural statement about the American movie musical on the eve of the Second World War. Branagh indiscriminately cannibalizes styles and conventions from musicals both early and late in their period of greatest popularity in order to create a kingdom of fantasy and aristocratic play. His method is Shakespeare's own. Out of

---

Mr. Bojangles, pp. 187, 269–71. For a discussion of Astaire's complex relationship to his heritage in African-American dancing styles, see Stanley Cavell, 'Fred Astaire Asserts the Right to Praise', in *Philosophy the Day After Tomorrow* (Cambridge, 2005), pp. 61–82.

[13] Eggert, 'Sure Can Sing and Dance', pp. 79–80.

[14] Altman, *Film Musical*, pp. 213–30.

[15] 'No Strings (I'm Fancy Free)', in *The Complete Lyrics of Irving Berlin*, p. 302.

faint but tantalizing historical allusions, wit games fashionable in the sixteenth century, and the old-fashioned conventions of 'poor Petrarch's long-deceasèd woes' – out of an eclectic mixture of history and linguistic fashion – Shakespeare created the play world of Navarre that Branagh aims to recreate.[16]

Because the mocking wit that provides so much of the play's verve and sass seems wholly untranslatable to a contemporary film audience, some reviewers praise Branagh's choice to cut 75 per cent of the play's language. But the substitution of dance for repartee has occasioned academic criticism.[17] Whereas Shakespeare's ladies turn their backs on the masked Russian visitors and refuse to dance, Branagh's ladies, when first introduced to the lords, dance their refusal to dance, then in the later masque episode they eagerly entwine their legs (clad in black fish-net hose) around their writhing partners (clad in skimpy white undershirts). Even though Branagh's ladies most certainly do dance while Shakespeare's don't, Branagh's final version of the masque of the Muscovites is nevertheless faithful to the play – only to a different part of the play. (The actual appearance of the lords disguised as Muscovites was mercifully cut.)

The duets of Fred and Ginger provide a physical and visual corollary to Shakespeare's lords' and ladies' linguistic sparks. The energy that propels the lame plots of Astaire-Rogers movies is bickering. When they first meet, Ginger poutingly rejects Fred's charm, then as Fred pursues and she resists, they dance the vicissitudes of courtship, creating their famous competition routines in which each tries to out-do the other's fancy footwork.[18] Likewise, in order to establish his ladies' oppositional stance at the first meeting, Branagh mimics a Fred and Ginger challenge routine. Biron's pick-up line only meets with a prickly riposte from Rosaline:

BIRON *(to Rosaline)*
Did I not dance with you in Brabant once?
ROSALINE
Did I not dance with you in Brabant once?
BIRON
I know you did.

ROSALINE   How needless was it then
To ask the question!

(2.1.114–17)

Then Rosaline immediately launches the four couples into their first dance number together, Jerome Kern and Oscar Hammerstein's 'I Won't Dance' (*Roberta*, 1935). Branagh has moved Shakespeare's ladies' pointed refusal to dance – from their later rejection of the lords' masque of the Muscovites to their first meeting – in order to establish the ladies' prowess in battles of wits.

In what appears to be a radical rewriting of Shakespeare's stand-offish ladies, however, Branagh replaces the aborted masque with Irving Berlin's 'Let's Face the Music and Dance'. Originally a self-contained story ballet from *Follow the Fleet* (1936), this number dramatized the choice of dance and 'moonlight and music, / And love and romance', even though Fred, a losing gambler, and Ginger, a suicidal beauty, know 'There may be trouble ahead . . . There may be teardrops to shed.'[19] Branagh's appropriation of this *carpe diem* lyric and use of highly erotic choreography may not be as radical a revision of his source text as critics have claimed.

As Boyet, Shakespeare's courtier-turned-1930s-butler, muses that 'The tongues of mocking wenches are as keen / As is the razor's edge invisible' (5.2.256–7), the camera moves in for a close-up and dissolve, which frame this interlude as another fantasy ballet. The *mise-en-scène* shifts to billowing fog illuminated by a garish red glow reminiscent of the 'blues' segment of Gene Kelly's dream ballet that ends *An American in Paris* (1951). Such dream sequences further the love plots in musicals by giving expression to the erotic desire smouldering beneath the surface of oppositional or

---

[16] See Charles Taylor, 'The Player', 9 June 2000, www.salon.com; Pendergast, *Guide*, pp. 5–6. Sir Philip Sidney, 'You that do search for every purling spring', from *Astrophil and Stella*.

[17] Crowl, '*Love's Labor's Lost*', p. 37. Friedman, 'I won't dance', pp. 134–43.

[18] Altman, *Film Musical*, pp. 160–77.

[19] 'Let's Face the Music and Dance', in *The Complete Lyrics of Irving Berlin*, p. 307.

repressed couples. Of course, this desire also lurks beneath the wit of Shakespeare's mocking ladies in their exchange with the 'old lovemonger' Boyet (2.1.254) about deer hunting:

MARIA

You still wrangle with her, Boyet, and she strikes at the brow.

BOYET

But she herself is hit lower – have I hit her now?

ROSALINE

Shall I come upon thee with an old saying that was a man when King Pépin of France was a little boy, as touching the hit it?

BOYET

So I may answer thee with one as old that was a woman when Queen Guinevere of Britain was a little wench, as touching the hit it.

ROSALINE (*sings*)

Thou canst not hit it, hit it, hit it,
Thou canst not hit it, my good man.

BOYET (*sings*)

An I cannot, cannot, cannot,
An I cannot, another can. (*Exit Rosaline*)

COSTARD

By my troth, most pleasant! How both did fit it!

MARIA

A mark marvellous well shot, for they both did hit it.

BOYET

A mark – O mark but that mark! A mark, says my lady.
Let the mark have a prick in't to mete at, if it may be.
. . .

MARIA

Come, come, you talk greasily, your lips grow foul.

(4.1.116–36)

Here the ladies heartily enjoy trading salacious witticisms with Boyet, and Branagh visually renders the eroticism of their arcane sexual innuendoes in his steamy dream ballet to 'Let's Face the Music and Dance'. Transported by Boyet's meditation, we enter a fantasy in which each lady, masked and prominently displaying a different lady's favour, dances the desire that Boyet teases out in word play. Thus Branagh does not mistranslate the ladies' rejection of the lords' masque in his source text. Rather he plays with movie musical convention, as Shakespeare plays with verbal wit, in order to suggest that the ladies are not wholly indifferent to masculine charms.

Their sexy dance features couples writhing on chairs with movements quite different from the romanticism of Gene Kelly and Cyd Charisse's *pas de deux* in *An American in Paris*. Indeed, Branagh's dream sequence recalls the open eroticism of Bob Fosse's choreography of 'Mein Herr' for the film of *Cabaret* (1972), in which Liza Minelli as Sally Bowles and the Cabaret chorines, in black hose and garter belts, bump and grind on chairs resembling Branagh's couples' props.[20] Like *Love's Labour's Lost*, *Cabaret* tells the story of the fragility of a fantasy world. Sally's hedonistic creed that 'Life is a Cabaret, old chum' is threatened by the rise of Nazism, just as Navarre's world of wit games, masques and pageants must confront the reality of death. Whether or not Branagh intended to telescope the soon-to-be-announced outbreak of the Second World War in the choreographic allusion to *Cabaret*, he did create a musical that comments on musicals – as *Cabaret*'s team of Masteroff, Kander and Ebb created a stage show that commented on stage shows, as Shakespeare created a play that commented on language play. All three revel in the glitter, while showing us its tarnish.

The indulgence of fantasy – as the music swells and characters launch into that other reality of song and dance – is what characterizes Branagh's Navarre as a retreat from news of an all-too-real world on the verge of war. As every social class in Shakespeare's Navarre enjoys some form of linguistic diversion, Branagh's comic characters share their betters' susceptibility to musical levitation, despite the newspapers and radio broadcasts about

---

20 Neil McDonald ('Branagh's Labours Lost') has also recognized the allusion to Fosse's style of choreography.

the worsening political crisis. The pretensions of Don Armado to being a soldier and lover take the form of imaginative transformations into a series of matinee idols. Singing Cole Porter's 'I Get a Kick Out of You', the Don suddenly metamorphoses into Maurice Chevalier with straw boater and cane ('fighting vainly the old ennui'), then into a gangster with striped suit and cigar ('Some get a kick from cocaine'), then into a dashing fighter pilot ('I get no kick in a plane'), then . . .[21]

Whereas Don Armado dreams of celluloid stardom, Branagh's version of Shakespeare's schoolman and curate display their pretentious linguistic excess in a musical flight of fancy – but not fantasy. Shakespeare's Holofernes openly boasts of his wit:

This gift that I have, simple, simple – a foolish extravagant spirit, full of forms, figures, shapes, objects, ideas, apprehensions, motions, revolutions. These are begot in the ventricle of memory, nourished in the womb of *pia mater*, and delivered upon the mellowing of occasion. But the gift is good in those in whom it is acute, and I am thankful for it.   (4.2.66–72)

Branagh's schoolmistress, Holofernia, makes good on this boast of 'a foolish extravagant spirit' when she and Nathaniel, the curate, become so enraptured by the lyrical beauty of Biron's sonnet – here Jerome Kern and Dorothy Fields's 'The Way You Look Tonight' (written for *Swing Time*, 1936) – that they launch into a hilariously bumbling set of leaps and turns. With the wench Jaquenetta, the clown Costard and Constable Dull prancing in the background, the schoolmistress and curate don't fantasize that they can dance like Fred and Ginger; they actually dance their rapture. The comic distance between their geriatric twirls and 1930s movie glamour not only mocks the pretension of scholars and curates, as does Shakespeare, but also testifies to the power of music and poetry to lift even ordinary dullards – like school teachers, churchmen and the movie-going audience – into a world of beauty and love beyond death, war and time: 'Lovely, never, never change'.[22]

The seductiveness of the alternate reality created in song and dance, which leads Branagh's

schoolmistress and curate to an amorous assignation, builds to a climax as his lords 'resolve to woo these girls of France' by devising 'Some entertainment for them in their tents' (4.3.347–9). With child-like glee, Branagh's lords exclaim the Shakespearian equivalent of 'Let's put on a show', trading the sophisticated grace of Astaire and Rogers for the frenetic energy of Judy Garland and Mickey Rooney. After the abortive masque of the Muscovites, Shakespeare's lords commission the Pageant of the Nine Worthies as entertainment for the ladies. Although Branagh only gives a newsreel account of the pageant, he does stage the final number of Navarre's amateur theatricals. As Master of Ceremonies, Costard, the vaudeville clown played by Nathan Lane, leads the entire cast, as chorus line, in Irving Berlin's Broadway show-stopper from *Annie, Get Your Gun* (1946), 'There's No Business Like Show Business'. But, instead of diverting attention from the worsening political crisis reported in the interpolated newsreels, both masque and pageant actually remind us of what the lords are trying to forget. The subtle allusion to *Cabaret* in the choreography of 'Let's Face the Music and Dance', and its reminder that 'There may be trouble ahead' preview the looming war. Likewise, Costard, mimicking Al Jolson's plaintive wail in 'My Mammy', sings that

You get word before the show has started
That your fav'rite uncle died at dawn.
Top of that your pa and ma have parted,
You're brokenhearted, but you go on.[23]

---

[21] 'I Get a Kick Out of You', in *The Complete Lyrics of Cole Porter*, ed. Robert Kimball (New York, 1983), p. 118.

[22] 'The Way You Look Tonight', in *The Jerome Kern Song Book*, ed. Oscar Hammerstein II (New York, 1955), pp. 169–72.

[23] 'There's No Business Like Show Business', in *The Complete Lyrics of Irving Berlin*, pp. 388–9. For Al Jolson, see Ethan Mordden, *The Hollywood Musical* (New York, 1981), p. 5. Eggert argues that Nathan Lane's allusion to Jolson's blackface performance of 'My Mammy' in *The Jazz Singer* reinscribes the American problem of ethnic and racial assimilation into this film: 'Sure Can Sing and Dance', p. 82.

At this climactic moment – when the whole population of Navarre is engaged in putting on a show – enter Marcadé who, complains the Queen, 'interrupt'st our merriment' (5.2.710).

Behind Biron's line, 'Worthies, away. The scene begins to cloud' (5.2.714), Branagh's audience may hear an abrupt reversal of the chorus that still echoes in our ears: 'Let's go on with the show.' Nevertheless, although news of the war forces them to leave the play world of Navarre, Branagh's lords and ladies turn even their parting into a Hollywood drama of loss. In *Shall We Dance* (1937), Fred and Ginger say goodbye on a ferry, shrouded by fog standing by their car, as Fred sings George and Ira Gershwin's 'They Can't Take That Away From Me'. Branagh's foggy goodbye scene also places his couples beside cars, this time at an airport, as they share lines from Gershwin's tune. But Branagh frames the nostalgia in the Fred and Ginger valediction with a visual allusion to the equally foggy airport goodbye scene that concludes *Casablanca*. In a film saturated with musical numbers – ten as compared to three or four in a typical 1930s musical – almost every number is, in turn, saturated with multiple allusions that, as we have seen, play off one another. This media saturation, comparable to Shakespeare's richly layered linguistic play, creates a complex ending – perhaps more complex than critics and reviewers have heretofore allowed.

Through allusive play Branagh suggests that his lords don't, in fact, abandon their musical retreat for the reality of war; they merely replace Fred and Ginger with Humphrey and Ingrid. By framing Fred's goodbye from *Shall We Dance* ('We may never, never meet again . . . Still I'll always, always keep / The mem'ry') with a visual allusion to the noblest war-movie goodbye in history, Branagh paradoxically undercuts nostalgia.[24] Our chuckling at the witty interplay of allusions stifles any sniffles, and distances us from the longing for a simpler, nobler past that defines nostalgia.

Criticized for extending his story beyond the parting of 'You that way, we this way' (5.2.914) in order to create the comic ending that Shakespeare deliberately rejected, Branagh adds real Second-World-War footage to a black and white, faux newsreel narrative of the characters' trials during the war and a joyous VE Day reunion.[25] But Branagh's epilogue does translate – in images without words – Shakespeare's concluding poems of winter, 'When blood is nipped, and ways be foul', and spring,

> When daisies pied and violets blue,
> And lady-smocks, all silver-white,
> And cuckoo-buds of yellow hue
> Do paint the meadows with delight.
> (5.2.901, 879–82)

Signifying the harsh reality, beyond the musical land of Navarre, through which the lords actually fulfil their parting vows of service, Branagh's black-and-white war sequence magically metamorphoses, in the film's final shot, into vibrant Technicolor. In his festive conclusion, Branagh merely extends Shakespeare's ambiguous representation of nature's cycle, in which bleak winter replaces spring's pied beauty. Marriages begotten in the parti-coloured spring, the cuckoo's song reminds us, often end in betrayal, and roasted apples and a pot on the fire temper winter's harshness.

Branagh's final shot actually captures some of the ambiguity in Shakespeare's concluding songs. As the merriment of Navarre is restored in the VE Day celebration, Branagh may seem to be conjuring an apocryphal lost play, *Love's Labour's Won*.[26] But when Officer Dull's camera flashes, and the scene suddenly shifts from black and white to Technicolor, we realize that we have been transported to Oz. Just as the tornado blows Judy from sepia Kansas to the fantasy land of Technicolor Oz, Branagh's return to the vibrant colours that have characterized Navarre suggests that this

---

24 'They Can't Take That Away from Me', in *The Complete Lyrics of Ira Gershwin*, p. 266.

25 For representative critiques, see Crowl, '*Love's Labor's Lost*', p. 38, and Friedman, 'I won't dance', pp. 139–40. For a defence, see Tuckett, '*Love's Labour's Lost*', par. 3.

26 '*Love's Labour's Won*: A Brief Account', in *William Shakespeare: The Complete Works*, ed. Stanley Wells *et al.* (Oxford, 1986), p. 349.

happily-ever-after ending, previewed in his added subtitle, 'A Romantic Musical Comedy', is a media fiction. Ending with one final leap into the alternate reality of musicals, Branagh reminds us, with an allusive wink, that we have willingly suspended our disbelief in order to enter an illusion created by a long history of 'wizards' behind curtains.

The play frame Branagh adopts allows this double stance of surrendering to the fiction, all the while watching the creation of the fiction from a knowing distance. Indeed, play (unlike irony) is always double. When playful otters chase, nip and scuffle – exhibiting behaviour that might signal 'This is a fight' – they are actually framing their behaviour to communicate 'This is play.' Giving a double message in a single nip, the playful otter speaks a paradox: 'This bite does not signify what a bite signifies.' Furthermore, because play conflates the defining frame (the communication 'This is play, not a bite') with what is inside the frame (the physiological bite), a single play action takes place simultaneously on two levels of reality: the player both participates in his action and stands apart framing the action.[27] In the play and film of *Love's Labour's Lost*, Shakespeare and Branagh take the double and paradoxical stance of players, not the arch stance of ironists.

Shakespeare both creates a play-world in the kingdom of Navarre through sparkling aristocratic banter, and plays with the very linguistic conventions that create this play-world, thereby simultaneously revelling in the fun and exposing the dangers of linguistic instability when death and time intrude. In *Love's Labour's Lost: A Romantic Musical Comedy* Branagh both creates a play-world in Navarre through the grace and sophistication of 1930s musical numbers and plays with the

conventions of musical comedy, thereby simultaneously revelling in the fun and exposing the fragility of retreat into celluloid glamour. The play frame allows for this rich mix of doubleness, indeterminacy and paradox.

Indeed, the interplay between Shakespeare, part of our distant past, playing with the cultural conventions of his own (to us, even more distant) past, and Branagh playing with the cultural conventions of our more recent past (the pre-Second World War film era) creates the kind of 'plural present' that, according to Ihab Hassan, is one characteristic of the postmodern sensibility. Such 'hybridization' produces 'a different concept of tradition, one in which continuity and discontinuity, high and low culture, mingle not to imitate but to expand the past in the present'.[28] Hassan's description matches both Shakespeare himself and Branagh who, in imitation of his predecessor, joyously cannibalizes past styles and genres at will.

So, what does my defence of Branagh's least commercially successful Shakespeare adaptation suggest? Merely that fans of Shakespeare's meta-linguistic comedy (of whom there have always been few)[29] can find much to admire in Branagh's meta-filmic appropriation of Fred and Ginger, Humphrey and Ingrid, Judy and Mickey.

---

[27] Gregory Bateson, 'The Message "This is Play"', in *Group Processes: Transactions of the Second Conference*, ed. Bertram Schaffner (New York, 1956), pp. 145–242. See also Anna K. Nardo, *The Ludic Self in Seventeenth-Century English Literature* (Albany, 1991), pp. 7–11.

[28] Ihab Hassan, 'Pluralism in Postmodern Perspective', *Critical Inquiry*, 12 (1986), 503–20; p. 506.

[29] Londré, *Critical Essays*, p. 3.

BOTTOM AND THE GRAMOPHONE: MEDIA, CLASS AND COMEDY IN MICHAEL HOFFMAN'S *A MIDSUMMER NIGHT'S DREAM*

PETER DONALDSON

Michael Hoffman's *A Midsummer Night's Dream* (1999) is one of a number of Shakespeare films in which media histories or sustained thematic attention to media regimes and practices play a central role. In such films as Olivier's *Henry V*, Mazursky's *Tempest*, Godard's *King Lear*, *Prospero's Books*, Loncraine's *Richard III*, Baz Luhrmann's *William Shakespeare's Romeo + Juliet*, *Titus* and Michael Almereyda's *Hamlet*, media themes rise to the level of subject matter, vying for attention with and sometimes supplanting the story line of the source play to such an extent that one may think of them as media fables or media allegories as well as Shakespeare adaptations. Not all of these films imply a narrative exclusively concerned with *cinema* – instead they often suggest journeys *across* media – from page or stage to screen, to be sure, but also, for example, from book to the magically animated and animating volumes in Prospero's collection in the Greenaway film, or from toy analogue video camera to complex digital editing suite in Almereyda's *Hamlet* or, in the case of Luhrmann's *Romeo + Juliet*, in the blending of many media, including billboards, newspapers and newsmagazines, and broadcast television into a ubiquitous, reality-challenging array of simulacra.

Like these films, Hoffman's *Midsummer Night's Dream* combines Shakespeare adaptation with media story. Though set in 1900, the year of Sarah Bernhardt's short film of the duel scene in *Hamlet* and just after the first Shakespeare film (Beerbohm Tree's 'Death Scene' from *King John*), the media narrative is not focused on film, but rather on recorded sound, and in particular on the role of the gramophone as a medium for recorded opera. The film constructs the advent of the gramophone as a democratizing event, rendering class-based canons of taste and cultural hierarchy more permeable in its fictional world than they are in the text of Shakespeare's play. The use of recorded opera – represented in the film by a small number of perennial 'greatest hits', including 'Libiamo ne' lieti calici' (*La traviata*), 'Una furtiva lagrima' (*L'elisir d'amore*) and 'Casta diva' (*Norma*) – structures key moments of cross-class and fairy/human community in the film, and opens a cultural space in which (among other effects) the artistic (as well as romantic/erotic) aspirations of Bottom and the mechanicals can be treated more sympathetically than they commonly are in productions of the play. Recorded opera gives Bottom, in particular a richer inner life, status within a tradition of lower-class characters ennobled by love, and an association with the wonders of human art and invention of the late nineteenth century. Opera – with help from Mendelssohn's music for *Midsummer Night's Dream* – also creates much of the magic of the fairy world in the film and gives that magic a human origin in the broadly shared musical world of an Italian town of the period, and in the technology that makes its reproduction possible. By shifting at key moments from opera as soundtrack accompaniment to shots in which records are actually shown playing on-screen within the narrative, Hoffman foregrounds the medium, calls attention to the historical moment of its introduction, and implicitly contrasts that moment with the more rigidly class-based cultural hierarchies of Shakespeare's play. This article will trace the opening up of such cultural space in Hoffman's *Dream*, the role of the gramophone in creating it, and will end with a brief look at the ways in which the film, like the play, ends by closing down some of the possibilities for class fluidity it opens.

THE GRAMOPHONE AT THE PALACE: THEFT AND SILENCE

The first on-screen appearances of the gramophone in the film take place during the opening sequence which offers an introduction to the Italian setting and a tour of the grounds and kitchens of the palace where preparations for the wedding of Theseus and Hippolyta are beginning. First, over the credits, we hear Mendelssohn's *Overture to Midsummer Night's Dream* as soundtrack accompanying the fairies, shown as tiny dancing lights against a broad expanse of the Tuscan countryside. As the palace itself comes into view, the music continues, lending a kind of fairy presence, a nimble delight, to the work of the palace groundsmen as they set out tables, tend the lawn and clear the great central fountain. The camera busily moves from lawn to kitchen, panning and tracking at counter-top height to show hands performing the varied tasks of preparation, rolling out dough, chopping tomatoes, carving roasts or carrying copper cooking vats. At one point, an eviscerated swan is carried through the kitchen (perhaps a Shakespearian emblem in a below-stairs register), and at this moment we see the fairy lights again, hovering about a pair of dwarfs merrily stealing silver tableware and serving platters, which they cart off, along with a large gramophone bell, as they sneak out of the palace and off into the woods. The camera completes its survey of the grounds with a shot of a satisfied and confident Theseus, loftily surveying his domains and his household from the centre of the second storey balcony. He turns thoughtful for a moment, plucks a white rose (i.e. one not yet 'purple with love's hue') from a vase and exits the shot, to appear again discovering Hippolyta, who is listening to a gramophone record. The camera first shows the

spinning disc in close-up, then the turntable and bell, then Hippolyta's intent reverie as she listens.[1] This is an important moment in several ways. Her listening defines her privacy: as Theseus moves into the shot and interrupts Hippolyta's concentration she is mildly startled and has to recover and recompose herself. Her silent listening and the withdrawal from the collective mood of the moment it implies, as well as her initial discomfort when Theseus arrives with the rose, all suggest that Hoffman interprets this encounter as one in which Hippolyta is ambivalent, is thinking of something other than the coming wedding and feels intruded upon. This interpretation is not uncommon in *Midsummer* productions – Hoffman's sequence might be read, for example, as a gentler replay, perhaps, of the comparable moment in the Reinhardt-Dieterle 1935 film, where Theseus alarms Hippolyta by suddenly encircling her waist from behind while she is wistfully gazing at the moon and presumably thinking of home. What is notable is that, in Hoffman, Hippolyta's ambivalence and emotional reserve are conveyed in terms of the protocols of the distinctively modern experience of listening to records. And since in the early years of the gramophone listening habits were somewhat more social than they are now, this moment also slightly anticipates the role that private listening and personal choice of music would later have as important markers of identity (especially among the young, the target audience for the film).

The contrast between Hippolyta's musical world and that of the palace is made possible by an intentional paradox in the sound design – the ambient music of the Mendelssohn soundtrack is diminished almost to inaudibility as the gramophone (which might otherwise be taken to be its

---

[1] As in web videos made by collectors of early operatic recordings, the close-up shot of the spinning turntable creates a presumption of period authenticity. See, for example, www.youtube.com/watch?v=ZBBH-u5Tv04 and other postings by YouTube user zciweslab. Consulted 13 October 2007.

on-screen source) comes into view.[2] This implies that Hippolyta occupies a space that is remote from whatever source the ambient music is coming from, and allows for the possibility that she may be listening to some other music entirely, inaudible to the others and to the screen audience. Even if the music is taken to be Mendelssohn's *Midsummer*, in this scene it is not heard as accompaniment to energetic labour, but as the object of thoughtful appreciation and reverie. This scene of individual listening contrasts with the use of music to this point as highly social, and also with the later moments in which the gramophone appears again, most notably when Titania and all the fairies listen in wonder to the forest-filling sound of Bellini's *Norma* played by Bottom. To this point, the gramophone has been presented as mildly enigmatic: do we hear the music Hippolyta is playing? If not, what might it be, and what does her visible response to the music mean? And who are those dwarfs? Where are they taking the record player they steal? Obscurely allied with the fairies, they seem benign media pirates, 'textual poachers', abetting the circulation of culture from the palace to the world outside.

THE PIAZZA: 'LIBIAMO NE' LIETI CALICI'

Following the introduction to the ducal palace and its grounds, Hoffman offers a second establishing sequence, a survey of the town of Monte Athena, where classes mingle more freely, with one character, Bottom, sometimes crossing over from artisan to gentleman, 'passing', in class terms, at least momentarily. Both sequences are accompanied by soundtrack music (Mendelssohn's *Dream* for the palace; Verdi's 'Libiamo' from *La traviata* for the town), which subsides once the survey function has been accomplished and the narrative settles on one character (Hippolyta; Bottom). In both sequences the camera moves freely and closely follows the rhythms of work, in the palace the work of groundsmen and kitchen servants, in the town of artisans plying their trades. But in the piazza, narrative point of view is not, as with the palace,

organized around the powerful, elevated and summative glance of the duke ('lord of all we've observed' as the published screenplay puts it),[3] surveying his estate from the centre of the balcony and of the cinematic image (a positioning that recalls the place of the ruler in the Stuart masque),[4] but instead shifts rapidly. First the omniscient camera descends into the square, lingering at the announcement of the competition for entertainment at the duke's wedding (which, unlike the text of the play, specifies a 'substantial recompense' for success),[5] then follows with tracking shots at the level of the tradesmen's carts, the level at which the work of hands takes place. Here we also see that work as the subject of on-screen spectatorship when, among numerous examples, the camera comes in close to the grinding wheel and then backs off to show the tinker and the appreciative glances of the gentlefolk watching the knives being sharpened.

Gentlemen and gentlewomen mingle with those who work in the square. They are distinguished by details of dress, and they come not to sell but to buy but also, in significant contrast with the palace, to watch and be watched. The piazza is a festive space in something like the full sense the term is given in Rousseau's account of the grape harvest in *La nouvelle Héloise*, or in the *Lettre à D'Alembert sur les spectacles*, a theatre without a stage where the activities of the community are the show, to be shared by all without tickets of admission, artificial

---

[2] In contrast, the volume is high and relatively constant through the survey of palace grounds and kitchen, unifying these spaces as soundtrack music can do. It diminishes somewhat for the shot of Theseus on the balcony, marking a distinction in mood, spatial location and social class, and then there is a further, marked diminuendo for the shot of Hippolyta and the gramophone.

[3] Michael Hoffman, *William Shakespeare's Midsummer Night's Dream: Love Makes Fools of Us All* [Screenplay] (New York, 1999), p. i.

[4] See Stephen Orgel, *The Illusion of Power: Political Theater in the English Renaissance* (Berkeley, 1975).

[5] The Italian phrase 'sostanziale riconoscimento' conveys a monetary expectation supporting the troupe's guesses as to how much a successful show will bring ('sixpence a day'?) but with a hint at the 'recognition' they are also after.

lights, hierarchical seating or rigid spatial segregation of performers and audience.[6] It is in this space that we meet Bottom and his crew and, though they share the piazza with the gentry, this setting allows them a rich social context much in contrast with the text, where the mechanicals appear as a small group with little established structure and few filiations bonding them to a world of their own. Indeed, they worry much about the *duke's* world, or more precisely that of the duke and the 'ladies'. They have no family, no neighbours, no non-comic grievances and no extra-theatrical pleasures. One might contrast them, in these respects, with the carriers in *Henry IV, Part 1* (2.1), whose brief lines establish their imbrication in a broad and complex set of social and historical contexts. One effect of Hoffman's portrayal of the town square in the idiom of cinematic realism is precisely to give the mechanicals of his *Midsummer* a wider world – each is introduced separately, with the tools of his trade, or emerging from his shop into the square; they are seen first as friends who greet one another warmly rather than suddenly appearing as awkward would-be theatrical performers. Bottom's life extends beyond the limits of work on the play perhaps more than the others: he has a wife (who speaks only Italian), frequents cafés, engages in several flirtations with other women, lives in an apartment near the square.

The soundtrack anthem of the piazza is the 'Brindisi' or drinking song from *La traviata*, 'Libiamo ne' lieti calici'.[7] This is soundtrack sound – there is no gramophone in sight – but the song sets the rhythm and mood for the busy life of the town, and there is one brief moment at which at least one character, Peter Quince, acknowledges the music directly, humming and keeping up the beat as if conducting while holding what is presumably a leaf from the playscript for 'Pyramus and Thisbe' in his hand.

'Libiamo' works in the scene as operatic intertext in several ways. First, it is a rousing drinking song, a communal praise of wine, pleasure and vitality. Then, it is among the arias most frequently heard outside the opera house, one of the songs taken up by street singers, organ grinders and others as part of the broad dissemination of opera as popular culture in the nineteenth century. When commercial distribution of sound recordings created possibilities for even wider access to operatic music, now performed by the opera house stars themselves, such pieces, 'Libiamo' among them, were recorded and continued as popular favourites.[8] Within the narrative of *La traviata*, 'Libiamo' already crosses class. It is a toast offered by one of the aristocratic men at a dinner in the home of the courtesan Violetta, and Alfredo, who offers it, uses the occasion not only to call for drink, but to profess his love for Violetta, and she replies by espousing a heedless pleasure, rejecting all else as *follia* (folly). As a drinking song/erotic duet that crosses class lines in a work of 'high' art that has at the same time been a vivid presence in popular media and settings since it was performed, 'Libiamo' helps to redefine Shakespeare's artisans as participants in a rich and in some measure democratic popular culture.

'UNA FURTIVA LAGRIMA' OR BOTTOM IN LOVE

Hoffman's Bottom wears a white suit and straw hat, an engaging smile, sits elegantly at one of the outdoor tables of a café, sips his drink and flirts with the gentlewomen passing by. Casting and costume are key elements in Hoffman's interpretation of the role, and they establish that Bottom's class ambitions are evident as soon as he appears. Men's

---

[6] Jean Starobinski writes of Rousseau's ideal of festive space:

> It is the place where the spectator, presenting himself as spectacle, will no longer be either seen (*voyant*) or voyeur, will efface within himself the difference between the actor and spectator, the represented and the representer, the object seen and the seeing object.

The Invention of Liberty, trans. Bernard C. Swift (Geneva, 1964), p. 100, cited by Martin Jay, *Downcast Eyes: The Denigration of Vision in Twentieth Century French Thought* (Berkeley, 1993), p. 93.

[7] See especially *La traviata*, dir. Franco Zeffirelli, perf. Teresa Stratas, Placido Domingo, 1982. DVD, Universal Studios, 1999 and excerpt ('Libiamo') at http://youtube.com/watch?v=NcKdnkGBSgA. Consulted 14 October 2007.

[8] See below, pp. 30–3.

'lounge' suits (jackets tailless, shorter than frock coats or morning coats) were worn across classes in 1900 in both Italy and England as they are in the film,[9] but variations in cut, fabric, colour and of course condition were class markers within a wide and fluid spectrum. But, whereas a workman might wear a good suit in this period, Bottom's outfit signals (perhaps now as much as then) a leisure class dandy. Kevin Kline, who plays Bottom here, has often played the clown before and often the fool (as in *A Fish Called Wanda*, *Soapdish* and other films), but if he is a clown he is usually a preppy clown and if he is a fool he is a well-educated and genteel one. Not only through his performance, but because of its continuity with these well-known aspects of his star persona, Bottom's social climbing in *A Midsummer Night's Dream* is poignantly plausible as well as comic. In the film, he seems to be passing easily for one of the aristocrats in the town square, but for the accident of a crude belch. This one defect in his self-presentation unfortunately coincides with the braying of a passing donkey, and the conjunction 'outs' him to the film audience in class terms, identifies him (if we didn't guess) as the film's Bottom, and hints at his eventual, textually mandated metamorphosis. Not privy to this joke for the audience, a pair of attractive young women notice him and one returns his flirtatious greeting, encouraging his attentions for a moment cut short by the appearance of a markedly plebeian wife who speaks only Italian and from whom Bottom quickly hides. The sequence transposes the fear the mechanicals have in the text of 'offending the ladies' (and therefore facing execution, as they repeatedly worry) to the more fluid class dynamics of an aspirant plebeian dandy faced with a double let-down as he is revealed as both married and working-class.

As the plan for 'Pyramus and Thisbe' unfolds in the town square, Bottom, of course, volunteers for all parts,[10] and as he tries out Lion and shows that he can speak as softly 'as any sucking dove', the open square begins to differentiate itself into a playing space (a shadowed area beneath the scaffolded wall of the town hall) and a sunlit audience space, inhabited by the gentry, white buildings behind them. Bottom is seen as belonging in both,

as the camera crosses the axis. The sequence suggests how easily Bottom *might* fit – though of course ultimately he does not fit – into the world of the gentry. The turning point comes when he is humiliated in the midst of a line by working-class boys who empty jugs of wine on him from above, drenching his white suit. (In the original plan, the director intended to use donkey manure, but relented.)[11] The moment marks the definitive failure of his flirtations with the woman to whom he tipped his hat earlier: she returns long enough to watch Bottom act, is amused and momentarily interested once again, but is visibly disgusted after the wine drenching. She casts a withering last glance, barely able to look at him, and leaves.

Bottom's pride, and certainly his commitment to keep working on the play, is patiently and sensitively restored by an intimate conversation with Quince (this is one of the glories of the production – all the lines are Shakespeare's, but Quince's words of support take on new meaning in the context of Bottom's humiliation and the scorn of his aristocratic audience). In Hoffman, the theatrical failures and exposure to ridicule for transgression of class lines (and especially for transgressions that might frighten or offend upper-class women) has already happened before rehearsals begin. Hoffman's version of this moment shows Bottom's decision to 'undertake' the role of Pyramus as a recovery of dignity after class-based humiliation, whereas in the play it is a moderation of his manic plan to play *all* the parts. The issue of class, never wholly absent in *Midsummer*, is not foregrounded at this point in the text, but it drives the scene in the film.[12] Restored (in some measure) by

---

[9] Farid Chenoune, *A History of Men's Fashion*. Trans. Deke Dusinberre (Paris, 1993 [Translation of *Des modes et des hommes: deux siècles d'élégance masculine* (Paris, 1993)]), pp. 121–4.

[10] As Kevin Kline did when approached by Hoffman: 'he had devised a way that he could play Oberon, Bottom and Theseus. I breathed a sigh of relief. He'd already begun his work', Screenplay, p. ix.

[11] Hoffman, Screenplay, p. 14.

[12] Shakespeare's artisans are so heavily stereotyped by class and so fearful of the nobles that the degree to which finding

his talk with Quince, Bottom takes a lonely walk out of the piazza to his home, to the accompaniment of Roberto Alagna's version of 'Una furtiva lagrima' from Donizetti's *L'elisir d'amore*.

The aria functions in several ways as intertext. On one level, its poignant, serious melancholy works, in concert with Rees's sensitive encouragement and Kline's nuanced performance, to dignify Bottom in his trouble. In a more general way, the aria works, as 'Libiamo' does, to elevate the portrayal of the mechanicals by associating them with the subject matter as well as the popular audiences of Romantic *bel canto*. Then there is the matter of 'the elixir of love'. The elixir of Donizetti's title is also the main plot device of the opera, as it is in *A Midsummer Night's Dream*. The lead, Nemorino, is a bumpkin who falls hopelessly in love with the local landowner, Adina, the most genteel of the young women in the village. She laughs off his advances and he seeks help from a travelling mountebank who sells him a potion to make him irresistible. This turns out to be cheap wine and only makes him drunk and more boorish than ever, but a coincidence (the death of a rich uncle and rumours of an inheritance) makes the false potion appear to work. In his drunken state he is quickly surrounded by the young women of the village, suddenly affectionate, who have heard the good news of which he is as yet unaware. They now see him as a changed man; he now has the air of a gentleman ('l'aria da signor'), as Adina looks on. While she is now still ignorant of his new-found wealth, she is determined to get him back (since she has been jilted by his rival) and, if confident, she can prevail with no other elixir than a tender glance.

As she exits, Nemorino imagines (or actually sees) a single tear in her eye, and as he ponders its meaning, his confidence rises by degrees until it is a firm and rapturous belief in her love and his own worth. Though this new confidence begins in misrecognitions (of the motives of the girls, of the power of the potion, of his own wretchedly inebriated state), it grows to something strange and admirable in the course of the aria, like the belief of the lovers in *Dream* in the story of their magically complex night in the forest, or Bottom's wonder at

his own dream vision. In Donizetti, that growth is marked by a shift in verb and tense in the course of the song – in the first lines Nemorino says her furtive tear *seemed* to prove her interest in him: 'A furtive tear appeared in her eyes . . . she seemed to envy those happy girls . . .' But, as this possibility begins to lift him from his melancholy, he reconsiders the meaning of the tear in the present tense: 'What more should I seek? She loves me, I see it',[13] and seeming is replaced by triumphant certainty as the key phrase 'She loves me, I see it' (*m'ama, lo vedo*) is repeated several times in the course of

---

them unproblematically endearing continues to count as a sign of good taste is surprising. But there is also a long tradition of political readings of the play, going back at least to Marx, who contrasts the 'Snug of accommodation' with the 'lion of contradiction'. Various aspects of their 'accommodation', exaggerated deference and fear of execution for minor violations of class-based codes of speech and decorum (especially in relation to sex) have been discussed in recent years by Theodore B. Leinwand, Annabel M. Patterson, Richard Wilson and Michael Bristol in the context of the history of artisanal rebellion and resistance in the later half of the sixteenth century. Bristol, *Carnival and Theater: Plebeian Culture and the Structure of Authority in Renaissance England* (New York, 1985), argues that the inadvertent malapropisms and other reversals of intent in their accommodations to the aristocracy encode a form of critique. For Leinwand, in '"I believe we must leave the killing out": Deference and Accommodation in *A Midsummer Night's Dream*', *Renaissance Papers* (1986), 11–30, their anxiety over the appearance of aggression ('we will *seem* to say we will do no harm with our swords' (21)) both rejects and evokes civil unrest and its sometimes cruel repression in the 1590s. Patterson, in *Shakespeare and the Popular Voice* (Cambridge, MA, 1989), pp. 52–70, finds a surprising avenue of approach to the question of the class implications of laughter in documents related to mid century uprisings, in which being made a 'laughingstocke to most proud and insolent men' is said to inflict 'such a stain of evil report as nothing is more grievous for them to remember, nor more unjust to suffer' (69–70). In 'The Kindly Ones: The Death of the Author in Shakespearian Athens', Richard Dutton, ed., *New Casebook On Midsummer Night's Dream* (Basingstoke, Hampshire, 1996), p. 215, Wilson suggests that the mechanicals' abjection is also that of Shakespeare himself, who 'collapses his own meaning into the diminutiveness of an aesthetic domain'.

13 'Una furtiva lagrima / negl'occhi suoi spunto. . . . / Quelle festose giovani / Invidiar sembro. / Che piu cercando io vo? M'ama, lo vedo' *L'elisir d'amore* [libretto] (New York, 1960), Act 2, scene 4

the aria, and often, in performance, with growing conviction.[14]

In Hoffman's use of the aria, however, the phrase *m'ama lo vedo* is only heard once, still in a doubting, melancholy key, during Bottom's confrontation with his wife, and works as irony – his wish, either to believe in the love of the 'festose giovani' with whom he has been flirting in the square, or in that of the love or even respect of his wife (who looks on his wine-drenched suit and defeated posture with disgust) is not realized here – though it will be in the forest. The counterpoint is clearest when he spreads his empty hands in an admission of defeat (he is just as foolish, just as disgraced as his wife believes, he seems to say), just as *m'ama lo vedo* / 'She loves me, I see it', is heard on the soundtrack. As his wife leaves the room, the scene ends as he looks out the window on a street that has turned dark and rain soaked, where, in the sequence to come, Helena will lament her own humiliation by love. But the story of Bottom's career as a lover that began with his first flirtations with the gentlewomen passing the café is not over, and Donizetti's aria aligns it with the deep sadness of Nemorino as lover's melancholy begins to change and dignify him.

This aria has additional associations relevant to the character of Bottom and to the film's foregrounding of recorded music: 'Una furtiva' launched Enrico Caruso's career as a major international star both in opera on stage and then on records. By 1900, the fictional date of the Hoffman film, Caruso had already performed in Russia, in South America and in lesser houses in Italy, but this season marked his debut at La Scala. His first performance (in *La Bohème*) was inauspicious. He was said to have been in awe of Toscanini, his performance was uneven, and his difficulty with the high C in the aria was often noted in reviews. Then came *L'elisir*, which had been extremely popular for at least twenty years following its premiere in 1832, but by 1900 had been absent from the repertoire of many houses for decades. Although Caruso had little time to learn the part, his performance of 'Una furtiva lagrima' brought down the house, made him famous. The aria also marked his

1 A self-caricature by Enrico Caruso in the role of Nemorino.

first success at Covent Garden in 1902 and subsequently at the Met in 1904. Caruso had in effect 'revived *L'elisir d'amore* . . . and had succeeded in restoring it to the front rank of the operatic repertory'.[15] He sang the part of Nemorino more than seventy times after that, ending his career with the Brooklyn Academy of Music production of *L'elisir*

---

[14] Alagna's own full performance of the aria at the Opera National de Lyon is an excellent example of this, among many others. *L'elisir d'amore*, perf. Angela Ghiorghiu, Roberto Alagna (1996), DVD, Decca, 2002.

[15] Michael Scott, *The Great Caruso* (New York, 1988), pp. 45–8, 51.

in 1920, shortly before his death.[16] The character resonated with Caruso's own public persona as
the son of an impoverished Neapolitan mechanic
who became a symbol of artistic refinement of
the highest order, but retained persistent traces of
crudeness. Caruso had a well-developed sense of
humour about this side of himself, but could not
always control the image he had in part created, as
when, in 1906, a scandal erupted over charges that
he had sexually molested a young woman in public – indeed, in the Monkey House of the Central
Park Zoo.[17]

Caruso was a gifted caricaturist, and a number
of his best self-portraits show him as Nemorino –
a self-satisfied meticulously but slightly absurdly
overdressed peasant striving for higher status, the
effect of his finery undermined by a broad grin,
wide stance with arms akimbo, sometimes with a
huge broad-brimmed hat.[18]

Caruso relished the role of the clown or bumpkin who, despite his common qualities and, as
time went on, despite his weight, could rise to
the heights of romantic rapture. The character
of Nemorino, then, and Caruso in the role of
Nemorino, overlaps with elements of Shakespeare's
portrayal of Bottom the Weaver, a proletarian who
is granted a 'most rare vision'. Hoffman works at
the intersection of these personae and these texts,
and in doing so deepens the romantic aspects of
Bottom's character, and moves him into a milieu
in which his dreams are nearly within reach.

'A RECORDING MAN'S DREAM'

Caruso's success at La Scala in 1900–1 also brought
him to the attention of the sound engineers of the
Gramophone and Typewriter Company (G&T) in
New York, and led in March 1902 to the first commercially and artistically successful music recordings in history.[19] 'Una furtiva' was recorded in the
first of these sessions. Fred Gaisberg, who travelled to Italy to record Caruso in a Milan hotel
room, called him 'the answer to a recording man's
dream':[20] not only was he a superb tenor, but there
was an unexpected technical match between his
qualities of voice and the capabilities as well as the

limitations of the new medium. The records were a
worldwide success, within weeks there were orders
from St Petersburg and Buenos Aires, G&T made
a profit of $90,000 (Caruso was paid $500 for these
first sessions, but went on to net over $2,000,000
in his career). On the strength of the early success of these 'Red Label' discs, G&T was able to
recruit seven opera stars from Covent Garden, and
the industry was in effect launched. As Roland
Gelatt puts it, 'Caruso made the record business
as much as it made him.' And the record business
could now fulfil its potential as a mass medium for
classical music. Gelatt writes:

Recording before 1902 can be classified as incunabula . . .
beginning with Caruso's recordings in March 1902, the
instrument at last began living up to the claims that had
been made for it. 'The most enchanting selections of the
world's greatest singers' could in truth be heard in the
home – and for only ten shillings a record.   (117)

I have suggested that Hoffman reshapes Shakespeare's *A Midsummer Night's Dream* so that it resonates with this pivotal moment in media history,
choosing music that was recorded in the earliest
days of the gramophone, showing the apparatus
playing on-screen. But perhaps the centrepiece in
Hoffman's recorded-opera-intensive *Midsummer* is
the scene in which Bottom actually plays a record
for Titania and we, the screen audience, actually
hear it – a scene that may be taken as a replay of
the moments of wonder experienced by the first
audiences for recorded classical music.

---

[16] *L'elisir* was most prominent in Caruso's stage career in the
years 1901–5 (39 performances), during which the only work
Caruso appeared in more frequently was *Rigoletto*, and again
from late 1916 until his death in 1920 (33 performances).
Caruso's Brooklyn Academy of Music Nemorino was his
final role. In this period, Caruso appeared in *L'elisir* more
often than in any other work with the exception of *Pagli-
acci*. (See 'Chronology of Caruso's Appearances' in Enrico
Caruso Jr. and Andrew Farkas, *Enrico Caruso: My Father and
My Family* (Portland, Oregon, 1990), pp. 655–98.

[17] Farkas, *Enrico Caruso*, pp. 128–9; Scott, pp. 93–6.

[18] Enrico Caruso, *Caruso's Caricatures* (New York, 1977), p. 59.

[19] See Roland Gelatt, *The Fabulous Phonograph 1877–1977*, 2nd
revised edn (London, 1977 [1954]), pp. 114–17.

[20] Fred Gaisberg, cited by Gelatt (p. 115).

The scene is prepared for by several earlier moments, including the sequence in which the dwarfs steal the gramophone from the palace. Later, as Titania prepares for sleep and Oberon plots her disgrace with Puck, we see the dwarfs enter Titania's precincts with their cart. They exchange European-style double kisses of greeting with their fairy customers as they unload their plunder. Like non-Western natives in narratives of colonial encounter, the fairies misunderstand the equipment as an assortment of trinkets and adornments[21] – some using the bell as a hat, others thrusting arms through record sleeves as if they were bracelets, some, bathing, apparently topless, in the nearby stream, use the discs as bath toys, floating them on the surface of the water as Titania orders music ('sing me now asleep'). Her 'bower', which like Peter Brook's can be drawn up into the air, is perhaps itself an acquisition made during a previous raid on the palace – it looks like a very large cooking vessel, and is drawn up by still other apparent borrowings from mortal technology – elevated by a series of vine-draped chains and pulleys connected to a tin contraption whose original purpose is hard to guess. The moment calls to mind Stephen Greenblatt's notion of the circulation of artistic energies through, for example, the repurposing of the clothing of the clergy and aristocracy in the Early Modern theatre.[22] The fairies appropriate many things from the human world in this *Midsummer*, the Indian boy, of course, but also table implements (which they use in the same way as mortals), primitive machinery, which they understand tolerably well and find new uses for, and now records and a record player, which they misunderstand quite completely, though charmingly.

When Bottom enters after his transformation, he is also, in a sense, misrecognized, as in the text: Titania's 'I pray thee, gentle mortal, sing again; my ear is much enamoured to thy note' follows a crudely sung tune that ends, as often in productions of this scene, in a donkey's bray. Yet it is important in a special way for this production that she looks to the mortal world for music. Her praise is of course partly delusional at this moment, a side effect of her potion-induced infatuation with Bottom. Her

followers don't share her taste at this point, but shortly they too will become enamoured by human song, reacting with wonder to a recording of Bellini's *Norma*. This occurs at the feast they prepare for Bottom ('Be kind and courteous to this gentleman'). With Bottom and Titania seated at an elaborately piled table, Cobweb presents Bottom with a silver covered dish. The cover off, the platter is revealed to be a record, whose grooves are covered with down and whose label is piled high with blackberries and raspberries. Bottom, wreathed in a golden laurel crown and robed like an ancient Roman aristocrat, indulgently smiles and blows the feathers off the disc, sets it on the turntable, cranks the mechanism and sets the stylus expertly, while punning on the servants' names as in the text – and suddenly the air is filled with the sounds of Bellini's 'Casta diva', provoking Titania's 'hail mortal', echoed by her followers, over whom a sacred hush seems to descend as fairy lights sparkle over the table and all look into the air for the source of the wondrous music.

Shakespeare's 'Hail mortal' is thus counterpoised with the Druid Priestess Norma's address to the Moon Goddess, the magic lights in Hoffman's forest correspond to the renewed splendour of the moon as Norma raises her arms in invocation,[23] and Norma's acknowledgement of the

---

[21] See for example Jeffrey Knapp, *An Empire Nowhere: England, America, and Literature from 'Utopia' to 'The Tempest'* (Berkeley, 1992).

[22] Stephen Greenblatt, *Shakespearian Negotiations: The Circulation of Social Energy in Renaissance England* (Berkeley, 1988), pp. 7–8.

[23] Stage direction: *Falchia il vischio; le Sacerdotesse lo raccolgono in canestri di vimini; Norma si avanza e stende le braccia al cielo. – La luna splende in tutta la sua luce. – Tutti si prostrano* (Eng.: Norma cuts branches of the mistletoe, which the Priestesses receive and deposit in their consecrated baskets. She then advances, upraising her arms on high. – The Moon beaming forth in full effulgence. – All kneel reverently). *Norma* [Italian and English Text], (Bryn Mawr, Pennsylvania, n.d.): Act 1, scene 4, p. 7.
In Monserrat Caballe's performance in Madrid in 1978, for example, stage lighting creates this effect: www.youtube.com/watch?v=RqbVILCYZmU [03:18 ff]. Consulted 7 March 2007. In the even more remarkable

goddess's response in the opening words of the aria: 'Chaste goddess who silvers these sacred ancient plants, turn thy beautiful countenance to us without cloud and without veil' ('Casta diva inargenti queste sacre antiche piante . . .'). Whereas it is the moon that shines in full splendour in *Norma* at the comparable moment, silvering the trees and moving the priestesses of the sacred precinct to homage, in the film this numinous moment arises as a reaction to the music Bottom plays, and for which he is hailed with awe and respect.

As is the case with *L'elisir*, *Norma* as a whole may be read intertextually as having many points of intersection with the play and with Hoffman's film. 'Casta diva' is a natural for *Midsummer*, since the play is suffused with English folkloric survivals of ancient beliefs, and the Moon/Diana is so present in the play: as timekeeper, needed source of light for Pyramus and Thisbe, divinity superior to the Fairy King and Queen, and many other roles. The aria easily fits, too, as anthem for Bottom's romance with the Fairy Queen, who herself invokes the Moon as deity several times, including the moment at which she leads Bottom to her bower, where the ambiguity of the chaste/unchaste associations of moonlight are strongest:

> The Moon, methinks, looks with a watery
>   eye
> And when she weeps, weeps every little
>   flower
> Lamenting some enforced chastity
> Bind my love's tongue. Lead him silently.

L'elisir also deploys its lunar motif in a shifting way – Norma as priestess is sworn to chastity but, even as she invokes the chaste lunar goddess and asks her to bring peace, her own role as priestess is tainted by unchastity and betrayal – she has borne two children to the Roman consul. Her people and her father want war with the Romans but Norma overrules them through her connection with the gods, giving the oracle a pacifist twist, in order to protect her lover from harm, even though his love for her is waning. The hymn to the moon and the sacred plants of the holy grove are

elements of a ritual practice over which she presides, but the beauty of the song derives, also, from a complex play of opposing motives and feelings that go beyond the ritual occasion and are at odds with her official role, suggesting her sad knowledge that her lover has transferred his affections to a younger priestess.

Though *L'elisir* shares with *Midsummer* the rich ambiguity that the chief devotee of the lunar *casta diva* in each is not herself chaste, what may be most important in Hoffman's use of 'Casta diva' is its association not with Titania but with Bottom, and with the plebeian experience of opera he instances at this moment in the film. Like 'Una furtiva', 'Casta diva' ennobles Bottom, reinforces his association with *bel canto*, and also makes him a representative figure for early recorded opera audiences and the new forms of access to art at its most 'lofty' (as Bottom might put it), which the new technology made possible.

This staging, within Shakespeare's magic forest, of an aria from Bellini's *Norma* resonates with a rich history of popular connection to Italian opera that has recently been studied in several major scholarly works, including Katherine K. Preston, *Opera on the Road: Traveling Opera Troupes in the United States 1825–1860* (Urbana and Chicago, 1993) and Karen Ahlquist, *Democracy at the Opera: Music, Theater and Culture in New York City 1815–1860* (Urbana and Chicago, 1997). Taken together, these books tell a story that is congruent with the one Lawrence Levine tells about nineteenth-century Shakespeare in *Highbrow/Lowbrow: The Emergence of Cultural Hierarchy in America* (Cambridge, MA, 1988), a story in which Shakespeare is regarded by Americans as a common cultural possession until mid century or just after, when Shakespeare

---

outdoor performance at the Theatre Antique d'Orange in 1974 (*Norma*, perf. Monserrat Caballe and Jon Vickers, 1974. DVD, Video Artists International, 2003) the warm south wind serendipitously began to blow at this moment, making Caballe's gown and the costumes of the chorus rise and float until the end of the aria. Here too, *inargenti* is taken as if it were a cue for the revelation of divine presence in nature.

in local and popular forms is (relatively speaking) squeezed out in favour of the high culture versions of the great cities. In the case of opera, the turning point is held by both Preston and Ahlquist to be the opening of the Metropolitan Opera in New York in 1860. This research also reveals how persistent the use of music of Verdi, Donizetti and Bellini, the three composers from whom Hoffman takes his opera selections, has been in popular culture. Preston quotes, for example, a mid-century description of the street singers and street organs in New York performing arias late into the night on Broadway, so numerous that their sounds overlapped:

At one corner the death-song in *Lucia* . . . in the next block the *Miserere* of *Trovatore* . . . Then the next moment we hear the *Casta Diva*, and as we pass on it merges into some of Verdi's passionate arias till frequently a night walk in Broadway is one continual concert. There is one air without which a street organ would be no more a street organ than a man without a head would be a man. After Verdi and Donizetti, the street organs fall back on the inevitable 'Mira Norma' of Bellini.

(p. 311, citing anonymous New York correspondent, *Dwight's Magazine*, 14 February, 1857, 156)

'To most Americans', Preston writes of this period, 'neither Shakespeare's works nor those of Rossini, Donizetti, or Verdi were solely Art. They were an integral part of popular entertainment, an everyday part of popular culture' (p. 316).

In the context of these histories: that of the early reception of Italian opera in America (and indeed of the wide reproduction of the very 'classics' Hoffman uses in his *Dream*) and their eclipse by the near monopoly in operatic production by metropolitan centres in the later part of the century, the playing of gramophone records in Hoffman's 'Tuscany at the turn of the last century' (Screenplay, vi) takes on the added resonance of a turning point in media history, when a new technology not only created a wider audience for opera than ever before, but also returned an art form to popular audiences that had been partly disenfranchised by the growth of metropolitan institutions of culture.

'IF IT PLEASE YOU!': ARTISTIC CLASS HIERARCHY, POPULAR MEMORY, SOUVENIR

But if Bottom has brought *bel canto* into the fairy world, he also in a sense leaves it there when he is expelled from Titania's bower. A shift in class control over culture is intimated by the way in which 'Casta diva' lingers in the fairy world not as Bottom's music but as celebration of the reunion of Titania and Oberon. First, we hear the aria play as Oberon discovers Titania and Bottom in their bed and applies the antidote to the love potion as Puck looks on slyly. At this point, Bottom and Titania being asleep, we hear this, I suggest, as soundtrack music rather than assuming that the record is still playing. Bottom, Titania and Oberon briefly form a threesome in the bed until Oberon asks for silence and the music increases in volume (without a diegetic hand at the controls) as they kiss and now the sleeping, slightly snoring Bottom has been pushed just below the frame line. As Titania turns in revulsion from the bower and asks 'how came these things to pass', 'Casta diva' is heard throughout the fairy world while she and Oberon, 'new in amity', walk solemnly through their realm (with insert shots of her followers washing her underwear in the stream). As the sun rises, Bottom, still asleep, is rather unceremoniously dumped. Chains and pulleys are shown in close-up suddenly letting go as the bed races to earth, spilling Bottom on the grass. Nearby is the gramophone, the record still turning, but silently now except for the needle scratching idly between the last groove and the post. The Bottom we now see is no longer the regally robed and crowned consort of the fairy queen. He has returned to casual mortal garments, lies in a meadow, and the fairy world has disappeared except for one tiny token, a miniature crown of gold, tucked into a tiny bird's nest in the meadow grass. He holds this and glances at it as he remembers his 'most rare vision', his ineffable/unspeakable 'dream'.[24]

---

[24] Many editions note the proximity of Bottom's claim to a unique vision, above mortal comprehension and expression

The final alternation of source and soundtrack sound comes as the mechanicals, Bottom having returned to them, prepare for the play, and then all assemble at the duke's palace for the wedding festivities. 'Libiamo' is heard in full force as Bottom commands 'every man look to his part', follows the artisans to the workshop, and seems, momentarily, to recapture even the palace where Philostrate seems to keep time to it with his staff of office – but the vocal line suddenly turns to echo and ceases as the mechanicals approach, now embarrassed and awkward in the upper-class milieu of the palace, and then comes to an abrupt halt as Bottom suddenly stops to admire a pair of nude classical deities in stone, the goddess, holding a cup with tiny yellow petals, metonymically recalling, in a more distant way than the miniature version we have seen him draw from the bird's nest in the meadow, the golden laurel crown of Bottom's dream, another of the traces it may leave in his waking life. He looks into the statue's face and reaches to touch her, as if remembering Titania, as Philostrate wards him off sharply – repurposing Shakespeare's line '*If* it please you!' as if it were the admonition of a museum guard protecting a masterpiece.

The final phase in the double pattern we have been tracing, whereby soundtrack and 'source sound' replays of operatic arias alternate, begins as the action returns to the palace grounds, where 'Libiamo' is heard again, not in the operatic version heard in the piazza at the beginning of the film, but by on-screen wedding quartet of guitar, bass, accordion and clarinet, played at a slower and more decorous tempo by men in dark suits and ties. Like 'Casta diva' shifting from its association with Bottom, the wonder of the forest and the sanctity of moon and plants to a celebration of the reunion and supremacy of Titania and Oberon, this is a privatizing replay, a reassertion of cultural hierarchy.

This central pattern in the film – the alternation and sometimes more complex interplay of opera as soundtrack and as 'remediated' gramophone music of the period – is not a central trope during the 'Pyramus and Thisbe' performance that follows or in the final sequences in which Bottom returns to his apartment and Puck (who appears now as street sweeper) ends the film with his rueful and indulgent wisdom, but the film's probing of the class dynamics of artistic privilege, participation and access continue by other means. In productions of *Midsummer* the question of how well the play within the play succeeds, for whom and on what terms, is often central. In this production there is an added complexity, as Bottom appears to fail (at least as an actor), while, in an original move, Hoffman has Flute succeed unquestionably, not despite himself or by turning the tragedy to farce, but by an impressive display of acting in terms that all can share – the troupe, the aristocrats and the film audience. Awkward at first, his squeaky Thisbe voice taunted by audience giggles, he finds himself in the moment, endows the somewhat ridiculous body of Pyramus with reality, removes his wig and finds his voice in grieving for a fallen comrade, transforming himself in the presence of the audience from cross-dressing boy to man, from a timid member of the troupe to the one who asserts his dignity most effectively, decisively silencing the scorn and nervous laughter of the court audience as they become immersed in the action.

This *tour de force*, improvisational performance is the turning point for the success of the play, and maps so closely to recognizable modern tropes of self-transformation in and through acting that it

---

(1.4.203–17), with St Paul's (1 Cor. 2:9; 2 Cor. 12:2–6). Its affinities with the tropes of courtly love have been somewhat less emphasized. Hoffman's take on Bottom's transformation by love brings his 'most rare vision' – with its promise of literary production – a bit closer to that of *Vita nuova* XLII: 'a miraculous vision appeared to me, in which I saw things which made me decide to write nothing more of this blessed one until such time as I could treat of her more worthily . . . so that if it pleases Him by whom all things live, that my life lasts a few years, I hope to write of her what has never been written of any woman'. Hoffman did graduate work in Renaissance literature at Oxford and used 'The Art of Courtly Love' (the common English rendering of Andreas Capellanus's *de amore et remedio amoris*) as the title of his own first screenplay (see Tara E. McCarthy, 'Michael Hoffman: A Renaissance Dreamer', *Written By: The Magazine of the Writer's Guild of America* (May 1999). Online version www.wga.org/WrittenBy/0599/hoffman.html. Consulted 22 February 2004).

helps to anchor the film's broader allegory of democratic participation in the sphere of art by staging a Stanislavskian breakthrough, in which theatrical depth and power depend not upon class or even craft codes of performance, but on an individual's access to the sources of his own emotional life.

However, it must be said that Flute's role in the film has been a minor one to this point, and has not been tied in, as Bottom's has, to a wider set of explicit class aspirations in the erotic and artistic realms. He saves the play, but the scope of his triumph is contained, in a sense, by the film's emphasis on Bottom, whose story ends less well. In the play he is confused on stage, the charm and poise he showed with gentlewomen in the piazza early in the film and with Titania in her bower is absent – here he is the source of exactly what the mechanicals feared, as the inadvertent sexual meanings of words slip out of control, and his sword can't seem to keep its tendency to phallic metonymy under wraps. Unlike the others he gets no encouraging winks or nods from the ladies.

Yet the play is 'notably discharged' (a double letdown here; there's no real praise and no money, nothing to make good the promise of 'substantial recognition'), and Bottom must sadly settle for that. In his final sequence, he walks to his apartment alone and we see him looking out of the window as the fairy lights appear again. He glances at the golden laurel crown he wore in the forest (now a tiny ring) with rueful acceptance of its belonging to another realm. Along with his love affair with the queen of fairies, Bottom's relation to culture is in a sense reduced to a memory, a token or – to extend the film's hints that the duke's palace is a kind of museum, perhaps one that would in a later period have a gift shop – a souvenir.

MAURICE EVANS'S *RICHARD II* ON STAGE, TELEVISION AND (ALMOST) FILM

RUSSELL JACKSON

Unrealized Shakespeare films have their peculiar attraction: Max Reinhardt's *Twelfth Night*, Laurence Olivier's *Macbeth* and Michael Powell and Emeric Pressburger's *Tempest* remain tantalizing possibilities, promising plans (some reaching an advanced stage of script development) that foundered for a variety of reasons, sometimes suggesting plausible additions to the roster of plays adapted for the screen.[1] *Richard II*, though, seems an unlikely proposition for a movie, with its hero who remains unheroic until late in the day and its lack of a decisive battle to be fought or imbroglio to be untangled in the final half-hour. However, on one occasion at least a film of the play has seemed possible – or at least plausible enough to engage its proposers in a search for funds and resources.

On 21 March 1951 the *New York Times* columnist Sam Zolotow announced that 'Stage Stars Plan Shakespeare Film. Maurice Evans and Margaret Webster Working on Movie of *King Richard II*'. Evans and Webster, 'considered tops in their respective Shakespearian departments as actor and director', would 'pool their know-how' on a film that was due to begin photography ('cameras are to start clicking') in New York during the summer, and the executive producer of the project, budgeted at $1,500,000, was to be Filippo del Giudice, whose credits included (readers were reminded) Olivier's films of *Henry V* and *Hamlet* and Noël Coward's *In Which We Serve*. Webster was to fulfil the same function as Alan Dent on Olivier's films – and Evans would supervise casting and 'treatment'. Zolotow noted that 'A Shakespearian film representation without the directorial services of

Miss Webster was thought to be inconceivable by one observer.' The team would adopt 'an entirely different approach' to that of Hollywood in filming Shakespeare, and 'the screen transcription would follow the stage offering, meaning the predominant emphasis would be placed on the Bard'. More discussions were to be held, and Evans expected to be able to say more after Easter.

Zolotow's reference to 'the stage offering' harks back to the 1937 Broadway production in which this English-born actor, directed by Webster, had

---

Television programmes referred to have been viewed at the Paley Center for Media, New York City. Other copies of the 'Hallmark Hall of Fame' productions are available in the UCLA Film and Television Archive's Hallmark Collection (which has a complete run of the series) and at the Los Angeles location of the Paley Center. In the UK, preservation copies of the Hallmark Shakespeares are held in the National Film and Television Archive, but at the time of writing, no viewing copies are available there. The Paley Center and UCLA viewing material is copied from original kinescope (film) transcripts. Tapes are called up at the Paley Center only in person through the computer database: consequently, catalogue numbers are not given here. Reference is also made (as 'Evans Collection') to the box and folder numbers of the Maurice Evans Collection, held in the Billy Rose Theater Collection of the Performing Arts Division of New York Public Library, Astor, Lenox and Tilden Foundations, at Lincoln Center.

[1] On Reinhardt's *Twelfth Night*, see Russell Jackson, *Shakespeare Films in the Making. Vision, Production and Reception* (Cambridge, 2007), p. 68; on Olivier's attempts to finance *Macbeth*, Clayton Hutton, *Macbeth. The Making of the Film* (London, 1960) and Terry Coleman, *Olivier. The Authorised Biography* (London, 2005), pp. 312–13; on the Powell and Pressburger's *Tempest*, Judith Buchanan, *Shakespeare on Film* (London, 2005), pp. 157–9.

staked a decisive claim to the character in the United States. The connection, by way of Del Giudice, with Olivier's films, suggested comparisons with that actor's success in turning theatrical experience in the title roles into prestigious feature films with considerable (if not spectacular) commercial viability. The announcement may have been prompted by a report in the same paper on 13 May that Evans and Del Giudice were scouting for locations in Florida.[2] After this, the *Richard II* plans disappear from the radar. There is no reference to them in a *Times* article by Webster on 12 August on Shakespeare's persistent appeal in the new media.[3] There are innumerable ways in which a film proposal can collapse – even after expense and effort in development – and without fuller inside information it is impossible to know exactly what went wrong, or how far work had progressed on the 'treatment' of the play. The published autobiographies of Evans and Webster include no references to it, and although Del Giudice figures in the negotiations for Evans's 1960 film version of *Macbeth* directed by George Schaefer, it seems reasonable to assume that this was one of the projects that as an independent producer he kept on one of his many back burners.[4]

However, the possibility of a cinema version of one of his greatest stage successes clearly continued to attract Evans, and a fully developed script, together with a draft and notes on scheduling and costing, are in the Billy Rose Theater Collection in the Performing Arts Division of New York Public Library at Lincoln Center. The film material has an intriguingly close relationship with Evans's performance for television, broadcast live by NBC in the 'Hallmark Hall of Fame' in 1954. Although it is not clear whether the television version influenced the film script, or *vice versa*, together they reflect an important Shakespearian actor's engagement with the new media. Like Laurence Olivier and Orson Welles before him and Kenneth Branagh in subsequent decades, Evans saw film and television (and, of course, radio) as a means of reaching new and wider audiences. There was not only an element of pardonable opportunism, in that these were plays he knew intimately and

which would attract finance because of his success in them, but also a strong sense of mission. Evans wanted to bring Shakespeare to a mass audience, and expended considerable energy and resources on doing so in his theatre work. The *Richard II* productions – both planned and realized – in the 1950s show how he hoped to do this and illustrate the sometimes difficult negotiations between the desire to perform the Shakespearian material and the cultural expectations of audiences and sponsors. The projects also suggest the potential of television as a new mass medium and its stimulating but uneasy position in relation to theatre and the cinema.

MAURICE EVANS AND AMERICAN SHAKESPEARE

Maurice Evans was born in 1901 in Dorchester, and became a professional actor when he joined the company at the Festival Theatre in Cambridge in 1926. After the usual vagaries of a jobbing actor's life, he made his mark in the first production of R. C. Sherriff's *Journey's End*, then appeared in a series of roles at the Old Vic. Evans was invited to New York in 1935 to succeed Basil Rathbone as Romeo to Catherine Cornell's Juliet. His performance was praised as passionate and lyrical, especially in comparison with what John Mason Brown called the 'Kelvinator' Romeo of his predecessor.[5] After further success on Broadway, Evans put together financial support for the first of what he hoped would be a series of Shakespearian revivals. In *Richard II* he was cannily choosing a play that had not been seen in a professional production in New York for some sixty years, and in which he had appeared at the Old Vic in 1934. Evans would

2 A. H. Weiler, 'By Way of Report', *New York Times*, 13 May 1951.

3 Margaret Webster, 'Why Shakespeare Goes Right On. A producer appraises the premier playwright of Broadway, the road, movies, radio and TV', *New York Times*, 12 August 1951.

4 On the 1960 film of *Macbeth*, see Hutton, *The Making of the Film*, pp. 18–28; and Maurice Evans, *All This . . . and Evans Too! A Memoir* (Columbia, SC, 1987), pp. 264–6.

5 *New York Post*, 4 March 1937.

be seen in a role that was new to most of the audience and the critics. His commitment to New York theatre led to a distinguished theatrical career, and well into the 1950s he was regarded as a leading Shakespearian actor – but only in the United States. He remained relatively unknown in Britain, apart from his appearances in a few films and his role as a suave warlock in the popular American comedy series *Bewitched*. His Shakespearian roles on television were never shown in his native country, except for the 1960 *Macbeth*, shown there in cinemas as a feature film.

From his earliest days in New York, Evans evinced a strong sense of mission, hoping to entice a wider audience to the Shakespearian repertoire. He told the journalist Lucius Beebe that despite the management's promotion of its 56-cent gallery seats, he was disappointed that audiences for *Richard II* were dominated by the 'carriage trade' in the stalls: 'That more people of modest means aren't accustomed to going to the legitimate theatre, I think, is the fault of a whole generation of producers and actors who, time and again, have failed to give the balcony trade its money's worth.'[6] In May 1937, under the headline 'Au Revoir to Broadway', Evans declared 'I am determined to have a shot at organizing a repertory theatre in the fall of 1938.' It would only be possible if it was preceded by a nation-wide tour to 'gain for us a national as well as a local reputation', and Evans outlined an itinerary to cover the continent from the Canadian cities to New Orleans, taking in the Midwest, Texas and California.[7] Plans were announced for plays by Sheridan and Goldsmith and more Shakespeare, including the possibility of a 'full-length' *Hamlet* and at least the first part of *Henry IV*.[8]

This idealism recurred in his Shakespearian ventures during the 1940s and 1950s, but Evans accepted the necessity for star performances on Broadway and beyond. Although regarded with real affection by Webster and his fellow-actors, he had a strong sense of the actor-managerial strategies and was careful to protect his own interests. Molly S. Berenger, Webster's biographer, points out that in engaging her rather than one of the 'rising young male British directors, such as Tyrone Guthrie,

John Gielgud or Michael Redgrave', he avoided the risk of 'losing control of the production, and possibly even the leading roles'. He could also influence her work and 'control the production from centre stage', although Webster was quite capable of looking after her own artistic interests.[9] As with most of his subsequent Shakespearian work, the billing was headed 'Maurice Evans presents'.

Webster's production was considered by New York critics to be in the current 'Old Vic' style. David Ffolkes, who had designed the sets and costumes for Henry Cass's 1934 Old Vic production, was able to prepare more substantial settings, but the principle of rapid movement from scene to scene was common to both versions.[10] With its well-paced speaking, and skilful use of the semi-permanent setting of stone arches dressed as appropriate with drapes and banners, the thirty-six scenes of the performed text moved swiftly. A note in the promptbook indicates that it began at the customary New York curtain time of 8.30 pm (effectively 8.35) and ended at 11.19 pm, with two intervals of ten minutes. A forestage was built over the orchestra pit of the St James's Theatre, to allow Evans greater proximity to the audience for the major speeches – including 'Of comfort no man speak' (3.2.144–77),[11] which elicited a thunderous and prolonged round of applause on the opening night.

The text was cut lightly, except for the removal of the scenes dealing with the discovery of Aumerle's

---

[6] Lucius Beebe, 'A King that Can do no Wrong', *New York Herald Tribune*, 21 March 1937.

[7] *New York Times*, 23 May 1937.

[8] 'Admirers of Evans Hope for Return Visit' (4 March 1937); 'Broadway May See Sheridan Comedies' (5 March 1937). Gilbert championed Evans with almost embarrassing persistence: an article on 21 March was headlined 'Theater Owes Debt to Maurice Evans'.

[9] Molly S. Berenger, *Margaret Webster. A Life in the Theater* (Ann Arbor, 2004), p. 66.

[10] The Old Vic staging was generally received as 'workmanlike but uninspired' (*New Statesman and Nation*, 20 October 1934) and made much use in the open-air scenes of 'built-up platforms and cycloramic effects in the [Max] Reinhardt manner' (*Truth*, 24 October 1934).

[11] References to *Richard II* are to the Pelican Shakespeare edition, *Richard II*, ed. Frances E. Dolan (New York, 2000).

2 *Richard II*, St James's Theatre, New York, 1937. King Richard (Maurice Evans) is restrained from striking John of Gaunt (Augustin Duncan) after the accusation 'Landlord of England art thou now, not king' (2.1.113).

part in the conspiracy against Bolingbroke (5.2 and 5.3) and a drastic abbreviation of the play's final scene, so that it began with Exton's entrance and the presentation of the dead king's coffin. The fourteen lines of conversation between the Abbot of Westminster, the Bishop of Carlisle and Aumerle were omitted from the end of Act 4. The script's only transposition placed York's description of the entry of Bolingbroke into London (5.2.1–40) after 3.4, immediately preceding the arraignment of Bagot, the challenges to Aumerle and the abdication scene. (In the revised lines, Scroop became York's interlocutor.) The play was divided into three acts, with intervals after 2.2 (after the news of Bolingbroke's imminent return), and 4.1, which now concluded with Bolingbroke's announcement of his coronation (4.1.320). A procession crossed the stage between 3.4 (the gardeners' scene) and 4.1.[12]

Stage-business was functional and effective. The seriousness of the accusation regarding Gloucester's death (1.1.100) was marked by a sudden lull in the 'buzz' of the court; Mowbray turned in towards his accuser and grasped his sword, and the King rose. In 1.4 Richard was selecting jewels and judging their effect in a mirror, aided by his entourage, with whom he exchanged knowing looks in all their scenes together and to whom he addressed such remarks as 'High-stomached are they both' (1.1.18). In 2.1, Richard threatened Gaunt with his riding crop on 'Landlord of England art thou, now '(2.1.113) and was restrained by Bushy

[12] 'Average playing time' recorded in a working promptbook of the 1937 production: Evans Collection: Box 6, Folder 1. The unbound pages, with the New Temple edition pasted in, have full notes on stage movement and cues, sketches of staging.

(illustration 2). A tolling bell marked Gaunt's offstage death. In the 'abdication' scene Richard raised the crown above his head and put it on with the first 'no' in 'Ay, no; no, ay' (4.1.201) causing a sensation in the court. After the Bishop of Carlisle's intervention ('Marry, God forbid') Bolingbroke did not sit in the throne, and it remained empty upstage centre as a focus for Richard's self-dramatizing performance.

The reception was rapturous: in the *New York Times* Brooks Atkinson applauded 'one of the most thorough, illuminating and vivid productions of Shakespeare we have had in living memory' (6 February 1934). A week later, Atkinson apologized for the 'too guarded' review and elaborated on the 'insight and virility' of Webster's direction and the excellence of the production (14 February 1937). Evans received most of the superlatives: John Mason Brown proclaimed him 'the finest and most accomplished actor at the present time' in the English-speaking theatre. Arthur Pollock in the *Christian Science Monitor* applauded 'the performance of an actor blessed by nature with abundance in the matter of expressiveness', and summarized the interpretation concisely in terms that would apply equally to the actor's later performances of the role:

In the early moments of the play he is rather a foppish fellow, proud of his appearance and his graces. When, after he has exiled John of Gaunt [sic] and Henry and reaped the fruits of his distrust in the realization that Henry, his rival, has come back to overpower him, he is that same young man struck with a bitter awareness of the cost of his errors and his easy weaknesses, a man facing the fact that he must at last pay for his character by renouncing all his ambitions.[13]

The abdication of Edward VIII lent a topical dimension to the play, which several journalists commented on and which Evans admitted had contributed to its success, but he was more interested in suggesting '[a]nother factor in the play's growing popularity' was 'the extraordinary modern slant on Richard's character'. He told another journalist that '[w]hat in another age was regarded as recklessness and wilfulness is, in these days of psy-

chiatry and neurology, looked upon with greater understanding and sympathy'.[14] On 18 October 1937 *Richard II* began a 35-week tour, with occasional performances of *Henry IV, Part One*.[15] For the tour, less than subtle newspaper advertisements promised 'The Dramatic Story of the First English King to Abdicate'.[16] The performance was even thought worthy of celebration on a cigarette card (illustration 3).

Evans's next Shakespearian ventures, all involving Webster as director, were a 'complete' *Hamlet*, which opened in New York in October 1938 (136 performances in New York and on tour), a New York production of *Henry IV, Part One* (January 1939), a revival of *Richard II*, which opened in New York and toured in May and June 1940, a production of *Twelfth Night* for the Theatre Guild, with Helen Hayes as Viola (November 1940, touring until June 1941), and, on the brink of the USA's entry into the war, *Macbeth*, with Judith Anderson (131 performances, with an additional 94 performances on tour). Evans had become a naturalized citizen of the USA in 1940, and his enlistment in the army led to a series of assignments in providing entertainment for the troops, the most remarkable of which was the fast-moving 'G. I. *Hamlet*'. Directed by Evans in collaboration with 'Sgt George Schaefer' – who was to be associated with him in many subsequent Shakespearian productions – this was performed in all sorts of more or less uncomfortable and occasionally dangerous situations. It provided the basis for a New York production in 1945, which in turn informed the

---

[13] 'Maurice Evans as Richard II', *Christian Science Monitor*, 16 February 1937.

[14] Russell Rhodes, 'Maurice Evans as "Richard II"', *New York Herald Tribune*, 14 February 1937. On the 'abdication' element in the production's promotion, see Lois Potter, 'The Royal Throne of Kings and the American Armchair: Deconstructing the Hallmark *Richard II*' in *Shakespeare on Screen. Television Shakespeare: Essays in Honour of Michèle Willems*, edited by Sarah Hatchuel and Nathalie Vienne-Guerrin (Rouen, 2008), pp. 107–27.

[15] Evans, *All This*, p. 129.

[16] Undated clippings of advertisements for various touring venues, Evans Collection, Box 33, folder 10.

HIGNETT'S CIGARETTES

MAURICE EVANS

3 Maurice Evans as Richard II in the 'abdication' scene (4.1).
Cigarette card published by Hignett's Cigarettes, *c.* 1937.

118 minutes of playing time, had to be delivered in no more than seventy minutes. 'If it was worth doing at all', Evans later wrote, 'it would have to be made intrinsically entertaining.'[19] In *Macbeth* the Hecate scene and the fight between Macbeth and Young Siward were cut, and Macduff did not produce the tyrant's head at the end.[20] In *Henry IV, Part One*, by contrast, Evans persuaded Webster to add a version of the recruiting scene in Shallow's orchard (3.2) from the play's second part, to 'give Falstaff more scope'.[21]

EVANS AND TELEVISION SHAKESPEARE: THE 'HALLMARK HALL OF FAME'

It is not apparent what progress had been made in scripting and planning a film of *Richard II* when it was first announced in the summer of 1951. Meanwhile, America was experiencing what was later regarded as the 'golden age of television drama', almost all of it produced in New York. Because broadcasts were live, and (before the advent of editable videotape) could only be repeated on air by being performed again, the producers were anxious to find material, either adapted or original. By his own account, Evans had been absorbed in plans for other theatre projects and had not seriously considered the possibilities of television until the spring of 1953, when two of his associates, Mildred Freed Alberg and Tommy Shand, raised the possibility of a *Hamlet* with sponsorship from Hallmark Cards.[22] This would be based on his Broadway recreation of the 'G.I. *Hamlet*' with the costume and set designs placing it in the same 'Ruritanian' nineteenth-century court. It would capitalize on work Evans had already

script for the 1953 television *Hamlet*. An illustrated edition of the script, with photographs and an essay by Evans, appeared in 1947.[17]

A common characteristic of all these productions was a willingness (except in the 'eternity' *Hamlet*) to trim the script in the interests of clarity and narrative drive. In the 'G.I. *Hamlet*', omissions included the graveyard scene, working towards a swifter, more action-driven second part of the performance.[18] This second part, which he knew from experience of the full-length text had a potential

---

[17] On the various productions and their reception, see Evans, *All This*, pp. 140–55.

[18] Evans, *All This*, pp. 183–4.

[19] *Maurice Evans' G.I. Production of 'Hamlet' by William Shakespeare, with a Preface by Mr Evans* (Garden City, NY, 1947), pp. 15, 11.

[20] Evans, *All This*, p. 151.

[21] Evans, *All This*, p. 125.

[22] Evans, *All This*, p. 235.

done and, when he was fifty-two, would capture his own performance before he was too old to be credible as the expectancy and rose of the fair state. (In the event, some reviewers did comment on his maturity.) As has been noted, Alberg and Shand seem to have made the initial approach to NBC, but a decisive factor was the participation of Albert McCleery, an innovative producer of TV drama whose 'arena' staging of *Romeo and Juliet* in 1949 had broken with the customary imitation of theatrical staging.[23] It was originally intended that Hallmark would share sponsorship of *Hamlet* with Sheaffer Pens, but when Sheaffer withdrew, Hallmark offered to meet $100,000 of the total cost. Although NBC lost some $50,000 on the broadcast, it effectively cemented a relationship that would benefit both parties for several seasons.[24]

The genesis and development of the *Hallmark Hall of Fame* Shakespeare productions have been described by Tise Vahimagi in Luke McKernan and Olwen Terris's *Walking Shadows* (1994), but the fullest discussion of the programmes themselves is Bernice W. Kliman's 1983 article 'Maurice Evans' Shakespeare Productions', which discusses staging and technique in *Hamlet* (26 April 1953), *Richard II* (24 January 1954), *Macbeth* (28 November 1954) and *The Taming of the Shrew* (18 March 1956).[25] Kliman's survey does not include *Twelfth Night* (15 December 1957), or the 1960 film of *Macbeth* – shown in the USA on television (20 November 1960; repeated 20 October 1961) and in the UK in cinemas. The Hallmark series continued (with a shift of emphasis and channels) into the twenty-first century, with an impressive record of strongly cast dramas, and Evans appeared in plays by other dramatists – including Shaw – but there were only two more Shakespearian productions: the 20 November 1960 version of *The Tempest* (the last of the live broadcasts and the last to involve Evans) and the production of *Hamlet* adapted by John Barton and directed by Peter Wood, transmitted on 17 November 1970.[26] Colour was used from *Macbeth* onwards, though the surviving kinescope copies of that and the *Shrew* and *Twelfth Night* are in black-and-white. (Until the early 1960s most viewers – and critics – could

see the transmissions only in black-and-white.) *The Tempest* was transferred to film in colour, and later had some currency as a VHS tape.

The *Hall of Fame*, inaugurated with the commissioning of Gian Carlo Menotti's opera *Amahl and the Night Visitors* for Christmas 1951, represents a kind of series, 'anthologies', which flourished in the USA in the years between the postwar resumption of television broadcasting and the industry's turn in the late 1950s towards filmed Westerns, situation comedies and detective series. Remarkably, it survived that major change.[27] Invariably linked with the sponsor's name and sometimes identified with a particular actor or performer, anthologies presented a succession of live television dramas, each with a different cast. For the sponsor, the principal benefit was what Erik Barnouw neatly describes as 'the gratitude factor', endearing their

[23] McCleery favoured a bare studio space with simple elements of furnishing and props and pools of light to demarcate locations, allowing freedom of movement to cameras and actors: see William Hawes, *Filmed Television Drama, 1952–1958* (Jackson, NC and London, 2002), pp. 48–51.

[24] Figures from Frank Sturcken, *Live Television. The Golden Age of 1946–1958 in New York* (Jackson, NC and London, 1990), pp. 59–60, citing personal interview with McCleery and report in *Variety*.

[25] Bernice W. Kliman, 'Maurice Evans' Shakespeare Productions', in J. C. Bulman and H. R. Coursen, eds., *Shakespeare on Television. An Anthology of Essays and Reviews* (Hanover and London, 1988), 91–107. See also Kliman's study of the 1953 and 1970 *Hamlet* productions in her '*Hamlet*'. *Film, Television and Audio Performance* (Rutherford, Madison and Teaneck, 1988), pp. 117–29 and 180–7; and '"An Unseen Interpeter." Interview with George Schaefer', *Film Criticism* 7.3 (Spring 1983), 29–37.

[26] Tise Vahimagi, '"When you care enough to send the best." Televised Shakespeare and the Hallmark Hall of Fame', in Luke McKernan and Olwen Terris, eds., *Walking Shadows. Shakespeare in the National Film and Television Archive* (London, 1994). On the Hallmark Hall of Fame Collection at UCLA, see the website www.cinema.ucla.edu/collections/Profiles/hallmark.html. This includes a link to an on-line version of the publication *Hallmark Hall of Fame: the First Fifty Years* (at www.cinema.ucla.edu/hallmark/index.html).

[27] Erik Barnouw, *Tube of Plenty: The Evolution of American Television*, revised edition (New York, 1982). See also the works cited above (notes 23 and 24) by Hawes and Sturcken.

brand to the appreciative audience.[28] Drama production, like most other programming, required a triangulation between network, producing company (unless NBC, ABC or CBS themselves were providing talent and facilities) and sponsors. (There was often a fourth constituency, represented by advertising agencies such as J. Walter Thompson.) The result was a style of programme title which seemed odd – indeed, comic – to British observers even after commercial television had begun on a different footing in the UK. Such series names as 'Gulf Playhouse', 'Ford Television Theatre', 'The Revlon Mirror Theatre' and 'The United States Steel Hour Presents the Theatre Guild of the Air', to take some titles from 1952 and 1953, suggested priorities alien to British and European broadcast culture.

The playwright's name, the standing of the leading actor and the comfortable distance between the plays and modern society made Hallmark's Shakespeares a safe investment. The 1953 *Hamlet* inaugurated the series of 'specials' with high production values and generous budgets, and the dominant message was clear: this was drama from the company whose slogan was 'Hallmark – when you care enough to send the very best'. As a guarantee of quality, the first Hallmark Shakespeare productions (*Hamlet*, *Richard II* and *Macbeth*) were introduced on-screen by Sarah Churchill, whose cut-glass English accent and social credentials as Sir Winston's daughter were more valuable to the series than her very limited acting ability. The 'Hall of Fame' itself was seen as a sort of crypt where homage was done to the notable personalities whose lives were usually dramatized: in the case of Shakespeare, it was explained at the beginning of *Hamlet*, the best way to honour him was by performing his work.

The ninety-minute broadcasts were divided into two acts, and the 120-minute presentations (*Hamlet*, *Richard II* and both versions of *Macbeth*) into three, with short intervals – no doubt welcome to the actors and technicians in the frenetically live performances – filled by commercials for the sponsor's cards and gift wares. Advertising breaks and 'wraparound' presentation claimed the dignity of

history and culture for the card makers themselves: in several a leather-bound volume 'The History of Customs' or a similar album from the company's own collection of vintage cards is taken from the shelf and opened with the same reverence as the copy of the play shown to the viewer. At the conclusion of *Hamlet*, Sarah Churchill (who has had time to slip into an appropriate ball gown since her demise as Ophelia) reads the names of the principal actors from a large folio on a lectern. The commercials are linked to whatever festive occasion is impending.[29]

The tendency of Hallmark's advertising, both here and in general, was to insist on the high quality of its product ('the very best' and 'the added touch that means so much') and to find ways of associating itself with tradition, courtesy and good citizenship. 'Yes', an announcer assures us after the first act of *The Taming of the Shrew*, 'a greeting card store is a friendly place, and whenever you're there you're being thoughtful and thinking of someone else'. Film footage common to several of the advertisements shows calm, well-dressed men and women (suits for the men, tailored coats with hat and gloves for the women) making judicious choices from spacious well-stocked displays and holding them up to the camera with delight and satisfaction. It is a vision of well-mannered consumerism emblematic of the Eisenhower era. Usually there is no explicit link in this or any other case with the play being presented. One of the few attempts at this preserved in the archive copies of the programmes occurs in a break in the 1956 *Macbeth*. An announcer

---

[28] Erik Barnouw, *The Sponsor. Notes on a Modern Potentate* (New York, 1978), p. 47.

[29] Marvin Rosenberg reported that a Mother's Day card was featured after the 'closet' scene between Hamlet and his mother: there is no commercial in the kinescope/video at that point, but the final advertisement announces that 'Hallmark is bringing back a charming old custom' by providing cards that will help to teach children 'the real meaning of May Day'. ('Shakespeare on TV: an Optimistic Survey', *Quarterly of Film, Radio and Television*, 9.2 (Winter 1954), 166–74; 168n.) In the USA Mother's Day is the second Sunday in May. Rosenberg was, after all, making notes on a live broadcast.

informs us that 'Macbeth was written in 1605, and at just about that time a custom equally lasting and enriching was being born across the channel [sic] in Germany.' After a shot of a young woman in a headscarf and a dirndl lighting candles on a wreath and attaching bible verses to it, we are told that this innovation, in its modern (and presumably less combustible) form as the 'Advent Calendar' has been brought to America by Hallmark. Generally speaking, though, in the 'gift' culture fostered by Hallmark, there is no need to make such crude connections: the plays are offered with the kind of generosity on the sponsor's part that the greetings cards themselves express. The company's president, Joyce C. Hall, insisted that 'good taste is good business', and responded to NBC's anxieties about low ratings for some programmes by pointing out that as a sponsor he would 'rather have 8 million people for me than 28 million against'.[30] At considerable cost, Hall authorized the distribution of 16 mm film copies of the kinescopes of *Richard II* and *Macbeth* to educational institutions, and underwrote a modest amount of printed educational material.[31]

Nevertheless, the accumulation of cultural capital should not deflect attention from the intelligence and innovation expended on the performances by producers, directors and actors. Although McCleery's preference for 'arena' staging was to some extent compromised by the imperative (from Evans) for conventional 'realistic' settings for *Hamlet*, *Richard II* and *Macbeth*, the productions keep the action fluid, establish fictional time and space by deft camera placing and a versatile 'floor plan' (especially necessary before editable videotape), and link sequences by skilful use of close-ups on gestures, objects or the back of an actor to facilitate a shift to another camera.[32] At the same time, the two-hour slot allowed Evans to present plays in a less brutally condensed form than that required by the one hour (effectively fifty or fifty-five minutes) enjoined on other series. Given that directors of the shorter programmes had to adapt ruthlessly, it is arguable that they felt freer to try out new ideas in staging: either in shifting the period of the play, or by using frankly artificial non-naturalistic presenters and narrators. The

bold modern-dress *Julius Caesar* directed by Worthington Miner in 1949 is a notable example of the former strategy and owed much to Orson Welles's 1937 Mercury Theatre production. Delbert Mann's 1953 Philco Television Theater *Othello*, played in nineteenth-century dress on a simple unit set and located entirely in Cyprus and with Montano as narrator, shows the potential of the 'presentational' element in overcoming restrictions of time and budget. (It also provides the intriguing experience of Walter Matthau as Iago.)[33] Some sequences in Evans and Schaefer's *Richard II* and *Macbeth* suggest inadequately budgeted movies, compromising the genuine skill with which cameras are placed, spatial and temporal shifts achieved and actors' detailed work is favoured. The 'studio realism' was abandoned in the stylized designs and presentation of *The Taming of the Shrew*, *Twelfth Night* and *The Tempest*.

RICHARD II: THE TELEPLAY

Salient aspects of the Hallmark Hall of Fame *Richard II* have been described in essays by Bernice Kliman and Lois Potter.[34] Evans's mellifluous

30 Cecil Smith, 'Hall of Fame's Famous Hall', *New York Times*, 22 October 1975. The occasion was a Television Academy luncheon honouring Hall.
31 Printed material included a special issue of *Listenables and Lookables* ('bringing information about network radio and video programmes to students, teachers and public service organizations') and a 'thank you' booklet with production photographs, delivered to Hallmark dealers. (Copies in Evans Collection.)
32 Kliman ('Maurice Evans' Shakespeare Productions') gives a good account of the editing techniques and other staging devices.
33 Worthington Miner's 1949 *Julius Caesar* was hailed by Jack Gould in the *New York Times* (13 March 1949) as 'the most exciting television yet seen on the home screen'. A kinescope of the production can be seen at the Paley Center. A tape of approximately half of Delbert Mann's 'Television Playhouse' *Othello* is also held at the Paley Center.
34 See Kliman, Maurice Evans's 'Shakespeare Productions', and Potter, 'The Royal Throne of Kings'. *Richard II* was broadcast on Sunday evening, 24 January 1954, from 4 to 6 pm. A full list of acting and technical credits will be found in the on-line catalogue of the UCLA Film and Television

delivery and elegant gestures reflect the period of his first successes and were already beginning to seem old-fashioned in the mid 1950s, but despite this – and his maturity – his performance has impressive simplicity, directness and musicality. With the exception of the excellent John of Gaunt (Frederic Worlock) and Gardener (Whitford Kane) most of the other performances are more or less adequate, although Bolingbroke (Kent Smith) is excessively stolid and the Queen (Sarah Churchill) has little beyond gentility to recommend her. The interiors (Westminster Hall, Ely House, the prison) are more effective and convincing than the exteriors, though the castle walls are indeed as impressive as NBC promised. As a presentation of a history play, the production seems constrained by adherence to 'studio realism', although at times it is as inventive and resourceful as the BBC's more radical *Age of Kings* (1960). Rather than focus on the production itself it seems appropriate for present purposes to examine its reception, which suggests the critical climate in which it was developed, and reflects the efforts of critics and programme-makers to negotiate between the imperatives of film and television technique.

The reception of *Richard II* – like that of *Hamlet* and the subsequent television *Macbeth* – included a good deal of comment on the relationship between the stage, television and the cinema. In the run-up to the broadcast much was made of the new facilities made available by NBC. The *Baltimore Sun*, reporting that Schaefer and Evans both made their own cuts of the play, then compared notes, was one of several papers to follow NBC press releases in drawing attention to the corporation's use of a converted film studio at 1268, E14th Street in Brooklyn (two blocks from the Brighton Beach subway), equipping it with a 60 ft wide screen (that is, a cyclorama) and laying a new concrete floor at cost of $53,000. Another paper relayed NBC's claim that the set 'was believed the largest ever made for a live dramatic program'.[35] After the broadcast, many critical responses included an element of celebration: this was a sign of the power of television, and the scale of the undertaking commanded respect. Comparison with the usual television fare

was in its favour: 'Watching this show is like gorging on a thick, juicy steak after days of bread-and-water starvation.'[36]

The medium itself was congratulated in the *New York World Telegram and Sun* by Harriet Van Horne, for whom Richard 'came back to life on television yesterday with the intimacy and incisiveness peculiar to the medium'. She admitted that 'true, we missed a certain vastness of view that comes across in the theater, and with it the pageantry and the pomp. But the all-seeing eye of TV enhanced the warmth and charm of King Richard, making us more tolerant of his folly.'[37] Ruse Dorin, in the New York *Telegraph*, considered the limitations were outweighed by other technical virtues, and the 'superb, daring use of the camera' in the scene at Berkeley Castle 'more than made up' for the moments when 'things seemed a little crowded'. The San Francisco *Chronicle*'s reviewer noted that 'The varied groupings of threes or fours, in two and three depths of focus, was proof that the director, the producer and the actor fully understood the intimate medium of TV without resorting to a tiresome series of close-ups and long-shots.'[38]

More serious reservations about the mimicking of cinematic production values were expressed by George Freedley in the New York *Morning Telegraph*, who complained that 'the production was

---

Archive. In addition to Evans the principal actors were: Kent Smith (Bolingbroke), Sarah Churchill (the Queen), Frederic Worlock (John of Gaunt), Bruce Gordon (Thomas Mowbray), Morton Da Costa (Aumerle), Richard Purdy (Duke of York), Louis Hector (Northumberland), Jonathan Harris (Exton), Ralph Clanton (Bishop of Carlisle), Whitford Kane (the gardener). Technical and production credits: director, George Schaefer; original music by Herbert Menges, conducted by William Brooks, directed by Jules Seidman; settings designed by Richard Sylbert; costumes supervised by Noel Taylor; associate producers, Emmett Rogers and Mildred Freed Alberg.

35 'Final Touch Put on *King Richard*', *Baltimore Sun*, 17 January 1954 (Donald Kirkley); *Boston Herald*, 25 January 1954 (William Buchanan).

36 *San Francisco Examiner*, 27 January 1954 (Dwight Newton).

37 *New York World Telegram and Sun*, 25 January 1954.

38 *New York Telegraph* and *San Francisco Chronicle*, 26 January 1954.

too cluttered and too "busy" which made the telecast look like a grade B film except in Mr Evans' solo speeches and his scenes with Kent Smith'.[39] Jack Gould's initial review in the *New York Times* observed that Evans had learned from his experience on the 1953 *Hamlet*, where (as the actor himself admitted) he tended to over-project: 'In an awareness of the medium's intimacy, his voice was carefully modulated for the living room's requirements and his gestures carefully disciplined.' Gould felt, though, that in *Richard II* 'the pursuit of tricky camera angles intruded on the meaning of the play'. He developed this argument in a subsequent article, with the headline 'Scenery and Props May Defeat Realism and Serve to Obscure the Play'. The production, fine in many ways, 'sacrificed added power because of its frequent preoccupation with effect rather than substance'. He objected to the shots across a flickering fireplace, the glimpses of Richard in the mirror during the 'abdication', and the deployment of horses: 'Such flashy De Mille-isms may be fun to do but they lose their purpose and point if they bewitch the eye at the price of the ear's understanding.' This was part of Gould's ongoing campaign to define the boundaries of television drama, together with an assessment of the medium in terms of its audience's expectations. The self-conscious techniques and would-be 'studio realism' of *Richard II* did it no favours, because 'for TV's mass following the characters in the Bard's works need not be figures on stage but living humans seen in the same atmosphere of intimacy as an Arthur Godfrey or a Lucille Ball'.[40]

In the trade press, *Variety* applauded the scale of the sets, 'which had a dimension that not only hurdled the more restrictive scope of a legit [that is, theatre] performance, but allowed for a continuing, uninterrupted flow of scenes'. It also noted a distinction between the tendency on stage and in films 'in the past decade' to 'modernize the Bard's works, either by set, dress or verbal projection', and praised Evans for clinging to the 'lyrical, melodramatic approach'. In the broadcasting magazine *CUE*, Philip Minoff complained that the play was 'dull, repetitive, far-fetched, postured, unconvincing and static', and made an interesting

comparison with a popular police series: '*Dragnet* is farcical because all its characters speak in the same low-keyed monotone. *Richard II* was tiresome for exactly the opposite reason. Very few in the large cast knew how, or bothered to throw away lines.'[41]

On balance, however, for every critic who objected to real horses, flickering fires and tricky shots in mirrors, there was another who appreciated the careful staging to the camera and the sense in some scenes of scale and depth, despite the limitations of the medium. In correspondence after the event, Evans and McCleery discussed the lessons to be learned from a viewing of the kinescope recording. On 3 February Evans wrote:

One position I feel still has to be tackled in any future Shakespearian telecast; namely, the desirability of coming closer to the main characters without chopping up the verse. I'm going to do some detailed homework on this point during the next few months and hope to come up with a solution . . .

One problem with the large sets had been the general wash of strong light needed to allow the three cameras mobility. McCleery emphasized the importance for any future production of 'cameo technique', keeping tight focus and concentration in lighting on figures rather than on the background:

Never have I been more convinced that my early recommendation to do Shakespeare in a modified form of the cameo technique is correct. Compare, for instance, the strength of the first page of the LIFE magazine spread with the rather flat, pedantic and undramatic shots that follow it. This is a black and white medium and black should be used in great masses to create dramatic contrasts that heighten and aid the story, rather than emphasizing the confused detail of would-be realism. It would still be

---

[39] *Morning Telegraph*, 3 January 1954. Perhaps inspired by the presence of Lightborn's lines, Freedley suggested that the $175,000 could have been used to present *Edward II*.

[40] *New York Times*, 25 and 31 January 1954.

[41] *Variety*, 27 January 1954; *CUE*, 6 February 1954 ('*Richard II* Gets a Handsome but Dull Presentation').

possible to have pomp and pageantry, height and distance without building great lumps of scenery.[42]

To some extent this advice was followed in *Macbeth*, which was broadcast in colour – Evans had rejected this in planning *Richard II* – and where the predominance of night scenes may have marshalled Evans and Schaefer the way that they were going. There, unfortunately, the 'studio realism' let them down badly in the final sequence, where the assault on Macbeth's castle seems to be achieved by a mere handful of troops armed with an unconvincing battering ram. (By comparison, *Monty Python and the Holy Grail* is truly epic.) The 'arena' staging of *The Taming of the Shrew* and the fanciful, Watteauesque *Twelfth Night* broke decisively with this kind of would-be cinematic effect, but the 1960 film of *Macbeth*, unsurprisingly, reverts to it. Evans and McCleery were not the only professionals engaged in assessing the lessons to be learned from *Richard II*. In London the *Daily Mail* reported that NBC had sent a copy for BBC executives to view:

The Americans use more cameras than we do. Some scenes are breathtaking. Long shots from an immense height wrung moans of anguish from our producers. They are still waiting for the equipment . . . At a cost of £2,500, with better actors in the subsidiary roles, the BBC could do as-near-as-makes-no-matter likewise.

As usual, the contrast with sponsored commercial television – which would not arrive in Britain for another two years – was a talking point, and the paper headlined the article: 'Lime Grove sees How the Enemy Does It. But Could Britain Have £60,000 Commercials?'[43]

RICHARD II: THE FILM SCRIPT

The relationship between Evans's television production and the script for a proposed film is not clear: it is entirely possible that the latter was prepared after the broadcast, and does not represent the project announced in 1951. The draft of the film script with accompanying production documents arrived in New York Public Library in 1989 as the gift of Harry Horner, who appears to have been designated as director. Two other copies of the script itself, evidently fair copies made from this draft, are in the Maurice Evans papers. The film and television scripts correspond at several points in much the same way as the 1954 television and 1960 film versions of *Macbeth*, both directed by George Schaefer, but neither he nor Webster is credited in any of the *Richard II* film material. Horner directed television drama – but none of the Hallmark specials – during the 1950s, then returned to his original metier as production designer. It is possible that his expertise produced the detailed breakdowns of casting and set requirements that accompany the script donated attached to his name.[44]

In any case, the adaptation of the play's text and the proposed directorial strategies in the film script correspond to those of the television version in ways that reflect the close relationship between television drama and the cinema. As might be expected, the film script 'opens out' the play more than would be possible in the medium of live, studio-bound television, and (like the 1960 *Macbeth*) takes advantage of the cinema's opportunities for larger casts and greater flexibility in staging and film editing. It is difficult not to read the film script as an elaboration on the television version, but we cannot be certain whether in comparing the two we are discovering evidence of the writer's 'reduction' of ideas to the format required for the smaller screen in the living-room, or of television ideas being expanded for the more expansive medium of cinema. In either case, the documents suggest the close relationship between the techniques of effective 'studio realism' in both media.

Evans's television production had opened with a prologue using film footage of the 1953 coronation

[42] Evans Collection, Box 33, Folder 8: Evans to McCleery, 3 February 1954; McCleery to Evans, 8 February 1954; *LIFE*, 8 February 1954.

[43] *Daily Mail*, 3 April 1954.

[44] On Horner's career, see International Movie Database: http://uk.imdb.co/name/nm0395105 (accessed 20 November 2007).

to introduce the story of a very different monarch and a different concept of 'the crown'. One suspects that, as in the opening of Olivier's *Richard III*, some explanatory information was thought necessary for citizens of the American republic – perhaps more than for British subjects of the Queen. A warm, authoritative (and male) voice-over describes the scene:

The pealing of joyous bells. The cheers of a mighty multitude – flags flying and all the world watching. As once again the gilded coach jogs through the teeming throngs, down over the time-honoured approach to Westminster Abbey. [Cut to interior of Abbey] Then in solemn pomp and splendour, as England's new monarch advances towards the ancient throne, a hush falls upon Westminster Abbey almost as though her loyal subjects were endeavouring to share their young Queen's thoughts. Thoughts of the lands and of the peoples over whom she would now rule. In the age of England's other Queen Elizabeth there lived a poet who expressed those thoughts in shining verse.[45]

Lines from John of Gaunt's speech in 2.1 – 'This royal throne of kings . . . This earth, this realm, this England' – are spoken as the coronation anthem 'I was glad' is heard in the background. After a close-up on the royal regalia as they are seen in the 1953 coronation broadcast, the voice-over continues: 'The Crown, now chiefly a symbol of dedication to duty was in other times believed to confer divine right upon the wearer.' After dwelling on the moment when the crown is placed on the young queen's head, the screen fades out to a parchment headed 'Instrument of Abdication' and the commentary announces the play's subject:

One of England's monarchs who lies entombed within this same abbey brought about his own downfall by thinking that kingship made him unassailable. Turn back the pages of history to the fourteenth century and with William Shakespeare for author let us see how one of England's rulers had to lose his crown so that he might learn to rule himself.

With a 'live orchestra trumpet flourish' (as the script describes it), the screen is filled by the first image of the production proper: a high shot looking down onto nobles assembling in Westminster Hall,

its angle and elevation recalling the camera placement from the 1953 coronation footage.

The film script opens with a simpler 'prologue' in which a 'model shot' of Westminster Abbey is followed by the image of Richard's tomb. Pages of a 'missal' on a lectern are turned to reveal a title-page, 'The Tragedie of King Richard the Second', and an illuminated representation of what is to be the first scene, 'the lists at Coventry'. Beneath the illustration we read 'The King commanded that two of the hostile nobles should be brought forth before his presence that he might hear what they would say' (Prologue, shot x).[46] This dissolves to a shot of the two combatants 'warming up their horses for a tilting tournament'.

The opening scene of the main narrative conflates the play's first and third scenes, so that matters seem already to have progressed to the trial by combat despite the inclusion in the first pages of elements of the accusations in 1.1. Richard shows little regard for the seriousness of the occasion, and is seen 'drinking with his companions' as Mowbray declares himself 'a loyal, just and upright

---

45 Quoted from the broadcast narration, which differs from the scripts in the Evans Collection. Box 17 has a 'Revised, Final' script, bound with a copy of the *Hamlet* script. Box 6, Folder 2 has a working copy accompanied by production documents, including props lists, rehearsal schedules and a timetable for the day of broadcast. There were twenty-eight actors and twelve extras.

46 Citations refer to scene/shot numbers in two of the identical fair copies of the screenplay in the Evans Collection, Box 6, Folders 3 and 4: 'William Shakespeare's / King Richard the Second. / As Adapted for Motion Pictures.' These are carbons of 91 double spaced text pages (plus title and cast list) on copy paper, and include 291 scenes/shots. In the prologues shots are given small roman numerals. Another version, apparently the source of these copies, is at NYPL, CTR file no. 1355. Its title-page identifies this as '*Richard II*. Treatment for a motion picture by Maurice Evans. Film Project, to be directed by Harry Horner.' The draft 68-page typescript is in single spacing, with some alterations by cutting and pasting, which the Evans Collection scripts adopt. There are 321 scenes/shots. Other documents in this file include: a breakdown of action into fifteen sets, with note of pages and scene to be filmed in them; a draft schedule for forty-eight days, plus one week each for process shots and second unit work.

4 *King Richard II*, Hallmark Hall of Fame, NBC television 1954. The opening scene. This view from a gallery shows only one of the cameras – at least two – used for this sequence: a second is out of sight to the right of the photograph, between the pillars and the microphone boom.

gentleman', but the mention of Gloucester's death clearly angers him (he 'rises') and when Green hands Richard a scroll ('Draw near / And list what with our council we have done') the implication is that, unless alternative 'scrolls' had been prepared, he had already made up his mind to banish them both. Much use is made of horses, which are in short supply – probably only one, in fact

– in the television production. Richard and his entourage arrive on horseback, and leave 'cantering' towards the 'exit', and the crowd of onlookers shows its displeasure by a 'marked contrast to the enthusiasm with which he was greeted . . . on his arrival' (scene 78). When Bolingbroke rides away, 'a woman presses a posy into the hand of the banished Lord'. (On television we see nothing of this

49

kind, and there are none of the film script's other reminders of the common people's feelings.) The moment is witnessed by the departing king and queen.

The transition to the next scene is made by way of neat symbolic device:

On to what at first appears to be a tapestry, a crown is bowled on its side and becomes a receptacle into which gold coins are being pitched. A hand reaches into [the] picture and scoops up the coins. Now we see that the crown is actually resting on a patterned carpet. We DRAW BACK to a MED. LONG SHOT of Richard and Bagot engaged in this game of chance.   (scene 81)

After the brief scene of Bolingbroke's leave-taking from Aumerle and Gaunt at the 'city gates' we return to the 'king's apartments'. The game has ended and Green is offering papers for the king to sign when Aumerle brings news of Bolingbroke's departure. The next sequence shows Bolingbroke embarking on a ship: as Gaunt waves farewell to him we dissolve to a shot of the old man 'standing on the parapet of a castle (One of the Cinque Ports)' (scenes 87–8, 89). Over a close-up of Bolingbroke on board the vessel, Gaunt's voice is heard off-screen, and a series of 'panorama shots' accompanies his speech until on 'less happier lands' the camera comes round to a close-up on the speaker. At the end of the speech (at line 66) 'physically shaken by the effort of his denunciation', Gaunt begins to descend a staircase, but 'staggers at the foot of steps and is assisted by an attendant'. An exterior shot in which Bushy is handed a letter by a monk, is followed by Gaunt's conversation with York (a rearrangement of the remaining lines of the scene). We return to Richard's apartments where he receives the news of Gaunt's illness: the queen protests at his levity ('My loving Lord') when Richard hopes that they may arrive too late (scenes 95–100). In his exasperation at Gaunt's reproof, Richard threatens him (as Evans had done on stage) with his riding crop but is restrained by Bushy (scene 106). After Gaunt's exit he 'throws himself petulantly into a chair' and after the brief moment of piety in response to the news of Gaunt's

death, on 'so much for that' he 'begins to examine the plate and other valuables set out in the hall' (scene 114).

The reordering of lines in the play's first scenes is more complex in the film script, but much corresponds to the television version – the king's levity and opportunism, his threat of violence against Gaunt and changes in the order of scenes so that Bolingbroke's departure could be shown. On television, Gaunt's farewell to his son takes place at a quayside and the scene ends with the substantial (but not wholly convincing) ship sliding off to the right as Bolingbroke waves from the stern.

The film script moves to a series of shots of 'troops on the march' as Richard sets off for Ireland: 'banners, drums, populace showing disapproval'. Priests bless the ships and the troops as they embark, as the queen and her attendants watch – but covertly members of the 'Northumberland faction' are also watching, and as the sequence ends we see them steal away. (There is no equivalent of this in the television version.) The scene in the garden of 'The Queen's Palace at Windsor' (scenes 112–13) begins with the first 8 lines of 3.4. Bushy, motioning the gardeners to retreat to a discreet distance, informs the queen of Bolingbroke's return. The scene is interrupted by shots showing a 'proclamation of taxes being affixed to a notice board' (scenes 123–4) and 'Ross and Willoughby beside their tethered horses' (scene 125) to establish the rebels' advance. Back in the garden, the impact of the news is felt and the scene there ends with Bushy, Bagot and Green making their way out of the garden gate and into a street where they mount their horses (scenes 126–8).

On television a similar order of events is indicated with a brief interpolated scene showing Bolingbroke's meeting with Northumberland and Hotspur. The queen and her ladies, together with Aumerle and a harpist, are trying to find some distraction. This short scene combines the opening 8 lines of the play's 2.2, augmented with seventeen of the first twenty-three lines of 3.4 ('What sport shall we devise here in this garden . . . ?'), before reverting to 2.2.38–40. The queen plucks a rose from a trellis close to the camera ("Tis nameless woe, I wot') and the gentle flute melody gives way to martial brass as the screen fades to Bolingbroke being greeted by Northumberland and Hotspur on his arrival in England, using lines from 2.3 (59–67, 21 and 41–50.): 'Welcome my Lords. I wot your love pursues / A banished traitor'. Returning to the garden by way of a fade to the rose in the queen's hands, the television production now moves to Bushy's lines of comfort – hopes dashed immediately by Green's arrival with news of Bolingbroke's return (lines 41 etc.). After a shortened version of the dialogue with York, omitting references to the Duchess of Gloucester, the scene concludes with a close-up on the clasped hands of Bushy, Bagot and Green as they decide on their courses of action.

In the film script, after the departure of Bushy, Bagot and Green a series of scenes (scenes 129–35) shows Bolingbroke's troops on the march, and 'peasants . . . throwing down their farm implements and falling in behind the column of soldiers'. By way of a 'process shot – wilds of Gloucestershire' the rebels arrive at Berkeley Castle, and in a scene in Bolingbroke's tent Bolingbroke argues his case to York: to illustrate his claim that he 'come[s] for Lancaster', Bolingbroke 'points to the emblem on his shield and banner which we saw in the prologue' (scene 135).

At this point the film moves to a scene (scene 137) in a 'Courtyard before Justice Shallow's House – Gloucestershire' and interpolates the 'recruiting scene' from *Henry IV, Part Two* that Evans had added in his stage production of *Henry IV, Part One*. (He may have expected to play Falstaff as well as Richard.) After this, the script returns by way of a close shot of a 'missal' with an illumination of ships at sea to a 'storm sequence' (scenes 137–8) representing the king's 'tossing' on the sea on the way back from Ireland. In a 'camp in Wales' the Welsh soldiers ('shadowy figures') are throwing their weapons down on a pile and 'slink[ing] away into the darkness' as they desert Richard – 'it is raining heavily' and the dialogue between Salisbury and the Welsh captain takes place at night 'beneath

a windswept tree'. Salisbury watches the king's ships on the horizon and mounts his horse and gallops away (scenes 140–2). This sequence of events is omitted from the television version, which moves directly to Richard's return.

On film more is made of the manner of his arrival. After shots of Richard in a 'long-boat' looking towards the shore, and Salisbury 'riding hard', we find Richard disembarking, 'touch[ing] the sand with his hand' to greet it. As Richard enters the castle, the reaction of the common soldiers is once again registered: 'FADE as King and Party move towards the castle gates. As the royal standard is run up on the castle tower, the soldiers outside the castle register disgust' (scene 151). After a long shot of the rebels marching along a 'coastal road' (scenes 152–3), Salisbury arrives outside the castle gate. From now on, darkness begins to fall, so that by the time Scroop arrives at the 'bivouac of bedraggled-looking troops' the sky is clouded and Richard is sitting by a fire. Richard is sitting beside Aumerle when he begins the 'For God's sake let us sit upon the ground', and – as if in imitation of Henry's meditation on the eve of Agincourt in Olivier's *Henry V* – the camera moves slowly in on him and then retreats at the end of the speech. (A similar camera movement is used for the television version.) By the end of the scene night has fallen and 'the surf pounds' in the background: 'A high wind creates a sense of desolation' and the scene fades out (scene 172). On television there is no corresponding suggestion of fading light and eventual nightfall, but the camera's relationship with the king is similar, including a move in towards him during his speech.

The ensuing scene (scenes 173–206), with the rebels' arrival in 'a clearing before Berkeley castle' – like the television version, the film omits all references to Flint – makes careful use of camera positions and angles to create a sense of spatial relationships and a pattern of dominance and subservience. A crane is specified to allow views down from and across the king's position on the battlements and to relate this to the 'real' political dominance of Northumberland. A long shot

5 *King Richard II*, Hallmark Hall of Fame, NBC television 1954. Camera rehearsal on the set for Berkeley Castle. The camera on the battlements is pointed at a shirt-sleeved technician standing in one of the king's positions: further cameras on the studio floor (which was more extensive than this foreshortened perspective suggests) included one behind the castle gates and another in the area behind the microphone boom to the right.

establishes the king's presence on the ramparts from Bolingbroke's point of view, and by the end of York's 'stain so fair a show' the camera 'has craned to behind the king'. A crane shot (scene 178) then looks down towards the rebels from above, 'hold[ing] the back of King Richard's crowned head big in foreground'. At 'duty to our presence' the camera 'swings round on the King' and on Richard's 'Yet know' we switch from this to a long shot 'from Northumberland's eyeline'(scene 180), before a medium close-up on Richard shows him looking down towards Northumberland and

answering his gaze as he speaks 'He is come to open' (scene 181). The same fluidity is maintained in the rest of the scene: the camera shows Richard in close-up as he sinks on a bench in an embrasure in the battlements, and then shoots over his shoulder to see Bolingbroke arrive and Northumberland move forward below (scene 186). At first Richard is seen from below as he responds to the instruction that he is waited for 'in the base court', but beginning with the line 'Wanting the manage of unruly jades' the 'Camera cranes slowly up to MEDIUM CLOSE on Richard', then while he descends (off-screen) a shot shows the lowering of the royal standard. The drawbridge is lowered and the portcullis is raised. After accepting that he must go to London, Richard mounts his horse and rides slowly off, while 'banners are lowered to the ground in solemn salute', and the scene ends with Bolingbroke and Northumberland exchanging 'looks of satisfaction'.

The television broadcast uses similar camera placements to suggest spatial relationships (necessarily more problematic even in a large studio) and the relative strength of the characters. For example, when Richard enters above on the castle walls he is seen first in a medium shot from the floor, with Northumberland still on horseback in the foreground, then in profile with a close-up from a camera on the battlements. 'What must the king do now' is seen from below. Later, as he turns to Aumerle with 'We do debase ourselves, cousin, do we not . . . ?' (line 127), Richard moves away from the edge of the battlements and sinks onto a bench against the upper wall with 'O God!' He returns to look down at Northumberland (who has dismounted), and as the king sinks to a seated position by the battlements we see Northumberland below with Richard's shoulder in the right foreground. During the following lines the cameraman racks focus to bring Northumberland and Richard alternately into sharper focus as appropriate. For 'Down, down I come' the camera on the battlements follows Richard as he moves to a door to make his off-screen descent.[47] At the end of the scene a slow march on brass instruments follows as Richard makes his exit towards and (it seems) under the camera, Bolingbroke follows on horseback. This marks the end of the first act of the television broadcast.

In the film, 'Panoramic shots of bells' introduce a montage: 'Ringing in belfries, cheering crowds, banners, cannonades, general rejoicing'. Much of York's speech describing the event (5.2.7–40) is used as voice-over as Bolingbroke is seen riding through the streets, followed by Richard 'in a cart' (scenes 207–9). In Westminster Hall Bolingbroke sentences Bushy and Green, then York announces Richard, who enters preceded by pages bearing the crown and the sceptre on cushions. When Richard speaks 'God save the king!' he addresses the empty throne (which Bolingbroke has not occupied after Carlisle's intervention), then swings round to confront the Lords with 'Will no man say "amen"?' As in the 1937 stage performance, Richard places the crown on his head with the second 'Aye', then he 'advances on the Lords flanking the hall' with 'Nay, all of you', singling out the clergy with 'Sour Pilates are you all.' Camera movements are as emphatic as the physical staging: Northumberland moves in towards him into a close two-shot to insist on Richard's signing the paper (scene 236), and when Richard dashes the mirror to the floor there is a 'PAN SHOT to Richard's reflection in broken mirror' (scene 245).

Much in this corresponds closely to the television production's staging and camera direction. The final scene of the play's third act is cut – lines of the Gardeners' dialogue will be used later – and after a commercial break pealing bells introduce the third act of the production, which begins in Westminster Hall with the abdication scene: the dispute between Aumerle and his accusers (lines 2–106) is omitted, and Bolingbroke condemns Bagot using lines from 3.1. In the scene's opening shot the television camera looks down on the barons as they pay homage to Bolingbroke – recalling the production's first moments. Bolingbroke is seated to one side of the throne, which is as yet unoccupied. When Richard enters, preceded by pages bearing the royal regalia on cushions, the courtiers then turn away from him. Richard goes up towards Bolingbroke, then turns and comes back to occupy the centre of the screen. His rebuke to the assembled lords (line 168: 'Were they not mine?') is contemptuous, and throughout he makes much use of the flowing robe and 'false' sleeves attached to it, his gestures becoming ever more histrionic as the emotional atmosphere intensifies. In what follows, Richard dominates the screen.

---

[47] Evans claims that this was facilitated by the use of a fireman's pole, but a photograph published in *LIFE* (8 February 1954) shows a more dignified descent by ladder.

On 'Here cousin, seize the crown', he takes off the crown and thrusts it in Bolingbroke's face. Bolingbroke, standing on the dais of his chair, looms above Richard. On 'ay, no' Richard sweeps towards the empty throne and there is a gasp from the lords as he raises the crown, puts it on and swings round to address Bolingbroke with 'Now mark me how I will undo myself.' Richard is framed by the pages standing on either side of him, and the camera is set at a low angle so that he occupies the centre of the screen. When the mirror is brought Richard sits on the floor, holding it so that the camera, looking over his shoulder, can see his reflection and then follow as he shifts the mirror to his left hand before flinging it to the ground.

Like the television version, the film follows the abdication with a brief scene in the 'Garden of the Queen's residence at the Tower of London' (scenes 259–62). In the film there is a dissolve to 'a drawbridge over the moat' and Northumberland and Hotspur arrive on horseback, escorting Richard. (In the television version Hotspur is not seen after the scenes at Berkeley Castle.) In the film the image of Richard's face reflected in the broken mirror is followed through: when Richard asks the queen to tell his story 'in winter's tedious nights', the camera 'focuses on reflection of King and Queen in the water of the moat'. Richard moves towards the 'tumbril-like cart which we saw before the deposition' and the queen tries to follow him, but Northumberland bars her way. The scene fades out as the procession moves off, 'reflected in moat' (scene 272). We fade in on 'a small stream' which is in fact 'a drainage conduit' in Richard's dungeon, and he speaks 'I have been studying how I may compare' to his reflection. At 'dies in its pride', he looks through the barred window and we see a gibbet beyond it, but he turns back to 'TRICK shot, of distorted images reflected in stream' for 'sometimes I am a king'. The speech breaks off after 'till he be eased / With being nothing' (lines 40–1).

Film and television versions share the same arrangement of scenes here, although on television there is no equivalent of the reflections. Common to both is an interpolated scene in which Bolingbroke explicitly commissions Richard's murder from Exton:

BOLINGBROKE
The Commons now begin to pity him
Have I no friend will rid me of this living fear?
EXTON
Meaning the King at Pomfret?
BOLINGBROKE
Exton, I would thou wert the man
That would divorce this terror from my heart.
EXTON
Am I not resolved?
BOLINGBROKE
And hast thou cast how to accomplish it?
EXTON
You shall not need to give instructions . . .

Exton continues with Lightborn's lines from Marlowe's *Edward II*, boasting of his expertise as a killer: 'I learned in Naples'.[48] We return to the dungeon: the lines on music and keeping time (lines 41–66) are cut, and Richard receives a brief visit from the groom who tells him of Bolingbroke's entry into London on 'roan Barbary' before being sent away by the keeper. After the spirited fight with his would-be assassins, Richard is about to make his escape through the open door when Exton stabs him. The final scene begins at line 30 of 5.6 as Exton delivers the coffin. The king insists 'I hate the murderer, love him murdered', but does

---

48 Lightborn's lines (and Mortimer's question) are adapted from *Edward II*, 5.4.29–40:

LIGHTBORN
You shall not need to give instructions,
'Tis not the first time I have killed a man.
I learned in Naples how to poison flowers,
To strangle with a lawn thrust through the throat,
To pierce the wind-pipe with a needle's point,
Or whilst one is asleep, to take a quill
And blow a little powder in his ears,
Or open his mouth, and pour quick silver down,
But yet I have a braver way then these.
MORTIMER
What's that?
LIGHTBORN
Nay, you shall pardon me, none shall know my tricks.

not disown and banish the murderer ('the guilt of conscience take thou for thy labour' (lines 41–4)) or vow a pilgrimage to the Holy Land 'To wash this blood off from my guilty hand' (lines 49–50). A note suggests a possible return to the images of the Prologue, but this is not included in the script. The television version ends strongly: the final shot is accompanied by organ music and as Bolingbroke comes into the foreground, the camera rises to look down onto the bier, which is raised and procession begins. To a solemn brass march it passes below the camera until the head is close up, and its position is held as the music rises to a final climax.

HALLMARK AND THE WAY FORWARD WITH TELEVISED SHAKESPEARE

As has been suggested already, the series' subsequent broadcasts of the comedies seem to have enjoyed freedom from the demand for realistic settings and period costumes considered appropriate to *Richard II* and *Macbeth*. It is unfortunate that Evans's work on Shakespeare for the screen should be represented for all but a handful of researchers by the 1960 *Macbeth* film: his eloquent but physically limited performance and the old-fashioned production values and direction suffer by comparison with Polanski's 1971 version. *The Taming of the Shrew* and *Twelfth Night*, available only in a few archives, are vigorously and inventively directed and acted. Even the 1953 *Hamlet*, in which performances and studio technique are by no means ideal, has the energy associated with the actor's earlier productions of the play and some of its individual performances (especially Joseph Schildkraut's feline Claudius) are original and effective.[49] With the *Macbeth* broadcast, Evans and his associates, anxious to profit from the lessons of *Richard II*, were exercised by the demands of adapting Shakespeare for the smaller screen. He was particularly anxious to achieve the right scale for the actors' performances, including his own. Evans was not complacent about the processes of television acting, and he found the technical questions both stimulating and frustrating. More general questions of the

productions' scale and scope also perplexed him. In a letter to Judith Anderson almost a year before the production, when he was anxious to persuade her to appear as Lady Macbeth, Evans seems to find himself working on the border between cinema and television:

One of the things TV is poorest at is exterior scenes and unfortunately all the plot development in *Macbeth* has to take place out of doors . . . I'm beginning to doubt the wisdom of attempting a full-length *Macbeth* without the aid of filmed sequences – not possible while I'm working in the theatre at night. Maybe it would be wiser to wait for a time of greater leisure or alternatively to do only sections of the play (the murder of Duncan and the sleep-walking for instance) on a program like *Omnibus*?[50]

In correspondence with other associates, Evans described the difficulty of devising sets and acquiring studio space for what he regarded as the minimum of three cameras, and in the event a composite set was devised that would allow free movement for cameras and sound equipment and fluidity of action.[51] An article in *Time* magazine (13 December 1954) quotes Schaefer as commenting that only three colour cameras on the set and one on a platform were used for *Macbeth*, comparing this with the five cameras used in *Hamlet*. For *Macbeth* the cameras were kept moving in and out of scenes, rather than (as in *Hamlet*) having the action move around the centrally positioned cameras. In the comedies the open studio floor bounded by a cyclorama, with stylized set elements disposed about the space, was effectively an adoption of the kind of 'arena' staging favoured by McCleery (who had now moved on to another network), and Evans's performances benefited from the change.

---

49 Kenneth S. Rothwell finds quite different occasions for praise and blame among the casts of these productions: *A History of Shakespeare on Screen. A Century of Film and Television*, 2nd edn (Cambridge, 2004), pp. 98–9.

50 Evans Collection, Box 37, Folder 1: letter to Judith Anderson, 25 July 1953. *Omnibus* was an arts programme which often included substantial excerpts from theatrical and other performances.

51 Evans Collection, Box 37, Folder 1: letters to actor Staats Cosworth (11 August 1954) and designer Otis Riggs (24 August 1954).

His Petruccio, a lighter version of Alfred Drake in *Kiss Me, Kate*, is vigorous, and his would-be gentleman of a Malvolio is engaging. Unfortunately by 1960, when *The Tempest* was aired, Evans in serious Shakespearian mode had begun to seem dated, his vocal and physical deliberation no longer in fashion. If it had been made, his film of *Richard II* would have engaged with the tensions between Shakespeare's histories and the cinema in terms more redolent of Olivier's *Richard III* than of Welles's *Chimes at Midnight*.

The unrealized film script documents an unmade film that exists alongside an achieved television performance few are able to see, and reflects the uneasy relationship between television and the cinema. The crucial move into stylized presentation of historical subjects for the screen was not one Evans was able to make, by temperament or through the influence of the sponsors' requirements. Paradoxically, an imitation in televisual terms of Webster's pacy 1937 production with its unit set and semi-stylized staging might have been more in tune with the tendencies of television drama. Perhaps the simpler more stylized methods of *An Age of Kings* reflected what those BBC executives had learned from the imported kinescope.

RICHARD II ON THE SCREEN

CHARLES R. FORKER

Cinema has been less kind to *Richard II* than to its companion plays of the second historical tetralogy. The two spectacular Technicolor versions of *Henry V* starring Laurence Olivier (1944) and Kenneth Branagh (1989) are familiar to everybody interested in the performance history of the play. And Orson Welles's *Chimes at Midnight* (1966), essentially an elegiac conflation of the two parts of *Henry IV* with a bit of *Henry V* added, is almost equally famous, partly because Welles himself played Falstaff with memorable warmth, enlisting John Gielgud for the role of Bolingbroke, who portrayed him as imperious and remote. Gus Van Sant's imaginatively free adaptation of the same three plays in *My Own Private Idaho* (1991) – a film about male prostitution in Portland, Oregon, featuring River Phoenix and Keanu Reeves (the Prince Hal figure) with William Richert as the Falstaff surrogate – is justly admired for its sensitive melding of gay underworld culture in 1990s America with Shakespeare's story of a ne'er-do-well son maturing, not without arrogance, into the privilege guaranteed by his pedigree. No one as culturally gifted or technically distinguished as Olivier, Branagh, Welles or Van Sant has yet succeeded in capturing the splendour or complexity of *Richard II* on film, although at least nine attempts to bring this most pageant-like of Shakespeare's histories to the screen have been recorded.

As early as 1950 Royston Morley directed a British TV version of the tragedy with Alan Wheatley in the title role, a production followed in 1954 by another television staging, directed by George Schaefer and starring Maurice Evans,

with whose name (along with that of Gielgud) the play had become especially associated.[1] The well-known BBC production of 1978, directed by David Giles and featuring Derek Jacobi as the deposed monarch with Gielgud as Gaunt and Jon Finch as Bolingbroke, was part of Cedric Messina's massive project that brought all thirty-seven of Shakespeare's plays into people's living rooms around the world.[2] Then in 1981 William Woodman's American production of the play, in which David Birney played the king, was released on videotape, purporting to present the drama in a manner approaching Elizabethan style.[3] Michael Bogdanov included *Richard II* in his seven-play marathon, *The Wars of the Roses*, acted by the English Shakespeare Company and featuring Michael Pennington in the title role. Dating from the late 1980s and costumed in Regency dress, this production was transferred to videotape in 1990.[4] A somewhat unsatisfying, visually modified, version of Deborah Warner's controversial 1995 National Theatre production of the play, with the Irish actress Fiona Shaw in the title

---

[1] See Charles R. Forker, ed., *Richard II*, Arden Shakespeare (London, 2002), pp. 98–100.

[2] Issued as a DVD produced by BBC and Time-Life Films in a boxed set entitled *The Histories of William Shakespeare* (Ambrose Video Publishing, New York).

[3] Re-issued on DVD as Volume III of a nine-play series, *The Plays of William Shakespeare*, a Century Home Video published by Kultur (West Long Branch, NJ).

[4] For an American review of this series, performed at the Stamford Center for the Arts, Stamford, Connecticut, see *The New York Times* (7 June 1988), C15. The videotape is available in the series, *Films for the Humanities* (FFH 4646).

role, was shown on British television in 1997 but never released commercially.[5] John Farrell directed a radically bare-budget American adaptation featuring Matte Osian as the abdicating monarch (2001), which was issued on DVD in 2004.[6] Costumed in army fatigues, jettisoning all traces of royal splendour, and shot in a crumbling abandoned fort near Boston with a hand-held video camera, this version portrays the vacillating monarch as the ruler of a third-world state that transforms England into something like a banana republic. Also in 2001 German television aired a production in German directed by Claus Peymann and featuring Michael Maertens as Richard. Two years later (2003) British TV broadcast an outdoor performance of Tim Carroll's Globe Theatre staging on the Thames with an all-male cast, starring the artistic director, Mark Rylance, as the mercurial king.[7] Of these nine productions, only Giles's, Woodman's, Bogdanov's and Farrell's are available for viewing on commercially obtainable videotapes or DVDs. Accordingly, this discussion focuses principally on them.[8]

THE BBC FILM (1978)

As in most of the films in Messina's multi-play Shakespearian panorama, Giles's approach to *Richard II* is conservative and traditional.[9] The costuming is medieval, the delivery of the verse classically articulate and musical, the characterization conventionally naturalistic and psychologically focused, and the physical movement, extending even to facial expressions, dignified, subtle and nuanced. Despite the deliberate artificialities of staging required by Shakespeare's text, Giles does not shy away from touches of realism, as, for instance, the use of genuine horses in the tournament scene.[10] Derek Jacobi brings to the title role a range of moods – haughtiness, levity, carelessness, royal imperiousness, paralysing self-consciousness, political ineptitude, grief, even physical stamina – without tasteless exaggeration; and Jon Finch plays Bolingbroke with dignity and restraint, never disclosing untrammelled ambition, and behaving in such a way as to preserve Shakespeare's carefully sustained ambiguity as to whether Richard is forced

from the throne or merely allows the crown to slip from his grasp through incompetence, overconfidence and a latent desire for martyrdom. Henry's guilt in the final speech and his stated intention to expiate it with a 'voyage to the Holy Land' (5.6.49) are played as genuine rather than as gestures of political expedience. The gifted Charles Gray makes a scrupulously imagined Duke of York, who, although weak with age and torn emotionally between loyalty to divine-right principle and political realism, never lets the character degenerate, as in some productions, into farcical senescence. Giles assists Gray's dignified characterization by cutting a few of the old man's dithering lines and by muting the comedy of his calling off stage for his boots when he intends to denounce the treasonous Aumerle. Wendy Hiller as York's duchess helps to humanize her husband in the almost impossibly problematic scene where they plead against each other for the condemnation and reprieve of their only son. Here too Giles resists the temptation

---

[5] Forker, ed., *Richard II*, 108–11. See also Paul Taylor's review in *The Independent* (14 June 1995), 23; Carol Chillington Rutter, 'Fiona Shaw's *Richard II*: The Girl as Player-King as Comic', *Shakespeare Quarterly* 48 (1997), 314–24; and Margaret Shewring, *Shakespeare in Performance: King Richard II* (Manchester: Manchester University Press, 1996), 180–4.

[6] The DVD was issued by Sub Rosa Studios, LLC (Liverpool, New York).

[7] For my review of this production, see 'Regime Change at Shakespeare's Globe', *Shakespeare Newsletter* 53.3 (Fall 2003), 71, 82.

[8] For a different but overlapping list of screen versions, see Kenneth S. Rothwell and Annabelle Henkin Melzer, *Shakespeare on Screen: An International Filmography and Videography* (New York, 1990), 230–6. See also *Shakespeare on Television*, ed. J. C. Bulman and H. R. Coursen (Hanover, 1988), 37–8, 89–91, 94–6, 120–1, 208–13, 239–40.

[9] Messina was succeeded in the project to film the entire Shakespearian canon by Jonathan Miller and Shaun Sutton whose approach turned out to be somewhat more experimental than Messina's.

[10] Ace G. Pilkington gives an extremely detailed account of this film in *Screening Shakespeare from 'Richard II' to 'Henry V'* (Newark, 1991), 29–63, 168–73. Although Pilkington's estimate is generally favourable, he mentions several negative reactions, citing Messina's somewhat restrictive conception of Shakespeare on TV as a 'front row in the stalls with two fine actors shouting at each other' (31–2).

to treat the competitive begging as comedy, even though Shakespeare might be thought to encourage it by allowing Henry IV to remark that 'Our scene is altered from a serious thing, / And now changed to "The Beggar and the King"', a popular ballad (5.3.78–9).[11] Gielgud is impressively grave and eloquent, especially in his famous aria on 'This royal throne of kings, this sceptred isle' (2.1.40). And, refreshingly, there is no attempt crudely to villainize the flatterers Bushy, Bagot and Green, or the dedicated self-seeker Northumberland, all four of whom are portrayed as unremarkable partisans – lesser men caught up in the toils of a political revolution.

Giles's moderate cutting of the play, while streamlining the action, simplifies its political issues and minimizes our consciousness of the circumstances that have led to Richard's plight, particularly as regards the responsibility for Gloucester's death, a matter about which Shakespeare's text deliberately leaves the audience in doubt. Although the truth behind the accusations and denials of treason in the opening quarrel remains unclear, Giles alienates us from Mowbray by having Richard Owens sneer venomously at his enemy while Bolingbroke (played by Finch) behaves with greater composure. Jacobi hints at Richard's guilt for Gloucester's murder by means of knowing looks when the subject arises in 1.1. And by cutting entirely the later action (4.1.1–107) in which Bagot accuses Aumerle and in which Carlisle announces that Mowbray has died in exile as a devout Christian and heroic veteran of the crusades, Giles leaves the putative stain on Mowbray's character unmitigated. By sacrificing the episode in which Bolingbroke presides over the hurling down and taking up of gages (as Richard had done in the opening scene), Giles abandons a significant structural parallel and diminishes the ritual formalism of the play in the interests of greater forward momentum. The cut also keeps us from reviving awkward questions about Richard's guilt for the death of his uncle and allows us to regard the fallen king more as a tragic casualty of Bolingbroke's rise than of his own dubious criminality.

Additional cuts have a similar effect, reducing formalistic and choric aspects of the dramaturgy for purposes of speeding up and clarifying the plot. The extended opening of 2.2 in which Bushy and Bagot converse with the Queen about her foreboding (including an elaborately complex simile on perspectives), and in which Green enters to impart the baleful news of Bolingbroke's return and Worcester's resignation from the royal household, reinforces a mood of gathering sorrow that increasingly affects the tonality of *Richard II*. But inasmuch as the episode slows the forward thrust, Giles excises it. Even a message concerning the Duchess of Gloucester's death (2.2.93–7) is omitted as unnecessary to the accelerating accumulation of woe. Similarly Giles cuts Salisbury's gloomy prophecy, comparing Richard's decline to 'a shooting star' (2.4.19), as well as the chief Gardener's emblematic speech about planting 'a bank of rue' in the place where the Queen had dropped a tear (3.4.102–7). Exton's valedictory speech over Richard's corpse, 'As full of valour as of royal blood' (5.5.113–18), is also sheared away, presumably because Giles judged the instantaneous remorse of a resolute assassin too incredible for twentieth-century audiences – audiences requiring psychological realism and unfamiliar with the Elizabethan conventions of choric didacticism. Giles also prunes a few extraneous elements of plot, as for instance Henry IV's enquiries to Harry Percy (the future Hotspur) about his 'unthrifty son' (5.3.1), where Shakespeare seems to be preparing for the introduction of Prince Hal in *1 Henry IV*, the next play of his sequence. Additional examples are the omission of the Abbot of Westminster's speech about plans to rescue and restore Richard (4.1.326–34) and details of the multiple executions after the conspirators have been rounded up (5.6.1–23). Giles clearly regarded such tangential information as distracting for audiences whose prime concern should be the relationship between Richard and Bolingbroke and the tragedy of Richard's fall. The film introduces a least one interpolation – the acclamation, 'God save the king!', at the point where

---

[11] Quotations from the play are taken from my Arden 3 edition; see note 1 above.

Bolingbroke announces his impending coronation and instructs his courtiers to 'prepare' themselves (4.1.319–20). The formulaic cry helps to define the moment, deliberately vague in Shakespeare's text, when Bolingbroke becomes officially Henry IV, although other features of Giles's direction make the matter somewhat more nebulous.

Certain features of Giles's staging invite comment. One of his most insightful is having Bolingbroke stoop down to touch the ground on the words, 'Sweet soil, adieu – ' (1.3.306), when he bids farewell to England. The gesture cleverly anticipates Richard's action upon arriving in Wales, 'Dear earth, I do salute thee with my hand' (3.2.6), thus helping to underline the symbolic parallel between the usurper's love of country and that of the monarch he unseats. When the King throws down his warder at Coventry, thereby aborting the combat, the unaltered text makes it clear that Richard 'Withdraw[s]' (1.3.121) briefly to confer with his nobles (including Gaunt) about the sentences of banishment he is about to pronounce.[12] Giles, like many directors before him, omits this momentary pantomime, giving the impression that Richard's decision is sudden, arbitrary, whimsical and entirely personal, thus making the King's pious words about the avoidance of bloodshed sound disingenuous and self-serving. Giles presents the well-spoken gardeners, who fulfil the role of an on-stage chorus, straightforwardly – not casting them as country bumpkins (as is sometimes mistakenly attempted) nor as monks (as was Barton's decision in his famous RSC production of 1974),[13] but as horticultural professionals from the secular world. Nevertheless, since the gardeners are among the few commoners in a drama focused largely upon aristocrats, Jonathan Adams, as the chief Gardener, speaks his lines with the merest trace of colloquial inflection or regional accent to distinguish himself from his betters.

Whereas the Elizabethan theatre marks off episodes from each other by simply clearing the bare stage, cinema allows the director to make transitions between sequential actions by changing the setting in a trice or by dissolving from one colloquy into the next as though an inde-terminate amount of time – hours, days or even months – had intervened. Giles takes advantage of the modern medium in his handling of the gap between Richard's confiscation of Gaunt's estates and Northumberland's news that Bolingbroke is already on his way back from exile – actions that, in Shakespeare's text, occur in the same scene and indeed within eighty lines of each other.[14] The radical telescoping of time in Shakespeare's original conveys – and seems intended to convey – the impression that Bolingbroke has gathered his forces to invade England before he could have known about the King's seizure of his inheritance, and that therefore his claim to be returning *only* for the purpose of claiming his rightful titles is at best a half-truth and at worst a lie. Giles's film shrinks the likelihood of such an inference by shifting the physical setting between the two events. The result is that Northumberland's announcement of Bolingbroke's expedition no longer seems to follow Richard's expropriation of the duke's properties so precipitously. And the change inevitably ameliorates our estimate of Bolingbroke's motives.[15]

Giles's handling of the climactic deposition scene (4.1) is equally interesting because here also the director refrains from portraying Bolingbroke, even after Richard has been taken prisoner, as openly lusting for kingship. Once the King has likened his crown to a well with two buckets and

---

[12] In Holinshed, the principal source, this council of nobles takes up two hours. See Forker, ed., *Richard II*, p. 217.

[13] *Richard II*, p. 178.

[14] See my editorial note on *Richard II*, 2.1.289–90 (Forker, ed., *Richard II*, p. 273).

[15] Sheldon Zitner is mistaken in claiming that 'the camera cuts to Bolingbroke in exile, informing us that before he returns to England he knows about the death of his father and about Richard's proposal to confiscate his property' ('Wooden O's in Plastic Boxes', in *Shakespeare on Television*, ed. Bulman and Coursen, p. 37). Giles, in fact, never shows us Bolingbroke in France. After he takes leave of Gaunt in 1.3, he remains off-screen until his return to England in 2.3. But Zitner is certainly correct to stress Giles's unShakespearian clarification of Bolingbroke's motives by separating the episode in which we learn of the duke's impending invasion from that in which his estates are expropriated.

reluctantly surrendered it to his adversary, Bolingbroke sets the emblem of royalty on a pillow and never puts it on his head. In fact we never see Henry IV wearing a crown in Giles's film. In the two scenes in which Henry appears after his coronation, the new king is shown either bareheaded (5.3) or wearing a head-dress based on historical portraits (5.6) – in the latter case, probably, on a portrait from Henry Holland's *Baziliologia* (1618). After York's statement that 'plume-plucked Richard' has willingly adopted Bolingbroke as his heir, the usurper responds, 'In God's name I'll ascend the regal throne' (4.1.109–14). But Carlisle's protest affirming divine right compels Bolingbroke to remain standing. By the end of this episode, where we see Richard on his knees with the mirror, Bolingbroke has seated himself uncrowned in a slightly raised chair. But whether this somewhat unadorned seat is meant to represent the official throne remains unclear. By means of ambiguous staging and by deliberately underemphasizing the iconic chair of estate in the deposition scene, Giles keeps Henry's status as a legitimately sanctioned monarch in doubt.

Still another ambiguous aspect of Giles's film centres on the possibility that Richard may be thought to be potentially homosexual. A long tradition in the stage history of *Richard II*, going back at least to Gielgud's famous revival of the role in 1929 and beyond that to Coleridge's observation that the character embodies an 'intellectual feminineness, which feels a necessity of ever leaning on the breast of others', has encouraged actors and directors to conceive of the title figure as gay – and this despite the fact that nowhere in Shakespeare's known sources is there any warrant for such an interpretation, although it is clear that Marlowe's *Edward II* almost certainly influenced the unsubstantiated charge that Bushy and Green have 'Made a divorce betwixt' Richard and his queen, breaking 'the possession of a royal bed' (3.1.12–13).[16] Giles raises the spectre of homoerotic attraction between the King and his favourites by setting the private scene involving Richard and his friends (1.4) in a bath house. We see Alan Dalton as Green, stripped to the waist, massaging the back of his half-clothed

sovereign, while Bagot (Damien Thomas) sponges his own naked torso in a wooden tub. Richard punctuates his reaction to the news about Bolingbroke's mood as he left reluctantly for France with bursts of laughter and childish giggling, the sense of locker-room intimacy, as well as unfeeling cattiness, serving to contrast markedly with the stiff formality of the two previous scenes in which Richard has royally officiated as judge. But if Giles raises suspicions of homoeroticism in this episode, he seems pointedly to contradict it later in the film, especially in the scene of parting from the Queen (5.1) where the physical devotedness of the couple and the prolonged pain of their forced severance is heavily stressed. When Bolingbroke condemns Bushy and Green for their various treasons, some of them obviously factitious (3.1.1–35),[17] the accusation that they have debauched the King sexually rings especially hollow. Giles underlines the point by directing York to show evident surprise at such a groundless slur. And at this point Gray (playing York) puts a hand on Bolingbroke's shoulder in a futile attempt to object to a slander callously invented to blacken the reputations and justify the doom of the favourites. Giles obviously encourages us to ask whether homosexuality should complicate our assessment of the title character, but Jacobi, as Richard, nowhere else in the film hints at such a proclivity, while York and the child-like Queen

---

16 Apart from Gielgud in 1929 and 1937, actors who have stressed Richard's effeminacy include Michael Redgrave in 1951, Harry Corbett in 1954–5, John Justin in 1959, Patrice Chéreau in 1970 and Ian Richardson in 1974. For details about actors and directors who have conceived of Richard II as homosexual or at least having homoerotic tendencies, see Charles R. Forker, 'Unstable Identity in Shakespeare's *Richard II*', *Renascence* 54.1 (Fall 2001), 20–1; for Shakespeare's sources in relation to homosexuality, see 'Unstable Identity', p. 21. For the quotation from Coleridge, see Charles R. Forker, ed., *Shakespeare: The Critical Tradition: 'Richard II'* (London, 1998), p. 131. For the influence of *Edward II* on Shakespeare's play, see my Arden 3 edition, 159–64, 310, 491–2.

17 Bolingbroke implies, for instance, that Bushy and Green are responsible for Richard's decision to banish him and expropriate his estates (3.1.18–27), a notion totally at odds with what we have seen and heard on stage.

(played charmingly by Janet Maw) both seem by their behaviour to reject such an imputation decisively.

Shakespeare structures *Richard II* by contrasting great public episodes such as the lists at Coventry, the confrontation at Flint Castle, and the abdication scene at Westminster with more private moments – Bolingbroke taking leave of his father, Richard chatting with his friends about his rival's departure, the subversive conversation of Ross, Willoughby and Northumberland anticipating Bolingbroke's return, and Richard's farewell to the Queen. Sometimes these contrasts occur within a single scene as well as between scenes, the purpose being repeatedly to narrow and widen the focus in a way that italicizes a tension fundamental to Shakespeare's histories – that between the urgencies of national responsibility and concern on the one hand and personal feelings and desires on the other. Cinema with its fluidity in regard to settings, its technique of flexible lighting, and its alternation of close-ups and wide-angle photography can obviously accentuate such contrasts, nor does Giles neglect his many opportunities to do so.

In the Flint Castle scene, for instance, when Richard appears on the battlements and addresses the rebels below, Giles breaks up the long scene by shifting back and forth between the King's imperious speeches to Northumberland and his more personal remarks to Aumerle and Carlisle. Richard's doom-eager fantasy of being deposed, 'What must the King do now? Must he submit?' (3.3.143), followed by his litany of objects to be surrendered (jewels, palace, apparel, goblets, sceptre), is often spoken to Northumberland (who has just returned from conferring with Bolingbroke to a position within earshot of Richard) as a public dramatization of royal frustration and grief. Jacobi, however, delivers the speech to Aumerle and the remnant of Richard's supporters on the upper level almost as a private meditation on kingly destiny. By the same token, much of Richard's bitter word-play on 'the base court' (3.3.180–3) is spoken, not as a histrionic display of his feelings to the enemy, but as private comments to his friends while descending an interior staircase – a staircase that would presumably be invisible behind the tiring house wall in an Elizabethan theatre. Thus Giles, through Jacobi's performance, undercuts the 'player-king' aspect of Richard's character in order to promote a concept of the tragic monarch as more private and introspective.[18]

The dark lighting in this scene is also surprising since the action occurs outdoors and since Shakespeare gives fresh prominence at this point to the sun-king imagery that suffuses the drama. Giles sets the episode at night – an unlikely time, one supposes, for Bolingbroke to be approaching a castle with an army – or perhaps just before dawn, in an effort to make visual Bolingbroke's florid reference to Richard as 'the blushing discontented sun' emerging from 'the fiery portal of the east' (3.3.63–4). And when York says, 'Yet looks he like a king. Behold, his eye, / As bright as is the eagle's, lightens forth / Controlling majesty' (68–70), we see Richard from a distance as an aureole of light surrounded by darkness. Later in the scene, when Bolingbroke, for mere protocol's sake, kneels before Richard in the courtyard and then takes him prisoner for the journey to London, it is still dark. Giles must have felt that darkness was symbolically appropriate to Richard's fall – a fall buttressed not only by the character's physical descent from a higher to a lower plane, but also by the mythological allusion to Phaëton (3.3.178), the sun-god's irresponsible boy who, losing control of his father's chariot, came, like Richard, to disaster. Striving for a more interior portrayal of the King and a more symbolic presentation of his surrender, Giles underplays the rhetorical and visual splendours frequently associated with the Flint Castle episode. Whether or not one concurs with this approach, it is obvious that his choices were determined by the recognition that cinema differs from the stage, having its own unique imperatives.

---

18 The concept of player-king is not entirely absent from Giles's film. As Peter Saccio observes, the opening shot of Richard shows him 'coming down a corridor, pausing at a door, and drawing himself up to enter', thus typifying the monarch 'as an actor' ('The Historicity of the BBC History Plays', in *Shakespeare on Television*, ed. Bulman and Coursen, 211).

Giles's penchant for shadowed interiors and dark settings carries over to later episodes, so that the entire second half of the drama is deprived of daylight. The deposition scene, which is often exploited as an opportunity for opulence and brilliant costuming, becomes surprisingly gloomy in Giles's film. Bolingbroke wears very dark robes, Carlisle's cope is black, and Richard enters in a subdued, mouse-coloured gown. Only York is allowed to wear off-white. Richard delivers the mirror speech *sotto voce* in a relaxed position, like a child playing on the floor, while Bolingbroke looks on impassively from a chair. Here Richard communes with himself, almost impervious to his onstage audience – an effect assisted importantly by the close-up camera. The scene in which Richard takes leave of the Queen is again set at night with a flickering torch in the background, while the cell in which Richard is murdered is once more shrouded in semi-darkness, the half-light disclosing only a crucifix on the wall and the bare suggestion of furniture.

Richard's only soliloquy, the lengthiest speech of the play, always poses a challenge for actors, being so difficult to sustain for its sixty-six lines in a confined space with no one on stage to react. Jacobi delivers it imaginatively as a segmented daydream, changing his physical position at various points. At the start Giles shows us only Richard's disembodied fingers drumming on a table; later we see Richard sitting down, lying on his bed, praying beside the bed, playing with straws (apparently from his mattress), and occasionally walking to the bars that separate him from the outside world. He reminisces to the Groom about 'roan Barbary' (5.5.78) through the grillwork of the cell, part of his face framed in a narrow window; and the violent action of the murder itself, once Exton and his men have entered the confined space, is shot in such a way as to make the identity of the murderers obscure and even the precise movements of the attack confusing. Darkness also characterizes the final scene. Bolingbroke is attired solemnly in black, and when the coffin is carried in and opened, we see only a small opening for Richard's face, a visual echo of the countenance at the cell window that the Groom had confronted.

Giles's emphasis on dark colours and settings has the effect of eliminating, or at least greatly limiting, our sense of the green world of England as the paradisal garden that Richard's overthrow so bloodily violates. Of course the colour contrast between red and green that infuses the play's imagery remains in much of the dialogue. But Giles confines our visual perception of the natural world to the garden scene (3.4), where political allegory is the *raison d'être* and where gothic architecture reinforces the sense of human artifice.

The BBC screening may be the most distinguished film version of *Richard II*, chiefly because of its superb classical acting. Jacobi, Finch, Gielgud, Gray and Hiller are particularly strong, but there are no weak performers in the cast. The strength of the film lies in its careful attention to the rhythms, sonority and intelligibility of the verse and in the credible, nuanced characterization of the principals. In its emphasis on the psychological interiority of Richard and on the opaque but dignified reserve of his antagonist, it somewhat slights the theme of divine-right kingship, undervaluing the colourful pageantry that traditionally embodies exalted royalty. There is also less probing of the larger questions of political stability and the nature of sovereignty than one ideally might hope for. But no production can do everything. For balance, taste and fidelity to Shakespeare's text, Giles's film remains exemplary.

THE BARD PRODUCTIONS FILM (1981)

The video film of *Richard II* directed by William Woodman was created for a series entitled 'Shakespeare in Performance' and apparently designed for use as a teaching aid at schools and universities. The same director also made similar 'educational' versions of *Romeo and Juliet* and *The Tempest* under the same auspices. Running for 172 minutes, it presents a very full text including eighteen of the play's nineteen scenes: Gaunt's interview with Gloucester's widow (1.2) is omitted, the Welsh captain is cut from 2.4, and Exton's role is expanded by substituting him for Ross in 2.1

and 2.3.[19] Seeking to flesh out the undeveloped character of Harry Percy (the Hotspur of *1 Henry IV*), Woodman introduces a few lines from the later play that adumbrate the character's relationship with Prince Hal.[20] By utilizing a bare-boards set with two basic levels connected by staircases that may be moved and reconfigured in various ways, the film is designed to give viewers the illusion that they are witnessing a stage performance.[21] For sound effects Woodman relies exclusively on drums, trumpet fanfares and lute music. He limits the scenery to such movable furniture as tables, chairs, heraldic banners and a wall crucifix (for the prison scene), so that spectators can appreciate the symbolic changeableness and fluidity of space as in an Elizabethan theatre, even if they do not see actors placing and carrying off these props as would have been the practice at the Theatre or the Globe. The camera technique is anything but static, and the audience is allowed to see much more than could ever be taken in from a seat in the stalls. Woodman's lens zooms in for close-up shots of actors delivering major speeches or angles up, down or laterally to focus on significant groupings of characters or particular areas of the platform at moments of heightened intensity.

One of the film's most effective devices consists of beginning a new scene with the close-up of a chosen symbolic property and then widening the focus to show the context in which it takes on meaning. Thus we see a looking-glass in which Richard's handsome face is reflected before the vanity of his behaviour materializes in the opening episode. Woodman, of course, is preparing us for the later scene in which the mirror becomes a complex symbol of Richard's destructive narcissism and deepening self-knowledge. A chess board with a toppled king-piece forms the background of the opening title and credits, an obvious portent of Richard's overthrow, which then returns as the close-up focus at the beginning of 2.2, where Bushy idly tries to lighten the Queen's sense of impending disaster. We see the chess-board close-up once more at the end of the same scene when Bushy, Bagot and Green split up. The allegorical garden scene begins with a close-up of flowers held in the Queen's hand (the episode offers no further props to establish a green location). Woodman then echoes the flower motif in the prison scene by having the Groom present Richard with a single white rose only moments before his murder. The emblematic blossom reminds us of the Yorkist badge during the Wars of the Roses, the dynastic carnage that Richard's deposition was to propagate in succeeding generations.

In accordance with Elizabethan custom, sumptuous costumes compensate for the minimalist set. On the whole, Woodman adopts fifteenth-century dress, styles a bit too late historically for Richard's reign but suited nonetheless to young actors with athletic physiques and a court given to 'fashions in proud Italy' (2.1.21). Both Richard and Bolingbroke wear tights under abbreviated tunics for most of their appearances, thereby showing off their legs to admirable advantage. And not content with revealing costumes, Woodman contrives to expose the naked chests and arms of some of the characters. Bushy and Green, having obviously been tortured, are shown bare-chested in the scene where they are condemned, and Woodman augments the

---

[19] All that remains of 2.4, a very brief episode, is Salisbury's concluding speech comparing Richard to 'a shooting star' (2.4.18–24).

[20] After Percy informs Bolingbroke about the 'dissolute' activities of his wayward son in 5.3, he soliloquizes briefly, importing four lines from Hotspur's role in *1 Henry IV*: 'All studies here I solemnly defy, / Save how to gall and pinch . . . / That sword-and-buckler Prince of Wales. / But out upon this half-faced fellowship' (1.3.206, 226–8). In another textual change, this one more difficult to justify, Woodman reassigns one of Richard's early lines to Mowbray. The King is reacting to the passion of Bolingbroke's charges against his opponent: 'How high a pitch his resolution soars!' (1.1.109). If the King speaks the line sarcastically or airily (as is usually the case), it reflects negatively on his supposed impartiality as a judge. In Woodman's film Jeff Pomerantz (Mowbray) utters the exclamation in straightforward surprise at Bolingbroke's vehemence. Perhaps Woodman reasoned that the unaltered text too much privileges Mowbray as Richard's agent in the matter of Gloucester's death.

[21] We learn from the credits that an 'Elizabethan stage' was built especially to serve as a set for the action. Although it has two levels and apparently several doors on the lower one, the architecture is more fanciful than historically Renaissance.

physicality of the episode by having Bolingbroke strike Green in shackles and rip off Bushy's shirt. In the scene where the King relaxes with his friends, Woodman conceives the action as a kind of levee during which the monarch dresses, Richard being mostly naked at one point.[22] Later, stripped to a loin cloth, Richard fights an assailant with a broadsword, and, when he 'sinks downward . . . to die' (5.5.112), is shown spread-eagled on the floor in the posture of the crucified Christ. Woodman then returns us to the image of crucifixion after Henry IV concludes his final speech with its reference to a purposed 'voyage to the Holy Land' – the means of washing 'blood from [his] guilty hand' (5.6.49–50). The prominence of the crucifix, the repeated image of the physically sacrificed King, and the frequency with which men make the sign of the cross all contribute to a Christological emphasis, justified by Richard's own conception of himself as a monarch by divine right and his deposition and death as constituting a latter-day Passion.[23]

Like Giles, from whom he appears to have borrowed several ideas, Woodman suggests an element of homoeroticism in the King's relations with his male courtiers without pursuing the notion in any dispositive fashion. One way in which he departs from Giles in this respect is to characterize Bolingbroke as a man who actually believes that Bushy and Green have seduced the King and 'Broke[n] the possession of a royal bed' (3.1.13). As mentioned already, Giles appears to present the charge of sexual deviance as an instance of cynical scape-goating on the usurper's part, whereas in Woodman's film, Bolingbroke treats the supposed seducers with a fury and physical savagery that betokens his crediting their misconduct. As for Richard's relationship to the Queen, Woodman (again like Giles) gives no sign that we should regard it as other than physically unexceptionable. Unlike Giles, however, Woodman casts a mature actress (Mary Joan Negro) in the role of Richard's spouse, thereby altering the emotional dynamic significantly. The historical Richard was married twice, first, to Anne of Bohemia (who predeceased him), and second, to Isabel of Valois (who was a mere child at the time of Richard's murder). As we learn from the cast list, Woodman

chooses to imagine Richard's queen as Anne rather than as Isabel, even though Shakespeare endows the adolescent Isabel with the speeches and attitudes of a young adult.

Given the self-imposed limitations of the platform stage on which all the action must take place, Woodman introduces a number of interesting touches. In 1.3, unlike Giles, he preserves the playwright's suggestion that Richard confers with his lords after throwing down his warder by making him exit rapidly and then immediately re-enter. The movement, which takes only a few seconds, is anti-naturalistic, but it illustrates Woodman's commitment to the Elizabethan convention of foreshortening time through the device of a stage emblem.[24] As in Shakespeare, he allows the tidings of Bolingbroke's return to follow the seizure of Gaunt's property without interruption or an obvious change of place, thereby fostering dark suspicions of the usurper's impure motives. When Gaunt takes leave of his son, he transfers his heavy metal chain of rank to the young man's shoulders, a chain that Bolingbroke later wears at important junctures, as for instance, when he protests to York, defending his invasion, that though 'banished Hereford', he has returned as 'Lancaster' (2.3.113–14). Gaunt is permitted to sit in the presence of the King when Richard visits him in 2.1 – a way of dramatizing his declining health as well as his status as a venerable counsellor whose warnings carry special gravity. Woodman follows Giles in setting many of the later scenes at night – notably Bolingbroke's

---

[22] Woodman appears to have derived the notion of nakedness from Giles's 1978 film (see the discussion above). But although David Birney plays the King as youthfully vain and shallowly self-centred, he avoids suggestions of effeminacy or foppishness.

[23] Richard explicitly compares himself to Christ and his betrayers to Judas (cf. 4.1.170–2).

[24] It might be argued that Richard's conference with his nobles before banishing Bolingbroke and Mowbray represents a monarch who craftily calculates the politics of a difficult situation – a monarch shrewdly bent upon ridding himself bloodlessly of an embarrassing threat to his authority. The extreme brevity of the council in Woodman's film, however, militates against such an interpretation in the present case.

confrontation with York after his return (2.3), Richard's disembarkation in Wales (3.2), the Flint Castle scene (3.3) and Richard's farewell to the Queen (5.1). In the episode where Northumberland parts the lovers, Woodman even imitates Giles by using a flickering torch for background atmosphere. Again, we must understand the decisions about lighting as intending symbolic rather than realistic effects, although it should be remembered that in Elizabethan London darkened stages resulted only from the position of the afternoon sun, assisted from the audience's point of view by the dramatist's poetic imagery, rather than from artificial illumination.[25]

David Birney invents a few unusual postures and gestures in his portrayal of Richard. When he descends to the base court at Flint Castle, for instance, he rushes down a flight of steps on the words, 'Down, down I come' (3.3.178), his long cloak billowing behind him. The effect is almost like a large bird swooping upon its prey. The loss of royal dignity at this moment is startling and the calculated staginess (which borders on caricature) somewhat off-putting, although it is clearly Birney's purpose to suggest an element of psychic breakdown in the character. More successful dramatically is the actor's decision to kneel in the deposition scene as he goes, step by step, through the ritual of self-divestiture, a coronation liturgy in reverse. During this passage, Bolingbroke stands silently to receive the crown and sceptre – a stage arrangement that movingly enhances the King's humiliation and, with splendid irony, inverts previous images of subjects (including Bolingbroke) who kneel to Richard. Instead of dashing the glass to the ground at the climax of the mirror speech (the traditional stage business at 4.1.289), Birney punches it with his fist, crazing the surface so that it distorts his reflected image – a way of literalizing his claim that his 'sorrow hath destroyed [his] face' (4.1.291). Curiously, Woodman films the prison scene from above, the camera focusing on Richard below through a wide grating in the cell's ceiling. The Groom positions himself on the ceiling bars so that a considerable space separates the two actors. Again the effect is anti-naturalistic, but it serves visually to symbolize a power inversion – the once all-powerful monarch now isolated and confined in a sort of pit while his erstwhile servant looks down from a position of freedom from on high. Initially, we see only a small corner of the platform stage in this scene and indeed hardly become aware that a larger acting area exists until the Keeper enters with Richard's food. Actually, the prison scene strains Woodman's meta-dramatic focus to the limit, illustrating the difficulty of presenting a cell with some degree of visual realism while also keeping us aware of a neutral theatrical space with variable uses and dimensions that can be shrunk or expanded in the viewer's imagination.

Paul Shenar, as Bolingbroke, also enriches his role with a few thoughtful strokes. At the beginning of Act IV, for instance, he presides impassively over the quarrels that ensue when Bagot accuses Aumerle, keeping his cool in a matter that revives the unpleasantness of Gloucester's death together with the memory of his own banishment. Unlike Giles, Woodman refuses to discard an episode so germane to the structural symmetry of the play, a balance that enforces through parallelism the important contrast between Richard and Henry as judges. But when York enters to announce that Richard has willingly agreed to Bolingbroke as his successor, an irrepressible expression of pleasure,

---

[25] Torches of course could be used in Elizabethan theatres as a means of suggesting darkness on a daylight stage, as for instance, in *Romeo and Juliet* (5.3.25) and Marlowe's *Edward II* (5.3.47–8, 5.5.37). The situation was obviously different for plays performed at enclosed theatres such as the Blackfriars where candles were used for illumination. Of the few literal references to evening or night in *Richard II*, none could reasonably be considered to determine setting. York's invitation to Bolingbroke 'to enter in the castle [i.e., Berkley Castle in Gloucestershire] / And there repose [him] for this night' (2.3.160–1), for instance, obviously tells us nothing about the time of day when York meets Bolingbroke for the first time after his return, let alone when Richard disembarks near a different castle (Barkloughly Castle in Wales) in 3.2 or confronts Bolingbroke at Flint Castle in 3.3. Giles and Woodman, who introduce dark settings for various scenes, do so conceptually, responding to dominant metaphors such as the King's plangent cry, 'From Richard's night to Bolingbroke's fair day' (3.2.218).

almost of relief, appears on the countenance of the *de facto* king. And after Richard has been forcibly returned to the Tower and Henry has announced his plan to be crowned within a few days, the new monarch strides in a wide arc around the stage, individually greeting his bowing peers as though to receive their accolades. In the semi-comic begging scene with Aumerle and his parents, Bolingbroke sits with administrative studiousness behind a desk, allowing himself the faintest smile at the bizarre situation of three family members kneeling to plead at cross purposes. In pardoning a would-be traitor, Shenar conveys the confidence of a man able to cope efficiently with danger and unexpected adversity, and to estimate his situation shrewdly. Although now officially king, however, Bolingbroke remains bare-headed. Woodman reserves the image of Henry IV crowned for the final scene when he confronts Exton bearing Richard's coffin. Only after his rival's death does Bolingbroke feel secure enough to wear the iconic emblem of royalty. Oddly, Exton enters with the coffin on the upper level of the stage so that Henry is required to ascend a staircase for his final speech over the royal figure whose assassination he had (unintentionally?) authorized. Awkward and improbable as this staging seems, Woodman appears to adopt it as a means of suggesting a symbolic reversal of the moment at Flint Castle when Richard had debased himself by descending to Bolingbroke in the courtyard.

Woodman's capable actors speak their lines with American accents, enunciating distinctly and without slighting intelligible sense or the cadences of iambic pentameter. Birney with his youthful, clean-cut bearing makes a glamorous Richard, clothed mostly in white, who effectively communicates the youthful self-indulgence of a careless, wilful and egotistical monarch in the first half of the play. His callous disrespect for the dying Gaunt extends to his nearly striking the old man with a riding crop when his uncle outspokenly blames him for Gloucester's death. He is less successful in the later scenes where he is required to wax more philosophical and self-pitying and to engage our sympathies as a man in the throes of a royal identity crisis. But few of the actors in this production, though professionally competent, have the emotional range and depth of Giles's BBC cast. Shenar plays Bolingbroke in a somewhat unfathomable and understated style except for the scene where he brutally abuses Bushy and Green. John McLiam, as Gaunt, delivers his great eulogy of England like an operatic aria but never gets much beyond his function as a built-in chorus; as a speaker of verse, he is no match for Giles's Gaunt, John Gielgud. Woodman's Mowbray (Jeff Pomerantz) gives us a more sympathetic reading of the part than his counterpart in the BBC film, while York (Peter Maclean) turns in a very bland performance, wisely eschewing the suggestions of encroaching senility that tempt some actors of the role. John Devlin, with jet black hair, portrays a sinister and conspiratorial Northumberland, while Mary Joan Negro, as Queen Anne, seems incapable of projecting sadness or grief with conviction and appears to rely almost wholly for emotional impact on the cadenced rhetoric of her speeches. Logan Ramsey makes a bombastic and over-the-top Carlisle, uttering his great defence of Richard's indefeasible right like a high-school oration. Nicholas Hammond plays the minor role of Harry Percy with considerable skill, drawing on a longstanding theatrical tradition that conceives of Hotspur as a stammerer.[26]

If Woodman's *Richard II* by no means represents a great or definitive reading of Shakespeare's tragedy, it nevertheless remains an effective and highly useful film, which seems indeed to have

---

[26] In *2 Henry IV*, Lady Percy, speaking of her dead husband, recalls that 'speaking thick (which nature made his blemish) / Became the accents of the valiant' (2.3.24–5) and was imitated by admirers. 'Speaking thick' means speaking hurriedly or indistinctly, but the words were misinterpreted by some to imply a speech impediment, and several actors have adopted stuttering as a feature of their characterization. Laurence Olivier, for instance, in a famous Old Vic performance of the role in 1945, stammered on the word 'w-w-w-worms' in delivering Hotspur's dying speech (*1 Henry IV*, 5.4.85–8). Actors seem to be attracted to the speech defect as a means of conveying the character's tragic vulnerability. Woodman regards Harry Percy in *Richard II* as an early study for Hotspur, which explains his interpolation of Hotspur's lines for the role in 5.3 (see note 20 above). Hammond stutters only two or three times in Woodman's film.

been an important aspect of its purpose. The some-what academic approach allows students and view-ers unfamiliar with Elizabethan drama to appreciate the historical distance that separates Shakespeare's stage not only from modern stages but also from the conventions of cinema. Woodman bridges this wide historical gap imaginatively, giving us the sense of an Elizabethan play with much of its artifice intact, as seen through the lens of a self-conscious modern movie maker who deliberately refuses to translate it more than minimally into a twentieth-century medium or to adulterate it with twentieth-century values. But neither does he attempt the impossible task of recreating a sixteenth-century performance with an all-male cast who double parts and play in an archae-ologically reconstructed theatre. The film stops well short of museum Shakespeare. If Woodman's experimental compromise with cultural archaism has obvious limitations, it nevertheless instructs without deadening our responses to the inher-ent theatricality of the play. Woodman proves that awareness of historical production values and dra-matic vigour, if inventively combined, can success-fully support each other.

THE ENGLISH SHAKESPEARE COMPANY FILM FROM 'THE WARS OF THE ROSES' (1990)

Michael Pennington's brilliant and varied interpre-tation of the role of Richard II makes the TV ren-dering of the ESC staging especially memorable. His range of costumes serves nicely to suggest the different facets of his personality. We see him first as a Beau Brummell dandy in a long brocaded dress-ing gown, chatting complacently about the quarrel between Mowbray and Bolingbroke until mention of Gloucester's death, when the accusers face each other, unexpectedly startles him into a frisson of anxiety. At Coventry he presides in an ermined robe of blue velvet, wearing his crown to show how commanding he can be as a public presence. Later he relaxes with his friends over port and cigars in shirt sleeves and waistcoat, arrives from Ireland in a furred overcoat to vacillate between

unrealistic optimism and despair, appears on the walls of Flint Castle in a military uniform of scarlet and gold, surrenders his crown in a floor-length coat of black velvet with green lapels (a costume that subtly reflects defeat mingled with vanity) and finally languishes as a prisoner, battered, barefoot and clad only in tattered underwear. Pennington's bravura performance takes us through a kaleido-scope of poses and moods – the complacent sybarite, the sneering puppy, the cruel sentimen-talist responsive only to his own feelings, the frus-trated child given to weeping and tantrums, the clever expert in word-play and paradoxical wit, the aesthete, the player-king, the dreamer, the would-be philosopher, the lonely victim craving personal connection, the outcast capable of intelligent self-reflection.[27] Pennington varies Shakespeare's lyric verse (often rhymed) by speeding up and slow-ing down his delivery. Magically, he can make us believe that the speeches and situations are gen-uinely human without pretending that the lines are other than conspicuously poetic and literary. Clyde Pollitt, as Gaunt, renders the great aria on England with unusual attention to musical detail, and the supporting cast, all seasoned professionals, play to and off each other in a style of seamless ensemble. Michael Cronin (Bolingbroke) – unsmiling, soberly dressed, reserved, inscrutably discreet, never raising his well-modulated voice – contrasts admirably with the volatile Penning-ton. The Gardeners and the Groom betray humble origin through their accents without destroying the clarity and artifice of their words, while Ross (wearing a tartan) and the Welsh cap-tain (in something like native dress) reflect Scotland and Wales through suggestions of regional pronun-ciation. This version, like Woodman's, makes it obvious that we are watching the filmed version of a stage production (the scenes are all played on an uncluttered theatre set). But the use of flexible

---

[27] Michael Manheim describes Pennington's Richard as 'at first foppish, then Werther-like'; see Manheim, 'The English His-tory Play On Screen' in *Shakespeare and the Moving Image: The Plays on Film and Television*, ed. Anthony Davies and Stanley Wells (Cambridge, 1994), p. 141.

lighting, close-up shots and modern and period music (Handel figures prominently) help director Bogdanov translate his stage conception to the new medium without strain.

Running nearly two and a half hours, this film projects the feeling of being based on a complete text. Bogdanov nevertheless dispenses with the interview between Gaunt and Gloucester's widow (1.2),[28] with the two scenes involving Aumerle and his family (5.2 and 5.3), with the Abbot of Westminster at the end of 4.1, and with the Gardener's concluding speech in 3.4 (on the intention to plant a bank of rue). He employs the upper stage, a utilitarian metal scaffold connected by stairs to the downstairs playing area, only for the viewing stand of the Coventry lists and the battlements of Flint Castle. Furniture is used sparingly – a bench and a single potted tree, for instance, to establish the garden setting in 3.4, and a desk with chairs ranged in front to suggest the judicial ambience of the confrontation between Bagot and Aumerle.

Bogdanov introduces inventive business to help characterize Richard. Offstage laughter, suggesting the frivolous tone of the court, precedes the King's entrance to the dying Gaunt,[29] and when York warns of the folly of confiscating his brother's estates, Richard ignores the seriousness of the admonition, absorbing himself with a pad and pencil in an impromptu sketch of his uncle's portrait. The action beautifully conveys Richard's incapacity to distinguish between national policy and private amusement, between life and art. Although Shakespeare carefully preserves an element of doubt about Richard's guilt in the matter of Gloucester's death, Bogdanov allows Pennington to signal Richard's discomfort with the topic, perhaps even his shame. When scolded by Gaunt, for example, he behaves with defensive spitefulness as though he feared exposure. Richard kneels to Bolingbroke in mock humility on the line, 'God save the King! Will no man say "Amen"?' (4.1.173), although we never see Richard's successor wearing a crown.[30] When asked straightforwardly if he is willing to resign, Pennington's monarch conceives the complicated 'Ay. No. No, ay; for I must nothing be' (4.1.201), not as a malicious teasing of Bolingbroke,

but, with appropriate body language, as a moment of agonized indecision. After Richard, luxuriating in the prospect of martyrdom, discharges his followers, Bogdanov marks the transition to Bolingbroke's ascendancy by a long stage pause during which we see the baggage of the royal entourage being sadly collected and hauled away. Unlike most directors, he plays down the violence of the murder episode. Exton's assistants, one of whom carries a garrote, enter Richard's cell wearing suits – a mark of their official status; and the royal victim manages to kill but a single assailant before being shot in the back bloodlessly. The corpses are dragged off stage, another reminder that a theatrical performance is being translated to the screen.

Bolingbroke in Bogdanov's film does not so much seize power as wait patiently with heavy-lidded forbearance until authority has been thrust upon him. There is no note of victory in his announcement that he intends to ascend the throne (4.1.114), only the protocol of the seated courtiers who suddenly rise to their feet. He seems reluctant and embarrassed to be handling the crown that Richard pushes towards him. The closest Cronin's Henry IV comes to betraying a personal emotion is just before what in the theatre would be the final curtain, when he gazes into Richard's coffin with unconcealed anguish, seeming to anticipate a reign fraught mercilessly with turmoil. The supporting characters are well acted but never allowed to upstage Pennington or steal the limelight from the centrality of Richard. Colin Farrell plays the bedevilled York as a dignified elder statesman, not as a comic weakling, while Northumberland (Roger Booth) comes off as surprisingly reasonable and level-headed, perhaps in order to contrast with his impetuous son, Harry Percy, played by Andrew

---

[28] Of the four films discussed in this survey, Giles's BBC version is the only one to retain the lone appearance of the Duchess of Gloucester (1.2).

[29] Bogdanov might have borrowed this idea from Giles, who also featured the sounds of court merriment at the same point.

[30] In this decision Bogdanov seems to be following Giles (see above).

Jarvis as a bald eccentric who wears a curious black band around his skull and speaks breathlessly in northern accents. Siôn Probert (Bushy) manages to make his difficult speech on perspectives (2.2.14–27) intelligible to lay listeners (he delicately wipes a tear from the Queen's cheek), while Hugh Sullivan (Carlisle) lends dignity without fanaticism to the role of Richard's episcopal ally. After counselling the King to take a more pragmatic and courageous stance when beset by calamitous news, the Bishop himself betrays in close-up how appalled he is by Scroop's report that even York has defected to the enemy. Bogdanov brings Bushy and Green on stage for their death sentences disheveled and bruised,[31] whereas Bagot, their coeval as an erstwhile royal favourite, appears before the same judge (Bolingbroke) in the formal attire of a political survivor and apparent convert to the new regime. The contrast in dress and situation makes a wry statement about the politics of changing with the wind, if not of betrayal. Bogdanov buttresses the irony by using as a national backdrop a gigantic flag of Saint George (a red cross on a white field). The emblematic flag becomes a staple of the production, being used also at earlier points – at the Coventry tournament, for instance, and in the abdication scene.

Clearly Bogdanov's choice of nineteenth-century costumes represents a compromise between the artificiality of Elizabethan staging and the naturalism of much contemporary cinema – a balancing of the need for a certain degree of historical distancing against the felt necessity of making Shakespeare more accessible to modern audiences than the remote world of men in doublet and hose can do. The device works well enough to make us accept the anachronism of a medieval combat between soldiers dressed as hussars rather than as armored or chain-mailed knights, and of courtiers in cravats and tail coats throwing down 'gages'. The joy of this film is its clarity of action and speech, embodied by skilled actors who know how to make the thrilling language sound credible, unstilted and sincerely felt. Pennington's enactment of the title role constitutes not only a theatrical *tour de force* but also proof that so flawed a ruler as Richard contains much to fascinate and admire.

THE JOSEPH ERICKSON / JOHN FARRELL FILM (2001)

Farrell's adaptation, reducing the playing time to ninety-three minutes (including a number of wordless pauses for atmospheric vistas of sea and landscape), represents an attempt to contemporize *Richard II* radically. Shakespeare's text is cut to ribbons. Gone are many of the more aureate speeches – Gaunt's praise of England (2.1.40–68), Richard's salute to his realm on returning from Ireland (3.2.4–26), Carlisle's defence of divine right (4.1.115–50), York's description of Bolingbroke with Richard as captive (5.2.7–40), and Henry IV's funeral speech over the dead king's coffin (5.6.38–49), for example. Surprisingly, in so ruthless a pruning, we are permitted to hear Sonnet 30 ('When to the sessions of sweet silent thought . . .'), read by Bushy as an entertainment for Richard and his queen. Farrell eliminates all of Shakespeare's medieval formalism, removes every trace of royal decorum and pageantry, and gelds the play of its religious symbolism, transferring the action to a grim secular world in which the only pressures that count are those generated by the struggle for power. Even what language survives from this all-verse play is often spoken like prose or shorn of its Elizabethan archaisms, not infrequently to the ruin of its stately music. Matte Osian, as Richard, either deliberately or in ignorance of the scansion, stresses syllables incorrectly in words such as 'revénues' (4.1.212), 'recórd' (4.1.230) and 'lámentable' (5.1.44). And when Bolingbroke comments on Richard's mirror speech, 'The shadow of your sorrow hath destroyed / The shadow of your face' (4.1.292–3), Farrell deems it necessary to have Richard respond with a heavy-handed 'How poetic!' in his fear that the literary conceitedness of the passage would demand too much of his unsophisticated audience.

Characters and plot undergo massive changes. Bagot, the Bishop, the Abbot, the Duchesses of Gloucester and York, Salisbury and the Welsh

---

[31] Unlike Giles and Woodman, Bogdanov makes nothing of the homosexual charge in Bolingbroke's indictment of Bushy and Green (see note 16 above).

captain are dropped altogether, while Exton's role is absorbed into Ross's[32] and, in at least one episode, Aumerle stands in for Bagot. Gaunt (in a wheelchair) acquires a nurse, who speaks a few of York's lines, while Aumerle, Scroop and the Groom are played as women. Kadina Delejalde (who acts Isabel) visits Richard in prison, although it isn't entirely clear, since he fails to recognize her, whether she is intended to be interpreted as the Queen in disguise or as an anonymous loyalist substituting for Shakespeare's Groom.[33] The female characters engage actively in battle, dressed in olive drab or camouflage, thereby remedying Shakespeare's marginalization of women. Curiously Scroop (Lisa Beth Kovetz) is played as a captured enemy of Richard, not as a follower, in the episode where she delivers adverse tidings to the King.

But Farrell does not scruple to alter the action in more important ways. Bolingbroke and Mowbray, struggling to get control of a vicious-looking knife, almost kill each other in hand-to-hand combat before Richard interrupts the violence to banish them. We never see the symbolic descent into the 'base court' (3.3.176), Richard's colloquy with Bolingbroke at Flint Castle being glimpsed in a grainy black-and-white flashback (as though on old-fashioned television) during a love scene with the Queen. Isabel herself is captured by ambush, but contrives to avenge herself on Northumberland by pushing him to his death off a parapet. She then escapes briefly to re-enter the guerilla combat and is finally stabbed to death in the aftermath of Ross's (i.e., Exton's) failed attempt to murder Richard in his cell. Meanwhile Richard, seizing a pistol from one of the intended murderers, shoots him in the throat, flees from the now open prison, continues to fight at large in combat territory, encounters Ross in battle (deciding however not to kill him when he has the chance), rushes down a rocky slope to the sea, and finally dies on the beach, picked off by a sharpshooter, as the tide washes over his corpse. The film ends with a sunset over the ocean in an apparent visualization of the sun-king imagery that Farrell has mostly eliminated from the script. We infer that Bolingbroke has seized dictatorial powers

(we never see him wearing the white officer's cap that substitutes for a crown), but there is no concluding episode, as in Shakespeare, to dramatize his remorse or feelings for his fallen enemy. Indeed he fades away as a presence at the denouement since his three final scenes (5.2, 5.3 and 5.6 in the original) are all discarded. There is no need for Henry IV to pardon Aumerle since her involvement in the plot to restore Richard is never shown – a simplification that also destroys the reason for portraying a crisis within York's family. In the falling action Farrell shifts the onus of anti-authoritarian sentiment onto Northumberland, played by Robert F. McCafferty as a malevolent rock star with spiked hair and earrings and the gloating laughter of a bogeyman from a teenage horror film.

Richard II is notable among Shakespeare's histories for its absence of battle scenes. The conflicts are personal and ideological, centring on political incompetence confronted by opportunistic efficiency, and the idea of venerable tradition challenged by pragmatic necessities. By turning the play into an anti-war film with chaotic noise and explosions (land mines, AK-47s, mortars, hand grenades, machetes, a helicopter and air-raid sirens dominate the screen and soundtrack), Farrell mechanizes the bloodshed, making it seem wasteful, devoid of honour, meaningless and abhorrent. In one of the extra features appended to the DVD, the director-adaptor voices his notion that the play is 'structurally flawed', chiefly because Richard is conceived of as 'a jerk' who can command but little sympathy. Consequently he directs Osian in the title role as a figure with little emotional depth or royal conviction – as a victim of forces he can barely understand, let alone control. As a spoiled creature of privilege, blind to the ugly dangers his stupidities have unleashed, he walks woodenly through the early episodes wearing a scarlet ascot under his tan uniform, evincing little royal demeanour or talent

---

32 For this conflation of roles, Farrell may have been influenced by Woodman (see above), who, although retaining the name of Exton, similarly combined Exton with Ross.

33 She speaks some scraps from the Groom's lines but never mentions 'roan Barbary' (5.5.78).

for command. At the beginning, Farrell shoots him in a dirty T-shirt, curled up in a foetal position on a prison floor. Here the prisoner scrapes the surface mindlessly with a stone, the grating noise interfering with the opening of his mumbled fifth-act soliloquy, 'I have been studying how I may compare / This prison where I live unto the world . . .' (5.5.1–2). The idea of filming as a flashback the events that have reduced a king to miserable captivity holds out a certain cinematic promise. But Osian seems entirely incapable of conveying the expanded or deepened self-consciousness that Richard's later speeches imply, so that the opportunity of showing growth in the title character is largely forfeited. When the King's full soliloquy returns late in the play, we have little sense that Richard's sufferings have taught him much, or even that the suffering itself has occasioned him more than inconvenience or physical discomfort. The tearful quality of Shakespeare's rhetoric and the histrionic self-pity that accompanies it in Shakespeare's text are either cut entirely from the script or so shallowly rendered as to leave us unmoved. Richard weeps only once – over the dead body of Isabel, an invented scene in which the King says nothing.

In a countercultural film so obviously aimed at avant-garde sensibilities, we are surprised, perhaps, that Farrell so totally ignores sexual themes. The relationship between Isabel and Richard, especially just before they separate, comes off as strangely lukewarm despite the amorous rhetoric (she regards him quizzically during part of the episode), and Farrell completely drops the imputation of homosexual relations between the King and his favourites, cutting Bolingbroke's lines to this effect and, unlike Giles or Woodman, avoiding any exposure of the male physique. Turning Aumerle, Richard's closest friend, into a woman helps also to destroy opportunities for a homoerotic ethos. The director's stress is almost wholly on the ugliness of war and the inhumanity it licenses. Here the horror-film tradition contributes to our revulsion – beginning in the opening sequence with a brief shot of a bloody figure who points accusingly at Richard as he contemplates his guilty past. Presumably the ghost is Gloucester for whose murder

Richard is blamed in Shakespeare's text. But since Farrell entirely cuts this background information, the ghost seems gratuitous. In any case, even Shakespeare eschews making Gloucester's death an ingredient in Richard's developing sense of his own misrule. The detail does, however, fit in with Farrell's delight in violence – in throat cutting, blowing off heads, stabbings, shootings, indiscriminate slaughter and summary executions. By stripping Richard of kingliness and by diminishing the stature of Bolingbroke, Farrell distances us from all the principals and sets them in a nightmare world of cynical nihilism.

As a cinematographer, Farrell is not without imagination. Fort Strong, the disused redoubt on a deserted island in the Boston harbor, makes an eerie setting with its cave-like bunkers, leaky rooms, winding corridors, dusty trenches, concrete walls, high-perched lookouts and overgrown surroundings. Admirably for Farrell's purposes, it suggests a regime in the final stages of decay and offers stunning visual opportunities for the cameraman. Unfortunately the editing and sound quality fall far below professional standards, and the actors are too untrained to speak Shakespearian verse with minimal clarity or projection, let alone believability as articulate aristocrats and politicians. Richard and Bolingbroke (played inertly by Barry Smith) confront each other in the tone of common soldiers rather than as members of a ruling family. A few individual effects are nevertheless commendable. When Richard, for instance, is forced to give up his crown, he proffers his West-Point-style cap to his cousin, deliberately letting it drop so that a disconcerted Northumberland must retrieve it. The technique of voice-over is put to interesting use when we see Bolingbroke departing for France to the accompaniment of Gaunt's attempt to cheer him up, heard on the soundtrack. Richard's mirror becomes a dirty shard of broken glass, part of the detritus of combat, wearily discarded rather than histrionically shattered. The secretive conversation between Northumberland, Willoughby and Ross, anticipating Bolingbroke's invasion, is shot in silhouette in a woodland with the use of binoculars as a significant prop. The garden scene (3.4), totally omitting the Queen, is reduced to a brief encounter with a local farmer, who appears with mosquito netting around his face. Farrell suggestively fragments Richard's prison soliloquy, skillfully conveying its improvisatory, stream-of-consciousness quality, enshrouding much of it in darkness and at one point allowing a brilliant shaft of light, as though a cell window had been briefly cracked, to illuminate part of the King's disembodied face. For lack of adequate funding, Farrell was compelled to film *Richard II* under grotesquely adverse conditions. Had he been able to afford better equipment and more classically experienced actors, he might have produced an 'alternative' or unorthodox version of Shakespeare's drama with better results.

The four films described in this survey present us with something of a paradox in estimating the success with which so formal a play as *Richard II* can be translated to the medium of the motion picture. Farrell's experimental attempt to re-imagine Shakespeare's drama as guerilla warfare in a repellent third-world setting is probably the most cinematic of the lot, judged merely in terms of the freedom with which the medium is employed. Unfettered from exaggerated respect for the literary quality of Shakespeare's play and uninterested in its historic or traditional values, Farrell endeavours to construct an entirely new work using the old text as a base. Altering language, context and plot wherever and whenever the spirit moves him, Farrell sets out to address a new, alienated audience and to say something entirely different from what traditionalists and purists expect. Such an aesthetic, of course, can be defended. We do not fault Vaughan Williams, a distinguished composer in his own right, from taking a sixteenth-century theme by Tallis and weaving it into a powerful symphonic work for twentieth-century listeners with its own appeal and integrity. Farrell, however, comes well short of Vaughan Williams in terms of taste and technical achievement, so that his film is largely a failure. But, in the final analysis, it is the execution rather than the approach that must be deprecated. The films by Woodman and Bogdanov that adhere very closely to the experience of live theatre and that subordinate physical setting to the importance of the spoken word come infinitely closer to what we customarily judge to be Shakespeare's intent, but are much less inventive cinematically. Bogdanov succeeds admirably, despite his filmic conservatism, because his company performs at such a high level of dramatic and verbal excellence and because his updating of the play through the use of Regency costumes brings it closer to contemporary sensibilities without fundamentally altering its sense of a recreated past. The BBC film, which combines classic Shakespearian delivery and expected period dress with greater freedom in the managing of the visual elements, falls somewhere between the revolutionary modernism of Farrell and the traditionalism of Woodman and Bogdanov. But we have yet to experience a filmed version of *Richard II* that fully explores the rich possibilities of cinema without destroying the play's reliance on verbal opulence and the artful symmetries of Elizabethan staging and structure. In the case of a tragedy about medieval kingship, so heavily dependent on the ritualistic, almost quaint, conventionalities of a remote time, it is interesting to speculate whether the ancient subject matter and modern cinematic freedoms are even potentially compatible.

'WHERE LIES YOUR TEXT?': *TWELFTH NIGHT* IN AMERICAN SIGN LANGUAGE TRANSLATION

PETER NOVAK

In 1998 a team of Deaf[1] and hearing artists set out to translate a full-length Shakespearian play into American Sign Language (ASL). Earlier attempts to translate Shakespeare, most notably those by the National Theater of the Deaf, had resulted in an adaptation of *Hamlet*, entitled *Ophelia*, as well as an hour-long version of *Macbeth* and a series of selected scenes and monologues from Shakespeare's best-known works entitled *Shakespeare Unmasked*. Deaf schools and theatres around the country have produced dozens of Shakespeare's plays over the years, but without any coherent methodology of translating his works into ASL and with few archives as examples. The aim of the ASL Shakespeare Project experiment was twofold. First, to translate one play, *Twelfth Night*, by means of a systematic and intellectually rigorous model, using digital technology to record the translation, and further to use the translation for a professional production of the play that was to open in Philadelphia almost two years after the translation process began.[2] The second goal of the ASL Shakespeare Project was to disseminate the play itself as well as information about the process on a website completely accessible to Deaf students in both ASL and English. The result is www.aslshakespeare.com, the first bilingual and bicultural website on Shakespeare on the internet, and a full-length production of *Twelfth Night* (on DVD) performed in American Sign Language with simultaneous English voice-over and optional captioning.[3] Translating one of Shakespeare's most musical of plays into a visual and manual language has created a new Shakespearian artifact that fuses text with performance and pro-

vides a new perspective on both. This paper not only details the practical and theoretical implications underlying a translation of Shakespeare's play into a visual/manual text, but also advocates for a re-envisioned definition of text itself.

This new translation by the ASL Shakespeare Project team was not the first attempt at rendering *Twelfth Night* into the language. In 1998, Luane Davis and John DeBlass directed an hour-long adaptation of *Twelfth Night*, for ages ten and up, at the Interborough Repertory Theater in New York. The piece, adapted by Robert Mooney, 'concentrated on the seven major characters', removed 'the long subplot', and was performed in a style coined by director Davis as 'Del-Sign', a new acting technique that combines the 'basic tenets of François Delsarte's (1811–71) codified movement technique and the foundations of American Sign Language'.[4] In 1985 an American Sign Language translation of *Twelfth Night* was produced in Los Angeles by

---

[1] I follow the convention in Deaf Studies of capitalizing 'Deaf' to signify the culture of people who use American Sign Language as their primary means of communication. Lower case 'deaf' indicates the audiological condition of hearing loss.

[2] The play was produced by the Amaryllis Theater in Philadelphia. The translation process and the production were both directed by the author but the translation was a collective one owing to the diligence of many, mostly to Adrian Blue (master translator and sign coach), Catherine Rush (dramaturg) and Robert DeMayo who formed the primary translation team, staying together throughout the sixteen months of translation.

[3] Published and distributed by Gallaudet University Press, 2006.

[4] Laurel Graeber, 'Signs of Shakespeare', *The New York Times*, 20 March, 1998.

American Theater Arts, directed by Don Eitner and translated by hearing actor, Tom Henschel, and hearing interpreter/actor Lou Fant.[5] Working from Shakespeare's original play, they updated the imagery throughout the translation process, rendering the more current thought or image into ASL. Wanting to create a universal experience for the entire audience, they decided to change Shakespeare's original text by back-translating their ASL translation into English, effectively rendering Shakespeare's original as an English translation of the ASL. Their translation of *Twelfth Night* was never recorded, and there are no published versions of their script, which was written in Fant's own method of transcription, making further study of it virtually impossible. The goal of the ASL Shakespeare Project was to develop a model of translation that could be replicated for future study, serve as a basis for additional translations and productions, and increase the study of ASL language and literature through the emerging field of visual poetics.

The translation of Shakespeare into ASL raises a host of questions about the practice of theatrical translation and forces a reconsideration of almost every standard practice involved in it. ASL conveys meaning by means of the three dimensions of a signer's body coupled with his movement through space. Because it is not fixed or static but requires kinetic movement, it exists in four dimensions, so that any attempt to transcribe this language in the height and width of a written text is not only impractical but ultimately unfeasible. Why bother trying to translate Shakespeare into ASL, some might argue, since Deaf people can always read the original in English. That argument rests on a common misunderstanding that conflates English with ASL and ignores ASL as a primary language. While distinctly American, ASL is nonetheless linguistically a separate language from English, distinct in its grammar and syntax. Many Deaf people in Britain, for example, may also know English, but would find an ASL translation of *Twelfth Night* as incomprehensible as ASL users would find a British Sign Language (BSL) translation. Complicating matters even further than the grammatical, syntactical and four-dimensional differences between ASL

and all other spoken/written languages, ASL is also a performed language. Any performance requires consideration of a dizzying number of variables, since description of even a simple, continuous, linear motion requires a means of plotting both movement through space and movement through time; however, ASL entails movement that is dispersed grammatically throughout the body.[6] Consequently, the structure of ASL requires a whole new consideration of writing, reading and literature itself.

There has been no standard process for ASL translations of Shakespeare. In most cases, individual actors are asked to translate their own lines from English to ASL – a practice that mitigates against any linguistic, stylistic or historical continuity. Even those within the community of signed languages question the possibility of translating a visual/manual language. As late as 2004 Peter Llewellyn-Jones, Programme Director of the Centre for BSL (British Sign Language) Translation Studies at the University of Leeds writes that 'if one distinguishes between translation and interpretation, the former working with written source and target forms and the latter the live interpretation of a spoken message in real time, the works of Shakespeare have never been translated into a signed language'.[7] His definition is too narrow because it rests on the assumption that both the source and target languages must be confined to the traditional notion of two-dimensional writing. There are, as he suggests, many productions of Shakespeare throughout England that are *interpreted* into BSL, a practice that requires great skill in instant manoeuvring between languages and cultures in

---

5 Fant is a Child of Deaf Adults, or CODA, a native ASL language user, and author of books on learning ASL and interpreting.

6 See H.-Dirksen L. Bauman's 'Getting out of Line: Toward a Visual and Cinematic Poetics of ASL', in H.-Dirksen L. Bauman, Jennifer L. Nelson and Heidi M. Rose, eds., *Signing the Body Poetic: Essays on American Sign Language Literature* (Berkeley, 2006), pp. 95–117.

7 Peter Llewellyn-Jones, 'Interpreting Shakespeare's Plays Into British Sign Language', in Ton Hoenselaars, ed., *Shakespeare and the Language of Translation* (London, 2004), p. 199.

the moment. However, interpreting is very different from translating and the differences between the two processes have profound implications for the final products. An interpretation is as ephemeral as the performance itself, but a translation remains stable and fixed and therefore promotes further study as a 'literary' document in and of itself. Rather than privileging written language, as Llewellyn-Jones does, I wish to subvert traditional notions of text by considering filmed or videotaped ASL as a 'written' text – fixed in time and space. This claim, prevalent in Deaf Studies, does not designate any film as text, but rather as the specific documentation of American Sign Language through videographic means.[8] This has major implications for the study of literature, challenging the very terms of writing, text and literature by re-framing the critical discourse in terms of bodies, presence and performance.

This practical distinction between the two processes, interpreting and translating, also forces a reconsideration of the performance products that these processes generate. Most often interpreters stand to the side of a stage and Deaf spectators must constantly shift their attention from the action on-stage to the adjacent interpreters, forcing a constant split-focus. Other interpreted performances incorporate both character and interpreter through 'shadow signing', in which interpreters, usually dressed in black, follow behind individual characters and sign the spoken dialogue. This second theatrical style allows Deaf spectators to see the action on stage and the ASL simultaneously without too much shift of focus, but both approaches privilege hearing audiences and the English text by making ASL secondary or peripheral to the spoken word and performance. A different technique, one pioneered forty years ago by the National Theater of the Deaf, makes ASL the primary performance language on stage by having all the characters use ASL while hearing actors 'voice' the spoken English text for hearing members of the audience. This technique eliminates the need for interpreters and makes English a secondary, though simultaneous, 'oral and aural' text that exists in tandem with the ASL translation. This was the target performance

method in translating *Twelfth Night*. Coupled with that choice is the assumption that the target audiences for this translation would be both Deaf and hearing. Two other assumptions were made explicit at the outset of the translation process: first, that all of the characters in the play would be Deaf, which creates not just an ASL translation, but an entirely Deaf theatrical world of Illyria; and second, all actors would only use ASL while other actors voiced the lines – no hearing actor would be allowed to voice and sign simultaneously as is often the case in other ASL-based productions.[9] Making the characters Deaf allowed us to translate sound-based images and stage directions into analogous visual images that are more appropriate to Deaf culture. The method also created unique and challenging translation cruxes. Separating ASL from English helped maintain respect for the language and simultaneously corrected the frequent error that supposes ASL to be a derivative form of English – simultaneous signing and speaking furthers that bias.

The translation team was careful at all times during the process to make sure that voiced English remained subservient to the ASL. That is, the ASL translation was not beholden to the vocal expression of the same lines. It is often easier to render an image more succinctly in ASL than in English. Moreover, sometimes the signs take longer so that

---

[8] See for example 'The Camera as Printing Press: How Film Has Influenced ASL Literature' by Christopher B. Krentz, and 'Textual Bodies, Bodily Texts' by Jennifer L. Nelson in *Signing the Body Poetic*, pp. 51–70 and 118–29.

[9] The bifurcation of character through separating voice and body elicits numerous additional critical vantage points: what emerges from the performance of this translation is a series of different but simultaneous texts, juxtaposed as sound (temporality) and presence (physicality), ASL and English, hearing and Deaf, each distinguished by the composition of the audience. The performance provides the Deaf audience with an ASL text, readable like any other, completely interpreted through the physicality of the performers. The hearing audience, on the other hand, hears Shakespeare's text at the same time as it sees the ASL translation. This conjunction creates for them a visual and aural dissonance at times – a recognition that they are hearing one language and seeing an altogether different one.

the spoken text is finished long before the ASL. Throughout the translation process the hearing members of the team would voice the text while another signed it, testing the timing of voice to sign, but the translation was never altered for fear that the hearing audiences would be bored by periods of silence. The exact timing of matching the voice to the sign must be worked out in rehearsal, not in translation. Indeed, in the performance of this translation, the speaking actors always attempted to match the signing actors, increasing or decreasing tempo and rate to match the ASL as closely as possible, not the other way around. Throughout both the translation and the rehearsal periods, however, the translation team vigilantly privileged sight over sound, approaching the play from a Deaf epistemological centre rather than a hearing one.

Transcribing a four-dimensional visual/manual language into two dimensions is the ASL translator's eternal dilemma. Resolving just one issue resulted in hydra-like growth of new ones. The translation itself took approximately eighteen months of work and was revised during the rehearsal period that followed. Primary was how to document the initial translation since ASL is impossible to transcribe in the two dimensions of written text, without special knowledge of the systems that some linguists have developed to write it. Numerous methods of notating three-dimensional movement have been attempted throughout the centuries, with varying degrees of success. In the 1970s linguist William Stokoe began his method of transcribing sign language on paper in an attempt to record the complexities of the language and to offer a method of reading ASL. However, none of the translators on this project was trained in Stokoe Notation or any other form of writing ASL, and to complicate matters, each one had a different method of glossing English words, ideas or sentences for themselves in ASL. Usually, the words that serve as glosses of ASL are written in English, providing another reason why many people wrongly consider ASL a reduced version of English. Others include short code in their glosses, like 'CL', which designate a specific type of handshape known as classifiers and then follow that code with descriptions of move-

ment. The following example of Sir Toby's first line that begins 2.3 shows Shakespeare's language on the left, followed by one translation team member's gloss on the right:

Approach Sir Andrew; Not to be abed after midnight is to be up betimes; and *diliculo surgere*, thou know'st – (2.3.1–3)	come, good night, prepare to 2CL LH, 'C' CL RH–(don't complete sign) (almost in bed) now past midnight – RH stand up(jump out of bed), good morning. f.s. 'diluculo surgere', your turn

This brief example cannot adequately convey the meaning of the ASL, which shows the sun setting and rising on the right hand, a sign that then resembles the bedcovers that Sir Toby 'almost' climbs into with a different classifier on his right hand. Translating the Latin interspersed throughout the play was also a challenge. In this example, Sir Toby supplies the beginning of the phrase *diliculo surgere saluberrimum est* (to rise early is very healthy) from William Lily's Latin grammar (1513).[10] The translation team decided not to translate the meaning of the Latin, since the phrase was incomplete, but rather to create an equivalent experience for Deaf spectators and hearing audiences, the majority of whom would know neither the Latin nor the phrase itself. Instead, the gloss reveals 'f.s.' which means 'fingerspell' (spelling the word with handshapes that represent the alphabet), and thereby providing the Latin for Deaf audiences who might know the original reference.

The translation team quickly realized that it was impossible to delay the videotaping by even a single day. Without recording a few pages at a time, immediately after translating them, even the glosses became difficult to decipher the following day. As a result, the team digitally videotaped the entire translation and analysed it as they progressed. Often, the translators would find a more appropriate translation for certain words or phrases later in the process, making earlier translations of the

---

[10] *Twelfth Night*, ed. J. M. Lothian and T. W. Craik, p. 42.

same word or phrase inconsistent with the new translation. Repairing the inaccuracy required re-filming and re-editing the earlier digital text, a time-consuming and complicated process.

Since sign language cannot be recorded effectively in writing, the resulting text is of necessity a visual one, greatly enhanced by advancements in recording and digital technology. The rapid expansion of ASL literature has arisen partly because of the proliferation of inexpensive digital video equipment that provides high-quality video for very little cost, a phenomenon that Deaf scholars like Christopher Krentz compare to the increase in written works after the advent of the printing press.[11] The final product was compiled on four CD-ROM disks that served as the base translation for the actors to use in rehearsal. Rather than a traditional read-through on the first day of rehearsal, the cast met for a 'watch-through' of the translation. Actors then used the CD-ROMs on a bank of computers outside the rehearsal hall to gloss and memorize the lines for themselves. Unlike hearing actors who read and then interpret a text, these actors quickly realized that some elements of interpreting a character have already been established in the ASL translation because ASL is a performance-based language. A key issue for the translation team throughout the process was to ensure that it was not completely 'performed', in order to afford the actors the freedom and flexibility to create the characters for themselves. The rehearsal process refined the translation even further by making corrections or emendations to the base translation and creating a unified whole through the performances of the actors. Like any text that progresses through stages of development, both the initial (or base) translation, as well as the final translation can be studied as separate literary documents to see where they diverge from each other.

The use of signed language in the United States can be traced back hundreds of years.[12] The Deaf population that inhabited Martha's Vineyard at the end of the seventeenth century, for example, used a sign language significantly different from that used in the US today, yet there is no recorded history of the language – which stifles any idea of rendering historical sign language in the translation of Shakespeare.[13] The focus of research then shifted towards an investigation into the historical use of gesture as it related to Elizabethan acting. Since there are few illustrations of Elizabethan performance practices, research was culled from various museums and catalogues from the seventeenth through nineteenth centuries and from a variety of sources: from John Bulwer's *Chirologia: or the Natural Language of the Hand* and *Chironomia: or The Art of Manual Rhetoric* published in a combined work in 1644, to 'the passions' of painter Charles Le Brun in 1702. Over sixty visual images were consulted in the research phase of the translation, including paintings and renderings of *Twelfth Night* itself.[14] Johann Heinrich Ramberg's (1763–1840) painting *Malvolio before Olivia* from the Boydell Collection of Shakespearian images was on display at the Yale Center for British Art during the translation process and served as the basis for an experiment. As we began to translate 3.4, where Malvolio first appears before Olivia, cross-gartered and in yellow stockings, the team replicated the gestures of the painting to see if it might have any influence on the translation.

---

11 Christopher Krentz, 'The Camera as Printing Press: How Film has Influenced ASL Literature', in *Signing the Body Poetic*, pp. 51–70.

12 See Nora Ellen Groce, *Everyone Here Spoke Sign Language: Hereditary Deafness on Martha's Vineyard* (Cambridge, MA, 1985). By the mid nineteenth century one in four inhabitants of the island was deaf. Oliver Sacks visited the island and found vestiges of sign language in older hearing members of the population who often subconsciously still use signs in conversation. See his *Seeing Voices: A Journey into the World of the Deaf* (New York, 1990), pp. 28–30.

13 The 1985 production discussed above located all of the action within a church on Martha's vineyard. It included a prologue for Lou Fant who played a minister who spoke about 'love and morality'. The remaining cast became members of the congregation: the hearing actors sat in the pews upstage and voiced for the Deaf actors downstage.

14 For the connection between Bulwer and the Deaf, see Jennifer L. Nelson, 'Bulwer's Speaking Hands: Deafness and Rhetoric', pp. 211–21. Sharon L. Snyder, Brenda Jo Brueggemann and Rosemarie Garland-Thomson, eds., *Disability Studies: Enabling the Humanities* (New York, 2002).

6 *Malvolio: Possibly a Self-Portrait in the Role*. John Boyne, c. 1750–1810.

7 Adrian Blue introduces the namesign for his character Malvolio. Video still from the Amaryllis Theater production.

Building upon the idea that all texts are related and surrounded by earlier and future texts, those still images of Shakespeare's plays were attempts at creating a visual intertextuality of sorts, much as other translations do when culling examples from known works. Although these images served to provide historically and visually for a dramaturgical understanding of the play, they had no impact upon the translation either for theoretical or practical reasons. Use in practice predicated the primacy of a static visual history over and above the linguistic complexity of movement in ASL by imposing two-dimensional images onto the translation rather than allowing organic images in ASL to emerge from Shakespeare's original text. Paintings and illustrations of dramatic literature present an individual artist's ideas about the scene (often separate from any theatrical production of it). They may provide more valuable information for a director,

designer or actor than for a translator since such paintings and illustrations are themselves interpretations of *Twelfth Night*. Therefore appropriating their movements, postures or gestures would have been a third or fourth remove from the original source.

Only two images of the sixty that were consulted in research had any effect on the translation. The first, a painting titled *Malvolio: Possibly a Self-Portrait in the Role* by artist John Boyne, (c. 1750–1810) depicts an effete rather than prudish characterization of Malvolio. The painting served as a visual prompt for the namesign of Malvolio, a gesture made as if brushing crumbs off the shoulder, or of brushing away an annoyance of some kind.

Namesigns are designated signs that serve as an individual's name in ASL and must be introduced first through fingerspelling. Namesigns often serve the same purpose that some of Shakespeare's character names do – they establish a physical trait or specific attributes of the individual character. Sirs Belch and Aguecheek provide good examples

8 Reproduction of three namesign drawings included in the programme of the American Theater Arts production of *Twelfth Night*.

as their namesigns reflect their respective traits of drinking and cowardice. Sir Toby's namesign is made by mimicking the enlargement of the oesophagus, and Sir Andrew's is made with the index finger that pushes up the side of the cheek to make it quiver. In production, each actor introduced his or her character's namesign at the very beginning of the production so that the Deaf audience would be familiarized with the invented namesigns that are specific to this translation. Simultaneously, the character name was projected as text onto the cyclorama upstage so that spectators equate the namesign to the person playing the character. The 1985 production of *Twelfth Night* at American Theater Arts used a different method. They introduced the audience to the specific namesigns by including artistic renderings of them in the programme for reference (see illustration).

Each of these names above was used by creating the first initial of the character name with an accompanying movement, 'V' for Viola, 'TB' for Toby Belch and 'M' for Malvolio. But these namesigns share iconic resemblances to other signs in ASL. Viola's name looks almost identical to the sign for 'VIRGIN', Toby's is an iconic representation of a belch, while Malvolio's namesign resembles the sign for 'STRICT'. All three names were conscious choices to reveal identity traits of the characters in the production.

In ASL, namesigns are only used when one is referring to a character who is not present; characters never use someone else's namesign in direct address, or to get someone's attention.[15] Instead, ASL users will point or index to a person to whom they are referring. Unlike the hearing population who call out a name to get that person's attention, Deaf people usually wave their hands to make a visual impact on the other person's peripheral vision. In some circumstances (when a person is turned with his back to another or is exiting the stage) a person may stomp on the floor to create vibrations that signal the interlocutor (or intersigner?) to turn around. These cultural methods of communication were added into the translation as often as possible, even though the blocking was yet to be solidified in the rehearsal process.

The second visual image used in the translation helped to solve a translation dilemma that was created by an idiomatic phrase spoken by Sir Andrew early in the play:

SIR ANDREW
Fair lady, do you think you have fools in hand?
MARIA
Sir, I have not you by th' hand.
SIR ANDREW
Marry, but you shall have, and here's my hand.
(1.3, 61–5)

The lines include implicit stage directions as Sir Andrew presents his hand for Maria to bring to the 'buttery-bar' a few lines later. It was the phrase

15 Samuel J. Supalla, *The Book of Name Signs: Naming in American Sign Language* (San Diego, 1992).

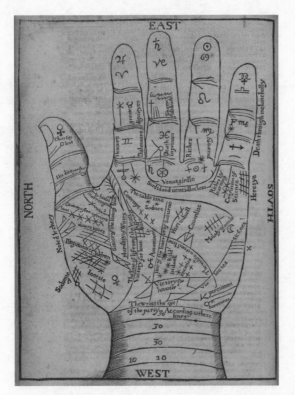

9 Untitled woodcut illustration in Richard Saunders
(1613–75), *Physiognomie, and chiromancie, metoposcopie, the
symmetrical proportions and signal moles of the body* (London,
1635), p. 38.

'fools in hand' that presented the difficulty. The
idiomatic phrase in English has no equivalent in
ASL and roughly translates to 'Do you think you are
dealing with fools?' (yet another idiomatic phrase).
Translating the line this way, Maria's next line, 'Sir,
I have not you by the hand' makes little sense.
Instead, the translators chose a common practice
in Elizabethan England, that they derived from
an image in Richard Saunders's book, *Physiognomie and chiromancie, metoposcopie, the symmetrical
proportions and signal moles of the body*, 1653. This
illustration depicts the art of 'chiromancy' or palm-
istry, foretelling the future through the study of the
palm.

Incorporating this practice into the translation,
these lines read something like, 'Fair lady, does my
palm say I am a fool?' Maria responds by saying, 'Sir
I cannot see your palm' and Sir Andrew presents

it for her to read, maintaining the implicit stage
directions and the following business that the scene
requires.

Chiromancy was but one manifestation of 'reading the body as text', a prevalent theme throughout
Twelfth Night that is not merely a critical conceit
but is rather manifestly literal in the ASL translation, where body and text are identical, and mis-
readings of the body have significant implications.
Malvolio's punishment, for example, is a direct
result of his misreading Maria's 'hand' (i.e., hand-
writing) for Olivia's. American Sign Language is
a performed language and as such, the physical
body is always required to convey semantic content. Semioticians like Keir Elam attempt to differentiate between a dramatic text (written *for* the
theatre, i.e., the script or written translation) and
the performance text (produced *in* the theatre).[16]
This distinction is untenable in the study of the
ASL translation of *Twelfth Night*. The performance-
related elements of the translation cannot be separated from purely literary ones for they share a
dialectical relationship. The ASL translation reveals
a new definition of the textualized body. It also
provides a new area of visual critical theory for the
study of Shakespeare, which is based on the understanding of the ASL performance as literature *and*
performance simultaneously.[17]

An ASL translation is bound, however, by the
practical considerations of how the source text
(Shakespeare) will be performed on the stage.
Indeed, the translation required that blocking, stage
directions (both implicit and explicit) and actual
production values (costumes, scenic design and
lighting) had to be decided in advance of, or
in the process of translation. For example, when
Malvolio signs, 'I frown the while, and perchance

---

[16] Keir Elam, *The Semiotics of Theater and Drama* (London, 1980),
p. 3.

[17] Some of these observations and analyses are drawn from my
previous work. See 'Shakespeare in the Fourth Dimension:
Twelfth Night and American Sign Language', in Pascale Aebischer, Nigel Wheale and Ed Esche, eds., *Remaking Shakespeare:
Performance Across Media, Genres and Cultures* (London, 2003),
pp. 18–38.

wind up my watch, or play with my – some rich jewel' (2.5.57–9) several questions needed to be answered. Would there be an actual watch? Where does Malvolio keep it? Is the jewel a part of the watch or separate from it, part of his chain of state as steward of the house? Where is it worn? By suggesting that the jewel might hang around his waist, the translation of these lines took on enormous sexual significance. As the translation progressed, Malvolio's language was revealed to be the most bawdy and sexually objectifying of all the characters, and in fact became a key to creating a Malvolio whose inner concupiscence always broke through his prudish exterior. Indeed, ASL manifests a much more physical relationship with Shakespeare's ribaldry and provides the Deaf spectators with a greater understanding of bawdy detail in performance than most hearing audiences understand through listening alone.

American Sign Language requires an almost architectural rendering of space. Signers create a spatially constructed world around themselves and are framed much as a camera frames a medium to medium-wide shot. Within that frame the signer drafts, on a smaller scale, the space that surrounds him and his relationship to that space, or to other objects, or between objects. Signers can manipulate that space as well as all the objects within it, literally creating illustrations of relationships to people and events by means of a moving mimesis. For example, if an actor points upstage, and gives that area a name, 'the coast', then that space upstage will remain as 'the coast' until the scene changes to another location, or when the signer changes subject or re-identifies that space. The signer can then illustrate another character entering from the coast, moving perhaps drunkenly along the street into town, and confronting other characters. From the beginning of the process then, the scenic elements of the play's production were necessarily dependent on the translation and how we established the physical location of the dramatic world and its inhabitants. Each entrance and exit, whether up, down, left or right, as well as the entire dramatic world of the play had to maintain a spatial logic consistent with the ASL translation.

Illustration 10 is a rendering of both the scenographic design for *Twelfth Night* and architectural elements of the Prince Music Theater in Philadelphia where the translation was produced. Three main playing spaces helped ground the translation in a three-dimensional reality. Two raised areas that flanked the stage in front of the proscenium became the household domains of Orsino and Olivia. The centre playing spaces were continuations of their respective houses as garden spaces, and as the seacoast or street. Maintaining an intense scrutiny of space was difficult to accomplish within the videotaped translation of *Twelfth Night* over the eighteen months of translation, owing to the extended period of time and different locations and conditions under which we videotaped. However, the final production maintains a spatial logic consistent with the requirements of the language.

Some scenes, though, created some enormously complicated problems specifically because of stage directions, but likewise compelled creative solutions. The dark house scene presented the most serious obstacle in the ASL translation. The stage direction from the First Folio, '*Malvolio within*' (4.2.21) indicates that he is most likely off stage, heard but unseen. Because ASL is a visual language, the spectators will not understand him if he is not visible to them. Complicating matters further, Feste appears at the dark house in disguise and Maria says 'Thou might have done this without thy beard and gown, he sees thee not' (4.2.64–5), suggesting that Malvolio and Feste cannot see each other, an impossibility in ASL communication. The disguise *is* necessary, therefore, so Maria's line was eliminated from the translation; but how to make Malvolio understood without being seen?

John H. Astington traces the production history of this scene and its staging in his essay, 'Malvolio and the Dark House'. 'Malvolio's prison is, literally, simply a dark place, but figuratively it is a hell . . . a fitting location for one possessed of the devil and given over to spiritual darkness.'[18] Throughout

---

[18] John H. Astington, 'Malvolio and the Dark House', *Shakespeare Survey 41* (Cambridge, 1988), p. 60.

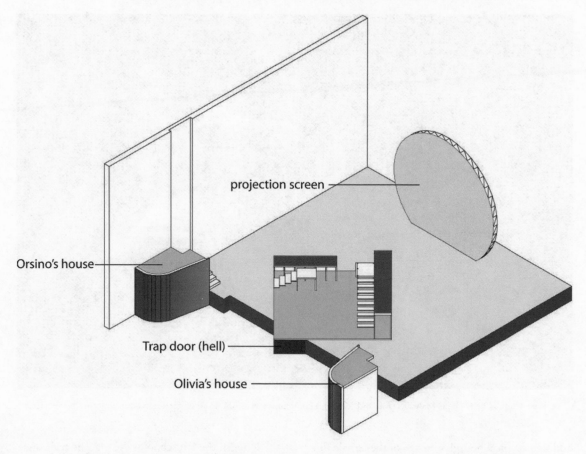

projection screen

Orsino's house

Trap door (hell)

Olivia's house

10 Rendering of scenic design of *Twelfth Night* and architectural elements of the Prince Music Theater, Philadelphia.

the production of the play, all references to hell and the devil were directed at the furthest point downstage centre, foreshadowing Malvolio's figurative hell by linguistically ostending it in the spatial syntax of ASL (see illustration 11). It was Jacques Copeau who first staged the scene in a trap under the stage in a 1914 production, and the tradition prevailed throughout the century.[19] The ASL translation stages the scene with Malvolio's hands and arms emerging through the trap door. The staging is more than a dark place for Malvolio – it is a linguistic hell.

ASL requires the body and face to produce meaning and so without them Malvolio's vocabulary is restricted to those signs and gestures that create meaning independent of the body. Having only his hands with which to communicate, Malvolio is trapped in a linguistic prison. The signs for 'my lady', for example, are created by touching the thumb of the open-handed 5-classifier to the chin and then to the sternum. Without his body, Malvolio's desperation to prove that he is not 'mad' is a frantic search for language conducted in physical improvisation. But his desperation only compounds his situation. Rather than making the sign for 'my lady', as he has throughout the play, he instead renders the term through the objectifying

---

[19] Astington, 'Malvolio', p. 55.

11 Peter Cook as Feste taunts Malvolio (Adrian Blue) who communicates in ASL from under a trap door underneath the stage.

and stereotypical hourglass image of the female figure, outlined by his hands. It is basis enough for Sir Topas (the disguised Feste) to accuse him of lechery and possession: 'Out hyperbolical fiend, how vexest thou this man! Talkest thou nothing but of ladies?' (4.2.26–7).

Having failed at his attempt to prove his sanity, Malvolio tries another tactic with Feste who has returned to the prison in his own 'voice'. Malvolio calls to him, 'Good fool, as ever thou wilt deserve well at my hand, help me to a candle and pen, ink and paper' (4.2.82–3). Lacking a fully realizable vocabulary in ASL, Malvolio answers the original letter with one of his own in the hope that writing will provide a body for his words that his hands alone (i.e., his presence) cannot. Maria's forged letter is countered with his own, which argues to Malvolio's claim to the truth. When Feste performs

the letter in the last scene of the play, he tries once more to perform Malvolio's madness by impersonating a mad 'voice' or, in ASL, an over-articulated and exaggerated signing. Once he is released from the dark room, Malvolio confronts Olivia with the forged letter, and she recognizes Maria's hand immediately. The written artifact remains the textual proof, something Malvolio's imprisoned body could never convey through a temporal and physical language.

When we are attempting to envision exchanges that occurred in Early Modern English, ASL translation is extremely useful because it draws attention to cultural and linguistic differences that contemporary usage of English has abandoned, as well as foregrounding the ability of ASL to resurrect and re-code those usages for contemporary Deaf audiences. Take for example, the you/thou dichotomy that pervades Shakespeare's work and has little bearing on today's casual listener to Shakespeare. ASL maintains the formal and familiar form of 'you' and can replicate that structure when characters shift from one form to the other, either to establish familiarity or some sense of distance. Likewise, ASL spatially locates those with higher status on a visual plane above those with lower status, making it easy to recognize status more clearly in ASL than in English, providing several ways literally to 'incorporate' materialist feminist or Marxist interpretations of power structures and status throughout the play. Throughout the ASL translation of *Twelfth Night*, Orsino's rank remained the highest of all the characters, while others like Malvolio jockeyed to change their status in relation to others. Olivia always located Orsino in space above herself, emphasizing her lower social standing to him, incorporating the paternalistic and oppressive social structure for women that permeated Elizabethan culture but that also reinforced Sir Toby's line that Olivia will 'not match above her degree, neither in estate, years, nor wit' (1.3.105–6).

The persistent problem for any translator of Shakespeare's plays is the issue of verse structure. French translations might use the Alexandrine line as an appropriate cultural and literary substitute for iambic pentameter; a choice suited to the rhythms and history of the language. Yves Bonnefoy criticized André Gide's translations of *Hamlet* for rendering the verse sections into prose. He viewed the translation as 'Shakespeare décorporé' or Shakespeare 'disembodied', because it lacked the power of verse to incarnate the words.[20] While ASL lacks the power of verse as an aural/oral function, it certainly embodies elements of verse structure through its own linguistic structures. In *Twelfth Night*, Shakespeare varies his use of language significantly between and within scenes, including blank verse, rhymed verse, song lyrics and extensive puns or plays on words. Each of these modes of language presents different challenges to a visual translation of the play and is translated using a variety of linguistic strategies, while maintaining appropriate cultural considerations in the target language.

In English, verse metre is essentially a convention of patterned stresses. Stress is a natural aspect of the sound of individual words. Metre, however, is an artificial construct imposed upon language. Verse metre entails co-ordinating a set of formal relations with the natural sound patterning of words. The task is whether or not one can find repeatable functions that can provide some co-equivalence to Shakespeare's patterns in the target language. While sound is what establishes the natural stress of a word in English, and some other spoken languages, sound cannot be the basis for word stress and therefore metrical structure in ASL. As an aural construct, metre has no parallel in Deaf culture or in ASL. Imposing an artificial rhythm onto the ASL as a means of approximating blank verse is neither linguistically nor culturally correct. ASL does, however, have a significant arsenal of methods to create visual rhyme, removing it from the oral/aural realm of production into a purely visual and performative model.

Every sign can be broken down into four basic components: hand configuration, location, movement and orientation. If two signs have identical hand configurations, movements and locations, then they have a strong visual rhyme. If they have a similar hand configuration only, the visual rhyme is weaker. However, if an entire story is told with the same handshape used for different signs, it has a strong rhyme. Because of its visual/manual modality and lexical and semantic use of space, the translation of Shakespeare into ASL took advantage of movement, location, and handshape in order to establish patterns of rhyme throughout *Twelfth Night* and used other registers and forms of ASL to create equivalent features of Shakespeare's varied uses of language.[21]

---

[20] Romy Heylen, *Translation, Poetics, and the Stage: Six French 'Hamlets'* (London, 1993), 97.

[21] See poet Clayton Valli's definitions of ASL rhyming structures according to a visual and kinetic model rather than an auditory and written one in his essay, 'Poetics of ASL Poetry', in *Deaf Studies IV* (Washington, DC, 1997), p. 253. Valli differentiates among six separate manifestations of ASL rhyme

The most easily identifiable of these elements of individual signs is handshape, and ASL has a category of signs known as 'classifiers', that are commonly defined as a set of signs that are made with a specific handshape and represent a noun's shape, size and location as well as other defining physical characteristics. Classifiers do not have precise counterparts in English, and transcribing them is often difficult because of their specific movements. They can represent individuals, vehicles or animals, and inanimate objects; they 'represent some mimetic elaboration to convey, for instance, a more precise description of an event or of a quality'.[22] Classifiers can be used in an infinite number of ways (within circumscribed boundaries), providing ASL users with enormous creative flexibility.

See, for example, how ASL elucidates an obscure meaning of the word 'revolve' by articulating it on the body, with the specific example of the 1-classifier. When Malvolio finds the letter that 'gulls him into a nayword' (2.3.130) he reads: 'If this fall into thy hand, revolve' (2.5.138). The *Oxford English Dictionary* cites Shakespeare's obscure usage of revolve in this sentence to mean 'to deliberate or consider; to meditate or think upon' (*OED*, v. 10). Editors of the recent Oxford edition of *Twelfth Night*, Roger Warren and Stanley Wells, provide a textual note believing that *revolve*

may be intended to sound like an affected novelty. The word is a great temptation to actors to gain an easy laugh by slowly revolving; but it is funnier if instead of this gag the actor points to what the line means. In Peter Hall's 1991 version, for instance, Eric Porter glanced up after revolve as if to say 'What an odd way of putting it' (thus neatly reflecting *OED*'s evidence), shrugged, and continued reading at once.[23]

Their description of Porter's performance relies again on the sound of the word, and the character's response seems more of confusion than clarity. In the ASL translation of the play, Malvolio reads his own body in order to fully understand the meaning of the word. He uses a 1-classifier for the word 'revolve' and watches his hand turn in a circle. As he begins to imitate that movement with

his full body he stops, realizing that the sign is correct, but in the wrong area of space – it is not his body that should turn. The three other characters behind him (Toby, Andrew and Fabian) see him sign 'revolve', and immediately think he will rotate and see them 'eavesdropping' behind him. They immediately run and hide. Malvolio then moves the same sign closer to his head to indicate 'to think about it, to revolve it in one's mind'. Throughout the translation there are these moments that foreground (and I use this word because of its spatial connotation) the visual/manual against the oral/aural narrative, as when the purely kinetic and physical action reveals aspects of historical meaning, production history, or cultural and linguistic complexity that are not present in contemporary productions or critical analyses.

The physical relationship of the signer to the world around her creates a discourse of narrative action that is purely visual, almost filmic. The characteristics of ASL narrative structure are not linear in function, giving the discourse a spatial logic comparable to the action of a camera. It's possible for the signer to 'cut from a normal view to a close-up to a distant shot to a close-up again, and so on, even including flashback and flashforward scenes, exactly as a movie editor works'.[24] The advantage of ASL as a performative language over more diegetic narratives is that it can easily manipulate proxemic relations between individuals and objects. Noted Deaf poet Bernard Bragg first created the phrase 'Visual Vernacular' as a label for an acting/signing technique that exploits the cinematic properties of ASL structure: 'The performer remains all the time within the film frame, so to speak, presenting a montage of cross-cuts

---

based on visual perception, defining rhyme as a repetition of 'handshapes, movements, non-manual signals, locations, palm orientation, handedness, or a combination of these'.

22 Edward Klima and Ursula Bellugi, *The Signs of Language* (Cambridge, 1979), p. 13.

23 Roger Warren and Stanley Wells, *Twelfth Night, or What You Will* (Oxford, 1994), p. 149.

24 William Stokoe quoted in Oliver Sacks, *Seeing Voices: A Journey into the World of the Deaf* (New York, 1990), p. 90.

12 Sir Andrew, Fabian and Sir Toby watch Malvolio ponder the word 'revolve'. Video stills from the Amaryllis Theater production.

and cutaway views.'[25] Both film editors and signers maintain a similar spatial logic in their construction of narrative, but ASL must also abide by grammatical and syntactic rules that films do not possess. ASL has linguistic complexity over and above images, even those that move.

ASL provides a signer with the ability to 'direct' her own narrative cinematically. In the context of the dramatic world of the *Twelfth Night* translation, individual characters create and direct their performances like film, aware at all times of an implicit, if not literal, audience. This cinematic narrative structure opens an enormous field of critical questions and perspectives. Does the gaze of the speaker have the power to objectify like a camera lens? How is the subject constructed visually? How do interlocuters function as audience within these self-constructed performances? Finally, how can the translator use these strategies when translating into ASL?

Just as Shakespeare varies his use of language from prose to blank verse and from rhymed couplets to lyrical songs, the translation incorporates several different methods of signing. ASL itself has a wide variety of registers and forms within it: 'In communicating among themselves, deaf ASL signers use a wide range of gestural devices, from conventionalized signs to mimetic elaboration on those signs, to

---

[25] I am indebted to H-Dirksen L. Bauman's article, 'Line/ Shot/Montage: Cinematic Techniques in American Sign Language Poetry', in *Conference Proceedings of Deaf Studies VI: Making the Connection* (Washington, DC, 1999), pp. 137–49.

mimetic depiction, to free pantomime.'[26] Everyday ASL is quite different from ASL on the stage which is naturally larger, more 'pronounced', and often more mimetic. Each of the songs in *Twelfth Night* was translated by taking advantage of this mimetic and also cinematic form of ASL poetry known as Visual Vernacular. Poet and performer Peter Cook, who worked on the translation for three weeks and played the part of Feste in the production, is known for his elaborately physicalized and visual metaphorical performance style, often repeating a sign several times to create a rhythmic effect. Cook is not nearly as bound by linguistic rules of ASL as other poets, enjoying instead the freedom and flexibility that visual and cinematic effects provide him. Peter's style is significantly more physical than other Deaf poets in that he makes use of his entire body, and often his voice, in his poems. Many people are attracted to Cook's physical style because it includes more mimetic features than most ASL poetry. Cook's vocabulary is based more on visual perception and physical context than in traditional ASL poetic narrative.

Songs often present difficult transitions in productions of Shakespeare's plays. In *Twelfth Night*, the song 'Come Away, Death' that appears in the middle of Act 2, scene 4 is intended to remind us of Orsino's craving for a lyricism that love elicits. In production, Feste is accompanied often by a lute or mandolin, and the song takes on a light and romantic mood for the Duke and Viola who are Feste's intended audience. While the lyrics of the song may be 'old and plain' (2.4.42), they do not dally 'with the innocence of love' (2.4.46), as Orsino suggests. Because ASL cannot present the tune that underlies the song, only the lyrics to the song are rendered visually, creating a picture of death and decay enhanced by unrequited love. Dark and deeply disturbing images of Death personified, a decaying corpse and deep isolation and loneliness are most present in this visual depiction of the song, showing both Orsino's distance from reality as well as his infatuation with the idea of love.

The songs were never voiced for the hearing audience during performance. Instead, Shakespeare's text was projected behind Cook so that the hearing audience was forced to read super-titles. Rather than depicting some sort of physical equivalent of music in ASL, which is essentially impossible and serves the hearing audience more than the Deaf spectators, the intention was to create the opposite of sound and music – silence. Except for the noises made by Cook's abrupt vocalizations and body movements, the songs were the only completely silent moments in the play, creating a purely visual and kinetic experience for every audience member without the intrusion of spoken text.

With an emphasis on the Visual Vernacular style, the base translation of 'Come Away, Death' takes two minutes and thirty-nine seconds to perform and contains approximately seventy different edits, creating a stunning montage of images. The translation also presents a darker undertone to the song than is traditionally interpreted on the stage. Cook begins by offering his heart to an 'off-screen' lover. The lover, whose gender is never specified throughout the song/poem, rejects the offering, and Cook returns his heart to his chest. His facial expression indicates that he sees something and the first edit is a reverse-angle cutaway to the image of Death, marching toward him. Moving back and forth between shots, we see Feste's reaction to Death's plodding march towards him. Death finally stops marching and stares down at the signer, and for the first time we realize how large and powerful the figure of death really is, looming over him. He reaches his giant hand towards the signer and throws him down a vast abyss showing the legs dangling in the air and then a close-up of the body's fall. The rhythmic relationship between camera shots changes throughout the poem/song. Rhythm changes by the number and speed of the edits, ending the first series of images with the poet's death at the bottom of a long tunnel.

Cook makes use of reverse-angle shots, incorporating cutaways and close-ups throughout the song for different effect. There are also two 'special

---

[26] Klima and Bellugi, *The Signs of Language*, p. 13.

13 Peter Cook performs the beginning of 'Come Away, Death'. Video stills from the Amaryllis Theater production.

14 Peter Cook depicts a decomposing body in 'Come Away, Death'. Video stills from the Amaryllis Theater production.

effects' in the song that create temporal shifts in the narration. The first depicts the poet's friends marching in single file to the grave. They collectively sigh and throw a flower on the grave, which the poet then rejects. As he throws the flower back to them, the film rewinds, depicting the same movements in reverse motion. Cook shows the reverse elements also in a reverse rhythm, illustrating the artificiality of movement that indicates a film in reverse motion.

The second special effect depicts a corpse decomposing in the grave. Cook begins by depicting the bulging of eyes from their sockets and then proceeds to illustrate the emaciated cheekbones, the bared teeth, articulation of ribs and finally clawed, skeletal feet.

The body decomposes before our very eyes as though the camera were recording the event through time-lapse. The song ends with the poet's decline into the bowels of the earth, towards his

eternal rest. These effects create a more chilling image of death and loneliness than traditional stagings of this song allow. Coupled with Cook's signature style of signing and the cinematic effects of Visual Vernacular, the songs are noticeably more elevated in presentation and style than other segments of the text. But the base translation of this song, and the final performance of it are quite different. Cook eliminates many of the editorial back-and-forth in the final performance of the song, reducing the rhythmic effect. Both 'versions' of the song are available for study – the original base translation can be found on the website www.aslshakespeare.com (under the Project and Challenges portion of the website, page 9) while the final translation in performance exists on the DVD of the production.

The ASL translation of *Twelfth Night* required a constant shifting – a simultaneous and delicate balance between cultures and languages, hearing and Deaf, presence and absence, sight and sound, time and space. From the initial translation through the filmed performance of the final translation, the ASL *Twelfth Night* has become a cultural product and a literary text fully documented for future study and critical analysis. This 'literature of the body', affording as it does a combined visual, kinesthetic and textual perspective on the play, rather than the commonly employed literary and theatrical perspectives, enables a more broadly conceived definition of text itself. The materiality of the actors' bodies as a textual element, and the four-dimensional structure of the language, brings a visual poetics to bear on the study of Shakespeare never before seen.

'THIS UNCIVIL AND UNJUST EXTENT AGAINST THY PEACE': TIM SUPPLE'S *TWELFTH NIGHT*, OR WHAT VIOLENCE WILL

ALFREDO MICHEL MODENESSI

Para Sarah, alma mía

Tim Supple's film of *Twelfth Night, or What You Will* (2003) begins with a familiar gesture of caution and ends with an equally well-known sign, now primarily – at least partly – of affection, just as often understood as a seal of joy and promise of happiness at the end of a 'romantic comedy'. In both cases a male touches the lips of one – the same – female. The first does it with the tip of his finger, quickly, not imperiously but firmly commanding her to 'hold her peace' lest a sound deprive both of their lives. The second does it with a kiss, after offering his hand no longer as that of a master to the now 'master's mistress'. To be accurate – and fair – in the latter scene man and woman lean towards each other in apparent, and tender, achievement of much repressed and delayed desires. This is what happy endings look like, they say. It is, however, also an action that makes the woman 'hold her peace' again.

A careful exchange of shots prior to the kiss contributes to this closing touch being uncomfortably more ambiguous than expected. Another woman is shown in close-up immediately before the newly acknowledged 'mistress' and her 'former master' hold hands and kiss; she says: 'A sister, you are she' (5.1.325),[1] with a hopeful smile. Supple and co-writer Andrew Bannerman chose Olivia's half-line to be the very last words in their adaptation of Shakespeare's play, relocating it at the end of the film, together with Orsino's 'Your master quits you' (5.1.320–5), so that both occur *after* the disclosure of identities and Malvolio's exit. It

isn't a huge move in adaptation – the film proceeds mostly in keeping with Shakespeare's text – but it may be hugely significant. Their decision probably derived from the fact that in Shakespeare's script Viola's last words come at 5.1.272–5 – i.e. should Shakespeare's design be punctually followed, she must remain silent on stage for roughly 120 lines, perhaps discreetly witnessing the revelation of Malvolio's plight and attentively listening to Orsino's last speech – unlikely to be a focal point, either way. Instead, the screenwriters' intervention ensured that Viola would be the last character to 'speak', however wordlessly.

Viola remains silent, then, but not unresponsive to Olivia, for what we see is her complex and eloquent filmic reply in three steps: first, Viola's dark eyes look briefly at Olivia, apparently in sudden realization of something to be wary of; then they turn to a void with growing doubt punctuated by a slight parting of her lips and a light swallowing in her throat – she seems to be checking whatever has come to her mind; finally, she blinks softly twice and looks to her right, where we know her 'former master' offers his hand. A cut makes our view turn 180 degrees to a general shot of the secluded corner in Olivia's garden where Orsino and Viola are sitting – and where

This article was first presented at the seminar 'Shakespeare's Comedy on Film', 35th meeting of the SAA (San Diego, 2007). My gratitude to Peter Holland, Sam Crowl and Adriana Bellamy.
[1] Act and scene references are to *Twelfth Night*, ed. J. M. Lothian and T. W. Craik (The Arden Shakespeare, 1975).

several key scenes have been played – with Olivia and Sebastian about to embrace in the far plane to the right. Viola takes Orsino's hand, and a quick cut to a close-up including only the two of them ends with the soft kiss; then we move rapidly to Olivia and Sebastian, who look into each other's eyes and caress, and then back to the kiss. Fade out and ending credits follow, with Feste's voice singing a 'sweet' arrangement of 'When that I was', his austere guitar introduction having served as musical background to the entire scene.

Thus ends a tale[2] that also started with a close-up of Viola's face, her lips being touched, her silence. Surely this deliberate coupling of actions where Viola's lips are twice sealed by a man's touch as bookends to a provocative rendering of Shakespeare's comedy in a contemporary setting may be read in a positive way: from life-saving though enforced silence to the quiet, physical, eloquence of love and *future* happiness. Supple's own view (however 'blurbish') seems to concur: '*Twelfth Night* . . . enthrals us with the sorrow of endings and the great hope of beginnings.'[3] But there's room for wariness, as Viola's final gestures suggest: a window for doubt inviting speech that nonetheless went checked added on to the prescribed, and doubtless hopeful, ending – a certain amount of fear in the light of accomplished love, at least. And hence the threat of narrative circularity: 'beginning', 'ending', 'hope' and 'sorrow' become hard to untangle.[4]

The opening sequence confirms it. The first image we see in Supple's *Twelfth Night*, after an austere presentation of its title in mobile and elegant blue lettering against a pitch-black screen, is a close-up of Viola, a woman in her twenties. This image belongs in a brief but crucial filmic narrative that prologues and frames Supple's take on Shakespeare's comedy. Viola is violently awakened from sleep by a full 90-degree blurry slow-motion zooming-in close-up of a young man of the same age and similar features who in the quickly ensuing shot immediately puts his finger on her lips to prevent her from making a sound. This image of her brother Sebastian we see from her sleepy eyes, but more significantly from an angle that suggests subordination in an atmosphere of utmost urgency

and confusion – there is great danger outside, neither unknown nor unexpected. Sebastian grabs an automatic hand-gun from under a cushion and goes to half-open a door. He peeps out as Viola, still shaken, makes sense of the situation and moves to stand up. The pace of the sequence is radically and meaningfully faster than that of the closing scene. The cutting is sharp, consistent with one of Shakespeare's favourite dramatic indices: the sudden interruption or nervous lack of sleep, which operates in *Twelfth Night*, of course, when Toby, Andrew and Feste 'gabble like tinkers' (2.3.89) and disrupt the nightly peace of Maria, Malvolio, the house.

In Supple's version, sleeplessness is also significant when Viola reflects upon Olivia's love for her (2.2.16 ff): at night, wearing only her manly shirt, after having evidently spent a while staring at the ring, Viola leaves her bed and stands in front of a three-way mirror, delivering her lines with restlessness, curiosity and confusion while looking at her body under the strange clothes she wears for protection. Although she moves back to lie in bed, she remains awake through the end of the sequence – the remainder of the night will bring little rest. Or none, as happens in the opening sequence, which ends with the twins running for their lives. With Shakespeare, restless nights go hand in hand with stress and violence, whether public or private, verbal or physical, often ultimately fatal to one and others or slowly self-consuming. Supple's powerful introduction to the state of affairs in Messaline – to be examined further – and his ensuing treatment

---

[2] Trevor Nunn's film of *Twelfth Night* (1996) begins with a song: 'I'll tell thee a tale', followed by a prologue underlining its deceivingly 'long ago and far away' design. Nunn's 'tale' – set in an unidentified yet recognizably nineteenth-century environment and played by a cast of English actors with flawless RP accents – coincides and contrasts with Supple's at many points.

[3] www.channel4.com/culture/microsites/T/twelfth_night/index.html.

[4] Peter Holland's conclusions regarding Nunn's film suggest an affinity: 'the film is . . . more than adequately alive to the text's awareness of the fragility and vulnerability of the possibilities of happiness' (www.shakespearemag.com/spring97/12night.asp).

of plot and characters, consistently suggest all those kinds of unrest through to the ambiguous ending of the film: in strictly Shakespearian fashion, 'peace' entails an irony everywhere it shows.[5]

Released as a TV film in 2003 by British Channel 4, *Twelfth Night* started to develop in 2001 as the central item in an educational project. To that effect, 4Learning, a branch of Channel 4, produced two companion pieces: a 'behind-the-scenes' documentary named *21ˢᵗ Century Bard: The Making of 'Twelfth Night'* (dir. John Butterworth, 2003), and a 65-page 'Online Extra' – a downloadable text-document containing much information, activities, links to online clips, and a bibliography. Both 'study-aids' were carefully designed to meet the requirements of British educational systems and markets. The central piece of this project originated at executive level, therefore, before becoming Supple's artistic responsibility, his first commission as a filmmaker.

A visually gifted director with a remarkable sense of the role of music on stage, Supple began at the York Theatre Royal in 1988, and then worked with the Crucible Theatre of Sheffield and Branagh's Renaissance Theatre. In 1993, he was appointed artistic director of the Young Vic, where he gained recognition for his ability to adapt and update classic pieces, a reputation that has carried on to his work with the National Theatre, the Royal Shakespeare Company and several opera-houses. Supple has a knack for working with non-dramatic sources, and has successfully staged narrative materials such as Faulkner's *As I Lay Dying* and Rushdie's *Midnight's Children* and *Haroun and the Sea of Stories*. His Shakespeare productions include *Coriolanus*, *The Comedy of Errors* and a stage *Twelfth Night*. More to the point, Supple has consistently employed multicultural perspectives and resources, mainly South Asian in origin. In 2006, for example, he travelled across India auditioning actors, performers, musicians and designers for his much praised contribution to the RSC's 'Complete Works': a multilingual and multi-ethnic *Midsummer Night's Dream* that toured India and Sri Lanka before playing at Stratford-upon-Avon and Verona.

In his first film, Supple's interest in multiculturalism is not only highly visible but also politically invested. The documentary *21ˢᵗ Century Bard: The Making of 'Twelfth Night'* is generally valuable but uneven, at times shallow. Still, regardless of their relative value, Supple's remarks in it, particularly when addressing his cast, suggest an awareness – or intuition – of stimulating issues underlying the play. Exploring his handling of filmic space and the play's language, his use of a modern-day setting and a multi-ethnic cast, his framing of the original story within a specific narrative of violence and his treatment of the female leads may help us see some of the implications Supple identified in Shakespeare's text, political or otherwise, and how he actualized them on film.

The possibility that the 'happy ending' may be a new starting point for an old tale of silence, mistrust and fear (or a combination thereof) locks on to Supple's spatial design: he underlines confinement and emphasizes isolation as much as he undermines privacy and stresses intrusiveness. As indicated, the final kiss occurs inside a trellised corner of Olivia's garden where other key actions have developed. Here Malvolio finds the letter and delivers his self-infatuated reading. Here Olivia seeks shelter from the madhouse her house has become, having given up on the impracticable privacy of the shrine she erected for her dead brother in the drawing room, continually intruded upon by her servants and uncle, and even by the *ghost* of her sibling.[6] Here, too, Viola and Olivia have their second exchange, after Malvolio's letter scene.

This confined spot, however, boxed-in by the trellis and vegetation, is also equipped with a CCTV system and microphones, the perfect

---

5 This is consistent with Sam Crowl's view that in 'our sceptical age . . . Shakespeare's comic pleasures result from how things fall apart not how the center, finally, holds.' ('Dark against Light in Shakespearian Comedy on Film', unpublished paper presented at the seminar 'Shakespeare's Comedy on Film', 35th meeting of the SAA (San Diego, 2007), p. 1.)

6 His appearence is probably meant to keep Olivia from mourning, however.

apparatus and setting for Toby, Andrew and Fabian (a plainclothesman in charge of surveillance) to enjoy the effects of Maria's 'device'. Moreover, here Olivia is found by cross-gartered Malvolio, and on top, after 'Why, this is very midsummer madness' (3.4.55), a servant walks in on them – while the steward's face is buried in his mistress's lap! However, earlier, after Malvolio's exit from the eavesdropping scene, as Toby and Andrew begin to pry on Olivia and Viola, looking to be even better entertained, Maria turns off the system and exceptionally restores the privacy of the place, a rare act of restraint and care inside a world running mad with intrusiveness and disregard.

Supple seems to have a simple but effective division of spaces in mind. On the one hand are sequences shot at obvious locations: outdoor exchanges such as Sebastain and Antonio's 'purse' scene (3.3), shot at a flea market, which provide a sense of direct, rough-coloured, 'cinematic realism', together with sequences shot in sets that are treated similarly, e.g. Toby's dark and messy den, a basement flanked by a small, cage-like wine-cellar with a strong metal door that eventually becomes Malvolio's cell or Fabian's surveillance booth, complete with crass pin-ups and similar paraphernalia, or the entrance to Olivia's house, with its heavily barred gate and obtrusive trees. Throughout, Supple emphasizes cage-like spaces by making his camera look through grates, bars, railings, tree-trunks in proximity to the lens, and the like, as in Olivia and Sebastian's scene of commitment, where each addresses the other from either side of the iron railing at the entrance to her home.[7] On the other hand are sets that yell out 'theatricality', with dream-like and misleading promises of freedom: Orsino's luminous living room and misty bathroom, for example, or Olivia's drawing room, mostly in darkness and converted to a chapel-like space where she keeps a shrine with a photograph of her brother, or the trellised corner in the garden.

Supple strives, then, to separate spaces conceptually: here, spots of fragile or vulnerable desires; there, spots of menace, violent intrusion, callous truths. His framing is well in keeping with both.

Crowded rooms and narrow spaces prevail. The basement and cellar are dimly lit and suffocating. The ship aboard which Viola and Sebastian escape is crowded with refugees from Messaline. The trellised corner looks smallish and squarely confined, until we realize it opens at one end to a very artificial balcony. The entrance and passage into Olivia's house create small squares limited by iron bars and wooden walls that function as traps – for instance, when Viola struggles to fend off Andrew, Toby and Fabian, whose tauntings to make her fight at a point resemble an attempt at gang-rape; and immediately afterwards, as Sebastian and then Antonio confront the ague-faced and belching knights. Only some timely shots of the horizon and the sea beneath, mostly from Orsino's balcony and the open end of the trellised corner, provide occasional relief from this atmosphere of near-incarceration and self-isolation.[8]

By the end of the film, the insistence on an oppressive atmosphere has played a major part. If a fundamental point in Shakespeare's *Twelfth Night* is that no member of Orsino's household other than Cesario ever enters Olivia's house prior to the last, continuous, act-scene (5.1), a simple but also crucial implication is that, for all his power, Orsino's access to the 'other' house is strictly limited. This cannot be overemphasized, of course, but it can be meaningfully stressed. As already mentioned,

---

7 Again, Supple's film coincides with – and surpasses – recent productions stressing the darker aspects of Shakespeare's comedy. According to Michael Hattaway, Nunn 'chose to foreground the conflict between Illyria and Messalina, and introduced an Illyrian army . . . filmed from low angles to make them more threatening' ('The Comedies on Film', *The Cambridge Companion to Shakespeare on Film*, ed. Russell Jackson (Cambridge, 2000), p. 89). This adaptative strategy isn't risk-free, however. Kenneth Rothwell, for instance, thinks that this 'Unfortunately . . . robs Viola of some of the mystery that Shakespeare surrounds her with, and turns Illyria into a police state' (*A History of Shakespeare on Screen* (Cambridge, 2000), p. 239).

8 Nunn's space is almost the opposite: wide-open spaces, beaches and rocky coasts, large castles and manors with sumptuous rooms and gardens, that nonetheless reveal how much 'Appetite lies underneath pretense' (H. R. Coursen, *Shakespeare in Space* (New York, 2002), p. 27).

Supple employed a multi-ethnic cast. However, he also carefully grouped his actors so that this wouldn't be a case of 'colour-blind' casting: Olivia's household is British while Orsino's is African and the twins are Indian. Since multiculturalism entails tension as much as integration, the limitations on the Duke's passage into Olivia's house or heart are made ever more significant in this 'colour-aware' scenario, no less because the one person (and then her twin) for whom Olivia's doors do open is not only Orsino's 'man' but, paradoxically, the more *recognizably alien* in the mix.

A concomitant *cinematic* point that cannot be overlooked is that Orsino's only visit to Olivia's house, an act of power, begins in broad afternoon light but ends in nightly darkness – on a fortuitous act of renunciation. The sequence containing Orsino's arrival and the ensuing rejection by Olivia, with the confusion of Viola before Antonio and the Countess, ending in the sudden appearance of Andrew, badly hurt, his head and shirt strikingly bloody, and the immediate entrance of Toby in even worse shape due to a greater wound and his permanent drunkenness and aggressiveness, is filmed in raw, 'realistic' fashion, with plain lighting and a soundtrack containing exclusively 'natural' sounds. Another salient strategy there is the menacingly mobile camera that tracks Orsino in his angry speech after Olivia's 'as howling after music' (5.1.108) to show the effects of his words on the faces of both his future wife and future 'sister'. So far, 'peace' looks evermore unreachable. But the set slowly begins to darken after Andrew and Toby burst in and music softly intervenes in this disquieting turmoil.

Olivia now walks at a much slower pace down the increasingly dark pathway to the trellised corner, and finds her recent husband sitting alone on the bench, deeply remorseful for his actions against the knights, tensely caught between his peaceful persuasions and choleric impulses. Throughout, Sebastian acts as if haunted by a violence that he cannot shun, no matter how hard he tries or how much he'd want to. A similar tension permanently haunts Toby and Olivia, who can rapidly shift from drunken stupor or anxious sobriety, respectively, to heavy tears for the death of their relation. The recognition scene takes place in highly theatrical fashion, with the sunset for a backdrop, and music distinctly punctuating the magic of the moment. Viola and Sebastian deliver and embrace as the set grows dark; Orsino and Olivia find relief.

Most characters now go to the basement, where Malvolio is freed and, once the 'device' is revealed, vows his revenge and leaves. No one responds to Orsino's command to 'entreat him to a peace' (5.1.379); Fabian finally acknowledges it but rapidly shrugs it off and exits. Violence remains strong beneath the newfound calm. A strong point in the film's highlighting of violence is that Malvolio's confinement in 'darkness' (4.2) is signified by a sack fastened over his head by Fabian, in cruel hostage, kidnapping, or POW style. He's also tied by the wrists to metal bars inside the wine cellar, which forces him to demonstrate his fury audibly by kicking on its iron door. Moreover, when visiting Malvolio as Sir Topas, Feste viciously grabs his head and bangs it against the door. Worse still, after that segment – played so totally against laughs that it makes Toby and Maria cry and repent in their drunkenness – Feste, now as himself, while promising through a narrow slot in the door to bring the things Malvolio needs to write, uses a knife to unfasten the sack but then points the blade at the steward's temple while delivering 'I'll ne'er believe a madman till I see his brains' (4.2.120–1). Malvolio's fearful reaction is eloquent, in contrast with his quietly dry, choleric self. Like violence and peace, throughout the film Feste is mercurial: fascinating yet sinister, at seemingly random intervals funny, aggressive, inscrutable, amicable and detestable, as mad as everyone and as sane as anyone, a raw comic spirit indeed, permanently disruptive and unpredictable, permanently in crisis, permanently critical, never just 'funny'.[9]

---

9 Supple's Feste (Zubin Varla), like Nunn's (Ben Kingsley), is Anglo-Indian and hence seems to fit Katherine Eggert's profile of 'non-white actors' cast in 'unassimilable roles' in recent films of Shakespeare's comedies. But while Kingsley's Feste 'wears the shapeless and worn clothes of a tramp . . . his accent is as upper class as [that of] the aristocratic characters', and may

By the time the couples leave the basement, night has fallen over idyllic Illyria. A tearful Olivia and a calm Orsino embrace and make *their* peace before he addresses his new love and she embraces her just-met husband. The visual backdrop to the closing kiss, then, is a sparsely starry sky, as melancholy as the music and voice that constitute its aural background. The transition from a violent beginning to a peaceful ending of the scene, act and play thus appears complete. But Supple's prevalent layout is ironic – half-tones, tense subtexts, internal struggle or doubt, delicately melancholic music juxtaposed with frantically melancholic music – and well reflected in the grey or twilight-reddish skies that abound in this film. This spreads to his treatment of language. The case immediately in point is Olivia's re-located half-line: she puts an end to the words in the play expressing happiness for the finding of a sister, for she's yet to know her husband other than carnally.

Supple seems to have directed his cast to assume a degree of tentativeness in most everything they say – to underscore the unactualized options lying beneath each word said and each action finally taken. In many speeches there is a sense of possible failure or error foreseen, implied; of saying and doing things either senseless, useless or impossible to correct once they are effected, but again just as inevitable. As so often happens with Shakespeare, in *Twelfth Night* words are at odds with deeds:

ORSINO   You uncivil lady,
To whose ingrate and unauspicious altars
My soul the faithfull'st off'rings hath breathed out
That e'er devotion tendered – what shall I do?

                              (5.1.110–13)

In Supple's view, and his Orsino's delivery, this 'do' plays the always brief yet always lethal villain's part in opposition to the tender 'off'rings breathed out' by a devout 'soul'. As we know, to Olivia's answer, 'Even what it please my lord that shall become him' (5.1.114), Orsino vows 'I'll sacrifice the lamb that I do love / To spite a raven's heart within a dove' (5.1.128–9).

Twelfth Night is full of threats, whether in earnest or in jest – which is to say in earnest. And so is

Supple's version: he takes advantage of the tension between nearly or eventually meaningless places, pointless words and futile actions; often, what is said may sound great and right, but what actually happens is not always in keeping and never for long. His cast follow suit: many actions and many speeches seem delivered with more than one meaning intended or at least entertained, more than the foregrounded purpose, or, if not, as if every word and deed should be promptly, and impossibly, taken back or reversed. In Illyria impulse and madness rule, frequently but all too briefly followed by a self-awareness that never amounts to future restraint.

Given this atmosphere of conflict, Supple apparently decided to draw on one of Viola's simple but crucial lines to bring her entire part against the general grain: 'My lord would speak, my duty hushes me' (5.1.105). Viola is the one character who almost never acts uncautiously, speaks tentatively or goes mad; instead, this young, bright, beautiful woman hardly ever speaks without a tinge or a bulk of contained fear well signified in the apparently empty spaces of her pauses – hardly ever, that is, for she looks relatively at ease and even risks some intensity whenever she negotiates her fiction of a male with Olivia, during the only moments in the entirety of *Twelfth Night* where Viola truly interacts with someone like her, although with the evident complication that in such scenes she is 'like' a man: not 'that' s/he plays (cf. 1.5.185) but a 'player'. Supple's filmic syntax at the ending, then, stresses what Viola's 'duty' involves well beyond the specifics of her situation as Orsino's servant: the recurrent act of silencing – of 'holding one's peace' or being forced to do so, or else forcing others – in order to define Viola as being at the core of a tale of violated privacy, concealment and confinement, ending in release, no doubt, but also in muteness, as hopeful as it may be and as it may *seem*, by means

---

be thus said to resist assimilation by being 'culturally fluid and culturally fluent' ('Sure Can Sing and Dance', *Shakespeare the Movie II*, ed. Richard Burt and Lynda E. Boose (London, 2003), pp. 83–4), Varla's Feste is unassimilable by virtue of sheer instability: everything about him is in permanently free motion.

of a kiss purporting everlasting faith, a promise of another meaning for 'peace'.

Still, a kiss is just a kiss? Perhaps, but there is reason for caution when a kiss is structurally bound to a different action – a finger placed on top of a woman's lips – that causes similar results, if to different purposes and degrees, at the very opening of this narrative. Let's go back there.

Interspersed with the visual narrative of turmoil in Messaline described above – the rude awakening and escape of the twins – are two extreme close-ups of a thirtyish man in another country: Orsino, the Duke of Illyria, who delivers his opening line, 'If music be the food of love, play on' (1.1.1), stressing the preposition as if responding to a challenge. As Sebastian cautiously peeps through the door in Messaline, in Illyria Orsino goes on to 'Give me excess of it that, surfeiting, / The appetite may sicken, and so die' (1.1.2–3), again with a hint of fierceness in his voice, a full stress on 'die'. More pointedly, the angle at which his face is set in relation to the shots of Viola's face suggests that, were they in the same room, he would look downwards on her, just as Sebastian did. Viola's quiet fear, throughout performed to indicate that it is not an unaccustomed feeling, lingers through the quick cuts to the point where she is up in her bed clothes and fumbling to put on a more appropriate outfit to make a getaway. The sequence carries on in a combination of the play's first scene and the frame narrative of the twins' escape, with a double soundtrack providing clues as to the route and destination of the film we are about to see.

What brings about this tense situation, powerfully punctuated and counterpointed by Orsino's aggressive plea for 'sweet sound'? Violence, the keynote to Supple's reading of *Twelfth Night*, is present in the soundtrack from the start as part of a splendid aural introduction and definition of what will follow. As the blue lettering of Shakespeare's name and the long title of his play appear on-screen, one of the musical themes of the film, unmistakably South Asian,[10] emerges subtly to find its captivating allure almost at once challenged and disrupted, though not overridden, by the sound of a car

stopping, its doors opening and hard, metal-tipped footfalls moving in haste together with the recognizable clicking of firearms. A door is banged on and shattered as the words '*or What You Will*' show and fade, before we see Viola's face an instant prior to her awakening. This is what precedes Orsino's 'If music', an exotic kind of 'sweet music' conflicting with the aural testimony of brutal assault.

Shortly, from Sebastian's point of view we find that strangers in military gear have broken into the twins' home and are now taking a middle-aged woman captive. She struggles mildly with her captors as inside Orsino's palace a slender, elegantly dressed and evidently nervous soprano sings an aria from *Die Zauberflöte*,[11] clearly dear to the Duke's heavy heart and discriminating ears. A man wearing a black beret throws a burning match on previously spilled fuel at the twins' home – the sound of the match and the flames magnified, much as in the gas-station sequence in *Romeo + Juliet* – and in a quick exchange of shots, through the fire that hurts his eyes, Sebastian sees the woman for the last time as she strives to look in his direction in slow-motion anguish while she's forcibly taken out of the frame. Throughout, she hasn't uttered a sound.[12]

---

[10] The work of Nitin Sawhney, an outstanding Anglo-Indian composer, performer and producer whose hybrid art fits Supple's multicultural approach perfectly. As already noted, Supple's use of music is among his greatest assets.

[11] Fittingly, Pamina's 'Ach, Ich Fühl's', her doleful response to Tamino's silence. Supple directed *The Magic Flute* for Opera North in 2003.

[12] Holland observes that 'there is something about the brutal bleakness of Supple that is a continuation of the darkening of the view of the play across [previous] versions, as if we have now to be prepared to see it as brutal as the play can be' (personal communication, 26 June 2007). Indeed, Supple's narrative framing and interpretation of *Twelfth Night* would be unfeasible without the historically dynamic awareness of the darker aspects of comedy mentioned by Crowl (see note 5), and the type and history of adaptative practice that releases dramaturgs and screenwriters from subservience to the intangible 'author', enabling present *and* creative engagement with a stimulating text. Otherwise, critical standards will continue to bow to stagnant prejudice. To illustrate, a review by Thomas Sutcliffe (*The Independent*, 6 May 2003), whose take on Supple's ideas is paradigmatically DOA: 'The suggestion that Viola and Sebastian were aristocratic asylum

At Orsino's palace, the Duke also strives but merely to hold back his tears: the soprano's voice, Mozart's poignant cadences, his love for fair Olivia, all well up in his eyes, along with other inexplicit feelings, frustration and impatience chief among them. Sebastian, on the other end, would cry, but there are more urgent matters at hand. Viola is now properly dressed, so they move from door to window; Sebastian opens it to reveal the same sparsely starry night that will preside over the final sequence — it is past midnight in Messaline — and she jumps out in slow-motion as within the strictly symmetrical shot he also vanishes. At the same time, the soprano reaches a crucial 'strain' in Mozart's exquisite aria and, while she negotiates its demanding notes, we go back to Orsino's palace. The singer's face tenses as she struggles to deliver the passage, and then we share her view of Orsino sitting on a single chair in a luxurious room that opens to a wide balcony framed with the same symmetrical accuracy as the twins' window to (temporary) safety. It is twilight in Illyria, its skies faintly red. The Duke delivers a line that confirms what the previous shots chronicle: the 'strain' he demands be sung again had a 'dying fall' (1.1.4). His remark makes the singer stop dead in her tracks. A tense pause ensues, and as the soprano resumes the aria, quick shots of Olivia, an elegant lady aristocratically sitting for a portrait, flash through Orsino's mind, seemingly leading him to make the noticeably intimidated soprano hold *her* peace for good with his blunt 'Enough, no more, / 'Tis not so sweet now as it was before' (1.1.7–8).

It never was 'so sweet' in fact, as we have presently and categorically been shown. Supple's overall take on Shakespeare's play is thoroughly and effectively advanced in this prologue. Profiting from the unique attributes of cinema to establish an appearance of simultaneity, he depicts worlds in high contrast regarding their levels of rest, comfort, safety, pleasure and so forth, with several underlying counter-strains in close association, a unified thematic cluster of varying degress of struggle, violence, frustration, fear, isolation, howsoever mutually contrasting as regards their objective conditions: relative or brutal, trivial or transcen-

dental, self-imposed or desperately out of control. In sum, 'sweet music' may have been sweet some time and some place other than *these* entangled times and spaces. To this aim, Supple made artistic choices that bespeak radical and radically important tensions and add interestingly diverse political dimensions to his *Twelfth Night*.

As said, the cast is not only multi-ethnic but purposefully so. On the Duke's side, the inhabitants of Illyria are black African: Orsino (London-born Chiwetel Ejiofor), Valentine (Burt Caesar), the soprano (Claire Wilde) and the piano player; significantly, a white butler appears briefly at the palace. Olivia's troupe are white British: she (Claire Price), Sir Toby (David Troughton), Sir Andrew (Richard Bremmer), Malvolio (Michael Maloney) and Fabian (Vincenzo Nicoli) are English, while Maria (Maureen Beattie) is Irish; furthermore, while the Captain explains Olivia's situation to Viola (1.2.36 ff), Olivia's dead father is conspicuously pictured in a kilt as his image transforms into that of her dead brother, shown to have died in a brutal car-crash.[13] Malvolio also wears a kilt when it's time to show his yellow stockings. Significantly again, the servant who walks in on Malvolio's attempt at seducing Olivia is black. The policemen who capture Antonio are white too, while the Captain who saves Viola (Vic Tablian, born in Egypt) has an eastern Mediterranean accent. With the exception of Maloney, most are primarily TV actors, while Feste (Zubin Varla, Anglo-Indian, best known for his work on stage and in musicals — he originated the role of Saleem Sinai in Supple's *Midnight's Children*) is an accomplished singer, and in the film a minor pop star.

'What means this . . . ?' (2.2.16). In this Illyria, Olivia's house is an island of a past sinking in anarchy since the demise of its late masters. Its current head is earnestly distressed and not whimsically but truly and unceasingly in mourning — even near the end she leaves the cellar in tears upon

---

seekers, fleeing a violent coup, made a kind of sense, I suppose — but this is a play about gender identity, not racial identity.'

[13] Perhaps resembling the Princess of Wales?

seeing a picture of her brother. In turn, Orsino is a contemporary avatar of *il cortegiano*. Yet Olivia 'cannot love him', a phrase she utters thrice in a short span during her first exchange with Viola (1.5.261, 266, 284), in this film with particular vehemence. Orsino's resolve to have her is just as firm and his refinement as much a fashioning of his cravings as that of his early modern counterparts. It's all in Shakespeare's text, of course. But in a twenty-first-century film that isn't 'colour-blind', where he *is* black and she *is* white, both attitudes become more specifically suspect. Her vehement rejection of 'Orsino's embassy' smacks of overdetermined prejudice, whether professed, mimetic or merely received. Then again, when Viola reveals to the Duke that Cesario loves *a woman* of his 'complexion' (2.4.26), Orsino's reply: 'She is not worth thee, then' (2.4.27) is made derisively so that it cannot be accounted free of a similar sin. Worse still, at Olivia's dwell two 'Gentlemen', one even a 'suitor', who might as well be trashing a pub after a defeat of their local team. For the Indian refugees, in turn, concealment means safety. Among other things, then, the tensions in this Dukedom epitomize the state of human affairs in many 'civil' societies.

All in Illyria suffer from some loss, lack or frustration, and act upon instinct without much regard for consistency or restraint. Impatiently or irresponsibly – or both – everyone seems unafraid to hurt others or themselves and is usually successful at it. Orsino is young and rules aggressively over young men, while Olivia's chaotic household is full of older men and one older woman, all unruly, with the relative exception of Malvolio – a despot who joins in the madness only when his class resentment is catalysed by Maria's letter. The Countess is an unwilling and inept ruler, save when she rescues Sebastian from the knavish trio, precisely at 'this uncivil and unjust extent / Against thy peace' (4.1.52–3), and gives them a loud piece of her mind. Otherwise, she is permanently anxious, and helpless when it comes to dealing with her uncle, who also suffers from the much emphasized absence of his aristocratic nephew. As in Olivia's shrine, in Toby's den there are a number of objects that used to belong to the noble kinsman, all strictly relating to a well-bred gentle-Englishman's recreational needs and habits – cricket bats, a dartboard, rowing paraphernalia – all now useless, ready to become relics of better days. On the other hand, while Ejiofor rightly plays Orsino as being more in love with obtaining Olivia than with Olivia herself, above all he stresses his enormous yet carefully contained frustration over his lost labours of love and the fruitlessness so far of that part of his otherwise mighty will. His anger, though aptly self-controlled (the politician in him?), is well suggested when he delivers 'O, she that hath a heart of that fine frame' (1.1.33 ff) while practising archery. Orsino is a man of huge and diverse appetites,[14] an equally large ego and desires not to be denied: he could indeed 'Kill what [he] love[s]' (5.1.109) – and yes, he hits the bullseye on his third shot, right at 'with one self-*king*' (1.1.39).

Conflict and anger abound in Illyria, and a good part of this may reflect on the stark ethnic and social contrasts therein. The contemporary British look of the town is established early on, when Viola arrives on a fishing boat to an isolated dock, in the company of the Captain and a group of male survivors, all unmistakably alien and illegal, who glance at her with dubious eyes that prompt her to seek a safer spot on board as they walk away after she gives the skipper a number of golden bracelets for his services: 'What should I do in Illyria?' (1.2.3). This introduction to the common conflicts in any major Western city is well supplemented by the age, conduct and habits of the aggressively crest-fallen knights, who spend most of their time in the basement – as if storing them away with the keepsakes of the family's former glory were the best option – and betoken the irrational prejudices and reactions that the rule of someone like Orsino might easily trigger in this multicultural dukedom. Toby is brutally disgusting – he not only belches loudly (and too often) and is never sober, but likewise noisily farts inside Olivia's shrine before

---

[14] He is far more at ease than Nunn's Orsino when having Cesario near – even slightly seductive.

announcing Cesario's presence at the gate. Olivia, however, seems sincerely worried over his explosive madness, substantially fuelled by the absence of their classier kinsmen, which seems to mark the end of some proper and dignified family and rule deserving more proper and dignified nostalgia than the knights downstairs can muster.

Significantly too, the knights are old-school heavy-metal heads – with very hoary heads that nonetheless command little reverence: Toby is ungraciously balding and Andrew keeps an ill-fitting mane. Former members of a band that once released an album of their own, they writhe in desperate nostalgia for a rock-scene (a rock-solid nation?) that is no longer there. Their follow-up on Sawhney's delicate arrangement of 'O Mistress Mine', brightly soloed by Feste with an acoustic guitar for the two old sots, who for a moment seem transported beyond their coarseness but just as soon relapse, is a heavily distorted, ear-splitting piece entitled, naturally, 'Hold Thy Peace, Thou Knave', the lyrics of which consist entirely of the same phrase repeated *ad nauseam*, at maximum volume. The moment is madly brilliant, filmed at great speed, with sharp angles and cuts, contrasting with the soft pace of the previous song and sequence. Toby dons sunglasses that make him look like an even worse-for-wear Townshend playing on a black Gibson Les Paul quite like Page's in his salad days, and Andrew uses his drumsticks against every possible surface in the room – a quick cut to the view from the CCTV camera isolates the horrid sound his sticks make against the basement pipeline – while Feste dictates maddening tempo and loudness on a programmed keyboard, singing at the top of his voice in brutal contrast with his (less than a minute earlier) former self. This musical juxtaposition of the two kinds of melancholy: heavy-hearted and subdued, and heavily disruptive, is perhaps the best summary of the state of affairs in Olivia's home and underscores the contrast between this old heavy-metal decadent world of old-timers and the operatically refined new rule of the newcomers from former insular and non-insular possessions – which is where this tale got started, after all.

The Messaline of Supple's initial narrative frame is pointedly Indian, and so are his actors: Viola is played by Parminder Nagra, significantly of *Bend It Like Beckham* fame, and Sebastian by Ronny Jhutti; both were born in England in the early 1970s and have been regularly featured in English films and on TV in dramas on Britain's present multiculturalism. The woman captured and presumably killed off-screen by the military brutes at starting – one of many Shakespearian absent mothers, herein made highly visible – is likewise recognizably Indian. The intruders can be easily spotted in numerous Bollywood films: a pack of heavily armed thugs at the service of some war-lord, big-time drug-dealer or political hot-shot. The Messaline that the twins leave behind poses many threats and dangers, social as well as personal, common to large, economically depressed areas of the world.

At a later point, for instance, Sebastian converses for the first time with Antonio (Andrew Kazamia, born in Cyprus) in the tense environment of an Indian café crowded with male patrons. Supple effectively emphasizes the nervousness affecting this odd couple as they sit at a table facing each other. Sebastian rejects Antonio's offer of company and moves to leave but is constrained to sit back by the older man, who eagerly grabs him by the hand. Although at first the youngster is firm in his rejection, he ultimately becomes self-aware and confides in the only person he knows outside his homeland. Sebastian, then, stays at the table partly because his multiply alien status demands caution and maybe his inexperience too: Antonio is much older and, like some of the customers, a rugged sailor. But he also stays out of gratitude: the man overly anxious to keep him there is the captain of the ship aboard which we earlier saw the twins with a group of Indian families and individuals seeking to enter Illyria illegally and who drowned trying. More importantly, having decided to resume their conversation, Sebastian exchanges a good part of Shakespeare's text with Antonio in Hindi – a strategy employed twice again later – to warn the sailor of the dangers into which *he* may run by keeping Sebastian's company. As the youth discloses the name of his father, we see a pair of quick flashback stills. The first one is of an older man in military attire posing for an official photograph; the other, of the same man lying on the ground, blood running from a gunshot wound to his head. By revealing the brutal origin of his escape from Messaline, Sebastian seems more mindful of the greater though supposedly remote violence that he has hopefully left behind than of the apparently smaller, present risks of befriending this 'notable pirate' (5.1.67) and mindful of the dangers that the outlaw may incur should he insist on desiring the fugitive's company. Either way, *un*conditional friendship is *un*sustainable.

The fears and restrictions affecting Viola and Sebastian are made greater, then, not only by their being in a strange land but also by being displaced, culturally uprooted, and yet controlled by widespread, cross-culturally shared factors. The case of the 'lost' sister is further complicated, of course, by the presence of the 'mournful' one. If regardless of her true gender Viola is identified as an outsider on account of her ethnicity, her status is made more vulnerable by factors that are inextricably linked to her gender, and hence with those that place her future 'sister' in similarly delicate, subordinate, conditions – e.g. their well-known lack of a male authority to back them. In the case of Olivia, there is the additional pressure of being the woman sought after by the current ruler of Illyria, whom she rejects with a firmness perhaps deriving as much from self-determination as from social over-determination, whether from prejudice or conflict.

These common factors create and support a connection between Olivia and Viola that is not restricted to the comedic attraction that the former feels for the latter, nor to the mourning Countess's confused state of mind or her inability to see through (or her desire *not* to see through?) Cesario, who, significantly, is not only 'male' and younger, but also dark, exotic and, for all 'his' swagger, frankly androgynous. In the case of Viola the link is not merely predicated on empathy or sympathy, either: it depends as much on mutual liking as on competition *and* inequality, with the additional pressure of her being a stranger to the ways

of Western love and yet in the exceptional position to experience and respond to the male world as an equally unequal insider.[15] Supple's Viola is not only a woman forced into cross-dressing by circumstance, but a culturally dislocated one – as much intimidated as encouraged by a liminality whereby she can be not only what she otherwise couldn't be but what she absolutely shouldn't be, howbeit provisionally. Viola loves Orsino as she loves what her unique position enables: to desire him, and just as much, to foil him, howbeit provisionally.

The definitive moment for the bond between the 'sisters' is Viola's sleepless scene. In Supple's treatment, the link between them transcends the tensely comedic situation of superficial disguise and becomes ambiguously deeper: gendered as well as genderless. Relocating the conversation between Sebastian and Antonio (2.1) to a later spot, Supple cuts straight from Olivia's drawing room in the evening (1.5) to Viola's quarters at night (2.2), so that, after Olivia urges Malvolio to deliver the ring, from a close-up of her face her voice can carry the lines 'Fate, show thy force. Ourselves we do not owe. / What is decreed, must be' (1.5.314–15) over the cut to the image of Viola in bed, wearing only her manly shirt, as mentioned before. As the voice of Olivia stops, Viola begins a much reduced version of 'I left no ring with her' (2.2.16 ff). She stands to stare at herself in the three-way mirror and delivers the main lines while unbuttoning the shirt. Looking at her breasts Viola realizes 'I am the man' (2.2.24) and with this, perhaps, the sense of 'ourselves we do not owe' and then she 'decrees' Olivia's 'Fate': 'she were better love a dream' (2.2.25) – and *her* fate too, for this also applies to her images in the mirrors, her elusive identity, her displaced gender and ethnicity, her cultural imperatives

---

[15] Contrastingly, 'Nunn's film . . . works through the equality and blend of genders predicted in [the twins'] opening performance, largely because his *Twelfth Night* reflects a particularly twentieth-century Western set of assumptions about gender equity' (Laurie Osborne, 'Cutting up Characters: The Erotic Politics of Trevor Nunn's *Twelfth Night*', *Spectacular Shakespeare*, ed. Courtney Lehman and Lisa Starks (Madison, 2002), pp. 105–6).

turned upside down. This is a remarkable translation of Shakespeare's 'poor monster' (2.2.33) into complex filming. Visually, aurally and elegantly, Shakespeare's 'Fate' and 'dream' come together across the cut to highlight another central issue in Supple's reading: the 'state . . . desperate for . . . master's love' (2.2.36) of *both* 'sisters' who eventually become the focus of the final close-ups in the closing and most telling exchange in this picture. Olivia's last line in the film, 'A sister, you are she', is, therefore, the arrival point of Viola's motion to unbutton her shirt, the end-point of her undressing, the site where Olivia finally 'sees' the images that Viola earlier contemplated in her three-way looking-glass. In Supple's film, then, the twins' reunion is effected through the sisters-to-be, not through the actual siblings. For as the disguise comes off – not only literally but verbally, symbolically and cinematically in Viola's final close-up – so silence, the touch of Sebastian's finger on her lips, comes back, now as a kiss from Orsino. Sebastian's mission seems accomplished: his sister has been delivered to safety: the 'peace' of a prescribed role.

Shakespeare's original design is brilliantly supplemented with the implications of the ethnic and cultural differentiation between Messaline and Illyria: a young maid arriving unchaperoned on a foreign, hostile and distant shore seeks refuge in the 'wickedness' of disguise, and as a 'monster' finds temporary, and ambivalent, release from an utterly different lifestyle to play a part in a madly strange scenario until she is reintegrated to her proper status by virtue of a miraculous twist of fate, whereby the fate of another woman, uncertain of her place in her own land, is delivered from the pressure of an otherwise inevitable imposition from a higher power, and maybe thereby, though not ideally, from her uncertainty. Making Viola an Indian woman underscores the poles of this pitch: outside her purdah, she must find her disguise ever more difficult to bear as well as more fascinating. Her wooing of Olivia is bold and assertive. Viola/Cesario relishes using a language that so far couldn't be but literature to *both* women (interloping shots of erotic paintings signify the process of Olivia's arousal), and hits home precisely when s/he touches Olivia's lips

with his/her finger, much in the way her lips were and will be touched: to bring ambiguous 'peace'. Olivia cannot but make her subdued 'You might do much' (1.5.280) a testimony of desire. But it all happens in a secluded environment (once later with the help of Maria), a space of generic intimacy where the unexpected and unaccustomed cross-gendered role may be played more comfortably and more truthfully. Viola also assists his/her master at bathing, and touches *his* body in an ambiguous exercise of her fictional selves, present and future.[16] Her love for Orsino, thus, is as much a fiction as a function of her temporary release from her cultural imperatives; once more, *inside* an otherwise inaccessible world.

Outside, instead, in the boxed-in spots where she is taunted, pushed and forced to confront the less 'dreamy' aspects involved in a mad-man's world, Viola becomes confused, intimidated and once undisguised finally relapses into silence. Her first conversation with Antonio at one point turns to Hindi but brings no relief from confusion. Instead, climactic words at the recognition scene, 'My father had a mole upon his brow' (5.1.240), are exchanged in Hindi, too, but now with her brother, which provides a chance at privacy and recovery of identity marks – the *mother* tongue, above all, a silenced one, as I noted earlier – that the trellised spot cannot totally protect, for as Viola and Sebastian approach each other and begin to speak, Orsino and Olivia who are their 'loved ones' but also strictly strangers to them also approach from either flank outside the squared area and look at them as fascinated spectators through the woodwork that reminds us of the bars and cages that have pervasively stood between most other actions and our gaze. 'And died that day' (5.1.242), still in Hindi, marks the original point of this journey: the reference to the death of the father prologues the end of the brother's duties as he begins a new stage while the sister retains her usual ones.

The image of the mother being taken to her death in the opening sequence gains in significance

---

[16] The same happens in Nunn's film, to different effects.

if coupled with Viola's earlier segue to Orsino's vow to 'sacrifice the lamb that [he] love[s]': 'And I most jocund, apt, and willingly / To do you rest a thousand deaths would die' (5.1.130–1). Not in 'jocund' fashion and hardly 'willingly', Viola's lines are all too close to what happens with her mother at starting – and more ironically, insofar as, however forcibly, she remains an Indian wife following her husband to death, as if to say 'My lord would speak, my duty hushes me.' It all seems to revolve around socially prescribed roles.

Viola's 'I am not that I play' stands behind the circularity of prescripted roles in Supple's treatment of Shakespeare's *Twelfth Night, or What You Will*. The categories that define a woman's part, like the designs of a playwright who among other things specialized in writing female parts to be played by males, are mostly externally configured with regard to herself; indeed, 'she were better love a dream'. This bias has historically invited questions and demanded answers that are hard to find, above all because most foundations for such answers are just as biased as the conditions that invite the questions. What Viola and Olivia ultimately share, beyond the conspicuously common letters in their names (though it cannot hurt to mention that they spell out the very root of the word) are the many forms of violence, including self-inflicted violence, that Supple manages to bring forth in his film. These forms of violence ultimately revolve around them, involve them, affect them, may make or mar them, and for the most part remain outside them and their control. There is one possible exception, however: Olivia's decisive intervention to stop 'this uncivil and unjust extent against thy peace', and her ensuing near imperatives: 'Thou shalt not choose but go: / Do not deny . . . Nay, come, I prithee, would thou'dst be ruled by me' (4.1.56–7, 63). Good. Except that – let's face it – two scenes later she loosens her sudden grasp on that particular situation by making the abused subject her new 'Lord and Master' in a hurry, so 'That [her] most jealous and too doubtful soul / May live at peace' (4.3.27–8). Will it? One cannot help but wonder. After all, she meant to keep Cesario's peace but kept Sebastian's instead and thereupon Viola's. Peace is always dearly bought. And sold. Supple's complex rendering of Shakespeare's comedy makes a stimulating and intriguing offer either way.

'THERE'S NO SUCH THING': NOTHING AND NAKEDNESS IN POLANSKI'S *MACBETH*

LINDSEY SCOTT

The 'nothing' that persistently haunts the images of *Macbeth* has been interpreted in terms of a condition of language and of self. After murdering Duncan, Macbeth appears 'lost' in thought and tells his wife, 'To know my deed, 'twere best not know myself' (2.2.69–71).[1] As he pursues a future foretold to him by the prophecies of the three Weird Sisters, he begins to identify less and less with his former self, until 'All causes . . . give way' (3.4.135) and life is no more than a 'walking shadow', absent of truth or meaning (5.5.23). Terry Eagleton writes that, in seeking to take possession of the throne, Macbeth will, in fact, 'become less than human in trying to become more', until eventually too much 'inverts itself into nothing at all'.[2] Malcolm Evans extends a reading of the protagonist's loss of identity to a more thorough exploration of 'the crisis of the sign and unequivocal discourse in the play'.[3] For Evans, the 'potentially baffling opacity' of the play's linguistic modes is a disorder that moves beyond the 'imperfect' speaking of the Witches to several other central characters in *Macbeth*.[4]

However, given the 'double' nature of the Witches in leading Macbeth towards a prophesized future that will both 'scorn / The power of man' (4.1.95–6) and bring about his own downfall, the most immediate explanation for the play's signified nothing lies with the Witches themselves, or more specifically, with the ambiguous territory of the female body.[5] For the male, to look on the naked female body and its external lack may provoke a sense of absence within the male himself, as the power of the incomprehensible female 'nothing' subsequently threatens to become everything:

'a yawning abyss within which man can lose his virile identity'.[6] It is an inversion of the natural order that takes root in *Macbeth*'s central thematic strategy, originating in the Witches' opening chant 'Fair is foul, and foul is fair' (1.1.10). In seeking to become more, Macbeth is reduced to less than a man, while the unknown female power of the Witches appears to operate in reverse; from nothing, they can perform 'A deed without a name' (4.1.65), and in the closure of Shakespeare's play, there is no indication of their punishment or indeed their end.[7]

---

1 All quotations and line numbers are taken from *William Shakespeare: The Complete Works*, ed. John Jowett, William Montgomery, Gary Taylor and Stanley Wells, 2nd edn (Oxford, 2005).
2 Terry Eagleton, *William Shakespeare* (Oxford, 1986), pp. 3–4.
3 Malcolm Evans, 'Signifying Nothing', in John Wain, ed., *Macbeth: A Casebook Selection of Critical Essays*, 2nd edn (London, 1994), pp. 271–80 (p. 275).
4 Evans, 'Signifying Nothing', p. 272.
5 While this concept has evaded *Macbeth* criticism, a psychoanalytical reading of the play exposes the same implications towards the female nothing that have previously been recognized in plays such as *The Winter's Tale* and *Othello*. See, for example: Kirstie Gulick Rosenfield, 'Nursing Nothing: Witchcraft and Female Sexuality in *The Winter's Tale*', *Mosaic: A Journal For the Interdisciplinary Study of Literature*, 35 (2002), 95–112; Eagleton's chapter on *Othello* in *William Shakespeare*, pp. 64–75.
6 Eagleton, *William Shakespeare*, pp. 64–5.
7 David G. Hale writes that the present tense, which is used in Macbeth's final reference to the Witches (5.8.19–22), suggests that they 'remain alive and presumably capable of further words of promise'. He also observes that Malcolm's closing speech (5.9.26–41) fails to mention the Witches or indicate any future punishment for their actions, thus concluding that

In these terms, *Macbeth*'s nothing becomes a projection of male anxiety regarding the unknown territory of the naked female body that results in Macbeth's crisis of identity and the deconstruction of the male self. The very nature of the Witches themselves comes to represent the threat of the female nothing's absence: their physical substance is shifting, unstable and indefinable; in appearance, they 'look not like th'inhabitants o'th'earth' (1.3.39), and their bodies vanish 'Into the air' and melt 'as breath into the wind' (1.3.79–80). But the most powerful absence that seems to render Macbeth himself as a 'false creation' (2.1.38), 'signifying nothing' (5.5.27), is the non-existent space of the Witches' prophecy. The prophecies not only palter 'in a double sense' (5.10.20) but are ultimately promises from which nothing can come, as Macbeth himself discovers when 'nothing is / But what is not' (1.3.140–1). Once submerged into the non-existent space of his possible future, Macbeth has no real care for the 'ignorant present' (1.5.56) – paradoxically, the cause for which he has 'fil'd' his mind in murdering Duncan does not exist. After his wife's death, and 'honour, love, obedience, troops of friends' (5.3.27) have disappeared, all that remains for Macbeth is the relentless pursuit of 'Tomorrow, and tomorrow, and tomorrow' (5.5.18) – a bloody passage to an absence that eventually succeeds in destroying the potency of his own bodily form. The 'whole space that's in the tyrant's grasp' (4.3.37) is, in fact, a 'no-where'.

These anxieties over the Witches' prophetic nothing are conveyed implicitly through the imagery of film adaptations such as Orson Welles's *Macbeth* (1948), where the nothingness of the Witches' cauldron both creates and eventually destroys Macbeth's bodily potency. In the film's opening sequence, Welles's camera plunges into the thick, black substance of the bubbling cauldron: the nothing from which Macbeth's deformed, simulated body will come. What is 'born' out of this cauldron is both warped and unnatural, and the Witches' evil infliction on Macbeth's body is symbolized by their creation of the clay doll; thrusting their hands into the belly of the cauldron, they claw and scrape away at its shapeless substance to form

an armless body with a slightly enlarged head, like a babe. In a perverse sense, the Witches in Welles's film are portrayed as giving birth to and nurturing Macbeth through their sculpting and manoeuvring of this child-like doll, whose bodily form they eventually destroy. At the end of the film, its body is decapitated, and the image of its head falling to the ground is juxtaposed with Macbeth's own beheading by Macduff.

Reading *Macbeth*'s prophetic nothing as a trope for the vagina and the threat it poses to man's autonomy would seem to provide an explanation for the exclusion of the female body in the play's literary references to 'naked frailties' (2.3.125). Instead of connoting vulnerability, the naked female body in *Macbeth* emblematizes the chaos and destruction that the play's women appear to instigate and the impending *absence* of the prophetic space. Roman Polanski's adaptation of *Macbeth* (1971) explores the theme of nakedness, literalizing Shakespeare's textual references and visually representing the naked body in a number of key scenes throughout the film. Given the source of the film's sponsorship, and the director's own extensive relationship with Playboy, this decision has hardly surprised critics. As Deanne Williams observes, 'Playboy underwrites the film in more than just the financial sense', and the nakedness of Francesca Annis's Lady Macbeth in her sleepwalking scene no doubt contributed to the opinion that her interpretation of the role was 'a perfect blend of the contradictions inherent in the Playboy *mythos*: the smiling acquiescence of the sex symbol, the persistent acceptance of helpful domesticity, and the transparent emotional manipulations of the *femme fatale*'.[8] However, despite obvious assumptions about the presence of the naked female body in a Playboy production, Polanski's *Macbeth* undoubtedly questions and unsettles the associations within the language of Shakespeare's playtext, prompting us to delve further into its indistinct

---

the new king 'may not know of their existence'. See David G. Hale, 'Order and Disorder in *Macbeth*, Act V: Film and Television', *Literature/Film Quarterly*, 29 (2001), 101–6 (p. 103).

[8] Deanne Williams, 'Mick Jagger Macbeth', *Shakespeare Survey* 57 (Cambridge, 2004), pp. 145–58 (p. 153).

boundaries of masculine and feminine, exposure and concealment, 'foul' and 'fair' (1.1.10), the male 'something' and the female nothing. By placing images of nakedness against a ruthless exploration of the play's violence, Polanski's film demands that we re-evaluate whether the play's signified nothing represents the chaotic absence of the female that overthrows 'Even till destruction sicken' (4.1.76), or the destructive nature of man's own 'vaulting ambition' (1.7.27).

The images of Shakespeare's *Macbeth* that relate directly to nakedness have been well documented, and they frequently exclude the female. After the discovery of the murdered Duncan, Banquo addresses those present on the stage and advises that their 'naked frailties', which 'suffer in exposure', must be hidden in order to question 'this most bloody piece of work' (2.3.125–7).[9] As Paul Jorgensen suggests, we can either take Banquo's words literally, as 'those present are hastily clad', or determine that '"naked frailties" well expresses the exposed feelings of all present'.[10] However, there is undeniably more to be perceived in Banquo's reference to nakedness, particularly after considering Macbeth's later instruction to 'put on manly readiness' (2.3.132). For Cleanth Brooks, 'manly readiness' is, in fact, 'a hypocrite's garment', as Macbeth 'can only pretend to be the loyal, grief-stricken liege who is almost unstrung by the horror of Duncan's murder'.[11] Therefore while nakedness here suggests frailty, innocence and exposure, the clothed body indicates pretence, disguise and concealment: the cloak that hides Macbeth's inhuman act with a show of 'manly readiness'.[12] Macbeth's statement describes a garment of disguise that is equally identified as masculine – to be dressed is also conveyed as to be ready for the necessary purpose of manly action. Immediately, then, Shakespeare's play provides us with a metaphor that projects gendered conceptions of the naked and the clothed body: references to nakedness seem to indicate a natural state of vulnerability – unclothed, and therefore weak or traditionally feminized bodies – while the clothed body projects an image of masculinity that is embedded within the play's representations of violent action.

The descriptions of the play's central women do not intimate the naked and vulnerable feminized body. Any verbal suggestions of nakedness are not directly associated with Lady Macbeth and the three Weird Sisters. Instead, their words and actions more readily identify them with the clothed body and the cloak of manly disguise: the Witches travel 'through the fog and filthy air' (1.1.11) concealed by mist; they are so 'wild in their attire' (1.3.38) that Banquo must question whether they are 'fantastical or that indeed / Which outwardly [they] show' (1.3.51–2). Lady Macbeth also assumes the cloak of disguise. Her call to the spirits that 'tend on mortal thoughts' is full of images that indicate her desire to hide her 'fell purpose', for the 'blanket of the dark' to cover Heaven in 'the dunnest smoke of Hell' (1.5.40–52).

Like the bodily representations of the boy actors on Shakespeare's stage, these female characters simultaneously embody masculine and feminine attributes. If the Witches signify the 'absence' of the naked female body, they also employ the disguise of the clothed body that connotes masculinity. In appearance they are equally androgynous: as Banquo beholds the Weird Sisters, he remarks 'You should be women, / And yet your beards forbid me to interpret / That you are so' (1.3.43–5); Lady Macbeth's call to the spirits to 'unsex' her and take her woman's milk (1.5.40–7) also associates her body with this genderless form. Her boldness in swaying her husband to commit the murder compels him to exclaim that her 'undaunted mettle' should 'compose / Nothing but males' (1.7.73–4).

---

[9] As Lady Macbeth has already been assisted off stage at this point, Banquo's talk of '*our* naked frailties' (emphasis added) addresses the all-male observers and therefore literally excludes women.

[10] Paul A. Jorgensen, *Our Naked Frailties: Sensational Art and Meaning in 'Macbeth'* (Berkeley, 1971), p. 104.

[11] Cleanth Brooks, 'The Naked Babe and the Cloak of Manliness', in Terence Hawkes, ed., *Twentieth-Century Interpretations of Macbeth: A Collection of Critical Essays* (New Jersey, 1977), pp. 34–53 (p. 45).

[12] For an extensive range of examples of clothing imagery from the play-text, see Caroline F. E. Spurgeon, *Shakespeare's Imagery and What It Tells Us* (Cambridge, 1935), pp. 324–35.

At no point do these bodily representations seem to suggest the naked vulnerability of Banquo's gendered metaphor. Instead, nakedness in relation to the *female* body can only connote its potentially destructive threat, never alluding to the possibility of helplessness or 'frailty'. Tellingly, this denial of naked vulnerability or exposure in favour of the cloaked or covered female body also appropriately colludes with the male desire to conceal a woman's private parts, to reconfigure the vagina as something monstrous or too 'obscene' for show.[13]

Although it would seem relatively straightforward to assume that Banquo's definition of 'our naked frailties' excludes the female, to conclude, as Rosalind Meyer does, that Lady Macbeth is 'truly fiend-like' and that the Witches 'conspire only to destroy', remains inconclusive.[14] If the naked female body does indeed signify the root and cause of the play's inversion of the natural order, how are we to understand the play's ending? What values and ideologies are promoted by an ending that sees the male usurper violently punished, a new male power succeeding the throne, and the fate of the Witches wholly undetermined? Janet Adelman asserts that the re-imagining of 'autonomous male identity' in the play's peculiar ending is entirely dependent on 'the ruthless excision of all female presence', ultimately offering a fantasy of escape from 'a virtually absolute and destructive maternal power'.[15] The crowning of the usurper's successor does indeed suggest a return to the harmonious order of the 'most sainted king' (4.3.110) Duncan, and brings to the throne a purity and virtuousness that is significantly 'yet / Unknown to woman' in the form of the untainted Malcolm (4.3.126–7). And yet the apparent satisfaction with the play's return of the traditional order is undoubtedly fragile, for while it is certain that the Witches have remained absent from the stage since their puzzling disappearance in Act 4, scene 1, the ambiguous nature of their departure ensures that they remain somehow outside the 'ruthless excision' that Adelman describes. This sense of ambiguity also adds to the element of doubt that we may infer from the indication that Malcolm is 'yet' unknown to woman, and therefore may encounter

still the prophetic words of these 'juggling fiends' (5.10.19).

What most crucially undermines the reverence of 'king-becoming graces' (4.3.92) in *Macbeth*'s closing scene is the action of man himself, not merely the actions of the 'abhorrèd tyrant' (5.7.11), but the actions of those who will govern over Scotland's *future*. Macduff's brutal severing of the 'usurper's cursèd head' (5.11.21) and Malcolm's praising of this act – which, ironically, symbolizes the end of this 'dead butcher and his fiend-like queen' (5.11.35) – only serves to indicate a perpetuation of the bloody and unrelenting violence that preserved Duncan's 'saintly' rule.[16] From the opening scene until the very end, Shakespeare's Scotland is a place that 'values butchery' and bloody brutality, where 'manhood is equated with the ability to kill'.[17]

Roman Polanski's *Macbeth* opens with a scene that focuses on what transpires from the 'fog and filthy air' (1.1.11) and in doing so, immediately addresses the ambivalent nature of the play's prophetic absence and the central characters' relationships to its all-consuming nothing. The scene begins with the Weird Sisters on a murky and deserted beach, a space that is both natural and 'unnatural', for their first meeting. Sounds of thunder and lightening have been replaced by the

---

[13] For an example of such an argument in relation to Shakespeare's plays, see Patricia Parker, 'Othello and Hamlet: Dilation, Spying, and the "Secret Place" of Woman', in Russ McDonald, ed., *Shakespeare Reread: The Texts in New Contexts* (Ithaca, 1994), pp. 105–46.

[14] Rosalind S. Meyer, '"The Serpent Under't": Additional Reflections on *Macbeth*', *Notes and Queries*, 47 (2000), 86–90 (p. 86).

[15] Janet Adelman, '"Born of Woman": Fantasies of Maternal Power in *Macbeth*', in Marjorie Garber, ed., *Cannibals, Witches, and Divorce: Estranging the Renaissance* (Baltimore, 1987), pp. 90–121 (pp. 90–1).

[16] For an exploration of the play's representations of manhood in terms of violent action, see Robin Headlam Wells's fourth chapter, '"Arms and the Man": *Macbeth*', in *Shakespeare on Masculinity* (Cambridge, 2000), pp. 117–43.

[17] Marilyn French, '*Macbeth* and Masculine Values', in Alan Sinfield, ed., *New Casebooks: Macbeth* (London, 1992), pp. 14–24 (p. 15).

natural sounds of seagulls and crashing waves, and while the verse structure and undefined location of Shakespeare's opening scene 'instantly construct a supernatural space', Polanski's film portrays the Witches as far more human than fantastical.[18] The domain they inhabit is unearthly – a liminal space caught between the land and sea – but their dress and appearance show them to be ordinary women. Tellingly, these women are of all ages; one young, one middle-aged, and the other elderly, thus representing the coming and passing of time in their physical appearance. Although the elderly Sister is without human sight, she predicts that the battle will end 'ere the set of sun' (1.1.5), and as the three depart across the sand with their backs turned toward us, their bodies part to form two dark shapes in the mist, like a pair of eyes that continue to see all. As they fade from our sight, the title 'Macbeth' appears on the screen, and the filthy air that consumed the Witches now turns blood red to the sounds and screams of battle. It is only once the titles have ended that the mist clears and we are finally permitted to see what lies beyond it. The location has not changed (we are still on the beach where the Weird Sisters left us), only it has now become a battle graveyard of bloody victors and dead bodies. The first image to greet our eyes is that of an injured rebel survivor, face down in the sand, being slaughtered. Quickly, then, we learn that enemies of Scotland's ruling power are defeated with savagery, where even the feeblest of survivors are murdered with brutal vengeance. The pivotal treatment of the consuming mist connects both the Witches' domain and the space of the battlefield to its threatening absence; 'Fair is foul, and foul is fair' (1.1.10) becomes the opening chant in Polanski's film, and the foulness of man's violence is the first thing to take shape out of its impenetrable nothing.

In this bloody and exceedingly violent portrayal of *Macbeth*, Scotland already appears as a 'grave', where 'sighs and groans and shrieks' fall on the air and 'violent sorrow seems / A modern ecstasy' (4.3.167–71). A tracking shot of the King and his royal followers shows them riding on horseback before a grey sky across a bleak and desolate land. Society under Duncan's rule promotes masculine

values where violence is second nature and men laugh callously at the bleeding Captain's story of how Macbeth's sword 'smoked with bloody execution' and 'unseamed' Macdonwald's body (1.2.18–22). Unlike the metaphors of Duncan's speeches that suggest nature, growth and harvest (1.4.28–9), nothing grows or thrives in Polanski's Scotland except man's lust for power. From this first stark contrast between the Witches and Duncan's men, we learn that the play's equivocal 'fair is foul, and foul is fair' has a far more integrated meaning in this film. Bernice Kliman writes that, in every drafted version of the screenplay, Polanski makes it clear that he intended for his Witches to 'appear foul in contrast to the warriors who look, in the main, fair'.[19] The women on Polanski's beach are filthy and haggard: their clothes and shawls are shabby; their skin blistered or wrinkled. The youngest sister is also silent and only seems capable of communicating with others by mouthing words or grunting. They do not belong to the realm of 'proper' Scottish society but instead form their own sisterly community outside it. In contrast, the words and actions of Scotland's ruling men demoralize the nature of their seemingly noble and valiant outward appearance. In Polanski's film, Duncan's inability to 'find the mind's construction in the face' (1.4.12) is a defect of a society as a whole, one that will extend beyond the world of the film to unsettle and challenge the spectator's own conceptions of 'foul' and 'fair'.

Macbeth's first appearance in Polanski's film is one of many instances that both promotes and rejects the preferred notion that Macbeth's path of destruction commences with the influence of demonic female powers. Jon Finch's Macbeth appears in close-up shot before a line of hanged

---

[18] Evelyn Tribble, '"When Every Noise Appalls Me": Sound and Fear in *Macbeth* and Akira Kurosawa's *Throne of Blood*', *Shakespeare*, 1 (2005), 75–90 (p. 77).

[19] Bernice W. Kliman, 'Gleanings: The Residue of Difference in Scripts: The Case of Polanski's *Macbeth*', in Jay L. Halio and Hugh Richmond, eds., *Shakespearean Illuminations: Essays in Honor of Marvin Rosenberg* (Newark, 1998), pp. 131–46 (p. 135).

men – an image that extends the remorseless aftermath of battle and simultaneously ties Macbeth to his own fate. The ominous beating of a drum at the hanging plays on the Witches' prophetic greeting, 'A drum, a drum – / Macbeth doth come' (1.3.28–9), only in Polanski's film, we first encounter Macbeth alone rather than in the company of Banquo. No words are spoken in this brief establishing scene, and Macbeth stands apart from the crowd of onlookers, staring sombrely into the distance before riding off with Banquo silently following him. Even prior to his initial meeting with the Witches, Macbeth appears distracted, as though his thoughts turn inward from the very beginning. Most of his soliloquies are spoken as internal monologue, and a substantial amount of dialogue spoken before other characters in the play is reworked as private thought.

Editors' stage directions for Shakespeare's playtext also indicate that Macbeth often speaks aside in early scenes, moving away from the other characters or occupying a removed space downstage to voice his thoughts out of earshot. While Macbeth is described by other characters as having a 'personal venture in the rebels' sight' (1.3.89), his onstage movements show that he desires to exist outside it, to occupy a space beyond the realm of constraint and the 'precise bonds of hierarchical allegiance'.[20] Polanski's portrayal of Macbeth seems to enlarge this point, drawing on the play's tensions between language and spatial representation and emphasizing the protagonist's desire to remove himself from the mortal sphere of his fellow countrymen, whose primary purpose is the 'kingdom's great defence' (1.3.97). Perhaps the 'imperial theme' already occupies his thoughts (1.3.128). Either way, Finch's Macbeth is portrayed as dissatisfied with his current function, and his lack of interest in the company of his own kind implies that he seeks to occupy a 'supernatural' space of power that exceeds his own natural bonds of allegiance, one that is, perhaps, not unlike the Witches' own. Tellingly, it is not the Witches who 'stop' Macbeth's path in this film (1.3.75) but the curiosity of the men themselves that leads them to investigate further the place 'Upon the heath' (1.1.6).

Unlike the exclusion that Banquo's definition of 'naked frailties' would seem to suggest, Polanski's representations of naked vulnerability do not exclude the play's central female characters. Macbeth's first encounter with the weird women introduces the theme of nakedness for the spectator, but with rather unexpected connotations for a film that announces itself as 'A Playboy Production' in the opening credits. While taking shelter from the rain, Macbeth and Banquo are suddenly intrigued by the strange sounds of the Witches' song and proceed towards the cave on horseback. It is almost as though the men stumble upon the women's private domestic space, even though the meeting with Macbeth – the time and the place (1.1.1–6) – was prophesied earlier by the Witches. The youngest of the three is stripped to the shoulders with her back exposed, and the eldest Sister, although unable to see, appears to be washing her. They sit together beside a dirty well, scarcely sheltered from the rain under a propped up thatch cover. Given the demonic or 'fantastical' powers that Shakespeare's Witches possess, this initial image of domesticity and nurturing seems unusual. The intimacy of the three women only gives further emphasis to the apparent lack of closeness between Banquo and Macbeth, and the simple act of nurturing and caring for the body also presents a sharp contrast to the bloody violation of the male bodies that we have just witnessed on Duncan's battlefield.

As the women begin to depart, Macbeth eagerly demands that they tell him more and as he follows them towards their cave, he calls to the youngest Sister, 'Speak, I charge you' (1.3.76), to which she responds by grunting in her usual manner and showing him the symbolic 'nothing' between her legs. In describing this moment in the film, Kliman notes that only Macbeth, not Banquo, 'follows them, only he sees the young one lift her skirts in an obscene gesture, only he sees them disappear into their cave with a bang of a door'.[21] However, the gesture is not coded as 'obscene'; rather,

---

[20] Eagleton, *William Shakespeare*, p. 3.

[21] Bernice W. Kliman, *Shakespeare in Performance: Macbeth* (Manchester, 1992), p. 130.

it visually demonstrates the Witches' silent, though undoubtedly forceful, response to Macbeth's own attempted intrusion into their world. The young woman's gesture is followed by her departure into the cave and her closing of the door that forbids Macbeth's entrance. Kliman also observes that, in lying to Banquo about the Witches' whereabouts, Macbeth has exposed his 'readiness to deceive'.[22] However, Macbeth's lie that the Witches vanish 'Into the air' (1.3.79) not only reveals his capacity for deceit, but also suggests implicitly that it is Macbeth who linguistically projects an image of the female nothing as 'secretive'. Symbolically, it also reveals his desire for the knowledge of its awesome power through his attempt to conceal the existence of the cave from Banquo. What was cloaked, hidden and coded as 'obscene' in Shakespeare's references to the female body has been laid bare in the visuals of Polanski's adaptation, so much so that in an entirely uneroticized image, the female nothing literally becomes ignorant of autonomous male identity rather than symbolically responsible for its destruction. Thus the film's first representations of nakedness overturn the play's conceptions by deliberately *exposing* the female body and associating the secretive and ambiguous aspects of its nothing, not directly with the women, but rather with Macbeth himself.

The film's images of nakedness are varied and complex in meaning. Unlike our first assumptions about a Playboy production may lead us to believe, they do not allude exclusively to the naked female body.[23] Neither do they attempt to simplify or overturn the play's definition of 'naked frailties' (2.3.125). After introducing images of the naked female body in Macbeth's first encounter with the Witches, Polanski's film moves quickly towards a representation of the naked *male* body in Duncan's murder scene. In a visual depiction that both mirrors and distorts Shakespeare's description of 'the bloody business' (2.1.48), Duncan's murder is constructed as rape. From the beginning of Shakespeare's *Macbeth*, women are presented as dangerously powerful, while men in power seem to be under threat or failing to maintain their rule; Duncan's inability to secure his kingdom and keep

enemies and traitors at bay has prompted many critics to refer to him as the 'feminized' or androgynous king.[24] Alongside the images of nurturance and growth that partly illustrate Duncan's rule, Macbeth's language prior to the murder implies 'a display of male sexual aggression against a passive female victim', as Macbeth imagines himself as moving towards Duncan with 'Tarquin's ravishing strides' (2.1.55).[25] Implications of nakedness also convey Duncan's natural state of vulnerability: Duncan's exposed 'silver skin' is 'laced with his golden blood'; his open wounds appear like 'a breach in nature' (2.3.112–13); prior to the murder his 'faculties' are 'meek' (1.7.17); his body 'unguarded' (1.7.70); and 'wicked dreams' abuse the 'curtained sleep' (2.1.50–1), threatening to violate both Duncan's unguarded body and the innocent state of unconsciousness. While Duncan's body is left vulnerable and exposed, the 'blanket of the dark' (1.5.52) conceals evil deeds and ill thoughts of 'black and deep desires' (1.4.51). Although the quality of naked vulnerability evades the central women of Shakespeare's play, it remains as a feminine attribute in the figure of the androgynous king.

If the image of the murdered Duncan, stripped of his royal robes, epitomizes the play's conception of the naked and vulnerable feminized male body, Polanski's film complicates such a reading by instead

---

[22] Kliman, *Shakespeare in Performance*, p. 130.

[23] Bruna Gushurst argues that Polanski's film indicates powerlessness through nakedness. See 'Polanski's Determining of Power in *Macbeth*', *Shakespeare on Film Newsletter*, 13 (1989), 7. Kliman also writes 'Those without power lack voice; those without power appear nude.' *Shakespeare in Performance*, p. 139.

[24] See, for example, Harry Berger, Jr, 'The Early Scenes of *Macbeth*: Preface to a New Interpretation', *ELH* 47 (1980), 26–8; Adelman, '"Born of Woman"', pp. 93–6; Dennis Biggins, 'Sexuality, Witchcraft, and Violence in *Macbeth*', *Shakespeare Studies*, 8 (1975), 255–77.

[25] Adelman specifically notes Duncan's 'womanish softness', and points out that the images surrounding his death, such as Macbeth's configuration of himself as the murderous figure of Tarquin in *The Rape of Lucrece*, transform Duncan into an emblem of female vulnerability. See '"Born of Woman"', p. 95.

presenting a strong, masculine king and connoting his murder as a rape of male potency. Unlike the other major film adaptations by Orson Welles and Akira Kurosawa (*Throne of Blood*, 1957), Polanski's *Macbeth* allows the spectator's gaze to penetrate the space of Duncan's bedchamber during the murder. This decision not only demonstrates the director's wish to exploit the play's violence, but also to show intimately Duncan's loss of power. Polanski's representation of Duncan prior to the murder is far from weak or vulnerable: Nicolas Selby is a 'strong and pitiless' king, and any textual implications of his meekness have been removed in order to maintain a powerful masculine image.[26] We first see him riding out onto the battlefield, not sidelined or safely removed from danger. Here he looks down at the disgraced Thane of Cawdor and callously removes the chain of honour from his neck with the point of his sword. Prior to the murder scene, Duncan's body is always distinctly covered or protected by his clothing: on arrival at Inverness, he is heavily shrouded in fur skins and thick robes; on the battlefield, he is covered from head to toe in armour, making the exposure of his body and his vulnerability in the murder sequence a far more unsettling context of nakedness for the spectator.

The film establishes Duncan's killing as sexual violation through several visual signifiers. The sequence begins with a voyeuristic camera shot through a window frame, which shows Duncan asleep in his private chamber, as his groomsmen remove his royal garments. The audience shares this view with Macbeth and his wife until one of the groomsmen closes the shutters, preventing any continuation of a penetrative gaze. After Lady Macbeth delivers the drugged liqueur to the servants' chamber and rings the bell to signal her husband, she is removed from the action that follows. While she waits anxiously in the courtyard and does not reappear until after the murder, the spectator is permitted to accompany Macbeth into the private space of Duncan's chamber, reintroducing the voyeuristic gaze that was earlier established. Once inside, Macbeth drags the unconscious bodies of the groomsmen from the doorway and, in a momentary error, begins to proceed with his own

dagger drawn. Realizing his mistake, he returns the blade to his belt-strap, and collects the daggers from the sleeping groomsmen before entering the bedchamber. Macbeth then watches his sleeping guest, to whom he should 'against his murderer shut the door, / Not bear the knife' himself (1.7.15–16), and, hesitantly, begins to pull back the bedcovers. Polanski has Duncan wake to see his attacker, and whisper 'Macbeth?' in bewilderment, just prior to the murder: what should have been 'done quickly' (1.7.2) becomes a desperate and disturbingly frenzied attack to silence a victim. Placing a hand over Duncan's mouth, Macbeth then straddles him, and stabs his body repeatedly. The sexual connotations of the attack are emphasized further by the spatial set-up of the scene. Polanski has already drawn the viewer's attention to the fact that Macbeth and his wife have provided their own sleeping quarters for their royal guest, as an earlier scene shows the servants clearing the room of its garments and Lady Macbeth strewing the newly made bed with herbs and petals. The fact that Duncan's murder takes place in the marital bed of the castle visually adds weight to critical arguments that imagine the murder itself as a sexual act, through which the union of Macbeth and Lady Macbeth is consummated.[27]

Polanski's murder scene plays with and disrupts the play's definition of 'naked frailties' by representing Duncan as a powerful figure of masculinity who is killed for his male potency, not because he is a suitably weak or feminized victim of 'meek' faculties (1.7.17). Duncan is not the androgynous parent who is both authoritative and nurturing, after whose death the 'wine of life is drawn' (2.3.94), but rather he is another perpetrator of male violence, himself an unjust king. Within the context of his own violent rule, his murder does not register with the spectator as a cruel injustice, but simply as another brutal exchange of power. Duncan's fallen crown does not signify the desecration of

---

26 Kliman, 'Gleanings', p. 137.
27 See, for example, Biggins, 'Sexuality, Witchcraft, and Violence in *Macbeth*', and James J. Greene, 'Macbeth: Masculinity as Murder', *American Imago*, 41 (1984), 155–80, for such arguments.

'The life o'th'building' (2.3.68) or that 'Renown and grace is dead' (2.3.93); instead, it spins uncontrollably until the murderous struggle is over, until one form of male greed for power has succeeded the other.[28] Likewise, his nakedness is not an image of sacred 'silver skin', but merely another slaughtered body that recalls the worthless corpses being looted on his battlefield. In Shakespeare's play, it is Duncan's union of masculine and feminine qualities that ultimately determines both his 'virtues' (1.7.18) and his undoing. Likewise, part of Macduff's strength resides in his understanding that he should not only 'dispute' but also 'feel' things 'as a man' (4.3.221–3). However, in Polanski's adaptation, gender boundaries are redefined. Banquo's talk of 'naked frailties' is deliberately removed from his speech in the following scene, where the naked body of Duncan's corpse is discovered. As if to fill its absence, Banquo inherits the line from Macbeth: 'Let's briefly put on manly readiness' (2.3.132). In Polanski's film, there is no space for frailty in ruling men.

Another crucial scene in terms of Polanski's examination of the relationship between gender, violence and nakedness is Macbeth's second and more ambiguous visit to the Witches, where he enters the underground cave to demand answers of their 'unknown power' (4.1.85). Here he is greeted by dozens of naked women of all different ages. Once again, there is nothing erotic about their nudity; rather, their nakedness is only unnerving for the viewer because it makes the women appear 'exposed in their humanity rather than all-powerful'.[29] Their appearance denotes the very nakedness of their words to Macbeth: 'Speak', 'Demand', 'We'll answer' (4.1.77). After his request to know more, Macbeth drinks the Witches' brew and then staggers forward to the cauldron for the 'visions' that will show him his future. Kliman observes that it is with 'psychological accuracy' that the first apparition to appear in the cauldron's murky surface is the reflection of Macbeth himself, 'for since he has already suspected Macduff it is reasonable that Macbeth's own image should warn him against Macduff'.[30] However, more significantly, this image also confirms Macbeth's own

place in the gloomy darkness of the film's prophetic space, for when Macbeth first looks into the nothingness of the Witches' cauldron, the 'Horrible sight' (4.1.138) that will 'grieve his heart' (4.1.126) and 'sear' his eyeballs (4.1.129) is the image of his own reflection.

As the reflection of Macbeth's face begins to dissolve in the water, the image of a spinning, severed head appears in its place, an early signifier of his own beheading by Macduff. Before any apparitions of bloody children or fatal visions of Banquo or Macduff, the prophetic space reveals both Macbeth's beginning and his end through the appearance of his own image. While Polanski's visualization of the prophecies finds the Witches' cauldron as its space of representation, the images that reveal the future also deliberately exclude the Witches themselves: a bloody newborn babe being ripped from its mother's womb signifies the birth of Macduff; a child in a suit of armour instructs Macbeth to be 'bloody, bold, and resolute' (4.1.95); and the murdered Banquo directs Macbeth's gaze towards a line of kings. When the visions end and Macbeth wakes, he finds himself alone in the cave. The Witches have disappeared, just as they were required to vanish from Shakespeare's stage. However, in Polanski's film, they have no visual presence or influence during the deliverance of the prophecies. Of all the images used to represent the film's prophetic space, the image most frequently shown is that of Macbeth himself: he stabs the armoured figure he believes to be Macduff, chases the

---

[28] At this point in the film, the fallen crown continues to balance awkwardly on its side, indicating perhaps that a just ruler is yet to come to Scotland's throne. However it also emphasizes another merging of male and female imagery: it becomes both a signifier of patriarchal authority, the male 'something', and the 'O' that traditionally signifies the female nothing. In Polanski's film, the crown is another image that symbolizes how Macbeth's violence creates his own 'nothing'. Consider also how Dunsinane itself becomes the space of Macbeth's created nothing. In the final scene, its interior is empty and deserted: all servants and soldiers have fled, its courtyard and halls filled with a vacant silence. All that remains is Macbeth himself – clinging to his crown and to the throne.

[29] Kliman, *Shakespeare in Performance*, p. 141.

[30] Kliman, *Shakespeare in Performance*, p. 132.

laughing Malcolm and Donalbain through the forest, and smashes Banquo's mirror with his sword. Significantly, the last thing Macbeth sees in the prophetic visions is the mirror held by the future line of kings that fails to reflect his own image. Macbeth's own body is now without substance, 'signifying nothing' (5.5.27), and the reflection of himself that first warned him to 'beware Macduff' (4.1.87) no longer exists. Similarly, the empty cave in which Macbeth wakes not only signals the Witches' ambiguity through their disappearance but, rather, the absence that Macbeth himself now represents.

In this scene, the nakedness of the women implies an exposed truth, even if it appears in a distinctly haggard or unpleasant form. In a reversal of outward appearances, it is the women's exposed bodies that reflect back to Macbeth the ugliness of Scotland's patriarchal society. Scenes of nakedness in Polanski's film extend to representations of frailty, innocence, vulnerability, pretence, power, rape, violence, humanity or truth. When the Macduff castle is 'surprised' (4.3.205), the naked bodies of Macduff's children appear as slaughtered lambs in the straw of their sleeping quarters. Polanski also uses, perhaps somewhat ironically, his most sympathetic representation of the vulnerable and frail naked body to illustrate Lady Macbeth's deterioration.

Annis's Lady Macbeth is portrayed with a soft femininity that is absent of the 'direst cruelty' (1.5.42) that has so frequently influenced interpretations of her character. As she watches Duncan and the royal party approaching from her standpoint on the castle battlements, her call to the evil spirits that 'tend on mortal thoughts' (1.5.40) seems unnatural, in that she herself is too gentle and naturally feminine to possess such 'unwomanly' thoughts or demand to be unsexed. With no reference to her woman's milk being taken for gall or having 'given suck' (1.7.54), the film's depiction of her femininity also entirely excludes motherhood.[31] She is young and attractive, but also child-like and foolish, and often acts without the conviction and self-government that Shakespeare's Lady Macbeth conveys. Annis's false smiles and talk of murder come far too easily; it is as if she is playing a game, longing

to dress up in the royal robes, and has no sense of consequence. The cracks in her 'undaunted mettle' (1.7.73) soon begin to show as she recoils from the blood on her husband's hand after the murder, turning her face away into his shoulder and consoling herself as much as him when she whispers, 'A foolish thought to say a sorry sight' (2.2.19). Her eyes widen with undisguisable terror as she embraces Macbeth and discovers the bloody daggers still in his right hand. The 'white' heart (2.2.63) that she so despises to wear is not merely her husband's but her own, and as she returns from Duncan's chamber with bloodstains smeared down the front of her white gown, a deliberate emphasis is placed on the naivety of her words: 'A little water clears us of this deed' (2.2.65).

However, Annis's Lady Macbeth is not entirely unlike Shakespeare's. For, while Polanski makes significant cuts to her soliloquies, he maintains the essential irony behind her convictions: Lady Macbeth is merely words without action. She may speak of concealing the wound that her 'keen knife' (1.5.51) makes, but as Joan Larsen Klein observes of her character, Lady Macbeth's 'threats of violence, for all their force and cruelty, are empty fantasies. It is Macbeth who converts them to hard reality.'[32] Although her words may connote a desire for masculine power, Lady Macbeth remains incapable of performing its violence. Polanski's chosen representation of Duncan's murder only reinforces this crucial point. Despite her faint words about how 'easy' murder is (2.2.66), Lady Macbeth is deliberately distanced from the murder itself. Polanski allows the viewer to *see* Macbeth committing the bloody deed in Duncan's chamber: we do not see Lady Macbeth there. We know that she visits the chamber to return the daggers, but her body is

---

[31] Williams comments that the play's references to motherhood are suppressed in Polanski's *Macbeth* because the 'physical realities of maternity and lactation contradict the Playboy vision of femininity: high voice, golden tresses, slender figure'. Williams, 'Mick Jagger Macbeth', p. 153.

[32] Joan Larsen Klein, 'Lady Macbeth: "Infirm of Purpose"', in Carolyn Ruth Swift Lenz, Gayle Greene and Carol Thomas Neely, eds., *The Woman's Part: Feminist Criticism of Shakespeare* (Chicago, 1983), pp. 240–55 (p. 244).

never placed at the scene of her husband's crime. While Shakespeare's play would have given both characters an involvement in the offstage space of the murder, Polanski clearly defines spaces of violence as masculine. Despite her call to the spirits to unsex her, Annis's Lady Macbeth is never shown to operate outside feminine domestic spaces or portrayed as unsettling the gender boundaries that seem frequently under threat in Shakespeare's play.

Annis brings a child-like naivety to the role of the 'fiend-like queen' (5.11.35) that is enhanced by Polanski's visual representations of nakedness. Her exposed body appears frail and brittle in the sleepwalking scene, which follows directly after the attack on the Macduff castle and thus associates the naked bodies of the murdered babes with Lady Macbeth's own naked vulnerability. In Shakespeare's play, Macduff receives the news that his family has been murdered just before the sleepwalking scene, making a causal link between his sorrow and Lady Macbeth's guilt. Polanski reorders the play's events to portray her as another victim of the film's escalating violence. Her story begins and ends with her husband's words, as we first see her reading Macbeth's letter and, after removing it from the treasure chest where she safely keeps it, she reads it again for her final scene. Her part in the plot's 'great business' is now over (1.5.67); she does not exist outside Macbeth's own narrative, and after his second visit to the Witches, her mental state begins to deteriorate, as if their marriage bond has now been broken and left her without function.[33] After the news of her death, we see her broken and partly exposed body lying in the castle's courtyard. Her face is then covered by a blanket (hardly suitable for a queen's body), while her muddied legs and feet are left exposed. This shot recalls Macbeth's crowning at Scone, and the image of his bare feet on the sacred stones during his 'marriage' to the land. Here, Polanski not only makes a visual reference to the play's metaphors of Macbeth as the 'dwarfish thief' (5.2.22) attempting to fill a giant's footsteps, but also to nakedness as a perversion of innocence. This is the film's ultimate perversion in terms of its representation of the naked body – not the filthy, haggard bodies of the Witches or the muddied legs and feet of Lady Macbeth's discarded corpse, but Macbeth's 'sacred' marriage to nature, to the earth and to Scotland.

By redefining the play's relationship between gender and nakedness, Polanski's film eliminates the threat of the female nothing from its depiction of the prophetic space. Instead, man's own reflection shifts into the cauldron's ambiguous, murky surface, and through the film's representations of the ruling power of Duncan's kingdom, Polanski connects an already bloody and violent masculine world to its future image. To say that the Witches' prophetic nothing gives birth to the 'bold' and 'bloody' Macbeth is certainly too narrow a viewpoint for the brutal patriarchal society that Polanski – and indeed Shakespeare – creates; it is a society of which Macbeth is, inevitably, already a part. Although the establishing scenes within Shakespeare's play and Polanski's film make this point abundantly clear, the desire to remove Macbeth's control from his own future course of bloody action is an idea that is strongly advocated in adaptations such as Welles's *Macbeth*, where the child-like voodoo doll that symbolizes Macbeth's own body is literally born from the 'hell-broth' of the Witches' cauldron (4.1.19). In signalling Macbeth as the Witches' own creation, Welles immediately eliminates any blame or notion of responsibility from his tragic hero.

The debate about Macbeth's own part in his prophesied future has undoubtedly been affected by interpretations of the play's female characters and their involvement in his fate, and the struggle between these two influences has perhaps never been fully rectified on film. For instance, in a discussion of Akira Kurosawa's *Throne of Blood*, Anthony Dawson is left asking who exactly is

---

[33] Polanski's portrayal of Lady Macbeth's role seems to echo Klein's interpretation of her character in Shakespeare's play; she writes that Macbeth 'exchanges the fellowship of his badly founded marriage to Lady Macbeth for union with the weird sisters'. With her husband 'out of reach and society in shambles, Lady Macbeth no longer has any reason for being'. Klein, 'Lady Macbeth: "Infirm of Purpose"', pp. 243 and 247.

responsible in a film that emphasizes 'the relentless destructiveness of human agency together with the malevolence of fate'.[34] Similarly, Neil Forsyth insists that Polanski's film remains 'caught between conflicting ideologies', arguing that the director wants the Witches to be seen 'from a political and feminist perspective as earthy and rebellious, healthily disrespectful of masculine and royal authority, but he cannot go very far along these lines without overbalancing the meaning of the whole film, which remains a serious and tragic engagement with evil'.[35] Indeed, Polanski's *Macbeth* explores a 'serious and tragic engagement with evil', but its focus shifts from an interrogation of the female to a wider exploration of the play's patriarchal violence. As a result, the film succeeds in maintaining the play's intriguing elements of fate without heralding the female body as its evil and destructive space of representation. By redefining Shakespearian conceptions of nothing and nakedness, Polanksi's *Macbeth* also exposes man's undoubtedly fragile relationship to innocence in the bloody warfare of Shakespeare's play, and demands that we re-evaluate its meaning.

Locating *Macbeth*'s nothing (and Macbeth's undoing) with the territory of the female body can lead to a reading that disregards the larger ethical concerns that arise throughout the play's political theme. The Witches themselves, though they equivocate to the very end, inhabit a space outside the immediate world of the play that persists in possessing, as Eagleton suggests, 'its own kind of truth'.[36] There is no evidence within the playtext to confirm that the Witches' words prophesy the murder of Duncan, only that Macbeth 'shalt be king hereafter' (1.3.48). Likewise, we can never be certain that Macbeth would have been crowned king had he not taken matters into his own hands and usurped the throne. While the combination of an ungovernable female power and an uncompromising male violence in the play's influences is absolute, Macbeth is 'bloody, bold, and resolute' (4.1.95) long before the Witches' instruction, as the bloody Captain's first account of how 'brave Macbeth' (1.2.16) unseamed his enemy on the battlefield 'from the nave to th'chops' readily testifies (1.2.22). In seeking to fulfil the Witches' prophecies, it is in fact Macbeth's own course of violent and bloody action that builds no future at all. Ironically, as Carol Rutter remarks, 'Macbeth wants both to possess the future – the one the Weird Sisters "gave" him – and destroy it – the one they "promised" Banquo'.[37] Thus the future 'absence' that reduces Macbeth's life to a walking shadow is an absence of his own making.

In Polanski's *Macbeth*, it is man's inevitable compulsion to violent action that ultimately determines Macbeth's future. Similarly, by choosing to act under his wife's persuasion and continuing to wade himself further into an ocean of blood (2.2.57–61), Shakespeare's protagonist creates *and* destroys the future that the Witches offer him and, in doing so, he succeeds in creating his own 'nothing'. Jan Kott argues that 'a production of *Macbeth* not evoking a picture of the world flooded with blood would inevitably be false'.[38] As this assertion seems to have become a staple quotation for critical discussions of Polanki's film, it is clear that the similarities between Shakespeare's vision and Polanski's have not gone unnoticed.[39] Macbeth destroys himself.

---

[34] Anthony Dawson, 'Cross-Cultural Interpretation: Reading Kurosawa Reading Shakespeare', in Diana E. Henderson, ed., *Shakespeare on Screen* (Oxford, 2006), pp. 155–75 (pp. 168 and 173).

[35] Neil Forsyth, 'Shakespeare the Illusionist: Filming the Supernatural', in Russell Jackson, ed., *The Cambridge Companion to Shakespeare on Film* (Cambridge, 2000), pp. 274–94 (p. 282).

[36] Eagleton, *William Shakespeare*, p. 2.

[37] Carol Chillington Rutter, 'Remind Me: How Many Children Had Lady Macbeth?', *Shakespeare Survey 57* (Cambridge, 2004), 38–53 (p. 39).

[38] Jan Kott, *Shakespeare Our Contemporary* (London, 1965), p. 90.

[39] This quotation is an important feature in Per Serritslev Petersen's essay, 'The "Bloody Business" of Roman Polanski's *Macbeth*: A Case Study of the Dynamics of Modern Shakespeare Appropriation', in Michael Skovmand, ed., *Screen Shakespeare* (Aarhus, 1994), pp. 38–53. See also Williams, 'Mick Jagger Macbeth', p. 149.

GHOSTS AND MIRRORS: THE GAZE IN FILM *HAMLETS*

SIMON J. RYLE

In this article I use the sense of rupture implicit in Jacques Lacan's theory of the gaze to explore film adaptations of *Hamlet*.[1] My discussion focuses on three well-known adaptations of the play: Olivier,[2] Branagh[3] and Almereyda.[4] I particularly employ Slavoj Žižek's conception of Lacan's 'anamorphic stain', and Henry Krips's reading of the points of rupture of the gaze to investigate the symbiotic relationship between the demands Shakespeare's text makes on film-production, and filmmakers' manipulation of libidinal-looking in conceiving diegetic space. My contention, that negotiation of concretized film space is the central issue to be confronted in the adaptation of Shakespeare to the genre codes of film, directs my attention to instances of what I term 'liminal space', sites of apparent filmic resistance to the concrete (visually defined, realistic, photographic, naturalistic) space of the film diegesis. Though psychoanalytic theory is central to my paper, I attempt to address the recent 'post-Theory' theses proposed by Bordwell *et al.*, by grounding theory always in discussion of filmic style, directorial technique and the various signifiers that compose the screen image.

MIRROR TRICKS AND SPECTRAL PRESENCES

To hold, as, 'twere, the mirror up to nature . . .

(3.2.21–2)

At the very opening of the era of cinema, theatrical productions begin to incorporate a series of special effects that uncannily seem to anticipate the future of new form – partially due to technological advances, and partly in order to maintain interest in customers wooed by forerunners to the silver screen. 'Pepper's Ghost', the use of two reflective screens of glass to make a ghost appear on stage, was developed by Henry Dircks in 1862 and perfected for theatrical use by Henry Pepper towards the end of the nineteenth century. The technique required that a second stage be constructed beneath the actual stage, and two reflective screens of glass put into place, the first set at a ninety-degree angle above the lower stage, the second in front of it. The effect generated public interest and Pepper invited Michael Faraday to his converted theatre at the Royal Polytechnic of London, where he explained the mechanics of the device. Such was the power of the effect that Faraday was, until Pepper laid a hand on the second pane of glass, reportedly at a loss to understand the generation of the apparition.

---

[1] Though of interest to psychoanalytically inclined Shakespearians, I will not pay particular attention to Jacques Lacan's conception of old Hamlet as 'anal father'. Lacan develops Freud's suggestion of the Oedipal myth structuring Hamlet's unconscious desire, yet never manifest on a literal level, in his suggestion of the play as 'a decadent form of the Oedipal situation, its decline' (49), in Jacques Lacan, 'Desire and the Interpretation of Desire in *Hamlet*', in Shoshana Felman, ed., *Literature and Psychoanalysis: The Question of Reading, Otherwise* (Baltimore, 1977), pp. 11–52.

[2] Laurence Olivier, *Hamlet*, Two Cities Films, Ltd, 1948.

[3] Kenneth Branagh, *Hamlet*, Castle Rock Entertainment, 1996.

[4] Michael Almereyda, *Hamlet*, Miramax Films, 2000.

One might note initially the way that Pepper's Ghost is generated for the spectator literally by conveying the mirror reflection of an alternative space into the spectator's perception of the space of the stage. I would argue that Pepper, in generating the ghostly reflection, exemplifies a theatrical parallel to my concept of liminal film space: a space between ontological planes, neither existing nor not existing. It is also worth noting that this importing of alternative space closely duplicates the effect generated by Pepper's main competition, the screen of the then-developing art of cinema.[5] Thus, my investigation of the potential of the mirror reflection and the ghost to disrupt the steady transmission of diegetic space in the Shakespeare film is not without precedent in theatrical tradition.

Important to this is the somewhat paradoxical ontology with which Christian Metz conceives the space of the film diegesis, simultaneously offering forth 'a small part of the real',[6] yet 'closer to fantasy' than the 'true space' of the theatre.[7] This paradox derives from André Bazin's 'integral' or 'undifferentiated homogeneity of space'[8] as the basic component of the matter that composes the cinematic shot, a concrete quality that sits uneasily with his rather poetic conception of film, elsewhere, as 'the night of our waking dream',[9] which in itself almost anticipates the theory of enunciation as used by Screen Theorists. Of course, this dual status of cinema closely parallels Hamlet's conception of the stage: of theatricality as both 'nothing' (2.2.559), the fraudulent tears of the actor, and the very 'thing' that will 'catch the conscience of the king' (2.2.606–7).

Though the cinema for Metz is a significantly more concrete presence than the imaginary space of theatrical diegesis, yet the space of the cinema is patently, unlike the play (but like Pepper's Ghost), not there in the auditorium: something less-than-real. It is precisely this quality of the film space that leads Mark Robson to delineate the ghost-making capacity of film: 'Flesh takes on the substance of celluloid . . . but this is no more than an inverted repetition of a spectral assumption of the flesh',[10] or as Bennet and Royle more succinctly put it: 'In a

film, everyone is a ghost'.[11] Of course, this formulation makes all ghosts and all instances of reflection on film, simultaneously as self-consciously meta-filmic, and also things at a further remove from reality, ghosts haunting ghosts.

It is the same simulacra-making capacity of mass media projection that informs Jacques Derrida's proposal of a 'hauntology' (a system he introduces with explicit reference to the ghost of old Hamlet):

What is a ghost? What is the effectivity or the presence of a spectre, that is, of what seems to remain as ineffective, virtual, insubstantial as a simulacrum? Is there *there*, between the thing itself and its simulacrum, an opposition that holds up?[12]

Indeed, it may be advisable to bear in mind the three ontological stages of hierarchy Derrida here seems to propose, 'thing itself' – 'ghost' – 'simulacrum', in investigating filmic instances of the less-than-real, ghosts and mirrors.[13] This is especially so when, as is the case in Shakespeare cinema, the film itself is haunted by an originary form, traces of the theatrical origins that the text was written for, that seem to resist adaptation to the genre codes of film. My object of investigation would, then, be

---

[5] A further connection between cinema and the mirror-trick ghost is that prominent pioneers of cinema, like Georges Meliès, often cut their teeth as magic-lantern illusionists. Significantly Meliès went on to direct an early film *Hamlet* (1907).

[6] Christian Metz, 'The Imaginary Signifier', in Robert Stam and Toby Miller, eds., *Film Theory* (Oxford, 1999), p. 414.

[7] Metz, 'Imaginary Signifier', p. 409.

[8] Dudley J. Andrew, *The Major Film Theories: An Introduction*, (Oxford, 1976), p. 157.

[9] André Bazin, *What is Cinema?*, trans. Hugh Gray (Berkeley, 1967), p. 107.

[10] Mark Robson, '"Trying to Pick a Lock with a Wet Herring": Hamlet, Film, and Spectres of Psychoanalysis', *EnterText* 1.2, University of Brunel, pp. 247–63; p. 260. http://people. brunel.ac.uk/~acsrrrm/entertext/hamlet/robson.pdf

[11] Andrew Bennet and Nicholas Royle, *Introduction to Literature, Criticism and Theory*, 2nd edn (Harlowe, 1999), p. 138.

[12] Jacques Derrida, *Spectres of Marx: The State of the Debt, the Work of Mourning, and the New International*, trans. Peggy Kampf (London, 1994), p. 10.

[13] Derrida also uses a quote from *Hamlet*, concerning Old Hamlet's ghost, to move into his discussion.

elegantly formulated by Robson: 'Hamlet as film . . . becomes the prosthetic body inhabited by the ghost of its own performance',[14] if one were to replace his 'performance' with 'theatrical origins'.[15]

It is worth considering here Yorick, not mentioned in the play's *dramatis personae*, the archetypal dead guy, someone never there. Branagh's treatment of Yorick in the gravedigger scene of his film well exemplifies the tendency of the Shakespeare cinematic adaptation to seek visual representation of verbal effects, a task both Brook and Kozintsev find as central to the adaptation.[16] I suggest this scene also provides succinct illustration of the paradox of cinematic space as set out by Bazin and Metz, simultaneously more concrete than the fluid meaning of the early modern stage space, and yet less real. Yorick's well-known place in stage tradition, as the skull upon which Hamlet meditates the inevitability of death, is somewhat usurped by the cinematic convention of flashback Branagh employs in this scene. The fade from the skull to the grinning face of Ken Dodd is automatically understood by the cinema spectator, well versed in flashback convention, to represent the subjectivized space of Hamlet's memories. In representing Hamlet's thoughts as diegetic space, Branagh gives body to Yorick's ghost: he literally fleshes out Yorick's skull. Yet, in reading the concrete spatial evidence of Yorick's past existence, the film spectator must process the flashback as another instance, this time stylistic, of the less-than-real within the film diegesis, a moment not directly a part of the continuous present of the diegesis. The flashback is thus the 'liminal space' *par excellence*, a level less real, in Derrida's hierarchy, than 'the thing itself' (the skull), that is to say, the ghost.

Here one might consider another dynamic of the flashback, apparent in Branagh's use of the technique to import erotic realism to the depiction of Hamlet and Ophelia's relationship, which Lehmann and Starks find as central to the dissipation of Oedipal tension in Branagh's *Hamlet*, that also precisely exemplifies the dual tendency of the genre codes of film to concretize the spatial nature of character interaction by the use of the spectral presences. As Richard Briers, playing

Polonius, reads Hamlet's love verse to Claudius and Gertrude, a fade-cut introduces the flashback as a visual explanation of the meaning of the words. The flashback is colour coded, in cold blue tones, to mark its temporal/spatial distance from the unfolding present of the diegesis. In calling explicitly on 'keyhole' point-of-view shots, Branagh seems to configure in his flashback both the spectator's scopic drive to see all, yet also to generate anxiety by hinting at the suppressed primal scene. Lehmann and Starks are right that the erotic flashbacks of the film fit Branagh's tendency to 'stress his [Hamlet's] status as normative male'.[17] Indeed, one might also question whether this erotic concretization in Branagh's film is not at odds with the play-text. Both Ophelia's emblematic self-'deflowering'[18] in Act 4, scene 4, and the bawdy songs which she sings as hysterical pathology – the hysteric naively embracing the forbidden, unknown, that in her sanity she so strictly avoided – seem to indicate, in the text, the unconsummated nature of their relationship.[19]

---

[14] Robson 'Hamlet, Film', p. 256.

[15] This haunting originary form is also implied by Fedderson and Richardson's use of 'excision' to characterize the removal of Renaissance concepts from the contemporaneous adaptation.

[16] See Grigori Kozintsev, '*King Lear': The Space of Tragedy* (Berkeley, 1977) and Peter Brook, *The Empty Space* (London, 1990).

[17] Courtney Lehmann and Lisa Starks, '"Making Mother Matter": Repression, Revision, and the Stakes of "Reading Psychoanalysis Into" Kenneth Branagh's Hamlet', *Early Modern Literary Studies*, 6.1 (May, 2000): 2.1–24; paragraph 8. http://purl.oclc.org/emls/06-1/lehmhaml.htm

[18] See Griselda Pollock, *Vision and Difference: Femininity, Feminism and the Histories of Art* (London and New York, 1994). Pollock writes: 'Flowers have often been used as a metaphor for a woman's sexuality, or rather their genitals . . . covering or masking the sexualized parts of the body which are traditionally erased' (135).

[19] See Carol Thomas Neely, '"Documents in Madness": Reading Madness and Gender in Shakespeare's Tragedies and Early modern Culture', *Shakespeare Quarterly* 42 (1991), 317–38. Neely writes: 'The context of her disease, like that of hysteria later, is sexual frustration' (325). Also see Kaara Peterson, 'Fluid Economies: Portraying Shakespeare's Hysterics', *Mosaic* 34 (2001). Peterson writes: 'Ophelia's illness seems like

This, then, one might read as the genre codes of film dominating and refuting the radical ambiguity of Shakespeare's text: the privileged glance back of the cinema spectator, onto a secret space that concretizes the meaning of the dramatic interaction. However, it is important to note that Branagh's use of the voice of Polonius speaking Hamlet's love poetry in voice-over, to enable seamless spatial and temporal contiguity in shifting between the present narrative to the time/place of flashback, explicitly borrows from the gendered flashback technique of 1940s and 1950s psychological melodrama. Susan Hayward notes the technique of the gendered flashback of structuring the subjective memory of the dysfunctional female psyche by the controlling male voice of analyst/detective:

So the flashback is not their subjectivity but others' subjective view of them – a return to the past provoked by a probing or electrifying of the female psyche . . . implicitly the ideological purpose being served here is that women do not control their unconscious, but men do.[20]

It is precisely in this form that the gendered 'acousmêtre' (to slightly reconfigure Chion's term) floats as a disembodied presence above the space of Branagh's erotic flashback, the unseen male voice that both defines yet maintains an ambiguous ontological relationship to the film's female visual element. More than noting how this parallel might suggest the reactionary gender ideology of Branagh's adaptation, as do Lehmann and Starks, I would focus on the way Branagh's technique, in structuring the erotic moment as neurotic male projection of the potential of female libidinal energy, in effect establishes two ghosts: the ghost of Polonius's voice that haunts the visually posited erotic moment, and the ghost of the event, the liminal space of the cinematic flashback, as visually realistic as any moment of the film, yet aurally marked as Polonius's subjective projection, that haunts the unfolding present of the film diegesis.

In this article, then, I propose to initiate a 'hauntology' of film *Hamlets* via investigation of these spectral ruptures to the screen space, which we might also term 'filmic lacunae', grouped around the motifs of ghost and mirror. This exploration of the mimetic disruption occasioned by film adaptation finds precedent in the play-text's rigorous interrogation of the essentialist humanist ideal of the stage. Bruce Danner, for example, asserts that Hamlet's 'essentialist, almost naive conception of theatrical performance' as holding 'the mirror up to nature' (3.2.22) is one refuted by various discordant episodes in the play itself, which work to destabilize the 'links between intention, representation and interpretation'.[21] I argue that, in the *Hamlet* film, such ruptures serve rather as *memento mori* of the theatrical origins of the film-text.

THE GHOST IN THE PEPSI MACHINE: FRAMING AND RUPTURING SPACE

O God, I could be bounded in a nutshell and count myself a king of infinite space, were it not that I have bad dreams.   (2.2.256–8)

It might initially seem contrary for a Lacanian analysis of the mirror in film to largely ignore, as this article does, Lacan's theory of the mirror stage, the formation of ego in the movement into the imaginary realm that allows for, or concurrently occurs with, the movement into the symbolic realm, precipitated by the (mis)recognition of the specular image in the reflection – especially considering Metz's widely applied use of Lacan's theory in characterizing the cinema as a 'strange mirror'.[22] In developing his conception of the cinema screen to be a 'new kind of mirror', Metz finds it lacks only one reflection: 'the spectator's own body'.[23] For Metz, it is the transition precipitated by the mirror stage that makes this absence psychologically

---

the indisposition commonly attributed to virgins desiring but not experiencing sexual release' (7).

[20] Susan Hayward, *Cinema Studies: The Key Concepts* (New York, 2000), p. 137.

[21] Bruce Danner, 'Speaking Daggers', *Shakespeare Quarterly*, 54 (2003), p. 29.

[22] Metz, 'Imaginary Signifier', p. 413.

[23] Metz, 'Imaginary Signifier', p. 410.

comprehensible. Whereas the child's ego is founded by identification with itself as object-reflection, in the strange cinematic mirror, 'it is always the other who is on the screen; as for me, I am there to look at him'.[24] Thus, the basic identification of the cinema spectator is as one who looks.

This being so, a Shakespearian facing the exciting possibility of a psychoanalytic approach to the mirror-strewn Elsinore of Branagh's adaptation might long to read this image-motif as 'an attempt to return *Hamlet* itself to the mirror stage',[25] as in Courtney Lehmann and Lisa Starks's overly literal conflation of the stylistic and psychic in analysis of Branagh's film. It is possible they suggest here that it is precisely desire for the lost object, *objet petit a*, which might be understood as an impossible desire to return to the pre-symbolic realm and from which derive all displaced drives, that structures the libidinous energy of Branagh's *Hamlet*. However, one might ask just how a work of verbal/visual art, itself a product of the symbolic realm, could be returned to the mirror stage, the very brink of the movement into the symbolic realm. As Metz himself puts it, with reference to the ontological division encoded in the mirror, 'the cinema is already on the side of the symbolic':[26] the cinema is always already the reflection.

To negotiate this difficulty, and to justify my neglect of the conceptually tempting mirror stage, I use Henry Krips's reading of Lacan's break with the Screen Theorists, caused by later period Lacan's reworking of the gaze, particularly as expressed in *The Four Fundamental Concepts of Psychoanalysis*. The use of the earlier mirror-stage theory allowed Screen Theorists to combine Lacan with politicized readings of the various ideologies of interpellation involved in the cinema spectator seeing her own life reflected in the screen image, which Krips terms 'a form of self-(mis)recognition'.[27] For Krips, this makes Screen Theory, and other uses of the mirror stage (such as Lehmann and Starks's) only anachronistically Lacanian, in that from the late 1950s onwards Lacan stressed, rather than the reflection of the self in the symbolic realm – which

for Screen Theory implies an uncomplicated transmission of ideology – the central importance of 'the Real': the points of rupture which disrupt the subject's relationship with the symbolic realm. The disruption of these 'anxiety-proving breaks or anomalies in the visual field'[28] brings about the self-scrutiny of the gaze. Because of his emphasis of rupture over specifically ideological meanings, Screen Theory criticized Lacan for being apolitical, a charge also levelled against advocates of 'post-Theory', whom I will discuss in greater detail later, such as Bordwell and Carroll.

For my purposes, it is important to note how the frame is implicit to the rupture of later-period Lacan's gaze. Two central examples serve to structure Lacan's formulation of the gaze in *Four Fundamental Concepts*: the dazzling sparkle of light he saw flashing from a sardine can in the sea one day during his youth while on a Breton fishing trip, and the strangely elongated skull with which Hans Holbein disrupts the system of spatial organization in his painting *The Ambassadors*. The similarity of the flash of light and the skull comes of the disruption they cause to visual orientation, yet both also implicitly rely on the frame. This is clearer in Holbein's painting, where the disruption of visual planes specifically calls upon the frame, which typically works to enclose an autonomous system of spatial organization in realistic art. In Holbein's painting the skull is only a rupture because it is located within a frame from which the codes of naturalistic art would exclude it.

Location of the frame is perhaps less clear in Lacan's account of the sardine can flashing with sunlight in the sea, which centres on a joke made by one of the fishermen, Petit-Jean, on the boat: 'You see that can? . . . Well it doesn't see you!'

---

24 Metz, 'Imaginary Signifier', p. 412.
25 Lehmann and Starks, 'Making Mother Matter', paragraph 7.
26 Metz, 'Imaginary Signifier', p. 411.
27 Henry Krips, *Fetish: An Erotics of Culture* (New York, 1999), p. 98.
28 Krips, *Fetish*, p. 99.

Writing on the incident more than twenty years later, Lacan comments:

The can did not see me . . . [but] it was looking at me all the same . . . and I am not speaking metaphorically . . . I, at that moment – as I appeared to those fellows who were earning their lives with great difficulty . . . looked like nothing on earth.[29]

In speculating how the rupture in visual perception caused by the bright flash of light becomes the gaze, the feeling of the universe looking back, Krips in effect attempts to bring issues of ideology back to the gaze. He suggests the strange anxiety young Lacan feels at the incident, remembered so long, derives from his 'unwelcome realization of himself as without a place among the men'[30] – that essentially the bourgeois Lacan senses, perhaps without locating the exact reason for the discomfort, that he was different from his working class colleagues on the boat. What is further interesting is Lacan's exact formulation of this discomfort, that he felt 'rather out of place in the picture',[31] specifically denotes the rupturing effect as deriving from the ontology of the frame. It is the framing effect of the working-class environment that structures the discomfort, from which derives the gaze.

I suggest a conceptual model that conceives the point of rupture as dependent on the existence of the frame can help throw light onto Lacan's assertion that, rather than a rare example of the rupture of the gaze, Holbein's painting is 'simply what any picture is, a trap for the gaze'.[32] It is by setting up a framed space that every picture, and indeed every film, encloses potential points of rupture: liminal spaces that, in seeming to resist the dominant symbolic organization of the framed space, serve to trap the gaze of the spectator. However, one should also relate this formulation to Žižek's suggestion that 'there is no "neutral" reality within which gaps occur, within which frames isolate domains of appearances. Every field of "reality" (every "world") is always-already enframed, seen through an invisible frame'.[33] Literally, it is by the 'gaps' that we know there is a frame. Žižek seems to broaden here Lacan's conception of every picture as a trap for the gaze – in fact, every observed thing is a trap for the gaze, for every 'reality' is viewed as a picture. Of course, this helps to clarify further the link between Holbein's *Ambassadors* and the flash of light from the can in the sea.

The symbiotic relationship between framed space and rupture perhaps also throws light on Hamlet's persistent musings on the theme of enclosure. Following the appearance of the ghost of his father, Denmark becomes for Hamlet 'a prison' (2.2.253). One might say the ghost opens up a psychic gap, causing him to reconfigure his psychic response to the enframing capacity of the space of Elsinore. One can read likewise Hamlet's enigmatic suggestion: 'I could be bounded in a nutshell and count myself a king of infinite space, were it not that I have bad dreams' (2.2.256–8). His hypothetical rejection of the nutshell as intolerable enclosure, a space that might otherwise potentially enclose the infinite in a limited domain of appearance (like the newly popular system of vanishing point perspective in early modern English visual art), is contingent on his 'bad dreams': psychic ruptures to that spatial organization.

However, if in this article my attention is attuned to the rupturing caused by these liminal spaces in Shakespeare film adaptation, I would like to go significantly beyond Krips's assertion of the perfect cinematic instance of the point of rupture as 'when viewers of a film see a fly bump into the camera lens'.[34] Krips's conception of the accidental rupture, for example, seems not at all to take into account the consciously designed nature of Holbein's skull. With reference to films of *Hamlet*, I would suggest the deliberate rupture

29 Jacques Lacan, *The Four Fundamental Concepts of Psychoanalysis*, trans. Alan Sheridan (London, 1977), p. 98.
30 Krips, *Fetish*, p. 103.
31 Lacan, *Four Fundamental Concepts*, p. 96.
32 Lacan, *Four Fundamental Concepts*, p. 89.
33 Slavoj Žižek, *The Parallax View* (Cambridge, MA, 2006), p. 29.
34 Krips, *Fetish*, p. 107.

can be located in conscious directorial departure from the text, for which Kim Fedderson and J. Michael Richardson co-opt the psychoanalytic term 'transference'.[35] However, perhaps even more revealing about the relationship between early modern theatrical drama and cinema, in that it does not specifically raise the problematic issue of directorial intent, is the possibility of the rupture as marking a spontaneous resistance to adaptation: some improvised site of negotiation arising from the occasional incompatibility of the genre codes of early modern drama and film, or a certain surplus that is left over in the translation between the two code systems.

I argue one should read a particularly enigmatic sequence in Almereyda's *Hamlet*, in which the ghost of old Hamlet, played by Sam Shepard, disappears into a Pepsi drinks dispenser, precisely as this type of filmic resistance to the theatrical origins. Important here is Douglas Lanier's delineation of the film's translation of the elements of the play to a modern idiom as Almereyda 'remaking . . . Shakespeare in the image of corporate ideology'.[36] One ingenious example of this translation process is the 'wire' Ophelia wears in the nunnery scene, which for Peter Donaldson 'recalls Shakespeare's habit of drawing metaphors from book and manuscript culture'.[37] What is perhaps particularly disturbing about the ghost in the Pepsi machine is its very refusal to conform to this system of visual substitution: rather than translating an early modern element into twentieth-century idiom, the Pepsi machine seems to eschew meaning on this level.

This difficulty of locating a precedent in the original text causes Fedderson and Richardson to remark, with some consternation, that the sequence 'appears extraneous to the film's translation of the play'.[38] Yet, despite their uncertainty as to the exact significance of the ghost in the Pepsi machine, they maintain the conviction that 'it nonetheless continues to mean'.[39] I argue the refusal of the sequence to fit a systemized understanding of the adaptation, coupled with the haunting feeling that it nonetheless means something, characterizes the sequence as a filmic instance of

Lacan's 'trap for the gaze', a rupture in the ontology of the film. Read this way, the ghost in the Pepsi machine provides a succinct example of the liminal space, a filmic improvisation that marks a rupture in the smooth translation of the elements of one code system to another.

One obvious question to ask of the ghost and Pepsi machine is: which is the rupture and which is the frame? To answer it is necessary to consider the ontological organization of material in Almereyda's *Hamlet*, including the proliferation of contemporary machines and media devices to be found in almost every shot of the film. Whether this indicates the monolithic culture industry that assimilates all forms of cultural expression that Adorno proposes, or implies a subversive attempt by Almereyda to reconfigure the canon to critique the logic of late capitalist society, has informed academic debate of the media-saturated space of his adaptation.[40] Rather, I would like to focus on the way the proliferation of mass media in the screen space of the film contributes to the self-conscious

---

[35] Kim Fedderson and J. Michael Richardson, 'Hamlet 9/11: Sound, Noise and Fury in Almereyda's *Hamlet*', *College Literature* 31.4 (2004), p. 153.

[36] Douglas Lanier, 'Shakescorp Noir', *Shakespeare Quarterly* 53 (2002), p. 171.

[37] Peter Donaldson, 'Hamlet Among the Pixelvisionaries: Video Art, Authenticity, and "Wisdom" in Almereyda's *Hamlet*', in Diana Henderson, ed., *Shakespeare on Screen* (Malden, 2006), p. 216.

[38] Fedderson and Richardson, 'Sound, Noise and Fury', p. 159. See also: Mark Thornton Burnett, '"To Hear and See the Matter": Communicating Technology in Michael Almereyda's *Hamlet* (2000)', *Cinema Journal* 42.3 (2003), pp. 48–69. In reading the scene along the lines of *fin-de-siècle* late capitalism, 'Hamlet's father . . . engulfed by the very energies that . . . he had earlier commanded' (51), Burnett explicitly acknowledges the distancing from the original textual meaning of the ghost.

[39] Fedderson and Richardson, 'Sound, Noise and Fury', p. 160.

[40] For example, Fedderson and Richardson look at the meaning of the film post 9/11; Burnett suggests the Almereyda 'reads the play through a late capitalist mindset' (48); Lanier and Donaldson, in separate articles, contribute interesting analyses of the ubiquitous media technology of the film; and Katherine Rowe explores specific ways the film investigates the technologies of memory.

process of spatial framing that Almereyda trails as a stylistic motif throughout his *Hamlet*.

I would argue a major component of this is the mass of extra-textual linguistic and visual signifiers that seem to invade the original text: the prices of items in a Kmart window, George Washington on a balloon held by Bill Murray as Polonius, the aisles of Action movies at Blockbuster, the definition of 'interbeing' given by Buddhist monk Thich Nhat Hanh from a screen within the screen. In one sense, Almereyda's *Hamlet* is a film about the encroaching media excesses of modern America. Particularly I would note here how the self-conscious excess of screen images in Almereyda's film is paralleled by his use of glass, the abundance of reflective surfaces, and his technique of compositional framing of characters in windows, a link which, Mark Thornton Burnett suggests, characterizes the film as 'a glasshouse of tinted windows, mirrors, lenses, and screens'.[41]

It is worth also briefly considering a sequence representative of the film's excess of reflective surfaces, a shot of Hamlet speaking to Gertrude, her face framed by the mirrored windows of her limousine. Her face becomes briefly an island in the centre of the screen, framed by reflections of the towering corporate skyscrapers of Manhattan. The ontology of this effect is paralleled semantically by the stylistic repetition of windows used to frame protagonists with extra-diegetic elements (cars driving by, skyscrapers glinting in the sun), occasioned by the modern steel and glass architecture of Almereyda's Hotel Elsinore, in the depth-of-field shots so favoured by André Bazin.[42] I posit it is useful to refer this technique to Žižek's claim, that 'Every "reality" . . . is always-already enframed, seen through an invisible frame'.[43] Almereyda's stylistic repetition of the framing shot works as self-conscious multiplication of the layers of existential framing that Žižek notes: the extra-diegetic screen elements serve as frames that are already doubly framed (by Žižek's 'invisible frame' and the frame of the screen).

Here it is worth returning to Hamlet's mirror, held 'as 'twere up to nature' (3.2.22). If the mirror becomes a metaphor for perfect mimesis within a discontinuous diegetic space – one that is refuted in the play's problematization of the potential for naturalistic theatre – might one not claim it exemplifies very well the potential for the frame-within-the-frame to rupture the domain of appearances? In this context, I argue the Pepsi machine should be read as precisely this type of frame-within-the-frame, a part of the excess of extra-diegetic elements that both frame and encroach upon Almereyda's narrative. Conceived this way, the disturbing nature of the sequence perhaps derives from the apparent victory of the frame, in subsuming the ghost of Shakespeare's text.

However, if Derrida's hauntology is applied to the sequence one is required to make another ontological judgement: is the ghost of theatrical origins subsumed by 'the thing itself' (the 'Real Thing', to borrow the well-known advertising slogan of another soft-drinks manufacturer), in the guise of the Pepsi machine, or the simulacrum? In invoking Baudrillard's conception of 'hyperreality' to depict Almereyda's protagonists confronted by a hostile symbolic universe, Burnett suggests 'the individual subject should be constructed as disoriented, at the mercy of floating signifiers, simulations, and imitations'.[44] Particularly the parallel of the subsumed ghost with Burnett's 'disoriented' subject seems here to indicate the implicit ontology of Burnett's reading: the Pepsi machine is the simulacrum, part of the unstable late capitalist symbolic realm. However, one might also conceive of the Pepsi machine as 'the thing itself', the monolithic culture industry that swallows up the ghost of theatrical origins. In this reading

---

[41] Burnett, 'Communicating Technology', p. 51.
[42] This is thus in direct contrast with Branagh's mirrored Elsinore, which encloses the film's protagonists with an inward directed gaze, a process that Sarah Hatchuel terms 'centrifugal' (paragraph 5), emphasized notably in an extended rotation shot used to move into the nunnery scene. Sarah Hatchuel, 'Leading the Gaze: From Showing to Telling in Kenneth Branagh's Henry V and Hamlet', *Early Modern Literary Studies*, 6.1 (2000), 3.1–22. http://purl.oclc.org/emls/06-1/hatchbra.htm
[43] Žižek, *Parallax View*, p. 29.
[44] Burnett, 'Communicating Technology', p. 49.

the Pepsi machine seems to become a metonymic reference to film itself (and perhaps in part a self-consciously deconstructive reference to the blatant product-placement required to finance his film): a curiously self-denying move on Almereyda's part.

I argue these potential readings of the framing effect of the film's excess of extra-diegetic elements is important in understanding Hamlet's narcissistic contemplation of his filmed reflection. For Fedderson and Richardson the excess of extra-diegetic elements causes the film to be saturated with 'an impending doom, coming upon the characters from somewhere other'.[45] However, rather than depicting the typical spectator's response, I would argue this dread of 'somewhere other' instead characterizes the response of Ethan Hawke's grunge Hamlet to the symbolic universe that encroaches upon his story. Thus, though I would argue Fedderson and Richardson conceive of an overly interpellated spectator (one who fully identifies with the emotions of the film's central protagonist), their formulation is revealing in considering the propensity of Almereyda's characters for the photographic recording of events. When read via the 'impending doom' of 'somewhere other', Hamlet's filmmaking and Ophelia's photography take on the function of resistance, via the framing of space, to the very extra-textual excess of contemporary America.

This idea is developed by Katherine Rowe, with her reference to corporate America's dominance of media technology: 'personal video is the technology of interiority'.[46] Indeed, much critical investigation has gone into Hamlet's use of the grainy, hyper-contrast of Fisher Price PXL 2000 'Pixelvision', which one might term a 'grunge', retro technology. However, critics have not yet noted how, in repeated shots of Hamlet (Ethan Hawke) watching a film he has made of Ophelia (Julia Stiles), Hamlet's filmmaking serves to cast a frame around the thing of importance, ontologically identical to the violent exclusion that for Žižek characterizes love as 'evil'.

One might term Almereyda's technique here the 'diegetic flashback', that is: a flashback occasioned by the actions of a character in the film, which occurs without chronologic/spatial interruption of the film's diegetic space. This technologically generated possibility thus opens a kind of framed liminal space, a past that is carried, via media technology, into the diegetic space of story's present unfolding, a rupture to the ontology of the film space. For Donaldson, the repeated Pixelvision shot of Ophelia 'in seductive close up'[47] visually represents an element of the play-text in suggesting 'Hamlet's doubts concerning the doubleness of female self-presentation'.[48] That Hamlet compulsively returns to the intimate moment suggests for Donaldson 'the shading of memory into auto-eroticism'.[49] Indeed, further investigation is perhaps required of the Baudrillardian implications of this fetishization of the technologically replicated love object. However, along the lines of Žižek's ontology of love as a violent choice, I would rather stress how his Pixelvision technology allows Almereyda's grunge Hamlet, in excluding other aural and visual events (the outside) from filmic preservation, to resist the constant invasion of the extra-textual.

I would also argue this technique entails significant spectral implications. Almereyda also makes use of the Pixelvision technology in playing with the peformative element of Hamlet's famous contemplation of suicide. From a shot over Hamlet's shoulder, the spectator is presented with two screens hooked-up to Hamlet's Pixelvision camera. Again, rather than the Baudrillardian implications of this multiplication of simulated images, I would like to focus on the screen rupture generated by Hamlet's resistance to corporate media. Hamlet repeatedly watches himself deliver the line: 'To be

---

45 Fedderson and Richardson, 'Sound, Noise and Fury', p. 162.
46 Katherine Rowe, '"Remember Me": Technologies of Memory in Michael Almereyda's *Hamlet*', in Lynda E. Boose and Richard Burt, eds., *Shakespeare the Movie II* (New York, 2003), p. 46.
47 Donaldson, 'Video Art, Authenticity, and "Wisdom"', p. 221.
48 Donaldson, 'Video Art, Authenticity, and "Wisdom"', p. 227.
49 Donaldson, 'Video Art, Authenticity, and "Wisdom"', p. 227.

or not to be' (3.1.58), while pressing a gun against his temple, then spools-back to the beginning of the soliloquy. On one level, Almereyda seems to joke with the extra-diegetic existence of this line, which has become quintessential Shakespeare, the cliché that everyone knows. Furthermore, this disruption to the forward progression of the narrative, made in the present playing-back of a 'diegetic flashback', seems to rework the postponement of action in *Hamlet* that critics so frequently note, framing Hamlet's self-destructive impulse as performative gesture. Almereyda's visual supplement to the text thus seems to emphasize the disingenuous in Hamlet's claim of disgust at 'the actions that a man might play' (1.2.84).[50]

More interestingly, by using the framed space of personal recording technologies narcissistically as mirror, in an attempt to cling to his personal narrative in a media-saturated America, Hamlet in effect makes himself into a point of rupture, a reflection less real than the present of the film diegesis. As well as the meta-drama implicit in the framed image within a screen space, Almereyda's filmmaker Hamlet seems here to haunt himself with a film ghost of his own potential suicide.

THE STAIN

Thou turn'st mine eyes into my very soul,
And there I see such black and grained spots
As will not leave their tinct.

(3.4.79–81)

Rather than the exaggerated Oedipal tension of Olivier's closet scene, commonly noted by critics,[51] I would rather consider the way Olivier constructs his diegetic space around the issues of self-reflection and staining that precede Hamlet's ambiguous second encounter with the ghost of his father. In the probing gaze that Hamlet casts upon his mother during the scene, itself visually derived from the comparison of two portraits, he vows to her to 'set you up a glass' (3.4.19). In his ensuing verbalization of her mirror reflection, her own view of herself becomes dominated by the stain of imperfection. One significant substitution Olivier makes in his film adaptation of the scene of Gertrude's unhappy

bemoaning of her spoiled self, is the word 'stain' for the more archaic 'tinct' of Shakespeare's text – a change that seems specifically to accommodate a Lacanian reading of the sequence. It is useful here to consider the 'anamorphic stain', a term Jacques Lacan repeatedly uses in *Four Fundamental Concepts* to refer to the point of rupture. In specifically applying this concept to refer to Hans Holbein's strangely elongated *memento mori*, Lacan formulates another term, the 'anamorphic ghost'.[52] The fact Hamlet's 'anamorphic ghost', to use Lacan's terminology, is in *Hamlet* literally a ghost might suggest Shakespeare was well versed, *avant la lettre*, in French psychoanalytic theory.[53] At least, this correlation promises fruitful analysis may follow from use of Lacan's conception of the stain, a disruption that traps the gaze, to read the manner in which Olivier uses the cinematic apparatus, and therefore the spectator, to parallel Hamlet's scopic longing for the ghost.

The ability of the cinema spectator to recognize easily the genre codes of subjective point of view offers much potential in film adaptation of the ambiguous early modern stage ghost. On a stage the ghost must either exist or not (unless a theatre is equipped with technology capable of replicating Pepper's Ghost), and so directors must choose where to align audience point of view. For example, in the banquet scene of *Macbeth*, Macbeth is driven to a wild madness by the ghost of murdered Banquo, whom none of the other guests see. On the stage either an actor must play the ghost, thus aligning the audience point of view with Macbeth's madness, or Macbeth must rage and scream at an empty space, thus distancing him from the

---

50 In suggesting the apparent disavowal of the theatrical, Danner finds Hamlet in fact threatens 'to bind his actions to the false theatricality he rejects', in Danner, 'Speaking Daggers', p. 31.

51 Perhaps the most impressive analysis of this theme is to be found in Peter Donaldson's 'Olivier, Hamlet, and Freud', *Cinema Journal*, 26.4 (Summer, 1987), 22–48.

52 Lacan, *Four Fundamental Concepts*, p. 89.

53 Or as Slavoj Žižek has it, with reference to an earlier play, '*Richard II* proves beyond any doubt that Shakespeare had read Lacan', in *Looking Awry* (Cambridge, MA, 1991), p. 9.

audience. On film, however, the ghost can, in simultaneous subjectively coded point-of-view shots, be there and not there, as in Kurosawa's *Throne of Blood*.

For Lacan the disorienting effect of the 'anamorphic lines' of Holbein's skull, which demand the viewer reformulate her way of looking, provides a 'rupture between perception and consciousness'.[54] Applying the ruptured meaning of the anamorphic stain to cinema, Slavoj Žižek finds it to be 'desire itself', which 'posits its cause retroactively as a blurred spot on its surface' and 'which can only be understood by "looking awry"'.[55] As I argue earlier, just as the stain in Holbein's painting is unintelligible unless one abandons the visual orientation demanded by the rest of the painting, a perceptional step which Žižek terms 'looking awry', so too Hamlet's conception of the meaning of Elsinore must be entirely reformulated with the appearance of the ghost. This is a conception Gertrude's subsequent stained view of herself indicates her son impresses upon her.

I would argue Olivier's principal technique in recreating in spectator consciousness the anamorphic staining of the ghost is the use of unnerving and ambiguously coded point-of-view shots throughout nearly all the scene. For example, as in the famous shot of the camera purportedly entering Olivier's head preceding the 'To be or not to be' (3.1.58) speech, to indicate the spectator's privileged witnessing of an internal debate, the coming of the ghost in the closet scene is signalled by a move into Hamlet's consciousness, this time marked by aural signifiers. The un-naturalistically amplified sound of a beating heart, presumably Hamlet's (it accompanies Olivier's wildly staring eyes), and eerie sounds swamp the audio track. For Olivier's Hamlet, the immediate context of his surroundings becomes dominated by supernatural noises, and the sudden climax of volume of an organ chord is accompanied by his collapse, indicating some kind of fall into a swoon. This is visually accompanied by a shot in which Gertrude appears to speak but cannot be heard by the spectator, which as well as seeming to imply a usurping of Shakespeare's text by filmic elements, impresses

upon the spectator the primacy of Hamlet's point of view.

From marking this shift to the subjective point of view of his Hamlet, then, Olivier undermines the effect by aligning his spectator, for the majority of the following scene, with the point of view of the ghost. This effect is underscored, in Olivier's *Hamlet*, by what Michel Chion terms the 'already visualised *acousmêtre*' of the ghost's voice, accentuated by the closeness of the voice track and its non-naturalistic reverb, so the ghost's voice appears to emanate from the very place of the cinematic apparatus. However, this aural effect is complicated by the gaze the camera casts on Gertrude, from the ghost's point of view, before the ghost says 'But look, amazement on thy mother sits' (3.4.102), emphasizing the possibility of the spectator as literally occupying the role of ghost, watching the drama.

By mixing codes that signify both objective and subjective shots, the ghost is at once Hamlet's imagination and the gaze that views his destructive imagination. To use Metz's terminology, the ghost becomes the 'first delegate' of the spectator look, whom the spectator sees through, yet does not see. This can be found when Olivier's Hamlet apparently addresses Gertrude, 'Do not look upon me!' (3.4.118), yet with his eyes transfixed upon the camera. Here Shakespeare's text is given a completely novel meaning, via the apparent recognition of the cinematic apparatus in Olivier's gaze, implicitly to include the cinema spectator in Hamlet's injunction. 'Whereon do you look?' (3.4.115) Gertrude asks, emphasizing the subjective status of the ghost. 'On him' (3.4.116), Olivier's Hamlet gasps, his finger pointed simultaneously at the camera/ghost and from the screen at the spectator. One might say that, though the soundtrack emphasizes the ghost as internal projection of Hamlet by visually aligning the spectator with the ghost's point of view, Olivier sites his spectator as simultaneously observing and

---

54 Lacan, *Four Fundamental Concepts*, p. 56.
55 Žižek, *Looking Awry*, p. 12.

observed, a figment of the imagination of the performance.[56]

It is tempting to read the disorienting effect of being addressed directly by Olivier, as if to the ghost, as paralleling Lacan's description of the gaze, for example, during the Breton fishing trip: 'The can did not see me . . . [but] it was looking at me all the same'.[57] This would fit with Screen Theory's conception of the gaze in cinema as effecting 'the construction of the spectator as fantasmatic entity (166).'[58] However, there is a problem in aligning Olivier's eyes staring wildly from the screen with the shining can. In further delineating the nature of his gaze, for example, Lacan writes: 'of all the objects with which the subject may recognize . . . the gaze is specified as inapprehensible'.[59] Though the intangible presence of Lacan's gaze corresponds ontologically with the uncertain presence of Olivier's film ghost (an ontological status that closely parallels that of my conception of liminal space), clearly Olivier's very visible eyes cannot be said to convey the sensation of Lacan's 'inapprehensible' gaze.

As the gaze cannot apparently explain the unnerving aspect of the scene, it may be tempting here to raise one aspect of the recent 'post-Theory' attempt to move film criticism beyond Screen Theory, that is, the suggestion that the Lacanian gaze is something never experienced by the cinema spectator. Stephen Prince, for example, argues that Screen Theory finds itself in the lamentable position of 'having constructed theories of spectatorship from which spectators are missing'.[60] In making his argument Prince differentiates between the 'model' spectator of Screen Theory, and the 'actual, "instantiated"'[61] spectator who sits in the cinema auditorium. For Prince, cinema criticism should pay more attention to the inattention of the average spectator, from whom (with regard to adult TV viewers) 'looks at the screen are extremely brief and are punctuated by regular glances away from the screen'.[62] I would argue, however, that the job of the critic is not, primarily, to keep an eye on the back-row lovers or attempt to identify how many pieces of popcorn the spectator consumes. Though Prince correctly identifies a problem pertinent to

a Lacanian reading of Olivier's adaptation of the closet scene, his thesis rather posits a fleeing from all theory, over the more 'piecemeal' use of theory suggested by his editor, Noël Carroll. It is certainly the case that the average spectator does not conceive of the ontology of her cinema experience as conforming to Lacan's gaze, but this does not mean, *ipso facto*, that Lacan's gaze cannot be useful in delineating the psychic mechanisms at work. Furthermore, whatever the sociological value of knowing spectator behaviour, I would affirm greater interest in an appropriate theoretical account of screen phenomena. That is to say, while the 'instantiated' spectator sips his cola, the critic must keep her eyes fixedly upon the screen.

In addressing this argument, Žižek suggests the impossibility of definitively experiencing the gaze causes the subject to accomplish 'a kind of reflection-into-self by means of which the object that fascinates him becomes the gaze itself'.[63] Žižek defines the clearest examples of this in film as 'the "subjective" shot from the standpoint of the murderous thing itself', which he terms the 'impossible subjectivity'.[64] Though, in the case of *Hamlet*, the ghost is not exactly murderous (it does encourage murderous revenge), Olivier's shot seems otherwise to provide an exemplary case of Žižek's 'impossible subjectivity'. Rather than the slightly ironic but otherwise unimportant ontological peculiarity of the film spectator at

---

[56] This cannot help but recall Stephen Heath's conception of the cinema spectator as 'the absent one', who haunts the meaning of the film, in *Questions of Cinema* (Bloomington, 1981), p. 87.

[57] Lacan, *Four Fundamental Concepts*, p. 96.

[58] Robert Burgoyne, Sandy Flitterman-Lewis and Robert Stam, *New Vocabularies in Film Semiotics: Structuralism, Post-Structuralism, and Beyond* (New York, 1992), p. 166.

[59] Lacan, *Four Fundamental Concepts*, p. 83.

[60] Stephen Prince, 'Psychoanalytic Film Theory and the Problem of the Missing Spectator', in David Bordwell and Noël Carroll, eds., *Post-Theory* (Madison, 1996), p. 83.

[61] Prince, 'Psychoanalytic Film Theory', p. 79.

[62] Prince, 'Psychoanalytic Film Theory', p. 77.

[63] Slavoj Žižek, *Enjoy Your Symptom!*, 2nd edn (New York and London, 2001), p. 202.

[64] Žižek, *Enjoy Your Symptom!*, p. 204.

once observing and observed, Žižek would affirm Olivier's scene affects the gaze by setting up a 'reflection-into-self' in the spectator, forcing the spectator to occupy the position of the ghost, and thus watch from the point of view of the 'murderous thing'. By using the ambiguous potential of the diegetic space outside the frame of the screen, one might argue Olivier replicates, in the spectator's gaze, the ghost as stain on Hamlet's consciousness.

Thus, by developing a verbal and visual dislocation in the signifying codes of the scene, Olivier seems to define the nature of filmic performance as necessarily haunted by the potential spectator. This is most dramatically found at the exit of the ghost, which, by alignment of spectator with the ghost's point of view, allows Olivier to end the scene unconventionally. Particularly interesting is a dynamic cut Olivier makes in building to this point, between two moving shots (itself a rarity in the studio era): from a close-up of Hamlet that tracks suddenly to the left with Hamlet's emotional surge at the ghost's imminent departure, to the longer final shot from the departing ghost's point-of-view, the dynamic camera work foreshadowed and underscored aurally by the introduction and sudden increase in volume of dramatic, menacing music. In arcing the camera left towards the ghost while angling back to the right, to keep Hamlet in the shot, Olivier both uses cinematic style to indicate the isolation of his protagonist, and plays with the spectator's desire to see that which Hamlet sees, the cause of his isolation. The quick cut to the ghost's point of view presents another moving shot, this time slightly shaky, perhaps to emphasize its subjective meaning, the camera all the while adjusting compositionally to keep Hamlet on-screen, prostrate on the floor, his gaze trapped by the departing ghost.

The scopic desire to see the ghost, cause of such anguish in Olivier's Hamlet, is thus largely frustrated in the spectator by the angle of the scene's shots. Olivier only briefly allows a reverse shot, towards the end of the scene, to show the space of the ghost. At Hamlet's question, 'Do you see nothing there?' (3.4.122), Olivier's camera cuts to a shot from behind Hamlet's shoulder, and Olivier fixes his gaze, and the spectator's, upon an indistinct shape floating in the dark shadow between two arches of the film's medieval Elsinore. The camera then pans to Gertrude, moves slightly behind her shoulder, to indicate a shift to her subjective point-of-view (and thus retroactively to mark the previous shot as subjectively Hamlet's point-of-view), and then pans back to the dark shadow. The change is a slight one, perhaps even liable to be missed by the inattentive spectator: this time the dark shadow contains no indistinct shape. To use Lacan's terminology, the stain of the ghost is no longer there. The effect of this retroactive revealing of the stain by its absence in the following shot offers ambiguous affirmation of Hamlet's point-of-view: while there was *something* there, it is difficult to say exactly what. We might note how this replicates the common critical response to the text, of the uncertain ontology of the ghost in this scene. By refusing to depict the ghost clearly, Olivier's direction emphasizes, rather than the material presence of the ghost (in Hamlet's perception), the way the blurred, indistinct stain has trapped his gaze.

In this way, the ghost as stain can help us understand Olivier's playful manipulation of the gaze in this scene. By aligning spectator consciousness with identification with the space of the ghost/stain, Olivier is able to develop a double mirror. The reverse shot of the ghost/stain reveals to the spectator what Hamlet has been gazing at, when he has gazed from the screen as if at the spectator. This is an unsatisfactory mirror reflection, as the spectator is unlikely to locate herself in the indistinct stain. However, the return to the position of the stain offers another mirror reflection: as the spectator gazes at the screen, Hamlet gazes from the screen. Thus, it is from the position of the stain that the film spectator gazes into the mirror of her gaze.

One might note here the way the ghost, as anamorphic stain, works to subjectivize cinematic space. By establishing the ghost as simultaneously there and not there, Olivier establishes the potentially unverifiable ontology of the conflicting subjectivities in cinematic montage. In effect, the ghost opens a liminal space, that is to say a space ontologically between existence and non-existence. Thus, it is by using the ghost to manipulate the spectator's expectations of the film's diegetic space that Olivier is able to replicate the anamorphic ghost that so disrupts Hamlet's place in the symbolic realm. Or rather, one might say, in adapting a dramatic motif for the big screen, Olivier is forced to disrupt the concrete reality of cinematic space – and, thus, via the liminal space the text resists the dominant ontology of its own adaptation.

SPY-TRAPS

Seeing unseen,
We may of their encounter frankly judge
(3.1.35–6)

A different kind of stain, and a different emphasis on mirroring, are to be found in Kenneth Branagh's *Hamlet*. In providing a hiding place for Polonius and Claudius to observe unseen, the baroque main hall of Branagh's *Hamlet* uses the one-sided mirror to concretize spatially the diegetic 'spy-traps' of Elsinore. At the culmination of the nunnery scene, his suspicions aroused by a sound, Branagh's Hamlet drags Kate Winslet, as Ophelia, from mirrored door to door, to attempt to discover the espionage. Inevitably, the metaphysical nature of Hamlet gets the better of him. Abandoning his frenzied search, he presses Ophelia against a mirrored door during a speech, the very door behind which the spies tremble. At this point, the camera cuts to a view from within, of her face squashed grotesquely against the glass (from the inside the mirror is transparent), which her father and Claudius watch powerless. For an instant, the screen is dominated by an anamorphic stain, of distorted flesh pressed against glass.

On one signifying level Branagh's stain functions as transferral to the visual plane of the destructive effects of Hamlet's nihilistic doubt. The succinct nature of Branagh's image is due to the fact it derives visually from the same device that inspires Hamlet's suspicion that he is observed, the mirrored doors of the film's reflective narrative space, made anachronistically possible by the two-way mirror. Such technology was not, in fact, available

during the period of Branagh's nineteenth-century setting (the two-way mirror was first patented by Emil Bloch in Ohio, 1903). Though the majority of the scene is filmed as reflection (the spectator sees Hamlet by seeing what he sees), yet Branagh evades easy identification with Hamlet's point-of-view because the spectator, unlike Hamlet, knows the eyes that observe from behind the mirror.

Rather than Lehmann and Starks's explicitly eroticized reading of the luminous interiors of Branagh's mirrored Elsinore as 'a total disavowal of the maternal body [. . . which] actively shun the horror of the womb',[65] I would concentrate on the manner in which Branagh's diegetic space replicates simultaneously the panopticonic device, and the paranoia of panopticon. Following this, one might also note the striking correspondence between Hamlet's suspicion of the doors as hiding secret observers (a paranoia that is, in this case, justified), and Lacan's concept of the gaze. Lacan writes:

I can feel myself under the gaze of someone whose eyes I do not see, not even discern. All that is necessary is for something to signify to me that there may be others there. This window, if it gets a bit dark, and if I have reasons for thinking that there is someone behind it, is straight-away a gaze.[66]

By reworking the 'spy-traps' of Elsinore for the specifically visual plane of the screen, Branagh seems to have unwittingly hit upon a solution, the one-sided mirror, which almost exactly replicates Lacan's darkened window of the gaze. Unlike the gaze of the film spectator that seems to haunt Olivier's *Hamlet* in the closet scene, then, the 'gaze of someone whose eyes I do not see' is cast in Branagh's *Hamlet* from within the diegetic space of the film.[67]

---

[65] Lehmann and Starks, 'Making Mother Matter', paragraph 5.

[66] Jacques Lacan, *The Seminar, Book 1: Freud's Papers and Technique* (New York, 1988), p. 215.

[67] A similar effect is generated in Almereyda's *Hamlet*, when Polonius delivers his asides on Hamlet's apparent madness to a CCTV camera, simultaneously invoking the impersonal gaze of the universe as manifest in surveillance technology, and the way such technology within the film

I argue Branagh (the director) reworks Olivier's manipulation of the spectator's gaze in a non-naturalistic seeming-to-know about what is behind the mirror that haunts Branagh (the actor). The dominant shot of the scene is filmed from over Hamlet's shoulder, and is framed by the reflective space of the mirror (which itself seems a meta-filmic reference to the frame of the cinema screen gazed upon by the cinema spectator). In Branagh's film, the ontological paradox of the contemplation of self-elimination as deriving from a reflective doubling in this scene is replicated stylistically in the simultaneous invocation and denial of the apparatus of film production, which Branagh somehow manages to keep out of shot.[68] Returning to Žižek's 'reflection-into-self', I suggest the effect can be found in Branagh's cut between two almost identical shots: from the dominant shot, the reflection of himself that Hamlet views, to a view of Hamlet from within the glass door roughly from Claudius and Polonius's point-of-view, an almost exact copy of the mirror image. Unlike Olivier's transfixed face, as recipient of the spectator's gaze, Branagh's Hamlet observes himself as he is unknowingly gazed upon. His own eyes have become aligned with the anonymous gaze of the universe gazing back.

As if he attempts to replicate Hamlet's ontological confusion spatially, Branagh's film works to undermine spectator certainty at the diegetic space as Hamlet prepares to deliver his most famous soliloquy. Particularly, one might note the rapid cuts between three establishing shots at this point, with which Branagh introduces the basic positions his camera will adopt during the scene. This uncertainty is heightened by a mismatch of shots between the first of the cuts. After entering ponderously the mirrored main hall of Elsinore, Hamlet stops before one mirrored door. From a medium close-up, a shot records his body twist slowly around as he gazes about the hall. This movement is interrupted by a cut to a view of the mirror reflection of Hamlet, gazing with unnerving fixity at himself in a mirror. Without any markers to suggest a jump forward in time, the mismatched shots seem to suggest, though perhaps unintentionally, that Hamlet's

gaze about the splendours of Elsinore is ontologically identical with his searching gaze at himself. The uncertainty is compounded by a second cut to the opening of a viewing hatch behind the mirror as Hamlet appears from Claudius and Polonius's view, and then the quick return to the shot of Hamlet's reflection, composed almost identically in *plan americain*, a three-quarter view of his head and torso. It is at the return to the mirror reflection that Hamlet begins his most famous soliloquy. On a stylistic level, like Almereyda's filmic play with the well-known speech, it is almost as if the shuffling of essentially the same view, with yet ontologically different meanings, serves Branagh as filmic drum-roll to the most quoted lines of the text.

Yet, one might also suggest that in this movement from one side of the mirror to the other, Branagh makes the spectator complicit in the spy-trap: she becomes a spy gazing upon the spies. Useful here is Stephen Heath's conception of suture as a 'stitching' of the spectator into the chain of discourse, while also making coherent the spectator relationship with the film: 'Suture names not just a structure of lack but also an availability of the subject, a certain closure'.[69] Heath develops the screen implications of the psychoanalytic mechanism of suture developed by Jacques-Alain Miller, where the suture 'names the relation of the

---

suggests meta-dramatically the gaze of the film spectator. It is possible Almereyda makes an ironic reference to the proliferation of mirrored surfaces in Branagh's film, and their masochistic-narcissistic potential, in having his Hamlet, Ethan Hawke, shoot Polonius while he is hiding behind the mirrored doors of a wardrobe.

68 One might consider here how Branagh's self-conscious use of the mirror seems to address Metz's suggestion of the powerlessness the spectator experiences, sensing the camera within the diegetic space of the narrative, yet forced to look where the camera looks, unable to look back. In Branagh's film, Hamlet approaches the mirror reflection as he debates the idea of self-elimination. Hamlet touches his dagger against the glass, and following a sudden cut to his face in extreme close-up Claudius jumps back. In bridging the gap between the reflective and actual in the shot, the dagger works as mediator of these two cinematic planes. The dagger with which Hamlet threatens (himself and the spies) thus also threatens the spatial organization of system he wishes to leave.

69 Stephen Heath, *Questions of Cinema*, p. 85.

subject to the chain of its discourse . . . it figures there as the element which is lacking, in the form of a stand in'.[70] It may be worth adding Žižek's elucidation of Miller: 'Lack is spatial, designating a void within a space', which designates suture as a process of desire, 'grounded in the constitutive lack'.[71] Transposed to cinema theory, Heath finds suture derives from the trauma of the gaze, which becomes in the film spectator anxiety generated by the potential for off-screen space in point-of-view anchoring. For Heath this is answered by the reverse-shot, which, in evoking absent space, takes the form of 'the surgical joining of the lips of a wound [. . . by which] the film ceaselessly poses an absence, a lack, which is ceaselessly bound up in and into the relation of the subject'.[72] By Heath's formulation, the topographical peculiarities of Branagh's scene become bound up in spectator consciousness.

Here it is useful also to consider Žižek's conception of the subject's 'blind spot': 'that which is "in the object more than the object itself"' . . . reinscribing the subject into its own image in the guise of a stain'.[73] Žižek's 'blind spot' can be read as an expression of the 'lack' implicit to suture. In failing to locate the 'blind spot', Hamlet's probing look requires spectator consciousness to complete the tension of unreturned looks in the scene. I would argue, rather than demonstrating the theoretical *bricolage* bemoaned by Bordwell and Carroll, this use of suture (though considered by some as a somewhat outdated facet of Screen Theory) works in this scene as particular response to Branagh's camerawork.

Like the mirror reflection which simultaneously invokes and denies the film apparatus, the confusion of diegetic space that derives from the quick montage of Branagh's establishing shots underlines the spectator's privileged view: only the spectator gets to see both sides of the glass. I would note here the contrast set up by the lush, melancholic non-diegetic music, which throughout Branagh's film works to define or underline Hamlet's emotional state and thus also aligns the cinematic events with Hamlet's point-of-view. The effect of this music, however, is undermined by the visual alignment

of the spectator with Claudius in this scene (like Claudius, the spectator gazes upon Hamlet gazing upon himself). I would argue the between-ness of the point-of-view offered to the spectator here is vital to her privileged view in this scene: it is the double complicity of spectator with a privileged point-of-view from both sides of the glass that allows the suture.

This privileged spectator suture is called into question by an uncanny seeming-to-know in Hamlet, at the end of Branagh's nunnery scene, as Hamlet returns Ophelia to the position of anamorphic stain. The lush non-diegetic music, which seems to define the meaning of Hamlet's nauseated reaction to the process of procreation and birth as a kind of pre-romantic sensitivity – 'We will have no more marriages' (3.1.150) – ends abruptly at 'Those that are married already, all but one shall live' (3.1.150–1). It is here Hamlet emphasizes his point, pushing Ophelia's face again against the mirror. This is followed by a quick cut, to a shot from behind the two-way mirror, of Claudius's view of the flesh-stain.[74] The return to the stain is marked

---

[70] Jacques-Alain Miller, 'Suture (Elements of the Logic of the Signifier)'. www.lacan.com/sympton8_articles/miller8.html

[71] Slavoj Žižek, 'Jacques Lacan's Four Fundamental Discourses'. www.lacan.com.zizfav.html

[72] Heath, *Questions of Cinema*, p. 13.

[73] Žižek, *Parallax View*, p. 17.

[74] Critics have noted how this scene, and I would argue particularly this shot, emphasizes the physical similarity of Derek Jacobi's Claudius and Kenneth Branagh, in Branagh's *Hamlet*. As noted by Lehmann and Starks, the shock of short, bleached blond hair that both sport works as visual signifier of the dissimilarity to Old Hamlet that Claudius and Hamlet share: for example, unlike Old Hamlet neither are warriors, working primarily in words. It is also worth noting the blond hair also seems pointedly to refer to perhaps the centrally canonical film adaptation of *Hamlet* in the English film industry, Sir Laurence Olivier's, for example see Fedderson and Richardson (157). Useful here is Harold Bloom's theory of the anxiety of influence, wherein the artist must measure himself against a series of father figures, in responding to the previous generation. Significantly, Branagh himself refers to this anxiety of influence as 'the ghosts of other performances', in Samuel Crowl, 'Hamlet "Most Royal": An Interview with Kenneth Branagh', *Shakespeare Bulletin*, 12.4 (Fall 1994), 5–8; p. 6. Lehmann and Starks use this to suggest

by the uncanny feeling that Hamlet knows his uncle is watching behind the mirror, and that, with 'Those that are married already' he makes a directly addressed threat. This uncanny feeling is generated, as well as by tone of voice, by the carefully matched eye-lines Branagh keeps in moving to the extreme close-up, a long-established cinematic convention used when cutting between single shot/reverse shot in a dialogue. Thus, Branagh manipulates screen codes to put his Hamlet, in Lacanian terms, in the position of the 'subject supposed to know'.

I would suggest Lehmann and Starks also detect the uncanny feeling of the suture called into question, when they suggest: 'no matter where we look or who we are looking for, Hamlet answers our gaze'.[75] However, I would contend that this gaze is not Lacan's gaze, 'the eyes of someone I do not see', which Žižek claims it is impossible to experience definitively. Lacan's unseen gaze cannot explain the uncanny nature of Hamlet's look, which the spectator very clearly perceives throughout this scene. Rather, I would argue, one should consider the brief transcendence of cinematic realism that Branagh's Hamlet seems to make at this moment. No matter how reasonable it might be for Hamlet to suspect he is spied upon, he cannot know Claudius is behind the very mirror he soliloquizes to, which he apparently chooses at random. Yet, the feeling he *does* know cannot help but mark his return of Ophelia to the position of anamorphic stain as performative gesture made for Claudius's benefit. It is the flesh-stain that marks the boundary of the mirror, the impossibility of Hamlet actually knowing he addresses Claudius. Yet, in the uncanny feeling that he seems-to-know, briefly Branagh allows his Hamlet to usurp the spectator's privileged perception of both sides of the mirror (as Hamlet/director, indeed, Branagh knows and does not know simultaneously).[76]

By applying Žižek's reading of the 'blind spot', it is the space behind the mirror, Hamlet's blind spot, that inscribes spectator consciousness in the film-object. The stain of Hamlet's seeming-to-know, marked visually by the flesh stain of Ophelia pressed against the very glass that previously sutured spectator consciousness in the film discourse. The priv-

ileged knowledge that binds the diegetic space of the scene to spectator consciousness is thus called temporarily into question. If the flesh-stain that has located the spectator point of view as aligned with Claudius's seems to become briefly an acknowledgement of Hamlet's awareness of his uncle, this locates the uncanny feeling in the spectator at Hamlet's gaze into the mirror. In effect, his seeming-to-know makes his look temporarily a lure, the anamorphic partial-object of the gaze or, as Lacan puts it, with reference to Holbein's skull, a 'singular object floating in the foreground, which is there to be looked at, in order to catch, I would almost say, *to catch its trap*, the observer, that is to say us'.[77] The spectator is literally caught by the look of Hamlet *qua* object, as his look senses the gaze from behind the screen (the two-way mirror) on himself. Thus, though the film spectator may not consciously locate the source of the uncanny feeling, like Olivier's self-consciously filmic closet scene, might one not suggest it nonetheless answers the 'post-Theory' denial of the existence of Lacan's gaze?

As this uncanny moment passes, Hamlet snaps out of his performative mode – the display he has made for the potential universal gaze behind the mirrored window – and decides to really check if Claudius is behind the glass. Like the spatial confusion that Branagh's unaligned cutting earlier

---

Branagh stages himself as heir apparent, in British theatre, to Derek Jacobi. This thesis is also forwarded by Robson: 'It is hard not to read this avoidance of the Oedipal reading as a thoroughly Oedipal attempt to supplant his cinematic "fathers"' (255). One might also consider Watson: 'Perhaps young Hamlet's tendency to think of suicide as an alternative to revenge reflects on a recognition that he is precisely what he must attack Claudius for being: the replacement of his father . . . the direct beneficiary of the process that necessitated the father's death', in Robert N. Watson, *The Rest Is Silence: Death As Annihilation in the English Renaissance* (Berkeley, 1995), p. 87.

[75] Lehmann and Starks, 'Making Mother Matter', paragraph 10.

[76] The correspondence of non-diegetic elements with Hamlet's mood, which Branagh uses to ensure Hamlet's point of view as dominant, cannot but help to impress upon the spectator Hamlet's seeming-to-know.

[77] Lacan, *Four Fundamental Concepts*, p. 92.

introduces, the scene ends with the improbably quick escape of Claudius and Polonius. They are behind the glass as Hamlet moves to open the door, yet literally no sign of them remains as Hamlet hurriedly enters their hiding space. It is striking how this spatially problematic pursuit of the spies seems to address Lacan's definition of the paranoiac, jealous husband who suspects his wife of having an affair, as suffering pathological psychosis, 'even if his wife really is sleeping around'.[78] Hamlet's simultaneously paranoid and correct suspicion of the spy-traps of Elsinore closely fits Lacan's example of the jealous, yet correct, husband. Thus, Branagh's Hamlet is, in this Lacanian reading, a paranoid psychotic. Branagh's success in this scene perhaps comes in the way this tension – psychotic/correct – reworks the ambiguity of Hamlet's real/staged madness. Transposed to a usurpation of the film spectator's sutured consciousness, I argue Hamlet's paranoid seeming-to-know about the spies behind the mirror thus replicates his ambiguous stage madness by rupturing the concrete diegetic space of the film ontology.

CONCLUSION: TEXT AND CAMERA

In recent work, Courtney Lehmann makes much of the diegetic space of the Shakespeare film, calling on Christian Metz in asserting 'cinema's ability to efface its own location in time and space is the very condition of its scopic seduction'.[79] I would suggest this claim sits uneasily with an odd shot that interrupts the rolling credits of Almereyda's *Hamlet*. As in Lurhman's *Romeo + Juliet*, a newscaster is used to translate the epilogue (Fortinbras's closing speech in Shakespeare's text) to a modern-day idiom. As if attempting to go one step further, Almereyda provides a final reverse shot, after the credits begin, of the very teleprompter the newscaster apparently reads from, the final words of the film scrolling up at the close. Rather than the 'ability to efface' the material conditions of its production of Lehmann's cinema, Almereyda seems to end his film with a sequence that implies quite the opposite. Thus, though Lehmann perhaps correctly identifies the dominant ideology of screen space, it is with reference to the filmic lacunae generated by sequences such as this that I have attempted rather to investigate the rupture of liminal diegetic spaces: that which does not quite fit in the picture.

The ambivalent meaning of Almereyda's final sequence wavers between conservative, apologetic revealing of the 'true' object, Shakespeare's text at the close of an interpretation so dominated by instances of the extra-textual, and that of a deeper level of irony, the 'pure' text confined to the apparatus of televisual production. Perhaps even more interesting is the meaning of this reverse shot, of the apparatus on the other side, at the close of a film so dominated by television screens. It seems to posit, as the ultimate ghost haunting all the screen ghosts, Shakespeare's text as the presence behind the camera.

This impulse in Almereyda, I would argue, is consistent with the pointed occurrence in Shakespeare film adaptation of the points of rupture that Lacan's gaze finds implicit to framed space. In this article I suggest a concentration of these rupture points can be found, in film *Hamlets*, in instances of the motifs of ghost and mirror. Their net effect seems to be that of resistance to the process of adaptation.

In the case of Almereyda's reverse shot, at the close of his *Hamlet*, we might claim, in his playful revealing of the text – the words that hold together the filmic ghost-world, the occupant of the unseen space behind the film apparatus – Almereyda simulates the magician who shows his audience the strings that hold together the universe. Ontologically, then, it is a move that parallels Henry Pepper's hand pressed against the second pane of glass, the anecdote with which this article began, and Faraday's exclamation: 'Ah, yes! Now I comprehend it . . .'[80]

---

78 Slavoj Žižek, *The Sublime Object of Ideology* (London, 1989), p. 48.

79 Courtney Lehmann, 'Dislocating Macbeth in Transnational Film and Media Culture', in Boose and Burt, eds., *Shakespeare the Movie II*, p. 231.

80 Quoted in Michele Pierson, *Special Effects: Still in Search of Wonder* (New York, 2002), p. 21.

'BEN, IT'S A TERRIBLE THING TO HATE YOUR MOTHER': MIND CONTROL IN *HAMLET* AND *THE MANCHURIAN CANDIDATE*

CATHERINE GRACE CANINO

In September 1950, a journalist for the *Miami News* ran a story that staggered the American imagination and intensified the anti-Communist feelings that were fostering the Cold War. Edward Hunter, who was also a CIA agent, warned Americans that post-revolutionary China was using insidious and heretofore unknown psychological techniques to force the Chinese into the Communist Party. He labelled these techniques with the term 'brainwashing', a derisive translation of the Chinese *his-nao*, which literally means 'to cleanse the mind'.[1] Hunter's theories not only reached a receptive audience, but were also quickly verified by other experts, who described similar techniques in Nazi Germany and the Soviet Union. Americans were alerted to the possibility that the Communists had 'cracked the brain's code' and were capable not only of controlling but of changing the will of their fellow citizens. Psychologist Joost Meerloo, a Dutch émigré from Nazi-occupied Holland, warned in his 1956 book *Rape of the Mind* that brainwashing techniques, which he dubbed with the far more sinister appellation *menticide*, were being used on an unsuspecting American public:

It is now technically possible to bring the human mind into a condition of enslavement and submission . . . the totalitarians [Meerloo's euphemism for any Communist government] . . . influence the mind so slowly and indirectly that we may not even realize what they have done to us.[2]

The reaction of Americans was rather spectacular. Quite rapidly, a panic over the threat of brainwashing spread throughout the country. Americans had already been conditioned to fear nuclear war, but the imagined loss of cherished American autonomy and free will was even more terrifying.[3] Brainwashing embodied cultural fears of losing control and Meerloo's paradigm for menticide became America's paradigm for anxiety.[4]

Meerloo's dire predictions and the resultant American fixation on brainwashing antedate the theories of Michel Foucault by several decades; however, they correlate nicely with his emphasis on the coercive nature of power and the resultant reconstruction of self-agency. Foucault's suggestion of the 'technology of self', in which the self is completely sacrificed to a master, as well as his theory of the interiorization of the gaze, in which the individual under power becomes his own overseer, echoes the 'enslavement and submission' terminology of Meerloo.[5] And, although Foucault's view

---

[1] Edward Hunter, *Brainwashing in Red China: The Calculated Destruction of Men's Minds* (New York, 1953), pp. 328–9.

[2] Joost A. M. Meerloo, MD, *The Rape of the Mind: The Psychology of Thought Control, Menticide, and Brainwashing* (New York, 1956), p. 35.

[3] For a modern study of this phenomenon, see J. Hoberman, *The Red Atlantis: Communist Culture in the Absence of Communism* (Philadelphia, 1998).

[4] For the purposes of this article, I am not engaging in the debate over whether brainwashing is a real phenomenon. However, I think it is unquestioned that it was, and is, a very real fear that has instigated a battery of psychological and sociological studies.

[5] Michel Foucault, 'The Subject and Power', *Critical Inquiry* 8 (1982), 777–95; 'Technologies of the Self', in *A Seminar with Michel Foucault*, ed. Luther H. Martin, Huck Gutman and Patrick H. Hutton (Amherst, 1988), pp. 16–49; and

of the reciprocal nature in the power relationship between a governing force and a recalcitrant will would seem to be in direct conflict with the robotic images of brainwashing, there is in fact a symbiosis between the two theories. Most psychologists in the field agree that the strongest wills are the most susceptible to subjugation; Foucault merely takes an additional step and claims that the will must not only be initially strong but continually resistant for the power relationship to be its most effective.[6] Although Meerloo and Foucault begin from opposite ideological points, they reach the same conclusion that individual identity faces a very real threat from the unseen but potent machinations of an external power structure.

Such theories, which argue the susceptibility of the human mind to external control, have had a tremendous influence on cultural and literary studies within the last fifty years. Nevertheless, there have been proponents of individual identity who have argued for the empowerment of the self and the ability of the human mind to resist ultimate subjugation. Even Foucault eventually, albeit reluctantly, acknowledged the power of 'selfhood'.[7] And even at the height of Cold War conformity there were those who questioned whether 'brainwashing' was an actual and measurable phenomenon or whether it was a societal fantasy induced by fears of a powerful and pervasive cultural adversary. This interrogation of the reality of brainwashing was located primarily in the arts – a safer forum, perhaps, than the political platform, but one that, in the McCarthy era, was still dangerous. This danger was especially felt in the film industry, and thus it is somewhat remarkable that it is a film, John Frankenheimer's The Manchurian Candidate,[8] which most successfully mocks and subverts the fear of brainwashing. The 1962 film fulfils all the prophecies of Rape of the Mind: it is the story of an American soldier who is brainwashed by the Communists and of an American political system and media that are infiltrated and manipulated by the Communists. Yet, at the same time, the film operates as a parody, undermining the fear of mind control through the successful (and often humorous) resistance of its main characters and, most particularly, through the satiric displacement of the source of the menticide onto the most American of symbols – the mother. Frankenheimer's recusancy is, of course, interesting from a socio-political-psychological standpoint. From an artistic standpoint, however, the most intriguing aspect of the film is that Frankenheimer has, by his own admission, restructured the satiric thriller into a modern-day retelling of Hamlet.[9]

Richard Condon's original novel[10] contains only bare hints of the Hamlet story: there is the protagonist's attachment to a dominant and despised mother, his lack of commitment to the innocent and weak-minded girlfriend, and the inevitability of a consanguineous slaughter. Frankenheimer, however, constructs the film to suggest an intertextual parallel with Hamlet in narrative form, characterization and, most significantly, thematic design. In seeing Hamlet as a template for a Cold War parable, Frankenheimer has provided us with an alternative, and I believe necessary, reading for Shakespeare's play. Both of these texts address the recalcitrance of spirit that Foucault described, and both raise the question of whether that spirit is trampled by the power structure, as Meerloo posits, whether it feeds the power structure, as Foucault suggests, or whether it in fact subverts both the power structure and the fear of it.[11] In this

Power/Knowledge: Selected Interviews and Other Writings 1972–1977 (New York, 1980).

[6] 'The Subject and Power', p. 790.

[7] Michel Foucault, 'What is Enlightenment?' in The Foucault Reader, ed. Paul Rainbow (New York, 1984), pp. 32–50 and Politics, Philosophy, Cultural Interviews and Other Writings, 1977–1984, ed. Lawrence D. Kritzman, trans. Alan Sheridan et al. (New York, 1988), pp. 25–6.

[8] The Manchurian Candidate, director, John Frankenheimer, screenplay George Axelrod, 126 min., United Artists, 1962, videocassette released by MGM/UA.

[9] John Frankenheimer. Interview. AFI's 100 Years, 100 Movies. Columbia Broadcasting System, 16 June 1998.

[10] Richard Condon, The Manchurian Candidate (New York, 1959). The novel is more of a political thriller than the psychological study which the film came to be.

[11] I realize that it is only recently that Hamlet has been seen to represent a watershed moment in the history of representing the self as separate consciousness (see Catherine Belsey,

alternative reading of Shakespeare's play, Frankenheimer questions the traditional view of Hamlet as
the quintessential autonomous Western hero, master of his own mind and seeker of his own truth.
Instead, he reconceives Hamlet's role, mirrored in
the protagonist of the film, to be one without free
agency – or, in the words of Joost Meerloo, he sees
Hamlet as a classic victim of menticide. However,
Hamlet differs from the typical Meerloovian victim, and from his cinematic counterpart, because
he never reaches a state of total submissiveness.
Hamlet instead remains in a state of constant and
tortured rebellion against the attempt to incarcerate
his mind – he is Foucault's recalcitrant provocateur.
Frankenheimer portrays the dichotomy of obedience and rebellion within Hamlet by bisecting it
between two characters in the film – the robotically obedient Raymond Shaw, who corresponds
to Hamlet as brainwashed victim, and the crypti-
cally defiant Ben Marco, who corresponds to Hamlet in rebellion. At the same time, Frankenheimer,
like Shakespeare, operates as the detached observer,
able to dissociate himself from the dilemma of his
characters and point to the ultimate absurdity of the
situation. When reading *Hamlet* through the lens
of Frankenheimer, we discover a more subversive
Prince of Denmark, and a more satiric playwright,
than we have seen before.

In order to appreciate more fully the parallels
between *Hamlet* and *The Manchurian Candidate* we
should first consider the fact that they were created in societies that were remarkably similar. The
England of the 1590s and the America of the 1950s
were both characterized by a pride of autonomy
and by a corresponding terror that that autonomy
would be snatched away. In postwar America, the
victory over Fascism became overshadowed by the
obsession over a new enemy, Communism. The
Communists were seen as more godless, more sinister and ultimately more evil than the Nazis, capable not merely of dominating the world but also of
dominating the minds and souls of freedom-loving
Americans. In what was to become one of the great
ironies of history, 1950s America, by its very fear
of mental enslavement, created its own tyrannical
overseer. The period is now seen as one of the most

repressed in modern American history, marked by
an almost slavish devotion to conformity and by the
abatement of individual rights and freedoms. Senator Joseph McCarthy and his followers gained an
expertise in mind control that may have surpassed
any of the Communist forces he vowed to destroy.

Like 1950s America, 1590s England was in the
grips of a post-victory paranoia after the defeat
of the Armada. The fear of a Spanish retaliation
seemed to be paramount in every mind. Rumours
of imminent invasions continued through the
remainder of Queen Elizabeth's reign, and neither
the death of the feared King Philip of Spain, the
accession of the diplomatic King James of England, nor the formal end to the war dimmed the
almost innate hostility and suspicion the two countries held for each other.[12] In addition to the threat
of all-out war, there was another, more insidious,
dread that the Spanish, in conjunction with their
Roman Catholic allies, would infiltrate and transform the English Protestant mind. This fear centred on the Jesuits, who were founded and sent
to England with the specific and singular purpose
of conversion. Tales of the nefarious methods of
the Jesuits, who might be called the 'programmers'
of the Catholic world, became legion. Quite simply, the Jesuits were said to use any means possible,
from employing witchcraft to perverting the law, to
return English Protestants to Roman Catholicism.
Once that was accomplished, it was reasoned, the
doors would be open to the Spanish invaders, who
would forever dictate the English way of life and
destroy the English freedom of thought.[13] This, of

---

*The Subject of Tragedy: Identity and Difference in Renaissance
Drama* (London, 1985) and Francis Barker, *The Tremulous Private Body* (London, 1985) and that this has spurred a debate
over how self-agency in *Hamlet* can be defined (see Andrew
Mousley, '*Hamlet* and the Politics of Individualism' in *New
Essays on Hamlet*, ed. Mark Thornton Burnett and John Manning (New York, 1994)).

[12] For a superb summary of England's relationship with Spain in
the post-Armada years, see Alison Weir, *Elizabeth the Queen*
(London, 1998), pp. 384–446.

[13] Of course, *Witches and Jesuits*, Garry Wills's seminal work on
the Jesuit scare and *Macbeth*, contains an outstanding synopsis
of the influence of the Jesuits (Oxford, 1995). For primary

course, is precisely what Americans in the 1950s believed about the Communists. Like their American descendants, the English valued their autonomy above all things, and the Catholics represented as great a threat to that autonomy as the Communists later did to the American independent spirit. And, in a similarly paradoxical twist, the fear of losing that cherished autonomy caused the English to set a spy network in motion that virtually destroyed the precious independence they sought.

In fact, both of these societal ironies are indicative of a psychological pattern in which fear itself can be the catalyst that triggers the very event that is feared. Psychologists and social scientists agree that stress is the key to any type of conversion of the mind, whether it is emotional or intellectual: those in a situation of extreme stress are more easily controlled and willingly persuaded than others.[14] Guy Arnold refers to this phenomenon as 'the crisis technique',[15] and it is used even today by religious, political and commercial proselytizers. This particular method of mind control is based on the supposition that someone who is experiencing a personal crisis or a stressful episode is far more susceptible to mental conversion – whether that conversion is to a religion, a political party or the latest pain reliever. On a communal level, the England of 1590 and the United States of 1950, facing the imagined crisis of imminent enemy infiltration, made themselves all the more vulnerable to 'domestic' infiltration through their own fear and self-imposed tyranny. William Shakespeare and John Frankenheimer appear to recognize this fundamental irony in their respective societies, and they respond to it in their respective masterpieces.

The protagonists of both *The Manchurian Candidate* and *Hamlet* begin their texts in equally vulnerable, and highly stressful, positions. Hamlet returns home to Denmark facing the death of his father and the well-orchestrated spectacle of his uncle's new court and marriage. After tending to more weighty affairs, Claudius turns to 'my cousin Hamlet, and my son' (1.2.64). Hamlet, ever in control, hides his anger in a sarcastic aside, and when his mother attempts to dismiss his melancholy, he responds with a thinly veiled, and yet controlled, warning

that he has 'something' within him that is being kept in check (1.2.85–6). Later, in soliloquy, Hamlet vents his true feelings, ending his diatribe against Gertrude and Claudius with the anguished 'But break my heart, for I must hold my tongue' (1.2.159).

We first come to know Raymond Shaw, the protagonist of *The Manchurian Candidate*, in a celebratory atmosphere as well. Sergeant Shaw returns home from guerilla warfare in Korea to a hero's welcome, disembarking from the plane to be met by a cheering crowd, military band and full media coverage. The celebration has been orchestrated by his mother and stepfather, Senator and Mrs Iselin, who make a theatrical and transparent entrance as they push their way through the crowd to be photographed with Raymond. Just as Hamlet becomes infuriated when Claudius refers to him as 'my cousin Hamlet and my son', so Raymond becomes incensed when he is photographed beneath a banner reading 'Johnny Iselin's Boy!' Ever in control, Raymond says nothing in public. In the car, Raymond angrily berates his mother for organizing 'this disgusting three-ring circus': Raymond's mother replies with as much condescension as Gertrude: 'Raymond, I'm your mother. How can you talk to me this way . . . my entire life is devoted

---

sources that illustrate the fear prompted by the Spanish in general and the Jesuits in particular, the State papers of Elizabeth's reign, particularly in the 1590s, are rife with examples. See *Cal. S.P., Dom. Reign of Elizabeth I* (1591–4; 1595–7; 1598–1601) (London, 1865). For the Jacobean view of the Jesuits, the best evidence is perhaps the pamphlets that were generated during his reign such as Christopher Bagshaw, *A Sparing Discoverie of Our English Jesuits* (London, 1603).

14 Denise Winn, *The Manipulated Mind: Brainwashing, Conditioning and Indoctrination* (London, 1983), p. 27. Charles Brownfield also points out that, during the Korean War, the Chinese would foster low morale among their American prisoners by allowing only collection notices, divorce subpoenas, 'Dear John' letters and other demoralizing mail to be delivered. Brownfield suggests that this made the prisoners much more susceptible to mind control (Charles Brownfield, *The Brain Benders: A Study of the Effects of Isolation* (New York, 1972), p. 55).

15 Guy Arnold, *Brainwash: The Cover-Up Society* (London, 1992), p. 29.

to helping you and to helping Johnny – my boys, my two boys.' Raymond has shown far less restraint than Hamlet in his mother's presence, and he dispenses approximately the same amount of vitriol in the car as Hamlet does in soliloquy. But Raymond's outburst is no indication of autonomy; when he tries to express his outrage, he is immediately and completely silenced by Mrs Iselin. The scene ends with Raymond's mother continuing to talk while Raymond covers his ears in anguish. We know the articulated reason for the barely repressed fury in both men: Hamlet is reacting to his mother's remarriage, Raymond to the fact that his mother is using him for political purposes. However, there is also an underlying reason for their rage. Both men are reacting to the subordination of their wills to someone they should love but in fact despise. Resistance to this subordination is futile. Hamlet must hold his tongue; Raymond must hold his ears.

The stage is thus set for menticide. The two men arrive to uncertain, stress-laden situations and are confronted by mistrusted people who silence even their most meagre attempts at rebellion. In addition to the circumstances, the personalities of the two men make them particularly vulnerable to mind control. Clinical studies on mental conversion indicate that people with strong and rigid temperaments are in fact the most easily and thoroughly converted.[16] Both Raymond Shaw and Prince Hamlet are initially depicted as men of severe, almost rigid, self-control. Despite his emotional outbursts (which are classified by the other characters as new phenomena), it is clear that Hamlet is a man who admires self-control in others and who takes some satisfaction in his own self-government. As he compliments Horatio on the latter's stoicism, he assesses himself as a man with a similar temperament (3.2.63). He uses the phrase '[s]ince my dear soul was mistress of her choice', to indicate that he prides himself not only on his independent spirit but also on his spirit's ability to remain at his command. Raymond Shaw is, at the beginning of *The Manchurian Candidate*, a man who strictly controls even the off-duty behaviour of his troops and who possesses complete mastery of his own desires. However, although Hamlet and Raymond are technically free-willed and apparently recalcitrant, they are, as we have seen, neither free enough nor rebellious enough to assert their independence fully, even in an ostensibly safe domestic environment. According to psychologists, both characters, so proud of their control and so infuriated by the confiscation of it, are ripe to be placed (or perhaps to place themselves) at the subservient end of a power relationship.

In both texts, the audience soon discovers the extraordinary degree to which they are subservient. We first learn of Raymond's true circumstances in the legendary scene of Ben Marco's nightmare. Frankenheimer is at his most brilliant in this scene, displaying not only the workings of the subconscious dream state but also evoking the fear that 'ordinary', 'all-American' situations could be fronts for Communist mind control. Ben, Raymond's second in command, has been in a mental decline since his return from Korea. One night, he dreams that he, Raymond and the other members of the platoon are sitting before a meeting of a ladies' horticulture society. As the dream/scene opens, the camera does a 360-degree tracking shot around the room, which is festooned with ferns, lace curtains and elderly women. On stage, a similarly festooned woman is speaking on the topic, 'Fun with Hydrangeas', while the platoon looks on with expressions of unrelieved boredom. When the camera finishes the tracking shot and returns to the stage, the woman has been replaced by a tall, bald, Chinese man, Yen Lo. Her voice and her words blend and then transform into his. The stage, rather than being surrounded by plants, is now back-dropped with posters of Stalin and Mao Tse Tung. Yen Lo, a Chinese doctor specializing in mind control, introduces the captured men, still looking bored, to the audience, now consisting of Communist officials. The scene shifts seamlessly from the brainwashing seminar to the garden party: the horticulture speaker and the Communist doctor alternately speak each other's lines; at times, we

---

[16] Winn, *The Manipulated Mind*, p. 23; Meerloo, *The Rape of the Mind*, p. 127.

look out over an audience of elderly ladies, at other times, at a caucus of soldiers and politicians.

The horticulturist, Mrs Whittaker, calls Raymond to the stage and the demonstration begins. Yen Lo asks Raymond who in the platoon he dislikes the least. Raymond chooses Ben Marco, and Mrs Whittaker notes, with some pride, 'Notice how he's always drawn to authority? That won't do, Raymond. We need the Captain to get you your medal.' Raymond promptly chooses another soldier, Ed Malvole. Yen Lo hands the duelling scarf to Raymond and instructs him to strangle Malvole to death. As the rest of the men, including Malvole, sit placidly by, Raymond slips the scarf around Malvole's neck and methodically strangles him. Marco wakes up in a cold sweat as he now remembers – the dream is reality. As the film progresses, we see how a 'brainwashed' person functions in society. Raymond spends much of his time in a state of either snarling belligerence or puzzling lethargy. He seems odd, but functional. However, Raymond is programmed with a 'post-brainwashing' suggestion, so to speak. Whenever his operatives initiate a game of solitaire, and pull the conveniently stacked queen of diamonds, he becomes an automaton, robotically fulfilling every command he is given. As Yen Lo delightedly tells his Russian compatriot, Raymond's 'brain has not only been washed, it's been dry-cleaned'. This is a crucial component in the brainwashing process, the jolly Communist explains, because 'without memory, he cannot possibly feel guilt' – which would of course be very useful in the creation of an assassin.

Hamlet's mission is revealed when he confronts his father's ghost. Although the ghost is neither a dream nor an illusion, it is as surreal and unnatural as the garden party's transformation into a Communist seminar. The ghost's directive to 'revenge his foul and most unnatural murder' (1.5.25) is a command that comes to consume Hamlet's mind and his life as completely as Yen Lo's brainwashing consumes Raymond Shaw's. Like Raymond, Hamlet becomes, in the space of an instant, transformed into an assassin. Of course, unlike Raymond Shaw, Hamlet does not fulfil his directive quite so promptly or obediently. Hamlet's inability

to fulfil his father's command in a timely manner is the crux of the play, and it is a crux upon which many a theory has hinged. However, if we consider Hamlet to be a man who prides himself on the notion that his soul is 'mistress of her choice', then we should consider how the removal of choice, or the imposition of the choice of another, might prove to be particularly debilitating. Claudius and Gertrude may, as king and queen, control Hamlet's actions but Hamlet's thoughts remain his own and he keeps them in active rebellion against his new family. His father's ghost, however, poses a far greater threat to his autonomy. Hamlet recognizes, as soon as the ghost vanishes, that his mind has been appropriated and is now being controlled by another. He also comprehends, as Yen Lo states, that the surrender of memory is requisite. Hamlet stresses that, in order to become the perfect killing machine, everything else in his mind must be 'wiped away'(1.5.97–104). Or, as Yen Lo might say, his brain must be 'dry cleaned'.

By the second act, Hamlet, like Raymond, is exhibiting nearly all the classic symptoms of an individual under mind control. Denise Winn lists these symptoms as anxiety, suspense, feelings of unfocused guilt, fear and uncertainty, bewilderment, increasing depression, fatigue, despair, a great need to talk, utter dependence on anyone who befriends, and a great need of approval of the interrogator.[17] The first eight of these symptoms are well documented in Hamlet's soliloquies. He exhibits a need to talk both with Horatio and with Rosencrantz and Guildenstern, although he knows the latter two cannot be trusted. He does seem to show a slight, if not utter, dependence on anyone who befriends him: he welcomes Rosencrantz and Guildenstern and even confides in them that he is not mad (2.2.377–81); he constantly refers to the players as friends (2.2.425, 537, 548); he eagerly brings Horatio into his confidence. If we read the ghost as his interrogator, we can certainly see Hamlet's need for his approval. Hamlet's own despair reaches its nadir in the third soliloquy when he

[17] Winn, *The Manipulated Mind*, p. 12.

contemplates death. This preoccupation with death is another condition of the indoctrinated individual. Brownfield reports that American prisoners in Korea were, according to eyewitness accounts, perfectly sane, but became 'passive, dependent, and anxious, [and] seemed to give up and accept death as an alternative to the frustrations and deprivations of the environment'.[18] This sounds remarkably close to a paraphrase of '[w]hether 'tis nobler in the mind to suffer / The slings and arrows of outrageous fortune, / Or to take arms against a sea of troubles / And by opposing end them' (3.1.59–92).

And yet, Hamlet falls short of being the classic victim of mind control because the remnants of his identity are in active rebellion against his programming. This is very different from the situation of Raymond Shaw, who loses all cognisant will to defy his directive. Unlike Raymond, there is a battle within Hamlet between the pre-programmed student, whose soul was 'mistress of her choice', and the programmed assassin, whose soul and thoughts must be 'bloody' and under the control of another. In Hamlet's case, this 'other' is his adored, critical and dearly departed father and king. From a filial, social and psychological standpoint, it is critical that Hamlet follows his father's command.[19] Yet Hamlet, on some level of his consciousness, refuses. We may posit many theories about why Hamlet hesitates, but we should remember that the act of hesitation is less about indecision than it is about resistance. Indecision, fear, conscience and timing may be reasons to hesitate, but hesitation itself is a purposeful action. Emily Bartels, among others, attributes Hamlet's resistance to a crisis of identity; she suggests that Hamlet tries to play the part of the avenger but that he 'never ceases to be Hamlet'.[20] In fact, he tries to play many parts but that which is Hamlet, whether we choose to call it his autonomous self or his subconscious identity, is blatantly refusing to co-operate with his father. Whether this leads to madness or liberation may be the real question.

Clinical studies on mind control suggest that this type of resistance is the key to mental and physical survival in a totalitarian environment.[21] More-over, these studies have demonstrated that the most effective method of resistance against mind control is humour, particularly humour directed against those in power. In the Korean War, captured American soldiers experienced very low morale and thus became not only more susceptible to brainwashing but to disease and depression. Consequently, hundreds of Americans died in Korean prisons. Turkish soldiers, receiving the same treatment, kept their morale high by openly deriding their captors; as a result, none of them became victims of mind control nor did any of them die.[22] Subsequent studies on prisoners in Argentina and Vietnam confirm these early findings.[23] So does Shakespeare. Hamlet uses derisive humour almost from the moment the ghost departs the scene. 'Ah, ha boy, say'st thou so? Art thou there, truepenny? . . . Well said, old mole! Canst work i th' earth so fast?' (1.5.152–64). In subsequent acts, he uses his irreverent wit to challenge anyone in authority, particularly Polonius, who represents a father figure to him (2.2.173–220). After he kills Polonius, he turns his wit directly onto Claudius, who, until then, had only been subject to veiled innuendo from his nephew (4.3.17–55).

Claudius and Polonius are only surrogates for the true demagogue in Hamlet's life, however. Although Hamlet's humour may help him resist total domination, he cannot escape that domination totally, because his particular demagogue is

---

[18] Brownfield, *The Brain Benders*, p. 57. He refers to this as an 'apathy death'.

[19] See Jennifer Law, 'Enacting Masculinity in *Hamlet*', *The Centennial Review* 43 (1999), 501–12, 502, and Eric P. Levy, '"Nor th'exterior nor the inward man": The Problematics of Personal Identity in *Hamlet*', *University of Toronto Quarterly* 68 (1999), 711–27; 718–19.

[20] Emily C. Bartels, 'Shakespeare and the Performance of Self', *Theatre Journal* 46 (1994), 171–85 (180).

[21] Arnold, *Brainwash*, pp. 23–4.

[22] Winn, *The Manipulated Mind*, pp. 202–3.

[23] William Sargant, *Battle for the Mind* (London, 1957), p. 231. Sargant also claims that 'the best way to avoid possession, conversion, and all similar conditions is to avoid getting emotionally involved in the proceedings' (109) – advice which would have fallen on deaf ears in Hamlet's case. Also Winn, *The Manipulated Mind*, pp. 206–11.

in absentia. In the direct presence of his father, as we see in the closet scene, his humour, as well as his passion, fail him. And so, the battle for autonomy must rage on. This battle is most clearly seen in his soliloquies. In 'O what a rogue', Hamlet displaces his true anxiety over his loss of autonomy with a superficial concern over his courage. By comparing himself to the players, he is acknowledging that this mission is not his own: 'Is it not monstrous that this player here, / But in a dream of passion, / Could force his soul so to his conceit'(2.2.552–5). Hamlet's true anguish here is that his soul is being forced to someone else's conceit. He is play-acting the avenger; he realizes it, and yet he cannot stop the performance. He postpones further confrontation by inventing a scenario to prove his father's spirit is genuine. If this were indeed a plan of action, Hamlet should be exhilarated. But because it is nothing more than a deferment, in his next appearance Hamlet is suicidal. In 'To be or not to be', direct mention of father/demagogue is completely repressed. Nonetheless, images of domination permeate the speech: 'slings and arrows of outrageous fortune', 'whips and scorns of time', 'the oppressor's wrong', 'the proud man's contumely', 'the pangs of despised love', 'the law's delay', 'the insolence of office'. Each of these images represents victimization or subordination at the hands of a superior force. Fortune, time, the oppressor, the proud man, love, the law and the office are all metaphors for the father/demagogue who cannot be repressed for long.

Because Raymond's and Hamlet's attempts at resistance are initially futile, it would seem that both texts argue for Foucault's theory of the reciprocal relationship between power and resistance. However, the two works situate resistance beyond the action of the protagonists and into a subtext of satire that serves to destabilize, even invalidate, the power of the established authority to control the mind. *The Manchurian Candidate* is, first and foremost, a political satire. Two political structures – both Communism and Democracy – are exposed as being corrupt, hypocritical, deceitful, frequently obtuse and generally indifferent to the people or ideologies they serve. Power is achieved for personal gain and, through tergiversating ways, always under the waving banners of patriotism. On the American side, this is best displayed in the character of the Senator Johnny Iselin, whose intelligence and insight are correctly appraised by his wife: 'I keep telling you not to think. You're very, very good at a great many things, but thinking, hon, just simply isn't one of them.' What Johnny is 'good at' is looking sincere yet affable at a podium and, not incidentally, implicating Communists in the United States Defense Department. The problem, for Johnny at least, is that he cannot seem to remember how many Communists there are supposed to be. After he complains that he is going to look 'like an idiot' if his wife keeps changing the number, Mrs Iselin notices the bottle of Heinz 57 Varieties ketchup in his hand. The next day, Senator Iselin proudly announces to the Senate that the Defense Department has hired exactly 57 card-carrying members of the Communist Party.

Even Yen Lo, the master of brainwashing, seems to have no real ideological loyalties. There is the distinct implication that Yen Lo is employing his considerable talents for the most capitalistic of motives – he is being paid for his skills by the highest bidder. As he examines a comatose Raymond in the hospital, he cheerfully warns a fretting Russian 'investor': 'Beware, my dear Zilkov, the fires of capitalism are highly infectious. Soon you'll be lending money out at interest.' Mrs Iselin also admits to her son, in their final scene together, that she is being paid handsomely for her efforts and that when she 'takes power', she will grind the Communists 'into the dirt' for making Raymond their pawn. The implications underlying the political satire of *The Manchurian Candidate* are clear. Incorruptible political ideologies exist in the same mythical realm as selfless public servants and a well-informed, caring citizenry. By presenting us with such a flawed image of the two dominant and competing hegemonies, the film succeeds in shaking two firmly held notions of the 1950s – first, that the Communists were fanatical pawns, and second, that the American government could protect us from them. With these notions and these institutions so undermined, the power that they pose over individual autonomy is substantially weakened.

Hamlet also functions as a political satire in that it vitiates established authority by revealing the pettiness and corruption within. As in *The Manchurian Candidate*, every regime within the play is exposed as being corrupt, hypocritical, deceitful, frequently obtuse and generally indifferent to the people or ideologies they serve. This is of course most obvious with Claudius. He reaches his goal of crown and queen through nefarious and cowardly means. Poison, not the sword, is his weapon of choice, and it is either administered to a sleeping enemy or through another's hands. He conducts his court through surveillance, secrecy and betrayal. Foucault argues that 'secrecy is indispensable to . . . [the] operation of power',[24] but Claudius is rather inept in the art of subterfuge. His act of murder is revealed by the ghost of his victim; his attempt to spy on Hamlet and Ophelia is recognized almost immediately by Hamlet (3.1.131); one murder plot is double-crossed by Hamlet and a second murder plot is exposed by Laertes (5.2.273). If power is achieved through secrecy, as Foucault suggests, then power through ineffectual secrecy must be its opposite.

And yet, if we can safely acknowledge that Claudius is corrupt, can we name any other authority figure in the play who is preferable? Old Fortinbras sacrifices his kingdom (as well as his life) for emulate pride. Young Fortinbras leads troops of men to die 'for a little patch of ground / that hath in it no profit' (4.4.9–10). The king of Norway is 'impotent and bedrid' and, despite assurances to the new court of Claudius, is unable to stop his nephew from his pillaging rampage (1.2.29). In each of these regimes, we see either a corrupt or incompetent leader who acts for his own self-interest, with absolutely no regard for his subjects or country. These characters are, to a large extent, medieval versions of Johnny Iselin and Yen Lo. Even Hyperion himself, King Hamlet, fails as a leader. His concern, when he returns from the grave, is not for his country or his son. He states that he wants revenge for his murder, but what he truly desires is revenge for the injury to his pride. Throughout his speech

to Hamlet, he displays an inordinately high opinion of himself (1.5.46–52). The ghost of King Hamlet is driven by self-interest – more precisely interest in his reputation – as well as revenge. There is no reason to think he was any different as a man and king. We know little of him before his death, and yet we do know that he was willing to put the fate of his country on the line for the sake of a duel with Old Fortinbras.

As we have discussed, Hamlet engages in humour, sarcasm and open rebellion to silence or mystify those around him. These can all be seen as acts of resistance to the enslavement of Hamlet's mind. However, the unflattering portrayal of the power structures of Denmark and Norway is not Hamlet's act of resistance; it is Shakespeare's. In most instances Hamlet is as taken in by the power structure as anyone else in the play. He sees the faults of Claudius well enough but, before the revelation of his father's murder, he was willing to accept quietly (if unhappily) his authority, and probably would have continued to do so if Claudius had *not* reacted to the play. Hamlet may comprehend the futility in Fortinbras's attack of Poland but, in the end, he hands the kingdom of Denmark over to him. He never recognizes his father's faults. Hamlet, with all his autonomy, does not appear quite cognisant of the problems with the power structure; so it is up to Shakespeare to provide the commentary. He, like Frankenheimer, shadows the text with hints and images that indicate the true absurdity of the institutions that command us and our independence. In doing so, of course, Shakespeare (and Frankenheimer) succeed in exposing them to ridicule and, ultimately, disempowerment.

Another level at which these texts strategically function as satire is by displacing the true source of power away from the political and/or patriarchal hegemony and onto the ultimate symbol of

---

[24] Michel Foucault, *The History of Sexuality: An Introduction*, trans. Robert Hurley (Harmondsworth, 1990), p. 42. For an interesting study of secrecy in *Hamlet* see Mark Thornton Burnett, 'The Heart of My Mystery: *Hamlet* and Secrets', in *New Essays on Hamlet*, ed. Mark Thornton Burnett and John Manning (New York, 1994), p. 46.

domestic security, the mother. In *The Manchurian Candidate* and in *Hamlet*, the main female characters – Mrs Iselin and Gertrude – initially appear to be traditional females. They are primarily wives and mothers, supporting players in the power structure, who serve only as attractive and optimistic appendages to their husbands. We soon discover, however, that from their sons' viewpoint they are the true sources of power. In both texts, it is Mother who becomes the umbilicus in each man's life. Raymond Shaw's mother has quite literally commandeered his autonomy since childhood. During an all-night drinking session, Raymond confesses to Ben Marco that this maternal control has been a lifelong and loathed burden for him:

My mother, Ben, is a terrible woman. A terrible, terrible woman. [Marco interjects: 'Rather like listening to Orestes gripe about Clytemnestra'] You know, Ben, it's a terrible thing to hate your mother. But I didn't always hate her. When I was a child, I only kind of disliked her.

In a flashback, Raymond recalls the summer before the war when he met and fell in love with Jocie. Jocie is, quite clearly, an Ophelia character. She is young, blonde, naive and completely devoted to her father, who happens to be the Iselins' political enemy. Raymond's mother confronts him and demands that he stop seeing Jocie. He admits to Ben that this encounter amounted to a maternal brainwashing session: 'She won, of course. She always does. I could never beat her. I still can't. I'm not loveable. But I loved her. I did love her. I do love her.' One of the subtler ironies of the film is that Raymond never defines the 'her' he loves.

As a young man, Raymond's chance of 'beating' his mother is, by his own admission, infinitesimal; when he returns from Korea it is non-existent. The audience is kept ignorant of the true extent of Mrs Iselin's power until three-quarters of the way into the film when, in one of Marco's flashbacks, we hear Yen Lo saying that the trigger to control Raymond's mind is the queen of diamonds playing card which 'is reminiscent in many ways of Raymond's dearly loved and hated mother'. The shocking truth, which we discover in the subsequent scene, is that Raymond's dearly loved and

hated mother is the Communist operative who detonates the control mechanism to Raymond's mind. Cruelly, she does so by initially providing Raymond with the illusion of momentary autonomy. At a masquerade party hosted by the Iselins, Mrs Iselin calls Raymond into the study and gives him the programming code: 'Why don't you pass the time by playing a little solitaire?' When she is called away, Jocie walks in wearing her costume: the Queen of Diamonds. When Mrs Iselin returns, Raymond and Jocie have eloped, and Jocie's costume is lying on the floor.

In the next scene, an ecstatic Raymond and Jocie announce their marriage to Ben Marco. Raymond is overjoyed with his accomplishment. He has defied his mother, not only by marrying the daughter of her enemy but also, in a nice psychoanalytic twist, by marrying a younger, prettier version of Mrs Iselin. But Marco suspects, and the audience knows, that Raymond's victory is a hollow one. In an earlier scene, Mrs Iselin had informed her husband of her decision that Jocie and Raymond should wed after all; the Iselins need Senator Jordan's approval for Johnny's vice presidential bid. Everything that had preceded the elopement – the masquerade party, the Queen of Diamonds costume – was arranged by Raymond's mother. The plan to elope was, we can assume, planted in Raymond's mind during the solitaire game. Raymond has not defied his mother at all – he has been horrifyingly obedient. The next morning, after Senator Jordan refuses to support the Iselins, Raymond has another meeting with his mother. He means for it to be an angry confrontation, which it is, until she pulls out the deck of cards. In the next scene, a hypnotically programmed Raymond enters the Jordan household in the middle of the night. In a remembrance of the death of Polonius, Raymond calmly pulls out a revolver and shoots Senator Jordan as he drinks from a carton of milk. Jocie comes running in, screaming, and Raymond methodically puts another bullet into her. Part of his programming is to kill any witnesses to his assassinations.

Gertrude is not the mastermind that the loathsome Mrs Iselin is. Nevertheless, she is, in many ways, her son's 'operative'. Although it is his father's command that has taken control of his mind, it is his mother's presence that seems to detonate his emotional charges. And, whereas Hamlet struggles continuously against the control of his mother, he does very little to cleanse his mind of his mother's constant presence. Like Raymond, Hamlet seems to have little use for his mother even before his 'brainwashing'. We have already seen his sarcasm and veiled criticism towards her in the convocation scene; in his first soliloquy, Hamlet situates all his anger for the remarriage upon the 'frail' woman who could not mourn as long as 'a beast that wants discourse of reason' (1.2.150). After the command for revenge is issued by the ghost, Hamlet's first thoughts are of that 'pernicious woman'. This pattern is repeated throughout the play. Whenever Hamlet is roused by thoughts of revenge, his first thought is always of his mother (3.2.381; 3.3.95). Although Hamlet, unlike Raymond, is able to confront Gertrude successfully in the closet scene, he, like Raymond, is never entirely able to defeat her power. He, like Raymond, has his moment of autonomy but in the end Gertrude is among his final thoughts. Hamlet's world, like Raymond Shaw's, remains a matriarchy behind the scenes.

Although these instances of maternal domination, because they have such tragic consequences, could be seen as a reaffirmation of the traditional patriarchy, this displacement of power onto the mother figure could also be a satiric strategy. The reconfiguration from patriarchy to matriarchy forces us to question the old power source and locate a new one. In other words, it raises the question 'where does the danger of menticide really lie?' The idea of mother connotes images of the home, which traditionally conjures up images of love and security. By transforming the traditional representation of mother, Shakespeare and Frankenheimer enervate the old demagogue and establish a new one within the very arenas of personal life that their audiences are, ironically, fighting to preserve.

In both Hamlet and The Manchurian Candidate, the protagonists ultimately achieve their own measure of successful resistance against the demagogues that seek to control their minds. In The Manchurian

Candidate, Frankenheimer portrays this victory for autonomy by bifurcating the struggle between two characters: Raymond Shaw and Ben Marco. Raymond Shaw, as we have seen, is like the programmed Hamlet who has wiped his mind clear of every thought but his father's directive. Marco is the side of Hamlet in rebellion who has 'bad dreams' (2.2.258). Marco has been brainwashed along with Raymond and yet, from the moment he returns home, he subconsciously rebels against the total surrender of his mind. He initially goes to the Army chief of staff and describes his dreams but he, like Hamlet, has his sanity questioned. When a colonel arrives at Marco's apartment to change his assignment to 'indefinite sick leave', he finds it strewn with books with a variety of unrelated titles. In a scene reminiscent of Hamlet's 'words, words, words' scene with Polonius, the Colonel asks if Marco has read them all. Marco replies, with a remnant of humour, 'Yeah, they'd be great insulation against an enemy attack.' In previous and subsequent scenes, Marco is always surrounded by opened books.

Marco's 'breakthrough' occurs at Raymond's apartment. He goes there for answers and is greeted by Raymond's houseboy Chunjin, a Korean who is being 'sponsored' on a work programme by Senator Iselin. Marco immediately recognizes him as the man who betrayed the platoon and led them to their capture. After a moment of shock, he greets Chunjin with a thundering punch to his face, and the two engage in a vicious, feral, no-holds-barred fight that virtually destroys Raymond's apartment. As they are eye-gouging and rib-kicking, Marco's repressed memories are released. He shouts out questions: 'What was Raymond doing with his hands?' 'How did the old ladies turn into Russians?' After the cathartic beating, Marco completely regains control of his mind. He is able to convince the Office of Army Intelligence of the reality of brainwashing and of the threat of Raymond Shaw. Most importantly, he is free.

Hamlet has his own breakthrough moment, which, in its own way, is every bit as feral as Marco's. This, of course, is the closet scene, where he vents his anger against his mother. Hamlet is in such a frenzy of rage against his mother that he physically threatens her; he goes one step beyond Marco and actually kills Polonius. During his paroxysm he, like Marco, receives confirmation of his fears when his mother acknowledges her guilt in marrying Claudius (3.4.9–95). His rage, if not his obsession, is only stopped by the appearance of the father/demagogue, who, acting as the 'interrogator', reminds him of his 'almost blunted purpose'. Hamlet calms down, but, although he has been subdued by the presence of his father, he has not been stifled. In fact, if we can read the closet scene not only as an expression of rage against the sexuality of his mother, but also as an expression of rage against the captivity of his mind, then we can see that, like Ben Marco, Hamlet is becoming victorious in his battle.

After the closet scene, Hamlet moves further and further away from his father's directive and by the fifth act, his father is put in his proper perspective. The graveyard scene is not only a contemplation of death but is also a recognition of his own father's condition. If imperious Caesar is dead and turned to clay, then so is Old King Hamlet. He is a ghost, he is a nightmare, he is dust. In this act, Hamlet begins to fight for himself, not his demagogue/father. He confronts Laertes in Ophelia's tomb with the cry 'This is I, / Hamlet the Dane!'(5.1.253–4) – not only a confirmation of his identity but also an admission that he has replaced his father as the sovereign of his soul. His duel with Laertes is his own fight for his own reasons – not his father's. He admits to Horatio that he, like Marco, had in his heart 'a fighting / That would not let me sleep' (5.2.4–5), but now that his father is his memory, not his psyche, he, like Marco, is released from that bondage. There may be indeed a divinity that shapes his end, but that divinity is *not* his father. Hamlet's admission to Horatio that Claudius 'Popped in between th'election and my hopes' (5.2.66) is the clearest indication that Hamlet's autonomy has returned – he is now concerned with his own ambitions and his father's directive takes a secondary stance. As George Walton Williams and others have pointed out, when Hamlet does finally accomplish the execution of

Claudius, he is not avenging his father's murder.[25] Hamlet is, in fact, avenging his own (5.2.326). Like Ben Marco, Hamlet is able to defeat his demagogue and regain his autonomy. He now fights and dies for himself, Hamlet the Dane. Raymond Shaw also receives a brief, albeit final, moment of victory. Raymond's last directive from his mother is to go to the Presidential Convention disguised as a priest and assassinate the presidential candidate. Raymond arrives, with Ben in hot pursuit, and climbs to a projection booth above the convention floor. He aims his high-powered rifle at the candidate. But, at the prearranged signal in the acceptance speech, he turns the rifle and shoots his mother and stepfather instead. Ben breaks into the projection booth at this moment. Raymond turns to Ben and states: 'You couldn't stop them – nobody can', whereupon Raymond turns the rifle and shoots himself in the face.

In the end, the empowered Hamlet, released from his mental captivity, and the victimized Raymond Shaw, still somewhat entrapped in his, meet the same fates. They also have the same epilogue. Hamlet begs Horatio to refrain from taking his own life so that he may live to tell Hamlet's story (5.2.298–301). After Hamlet's death, Horatio grants his friend's last wish, asking Fortinbras to let him tell the world of the 'unnatural acts' he has witnessed. (5.2.335). Ben Marco, who ends the film as Raymond's only friend, is also left with the responsibility of telling Raymond's story. In the closing scene of the film, he stands at a rain-splattered window reading the citations for the various Medal of Honor winners. He invents an appropriate citation for Raymond Shaw:

Poor Raymond. Poor, friendless, friendless Raymond . . . Made to commit acts too unspeakable to be cited here, [by an] enemy who had captured his mind and his soul, who freed himself at last and in the end, heroically and

---

[25] George Walton Williams, 'Hamlet and the Dread Commandment', in *Shakespeare's Universe: Renaissance Ideas and Conventions: Essays in honour of W. R. Elton*, ed. John M. Mucciolo (Aldershot, 1995), pp. 60–8.

unhesitatingly, gave his life to save his country. Raymond Shaw. Hell, Hell. [A crack of Thunder]

Hamlet is given a soldier's funeral by Fortinbras. Raymond Shaw is wearing his medal of honour when he dies. Both men have paid the ultimate price for the retention of their minds, but both men die heroes.

Frankenheimer's *The Manchurian Candidate* is a film that, on one level, illuminates the dangers and tragic consequences of mind control and thus endorses the fear that was rampant in post-war America. On several other levels, however, Frankenheimer satirizes and destabilizes that fear, while pointing the finger at other, less obvious, but more likely sources for mind control. By using *Hamlet* as the prototype for his artistic vision, Frankenheimer has provided us with another reading of the play in which Hamlet's own struggle against the assault on his autonomy, reflected within Shakespeare's post-Armada society, can be seen. What we see in *Hamlet*, if we read it through Frankenheimer's lens, is a character whose identity and autonomy fall victim to the power structure but who, through his own resistance and Shakespeare's satirical strategies, is able to regain his self-mastery. His resistance, and Shakespeare's, does not enable the power structure, as Foucault suggests, or succumb to it, as Meerloo posits, but in fact successfully subverts it.

CHANNELLING THE GHOSTS: THE WOOSTER GROUP'S REMEDIATION OF THE 1964 ELECTRONOVISION *HAMLET*

THOMAS CARTELLI

'THE PARTICULAR INTENSITY AND NERVES OF THIS'

In early February 1964 when the buzz around the scandalous affair between Richard Burton and American screen goddess Elizabeth Taylor was at a fever-pitch, a new Broadway-bound production of *Hamlet* began to take shape in Toronto under the direction of the already legendary John Gielgud and starring Burton in his third go-round in the title role. Rehearsals with a uniformly accomplished supporting cast of British and American actors – which included such then and later-to-become stage-luminaries as Hume Cronyn, George Rose and John Cullum – proceeded at a speedy clip, though not without distractions prompted by occasional sightings of Ms Taylor. Sources indicate that Burton accepted instruction from Gielgud in an understatedly deferential manner – amicably trading anecdotes with him about fellow stage-legends, Ralph Richardson and 'Larry' Olivier – but seldom followed the old master's directives, much less seemed to work very hard at mastering his lines.[1] Although the cast uniformly evinced respect and admiration for Gielgud – who seemed to know all their parts by heart and could rehearse them backwards and forwards – they also found themselves at sea without a rudder as opening night beckoned, lacking any determinate sense of an overarching concept or sustained interpretive focus for the production itself.[2] Seriously professional to a fault, the cast was often bewildered by the variability of Gielgud's daily notes and directives, which would require, for example, the actor play-

ing Guildenstern to be meekly obsequious in one scene, aggressively inquisitorial in another, without developing a consistent through-line of interpretation that would render his changes in tone coherent. Equally bewildering was how to reconcile Sir John's insistence on their mastery of the musicality of the verse and constant tinkering with blocking and stage-properties with the one definite concept at the heart of the play's production: that is, the decision to stage the play as a rehearsal of *Hamlet*, performed on a more or less bare stage by actors dressed in what were supposed to be the kind of clothes actors would wear to rehearsals.

The anxieties that beset the cast during their rehearsals and first two weeks of under-applauded (but financially rewarding) performances in Toronto, and that continued to preoccupy them in their next two-week run in Boston, gradually receded as Burton's celebrity and growing mastery led to a record-breaking total of 138 performances in the part by the time the production's run concluded eighteen weeks later, on 8 August, in New

---

[1] Most of the information I've gleaned about the Gielgud/Burton production derives from books written on the subject by two fellow cast members. See William Redfield, *Letters from an Actor* (New York, 1967) and Richard L. Sterne, *John Gielgud Directs Richard Burton in Hamlet: A Journal of Rehearsals* (New York, 1967).

[2] Though rather differently positioned, Redfield and Sterne both provide intimate insights into the rehearsal process and offstage discussions of the 1964 stage production that indicate just how under-conceptualized, under-rehearsed and mutable it was.

York. Just prior to the last month of that run (on 30 June and 1 July to be exact), the production was recorded in live performance on three occasions from seventeen different camera angles and edited into a film that was shown for two days (23–24 September 1964) in 2000 movie houses across the United States, and reportedly rewarded Burton and its producers with a $4 million gross return.

The idea of bringing a live theatre experience to thousands of viewers in different cities was trumpeted (by Burton among others) as a new art-form called 'Theatrofilm', made possible through 'the miracle of Electronovision', which was, in fact, one of several technological predecessors for recording moving pictures on videotape. The Electronovision process deployed 'was basically a multi-camera TV-style recording' for which 'Studio video cameras were positioned in the orchestra, boxes and balconies to mimic the audience point of view', with a 'kinescope film recording [later being] made of the video image for theatrical release'.[3] As such, the points of view captured and conveyed were essentially the same as would be deployed in most early televised recordings of live theatre productions when 'all shows were shot "in proscenium"' and 'the limited camera work possible in early television created an effect of spatial continuity more comparable to the theatre than the cinema'.[4] In this respect among others, the Electronovision *Hamlet* effectively worked within the parameters established in 'a spate of drama anthology shows with theatrical names, including The Kraft Television Theatre, Ford Theatre [and] Playhouse 90' throughout the 1950s in the 'so-called "Golden Age" of television'.[5] Indeed, the last of these shows, Playhouse 90, had, by 1957, already begun to use an even earlier form of videotape recording technology, to substitute pre-recording for live production, and to follow cinematic practice by recording individual scenes in discrete takes on different sets. By contrast, the only concession to conventional filmmaking practice made in the Burton 'theatrofilm' was the distillation of a composite edited product from the footage of three

recorded live performances.[6] Though bruited as employing a new technology to bring a new kind of live-theatre immediacy to what would become a cinematic event, the Electronovision *Hamlet* could thus be said to operate as both an anomalous and nostalgic throwback to the already superseded days of live television recording.

Burton nonetheless insisted on the immediacy and 'liveness' of the reproduced theatre

---

[3] See www.braintrustdv.com/essays/back-to-future.html. The next year the Electronovision process was deployed in an eight-day black-and-white shoot of a biopic about Jean Harlow in an effort to beat a Technicolor version of the same subject into the theatres. Though the Electronovision *Harlow* won its race, it was, according to our web essayist 'braintrustdv', considered 'more of a curiosity than a movie and was pulled from its few bookings about as quickly as it had been shot'. In the aftermath of this and a few additional experiments, 'the Electronovision cameras were relegated to video-movie history'.

[4] Philip Auslander, *Liveness: Performance in a Mediatized Culture* (London, 1999), p. 20.

[5] Auslander, *Liveness*, p. 22. See Erik Barnouw, *Tube of Plenty: The Evolution of American Television*, 2nd revised edition (New York, 1999), pp. 154–67.

[6] Some twenty-eight years later – on 26 May 1992, to be exact – Richard Eyre and Ian McKellen would seek to replicate this experiment in an even more austere manner by training three cameras on their stage production of *Richard III* at the Lyttleton Theatre in London in order to produce 'three separate videotapes [that] would never be edited and could only ever be viewed simultaneously [on three separate screens] by a visitor to the [British Theatre] Museum in Covent Garden. The adjacent screens show the full stage, the principals in each scene, and a close-up of whoever is speaking, so that the viewer, rather like a theatre audience, can "edit" the production, by switching attention between the three images'. Ian McKellen, *William Shakespeare's Richard III: A Screenplay Written by Ian McKellen and Richard Loncraine* (Woodstock, NY, 1996), pp. 7–8. No doubt persuaded by his own observation that 'the most obvious way of preserving a live performance is the least satisfactory' (p. 7), McKellen would collaborate with director Richard Loncraine three years later on a screenplay and celebrated film version of *Richard III* (1995) inspired and shaped by the earlier stage-production. For astute commentary on McKellen and Eyre's 'triple record' and Burton's earlier 'theatrofilm', see Laurie Osborne, 'Speculations on Shakespearean Cinematic Liveness', *Shakespeare Bulletin* 24.3 (2006), 49–65.

performance in an interview he expressly gave to promote the American screenings of his 'theatro-film' (and which, given the new miracles of the internet, can now be seen on YouTube). As Burton contends:

The film was shot . . . with an actual live audience and with the actors performing and either being adept or inadequate, or good or fluffing, or being articulate, just as they would if you went to see [the] production . . . none of the actors make any concession to this new process . . . [W]e don't tone it down in order to seem like film actors or play it up because the cameras are perhaps a little further away than they would be in a film studio. It's played exactly as is, and the result will be certainly unique, possibly extraordinary, and perhaps epoch making. That is something for the audience to decide. You get the immediacy of a live production of *Hamlet* on Broadway in the nervousness of the actors, knowing that they can't go back on it, that this is it for all time, unlike in films, where you can, if you make a mistake, go back and do it again. I think the particular intensity and nerves of this is probably the same kind of thing that excites a real life audience in a real live theatre.[7]

Given the promotional bias of Burton's remarks – and the extent to which they differ from a later reported comment that Shakespeare is 'poison' in the film box-office – it's hard to know how much we should credit his assurance in the unique-ness and epoch-making nature of this undertak-ing, much less his confidence in the capacity of the Electronovision *Hamlet* to sustain the 'immedi-acy' of live performance.[8] Burton's apparent con-viction that the 'particular intensity and nerves' of this minimally mediated translation of 'real live theatre' could, when screened, continue to excite 'real life' audiences notably depends on his claim about the *un*likeness between the precarious 'once and forever' conditions that informed the video-taped recording and the more deliberative, repeat-edly revised-until-perfected conditions that obtain in filmmaking. He sees (or pretends to see) this mode of capturing a stage performance on the fly as a faithful or effectual substitute for the experi-ence of live theatre as well as a preferred alternative to dismantling the theatrical dynamic in order to service a play's adaptation to the more discontinu-ous and distancing practices endemic to the film-making process. Whether because Burton honestly believed that the miracle of 'liveness' conveyed by Electronovision could not (or should not) outlive its moment of production, or came to feel that such experiments were not, in the end, so momen-tous that they required preserving, all but two copies of the Electronovision *Hamlet* were even-tually destroyed, one of which was consigned to the BFI archives in London, the other only recov-ered in an attic and made public by Burton's widow, Sally, in 1988.[9]

'CHANNELLING THE GHOSTS'

Our scene now shifts to early March 2007 and St Ann's Warehouse in the recently gentrified waterfront neighbourhood of DUMBO in Brook-lyn, and then to late October 2007 and the New York Public Theater, where the Wooster Group has undertaken a sustained 'emulation' of the 1964 'theatrofilm' of *Hamlet*. One of the first experi-mental theatre companies to bring video moni-tors on stage and enter into dialogue with them in the course of a production (their first efforts summoning up some of the same indignation from their audiences that Bob Dylan did from his when he first went electric at the 1965 Newport Folk

---

[7] Burton's promotional interview is available as an extra fea-ture on the DVD version of the videofilm, currently mar-keted as *Richard Burton's Hamlet* (dir., John Gielgud (1964) Onward Production. Sound, b/w, 191m), which also includes the text of the quoted passage in its accompanying booklet. Video footage of the Burton interview is also available at www.youtube.com/watch?v=sLQDW4ZqckQ.

[8] As Laurie Osborne observes, 'Burton implicitly invokes the irremediable flaws that the reproduced performance will rep-resent as a significant factor in the production's "liveness"' ('Speculations', p. 50).

[9] Ironically, as Osborne writes, 'What was a stage *Hamlet*, tem-porarily envisioned and filmed as "theatrofilm" that "will never possibly be shown again"' (Burton, Interview) is now only a DVD production which includes the interview and the ad 'extolling the "liveness" and immediacy of the experience' ('Speculations', p. 52).

Festival), the Wooster Group has recently begun to employ video footage in an even more singular manner, that is, as a visual prompt or model for their own efforts at imitation or emulation.[10] Their 2004 production, *Poor Theater*, for example, featured not only a stirring side-by-side emulation of sections of Jerzy Grotowski's *Akropolis*, but a painstaking effort by Group members to perform a dance-piece designed and described by choreographer William Forsythe, whose videotaped presentation was replicated by the Wooster Group's Scott Shepherd as other members of the Group moved through their paces. While the tone, and mode of attack, of the Grotowski emulation was well-nigh reverential, and delivered a secondary 'live' performance that arguably superseded in power and effect its videotaped 'original', the representation of Forsythe and execution of his dance-piece seemed doubly ironized, with Shepherd assuming the guise of a self-absorbed new-age guru, and the other Wooster actors demonstrating, despite their adeptness and commitment, the obvious difficulties involved in mastering someone else's art and craft.[11]

By contrast with the mixed modalities of *Poor Theater*, the mood and mode of address of *The Wooster Group Hamlet* in its St Ann's performances seemed structurally, if not designedly, parodic despite the reverential claims advanced about the performance in the programme notes. In the notes, the Group rather portentously identifies their production as 'an archaeological excursion into America's cultural past, looking for archetypes that shadow forth our identity', which 'attempts to reverse the process' of transforming a theatre performance into film by

reconstructing a hypothetical theater piece from the fragmentary evidence of the edited film, like an archaeologist inferring an improbable temple from a collection of ruins. Channeling the ghost of the legendary 1964 performance, the Group descends into a kind of madness, intentionally replacing its own spirit with the spirit of another.

These passages gesture towards a channelling of the ghosts of the theatrical past in a combined

act of cultural recovery, subjective dispossession and collective *hommage*. But in claiming that the 'fragmentary evidence of the edited [Burton] film' constitutes 'a collection of ruins', the Group also appears, somewhat disingenuously, to conflate the purportedly 'faithful' film of the 1964 stage-performance with their own elaborately reconstructed version of it, which (a technical note in the programme tells us) has been 'digitally re-edited . . . so that the lines of verse, which were spoken freely in the 1964 production, are delivered according to the original poetic meter', and from which 'some figures have been erased and obscured, . . . the duration of the play [having also been] shortened using fast forwards and jump cuts'. This re-editing process effectively precludes the staging of a sustained side-by-side dialogue with the Burton film by (literally) opening the film up for the Wooster actors themselves to displace, enter into, colonize, speak over and re-inhabit. Having deconstructed and reassembled the film that records the otherwise irrecoverable stage performance, the Group more often than not surrogates its rehearsal of the 1964 *Hamlet* to its re-edited version of that film, thereby doubly displacing the 1964 *Hamlet* and *making* ghosts of the actors it sets out to channel.

At both the St Ann's and the Public Theater performances, the re-edited theatrofilm was projected

---

[10] Comprehensive studies of the work of the Wooster Group have been undertaken by David Savran in *Breaking the Rules: The Wooster Group* (New York, 1988) and in a more recent essay-collection edited by Johan Callens, *The Wooster Group and Its Traditions* (Brussels, 2004). See also the chapters devoted to the Wooster Group in Arnold Aronson, *American Avant-Garde Theatre: A History* (London, 2000), pp. 144–204 and Philip Auslander, *Presence and Resistance: Postmodernism and Cultural Politics in Contemporary American Performance* (Ann Arbor, 1992), pp. 83–104.

[11] The differing tones of the two main pieces (a third, presented as a coda to the first, involved an emulation of the artist Max Ernst) evoked two differing takes on *Poor Theater*'s identification as 'a series of simulacra', the term itself being given a broad range of dictionary definitions in the programme, which extend from 'a material image, made as a representation of some deity, person or thing', to 'counterfeit; travesty; sham'.

15 Scott Shepherd channelling Richard Burton in *The Wooster Group's Hamlet*.

on a large backcloth screen and on several smaller monitors, three of which remained visible to the audience throughout the production while others were placed in the sightlines of the actors in order to prompt their performance. The audience was not encouraged to notice the additional monitors above their heads (at St Ann's), though the head-set mikes worn by the actors at both sites were as conspicuous as they would be at a Madonna concert. At the Public Theater performance in October, I registered the presence of two recessed monitors set at the edge of the stage to help cue the actors, but could not discern the presence of any overhead monitors, and noted that two of the three smaller, rectangular monitors onstage (those with their longer sides up) were mainly used to display images of the Wooster actors themselves, sometimes held in static poses that did not always synchronize with the forward movement of the drama. (In one instance, halfway through the performance, the stage-right monitor held an image of Shepherd holding the skull of Yorick, something we did not actually see Shepherd do later in the performance, most of the gravediggers scene having been skipped or fast forwarded. In another, an image of John Gielgud was projected in the role of Hamlet's father's ghost from a 1970 Hallmark Hall of Fame televised production.)[12] In both venues, the live actors spoke in synchronic relation to the film-actors' performances, but mostly over the sometimes muted but more often altogether suppressed spoken dialogue of Burton *et al.*,

while displacing with their own bodies the often editorially erased bodies of the actors represented on-screen.

Although often as deferentially emulative and occasionally as dialogic as it claimed to be, the Group's performance was, in these and other respects, just as often interventionist and exaggeratedly reiterative. (The movements forward, backward and to the sides of a chair and table on rollers to approximate the shifts in camera angle from long-shot to close-up and back again in the theatrofilm were among the most pronounced examples of the Group's often amusing, occasionally gratuitous, literalism. Why, after all, try to imitate something that is clearly inimitable?) Rather than embodying a sense of dispossession by, and ceding of control to, the ghosts of the theatrical past, the effect more closely resembled a calculated act of seizure or appropriation, the actors going so far as to order fast-forwarding of the videotape, the skipping of allegedly 'unrendered' scenes, and even the substituting of scenes from recent *Hamlet* films directed by Michael Almereyda (2000) and Kenneth Branagh (1995), which were twice granted a freedom to speak directly to the audience seldom allowed to the Burton production. (Briefer, silent clips and images from earlier *Hamlet* films

---

[12] Gielgud played the same role in the 1964 production, but his lines were delivered by means of pre-recorded audio transmission, with the ghost's physical presence conveyed only by an ominously outsized shadow.

directed by Zeffirelli (1990) and Kozintsev (1964) were consigned to the smaller monitors.) And as noted above, what we saw of the Burton film in the Group's 'revival' was a screen haunted by ghosts: the actors' images often erased by the Group editors, and their words and gestures variously suppressed, emulated or parodied by the Group actors.

This repossession of the space of the dead by the living often generated oddly mechanized modes of emulation. As the Group actors painstakingly tried to record at the level of physical movement and gesture every move made in the Electronovision recording, they seemed more intent on reconstituting the final cut of the Burton video-film than on 'reconstructing' the performances to which it claimed to be roughly commensurate. In the St Ann's version in particular, this effort involved the cultivation of a rigidly choreographed series of bird-like facial tics, splayed gestures and spastic movements on the part of the actors, who came to resemble marionettes pulled in opposing directions by an unseen string. (The deployment of such gestures and movements seemed less pronounced, and more nuanced, in the Group's Public Theater performance, which may have represented a refinement in the Group's approach to the material.) As they tried to keep pace with the audio portion of the film playing directly into their ears, the actors engaged in an increasingly fevered competition with the film itself. What seemed to start out as a kind of stage-actors' revenge against the threat posed to 'liveness' by innovations like 'Theatrofilm', in which living actors control the speed and pacing of the painstakingly 'distressed' video recording, and living bodies erase and displace the fading shadows of electronic reproduction, devolved (particularly in the St Ann's performance) into a collective 'descent' into much the 'kind of madness' of relentless replication described in the programme notes. This impression became especially pronounced after the intermission at St Ann's, as we watched the actors sustain their emulative experiment (with only slight variations) to the bitter end of the Burton film, rather than end it once its manifest point had been made (as was refreshingly the case in *Brace Up!* (2003, 1991), the Group's earlier adaptation of Chekhov's *Three Sisters*, which abruptly ended a step or two short of textual closure).

'THE MEDIA'S THE THING'

Not quite seeing the point of the performance's second half became a common refrain in responses to and reviews of the Group's performances at the Public Theater, Ben Brantley's remark that the performance 'crossed the line from hypnotic to narcotic' after intermission being representative (*New York Times*, 1 November 2007). Since arguing this point is where my own capacity for comparative recall will come most into question, I would like to delay that moment for now in order to entertain a related line of inquiry.

In some quarters – particularly in the experimental theatre community and among academics working in that area as well as in performance studies – the Wooster Group commands what amounts to a cult following (entirely deserved in my opinion). This following is especially evident when the Group performs on its home-turf, the Performing Garage on Wooster Street in New York's Soho, and in their recently annexed home-away-from-home at St Ann's. Though their move to the Public Theater in October led to sold-out houses and a two-week extension of their run, the audience that attended their performance on 26 October was half as large after intermission as it was at the start, and rewarded the actors with a comparatively weak smattering of applause. This decidedly unenthusiastic reception might well have been more the exception than the rule during the extent of their run, but, combined with the diminished house, might also indicate that many of those who came to the theatre in search of Shakespeare's *Hamlet* – like the *Times*'s Ben Brantley – left with empty stomachs.

It's possible that the Wooster Group's studied avoidance of Shakespeare (until this year) has allowed them to fly under the radar of the kinds of audiences who were drawn to their *Hamlet* production at the Public Theater. This is not, of course, the Group's first effort to subject a classic play to their at times mesmerizing, at times clinically dissective, deconstructive techniques. Indeed, deconstructing classic plays, or 'colliding' them with B-movies or pulp novels, is the Group's primary business. In the past twenty years, plays as differently oriented as Thornton Wilder's *Our Town*, Eugene O'Neill's *Hairy Ape* and *The Emperor Jones*, Arthur Miller's *Crucible*, Racine's *Phèdre* and (as noted above) Chekhov's *Three Sisters* have become, in the words of *Village Voice* critic Michael Feingold, 'grist for its postmodern mill'. And as Feingold rightly observes, 'the results [the Group] ground out were never simply the play the author wrote, but what might be called its continuation by other means, like Clausewitz's definition of war and politics'. 'But with *Hamlet*', Feingold adds, 'the Wooster Group has put its commitment on the wrong foot. The media's the thing wherein they hope to catch – well, it's hard to say whose conscience, or even whose interest, they expect to catch by what they've chosen to do' (*Village Voice*, 6 November 2007). Feingold has more to say of interest to the argument I am seeking to develop, particularly regarding why the Woosters chose the Burton *Hamlet* production out of all others of greater theatrical and historic significance to emulate, and we will return to him later. But for now, I want to highlight what is clearly the chief target of his objection, namely, the Group's foregrounding of electronic media, both new and old, in their production of *Hamlet*, which, for Feingold, is for that reason alone a production pursued for no rhyme or reason that he can discern. Indeed, it barely merits the word 'production' at all. Just so.

As noted earlier, the Wooster Group has achieved much of its renown, indeed has become notorious, for bringing to the stage and deploying in more or less prominent ways electronic media – mainly video monitors and pre-recorded sound – that become collaborative players in performances with which its live actors often interact.

This practice has become more pronounced in the last few years and has become (for obvious reasons) particularly integral to the experiments in emulation it has recently been pursuing. For these reasons alone, the choice to build a Wooster Group *Hamlet* on and against the recording of the Electronovision *Hamlet* – and not, as Feingold might wish, 'the 1930s Old Vic rendering that made Gielgud London's hero' – should be obvious. Since the Group's prevailing 'method' of performance is, at this point in time, equally committed to emulation *and* mediatization, it required a recorded theatrical performance to emulate and remediate. What's more, it no doubt found in Burton's promotion of Electronovision's avowed capacity to sustain the *liveness* and immediacy of stage-production the perfect opportunity to engage and elaborate on its own evolving efforts to bring living bodies and electronic media into interactive commerce with each other on the stage.

Earlier in this article I referred to two established aims that would appear to cross or overlap in the Group's choice of subject matter: namely, the attempt to distil and reconstitute 'liveness' through the medium of electronic reproduction (in this instance, through the 'miracle of Electronovision') in the mid 1960s, and the Group's efforts to integrate what were then 'new media' into their stage performances in the early 1980s. Both efforts variably focus on emerging challenges posed (and opportunities afforded) by contemporaneous developments in film, television, video, musical performance and recording, the manipulation of sound, digital reproduction and computer technology, and even the growing ubiquity of 'surveillant and regulatory double imaging systems'.[13] These challenges and the adaptational strategies they provoke – which Philip Auslander would characterize as collateral developments in 'mediatization' – have been held to unsettle the 'ontological integrity' of

---

[13] Jennifer Parker-Starbuck, 'Framing the Fragments: The Wooster Group's Use of Technology', in Callens, *The Wooster Group and Its Traditions*, p. 225.

'live performance' by subjecting it to a form of 'contamination' against which it is unable to compete.[14] Though Auslander sees no reason to view 'the historical relationship of liveness and mediatization' as a relation of 'opposition',[15] he nonetheless concedes that

The ubiquity of reproductions of performances of all kinds in our culture has led to the depreciation of live presence, which can only be compensated for by making the perceptual experience of the live as much as possible like that of the mediatized, even in cases where the live event provides its own brand of proximity.[16]

This, of course, is exactly what the Electronovision *Hamlet* fails to do, and could not do other than fail to do, given its avowed commitment to a theatrically defined performance and reception aesthetic (see the Burton interview) and its choice of a newly available technology that promised to make the translation to film as seamless and transparent as possible. By contrast, compensating for the 'depreciation of live presence' by 'making the perceptual experience of the live as much as possible like that of the mediatized' is exactly what the Wooster Group has been moving towards over the last twenty years, though the Group would no doubt quarrel with the notion that there is anything compensatory in its embrace of mediatization. Indeed, in answer to the question posed by Susan Sontag in a special 1966 issue of the (then) *Tulane Drama Review* devoted to the challenge of cinema – 'Is cinema the successor, the rival, or the revivifier of the theatre?'[17] – the Group would be likely to respond that cinema is at once its contemporary and accomplice, and but one medium among many it seeks to accommodate to its conscientiously hybrid approach to theatrical representation.

Depending on one's point of view, then, the Group has either brought what might have begun as a compensatory strategy to the level of a highly evolved and 'progressive' aesthetic practice in works like *The Wooster Group Hamlet*, or has taken its established theatre practice to a point of crisis by allowing it to become little more than a sophisticated form of mechanical reproduction. If I had

to select my own point of view from these alternatives, I'd say that *The Wooster Group Hamlet* does not, as Feingold would allege, subordinate or surrender what we still think of as *theatre* to the tyranny of *media* so much as submit itself to a series of *remediations* that do not merely involve 'the representation of one medium in another'[18] but, rather, the imbrication or overlapping of one medium by another. In this respect, the Wooster Group's aesthetic practice is 'progressive' not only insofar as it refuses to deny or ignore its already mediatized condition, or to lament the inevitability of its embrace of, and embrace by, collateral developments in new media, but also for its effort to integrate these elements in the development of new theatrical forms.[19]

---

[14] Auslander, *Liveness*, pp. 41–2.

[15] Auslander, *Liveness*, p. 53.

[16] Auslander, *Liveness*, p. 36.

[17] Susan Sontag, 'Film and Theatre', *Tulane Drama Review* 11 (1966), 33.

[18] Jay David Bolter and Richard Grusin, *Remediation: Understanding New Media* (Cambridge, MA, 1999), p. 45. As deployed by new media theorists, the term *remediation* points not to continuous progress towards ever more sophisticated forms of representational practice (such that the new always requires the supplanting of the old) but to the imbrication of all forms of media, with theatre itself figured as one medium among many.

[19] One may compare the Wooster Group's practice of representing, embedding and interacting with other forms of media (both old and new) on stage with what the more adventurous directors of Shakespeare on-screen (Michael Almereyda, Baz Luhrmann and, particularly, Julie Taymor) have recently been doing: that is, not only gesturing to the many ways everyday life has become mediatized, but deploying different media in the development of increasingly hybridized artforms. Rather than reject the sources, materials and representational practices of the past, artists like Taymor find new ways of recycling and deploying them in the present. Note, for example, the remarkably inventive (and powerful) ways that Taymor deploys computer-generated visual effects to recycle Ovidian myth, indeed, to embody the genius of Ovid's metamorphic art, in *Titus* (1999), her recent film-version of Shakespeare's *Titus Andronicus*. For more detailed commentary on this subject, see Thomas Cartelli and Katherine Rowe, *New Wave Shakespeare on Screen* (Cambridge, 2007), especially pp. 45–96.

The Group is, of course, deeply invested in the myth of its own redoubtable *avant-gardism*, in the belief that its work has been 'pivotal' and 'radical' in assimilating new media, thereby boldly advancing the theatrical medium. Indeed, in one of its many more or less official efforts at self-definition and genealogical identification, the Group describes itself as having

played a pivotal role in bringing technologically sophisticated and evocative uses of sound, film, and video
into the realm of contemporary theater . . . [and in
combining] radical restagings of classic texts, found materials, films and videos, dance and movement works,
multi-track scoring, and an architectonic approach to
design. Through a process of overlayering, colliding, and
sometimes synchronizing systems, the structure of a piece
gradually emerges during an extended rehearsal period
as the various elements fuse into a cohesive theatrical
form.[20]

However self-congratulatory they may appear, the claims the Woosters make for their multi-mediatizations genealogically resonate with a host of similar claims made for theatre throughout the twentieth century as potentially the consummate, because most all-inclusive, art form of them all, a 'total art, potentially conscripting all the arts into its service'.[21] Such claims, as Susan Sontag writes, often fastened, in the first decades of the twentieth century, on the call for the emulation, and practical incorporation, of cinematic technique in theatrical production, as in Meyerhold's summons to '"cinematify" the theatre', to 'use in the theatre all the technical means of the screen – but not just in the sense that we install a screen in the theatre'.[22] Some may argue that the Woosters have, in their emulation of the Electronovision *Hamlet*, failed to take that last qualifying proviso to heart. But their inspired remediation of cinematic conventions, particularly in such works as *House/Lights* (2005, 1999), a 'colliding' of Gertrude Stein's *Doctor Faustus Lights the Lights* (an allegory of mediatization in its own right) with a campy 1964 film entitled *Olga's House of Shame*, plainly suggests otherwise. As Ben Brantley himself writes

in a review of *House/Lights*, 'The company has become the American theater's most inspired and articulate interpreter of an age in which machines mediate between the perceiver and the perceived, between subject and object', and may well be 'the only troupe in the world in which theater beats the movies at their own game' (*New York Times*, 28 February 2005).[23]

Though Brantley's admiration of the Group's mediatized translations of the *Zeitgeist* seems diminished now that Shakespeare has become their objective, much the same may be said of the company's performance in *The Wooster Group Hamlet*. The Group not only deploys multiple screens and monitors, dense supportive soundscapes, speech-acts delivered into standing-mikes in ways that resemble the stylings of rock bands, torch-singers and stand-up comics, but remnants of the Electronovision film that are so painstakingly 'distressed' that they begin to 'read' like staticky postings from a nightmarish David Lynch film as well as providing a visual archive of most inscriptions of the play made on screens large and small in the last forty-odd years. Auslander observes that in earlier 'intermedia experiments' like Robert Blossom's 'Filmstage', which 'combin[ed] live actors with film', the 'filmed images were inevitably more compelling' than the live actors, most likely because the actors seemed 'only pale reflections of the mediatized representations that dominate the cultural landscape'.[24] But this effect is only discernible in *The Wooster Group Hamlet* in its very last moments, and only because most of the actors have abandoned the stage to allow the Electronovision

---

[20] The Wooster Group, *House/Lights*: after Gertrude Stein's *Doctor Faustus Lights the Lights* (New York, 2000), p. 69.

[21] Susan Sontag, 'Film and Theatre', p. 36.

[22] Vsevolod Meyerhold, 'Reconstruction of the Theatre' (1930), trans. Margorie L. Hoover, *TDR* 11 (1966), 187.

[23] For an especially illuminating account of how differently Wooster Group projects like *House/Lights* 'play' and are received in different venues, see Ric Knowles, 'The Wooster Group's *House/Lights*', in Callens, *The Wooster Group and Its Traditions*, pp. 189–202.

[24] Auslander, *Liveness*, p. 37.

film the last word. Until then, the live actors, through their fast-forwardings and editorial elisions and erasures, not only control *how* we see the film, but serve as mediatized extensions of it, physically emulating shifts in focus and vocalizing the film dialogue their sound editors have suppressed. (*They* 'control the vertical', *they* 'control the horizontal', in a marked inversion of Rod Serling's ominous claim of control over televised transmissions of *The Twilight Zone* (1959–64).) At the same time as the Wooster actors, in Auslander's terms, '*perform* the inscription of mediatization within the immediate', for example, by speaking the dialogue through their headset mikes, they also reserve the right to alter or 'edit' the production to suit their purposes as actors.[25] After the Mousetrap scene is concluded, for instance, we watch as Scott Shepherd orders the film fast forwarded to 'the recorders', not just so that he might enjoy replicating Burton's (and Hamlet's) masterly dressing down of Rosencrantz and Guildenstern, but so that he might make the moment his own and, for that matter, *ours* as he defies anyone to 'play upon' *him*.[26]

'THE BEST IN THIS KIND'

That said, it seems crucial to reassess in closing the often parodic position *The Wooster Group Hamlet* assumes in performing its surrogation of what is, after all, not only an earlier exercise in mediatization but arguably the central play in the Western dramatic canon. Despite its avowed commitment, at this stage in its development, to imitation and emulation, the Wooster Group betrays, both in its mechanical and occasionally more freewheeling replication of the Electronovision *Hamlet*, a decidedly less deferential attitude towards the theatrical practices put on display there than it does, for example, in its 2004 replication of Grotowski's *Akropolis*. Much of this difference in tone and mode of attack no doubt derives from the fact that, in the present instance, they have set out to emulate the performance of a classic play that is rendered in an unexceptional manner, as opposed to a strikingly inventive contemporary piece that was already rendered in a cutting-edge fashion. The

mere structural juxtaposition of their mediatized stage and of actors exclusively focused on performing a rigorously ordered series of tasks with a modestly staged and even more modestly filmed (albeit, star-centred) 1964 production of *Hamlet* often makes the earlier production seem superannuated.[27] Indeed, the Group's mastery of new media technology – particularly as evinced in the physical erosion and manipulation of the Burton film – combined with the characteristic intensity and discipline its actors bring to bear on their replications, make the juxtaposed 1964 production appear to operate in an antiquated manner and with a discernible lack of momentum (exacerbated, no doubt, by the Group's editorial excisions, elisions and interruptions). Speaking theatre-to-theatre as opposed to theatre-to-film, the physical discipline, energy, intelligence, self-consciousness and overall theatrical command of the Group actors make the professedly 'daring' 1964 'live' production seem comparatively conservative in its bearing and execution, more the product of established mid-century Anglo-American dramatic conventions than of anything that could pass for originality or risk-taking in the heady experimental theatre atmosphere of 1960s New York. Indeed, in taking on such a Janus-headed production in the first place – with Gielgud looking squarely back to Edwardian traditions, and Burton, one of the

---

[25] Auslander, *Liveness*, p. 54.

[26] Shepherd's order, 'come to the recorders', seems to me a profoundly purposive and uncannily apt emulation and remediation of Hamlet's order to the First Player to 'Come to Hecuba', and 'replicates' some of the same dramatic effects. Just as Hamlet requires the reproduction of the Player's depiction of a noble king-father's brutal murder and a loyal queen-wife's deep lamentation to 'spur his dull revenge', Shepherd requires the reproduction of this scene (both by Burton on film and himself on stage) to demonstrate his (and Hamlet's) achieved mastery of his dramatic instrument.

[27] Recounting a 1985 interview he conducted with co-founding Group member and film-star, Willem Dafoe, Philip Auslander notes that Dafoe said that 'from his point of view as a performer, what he does when performing in a Wooster Group piece is virtually identical with that of acting in films – to him, both are primarily [forms of] task-based performing' (Auslander, *Liveness*, p. 29).

last angry young men of the 1950s, playing bitter and caustic throughout and often wildly emoting – instead of something more overtly venturesome (like the closely contemporaneous Peter Brook *King Lear* featuring Paul Scofield), the Group may even be targeting the superannuated convention of the star-centred Broadway Shakespeare production head-on.[28]

Intense, intelligent and inspired as his performance often is, no one today watching the 1964 film, for example, can fail to notice how little effort Burton expends in seeming to think the thoughts that he delivers, or in pursuing a performative through-line that demonstrates imaginative logic or intellectual rigor. Unlike the rest of the cast, Burton often performs his lines in a palpably pre-meditated form of casual recitation, as if focused more on how to deliver a speech or line with sufficient idiosyncrasy, speed or volume to maximize its uniqueness or singularity of address than on what the line or speech might signify or advance. Complicating their studied emulations by flattening, speeding up, or melodramatizing their lines' delivery (a speciality of the inimitable Kate Valk, here doubling as Gertrude and Ophelia), the Wooster actors, for their part, make stage-acting itself an object of critical interest – and concern. Indeed, they take their company's prevailing ethos of imitation to, and beyond, its limit, isolating it as a form of restored behaviour *in extremis*, thereby rendering it both strange and estranging, at once oddly compelling and alienatingly robotic. Rather than 'play' a character, they seek to reiterate physically, with tonal and rhythmic variations, that character's earlier playing, in the process subtracting or emptying out the earlier effect of dramatic embodiment by, as it were, doubling the surface focus of our attention. By reproducing Burton's performance of Hamlet, for example, instead of attempting to inhabit or 'speak' the character Hamlet directly – that is, by holding a mirror up to another mirror as opposed to nature – Scott Shepherd could be said to deny 'the purpose of playing' itself, though, given our age's preference for simulacra, he could just as well be trying to show 'the very age and body of the time his form and pressure'.[29]

Although the simulating actors claim our attention with an intensity of address that exceeds whatever residual claim to immediacy the 'distressed' filmed performers can make, they generate that effect with a machine-like rigour that turns *Hamlet* itself into a pre-scripted race to the finish to no apparent end, the play also having been largely emptied out of any point or purpose beyond studied and sustained replication. The mechanized manner in which the Group pursues its emulative aims seems, in this respect, symptomatic of the fact that it is specifically *Hamlet*, and not just the star-centred Broadway or Electronovision *Hamlet*, that the Group is also channelling and targeting head-on. While *Hamlet* no doubt remains in many quarters Shakespeare's most revered and celebrated play, for actors and academics who are compelled to turn and return to it again and again, it has no doubt lost much of its mystery, making it arguably the most difficult piece in the Shakespeare repertory to render 'new' or work compelling changes and variations on. As Marvin Carlson observes:

Our language is haunted by Shakespeare in general and *Hamlet* in particular, so much so that anyone reading the play for the first time is invariably struck by how many of the play's lines are already known to her. Even more experienced readers (or viewers) can hardly escape the impression that the play is really a tissue of quotations. Our iconic memories are haunted by *Hamlet*. Who does not immediately recognize, in whatever pictorial style he may appear, the dark habited young man gazing contemplatively into the sightless eyes of a skull he is holding

---

28 Brook was, at this time, not only touring with his 1963 RSC production of *King Lear*, but premiering his even more provocative production of Peter Weiss's *Marat/Sade*.

29 In an intriguing note added to the Public Theater programme, Oskar Eustis, the current artistic director of the Public Theater, writes that he sees 'the Wooster Group looking back at Burton's Hamlet with the same elegiac perspective' with which Hamlet views Denmark after his return to Wittenberg, knowing that he 'can never fully belong in his world again'. He then asks, 'Were we ever that innocent? Were we ever that capable of direct, unmediated action, or acting?' For what it's worth, I doubt that the Woosters would reply in the affirmative to Eustis's questions.

(and who, seeing that image, can keep from her mind the phrase, 'Alas, poor Yorick')?[30]

For such reasons among others, *Hamlet* has variably served, for much of the last century, as both a favoured site of radical transformation and of 'numbing, repetitive enactment'.[31] As Richard Halpern observes, 'Not only does Shakespeare's play empty out its own meaning through constant performance, but in doing so it symbolizes the performance of history, which has become unendurably routinized, and thus caught in the toils of the Hamletmachine.'[32] The Hamletmachine is, for Halpern, not just the title of the radically transformative Heiner Müller play (though it is that as well), but an historicized conceit premised on the 'deepening [of] the cultural petrification' that had already settled over the post-romantic conception of Hamlet in the nineteenth century. Contending that the machine 'paradoxically' represents 'both tradition as repetitive propagation . . . and the ceaseless innovating drives that followed in the wake of industrial modernization', Halpern extends the paradox to the figure of the ceaselessly questioning Hamlet himself 'because he represents in a particularly oppressive form the burden of tradition for modernist culture'.[33]

Adapting these terms to our discussion of the Wooster Group's recent exercises in mechanical reproduction, we may well see the Group's own paradoxical commitment to 'repetitive propagation' and 'ceaseless innovating' brought to the point of crisis or contradiction by the 'oppressive . . . burden of tradition' *Hamlet* represents for a company so committed to building on the experimental cultures of modernism. Had the Group decided to faithfully replicate the entire version of *Hamlet* reproduced in the Electronovision film, it might have achieved a level of reproductive efficiency comparable to the mechanical regularity of the clockwork Hamlet and Ophelia of W. S. Gilbert's 1892 literary satire, *The Mountebanks*, that Halpern discusses in *Shakespeare Among the Moderns*.[34] But however devoted the Group may be to making their bodies the media through which earlier performances circulate – what Marvin Carlson

terms 'body ghosting'[35] – the temporal disconnect between where they are now and where the Electronovision performance was then opens up a space that they often fill with sudden and unanticipated interpolations, including the incorporation of two haunting songs sung by the actor Casey Spooner concurrent with his performance as Laertes.[36] The Group clearly does not follow Heiner Müller's example of completely dismantling and rewriting the play, much less bring anything close to Müller's engagement with politics and history. But it engages in sufficient (if not 'ceaseless') 'innovating' to avoid the effect of 'numbing repetitive enactment' Halpern describes. Although technical prompts and the actors' repertoire of physical movements, tics and gestures are rigorously scripted, blocked and executed in synchrony with the Burton film, enough improvisatory energy is invested in the vocal delivery of reproduced text that marked differences may be registered in variations of tone, speed, volume and rhetorical attack, as well as on the level of attitude or mood. Indeed, by having her small cast double their roles (Kate Valk playing both Gertrude and Ophelia to often moving, often comedic, effect) and occasionally serve as voyeuristic stage-hands, lip-synch lines that are spoken by a laconic Bill Murray in the *persona* of Polonius and play awed witness to Charlton Heston's thunderous delivery of the First Player's 'Hecuba speech' (in cameo appearances drawn from recent *Hamlet* films), director Elizabeth

[30] Marvin Carlson, *The Haunted Stage: The Theatre as Memory Machine* (Ann Arbor, MI, 2001), pp. 78–9.

[31] Richard Halpern, *Shakespeare among the Moderns* (Ithaca, NY, 1997), p. 273. Radical transformations of *Hamlet* are many and varied, both in terms of seriousness and quality. In addition to Heiner Müller's *Hamletmachine* (1979), among the better-known are Joseph Papp's *The Naked Hamlet* (1968) and, of course, Tom Stoppard's *Rosencrantz and Guildenstern are Dead* (1966).

[32] Halpern, *Shakespeare among the Moderns*, p. 273.

[33] Halpern, *Shakespeare among the Moderns*, p. 235.

[34] Halpern, *Shakespeare among the Moderns*, esp. pp. 227–38.

[35] Carlson, *The Haunted Stage*, p. 169.

[36] True to the Group's collaborative aesthetic, Laertes's songs were composed by Spooner himself in collaboration with Warren Fischer.

LeCompte brings more humour, irony and playful-ness to the production than has yet to be credited. (She even adds an unscripted character, dressed in the garb of a nurse, who hovers protectively, if silently and ineffectually, over the proceedings, and whose very appearance may be designed to evoke the appropriative motive at the heart of the per-formance.)[37] What's more, she also alters, in the Public Theater production, the disproportionate privileging, in the St Ann's version, of her own actors' performances over those of the ghosts of the 1964 production.

When members of the Group were queried about its aims at a post-performance talk-back last March (2007), the actors uniformly claimed that the aim was the process itself, the work or exercise of imitation/emulation, which was ongoing and subject to change and new discoveries: an explana-tion that several auditors found somewhat unforth-coming. But in light of changes the Group seems to have made in the last seven months, I am much more willing to take them at their word. Though the nature and content of reception and attention will differ in all of us from eye to eye and ear to ear and, in performances like this one, even from gen-eration to generation, I became aware, during the closing movement of the 26 October performance, that my own attention had begun to shift from the stage to the increasingly active and often stat-icky backcloth screen, prompted, no doubt, by the insistent rise in volume of the soundscape, which served as the screen's commensurate audio accom-paniment.[38] The screen – then and, in my mind's eye, now – was not so much opaque or impene-trable by reason of the static as rendered mutable, and made me think of the amoeba-like permu-tations of the thought-shaping sea on the planet Solaris in Andrei Tarkovsky's brilliant 1972 film of that name. Snapped back to attention by the playing out on stage of the duel between Laertes and Hamlet, and the dying words of the Prince, I just as quickly found myself redirected to the screen where the final scene of the Burton film was played out in full, without any replicative help from the Woosters. Failing to notice, much less consider, where the replicants had gone, and for

the first time that evening being permitted direct access to the screen actors, I discovered what I ini-tially took to be the Group actors again, a few seconds before the film's (and performance's) end, casting their irregularly sized shadows across the lower section of the screen. They had, in fact, left the stage while my attention was otherwise engaged

---

[37] In the production's programme and promotional materials (postcards and posters), the Nurse ('played' by Dominique Bousquet, who doubles as one of the Players) is, in fact, the only character from the cast who is depicted. Her eyes and the top portion of her face are portrayed above a pile of books and a DVD case that obscure the rest of her body. Four of the books are different editions of *Hamlet*. The DVD is *Richard Burton's Hamlet*. The fifth book is titled *Hollywood Nurse*, one of a series of 'naughty-nurse' novels (*Tropics Nurse, Desert Nurse*, etc.) published by Marguerite Nelson in the 1960s. However, the Group was apparently inspired to deploy the Nurse in their performance and this image in their postcards in direct imitation/emulation of Richard Prince's 'Nurse paintings' and promotional post-cards produced and distributed by New York's Guggen-heim Museum to promote their 2003 exhibition, 'Nurse in Hollywood: Richard Prince: Spiritual America', in which the Nurse paintings were featured. Prince is, revealingly, an 'appropriation artist' who is both celebrated and cen-sured for his photographing of 'public domain' advertise-ments, and then enlarging and representing them as his own 'product'. The Nurse-series is differently rendered. Accord-ing to www.guggenheim.org/exhibitions/richard prince/prince.html, 'The Nurse paintings are premised on medi-cal romance novels, a genre of pulp fiction that has its own section in Prince's upstate New York library. For this recent series, the artist transfers enlarged inkjet reproductions of book covers to canvas, masking out all the supporting char-acters and text other than the titles by applying smudged and dripping pigment.' The similarity of Prince's process to the Group's elisions and 'distressings' of the 1964 Electronovision film should be obvious. Thanks to Katharine Goodland for bringing the connection with Prince's work to my attention.

[38] One of my undergraduate students, Mallory Musallam, who attended the Public Theater production, offered this intrigu-ing take on the film vs. theatre debate: 'I felt that the char-acters behind their black and white barrier were intimately close, whispering pieces of their souls, while the charac-ters on the stage seemed so distant . . . I saw the menaces on the stage as a representation of advanced technology: an overbearing force in society that's hyper-active, less emo-tional and more mechanical, ostentatious and unnecessary, and ultimately seeking to outdo things from an earlier time.'

to simulate the taking up of positions behind the screen by their (actually pre-recorded) shadows, presumably to allow the ghosts of 1964 a comparatively unmediated hearing, and, possibly, a belated *hommage*. The gesture seemed out of keeping with the Woosters' reputation for being aloof and diffident, cool and remote. It also served as yet another in a series of inspired remediations: in this instance, a carefully designed channelling of themselves into the tributary stream of the ghosts of *Hamlets* past, passing, present and to come, shadows replaying shadows, the best in this kind.[39]

[39] In a wonderfully apposite passage, Gerald Siegmund writes that 'The theatre of the Wooster Group is a theatre of voices that adds to the presence of the theatrical event moments of absence in which it repeats those who are absent, dead, or forgotten via voice-masks. The use of media in this context furthers an understanding of the media in the old sense of "medium", of a link with this spirit world. . . . The voices without bodies, the missing bodies . . . open the theatre towards a history that is always also the history of the theatre. This is what the mask stands in for . . . it grants ghosts . . . potential bodies and voices.' 'Voice Masks: Subjectivity, America, and the Voice in the Theatre of the Wooster Group', in Callens, *The Wooster Group and Its Traditions*, p. 178.

LISTENING TO *PROSPERO'S BOOKS*

EVELYN TRIBBLE

Peter Greenaway's 1991 *Prospero's Books* has received critical attention primarily for its extraordinarily dense rendering of the visual field. The twenty-four books of Prospero – an allusion, Greenaway admits, to cinema's twenty-four frames per second[1] – provide a powerful structuring device for the film's exploration of the inter-connected materiality of book and cinematic frame. The result is an extraordinarily complex and imagistic film, and the viewer is at first nearly overwhelmed by the level of visual detail and layering. Claus Schatz-Jacobsen's discussion of the film provides an example of the critical preoccupation with the visual in the film: 'It seems as if Greenaway has been inspired by Prospero-Shakespeare's potent magic to pursue every conceivable visual possibility offered by the state of the art in film and television technology... Nothing seems finally alien to Greenaway's painterly urge to emulate by purely *visual* means the potent *verbal* magic of his ideal reflection in the mirror of the *Tempest*, Prospero-Shakespeare.'[2] While it is of course correct to call attention to the painterly nature of the film, the contention that it is 'purely visual' represents a misunderstanding of the full implications of its nature which, far from being exclusively visual, depends upon setting into play tensions and potential rivalries among cinematic image, post-production digital image, dialogue, sound and music.[3] Moreover, it is also a mistake to conceive of *The Tempest* primarily as a 'verbal' accomplishment, since the play's emphasis upon spectacle, illusion and, especially, sound, is perhaps more marked than that of any other Shakespearian play. Rather than being a sim-

ple adjunct to the visual elements of the film, as is often assumed, the acoustic dimension of *Prospero's Books* is one of the most complex areas of intersection between the play and the film.

In a 1992 interview on *Prospero's Books*, Peter Greenaway remarks upon the extraordinary experimentation of *The Tempest*. Likening Shakespeare's late play to the last works of Titian and Beethoven, Greenaway remarks that such late works 'somehow take an enormous leap and lurch into the future and... create whole new worlds and universes worthy of exploration, which may only come fully into fruition many, many years after the deaths of their creators'.[4] *The Tempest* is indeed an experimental play, especially in its exploration of the potential – and limitations – of the masque and its associated spectacle, and Shakespeare pushes the embodiment of imagination to its limits, at least within the theatrical vocabulary he had available at

---

[1] Peter Greenaway makes this point in two interviews: Suzanna Turman, 'Peter Greenaway', in Vernon Gras and Marguerite Gras, eds., *Peter Greenaway: Interviews* (Jackson, 2000), p. 150, as well as Dylan Tran, 'The Book, The Theater, the Film, and Peter Greenaway', in the same volume, p. 132.

[2] Claus Schatz-Jacobsen, 'Knowing I Lov'd My Books: Shakespeare, Greenaway, and the Prosperous Dialectics of Word and Image', in M. Skovmand, ed., *Screen Shakespeare* (Aarhus, Denmark, 1994), p. 144.

[3] As Julie Sanders points out in her brief discussion of *Prospero's Books* and the ballet, the rivalry extended to a public falling-out between Greenaway and Michael Nyman over the director's additions and alterations to Nyman's score. See *Shakespeare and Music: Afterlives and Borrowings* (Cambridge, 2007), p. 65 and 71n5.

[4] Turman, 'Peter Greenaway', p. 148.

the time. In this play, however, Shakespeare's true innovation and experimentation lies in the acoustic dimension: his creation of a distinctive soundscape that exploits the full spectrum of sound from silence, music and noise.

It has long been recognised that *The Tempest* is one of the most acoustically rich and complex of all of Shakespeare's plays. Indeed sound, heard and unheard, drives much of the action of the play; as Virginia and Alden Vaughan note, the play makes a 'magical island out of sheer sound'.[5] Robert Johnson composed the art songs 'Full fathom five' and 'Where the Bee sucks' expressly for the King's Men,[6] but the play contains many more references to sound and music throughout: 'The isle is full of noises / Sounds and sweet airs' (3.2.135–6). The play is also rife with both explicit and implicit sonic stage directions. These include Prospero's call for 'heavenly music' (5.1.52) prior to his vow to drown his books; the offstage marking of the destruction of the ship in the first act by *a confused noise within* (1.1.60 SD) and calls for *solemn and strange music* (3.3.17 SD). Extended stage directions also call for elaborate musical and sonic sound effects. For example, thunder and lightning, sounds associated throughout Shakespeare's plays with the supernatural, mark the transformation of the banquet in Act 3: *Thunder and lightning. Enter ARIEL, like a harpy; claps his wings upon the table; and, with a quaint device, the banquet vanishes* (3.3.52 SD). The text explicitly calls for 'strange noises', the best known of which is the 'strange, hollow, and confused noise' that marks the interruption of the marriage masque: 'Enter *certain Reapers, properly habited. They join with the Nymphs in a graceful dance; towards the end whereof Prospero starts suddenly, and speaks . . . To a strange, hollow, and confused noise, the spirits in the pageant heavily vanish*' (4.1.138 SD).

Bruce Smith and Andrew Gurr, among others, have attributed this preoccupation with sound in the play to Shakespeare's experimentation with a new sonic environment: the indoor space of the Blackfriars Theatre. The Blackfriars provided a markedly different sonic environment from that afforded by the outdoor amphitheatre of the Globe. Earlier in Shakespeare's career, Smith argues, Shakespeare's acoustic palette featured 'high-energy percussive sound effects'; however when writing for the new theatre Shakespeare produced a play that 'exploits the acoustic possibilities of the new space to the full. The script presents an acoustic design with a complexity and subtlety approaching consorted music.'[7] Gurr, writing of the 'unique exploitation of instrumental music as well as song, [and] the plethora of magic and stage effects dependent upon the music', suggests that the opening storm is 'a bravura piece of staging',[8] particularly in the way that it employs the intimate indoor space of the Blackfriars to stage a sonic effect more closely associated with outdoor amphitheatres such as the Red Bull. In *The Tempest*, then, Shakespeare explores his new acoustic technology with an enthusiasm that we might compare to the experimentation of film directors with new sound technologies such as Perspect-a-Sound or Dolby Surround-Sound. As Greenaway has remarked, artists tend to experiment with new 'aesthetic technologies'; in the case of *The Tempest*, the new technology is primarily acoustic, enabled by the infrastructure of the indoor theatre.[9]

For Shakespeare sound and music was the essential element in creating a supernatural space, and in this play, the acoustic element is persistently associated with dislocation and disorientation.[10] As Peter

5 William Shakespeare, *The Tempest*, ed. Virginia Mason Vaughan and Alden T. Vaughan (Walton-on-Thames, 1999), p. 19.

6 Howell Chickering, 'Hearing Ariel's Songs', *Journal of Medieval and Renaissance Studies* 24 (1994), 131–72; David Lindley, *Shakespeare and Music* (London, 2006).

7 Bruce Smith, *The Acoustic World of Early Modern England* (Chicago, 1999), p. 233.

8 Andrew Gurr, '*The Tempest*'s Tempest at Blackfriars', *Shakespeare Survey 41* (Cambridge, 1989), pp. 91–102; p. 93, p. 95.

9 Greenaway's argument about 'aesthetic technologies' was made in his keynote address, as yet unpublished, at the CENDEAC Conference on 'Peter Greenaway: The Impure Image', 23 November 2006, University of Murcia, Murcia, Spain.

10 I have discussed this issue at greater length in '"When Every Noise Appalls Me": Sound and Fear in *Macbeth* and *Throne of Blood*', *Shakespeare* 1 (2005), 75–90.

Seng remarks, 'all the music in *The Tempest* seems to have this mysterious character, performed as if it came from all over the stage'. Seng also notes that no other play uses 'dispersed music' as extensively as *The Tempest*.[11] Ariel's song, with which he '*invisible, playing and singing*', (1.2.376 SD) leads Ferdinand into the view of Miranda, calls upon the spirits to sing 'dispersedly within' (1.2.383 SD). The effect on Ferdinand is profoundly disorienting, as he struggles to understand the source of the sound: 'Where should this music be? i' the air or th'earth?' (1.2.390):

> It sounds no more: and sure, it waits upon
> Some god o' th' island. Sitting on a bank,
> Weeping again the king my father's wreck,
> This music crept by me upon the waters,
> Allaying both their fury and my passion
> With its sweet air. Thence I have follow'd it,
> Or it hath drawn me rather. But 'tis gone.
> No, it begins again . . .
>
> Hark, now I hear them . . .
>
> The ditty does remember my drown'd father.
> This is no mortal business, nor no sound
> That the earth owes. I hear it now above me.
>   (1.2.391–8; 407; 408–10).

The inability to localize sounds and music, its haunting and elusive nature, is underscored by this speech, which draws attention to the rich acoustic environment inhabited by the audience, as well as to the skill of the famous group of musicians who played at the Blackfriars. Paradoxically, only within a contained indoor environment is it possible to achieve the effect of dislocation and dispersal, for to experience sound as dispersed requires a precise acoustic environment in which one expects to be able to distinguish its source.

If the role of sound in the sensorium has only recently been explored in Renaissance studies, it is even less commonly given a central role in cinematic studies, which have historically been preoccupied with the visual. Standard textbooks on film tend to treat film sound in stand-alone chapters rather than as an integral part of the cinematic experience, and standard shot analysis techniques such as those outlined in Brian McFarlane's book

on adaptation neglect sound as a unit of analysis.[12]

Moreover, the dominance of psychoanalytic approaches in film theory has resulted in an emphasis upon the visual that has overshadowed attention to the aural elements of cinema. Laura Mulvey's enormously influential 'Visual Pleasure and Narrative Cinema'[13] established the dominance of the 'gaze' as the dominant mode of analysis. Even so spirited a challenge to psychoanalytic film theory as Vivian Sobchack's *The Address of the Eye: A Phenomenology of Film Experience*[14] re-directs attention to an embodied mode of sight rather than attending to the full range of sensory modes experienced by the cinema-goer.

Certainly a large literature now exists on the elements of sound and music in cinema, particularly on music. The call for a theoretically inflected account of film sound can be traced to a special issue of *Yale French Studies* in 1980,[15] edited by Rick Altman, which contained contributions from Altman, Christian Metz, Mary Ann Doane, Kristin Thompson, David Bordwell and Claudia Gorbman, among others. In 1992, Altman revisited the question of cinematic sound from a more material, historical and culturalist perspective in his collection *Sound Theory Sound Practice*.[16] While this work has been influential, sound continues to be seen as a supplementary rather than a central category as critical analysis, as Anahid Kassabian has argued in his recent book on *Hearing Film*, and the literature on sound dwarfed by work on the film image.[17]

Perhaps the most influential of theorists of cinematic sound is Michel Chion, whose *Audio-Vision:*

[11] Peter Seng, *The Vocal Songs of Shakespeare* (Cambridge, 1967), p. 252.

[12] Brian McFarlane, *Novel into Film: An Introduction to the Theory of Adaptation* (Oxford, 1996).

[13] Laura Mulvey, *Visual and Other Pleasures* (Houndmills, Basingstoke, 1989).

[14] Vivian Sobchack, *The Address of the Eye: A Phenomenology of Film Experience*, (Princeton, 1992).

[15] Rick Altman, ed., *Yale French Studies 60* (1980).

[16] Rick Altman, *Sound Theory Sound Practice* (New York, 1992).

[17] Anahid Kassabian, *Hearing Film* (New York and London, 2001).

Sound on Screen[18] (1990, 1994) and *The Voice in Cinema* (1999)[19] constitute a manifesto for theoretical analysis of sound. Chion's books are to some extent extended glossaries of sound terminology, designed to supply a theoretically sophisticated vocabulary for analysis of sound in film. Chion's central claim is that sound remains a neglected element in cinema theory, either ignored or 'relegat[ed] to minor status'.[20] Generally, when sound is discussed, it is on the basis of an 'additive model'[21] rather than as constitutive or transformative. The additive model simply adds on the element of sound, implicitly suggesting that 'witnessing an audiovisual spectacle basically consists of seeing images plus hearing sounds. Each perception remains nicely in its own compartment.'[22] Instead, Chion argues for *audio-vision*: 'one perception influences the other and transforms it'.[23] One of Chion's most important insights is that sound is never natural, that there is no so-called 'natural harmony' between sound and image.[24] Rather, the yoke between sound and image is an *illusion* of a 'spontaneous and irresistible weld' that Chion terms 'synchresis'.[25] As will become clear, 'synchresis' is an important conceptual category in understanding the constructed nature of the relationship between sound and image.

The renewed interest in film sound is part of a larger scholarly revival of interest in the auditory dimensions of human experience, of which Smith's work, discussed earlier, is a prime example, as is the work of Wes Folkerth.[26] The pioneering work of Murray R. Schafer[27] on soundscape studies has provided models for scholars working in a wide range of disciplines and historical materials to study what Jonathan Sterne has called 'the audible past'.[28] The term 'soundscape' describes the relationship between the acoustic environment and the perceiver of that environment: as Barry Truax puts it, soundscape is 'An environment of SOUND (or sonic environment) with emphasis on the way it is perceived and understood by the individual, or by a society. It thus depends on the relationship between the individual and any such environment. The term may refer to actual environments, or to abstract constructions such as musical compositions and tape montages, particularly when considered as an artificial environment.'[29] This relational quality of the soundscape has made the concept a useful tool for exploring historical acoustic environments such as early modern London.

It is important, however, to emphasize that sounds of Shakespeare cannot simply be reproduced on film. The works of Truax, Schafer and Chion remind us that the relationship between sound and image is never natural, that it is always embedded in a culturally determinate soundscape. If we understand soundscape as relational, we realize that it is a product of a particular set of relations among auditors. Shakespeare's company constructed a soundscape for its auditors within the context of a particular set of culturally determinate sounds heard in London, in which certain sounds – e.g. church bells,[30] thunder – had a very specific meaning, and within the acoustic possibilities of constraints of the built environment of the Globe, the vocal abilities of the players and the ambient sounds produced by the audience. Audiences at the cinema are products of very different soundscapes and are particularly influenced by the ubiquity of sound recording and amplification devices. They have naturalized certain sounds in the cinema, which have been, in turn, the piano

[18] Michel Chion, *Audio-Vision: Sound on Screen*, trans. Claudia Gorbman (New York, 1994).
[19] Michael Chion, *The Voice in Cinema*, ed. and trans. Claudia Gorban (New York, 1999).
[20] Chion, *Audio-Vision*, p. xxv.
[21] Chion, *Audio-Vision*, p. xxvi.
[22] Chion, *Audio-Vision*, p. xxvi.
[23] Chion, *Audio-Vision*, p. xxvi.
[24] Chion, *Audio-Vision*, p. 95.
[25] Chion, *Audio-Vision*, p. 63.
[26] Wes Folkerth, *The Sound of Shakespeare* (London, 2002).
[27] Murray R. Schafer, *The Soundscape: Our Sonic Environment and the Tuning of the World* (Rochester, VT, 1977).
[28] Jonathan Sterne, *The Audible Past: Cultural Origins of Sound Reproduction* (Durham, NC, 2003).
[29] Barry Truax, *Acoustic Communication* (Westport, CT, 2001), soundscape.htm. CD-ROM.
[30] David Cressy, *Bonfires and Bells: National Memory and the Protestant Calendar in Elizabethan and Stuart England* (London, 1989).

and/or orchestral accompaniment to silent film; in Japan, the vocal commentary of the *benshi*; the monoaural sounds of early sound cinema; and the ear-shattering surround-sound of the contemporary cinematic experience. All this is to say that to merely reproduce Shakespeare's sounds in a cinematic medium is inevitably to distort them. The 'same' sound will be heard very differently by a sixteenth-century playgoer and a twenty-first century cinema-goer, just as the doublet, hose and breeches that would seem natural to the early viewer seem antiquated and strange now. Thus I argue for attending both to the technologies and conventions of sound available in the early modern theatre, and to the very different technologies and conventions of sound production in the cinema. Studying sound as a crucial element of adaptation forces us to see that sound is neither a natural nor a transparent phenomenon. Sounds are both physiologically determinate and culturally embedded, meaningful only when placed within a particular soundscape.

In *Prospero's Books*, Greenaway, Garth Marshall (production sounds) and the minimalist composer Michael Nyman create a dense and unsettling cinematic soundscape through a sometimes uneasy collaboration. Greenaway and Nyman have both acknowledged the rivalries and tensions that beset the relationships among sound, music and image in film.[31] In an interview on the topic of 'Sound and Vision', Greenaway, asked if he would be interested in 'making a movie without any text at all, no dialogue, no words on the screen, just images', at first replies that he would 'feel like I'd be chopping off this arm'. But he elaborates: 'I suppose this is one of the quarrels I used to have with Michael Nyman, which takes precedence, the dialogue or the music? There's an inevitable battle. Unlike the eye, which has the ability to sort things out, the ear doesn't have that ability. So unless you organize things very well, you just get a whole cacophony of noise that is very difficult to sort.'[32] Despite his emphasis upon film image, Greenaway acknowledges that 'in cinema, it is rare to come across a truly satisfying equivalence between image and music. Traditional film-editing procedures and practice normally push, cajole, persuade or relegate music into a secondary or tertiary role, essentially making it function as a prop for providing emotional mood. Music used as structure in film, outside of being merely a vehicle to illustrate, is exceptional.'[33] Sound is the unacknowledged underpinning of the cinematic experience, as Greenaway suggests:

Cinema is believed traditionally to operate through pictures. Does cinema communicate through pictures? I doubt it. The average cinema-film, like the average television programme, is a poor communicator without a sound track, without dialogue, without text. Turn off the sound track of a film or a television programme and this fact can be observed very quickly.[34]

Listening to *Prospero's Books* reveals Greenaway's intense preoccupation with sound and music in his film. In the opening sequences, Greenaway yokes sound, magic and the aesthetic, drawing particular acoustic attention to the sounds of quill on parchment, pages turning and, most importantly, of water. Greenaway evinces an interest in both the visual and sonic properties of water throughout his career, demonstrated not only by *Prospero's Books*, but also by the 1978 *Water Wrackets*, the 1984 *Making a Splash*, the 1986 *Drowning by Numbers*, as well as his *Watching Water*, the catalogue for the Venice Bienale exhibition at the Palazzo Fortuna in 1993. In an interview with Marlene Rodgers, Greenaway discusses the properties of water:

On a practical level, water is fantastically photogenic. But of course, the world is four-fifths water, we're all born in amniotic fluid . . . it literally is the oil of life, it is the blood

---

[31] Marlene Rodgers and Peter Greenaway, 'Prospero's Books: Word and Spectacle: An Interview with Peter Greenaway', *Film Quarterly* 45 (1991–2), 11–19; p. 11.

[32] Peter Greenaway, 'An Open Discussion with Peter Greenaway', August 2002, European Graduate School, Switzerland, www.egs.edu/faculty/greenaway/greenaway-sound-and-vision-2002.html. Acccessed 25 August 2007.

[33] Michael Nyman and Peter Greenaway, *Sleevenotes to The Nyman / Greenaway Soundtracks*, 1989 Virgin Venture DVEBN 55. www.michaelnyman.com/disco/17. Accessed 2 November 2007.

[34] Peter Greenaway, *Watching Water: Venice Bienale* (Venice, 1993), p. 48.

life, which splashes, dribbles, washes, roars – it's a great friend and a terrifying enemy, it has all those significances.[35]

While the question Rodgers posed is about water *imagery*, Greenaway's response is alert to both the visual and acoustic properties of water – 'fantastically photogenic', water is a shape-shifter characterized also by its chameleon-like acoustic qualities – splashing, dribbling, roaring, all of which are exploited in the film. Thus while water visually dominates *Prospero's Books*, it is also omnipresent acoustically, from the opening bathing/pissing scene to the final drowning of the books. Greenaway creates a series of ambient sounds of enclosed watery spaces, including the Bathhouse and Caliban's pit, which results in an echoic and reverberant soundscape. As Barry Truax defines it, reverberation is the result of 'multiple reflections. A sound wave in an enclosed or semi-enclosed environment will be broken up as it is bounced back and forth among the reflecting surfaces. Reverberation is, in effect, a multiplicity of echoes whose speed of repetition is too quick for them to be perceived as separate from one another'.[36] In its multiplicity, reverberation might be seen as the acoustic counterpoint to the layering of visual images that renders the experience of Greenaway's work multiple and simultaneous as much as sequential.

While Nyman's scoring has been the acoustic element that has received the most attention in critical work on Greenaway's films, Garth Marshall's inventive production sounds are at least as important in establishing the aural dimensions of the film. Indeed, the intertwining of sound and score, and the difficulty in distinguishing between them, is a key feature in Greenaway's unusual use of sound and music. Greenaway begins the film with a deliberately sparse and miniaturized soundscape that belies the coming cacophonous use of sound. There is no underscoring at all until several minutes into the film; instead a gradual and intense build-up of sound marks the opening eight minutes of the film.

The opening shots of the film isolate three sounds that will be placed in continual play: water,

the scratch of pen on paper (a 'delightful sound', as Greenway remarks in *Watching Water*)[37] and the human voice, or, more specifically, Gielgud's voicing of Prospero. In contrast to the cacophony that characterizes much of the film, the very early 'establishing sounds'[38] in *Prospero's Books* are almost miniaturized, and the first few minutes of the film are noteworthy for their spareness and the isolation. Cut with the opening credits, a water drop is seen in extreme close-up and in slightly slowed motion. As it falls, we hear the distinct and amplified sound of a water drop. Michel Chion terms this sort of effect an 'acoustic close-up', arguing that the soundtrack acts like a close-up in 'diminishing all competing sounds within the mix and punctuating the contrast of volume and texture within the soundscape.'[39] The combination of the close association of the framing of the shot and the amplified sound of the water-drop acts as a 'synchresis', an example of the weld between the auditory and the visual that is of particular interest to Chion. In this case, sound and image have an apparently mimetic relationship, since the distinct sound of the drop matches the expectations established by the visual close-up of the water drop. That is, despite its obviously constructed nature – no water drop has ever sounded so distinct – the weld seems natural, a sound effect of the sort that is customary and expected in mainstream cinema. Yet Greenaway's use here of mimetic sound is simply a means of setting up the startling discontinuities between sound and image that are soon to come.

As the opening sequence continues, the scratch of pen on paper is heard, a normally indistinct and 'small' sound that is here given acoustic prominence. Like the water drop, this sound is isolated and welded with an image, in this case that of a quill moving over a piece of parchment. Gielgud's

---

35 Marlene Rodgers in *Peter Greenaway: Interviews*.
36 Truax, reverberation.htm
37 Greenaway, *Watching Water*, p. 42.
38 Rick Altman, *Sound Theory Sound Practice*, p. 250.
39 Chion, *Audio-Vision*, p. 95.

famous magisterial voice now is heard voicing the words on the parchment: 'Knowing I lov'd my books.' As is well known, Gielgud voices the entire script, up until the moment that Ariel (or the Ariels) urge Prospero's 'affections' to become 'tender' towards his enemies. The superimposition of the sound of writing with the image of the first words of *The Tempest*, 'Boatswain', and the *Book of Water* has been described by Greenaway himself as part of the disjunction of sound, image and text:

The first word of the play is 'Bosun', which is a very interesting word because it is one that is never written down. It was used by seamen who were basically illiterate, so that when they came to write the word down it was 'boatswain'. It's a nice opening point about the topsy-turvy use of oral and written language.[40]

As Amy Lawrence suggests, 'the pre-credit sequence is an idyllic moment where words-as-sound and words-as-image coexist, the image playfully intertwined with the word, the voice with music'.[41] The concept of watery beginnings and generation is also represented through the 'synchresis' of the image of the inkwell and the slight ring of the quill against its sides as it dips into the watery fluid, which David Pascoe describes as 'the sap that nourishes the images and permits the spectacle to develop'.[42]

As the film continues, these distinct and miniaturized sounds begin to interplay with louder, indistinct and less identifiable noises and a growing tension develops between foreground and background sound. No longer is it possible to identify sounds clearly, as they are not welded to images with the mimetic precision that characterize the first few minutes of film. The rhythmic sound of the water-drop acts as a form of acoustic punctuation, fading slightly as it acts as a counterpoint to an emerging new set of sounds. These include the sounds of writing, the joyful and reverberant voices and laughter of Prospero and Ariel as they 'savour' the word *Boatswain*, along with unidentifiable low rumbling sounds, claps of thunder, rainfall, pissing, howling and the rhythmic tolling of the mariner's bell.[43] Having painstakingly associated sound and image in the early shots through acous-

tic and visual close-up, Greenaway rapidly destabilizes these connections, layering filmed image, digital overlays and effects, Nyman's score, and an increasingly cacophonous array of sounds.

In the film script published after the release, Greenaway explicitly identifies Prospero's magic as acoustic:

At once, far off . . . begins a rumbling, droning noise – like a thousand distant flying machines . . . It is not one sound but many sounds combined. This is the sound of Prospero's magic. It always precedes every act of magic that Prospero performs and is the slow prelude – ever increasing in noise – that always prefaces a massive burst of aggressively musical sound when the peak of magic is attained.'[44]

Greenaway's description points to the complexity of the acoustic framework of the film. As he disrupts the visual field, so he re-imagines the acoustic field, eschewing the traditional division between so-called 'on-screen' and 'off-screen' sound, otherwise described as 'diegetic' and 'non-diegetic'. Traditionally, in cinema, 'diegetic' sounds are associated with production sounds, as well as with music that clearly proceeds from an identifiable source within the fiction of the film. If cinema-goers watch a couple dancing to music played on screen by an orchestra or radio, the music is diegetic, as are any other mimetic production sounds such as the rustle of a dress or applause. If the couple instead dances outside in a field, with no source of music apparent within the film's fiction, the audience understands the music heard as underscoring and does not understand it as part of the fiction. This expectation can be played with by the director, as when in the 1935 Reinhardt-Dieterle *Midsummer Night's Dream*,

[40] Adam Barker, 'A Tale of Two Magicians', *Sight and Sound* n.s. I (1991), 27–30; p. 28.

[41] Amy Lawrence, *The Films of Peter Greenaway* (Cambridge, 1991), p. 142.

[42] David Pascoe, *Peter Greenaway: Museums and Moving Images* (London, 1997), p. 191.

[43] Peter Greenaway, *Prospero's Books: A Film of Shakespeare's* The Tempest (London, 1991), p. 43.

[44] Greenaway, *Prospero's Books*, p. 43.

a gnome orchestra is discovered to be playing Mendelssohn's famous score within the cinematic frame. Because of the complexity and indeterminacy of its fictional frame, sound in *Prospero's Books* cannot be categorized according to this neat distinction between diegetic and non-diegetic sound. Indeed the very terms have been critiqued as a 'dichotomous schema' that reduces the complexity of the relationship between sound and space.[45] In both *The Tempest* and *Prospero's Books*, the emphasis upon magic and upon Prospero's and Ariel's ability to manipulate their acoustic environments renders futile attempts to map sound and score onto a simple diegetic/non-diegetic framework. Such neat polarities fail to account for a sonic environment that depends precisely upon the elusive nature of sound and the overdetermination of its relationship with the image.

The acoustic nature of Prospero's magic in Greenaway's film means that the traditional distinction between soundtrack and score is deliberately violated. Nyman's music is marked by a high degree of repetition and cyclic movements. In this film, the production sounds mimic the repetition and rhythm of the score. Normally soundtrack/score is mapped onto the non-diegetic/diegetic dichotomy. However, in the film the use of rhythmic production sounds such as the tolling of bells, metallic hammering, dripping water and skipping rope mimic and continue the patterns set up by Nyman's score, which are in turn disrupted by disjunctive and unidentifiable non-rhythmic sounds.

By the time Nyman's underscoring is introduced, about four minutes into the film, Greenaway and Marshall have already established a rich and at times confusing sonic environment. The 'sound of magic' is not located within a specific agent and resists attempts to contain and identify it. Indeed, the famously long tracking shot of Prospero walking through his palace is notable for its deliberate confusion of score and soundtrack. The crescendo of sound begins with Prospero's command to 'use your authority', and the cacophony of thunder and the mariner's bells gives

way to Nyman's extraordinary and mesmerizing score. But both score and sound refuse to be confined either within or without the fictional frame. The dancers move in time to Nyman's score, placing the underscoring within the fiction of the film as assuredly as the production sounds. Nyman's score recedes at 8:44 or thereabouts, yet the dance continues to its now silent rhythm. At the same time, sounds that mimic that rhythm are heard, such as hammering, as are strange and indistinguishable sounds that contribute to a rich yet indeterminate soundscape.

Yet Greenaway is not simply reproducing the sounds of Shakespeare. The decision to imagine Prospero's magic as acoustic has important implications for the representation of sound elsewhere in the film. While these sounds have affinities with the repeated calls for 'strange' and 'confused, hollow' sounds in Shakespeare's play, they do not simply imitate the sounds heard in *The Tempest*, but instead cinematically re-imagine and reposition that soundscape within the cinematic frame. Put simply, both the visual and the acoustic fields are so dense and crowded that Greenaway can only represent rupture through a sudden reduction in those fields. The best example of this strategy can be found in the masque sequence, which provides a set-piece of superabundance of visual and verbal spectacle. In the play, the masque is interrupted by Prospero's sudden 'start', followed by the famous stage direction: *To a strange, hollow and confused noise, the spirits in the pageant heavily vanish* (4.1.142 SD). Such discordance balances the elaborate song of Juno and Ceres, as well as the 'graceful dance' of the Nymphs and reapers just preceding. However, given the set of associations Greenaway establishes among music, noise and magic, the logic of the soundscape of *Prospero's Books* cannot support an increase in the level of sound or confusion at this point. Instead, Greenaway uses a simple device: Gielgud's voice intones 'I had forgot that the foul conspiracy' (4.1.139). His lines freeze the actors, and the distinct tolling of a single bell is heard, a

---

45 Kassabian, *Hearing Film*, p. 42.

sound distinct from the tinnier and more frantic mariner's bell heard earlier. As Gielgud begins to utter the famous 'Our revels are now ended' speech (4.1.148), the unusual spareness of the acoustic framework is mirrored by a gradual reduction in the visual field. Followed by Ferdinand and Miranda, Prospero advances to the camera, slowly, in time to the bell. As he moves into a medium shot, a curtain is abruptly drawn behind him, cutting Miranda and Ferdinand out of the field. The lines 'We are such stuff as dreams are made on' are directed in medium close-up directly to the camera, and the speech is framed both visually and acoustically by the curtain, which draws attention to the theatricality of the scene. Thus the relationship of film and play is constructed not mimetically, through a reproduction of the sounds of the theatre, but relationally, through manipulating the cinematic soundscape.

The final sequences of the film are equally inventive in their use of sound. Prospero's abjuring of his 'rough magic' and his promise to 'drown his books' are marked by a simultaneous use of the production sounds of the slamming shut of books and Nyman's score. As the water drops punctuated the beginning of the film, the slamming books punctuate the end. It is in the book-drowning sequence that Greenaway plays with the use of 'synchresis' and shows the constructed nature of Chion's world. Greenaway is known for his revision of the ending of *The Tempest*, especially for his decision for Caliban to rescue the drowning books. As Prospero flings the books into the water space of the pool, Greenaway and Marshall play with synchresis by welding the image of the books with the sound of breaking glass, explicitly demonstrating the non-natural relationship of image and sound.

In many ways Greenaway is among the least likely of British directors to undertake an adaptation of a Shakespearian play, that complex admixture of homage and rivalry more usually associated with the work of Laurence Olivier and Kenneth Branagh. Greenaway is known for his persistent and vitriolic critique of the enslavement of cinema to narrative conventions born of print. 'Most cinema is illustrated text' is a statement Greenaway has repeated numerous times over the past decade.[46] While it might at first glance seem contradictory to have adapted a Shakespearian text, *The Tempest* is perhaps a special case. Greenaway was attracted to it in part because of its lack of plot: in this late play, he suggests, 'Shakespeare begins to eschew narrative'.[47] In the absence of the need to reproduce the narrative modes of another, alien, medium Greenaway instead re-imagines the text as a native cinematic artifact. And this in turn involves much more than a simple translation of the verbal into the visual; indeed, for a director such as Greenaway, listening to *The Tempest* requires a re-imagination of acoustic cinematic techniques and vocabularies. The result is a profound revision of the relationships among word, sound, music, text and image.

---

[46] See, for example, this interview given to the BBC on 22 February 2002: 'Cinema is Dead, Says Greenaway' http://news.bbc.co.uk/1/hi/entertainment/1835469.stm. This was also Greenaway's argument in the unpublished keynote speech to CENDEAC on 25 November 2006.

[47] Rodgers, 'Prospero's Books', p. 148.

LEND ME YOUR EARS:
SAMPLING BBC RADIO SHAKESPEARE

MICHAEL P. JENSEN

The British Broadcasting Corporation's first Shakespeare radio programme was on 16 February 1923.[1] Since then, the Corporation's output has been too vast, the numbers of people involved too large, and the variety of shows too varied for this article to give more than a sampling. We can see the broad outlines of this work by considering three carefully chosen directors whose Shakespeare productions seem intrinsically interesting, and noting the range of broadcasts they produced.

Critics have lately problematized an old and simple concept, that of retelling stories, in this case stories created for the stage retold on radio. Perhaps they are correct to do this, for adaptations take on different characteristics over time, in different media, at the hands of different adapters, and as Courtney Lehmann points out, there are vastly different degrees of adaptation.[2] For the sake of simplicity, I mean here by *adaptation* what the BBC and its directors usually mean when they use the word: putting a more or less full-length Shakespeare play on the radio, with adjustments made for time and radio's non-visual needs.

The BBC was the first to broadcast Shakespeare, and has done so more than anyone else. The US had several broadcasts in the nineteen twenties and two short Shakespeare series in the thirties, but the plays all but disappeared by the nineteen fifties, except for the annual broadcasts by the Oregon Shakespeare Festival on the National Broadcasting Company and National Public Radio. Canada could boast of the first North American Shakespeare broadcast, and there were regular productions in the nine-teen thirties, forties, fifties and nineties.[3] Australia may be the first country to produce the canon as it was then constituted, which they did from 1936–8. These ninety-minute broadcasts had impressive ratings, but future shows were sporadic.[4] The BBC has produced multiple Shakespeare broadcasts nearly every year since the beginning.

The Corporation had a Shakespeare unit in the earliest years, run by Cecil A. Lewis with Cathleen Nesbitt as the principal adapter and star. Though he stayed on for two more years as Program Advisor, Lewis left his regular duties in 1926.[5] The unit was soon replaced by a staff of directors who might produce a Dickens novel for radio, followed by a

---

[1] For a description of this show, see Asa Briggs's *The History of Broadcasting in the United Kingdom, Volume 1: The Birth of Broadcasting* (Oxford, 1961), p. 256. Alan Beck's alternative claim may be found at www.kent.ac.uk/sdfva/invisible/shakes.htm.

[2] See her introduction to the section of Shakespeare film adaptations in Richard Burt, ed., *Shakespeares After Shakespeare: An Encyclopedia of the Bard in Mass Media and Popular Culture*, 2 vols. (Westport, Connecticut, 2007), vol. 1, pp. 74–9. While Lehmann, pp. 75–8, shows how varied adaptations are and that this variety compromises the meaning of the word, her well-meant attempt to create new labels to identify different types of adaptation may be doomed for the same reason – adaptations are too varied to be contained in her new categories.

[3] For Michael P. Jensen's descriptions of most US and Canadian programmes, see Burt, *Shakespeares After Shakespeare*, vol. 2, pp. 508–84.

[4] K. S. Inglis, *This is the ABC: The Australian Broadcasting Commission 1932–1983* (Melbourne, 1983), p. 53.

[5] Briggs, *History of Broadcasting*, p. 358.

Shakespeare play, followed by a Jane Austen adaptation. They often created their own programmes, but also took on whatever the Head of Drama assigned them. It just happens that some directed a lot of Shakespeare, even if they did not think of themselves as Shakespeare directors. Until recent decades, directors were usually their own producers or, to turn it around, producers directed their own shows, with only occasional exceptions.[6] One of these producers was Mary Hope Allen.

Allen began her radio career in 1927, after reviewing theatre for the *Weekly Westminster Gazette* and the *Manchester Guardian*. She read through every play in the then repertoire to judge which were suitable for radio. That done, she began to write programmes, and later directed the programmes she wrote, though Herbert Farjeon became the main writer for her broadcast team during the war. Farjeon was critical of the BBC's Shakespeare adaptations in his reviews for *The Listener*; so the Corporation hired him to do better.[7]

Allen did not give up writing. She was the producer of J. B. Priestley's wartime broadcasts, which led to an intimate relationship with him and collaboration on the play *Good Night Children* (1942), which Evans calls 'a satirical comment on the establishment of Broadcasting'.[8]

Allen's first producing assignments were not for the Drama Division, but for the Features unit, which allowed a degree of creativity that the Drama did not share. Features was to experiment with the possibilities of radio, finding new ways to create and mix sound, new kinds of stories to tell and innovative ways to tell them. The showcase was *The Experimental Hour*. Her first Shakespeare broadcast shared the second episode.[9]

Allen and Barbara Burnham co-directed the 1937 episode, *Take Your Choice: Twelfth Night*. The choice is modern or early modern performance. 1.5 is spoken in modern English with women acting the female roles, followed by the same scene in early modern accents with men playing all the parts. It is likely that Allen directed one segment and Burnham the other. The cast included Carleton

Hobbs as Malvolio in both parts, an actor Allen would use repeatedly over the years. Despite the programme's title, the broadcast was thirty minutes long.

Allen put a touring production of *Twelfth Night* on the air in 1943. The Council for the Encouragement of Music and Arts was created to make sure that Britain had ballet, opera and drama despite the many resources diverted to fight the Second World War. Shows were staged in camps for soldiers and in cities for civilian audiences. Some of these programmes were abridged on the series *From the Theatre in War-Time*. The script was by Walter Hudd, the stage director who also played Malvolio. Allen produced from the Theatre Royal, Bristol.

Head of Drama Val Gielgud merged the Feature and Drama Divisions as Britain became more deeply involved in the war, essentially eliminating Features and many feature broadcasts to make time for war news.[10] The BBC had produced two or three full-length plays a week, but for the duration

---

6 An obvious exception is any programme with multiple producers, such as the 1943 *Peer Gynt* mentioned below. This probably accounts for the confusion over who directed it. For an overview of how BBC radio Shakespeare evolved, see Susanne Greenhalgh, 'Shakespeare overheard: performances, adaptations, and citations on radio', in Robert Shaughnessy, ed., *The Cambridge Companion to Shakespeare and Popular Culture* (Cambridge, 2007). See especially, pp. 175–88.

7 Farjeon had a varied career. In addition to writing for Allen, according to Amy Scott-Douglass, he published the Nonesuch Press editions of Shakespeare's works and managed the Little Theatre in London. See Burt, *Shakespeares After Shakespeare*, vol. 2, p. 802.

8 Gareth Lloyd Evans, *J. B. Priestley – the Dramatist* (London: 1964), p. 153. Evans adds that the play 'hardly raises itself above the level of an idle entertainment'. Evans nowhere acknowledges Allen's hand in the play, which is typical of surveys of Priestley's work.

9 *The Experimental Hour* was inspired by *The Columbia Workshop* on the Columbia Broadcasting System in the United States. *Workshop* ran from 1936–42, and was revived under the title *CBS Radio Workshop* from 1946–7. There is more on *The Columbia Workshop* below. For the BBC's debt to the CBS series, see Val Gielgud, *British Radio Drama 1922–1956* (London, 1957), p. 69.

10 Gielgud, *British Radio Drama*, p. 69.

there were only several a year. Short versions were presented instead, usually in abridgements of an hour or less. For Shakespeare, this meant concentrating on part of a play with the stories retitled to reflect this change. Programmes such as *Henry at Agincourt* (1939), *Put out the Light* (1939),[11] *Prospero's Island: Scenes from The Tempest* (1940) and *This is Illyria, Lady* (1940) are examples.

Though it came late in the cycle, 1943, Allen made a series that used this approach. Each episode of *Shakespeare's Characters* featured the scenes of just one character, or paired characters in the cases of Rosencrantz and Guildenstern and Touchstone and Audrey, plus added context. Stories usually involved important minor characters, such as Capulet, or major characters from a subplot, such as Beatrice. This allowed the economy of small casts, and running times of thirty minutes. Herbert Farjeon made sure that any loose ends were tied. Unusually, some episodes were presented on the BBC proper, now called the Home Service, while others were presented on their new General Forces Programme, for the armed forces. This was not the BBC's first series dramatizing Shakespeare's characters. That was *Shakespeare's Heroines* in 1926.

The total number of episodes has eluded researchers since the show did not have a regular time slot to check. We know there were at least sixteen episodes, possibly more, including three certain repeats, but the characters in only twelve episodes have been identified.

We know what these shows were probably like. The *Radio Times* listing for 9 April 1944 indicates that the supporting characters in the *Polonius* episode are Hamlet (Marius Goring), Ophelia (Sarah Jackson) and Gertrude (Lydia Sherwood), but there is no mention of Claudius, Laertes, Reynaldo or the Player-King. The listing for the *Capulet* episode (20 February 1946) mentions Paris (Lewis Stringer) and members of the Capulet household, but not Romeo. Assuming the listings are correct, these programmes do not attempt to cover the plots of the plays, or even the complete stories of the featured characters. Since Capulet (Carleton Hobbs) does not interact directly with

Romeo, Romeo is cut. References to him must have been handled by the narrator (Leslie Stokes). Listeners do not hear Polonius (John Ruddock) lecturing Laertes, or interact with Claudius, putting the emphasis on his scenes with his daughter, the verbal abuse received from Hamlet, and the scene in Gertrude's closet.

The series must have been well received, because Allen's Shakespeare output increased. She made full-length adaptations of *Romeo and Juliet*, *As You Like It*, *King John*, *Julius Caesar* and *The Tempest* between 1944 and 1945, all adapted by Farjeon.

The influence of *Shakespeare's Characters* on these full-length adaptations must be a matter of speculation until more is known about the series, but two episodes are confirmed to have preceded their adaptations. *King John* aired a few months after the *Faulconbridge* episode. The cast featured many of the actors Allen used before in the same roles. For example, Carleton Hobbs played the King and Norman Shelley was Hubert in both programmes. Aside from using fuller scripts, the main difference between these shows is that the longer programmes allowed Allen to import a star; so Ralph Richardson replaced Robert Speaight as the Bastard. *As You Like It* followed *Touchstone and Audrey* by three months. John Ruddock and Eileen Beldon played these roles in both broadcasts, but since the *Shakespeare's Character's* episode had few of the major characters from the play, Allen did a lot of new casting. She mostly used her usual contract actors, but cast stars Michael Redgrave as Orlando and Edith Evans as Rosalind.

The Tempest closed out this cycle of adaptations. The script, as usual, was by Farjeon, who died between finishing it and the broadcast. The play used to be thought of as Shakespeare's farewell to the theatre. In an unintended sense, this was Farjeon's farewell.

As *Shakespeare's Characters* ended its original run, Allen produced *O Rare Ben Jonson* (1945), a dramatic biography of Jonson (Arthur Young) written

---

[11] Gielgud, *British Radio Drama*, p. 98, says that he directed these two, and identifies them as 'the Agincourt sequence from *King Henry V*, and the final act of *Othello*'.

by L. A. G. Strong, with a number of early moderns as supporting characters, including Shakespeare (Hobbs), Inigo Jones (Alexander Soafer), Francis Beaumont (Sebastian Cabot), James Shirley (Roger Snowdon) and John Marston (Malcolm Greame). *Shakespeare's Country* was two years later, a biographical play that took Shakespeare through his early days in London. Anthony Marlowe was the young Shakespeare.[12]

Allen did less Shakespeare after this, but stayed busy with other projects, including returning occasionally to experimental radio. The experiments with Shakespeare capture different aspects of her first Shakespeare assignment. *Hamlet: The Closet Scene* (1947) runs 3.4 three times: in English, French and Spanish. A 1949 programme called *The Elizabethan Tongue* is 45 minutes of excerpts from Shakespeare pronounced the way scholars think the language sounded in Shakespeare's time.

There were three later adaptations from Shakespeare. At 75 minutes, *King John* (1947) was a shortened version of the play Allen had produced at twice the length in 1944. Carleton Hobbs and Norman Shelley were back in their familiar roles, and jobbing but gifted actor Howard Marion-Crawford replaced Richardson as the Bastard. M. R. Ridley wrote narration to cover the cuts, which was read by Christopher Pemberton. Allen directed Christopher Marlowe's *Tamberlaine, the Great* the same year.

It was nearly five years before Allen's next Shakespeare production, a remounting of *The Tempest*. This is the second of three times John Gielgud played Prospero on the radio,[13] and others in the cast were also impressive: Leon Quatermaine, Hugh Manning, Leslie French, William Devlin and Eric Porter, amongst them.[14] Farjeon's old script was used again. Allen's last Shakespeare work was an adaptation of *All's Well That Ends Well* in 1954, which she adapted herself. Irene Worth led the cast.

Allen produced other shows until her retirement in 1958. That retirement was busy for many years, as she worked for the BBC on a freelance basis, most notably on a series of adaptations from Henry James that lasted well into the nineteen seventies.

Allen lived through the entire twentieth century, born in 1898 and dying in 2001.[15]

Allen's *From the Theatre in Wartime* episode was one of the BBC's infrequent broadcasts of staged Shakespeare. The only theatres to have long associations with the BBC are The Shakespeare Memorial Theatre (now called The Royal Shakespeare Company)[16] and The Old Vic. John Burrell did not have a notable radio career, but he is interesting for the purpose of this article: his broadcasts run the gamut of how theatre companies were put on the air. He was a director of The Old Vic for five years.

The word 'Company' was added to Old Vic when damage to the roof by German bombs forced the theatre to close and the Old Vic Company relocated to the New Theatre (now the Albery) in the West End.[17] 1944–9 are the years of what is usually called the triumvirate, for the Company was led by Burrell, Laurence Olivier and Ralph Richardson. It is when the latter two played some of their most renowned roles. Richardson put his indelible stamp on Peer Gynt and Falstaff. Olivier was Richard III, Hotspur, Shallow, plus Oedipus and Mr Puff in the double bill of Sophocles and

---

[12] Though this programme is not extant, the script is in the BBC Written Archives, Caversham, Reading. The name of the writer is given only as Blair, according to Eve-Marie Oesterlen of the British Universities Film and Video Council, whose assistance with research for this article has been great and is greatly appreciated.

[13] The others were broadcast on 22 February 1931 and 20 December 1948.

[14] Unfortunately, neither *The Times* nor the BBC Programme Catalogue lists which parts these actors played.

[15] Biographical information on Allen was drawn from Vincent Brome, *J. B. Priestley* (London, 1988), and the superb obituary in *The Independent* (London) by Julian Potter, found at http://findarticles.com/p/articles/mi_qn4158/is_20010410/ai_n14380779. Allen's only known extant Shakespeare productions are the adaptations of *Romeo and Juliet*, *As You Like It* and the 1953 *Tempest*. These are held in the BBC Sound Archive.

[16] The earliest broadcast found is *Much Ado About Nothing* in 1936.

[17] J. C. Trewin and Stanley Wells, *The Pocket Companion to Shakespeare's Plays* (London, 2005), p. 192.

Sheridan. Burrell is nearly forgotten, remembered, if remembered, for staging some of these shows. To understand Burrell's radio work, we must know what happened with the Old Vic Company under the triumvirate.

Burrell trained with Michel Saint-Denis, and worked briefly at small theatres before joining the BBC. He assisted BBC director Peter Creswell with a production of *Peer Gynt* that featured Richardson as Peer, in an adaptation by Tyrone Guthrie.[18] As for directing, the few dramas listed in the BBC Programme Catalogue are all non-Shakespearian, though he directed Ben Jonson's *Volpone* in 1944, which the Catalogue missed. There seems to be only one Shakespeare programme, *Shakespeare's Birthday* (1942), described as honouring Shakespeare, broadcast on the traditional date of his birth, 23 April. It featured Peggy Ashcroft, Robert Donat, Edith Evans and Ralph Richardson again. The show was 'devised' by Audrey Jones with Shakespeare credited as the writer, so we know that the actors read excerpts from some plays or poems, though they may have done more. There is no other information about the content, but the Catalogue states that the show went out on the BBC World Service, so it was programming intended to help define Britain's image to the world. Richardson worked with Burrell on other broadcasts,[19] and requested that Burrell round out the directorship of the Vic, despite his relative inexperience. The Company had a recurring radio presence during the years of the triumvirate, appearing five times. Burrell had some kind of participation in four of these broadcasts, even if he was just the stage director of a show broadcast by another.

Creating original radio content was unusual for a theatre company. Most of them broadcast productions at the end of their runs or a couple of scenes to tempt potential audiences. The Vic produced new content beginning with their first programme, a 1934 *Merchant of Venice*, and did so again with Burrell's first broadcast for the Vic.

That show was delayed because of the war — the end of the war. An eight episode serial of both parts of *Henry IV* was scheduled to begin on

10 May 1945, but the German surrender occasioned a replacement variety programme celebrating the Allied victory, so the start date was pushed back. It aired Thursdays from 31 May to 19 July.

The adapter was Robert Gittings, who in an article in the 4 May *Radio Times* wrote that his challenges were to make the themes of these plays come across and give the comedy room to work, while keeping the historical setting clear. To do this, he dropped and transposed scenes to focus on certain characters, and added a narrator to guide the audience to where he wanted them to go. Richardson was Falstaff, and Olivier narrated, which is interesting because he had just played the Prince Hal/Henry V character to acclaim in a motion picture. Other roles were filled by members of the Old Vic Company, including Michael Ware as Hal. Burrell directed. He was also the stage director when the plays opened at the New two months after the end of the series, 26 September (*Part 1*) and 3 October (*Part 2*). Richardson and Ware repeated their roles, while Olivier took Hotspur and Shallow.[20] The series was an event at the time, but has been long forgotten. Scholars still write only about the stage version.[21]

Though it briefly takes us away from the BBC, the next Old Vic broadcasts were unusual in reviving retired productions. An offer came while the Company was on tour in the United States. *Peer Gynt* (staged by Tyrone Guthrie) and

---

18 This broadcast is commercially available as a bonus feature on the BBC's *Henrick Ibsen Collection* of television adaptations, released on DVD in 2007. Burrell is not mentioned in the on-air credits.

19 In addition to the two just mentioned, Burrell directed Richardson as the title character in a seven part adaptation of *The Adventures of Don Quixote* in 1944.

20 Dates and casting for Old Vic shows are found in Audrey Williamson, *Old Vic Saga: A Twelve Years' Study of Plays and Players* (London, 1948), and *Old Vic Saga 2: 1947–1957* (London, 1957). Williamson gives excellent contemporary commentaries on the strengths and weaknesses of these productions.

21 For two examples, see Herbert and Judith Weil, *The First Part of King Henry IV* (Cambridge, 1997), pp. 47–8, and Scott McMillin, *Henry IV, Part One* (Manchester, 1991), pp. 14–34.

Richard III (by Burrell) opened at the New in 1944. They toured, and were eventually taken off the boards for new work. On a 1946 trip to New York to present the *Henry IV* plays, *Uncle Vanya* and the double bill of Sophocles and Sheridan, the Company was asked to do two broadcasts for *The Columbia Workshop*. They chose *Peer Gynt* and *Richard III* because they had been successful on stage, and old shows would not discourage audiences from attending the current productions. The one hour programme expanded to ninety minutes for these broadcasts.

Burrell was running things in London and did not participate in these shows, which were handled by CBS staff director Richard Sanville. Actors still with the company repeated their stage roles. Burrell is credited as the stage director of *Richard III* on the air, though some of his innovative touches, such as putting a silent Jane Shore on stage in some scenes, could not be effectively duplicated in the voice-only medium.[22] Audiences were small, but the broadcasts were highly regarded.

1947 was an off year and the Old Vic board was not happy. Olivier was away filming *Hamlet* (released in 1948) and Richardson was making money in Hollywood. The board complained that the Vic was losing prestige as a result of its star attractions being away for extended periods. To placate the governors, Alec Guinness was promoted from featured to leading actor, and Richardson returned to direct him and take the role of John of Gaunt in *Richard II*. Guinness himself called his performance a 'partly plagiarized, third-rate imitation of Gielgud's definitive Richard'.[23] The BBC treated it as an event, recording the Company for broadcast under Burrell's direction. The programme was presented at the same hour that the show opened at the New Theatre. The only known accommodations for broadcasting are that Richardson introduced the play, and interrupted the action to read the stage directions. This was presumably done in order to relate the action that listeners could not see, but was inadequate because the stage directions do not describe everything, and certainly do not describe Richardson's blocking. The stage notices were mixed, but the show was popular enough to be revived at the New Theatre the next year, though without Richardson, who was away again.

BBC news and magazine shows cover theatre openings to this day. Burrell's last programme was a half-hour special featuring his stage production of *The Taming of the Shrew* for the Vic's 1947–8 season. Olivier and Richardson were not seen that year, so film star Trevor Howard was cast as Petruccio in another attempt to keep the governors happy. The pre-London opening was at the first Edinburgh Festival. The BBC covered it in a production entitled *The Old Vic at Edinburgh* (1947), which featured interviews with some cast members who performed excerpts from the play. Burrell did not direct the broadcast. That was handled by Ayton Whitaker.

The contracts of the triumvirate were not renewed. Guthrie blamed this on a combination of Olivier and Richardson's prolonged absences, and Burrell's inability to run things effectively when they were gone.[24] Shortly after leaving the Vic, Richardson suggested that Burrell be hired to direct Ruth and Augustus Goetz's adaptation of *The Heiress* from Henry James's *Washington Square*, to feature Richardson and Peggy Ashcroft. Burrell was fired five days before the road opening for muddling the blocking, and John Gielgud was brought in to rescue the production.[25] Burrell came to the United States, where he directed *Peter Pan* on Broadway in 1950, founded the Academy of the ill-fated Shakespeare Festival Theatre in Stratford, Connecticut and worked for CBS

---

[22] For a comparison of what this broadcast does and does not share with Olivier's film, and some briefer comments comparing it to Burrell's stage production, see Michael P. Jensen, 'Olivier's *Richard III* on Radio', *Shakespeare Newsletter* 54:4 (2004–5), pp. 101–2.

[23] Alec Guinness, *Blessings in Disguise* (New York, 1986), p. 20. My thanks to Susanne Greenhalgh and Eve-Marie Oesterlen for helping me piece together the elusive facts about this broadcast.

[24] Tyrone Guthrie, *A Life in the Theatre* (New York, 1985 [1959]), pp. 226–7.

[25] Sheridan Morley, *John Gielgud: The Authorized Biography* (New York, 2002), pp. 223–4.

television. He ended his days teaching at the University of Illinois.[26]

If Burrell is better remembered for his work on stage than on the radio, Martin Jenkins is a consummate broadcaster, with many fascinating and prestigious programmes. He briefly joined the Royal Shakespeare Company in 1963 serving as an assistant director, and performing in *Julius Caesar* and John Barton's adaptation of the first tetralogy, *The Wars of the Roses*. He left the RSC and co-founded the Everyman Theatre in Liverpool with future RSC Artistic Director Terry Hands, building their reputation on new plays. Jenkins moved to the BBC in 1966. His radio productions are said to number more than one thousand, of which his Shakespeare work is a small fraction, but he has still managed to produce more Shakespeare than most radio directors, including some of the best work of the seventies and eighties.[27] Like Allen, Jenkins likes to use the same actors again and again, versatile performers with expressive voices.

His Shakespeare adaptations are virtually uncut, the scripts merely adjusted for radio's non-visual needs. Jenkins explained his ideas about audio adaptations to Janet Clare, who paraphrased them.

A minor adaptation will usually overcome any problems caused by the introduction of new characters. The quick succession of scenes in Renaissance drama . . . is an ideal framework for the aural medium. Radio, moreover, brings a particular performance into close focus; the soliloquy becomes a still more potent dramatic device . . . the visual element in modern productions can obscure the text.[28]

Jenkins has directed some of Shakespeare's best known works, starting with *Julius Caesar*, which Jenkins adapted himself (1972), *The Winter's Tale* (1982), *Macbeth* (1984) and *The Merchant of Venice* (1987). He added some plays that are rarely performed on the radio: *Titus Andronicus* (adapted by Jenkins, 1973), *Sir Thomas More* (1983)[29] and *All's Well That Ends Well* (1986).

He has a penchant for history plays. Both parts of *Henry IV* were broadcast a week apart in 1973, produced and cast as a unit. John Rowe was Hal.

Jenkins and Rowe returned to the character in a superb 1976 production of *Henry V*, which featured John Gielgud as the Chorus.

Though not conceived as a trilogy, these shows play that way, partly because of the consistent casting of Jenkins's regular actors such as Rowe, Peter Jeffrey and Julian Glover and partly because the shows have a cynical tone, an interpretation that was popular in the seventies, perhaps most famously in the 1975 RSC productions by Terry Hands. The close dates raise questions of influence between Hands and Jenkins that I have not yet been able to answer. By the time he produced *Henry V*, Jenkins had mastered aural drama. The container of tennis balls is heard opening in 1.2. There is a line followed by the sound of the King bouncing a ball three times, another line, two bounces more, the anger in Henry's voice growing as he delivers his next line. The entire programme shows this kind of thoughtful sound design.

Jenkins revisited these plays the next year in *VIVAT Rex*. The 26-part series covers 226 years of English history as told in several chronicle plays: Marlowe's *Edward II*, the perhaps semi-Shakespearian *Edward III*, the anonymous untitled play commonly called *Thomas of Woodstock*, *The Famous Victories of Henry V*, both of Shakespeare's tetralogies, John Ford's *Perkin Warbeck* and *Henry VIII* by Shakespeare and John Fletcher. Jenkins adapted every episode and directed most,

---

[26] The known extant broadcasts by Burrell mentioned in this article are *Shakespeare's Birthday*, *Peer Gynt*, *Richard III* and part 3 of *The Adventures of Don Quixote*. Also extant is *The Columbia Workshop* episode of *Peer Gynt* in which Burrell had no involvement.

[27] Facts about Jenkins's life are culled from a 30 June 2006 press release from the University of Liverpool announcing honorary degrees for Jenkins and others, and a BBC booklet by Robert Cushman, *VIVAT Rex* (London, 1977), p. 2.

[28] Janet Clare, 'Theatre of the Air: a Checklist of Radio Productions of Renaissance Drama, 1922–86, with an Introduction', *Renaissance Drama Newsletter*, University of Warwick, Supplement 6, 1986, p. 4.

[29] *The Times* (24 December 1983) implies that adapter Penny Gold directed the play, but does not say so plainly. The BBC Programme Catalogue confirms that Jenkins directed.

with director Gerry Jones handling direction of the rest.

Jenkins writes that his involvement in the RSC *Wars of the Roses* led to his fascination with English history plays. His description of how he adapted the texts for broadcast reads as if his process was similar to John Barton's as he prepared the first tetralogy for the RSC's production:

To condense these fourteen plays . . . involved a complete job of cutting and editing. Scenes have been transposed to give each episode an individual unity; numbers of smaller characters have been cut and others have been combined . . . to overcome some of the cutting and to highlight certain vital points in scenes of character development, it has been necessary to write several extra passages of verse.[30]

These plays are not independent. *Edward III* ends and *Thomas of Woodstock* begins in episode four. *Woodstock* ends and *Richard II* begins in episode five. Jenkins reshaped the originals, showing one reign rolling into the next. The cast features some of the most respected actors of that era, including Peggy Ashcroft, Richard Burton, Robert Hardy, Michael Redgrave, Diana Rigg, Paul Scofield and, in roles they would soon play for the *BBC Television Shakespeare*, Derek Jacobi as Richard II and Anthony Quayle as Falstaff.

Jenkins has been drawn to non-Shakespearian drama at other times. He broadcast *Volpone* in 1971, Thomas Middleton's *A Chaste Maid in Cheapside* in 1979 and Michael Drayton's *Sir John Oldcastle* in 1985, the first time the BBC broadcast the latter plays.

Jenkins has dabbled in other forms of Shakespeare broadcasting. The original radio play *An Epiphanous Use of the Microphone* (1998) was commissioned from David Pownall to celebrate the 75th anniversary of the BBC's first full-length dramatic broadcast, *Twelfth Night* in 1923. Pownall's script skips in time between preparations for the 1923 broadcast and the first performance of the play at the Inns of Court. He sets the Inns performance on a sultry evening, so the windows are open when

a gust of wind blows the candles out. The play is then heard very like a radio show with the actors conveying a woman dressed as a man and twins vocally, not visually. It is not just a tribute to the first broadcast, but a meditation on the nature of audio drama.[31]

Jenkins is not above conducting celebrity interviews, especially when they involve famous Shakespearians. The two episodes of *Sir John Gielgud in Conversation* featured the star discussing several of his Shakespearian roles in addition to other matters, with particular emphasis on Hamlet in part one. This was broadcast in 1975, the year before Jenkins cast Gielgud as the Chorus in *Henry V*.[32] Two years later came Peggy Ashcroft in the programme *Shakespeare and the Histories*, created to publicize *VIVAT Rex*.[33] She discusses playing Margaret in *The Wars of the Roses* and *VIVAT Rex*, noting the different techniques she uses for the stage and microphone. *See the Players Well Bestow'd* (1982) is described in the BBC Programme Catalogue as 'A celebration of the 50th anniversary of the Shakespeare Memorial Theatre in Stratford-upon-Avon and the opening of the Royal Shakespeare Company's new home at the Barbican in London.' Terry Hands contributed to the programme. Jenkins conducted these interviews in addition to directing the programmes. Jenkins was off microphone when he directed *Memories of Ralph Richardson*, which included Michael Meyer reading an excerpt from his book *I Am Not Prince Hamlet* (1986). Jenkins even wrote a Shakespeare documentary, *King Lear Thro' the Ages*, which examines the play's reception since its first performance. This was directed by Ian Cotterell, who also has an impressive résumé

---

[30] Cushman, *VIVAT Rex*, p. 2.

[31] The play is published in David Pownall's, *Radio Plays* (London, 1998).

[32] They worked together again in 1982 when Gielgud played Time in *The Winter's Tale*.

[33] The BBC Programme Catalogue gives the title as *Dame Peggy Ashcroft*, but the catalogue often lists celebrity interviews as if they are titled after the person interviewed. An episode of *VIVAT Rex* aired later that day.

of broadcasting Shakespeare and other early modern writers (1977).

After many years away from early modern drama, Jenkins revisited the play of his first Shakespeare broadcast, *Julius Caesar*, with a well-known American cast that included Richard Dreyfuss, Kelsey Grammer, Stacy Keach and JoBeth Williams. This co-production of the BBC, L.A. Theatre Works and KCRW Radio in Los Angeles was broadcast by the BBC in 1995. This was Jenkins's last Shakespearian production to date, though he is still an active broadcaster.

Without wishing to disparage Jenkins's Shakespeare work, which I admire, the times have perhaps passed him by. In his conversation with Clare, Jenkins said (in Clare's paraphrase) that radio is not 'a director's medium; there is no place for the exhibition of directorial inventiveness'.[34]

Yet, that is what current BBC Shakespeare broadcasters do. Director's radio Shakespeare is at least as old as Nigel Bryant's Caribbean flavoured *Twelfth Night* in 1995. The BBC's most recent series, *The BBC Radio Shakespeare* (1999–2001), has quite a bit of it, with a *Romeo and Juliet* (1999) that pointlessly adds car sounds and the grunting of Capulet and someone (who does not seem to be his wife) having sex. The imaginative *Othello* (2001) was also set in the twentieth century, with sound patterns that indicate jazz broadcasts, the Duke getting war news on a teletype, and Othello and Cassio speaking on the phone at the beginning of 2.3. Though the modern touches seem phony in *Romeo and Juliet*, they are thoughtfully integrated into *Othello*, focusing listener attention. These programmes are traditional in the way they adapt Shakespeare's dialogue, yet young directors add their own sensibility to the sound patterns. It is not what Mary Hope Allen, John Burrell and Martin Jenkins did, but it is the current state of BBC radio Shakespeare.[35]

RADIOGRAPHY

(All programmes were broadcast by the British Broadcasting Corporation unless otherwise indicated.)

ALLEN, MARY HOPE (DIRECTOR)[36]

The Experimental Hour – Take Your Choice: Twelfth Night (Co-director. 30 minutes. 6 December 1937)

From the Theatre in War-Time: Twelfth Night (30 minutes. 1 November 1943)

Shakespeare's Characters: Fluellen (30 minutes. 13 March 1944)

Shakespeare's Characters: Polonius (30 minutes. 9 April 1944)

Shakespeare's Characters: Hotspur (30 minutes. 7 May 1944)

Shakespeare's Characters: Touchstone and Audrey (30 minutes. 4 June 1944)

Romeo and Juliet (150 minutes. 30 June 1944)

Shakespeare's Characters: Beatrice (30 minutes. 2 July 1944)

Shakespeare's Characters: Faulconbridge (30 minutes. 30 July 1944)

Shakespeare's Characters: Rosencrantz and Guildenstern (30 minutes. 27 August 1944)

As You Like It (150 minutes. 8 September 1944)

---

[34] Clare, 'Theatre of the Air', p. 4.

[35] Probably all of Jenkin's early modern and Shakespeare related broadcasts are extant somewhere. Those I can confirm are *Volpone, Julius Caesar* (1972 and 1995), *1 and 2 Henry IV, Titus Andronicus, Sir John Gielgud in Conversation, Henry V, VIVAT Rex, Shakespeare and the Histories, King Lear Thro' the Ages, A Chaste Maid in Cheapside, The Winter's Tale, Sir Thomas More, Macbeth, Sir John Oldcastle* and *All's Well That Ends Well. Julius Caesar* (1972), *Henry V* and *The Winter's Tale* were released on cassette to schools in Australia by the Australian Broadcasting Commission in 1986. *Macbeth* was released commercially by the BBC in Britain and The Mind's Eye in the US in 1988. The 1995 *Julius Caesar* is currently available from L.A. Theatre Works.

[36] Clare, "Theatre of the Air," p. 32, lists Allen as the director of a production of *Macbeth* aired on 14 September 1942. If true, and if it is an adaptation, it would be her first. Neither the BBC Programme Catalogue nor *The Times* listings support this. Clare makes a number of errors, but presumably found something or would not have created the listing. For the sake of inclusion, this production is moved to this footnote. No Allen-directed broadcast of *Macbeth* has yet been found on another date.

Shakespeare's Characters: Emilia (30 minutes. 24 September 1944)

King John (145 minutes. 29 December 1944)

Julius Caesar (120 minutes. 9 February 1945)

The Tempest (130 minutes. 25 May 1945)

Shakespeare's Characters: Orsino (Probably a remounting; original air date unknown. 30 minutes. 5 August 1945)

O Rare Ben Jonson (40 minutes. 12 August 1945)

Shakespeare's Characters: Capulet (Probably a remounting; original air date unknown. 30 minutes. 20 February 1946)

Shakespeare's Characters: Sir Toby Belch (Probably a remounting; original air date unknown. 30 minutes. 14 July 1946)

Tamberlaine, the Great (Two episodes, 60 minutes each. 7 and 14 January 1947)

Shakespeare's Country (50 minutes. 23 April 1947)

Hamlet: The Closet Scene (25 minutes. 11 August 1947)

King John (75 minutes. 3 September 1947)

The Elizabethan Tongue (45 minutes. 28 December 1949)

The Tempest (116 minutes. 1 June 1953)

All's Well That Ends Well (150 minutes. 5 September 1954)

BRYANT, NIGEL (DIRECTOR)

Twelfth Night (145 minutes. *c.* 1995)

BURNHAM, BARBARA (DIRECTOR)

The Experimental Hour – Take Your Choice: Twelfth Night (Co-director. 30 minutes. 6 December 1937)

Prospero's Island: Scenes from The Tempest (45 minutes. 4 February 1940)

This is Illyria, Lady (60 minutes. 14 July 1940)

BURRELL, JOHN (PRODUCTION ASSISTANT/DIRECTOR/STAGE DIRECTOR)

Production Assistant

Peer Gynt (Peter Creswell, director. 173 minutes. 10 August 1943)[37]

Director

Shakespeare's Birthday (30 minutes. 23 April 1942)

Volpone (90 minutes. 19 March 1944)

The Adventures of Don Quixote (One 35 minute and six 30 minute episodes. 29 April–11 June 1944)

Henry IV (Eight 45 minute episodes. 31 May–19 July 1945)

Richard II (150 minutes. 23 April 1947)

Stage director

Richard III (Richard Sanville, dir. CBS Radio. 90 minutes. 2 June 1946)

The Old Vic at Edinburgh (director: Ayton Whitaker. 30 minutes. 2 September 1947)

GIELGUD, VAL (DIRECTOR)

Put out the Light (30 minutes. 12 February 1939)

Henry at Agincourt (55 minutes. 5 November 1939)

GUTHRIE, TYRONE (STAGE DIRECTOR)

Peer Gynt (Richard Sanville, dir. CBS Radio. 90 minutes. 9 June 1946)

JENKINS, MARTIN (DIRECTOR/AUTHOR)

Director

Volpone (120 minutes. 15 August 1971)

Julius Caesar (140 minutes. 30 July 1972)

1 Henry IV (170 minutes. 18 March 1973)

2 Henry IV (185 minutes. 25 March 1973)

Titus Andronicus (165 minutes. 28 October 1973)

Sir John Gielgud (30 and 20 minutes. 22 and 26 March 1976)

---

37 Garry O'Connor states that the programme was directed by Tyrone Guthrie in *Ralph Richardson: An Actor's Life* (New York, 1982), p. 110. The BBC Programme Catalogue disagrees. The programme survives in the BBC Sound Archive, which credits Guthrie as co-producer, which may be the source of confusion.

Henry V (195 minutes. 18 April 1976)

Shakespeare and the Histories (20 minutes. 19 June 1977)

VIVAT Rex (Twenty-six 55 minute episodes. 13 February to 7 August 1977)

A Chaste Maid in Cheapside (120 minutes. 24 June 1979)

The Winter's Tale (180 minutes. 21 January 1982)

Sir Thomas More (120 minutes. 25 December 1983)

Macbeth (130 minutes. 23 April 1984)

Sir John Oldcastle (115 minutes. 14 April 1985)

All's Well That Ends Well (135 minutes. 24 October 1986)

The Merchant of Venice (135 minutes. 3 July 1987)

Memories of Ralph Richardson (20 minutes. 17 December 1989)

An Epiphanous Use of the Microphone (58 minutes. 15 May 1998)

Julius Caesar (120 minutes. 26 February 1995)

Author

King Lear Thro' the Ages (Ian Cotterell, director. 85 minutes. 27 April 1977)

KAVANAUGH, PETER (DIRECTOR)

Romeo and Juliet (180 minutes. 19 September 1999)

LEWIS, CECIL A. (DIRECTOR)

Scenes from Shakespeare (30 minutes. 16 February 1923)

MORTIMER, JEREMY (DIRECTOR)

Othello (185 minutes. 30 September 2001)

ROSE, HOWARD (DIRECTOR)

Twelfth Night (135 minutes. 28 May 1923)

Much Ado About Nothing (105 minutes. 12 July 1936)

WOOD, CYRIL (DIRECTOR)

Merchant of Venice (30 minutes. 13 May 1934)

AN AGE OF KINGS AND THE 'NORMAL AMERICAN'

PATRICIA LENNOX

In the early 1960s the BBC television Shakespeare series, the fifteen-episode *An Age of Kings*, was a 'stupendous' success in America and England, seen by millions of viewers. It received England's prestigious British Guild of Directors award for Excellence in Directing. Broadcast in America by National Educational Television (NET) it received the Peabody Award for 'a brilliant and imaginative portrayal of Shakespeare's rich pageant of English history'. Its 'magnificent panoply' was 'the most exciting drama seen on television' in 'an extraordinary piece of work – marvelously made and presented with intelligence and dignity'.[1] Much loved, highly praised, *Kings* then seemed to disappear from memory for the next forty years, overshadowed by the more visually sophisticated filmed-for-television *The Wars of the Roses* (1964), the Royal Shakespeare Company's adaptation of the history plays,[2] and the BBC/Time-Life Shakespeare Series (1978–85). *An Age of Kings*, which marked significant developmental stages for both the BBC and NET, was rebroadcast only once again in England (January–April 1962) and never issued in video, but kinescopes of the BBC and NET broadcasts have been preserved. It is only now that *Kings* is beginning to re-emerge through the efforts of the British Film Institute, scholarly articles, memoirs of youthful television viewing, internet web pages and, sadly, in the obituaries of its participants.[3]

This article examines the trajectory taken by the first major BBC Shakespeare series – from its creation as an ambitious work of television entertainment to its final incarnation on American television as an educational programme. It looks closely at NET's financially successful marketing of *Kings* as a pedagogical tool where an important component was the addition of a wraparound commentary by University of California professor Frank Baxter who introduced each episode with a genial explanation of Shakespeare for the viewer he refers to as 'the Normal American'. His is an intriguing example of mid twentieth century Shakespeare teaching that presents the text as neither high brow nor low brow, but instead as the work of America's literary ancestor. Baxter's 'normal American' also represented the audience the newly formed NET needed to attract if its role in educational television was to succeed.

---

1 'The Bookshelf', *Wall Street Journal*, 20 April 1964 (Edmund Fuller); *Los Angeles Times*, 22 November 1961 (Cecil Smith); 'TV Translates Shakespeare', 21 October 1961; 'Critic Chooses Season's Best TV Offerings', 17 June 1962; 'An Age of Kings Abdicates, Alas', 2 March 1962.

2 See Stanley Wells, 'Commentary: Television Shakespeare', *Shakespeare Quarterly*, 33 (1982), 261–77.

3 See Emma Smith, 'Shakespeare serialized: *An Age of Kings*', in Robert Shaughnessy, ed., *The Cambridge Companion to Shakespeare and Popular Culture* (Cambridge, 2007), pp. 134–49; Patricia Lennox, 'Henry VI: A Television History in Four Parts', in Thomas A. Pendleton, ed., *Henry VI: Critical Essays* (New York, 2001), pp. 235–52; ActionTV (www.startrader.co.uk.); Internet Movie Data Base (www.IMDB.com); BFI (www.bfi.org.uk).

THE BBC'S EPIC PAGEANT

BBC producer Peter Dews's *An Age of Kings* is made up of Shakespeare's history tetralogies presented in fifteen episodes, each one running between sixty and seventy-five minutes, with the episodes arranged in order of reign: Richard II, Henry IV, Henry V, Henry VI and Richard III.[4] Its place in the annals of televised Shakespeare was significant in England and America. It was television's first serialized Shakespeare, the BBC's first big budget Shakespeare television production, the first 'classic serial' to be purchased from the BBC for American television, NET's first major arts programme distributed nationwide to its loosely affiliated network of independent stations – and the first NET programme to have a major corporate underwriter.[5] In England the press treated the BBC series as a national theatre event, a further extension of the previous decade's coronation pageantry and Festival of Britain, which celebrated not only the country's heritage, but the long-awaited end of postwar austerity. At the BBC, now housed in its new Television Centre with expanded studios and upgraded technology, the Shakespeare history series was a major commitment of time and money, but it offered an opportunity to show that television could do something that live theatre could not afford to do: dedicate several months to 'an epic pageant'. In the booklet-size programme produced for the series,[6] the BBC's head of television drama, Michael Barry, points out the near impossibility of presenting all eight of Shakespeare's history chronicles in a single theatre season, something done only in Frank Benson's 1900 production at Stratford-upon-Avon; *An Age of Kings*, he explains, is unique in part, because it is the first time a group of Shakespeare plays has been televised as a series that emphasizes the overlapping and continuing roles of characters and issues. Barry points out that the hour-long format chosen for *Kings* can be long enough to move action and character well along in a story, yet short enough for viewers to make the commitment to watch or listen, with the added advantage that, unlike attending the theatre, there is no 'difficulty of many visits away from home'. Seeing Shakespeare's English history plays serially 'the audience can ask what next' as 'the story surges' from father to son, from establishing to destroying family dynasties. Barry makes *Kings* sound like an up-scale version of the enormously popular show on the rival commercial station ITV, *Coronation Street*. Perhaps it was. BBC viewers and critics loyally and enthusiastically followed Shakespeare's kings and company in *An Age of Kings*, for nearly three-quarters of the year, in live broadcasts at primetime, 9 pm, every other Thursday evening between April and November.

Epic pageants are expensive. *An Age of Kings* had a working budget that was lavish for its time but now seems very modest. For example, the total cost for all three parts of *Henry VI* – over five hours of programming – was £9,000, with Part 1 costing a mere £2,000.[7] The permanent set with its warren of hallways and multi-level rooms was a long-term economy, as was establishing a repertory company. The permanent company consisted of more than two dozen actors whose regional origins represented 'the range of Great Britain'. The casting was canny for a national broadcast because, as Dews says, 'the citizens of provincial towns where the live theatre flourishes will know their own

---

[4] Each play was divided into two episodes (*Henry VI, Part 1*, done in one); *Richard II*, Acts 1, 2 and 3, 'The Hollow Crown'; Acts 3, 4 and 5, 'The Deposing of a King'; *Henry IV, Part I*, Acts 1 and 2, 'Rebellion from the North'; Acts 3, 4 and 5, 'The Road to Shrewsbury'; *Part II*, Acts 1 and 2, 'The New Conspiracy'; Acts 3, 4 and 5, 'Uneasy Lies the Head; *Henry V*, Acts 1, 2 and 3, 'Signs of War'; Acts 4 and 5, 'The Band of Brothers'; *Henry VI, Part I* 'The Red Rose and the White'; *Part II*, Acts 1, 2 and 3, 'The Fall of the Protector'; Acts 3, 4 and 5, 'The Rabble From Kent'; *Part III*, Acts 1, 2 and 3, 'The Morning's War'; Acts 4 and 5, 'The Sun in Splendour'; *Richard III*, Acts 1, 2 and 3, 'The Dangerous Brother'; Acts 3, 4 and 5, 'The Boar Hunt'.

[5] For later history of public television and corporate underwriters see Laurence Jarvik, *Masterpiece Theatre and the Politics of Quality* (New York, 1998), p. 132.

[6] Michael Barry, 'Presenting our epic pageant' in *An Age of Kings: presented by BBC Television* (London, 1960).

[7] Kenneth Rothwell and Annabelle Henkin Melzer, *Shakespeare on Screen* (New York, 1990), no. 103.

favourites'.[8] It also gave actors a chance to use – and viewers to hear – a variety of regional accents, further emphasizing the national agenda of the project.

This 'pageant' also relied on far more people – directors, designers, technicians, actors, musicians – for a longer period of time than any of the BBC's sixty previous Shakespeare productions during the past thirty-seven years. Producer Peter Dews, who received the lion's share of praise for his intelligent, lively translation of 'verbal imagery into pictorial'[9] was also the production director responsible for concept, casting and performance.[10] As television director, Michael Hayes was in charge of the camera work and live 'edit', deciding which cameras and which shots to use during the broadcast. He would later win awards for similar work on the televised RSC *Wars of the Roses*.[11] *Kings*'s text editor Eric Crozier's extensive BBC experience included a 1958 adaptation of *A Midsummer Night's Dream*. The incidental music that was so integral to each episode was composed by Christopher Whelen, who was credited on-screen but not in any of the printed materials, while Sir Arthur Bliss, Master of the Queen's Musick, was commissioned to write theme music, suitably stirring for a national pageant.

Producer Peter Dews, who conceived the idea for the series, shared Michael Barry's enthusiasm about television's unique ability to handle a lengthy series. Discussing the challenges he faces in putting Shakespeare's history plays on the small, domestic television screen, Dews acknowledges that the grandeur of crowd scenes would be reduced, and he echoes language used to describe the recent coronation when he says the black and white broadcast will lose the 'blaze of reds, golds and blues of heraldry'. However, he adds, there is an advantage in a broadcast: the microphone allows actors to speak in 'a normal voice' with 'a more rapid and cogent delivery', and cameras make it easier to pinpoint significant details – and reactions. For Dews, 'Shakespeare is primarily about people, and for TV, people are faces.' Majestic battle scenes might be lost but individual characters would be strong. What he doesn't point out is that millions of viewers would also be seeing a changing style in

Shakespeare performance. Most of *Kings*'s actors, many of them with Old Vic experience, were performing in the still controversial 'new style' with television-friendly intimacy, naturalness and, as some critics complained, with less emphasis on the 'poetry of language'.

For Dews the 'watchword' for the production was 'Great Men in Small Rooms' and the TV screen provided just such a 'room'. His shooting plan basically was 'when in doubt close in. Let the faces do the work.' The close-up is the dominant visual pattern in the series. In scene after scene the screen fills with a headshot, the camera stays steady, capturing details such as blood trickling down the dying Richard II's lip; Hotspur's eyebrow raised in amusement at his Kate, and later, the flash of panic in his eyes as he dies; Princess Katherine's slight moue of disapproval as her suitor, Henry V, awkwardly puts a foot on the bench where she sits. In close-up these faces appear on-screen with a depth that is lost in the mid distance shots which must be brightly lit for technical reasons. The close-ups are cinematic, but the longer shots remain shadowless reminders of the television studio.

Kings's actors were chosen for their strong faces – and their ability to disguise them – some of the company would play as many as a dozen named roles, plus carry the spear when needed. Major characters are played by stage actors with solid reputations, including Jack May (York), Robert Hardy (Henry V), Paul Daneman (Richard III), Frank Pettingell (Falstaff), Eileen Atkins (Joan of Arc) and Angela Baddeley (Mistress Quickly), but there were no major stars. Judi Dench (Katherine of France)

---

[8] Unless otherwise cited, all quotations from Dews are from Peter Dews, 'The Producer's View', in *An Age of Kings: Presented by BBC Television* (London, 1960).

[9] *News Chronicle* (13 May 1960).

[10] Dews's later career included managing the Birmingham Repertory Theatre and directing plays in England, Canada (Stratford, Ontario, Shakespeare Festival) and the United States.

[11] The stage production was filmed on a specially adapted stage, performed specifically for the camera and then edited before being broadcast. With *Kings* Hayes was directing a live broadcast televised at the moment of performance.

was just beginning her career and (Hotspur) Sean Connery's James Bond fame was still two years away, his career launched in part by the charismatic performance here. Further, *Kings* offered viewers the satisfaction of watching actors in a repertory company play a range of roles, 600 in total if you include spear carriers. At the same time clarity and continuity were gained by having actors play the same character from play to play – for instance Fleming's Bolingbroke/Henry IV, Hardy's Prince Hal/Henry V, Daneman's Richard, Duke of Gloucester/Richard III.

For *An Age of Kings* the matrix where the strengths of television and theatre met was in the live broadcast. Like a theatre audience, BBC viewers saw each episode at the moment of performance. This audience of over three million shared the immediacy and energy of a live transmission, cameras running, no room for revision or covering up mistakes – an immediacy that sports events still retain. The actors brought the adrenaline of being on live camera to that performance. In his autobiography actor/director Michael Blakemore describes his own experience with live television drama in the 1960s, acting for an invisible audience and without second chances. It must have been the same in the BBC studio as *Age of Kings* moved swiftly from scene to scene during each of fifteen intense, non-stop broadcasts.

The countdown on the studio floor had a colder terror than a first night because it was impossible to visualise, let alone negotiate with your audience. The floor manager signalled 'Go' with a silent stab of his forefinger and the show was off and running . . . There was enough adrenalin pumping through the studio to service an Olympic Games and no one was exempt from the pressure.[12]

With *Kings* the momentum of a performance every other week and an intense rehearsal schedule in between added to that adrenalin. The BBC scripts in the Birmingham Shakespeare Library include the rehearsal schedules for all but one of the fifteen episodes. For seven months they followed the same pattern. After a Thursday performance the actors had four days off to learn their lines, followed by rehearsals from 10:30 to 5:30 from Tuesday to Tuesday, with a day off on Sunday and a half day on Saturday. The day before the broadcast there were camera rehearsals from 2 pm to 10 pm. On the day of broadcast there were more camera rehearsals from 2 pm to 7 pm, a two-hour break and a performance at 9 pm. Dews was not exaggerating when he worried about keeping the energy up. Somehow everyone did, and the final episodes were as intense, polished and engrossing as the first.

Within the plays the pace was swift. Designer Stanley Morris's multipurpose set was a key to fast movement from scene to scene, with only a momentary fade to black between, just enough to let the viewer know a change was coming. The style was 'unashamedly theatrical because the plays were'.[13] Still, everything had to work in a live broadcast using between three and five cameras. The set consisted of generic units that could be reused throughout the series: a collection of steps, platforms, corridors – which the designer and producer were especially proud of – plus gardens, pillars and window frames. There were almost no long or middle-distance establishing shots. Scenes began with people, arriving and speaking, with the camera's close-up catching the subtle glances that often belied the words. Exterior scenes were played against a scrim with a few set-pieces in front, and relied on sound effects to set the scene. There are seagull calls and the splash of distant waves when Richard II arrives on an English beach consisting of nothing more than a pile of sand and a few blades of sea grass. On the television screen the city walls of Harfleur are limited to a couple of feet of worn stones on either side of the unimposing city gates. The Governor's voice is heard off-screen, thus avoiding the need to shift to the top of the wall. A half-dozen soldiers face the gates, backs to the camera, positioned very close together, as though pushed forward by the troops. Finally,

---

[12] Michael Blakemore, *Arguments With England* (London, 2004), p. 247.

[13] Peter Dews, 'TV Shakespeare', *Plays and Players* (July 1963), p. 18.

just before they surge into the city, they turn, look directly at the camera as though encouraging invisible soldiers just out of range to follow. The scene's strategy is economical, fast, dramatically effective – and used with slight variations many times during the series. Most battles were fought within a very small space, but one of the more elaborate sets was a boggy mud pit for Richard III's death. This swampy place of tall weeds growing in something squishy was large enough for a two-man duel and deep enough for Richard's corpse to sink into and nearly disappear under the surface.

The most basic component of the sets though was the multipurpose room, with details vaguely suggesting the medieval – stone walls, arched windows, heavy doors, wall hangings. Wall decorations, tapestries and flags helped established a location, sometimes unexpectedly, as with the bucolic scene of pastoral lovers painted on the walls of Glendower's Welsh banqueting room in *Henry IV, Part 1*. A five-foot high crucifix with a tortured Christ hangs on the wall behind Henry V's bishops as they debate the king's right to invade France. More often than not the exterior backdrop is a bare stone wall.

Often a single piece of furniture is used as a focus to tie the set together, an economical device that Dews had been praised for in his 1958 television *Henry V*. Hotspur's farewell to his wife is set in their bedroom where their lovingly teasing skirmish takes place on the bed. Nothing else is seen of the room, only this bed-sized surface covered with a lambskin where Kate reclines and Hotspur embraces her. It is the epitome of Dews's strategy: great men in small rooms. In a larger room, *Kings*'s central piece of furniture was not the throne, but the long table where the monarch, sitting in a slightly more exalted chair, met with his counsellors and conspirators. With each reign the new king would enter from the door directly behind the table and take the monarch's chair. A wonderful example of the economic use of this table occurs in *Richard II* where to make the king's downfall clear, the camera pans slowly across the litter-strewn table, where live white mice now run about under a veil of cobwebs. The camera con-

tinues a couple of feet to the right and another set, the garden where Queen Katherine walks with her ladies.

Sometimes, however, the 'room' needed to be larger, for instance, in *Richard II*, Bolingbroke's meeting with York, which was played as a public, political conference witnessed by the rebel soldiers who menaced and cheered. The effect of larger numbers of people was created by placing a relatively small number of soldiers, pikes in hand, with backs to the camera, but when cheers went up adding a much larger number of voices – probably everyone on the TV set from cameramen to production assistants.

For *Kings* the signature picture for the opening of each segment, on screen as the credits roll and Bliss's theme plays, is a marble sepulchre, whose rectangular shape and angle is a visual echo of the king's conference table. The row of five crowns placed there suggests 'sad stories of the deaths of kings'. Each hollow crown contains a model of the emblematic animal or object identified with a king: *Richard II*, a white hart; *Henry IV* and *Henry V*, a swan with outstretched wings; *Henry VI*, Parts 1 and 2 a dagger, Part 3 a sunburst; *Richard III*, the boar. Although the kings might be represented in death by a single tomb, each play presented different challenges in televising. *Richard II*'s soliloquies and close encounters between characters seem almost made for the television close-up. The 'rollicking' tavern scenes of *Henry IV* appeared less so, especially since this Boars Head Tavern is occupied by only the Falstaff followers. It is left to viewers to conjure up images of the merrymaking crowd from hearty noises coming from another room – though occasionally a wench enters and exits pursued by a drunk. *Henry V*'s problem was two-fold: battle scenes and the memory of Laurence Olivier's film. Dews made it clear that he had decided no film would be used in the series: 'When the author has apologized for the absence of horses, who are we to put them back into the scene?' Special effects are limited to superimposed images: notably the demon figures that dance on the pupils of Joan of Arc's eyes, and the montages of bodies of soldiers dead and dying during *Henry V*'s battles, but those were achieved with clever camera work in a live broadcast.

What made *Kings* unique was the connection from play to play. It worked as a real television series. It had many of the elements that define television programming: it was a serial story with characters who reappeared and where events had later impact. The chronological arrangement of rulers meant that the series's penultimate plays were the little known, seldom performed, three parts of *Henry VI*, which proved to be an exciting discovery for audiences. Dews's devices for 'bridging the old gaps between plays to make a continuous, irresistible serial' were highly praised. These included Henry IV's dagger stabbing into a pile of state papers at the end of *Richard II*, and having a young actor in *Henry IV* who had been heavily disguised as Justice Shallow take off his make-up and 'emerge' as Epilogue to close the play. The same actor then opened *Henry V* as Chorus. At the end of that play the death of Henry was brought forward from *Henry VI* 'in order to avoid the joyful, everyone-lived-happily-ever-after conclusion . . . which would have split the serial in two'.[14]

Further, in television terms the series was an anomaly because normally network series and serials use a team of writers, while the 'single author' show defines the unique TV drama. While officially this is a single author show by Shakespeare (Eric Crozier's editing and cuts were scarcely noted), *An Age of Kings* was also that television staple – a serial. Discussing *Kings* in terms of expectations of serial narratives, Emma Smith measures it using Sarah Kozloff's list of 'formal properties particular to television serials'.[15] The list of properties of a serial include regular schedule slot, recapitulations to bring viewers up to date, identification of protagonists and flash forwards to 'tease the viewer with bits of upcoming action'. Smith points out that for *An Age of Kings* on BBC, only the first was applicable, while minimal attempts were made at flash forwards. At the end of *Henry V*, for example, the battles to come were suggested by the camera's return to the battlefield carnage, bodies fallen everywhere, as the credits rolled.

There was, however, some attention paid to ending episodes with 'open or proleptic forms rather than closed ones', such as those discussed above. The most familiar form of television serial, the soap opera, moves forward with repetition of problems and no clear end in view. Shakespeare's histories had a clear end in view, the Tudor dynasty; yet the audience of *Kings* experienced the progression through the story as it unfolded chronologically for the first time, which meant that well-known and obscure plays changed place. The power of the penultimate plays, the three parts of *Henry VI*, impressed many who watched the doleful king, played by Terry Scully, move from tremulous piety to dignity, crushed by the ruthless Margaret (May Morris). When Henry, safe in his windmill refuge at Towton, looks out through the broken window and down at the deaths below, his is the saddest face in the entire series.

An Age of Kings may conform to only a few of the standard properties for a television serial, but it still generated a loyal following who returned broadcast after broadcast and remembered it decades later. The key to all serials is that the programme runs over a period of weeks and months, long enough for the viewers to incorporate it into their lives. Later Shakespeare series, though, have showed it is more complicated than that. In 1985, when PBS re-packaged some of the BBC/Time Life productions as *The Shakespeare Hour*, hosted by comic actor Walter Matthau, they followed *Kings*'s fifteen-week format, divided five plays linked by a common theme, such as love, into two or three segments of approximately one hour. It failed to capture anyone's imagination and was dismissed as ineffective. Even Dews's own 1963 BBC series of Shakespeare's Roman plays, called *The Spread of the Eagle*, failed to soar, so most critics argue, because there actually was little to link the plays with one another.

Only Shakespeare's English history plays, gathered together as *An Age of Kings* and later by John Barton and Peter Hall as *The Wars of the Roses* for

---

[14] Purser, 27 December 1969.

[15] Emma Smith, 'Shakespeare serialized', pp. 136, 143, 148, 149.

the Royal Shakespeare Company, have succeeded as weekly (or bi-weekly) television series. Despite Dews's fears that the show would fail, the reviews indicate that the series was seen as thrilling stuff from the very beginning and continued to be so. Viewer numbers increased from three to five million. During the seven-month run a tone of fond familiarity crept into the reviews – though a cartoon in *Punch* did dub it *An Age of Eternity*. Generally, each episode was treated by the press as if it was a new show and reviewed by the television critics, with no attention at all from theatre critics. For the first programme, 'The Hollow Crown', *Richard II*, Acts 1, 2 and 3, critical response was generally one of relief, 'this bold venture will not be the glorious failure some have prophesied',[16] and anticipation, 'Perhaps the greatest serial to be launched on television has begun.'[17] With the second instalment of *Richard II*, Acts 3, 4 and 5, 'The Deposing of a King', the series was seen as going from strength to strength. Most important, for a BBC facing competition from the independent commercial station ITV, *Kings* not only 'vindicated the peak-time showing of classics on television', but was strong enough to entice viewers away from the commercial station's detective series *No Hiding Place*, which also dealt, 'though on a lower level with dirty work including murder'.[18] *Henry IV* left many reviewers disappointed in Frank Pettingell's often serious Falstaff and the under populated Boars Head Inn, but they all praised the continuity as the actors moved to *Henry V*. After *Henry V*, and a total of seven hours, the '"pieces" were now beginning to click into place'.[19]

The real hurdle was the three parts of *Henry VI*. Most critics had been sceptical about placing the lesser-known plays, traditionally seen as Shakespeare's prentice work, towards the series' end – where they fit in terms of the kings' chronology. Happily, when they were broadcast, it was declared that there was 'no loss of the sense of continuity which Mr Peter Dews's productions have achieved' (*The Times*, 26 August 1960). If the two final instalments, *Richard III*, 'The Dangerous Brother' and 'The Boar Hunt' (Acts 1, 2 and 3 and Acts 3, 4 and 5), seemed anticlimactic to many

critics who complained that it was a series of too many bloody murders, that may be the effect of watching the play at the end of the full tetralogy, especially because *Henry VI* proved more exciting than expected. Reactions to *Richard III* were similar twenty years later when Jane Howell directed *Henry VI* and *Richard III* for the BBC Shakespeare Series. Reviewers who had been elated by *Henry VI* felt a similar let down, as did recent reviewers of Michael Boyd's production at the Royal Shakespeare Company. *An Age of Kings* ended triumphantly; the great pageant had fulfilled its promise. It had also done something that the BBC had been trying to achieve for several years: they finally sold a major programme to American television. In fact, *An Age of Kings* was such a success that they sold it to two separate American broadcast groups, each with a very different agenda.

AMERICAN BROADCASTS: CAPITALIZING ON SHAKESPEARE

Although NET has the most enduring and widest-reaching connection with *An Age of Kings*, it was not the first to broadcast this Shakespeare series in the States, nor was Humble Oil the first corporation to 'sponsor' it. Several months before *An Age of Kings* was swept up as its own by NET, the series was broadcast in New York, Washington (10/18 Jan to 21/23 April) and Los Angeles (beginning in November) on Metropolitan Broadcasting System's independent commercial stations WNEW, WTTG and KTTV.[20] It should be noted that the 1961 reviews in those cities' papers refer to Metropolitan's broadcasts, not NET's – and there was a difference in framing, if not in actual content, of the programmes. Based on the available information, public broadcasting historian Laurence Jarvik's suggestion[21] that the series was

---

16 *The Birmingham Mail*, 29 April 1960.
17 *The Guardian*, 30 April 1960.
18 *The Guardian*, 13 May 1960.
19 *The Guardian*, 22 November 1960.
20 Metropolitan also broadcast the RSC *Wars of the Roses*.
21 Jarvik, *Masterpiece Theatre*, p. 132.

purchased from BBC by NET for dual distribution with Metropolitan seems unlikely, despite the fact that their programme booklets are nearly identical. However, as discussed below, the contents of the booklets reflect two very different approaches to televising Shakespeare. Records are scarce here, but the *Christian Science Monitor*'s December 1960 article, announcing *Kings*' scheduled (Metropolitan) showings in New York and Washington supports the argument of two separate purchases when it reports that National Educational Television is '*also*' (my italics) negotiating with the BBC for the series 'on behalf of some 50 ETV stations in the United States'.[22]

In 1961 the well-established Metropolitan Broadcasting Corporation, with its urban-based stations, was continuing to mix standard television fare with sophisticated music and theatre programmes, much as the three major networks (CBS, NBC, ABC) had done in the previous decade's 'Golden Age of Television'. Metropolitan classified the Shakespeare series as 'a public service feature'[23] but, more importantly, 'valued' *An Age of Kings* for its theatricality and entertainment – elements needed to attract audiences and sponsors.[24] The show was 'presented' by the Standard Oil Company (New Jersey), 'principal US operating affiliate: Humble Oil and Refining Company' and by the nationwide chain of local filling stations, 'your Esso dealer'. The choice of programme and the method in which it was presented bore the stamp of the company's culturally minded president, M. J. Rathbone.[25] He wrote that this was 'a definite step forward in providing intelligent, cultural programs on television . . . Shakespeare can be, and is, exciting . . . and no more tempestuous period of time exists than during the violent reigns of these English monarchs'. As at the BBC, this is Shakespeare, competing with other prime time programming, presented for the audience's enjoyment, 'to help satisfy the taste of many people for classic drama'. The oil company president emphasizes that 'the company's policy of keeping hands off program content' means the audience is seeing these 'splendid' plays just 'as the farsighted producer and capable cast of English actors believe they should be'.[26]

Rathbone's comments are in sharp contrast with the newly formed Fourth Network's strategy. NET was 'eager to emphasize its educational value, not its entertainment potential'.[27] One of the most telling examples of the shift from epic pageant to history lesson is the variation in the BBC programme booklets as provided by Standard Oil, and NET/Humble Oil. The two American versions of the free, 28-page *An Age of Kings: Shakespearian Pageantry Depicting the Turbulent Reigns of Seven Monarchs* look identical – same size, cover, paper, graphics – but the textual changes represent the shift from recreational Shakespeare to educational Shakespeare. In New York and Washington where *Kings* was seen by an estimated more than two million viewers, the response was 'little short of sensational', with the result that requests for the booklet were so overwhelming that Standard Oil had to discontinue supplying copies, and instead 'some 15,000 booklets' were distributed through 'local public libraries, book and department stores'.[28]

Adapted from the handsome eleven-page BBC booklet, both American versions make only minor changes to the BBC material describing the individual plays. One major change is that each episode is now given an individual page, instead of the BBC's single-column summaries placed three to

---

22 'Britain Exports "Kings"', 27 December 1960. On 28 March 1961, three months before the end of the New York/Washington commercial broadcasts of *Kings*, *The Christian Science Monitor*, generally regarded as a reliable source, reported ('An Age of Kings to Widen Impact') that 'next autumn' *Kings* would be shown on 'stations affiliated with the National Educational Television network in the United States'.

23 'TV and the Broad "A": An Intimate Message from Washington', *Christian Science Monitor*, 18 Febuary 1961 (Josephine Ripley).

24 Gilbert Seldes, *The Public Arts* (New York, 1956).

25 Among his honours was a 1964 award from the Stratford Shakespeare Theatre (Stratford, Connecticut) to Rathbone for his and Standard Oil's contribution to the arts.

26 *An Age of Kings: Shakespearian Pageantry Depicting the Turbulent Reigns of Seven Monarchs* (New Jersey: Standard Oil Company), p. 17.

27 David Stewart, *The PBS Companion: a History of Public Television* (New York, 1999), p. 23.

28 'TV and the Broad "A"'.

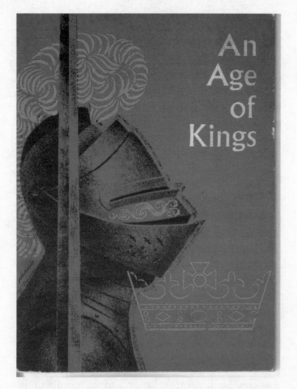

16 The red cover of the booklet for the New York and Washington area broadcasts sponsored by Standard Oil of New Jersey, later used by NET.

8. THE BAND OF BROTHERS

On the eve of battle, the King searches his soul. The battle brings vindication and victory. Peace is sealed when Henry woos and wins the attractive Katherine in marriage.

Before the battle at Agincourt, the pensive King wanders unrecognized among his soldiers, talking and even quarrelling with some of them. Assailed by responsibilities and doubts, Henry V finds it very bitter to be a King. He prays for forgiveness for his own and his father's sins, and asks for strength for the morrow. In the morning a final French offer of terms is refused.

The battle brings brilliant victory—the French dead number ten thousand, the English only twenty-nine. Henry V, attributing his victory solely to God's will, returns in triumph to London.

Peace between France and England is negotiated by the Duke of Burgundy and sealed with Henry's courtship of, and marriage to, Princess Katherine of France. The two kingdoms of France and England are to be united by the promise of an heir.

1415
HENRY V
ACTS 4 & 5

17 Henry V (Robert Hardy), Princess Katherine of France (Judi Dench), Alice (Yvonne Coulette); 'The Band of Brothers' (*Henry V*, Acts 4 and 5), from the Standard Oil booklet.

the page. Further, unlike the BBC's, the US booklet is illustrated with a stamp-size historical portrait of each king, a production photograph for all but two episodes, and eight 'cast photos', headshots of actors in character. The episodes without production pictures are the two parts of *Richard III*; engravings of the Tower and Henry VII are used, suggesting the booklet went into production before the series ended its BBC run. Some changes reflect the needs of American viewers who would be less familiar with the British kings. A three-colour centrefold map of England 'during the kings' is added; major sites are marked with icons representing city, castle or battlefield. The BBC's genealogy table is slightly simplified and illustrated with the kings' portraits. The BBC programme booklet has a page listing the members of the permanent company, without identifying their multiple roles (these

can be found only in the American paperback) and identifies roles for only eight actors: David William (Richard II), Tom Fleming (Henry IV), Robert Hardy (Henry V), Terry Scully (Henry VI), Paul Daneman (Richard III), Frank Pettingell (Sir John Falstaff), Angela Baddeley (Mistress Quickly), Patricia Heneghan (Lady Percy). The American programme booklet drops the list of the permanent company, of greater interest to the British theatregoer, but adds a page of photos, in character, of actors in twelve major roles: all the kings, plus Hotspur, Falstaff, Earl of Northumberland and Richard II's Queen.

Standard Oil's copy includes a brief, fourteen-line introduction, 'the plays', which is replaced by NET/Humble Oil with a two-page essay by Frank Baxter and a note that each play will be introduced by his 'filmed commentaries', produced for NET by WQED-TV, San Francisco, California. The BBC booklet had no introduction *per se* to the plays, but included two brief essays about the series: one by the Corporation's Michael Barry, 'Presenting our epic pageant' and the other by the series's creator Peter Dews, 'The Producer's View'. Standard Oil's president Rathbone's 'sponsor's view', quoted above, replaces Barry's, and Dews's comments remain in a slightly shorter version. In the NET/Humble Oil version an essay on 'the fourth network', as NET called itself, replaces Rathbone's. More significantly, Dews's production notes are replaced by 'What An Age of Kings can mean to educators and students', which includes the suggestion that the broadcasts can 'open the door to many educational uses' including class 'viewing sessions', and neighbourly 'discussion groups'. Prepared to accompany broadcasts made over an unspecified period of time by a national network of educational stations, the booklet accommodates different time slots and dates, by advising interested viewers to contact their local stations. At the bottom of the page there is information about 'important study aids': a book-length study guide (available at cost from NET in New York) and an inexpensive (seventy-five cents) paperback version of *An Age of Kings* published by Pyramid books, 'available wherever paperback books are sold or (in quantity) from NET'.[29] Copies of the booklet were available from Humble Oil and Refining Company's Public Relations Department in Houston, Texas.

Not only was the newly formed National Educational Television 'fourth network' establishing its identity and creating a financial base, it was also creating a pedagogical structure that would be adapted for future Shakespeare programmes, including the BBC/Time-Life series. The most visible component in NET's transformation of *An Age of Kings* into an educational package was their addition of Frank Baxter's commentary. Because that addition is so closely tied to the actual survival of NET and its financial structure as a not-for-profit organization, it is helpful to have some background on the creation of NET in order to understand the necessary role played by an educational packaging of Shakespeare.

HOW SHAKESPEARE SAVED NATIONAL EDUCATIONAL TELEVISION

In England, where any whiff of pedagogy would have been fatal to its success, *Kings's* viewers had tuned in for a great show. Theoretically, both British and American audiences saw the same *Age of Kings*, but because of transmission, marketing, placement, editorial intervention and segmentation the viewing experience was structured so that it was very different on each side of the Atlantic. For critics and audiences in Britain, *Age of Kings* was part of typical BBC programming that mixed a range of programmes – dramas, sports, comedies, quiz shows, ballroom dancing, American Westerns and detective shows – in a single evening's viewing. In America it was presented as part of a similar mix on Metropolitan Broadcasting stations where in New York, Washington and Los Angeles Shakespeare's kings had to compete in this three-programme time slot with *Father Knows Best*, Westerns, *Dobie Gillis*, 'Alfred Hitchcock Presents' and 'The Million Dollar Movie'. On 18 April 1961, the day of the final show (*Richard III*, Acts 3–5), the New York station had shown earlier the dramas *Mr. District Attorney*, *City Assignment*, and cartoons, including *Heckle and Jeckle*.

Across the Atlantic those outside of the areas reached by Metropolitan Broadcasting still got the great show, but most American viewers saw it on NET-wrapped in pedagogical virtue, part of an educational programme offering viewers 'an experience in historical and cultural understanding'.[30]

---

[29] *An Age of Kings: Shakespearian Pageantry Depicting the Turbulent Reigns of Seven Monarchs* (New York: National Educational Television and Radio Center, 1961); Albert B. Weiner, *Shakespeare's An Age of Kings: Presented by National Educational Television* (New York, 1961); Nathan and Ann Keats, general editors, *An Age of Kings: the Historical Plays of William Shakespeare* (New York, 1961). The 'Introduction' was by Professor Oscar Campbell, Columbia University.

[30] Stewart, *PBS Companion*, p. 23.

The NET 'packaging' of the programme for American distribution effectively placed the British director and actors within an American educational format that illustrates both Michael Bristol's argument that Shakespeare is 'continually re-inscribed as an American institution' and Frances Teague's observation that Americans take 'great pleasure in using Shakespeare and summoning the authority of Shakespeare to support their positions'.[31] In 1961 NET, poised on the brink of existence, used Shakespeare's plays in *An Age of Kings* to establish their position as an American institution. They acquired *An Age of Kings* as the showpiece of 'a brassy "go for broke" gamble'; that Shakespeare purchase 'may have saved' American educational television.[32]

The newly established National Educational Television (NET) was a programme distribution centre with neither plans nor license to produce shows.[33] It used the award-winning, prestigious *Age of Kings* for its first steps towards its goal of connecting the independent non-profit television stations under a unified identity based on quality broadcasting, built around shows produced for distribution to this 'fourth network'.[34] In retrospect, the experimental arrangement between BBC and NET seems inevitable. Certainly NET's goal for its American audiences was the same as Lord Reith's for the BBC: entertain, enlighten and instruct.[35] NET's goal was to lift the local stations out of their backwater status by providing programmes that could compete with the three commercial networks' programmes. Like many theatre companies, it turned to Shakespeare for a great show, prestige and fundraising. The BBC series became television's first non-commercial programme underwritten by a corporate sponsor, a financing formula that became a crucial factor in NET's survival. Shakespeare's cultural agency helped sanitize what, although labelled an underwriting grant, was basically a form of commercial sponsorship.[36] Further, the highly acclaimed series was a major component in NET gaining major grants: an additional $3.5 million in funding from its main underwriter, the Ford Foundation, and, two years later, $25 million from the Federal Government.[37]

Soon after the series' success in Britain, between April and November 1960 and, probably during its broadcast in the New York/Washington area, NET (still calling itself NETRC, National Educational Television and Radio Center) with the help of Humble Oil and Refining Company[38] purchased the North American rights to the show. A key word here is 'rights' which meant that NETRC could basically do what it wanted in

---

[31] Michael D. Bristol, *Shakespeare's America, America's Shakespeare* (London, 1990); Frances Teague, *Shakespeare and the American Popular Stage* (Cambridge, 2006), p. 174.

[32] James Day, *The Vanishing Vision: The Inside Story of Public Television* (Berkeley and Los Angeles, 1995), p. 74.

[33] The broadcast credits include the National Center for Educational Television and Radio, but all of the print materials use only NET or National Educational Television, which is NCETR's re-branding as a central distribution centre and its relocation to New York City, under president Jack White.

[34] Independent stations broadcast locally, while the three major networks broadcast nationally. Non-commercial stations had been granted broadcast licenses by the US government's Federal Communications Committee (FCC) only nine years earlier and were still struggling to produce local shows with limited resources. *An Age of Kings* was also sold by the BBC to Australian television.

[35] For BBC see Robert Giddings and Keith Selby, *The Classic Serial on Television and Radio* (New York, 2001). For NET see James Day, *The Vanishing Vision*; Stewart, *The PBS Companion*, chs. 1–4; Jim Robertson, ed., *Televisonaries* (Charlotte Harbor, FL, 1995).

[36] This was a legal consideration for stations licensed by the Federal Communications Commission as non-profit, but based on the negotiations for *An Age of Kings*, a formula was established: stations could ask a corporation for funding for a show the station was planning, but a corporation could not go to stations and request that a particular show be done.

[37] The Ford Foundation was the major source of funding for non-commercial television. The original grant offered each new station a matching grant of $30,000, half the amount of start-up costs. *Kings* was quickly followed by *Ragtime Era*, with pianist-storyteller Max Morath; *Prospects of Mankind*, a socially significant programme with Eleanor Roosevelt talking with a series of world leaders, *Appalachian Spring*, featuring the choreography of Martha Graham, and a Pablo Casals master class.

[38] For White and early NET see Day, *The Vanishing Vision*; Stewart, *The PBS Companion*, for first-hand reports. See also Jarvik *PBS: Behind the Screen*; for financial information see David Horowitz and Laurence Jarvik, eds., *Public Broadcasting and the Public Trust* (Los Angeles, 1995).

terms of sales, distribution and packaging in America. The prestige of this 'monumental' Shakespeare series had attracted the attention of NETRC president and future NET president, John F. White, who was looking for a programme that would put educational television on the broadcasting map of America and found it in Shakespeare's history plays brought together as *An Age of Kings*.

This was a crucial time for independent, non-commercial television stations.[39] Eight years earlier, 1952, the Federal Communication Council, after years of petitions for non-commercial station licenses, and a licensing freeze of three and a half years, had finally been persuaded to grant broadcast licenses to 242 independent non-commercial stations, along with 2,043 newly licensed commercial stations. By 1961 there were only fifty-seven non-commercial stations, each one struggling alone with a small budget and local programming. White's goal for NET was to provide these independent stations with major programmes that far exceeded anything they could produce locally, particularly in the arts. Potentially this could allow the stations to fill the gap left by the severe drop in quality material on television created by the networks' move to Hollywood and reliance on made-for-television films.

NET's timing was perfect. In 1961, FCC Chairman Newton Minow stunned the television networks by loudly and very publicly denouncing television as 'a wasteland of westerns and detective shows'. Minow, who had been a law partner with Adlai Stevenson, was part of the Kennedy presidential intellectual 'egg-head' appointments. Minow's observation were seen as a serious attack at the time, partly because the networks feared government regulation. The industry's shocked and indignant reaction resulted in feeble attempts to rectify the situation. However, the flurry of quality shows was as short lived as an April snow, and the networks quickly returned to the vastly more profitable commercial favourites. It had been different in the previous decades when television had offered a mix of commercially popular shows along with political and cultural public service shows, including the legendary anthology series *Omnibus*,

Philco Playhouse, *Hallmark Hall of Fame*, *Playhouse 90* and *Kraft Television Theatre*, many of which had presented Shakespeare plays. (For details on *Hallmark*'s productions see Russell Jackson on Maurice Evans in this volume.)[40] Minow's attack was, however, a gift for the struggling independent stations, a bargaining chip for stations to fill the gap with programmes for smaller, but valued, audiences – and help protect the major networks from government interference. In 1961 in America the BBC series was welcomed – and promoted – as an antidote to the growing 'wasteland' of commercial programmes. *An Age of Kings* became the touchstone of nearly every plea for better quality American television programming. It was held up as an example of what the medium could achieve, 'TV Groping Upward from Its Low Estate',[41] and, for better or worse, an icon of educational television.[42] NET's first major venture established a type of programming that today is standard broadcast practice for NET's successor, the Public Broadcasting Corporation Stations (PBS).

Typical of arts programming, and the previously televised network Shakespeare plays, Metropolitan Broadcasting included a brief introduction to each episode. In New York and Washington Jim Fleming, a smooth-voiced television announcer with a low-key manner from the *Today Show* summarized the play, said something about what was coming next, and spoke with moderately phrased praise of the corporate sponsor. In fact, Standard Oil was not only praised by him for the company's contribution to culture, but its president James Rathbone appeared with him at least once to say a few words. Washington columnist Robert Spivack noted with pleasure, 'It isn't usual for a huge industrial giant, or its President, to appear on a Shakespeare

[39] See Jarvik, *PBS Behind the Screen*, pp. 11–14.
[40] In US terminology 'anthology series' refers to unrelated plays united by a time slot, sponsor and production team.
[41] *Chicago Daily Tribune*, 19 October 1961 (Larry Wolters).
[42] See Louis Marder, 'Round Table: Shakespeare's Age of Kings', *College English*, 23:1 (1961), 38–40; reprinted in 'The Public Arts', ed. Frederick S. Kiley, *The English Journal*, 50 (1961), p. 566.

program.'[43] In Los Angeles, Metropolitan's KTTV presented the Shakespearian cycle in 'splendid trappings' with Hans Conried, an actor noted for sophisticated charm, an 'ideal choice as host and narrator' in a medieval setting.[44]

Despite enormous popularity, there were some complaints. For American audiences the height of Shakespeare performances was defined by a triumvirate of John Gielgud, Maurice Evans and Laurence Olivier.[45] *An Age of Kings's* range of accents, that had been so important to Dews, was a potential problem for American viewers. Critics complained that many 'of the actors adopt North country, Welsh or Scots dialects which are unfamiliar', and the show suffered most seriously from words 'so mouthed and so rushed by several members of the company that they bordered on total unintelligibility'.[46] Though many of the actors were highly praised, especially Sean Connery's Hotspur and Frank Pettingell's Falstaff (which had not been as popular in England), the emerging style of naturalistic acting left some critics feeling the performances were a let down and would not hold up to the 'very best' of Maurice Evans or Sir Laurence Olivier.[47] One reviewer, in *Variety*, missed the point about the show being filmed (really a videotape record of a live broadcast) and felt that since 'the BBC has put the series on film and considering too, the added dimensions afforded by celluloid' it had sacrificed too much to keep 'the studio look'.[48]

NOT-FOR-PROFIT AND THE NON-SPONSOR SPONSOR

It was Metropolitan Broadcasting/Standard Oil's combination of Shakespeare and a discrete sponsor that gave NETRC/NET a model for the financial format it needed. They could transform the 'sponsor' into an underwriter, have no commercials, but keep the company name visible in the ads and at the beginning and end of the programme. When, late in 1961, NET began *Kings's* three-year journey to nearly all of the educational stations across the United States, the nationally distributed programme was financed by a 'grant' from Humble

Oil and Refining Company, Standard Oil's parent company. The total was between $150,000 and $400,000, depending on whose report one reads.[49] This covered the costs of purchasing the rights to the programme from the BBC, filming additional commentary by Baxter, printing the illustrated booklet and a 92-page study guide. NET made the programme more visible and accessible by paying for local advertising, something educational television stations found impossible to do with budgets based on local donations. The arrangement with Humble Oil was a delicate negotiation for the public broadcasting executives because, according to their FCC licenses, independent stations' public broadcasting could not accept commercial sponsors. However, the FCC had been persuaded to allow non-commercial funding grants.

Part of the negotiations with Humble Oil led to Frank Baxter. The professor became the lynchpin of the educational packaging of *An Age of Kings*. Baxter is not a host; he is a professor delivering a series of lectures which occupy a comparatively large 20–25 per cent of broadcast time. The amount of time allotted to Baxter may represent the degree of anxiety on the part of Humble Oil about the extent of American interest in a British Shakespeare production of epic proportions, A great deal of Humble Oil's money was involved in what was, at that time, an experimental financial arrangement with a newly created central distribution centre for educational television. He had many admirers

---

43 15 March 1961.

44 10 November 1961, *Los Angeles Times* (Cecil Smith).

45 Although all three were British by birth, they were in America through film and television.

46 *Los Angeles Times*, 22 November 1961 (Robert Kirsch). *The New York Times*, 11 January 1961.

47 *The Morning Telegraph* (Leo Mishkin).

48 11 January 1961.

49 In his somewhat informal, but very informative, history of educational broadcasts Stewart quotes the men involved with the 'deal' remembering the BBC was paid a quarter of a million and that Humble Oil came up with $400,000. Jarvik (p. 132) bases his numbers on the BBC archive files and sets it at $150,000: $60,000 for NETRC advertising, $90,000 to the BBC for North American rights, with an additional grant for Baxter's 'wrap-around segments'.

among educational television executives. Jim Day, founder of San Francisco's KQED, talking about the difficulties of raising money for independent stations, tells how he discovered early on that 'being in favor of educational television was not sufficient motivation to send money'. There had to be a factor of surprise. 'It may not have been controversy. It may have been Frank Baxter saying, "Wow! That's exciting!".'[50] Baxter was celebrated as a man who made the talking head a viable concept – someone worth watching. Surprisingly, though, the suggestion to include Baxter came not from the television executives but, according to public television executive David Stewart, after NETRC development directors, Nazaret ('Chick') Cherkezian and Warren Kraetzer met with 'the money' decided the 'people' at Humble Oil's headquarters in Texas, Baxter's role in NET's *An Age of Kings* to explain the plays for 'the normal American'.

Now packaged as an educational programme, *An Age of Kings* would be viewed between 1961 and 1964 on television broadcasts by over five dozen stations, and still later be shown in countless schools through an NET film rental programme.[51] NET's early economy was such that only a few copies of the programme existed. They were 'bicycled' from one group of stations to the next group at the completion of the series. The shows were so successful, though, that by 1963 stations were beginning to rebroadcast them. Generally, the kinescope episodes were shown weekly, often in a Thursday or Friday night prime time slot, and repeated on Sunday. As with the initial New York/Washington broadcasts by Metropolitan, the NET programme continued to garner highest praise. Everyone seemed pleased with Dr Baxter's performance.

DR BAXTER EXPLAINS SHAKESPEARE'S KINGS TO 'THE NORMAL AMERICAN'

Peter Dews felt that audiences would warm to the stories just as the schoolboys he had taught did. The BBC trusted its audiences, many of whom were not necessarily expected to know the historical backgrounds or even the plays themselves. There the *Radio Times* printed summaries of the shows; the booklet described above was made available. Metropolitan Broadcasting followed a similar pattern. NET and Humble Oil executives felt they needed more if they were to secure the largest possible audience.

'Dr. Baxter will provide animated, informative, and far from pedantic commentary on the historical, geographical and genealogical backgrounds of the plays' (NETRC announcement). (The title Dr was always included in the announcer's introduction though not in the credits.) Baxter said he was merely a 'footnote'[52] to the proceedings – but he was an unusually lengthy footnote. Generally the host on a drama show was expected to speak for only for a couple of minutes and often the real role was to be a tasteful representative of the programme's sponsor. The length of Baxter's pre-show lecture was unique to NET and was not repeated for Shakespeare programmes after *Kings*. The broadcast times seem to have been adjusted to make room for him without undue cutting of the BBC kinescope. The 'Procrustean chopping' that Dews complains about,[53] done to fit his slightly more flexible length shows into the standardized American broadcast hour, seems to be a later addition. However, the insertion of Baxter's concluding remarks before the final credits breaks into Dews's use of that time to provide a final, often subtle, coda for the play, memorably the abandoned Richard II's look of increasing dismay and the camera's return to the bodies of soldiers at the end of *Henry IV*.

[50] Robertson, p. 155.
[51] The Paley Center for Media Studies, New York and Los Angeles has a nearly complete copy of the NET broadcasts. The British Film Institute BFI has a webpage that includes clips from some scenes and the full 'Road to Shrewsbury', *Henry IV Part I*, Acts 3, 4 and 5, but although the home page can be brought up viewing is restricted to subscriber schools in England.
[52] The best known and most enduring of all public broadcasting hosts, Alistair Cooke for *Masterpiece Theatre*, identified his role saying, 'All the work is really done by others, I'm merely the headwaiter.'
[53] Dews, *Plays and Players*, p. 18.

One notable cut in the NET version may have been made to make the programme more suitable for family viewing. In *Henry VI*, they shortened (Eileen Atkins) Joan of Arc's agony at the stake. In the BBC version the camera moves in closer and closer until all that is on the screen are the terror-filled eyes and all that is heard is an unearthly scream that seems to go on and on. NET cuts away sooner.

One of the keys to the Humble Oil executives' interest in Baxter is that he was much-loved, 'a television pedagogue of great experience', with an 'unfaltering' manner: 'a sort of distinguished avuncularism and a gleeful excitement with his subject, and the happy opportunity of communicating it to millions of others'.[54] In 1956 cultural arbitrator Gilbert Seldes wrote about 'the kind of people who would have been sure that a college professor talking about Shakespeare was not for them; when the professor was Frank Baxter, they discovered it was very much for them'.[55] Baxter had come to national attention in 1949 when *Time* magazine named him one of America's outstanding teachers, someone who could make literature come alive. His television career began in the early 1950s when his forty-five minute 'classroom' lectures on the Los Angeles CBS affiliated station[56] 'were considered to be unusually interesting and appealing and attracted viewers who previously had no knowledge or interest in Shakespeare'.[57] Initially broadcast by CBS station KNXT (Channel 2) in Los Angeles as part of a credited college course, they were later shown nationwide on both commercial and non-commercial television These highly successful television lectures on Shakespeare gained an Emmy-winning reputation for this enthusiastic educational performer. Baxter was also featured as an intermission special during the 1954 broadcast of Laurence Olivier's *Richard III*. In 1955 *Time* reported that 'since he started reading Shakespeare on TV' Baxter 'has won the dubious title of "The Liberace of the Library"'.[58] Later he played the role of 'Dr. Research' on four educational science films, produced and directed by Frank Capra.[59] Baxter was so well known by 1962 that in the *Chicago Daily Tribune*'s article[60] about overlapping broadcasts of

Maurice Evans's *Macbeth* and *An Age of Kings* Baxter's was the only photograph used.

The NET presentation of *An Age of Kings* opens with their own designed background, medieval figures on a chessboard, with the knight on horseback, lance pointed, at the centre. The words 'An Age of Kings' is followed by the credit for the corporate sponsor, Humble Oil. As the company's name appears on the screen, the announcer says 'An Age of Kings is made available in the United States under a grant from the Humble Oil Company. Your host is Dr Frank C. Baxter' before the BBC title appears over the iconic row of 'hollow' crowns accompanied by Bliss's theme music. Baxter, in an abridged version of his earlier television lectures, though some of the plays are new to his 'syllabus', tells *Kings*'s audiences about the historical background, the relationship between characters and, events in the play. He returns at the end with a summary of what has just been seen.

Baxter describes his role: 'I exist only to make clear certain things that are not really part of the natural background of any normal American, something about the relationships of all these people, what the struggles are in which they are involved. In a sense I am the scorecard of the game,

---

[54] *Christian Science Monitor*, 2 February 1963 (Donald Mainwaring).

[55] Gilbert Seldes, *The Public Arts* (New York, 1956), p. 271.

[56] The course 'Shakespeare on TV' (English 356 A and B) could be taken for college credit through the broadcasts. The university published Baxter's 'Outline Guide' to supplement the assigned textbook *Shakespeare: Major Plays and the Sonnets*, ed. G. B. Harrison, published by Harcourt Brace. A two hour final exam was given at the university's Bovard Auditorium on Saturday afternoon at the end of term.

[57] Robertson, p. 184.

[58] 'Invitation Only', *Time*, 23 May 1955.

[59] Capra was trying to re-establish his career after the McCarthy hearings. The programmes were *Our Mr. Sun* (1956), *The Strange Case of the Cosmic Rays*, atoms, gamma and ultraviolet radiation (1957), *Hemo the Magnificent*, the body's blood system (1957), *Unchained Goddess*, the weather (1958). The films became an audio-visual staple in classrooms for the next decade and beyond.

[60] 20 October 1961.

without which you can't follow the action.'[61] To help clarify there is a map and a family tree for descendants of Edward III, where the image of the actor playing the role appears beside the king's name. Baxter moves about, standing in front of the camera, sitting in an Elizabethan chair behind a table holding a sword and a crown – the backdrop consists of a medieval banner, a draped curtain and a shield – or stepping a few feet to his right in front of what looks like the stage for a puppet show. The curtains on this 'stage' are opened by Baxter at various points to reveal the family tree, a map, a drawing of a castle, drawings of kings in tabards – the only actual portrait appears at the very end of the series and it is Queen Elizabeth I.

According to the professor, some of the things the 'normal American' was not expected to have any knowledge of were feudal society, the anointment of kings, the political role of clergy, the succession of kings, the English claims to France, the relationships of Scotland, Wales and Ireland (for *Henry V*), and the emerging national identity under the Tudors. Baxter is a skilful speaker and covers a lot of territory in his allotted ten-plus minutes, guiding the viewer through the intricacies of the monarchies with the use of charts and graphs and a gently persuasive enthusiasm. There are props: a child's toy figure (a head perched on a ball-shaped body) with a white beard that rocks and rights itself is used to illustrate Falstaff's equanimity, his ability always to come up right. Elizabethan coins are casually produced by Baxter from his pocket and laid on the table for a close-up of the inscription to show that even as late as the 1590s England still listed France as its own. Some of the history lesson might be useful, some of it is misleading: battles were fought by knights and kings, not the common man; the besieged castle, such as Harfleur, always had the advantage because 'they would have stored up food' while the besieger will have to go out into the countryside.

Key to the discussion is making Shakespeare's plays something the 'normal American' can relate to by explaining them in an American idiom. Seizing the crown is not like taking a senatorship or a governorship in an American election. A discussion of comedy and tragedy includes an extended metaphor of baseball and stealing home from third base. Introducing the first programme, 'The Hollow Crown', Baxter asks the question 'Why should Americans be interested in plays about English kings?' The answer is first that 'all history flows towards us out of the past like a great river and all that we have and are is conditioned by the past'. But more specifically, for those normal Americans, without the end of feudalism (chronicled in these plays) we would have been without the growth of 'the steadying middle class' and 'without the importance of power of parliament our political system would never have been possible'. He gives his viewers a vision, 'Isn't it interesting to think that in Shakespeare's audience back there so many hundreds years ago, the groundlings who paid their penny in the pit included many an Elizabethan apprentice who was to journey far across the Atlantic, live out his life, achieve some competence and success in life and leave his bones in the soil of Plymouth Colony, Massachusetts, or Virginia, or become important in Maryland or Pennsylvania.' In other words, normal working Elizabethans saw these plays, came here and brought the memory with them. It's not quite true, of course, but it is part of a programme to somehow reassure the viewers that the plays will not be too alien for them to grasp.

Much of Baxter's time is spent providing character studies – with no suggestion whatsoever that there might be differing opinions or alternate analysis. Hotspur is 'magnificent . . . one of the most delightful, complex and interesting characters invented by Shakespeare'. His qualities include being a man of honour, chivalric, a warrior, humorous, 'he's fun and he's, well, Hotspur'. Bolingbroke is 'masculine', 'extroverted, a leader, someone behind whom men could rally'. Richard II, on the other hand, is 'sensitive, in love with beauty, dresses exquisitely'; unfortunately, he is also a 'somewhat wasteful king' is 'a

---

[61] All Baxter quotes have been transcribed from the NET tapes at the Paley Media Center, New York.

connoisseur of emotions, an amateur [sic] of life, sensitive, gifted, handsome, but miscast badly as a royal king.' A very 'impressive' success with words is seen by Baxter as problematic, something that enables Richard to always 'steal the show'. Despite Richard's early promise, 'whatever the gods had intended him for, it was not the king of troubled England'. For Baxter the difference between the contenders for the crown is summed up in the 'symbolic gestures' on their return to England. Richard, back from Ireland, is 'weak, almost feminine' as he takes the earth in his 'delicate, royal palm' while the 'masculine and extroverted' Bolingbroke boldly asks the way to the castle. Later, Baxter's explanation of Henry V is without any shadow on the young king's reputation.

However, by *Henry IV*, Baxter acknowledges sadly that Henry IV is not really a successful king, but was 'uneasy, cold, and never popular'. Henry V 'like all feudal medieval kings had a dream to leave a name behind him. This means conquest'. Baxter points out how 'honourable' Henry's motives are, reviewing the inheritance with his bishops, informing the French of the impending attack, but the introduction focuses even more attention on the representatives of England, Scotland, Ireland and Wales who, for Baxter, epitomize national types (though in fact he is talking about stereotypes): Gower 'mannerly, good humored in a quiet way, a sportsman who wants fair play is as English as a pork pie'.[62] Jamy is a 'dour Scot, with long upper lip and long thin nose and a brogue like Dundee jam' but 'is a good solider' who doesn't say much. MacMorris, in contrast, is 'as professionally an Irishman as a modern Irish playwright [Baxter here gave a contemptuous sigh] who rages, shouts, beats his breast, foams at the mouth, and is tender and gentle the next moment'. 'Last but not least' is Fluellen, 'an amazing fellow' who 'joys in being a Welshman, talks with a magnificent Welsh intonation', and 'is a good dedicated soldier, "look you things must be done . . ."'

Falstaff receives more close attention than any character in Baxter's introductions. 'Rowdy, noisy, bawdy' Cheapside is really a 'Skid Row' and 'low life' with a vengeance.[63] Falstaff, he informs

viewers, 'is considered with Don Quixote one of the two greatest of all figures in comic literature of the Western world'. After noting that endless books, critical articles and essays continue to be written about Falstaff, Baxter spends several minutes, more than for any other character, dissecting what makes the character funny. He decides it is the way the 'comic hero gets away with it' for a successful rebellion. 'We all want to be doing something else' in life, but Falstaff's 'free until the last moment when life catches up with him'. It is a description that is at odds with Frank Pettingell's Falstaff who is not quite the great comic character and in the second part of *Henry IV* is far from an appealingly free comic spirit. Throughout Baxter's lectures there are very few references to the actual performances and choices made in *An Age of Kings*. Although Baxter makes frequent references to the productions, sometimes his comments are actually at odds with it. For example, Robert Hardy's Henry V is actually a much darker and less heroic interpretation of the role. Sometimes it does not match what appears in the production. In the final part of *Richard II*, Baxter goes to pains to point out that the Tower is not really a jail but a royal residence; however, audiences see Richard not in the Tower but in Pomfret in a straw-filled cell.

It is difficult to judge how much of an impact Baxter had on the programmes' success, but whether he was welcomed or merely found acceptable by American audiences, it is clear from reviews and viewer response that he was not obtrusive. Nor did anyone at the time point out that Baxter's – and NET's – 'normal American' was assumed to have an English heritage.

An Age of Kings would come full circle in 1964 when it was shown on New York's newly licensed educational television station WNET, Channel 13, which remains the New York area PBS station today. By that time all of the parties involved

---

[62] In the outline guide to his course Shakespeare on TV: English 356B, Spring Semester 1954 Baxter says that Gower is 'as unimaginative as a pork pie' (Los Angeles, 1954), p. 25.

[63] The warts, bumps and syphilitic sores on Bardolph's face support this idea.

had used Shakespeare's plays to achieve their goals. The BBC had established a mutually beneficial link with American educational television, initially not as lucrative as major networks might have been, but far more enduring. NET survived as the Fourth Network, thrived and nourished local educational television stations with its programmes. Other Shakespeare series would follow: the RSC's *Wars of the Roses* and, a decade later, the BBC would launch an even more ambitious Shakespeare television project, the complete works in 'The BBC/Time-Life Shakespeare series'. In the 1950s, television's fabled Golden Age, Shakespeare plays had been presented as part of network television's cultural mix. Once educational television stations became the only place they would be shown, they became segregated away from mainstream entertainment. Epic pageant was redefined as an educational event. Fortunately, the American viewers responded to *An Age of Kings* with the same enthusiasm that Peter Dews had seen in his schoolboys and the BBC in its audiences. NET's study guides and Frank Baxter's encouraging explanations may have helped – but it may also have been simply that Shakespeare's plays captured the imagination of the 'normal American', millions of whom tuned in week after week just to see what was going to happen next.

SHAKESPEARE AND BRITISH TELEVISION

OLWEN TERRIS

'Cultural values refer to our whole living, and not to a grace note on the margin'

Raymond Williams, *Communications*

INNOVATION AND OPTIMISM
1936–1950

Shakespeare and British television were close companions from the beginning. On 26 August 1936, *The Times* (London), under the heading 'First Television Broadcast', reported on a demonstration at Radio Olympia where the first experimental transmissions could be seen. Two programmes, lasting approximately ninety minutes, were transmitted daily from Alexandra Palace by the Baird system. At 12.49 and 5.19 visitors could see film excerpts, and among the films selected was Paul Czinner's *As You Like It* (1936). Elisabeth Bergner's name was mentioned as the selling point, Shakespeare's, the BBC's and Olivier's were not. Five months later on 5 February 1937 the first Shakespeare lines were spoken live on BBC television by Margaretta Scott (Rosalind) and Ion Swinley (Orlando) in *Scenes From Shakespeare's 'As You Like It'* (3.2) lasting eleven minutes.

Scenes from Shakespeare were transmitted monthly throughout television's first year of broadcasting. Shown in the mid afternoon, they employed actors and actresses well known from the stage, Michael Redgrave as Romeo, Celia Johnson as Desdemona. The scenes appear to have had no linking narration, audiences being expected to derive pleasure with no explanation of plot or setting, the BBC perhaps assuming that audiences would be familiar with the text, or if they were not then presenting famous passages from the greatest dramatist needed no apology or explanation, or perhaps they simply didn't think of their small audiences very much at all.[1]

The advent of television was regarded as miraculous.[2] The *BBC Handbook 1938* proclaimed 'Trains were an improvement upon stage coaches, mechanized flight on ballooning; but television is an improvement on nothing. It is something new under the sun.'[3] From the beginning producers and directors pushed hard at the technical boundaries of television dispelling any twenty-first century notion that plays in the 1930s and 1940s were wholly studio bound recreations of stage performances where the technology was there to record,

---

This article is the result of research conducted as part of 'An International Database of Shakespeare on Film, Television and Radio' (2005–8), funded by the Arts and Humanities Research Council at the British Universities Film and Video Council at www.bufvc.ac.uk/shakespeare.

[1] Around 2000 households had a television set by the end of 1937.

[2] BBC Television began transmission in 1936 as part of the BBC, a monopoly public corporation funded by a licence fee paid by each viewer or listener. Independent Television (ITV), funded by advertising revenue, became the BBC's first competitor in 1955. Channel 4, a public corporation funded by advertising, began broadcasting in 1982. For a detailed, if uncritical, account of British broadcasting (chiefly seen from within the BBC) see Asa Briggs, *History of Broadcasting in the UK*, 5 vols. (London, 1995). For a history of Independent Television see *Independent Television in Great Britain*, 6 vols. (London, 1982–2003).

[3] *BBC Handbook 1938* (London, 1939), p. 40.

not to shape, the aesthetic. Many were of course, but in 1938 Dallas Bower produced a modern dress version of *Julius Caesar* employing stock news footage and incidental music, and in January 1939 *Twelfth Night* (Peggy Ashcroft as Viola) was relayed live from the Phoenix Theatre, London. Plays were repeated the same week because it was felt that single performances to a small audience were uneconomic, an astonishing achievement considering that broadcasts were live, actors had to be brought back, studio crews reassembled and the show directed again. Shakespearian drama put back the time of close-down for the first time in 1947 as broadcasting was extended by thirty minutes to accommodate a full performance of *Romeo and Juliet*.

Producers and directors, perforce with a background in radio, stage or cinema, understood from the start that producing plays for television demanded a different art and craft and these issues were frequently debated in the *Radio Times*. In 1937 producer George More O'Ferrall wrote 'I believe television is a medium of its own and it is a mistake to try to copy the films'. Yet for O'Ferrall the camera was there primarily to record performance; as he continued, 'We should regard fine acting as our chief asset and use the camera to show it to its best advantage.'[4] He believed actors should play more slowly for the television camera, holding the point, not over-emphasizing it. Ten years later producer Michael Barry was looking for a greater urgency, at least in speech delivery, stating that 'television brings the actor closer to the audience as on an Elizabethan stage', the intimacy of television allowing for a 'much quicker pace in speech'.[5] The same year O'Ferrall echoed Barry's sentiments and in a *Radio Times* feature article 'Televising *Hamlet*' he asked, 'But why should we claim that television is especially suited to Shakespeare? Because in its method of presentation it comes nearer to the Elizabethan theatre, for which the plays were written than the modern theatre can do.' Certainly the small studio space, and the proximity of the actors, encouraged the extensive use of medium and close-up shots which captured the intimacy, if not the simultaneous quality of the character's isolation, so often felt in the theatre. O'Ferrall was concerned about the attention span of his viewers too: 'anything over an hour-and-a-half is (in my opinion) a strain on television audiences. So *Hamlet* will be presented in two halves.'[6]

Most interestingly the public felt that they too were an integral part of a new era of technological experimentation and cultural adventure and had the power to shape it. Jean Bartlett, identified as a 'housewife', reported in the *Radio Times* in 1937 on her experiences of watching the first months of television broadcasting and offered a timely and thoughtful critique: 'The most important element of the television picture is obviously movement. The artists may be shatteringly beautiful, the lighting perfect, the scenery just right, but without constant movement it completely fails.' Of the short *Scenes from Shakespeare*, the only Shakespeare to be broadcast in 1937, Mrs Bartlett was sceptical. Commenting shrewdly on an audience's ability to assimilate the uncontextualized scenes at speed and criticizing the position of the camera which recorded them, she noted: 'Shakespeare on the other hand, invariably falls flat even when distinguished artists are playing the selected parts. Non-Shakespearians are frankly bored – they cannot get the hang of the thing before it is over; and lovers of Shakespeare are irritated by brief episodes suspended in mid-air and inevitably devoid of the play's original stagecraft, and viewed from two cameras alternately at rather uninteresting angles.'[7]

'Television is Here to Stay – You Can't Shut Your Eyes to It' heralded a full page advertisement for television sets in the *Radio Times*, February 1939. 'Television is here to widen your horizon, to give a new depth, a richer meaning to life.' If Shakespeare did have a significant role to play in nourishing the

---

4 George More O'Ferrall, 'The Televising of Drama', *Radio Times*, 19 March 1937, pp. 4–5.

5 Michael Barry cited in the *Radio Times*, 3 October 1947, p. 33.

6 George More O'Ferrall, 'Televising *Hamlet*', *Radio Times*, 5 December 1947, p. 30.

7 Jean Bartlett, 'Views of a Viewer', *Radio Times*, 4 June 1937, p. 3.

nation's spiritual life he took his place in a broad and colourful tapestry.

Television broadcasting was suspended in September 1939 for the duration of the War and resumed in June 1946. In December 1947, *Hamlet* was broadcast over two weeks in ninety-minute episodes. Part 1 was prefaced by a thirty-minute documentary on penicillin and followed by the news; viewers that day could also have watched a documentary on sea scouts, London bus drivers training on skid tracks and a Russian newsreel entitled *Sunday in Moscow*. Norman Collins, Controller BBC Television Service, writing in *BBC Quarterly* in 1949, supported this integration of Shakespeare into the nation's viewing life: 'But television must never be a gigantic stage for showing Shakespeare. There must be fun as well as fineness in the service, and a place for the Lido Cabaret as well as for *King Lear*.'[8] Collins's warning that Shakespeare was fine but no fun was a premonition of the segregation and elevation of Shakespeare in broadcasting schedules which was to come. Many cultural historians have not shared Collins's evaluation of television as a medium which could embrace Shakespeare on an equal footing. Constructing cultural hierarchies and starting from the premise that television is low-brow (the most degraded of the mass media) and Shakespeare its redeemer is an assumption that has bedevilled debate, muddled thinking and poorly served both the medium and the message for decades.[9]

THE FEAR OF COMMERCE 1950–1960

The excitement of the technical, entertainment and educative possibilities of television felt by producers and audiences in the 1930s and 1940s, in the 1950s began to be tempered by fear – fear of being unable to fill the broadcasting hours available, fear of the onset of competitive television, fear of technical advances being made in America, fear that lack of money and studio space would curtail ambition and fear of the effect television might have on family life.

In 1954 radio listeners still outnumbered television viewers by three to one but the number of combined radio and television licences had passed the three million mark. An increase in the number of transmitters meant that signals could now reach 90 per cent of the population, and television was no longer the prerogative of the upper-middle classes in London and the Midlands who could afford a set. *The BBC Handbook 1954* cited a letter to *The Times* which reported a skipping rhyme, chanted by a small child in a London street:

> I like coffee
> I like tea
> I like radio
> And tv[10]

Television was now pervasive although surveys suggest strongly that the acquisition of a receiver was as much to do with a desire for social status and modernity as it was a wish to expand personal cultural horizons.[11]

Television had reached the masses but the democracy which this entailed began to be questioned, the culture of 'ordinary people' always seeming an issue of concern to those in social and political power who construct cultural distinctions and then police the boundaries to maintain them. The phrase 'popular culture' has frequently been interpreted as an aesthetic judgement, not taken literally, anything which millions enjoy and understand 'for free' becoming immediately artistically suspect. As cultural historian Lawrence W. Levine

---

[8] Norman Collins, 'Television and the Future', *BBC Quarterly* 4 April 1949, pp. 30–1.

[9] There are surprisingly few historical surveys of Shakespeare on British television. Readers are directed to Susanne Greenhalgh, 'U.K. Television', in Richard Burt, *Shakespeare After Shakespeares: an Encyclopedia of the Bard in Mass Media and Popular Culture*, vol. 2 (Westport, CT, 2007), pp. 651–732. A survey of Shakespeare on British television is followed by 500 annotated entries of television adaptations and a comprehensive bibliography. J. C. Bulman and H. R. Coursen, eds., *Shakespeare on Television: an Anthology of Essays and Reviews* (Hanover, 1988) offers a selection of essays addressing the challenges of presenting Shakespeare on the small screen.

[10] *BBC Handbook 1955* (London, 1956), p. 82.

[11] Tim O'Sullivan, 'Television Memories and Cultures of Viewing', in *Popular Television in Britain: Studies in Cultural History*, ed. John Corner (London, 1991), pp. 164–7.

observed, it was believed by those in power that 'culture cannot come from the young, the inexperienced, the marginal' and is 'recognisable only by those trained to recognise it, comprehensible only to those qualified to comprehend it'.[12] Raymond Williams, academic and critic, also saw the dangers of a ruling body dividing culture into 'mass' and 'minority' and failed to see that it was a permanent and reliable way of safeguarding excellence. Writing in *Communications* he observed, 'At best, a minority culture is keeping the works available, often the best that has been said and done in the world. At worst, it translates into its own accents.'[13]

In 1950, R. W. Moore, Headmaster of Harrow School, was one of those who was worried that mass education, a necessary consequence of democracy, pointed to barbarism and wrote in *BBC Quarterly*, 'there is an element of evil in all mass-spread entertainment'. Deploring the development, he continued, 'one of the saddest aspects of broadcasting arises from the thought that one can walk down a street and hear in almost every house the same programme pouring into the ears of the inmates'.[14] By giving everyone the opportunity to enjoy Shakespeare, he implied, the class structure supporting and celebrating him would collapse, the work was devalued, and the individual's personal relationship with the poet undermined and under threat.

The early 1950s saw a growing fear of the onset of commercial television. Whether the public wanted or needed broadcasting competition seemed irrelevant; the forces of political economy were strong and by October 1955 Britain's second television service, and first commercial one, had arrived, a presence which had an immediate and long-lasting impact on the nature of the drama transmitted in the UK. The name 'Independent Television' (ITV) was an intelligent choice, the word 'independent' distinguishing it from the state-linked BBC and suggesting an objective and dispassionate stance, so masking its true objective which was to make money. Championed by the Conservative Party, ITV's stated aim was to break the BBC's monopoly and establish competition.

Lord Reith, the first Director-General of the BBC, had five years previously predicted the arrival and impact of commercial television and his remarks were prophetic. A diary entry for 1950 reads, 'If there is to be competition it will be of cheapness not goodness.'[15] Over ten years later, embittered by the BBC and all who ran it, he felt that the organization had succumbed to the lowest common denominator – i.e. giving the public what it wanted in order to survive. An entry in 1964 illustrates that Reith believed his prophecy had come to pass 'he [Sir Hugh Carleton Greene, the Director-General] is, in fact, in favour of what is a negation of almost all that I stand for. He gives the public what it wants. That is his price. It is exactly what I utterly repudiate.'[16] Later the same year he concluded that the BBC and God had finally parted company: 'the BBC has lost its dignity and repute; in the upper reaches of intellectual and ethical and social leadership it has abdicated its responsibility and its privilege . . . it is no longer on the Lord's side'.[17]

The effect of giving the public what it wanted was felt within weeks of ITV's first broadcast. A piece in the *Daily Mirror* headed 'ITV Cuts the Culture to Stop Viewers Switching Off' reported that, when a concert or talk was broadcast, viewers turned off or switched to the BBC.[18] The regular Hallé Orchestra concerts, conducted by Sir John Barbirolli, were moved from 8.30 pm to 10 pm to make way for the American Western series *Gunsmoke*. 'Brahms Will Not Sell Boot Polish', reliably reported the *News Chronicle* the same day.[19] The same issue, quoting an ITV spokesman, noted 'a

---

[12] Lawrence W. Levine, *Highbrow/Lowbrow: The Emergence of Cultural Hierarchy in America* (Cambridge, MA, 1988), p. 252.

[13] Raymond Williams, *Communications*, rev. edn (Harmondsworth, Middx, 1962), pp. 100–1.

[14] R. W. Moore, *BBC Quarterly* 5, no. 1 (Spring 1950), p. 8.

[15] John Reith, *The Reith Diaries* (London, 1975), p. 470.

[16] Reith, p. 512 (Letter to Mr Oliver Whitley).

[17] Reith, p. 514 (Letter to Sir Arthur fforde).

[18] Clifford Davis, 'ITV Cuts the Culture to Stop Viewers Switching Off', *Daily Mail*, 24 November 1955.

[19] James Thomas, 'Brahms Will Not Sell Boot Polish', *News Chronicle*, 24 November 1955.

survey of our audience over the first eight weeks has proved that they are exactly like the public in the US. They want good stories in plays, boxing and other blood sports, and smart personality musicals.' Shakespeare did not fit well into the perceived public demand. In 1956, Desmond Davis, Head of Drama at Associated Television, resigned claiming there was no drama left for him to produce.

The first Shakespeare play transmitted by Independent Television was Peter Brook's celebrated production of *Hamlet* at the Phoenix Theatre, London with Paul Scofield in the title role. It was broadcast live from a studio to audiences in London and the Midlands on 27 February 1956. This broadcast is extremely instructive for what it reveals about the friction between culture and commercialism in the very early days of ITV. The play was shown with two commercial breaks – in the first Alexander Gauge (Friar Tuck in ATV's *Robin Hood* series) promoted sausages, and the second advertised MacDougall's flour directly after Ophelia's mad scene. What caused the greatest commotion, however, was that at the close of the play the sound was deliberately faded thirty seconds before the end of Fortinbras's final speech as the audience was led into a carefully timed jingle advertising Sunfresh orange juice. Worse, the announcer declaimed 'and there we must leave Hamlet'. This unkind cut outraged Peter Brook who sent a telegram to Sir Kenneth Clark (then Chairman of the IBA) threatening never to work with commercial television again. One critic, however, was unruffled by the intrusion of advertising, feeling commercial breaks to be no more disruptive to ruminative silence than the interval at the theatre, and wrote 'I thought the alliance of sausages, the *Daily Mail*, more flour, more coffee and Shakespeare splendidly realistic and much more interesting than the fight to get to the bar that goes on during the intervals in a theatre.'[20]

Audience reaction to the play was not promising. Bernard Sendall in his history of independent television notes that 16 per cent of 'so-called' Band III homes (homes that could receive both BBC and ITV channels) tuned in, but audiences fell to 8 per cent in the first quarter of an hour and never rose above 15 per cent.[21] The BBC meanwhile was showing the panel game *What's My Line*, the current affairs programme *Panorama* and *Off the Record* (popular dance music) and audiences switching channels helped viewing figures for *What's My Line* to reach new heights for this episode, Lady Barnett and Gilbert Harding receiving as much praise from the public and critics for their performances as did Scofield.

If ITV primetime had abandoned Shakespeare at the first hurdle, then ITV schools broadcasting did not. The quality and quantity of educational output by Associated-Rediffusion and ATV in the 1950s and 1960s was remarkable; tackling comedies, histories and the tragedies, the programmes, typically shown in seven or eight parts to accommodate the school term, introduced children to aspects of stage production, textual analysis, dramatic structure, acting technique and history. In 1958, for example, Associated-Rediffusion broadcast a nine-part series *Producing Macbeth* and in 1960 an eight-part series entitled *Terrible Choice* examined good and evil in medieval drama. Sadly these programmes have not survived.

As ITV struggled to reconcile Shakespeare to its cultural and economic remit, at least in primetime, the BBC continued to produce a steady and innovative stream of Shakespeare's plays throughout the 1950s. Never underestimating an audience's capacity for intellectual challenge in 1950, and in days when *entente* with the French government was clearly more cordial, the broadcasters treated the British public to the last scene of *Othello* in French. The scene was from Jean Meyer's Comédie Française production staged at the Old Vic Theatre, London. The staging was re-enacted for television, after a two-day rehearsal, and broadcast to mark the state visit to the United Kingdom of the President of the French Republic. Despite the enticement in the *Radio Times* that *Othello* is 'the most Racinian of plays' this bold move did not go down well with

---

[20] Peter Black, *Daily Mail*, 28 February 1956.
[21] Bernard Sendall, *Independent Television in Britain. Vol. 1: Origin and Foundation, 1946–62* (London, 1982), p. 168.

viewers, reaching a Reaction Index (RI)[22] of only 54, the official summary in the Audience Panel Viewing Report concluding 'for the majority of viewers the language barrier proved a serious deterrent to enjoyment'.[23]

Two years later the BBC offered *The Merry Wives of Windsor*, one of the earliest live studio broadcasts. This production fared worse with audiences securing a RI of 41 – the lowest yet for a Shakespeare play where the average for a Sunday evening drama was 75. One local government official, contributing to the Audience Panel Viewing Report, commented 'not one of Shakespeare's best. It always seems to me to take a long time to get nowhere.'[24] Other comments on the production were typical of viewer reaction to Shakespeare in the 1950s – I couldn't follow the plot, the actors 'gabble', it looks cramped, I liked the scenery, the amount of concentration outweighs enjoyment, I don't much like Shakespeare anyway and especially not on Sundays.

The *Radio Times* would usually allocate a full or half page to a Shakespeare production giving the plot and the full cast. There would be an illustration (often pen and ink drawings), stills of the actors, and generally a short piece from a critic on the history of the play and its production. It has been noted by writers on Shakespeare on television that this isolated Shakespeare from the 'flow' of broadcasting, setting Shakespearian drama apart as something culturally elite. This is true, but the BBC treated all classic drama the same way in its *Radio Times* presentation; plays from the great writers were special and should be highlighted and celebrated as events worth preparing for and investing in. Perhaps the biggest problem was that Shakespeare began to be presented not as entertainment, a programme mixed in with boxing, a variety show and the weather, as an extension and illumination of experience but as something potentially difficult and set apart, revered by the educated and disseminated to the ordinary man and woman as an elite supplement to their modest cultural fare. This turnabout was to have long-term damaging effects on the quantity and quality of Shakespeare on television.

Watching television is frequently a casual experience – 'is there anything on telly tonight?' – unlike going to the theatre or cinema where plans have to be made and money changes hands. In the small sitting room interruptions are frequent. The television technology itself in the 1950s caused its own distractions – no remote controls, switching on five minutes before a show to allow the set to 'warm up', getting up and down every two minutes to adjust the horizontal and vertical holds as pictures wobbled out of view, and twiddling knobs at the back of the set in frequently hopeless endeavours to rid the small grey screen of its snowstorm. Watching drama, particularly Shakespearian drama where intense concentration is required over two hours, is not, and never has been, easy.

Television playwright Dennis Potter in an interview conducted in 1970 saw dangers in television viewing, believing that watching, for example, commercials, pop shows, the news and Shakespeare in a seamless flow ironed out emotional response resulting in a generalized, not particular, experience. He was in sympathy with Raymond Williams who, in his seminal work *Communications* published eight years earlier, had questioned 'But isn't the real danger of "mass culture" – of things like television . . . that it reduces us to an endlessly mixed, bored reaction? . . . You're not exactly enjoying it, or paying any particular attention, but it's passing the time.'[25] Potter knew that watching television is often random and its pervasive nature can work against informed choice – 'the theatre is a kind of middle-class privilege, a dying sort of minority thing . . . but only television is classless, multiple, and of course people will switch on and people will choose. On the whole I suppose I'm very pessimistic. People will tend to choose crap

---

[22] Reaction Index (RI) is a five-point scale measuring viewers' enjoyment of a programme, ranging from extreme enjoyment/pleasure to extreme dislike.

[23] Audience Panel Viewing Report 8/3/1950. BBC Written Archives Centre, Caversham.

[24] Audience Panel Viewing Report 16/11/1952. BBC Written Archives Centre, Caversham.

[25] Williams, *Communications*, p. 99.

rather than not. But on the other hand you do just have the chance to grab them.'[26] Sceptical about an audience's conscious appetite for culture, he nevertheless refused to relieve broadcasters of their obligation to provide it.

REALISM AND NATURALISM
1960–1970

Media historians have deemed the 1960s to be the 'golden age' of British television, although this value judgement is often a reflection of the nostalgia of middle-aged critics for the time when they first became acquainted with, and responsive to, television drama. In the case of Shakespeare productions, however, the historians may be right as the decade (which embraced the quatercentenary) brought audiences *An Age of Kings*, *The Spread of the Eagle*, *The Wars of the Roses*, *Hamlet at Elsinore*, plus an adaptation of *Macbeth* for schools and a steady stream of productions within the *Play of the Month* banner.

An Age of Kings, broadcast in 1960, was an audacious concept and the most ambitious Shakespeare project the BBC had undertaken. In fifteen parts it encompassed *Richard II*, *Henry IV Parts 1 and 2*, *Henry V*, the *Henry VI* cycle and *Richard III*. Each episode cost £4,000, a sizeable proportion of the drama budget. Peter Dews, the producer, stated his lofty objectives: 'all I aim to do is to present this great sweep of plays in a manner that will intrigue the Specialist, gratify the Lover, and introduce to the yet un-knowing Spectator, some of the Glories, tragic and comic, of the Crown Jewels of our Language'.[27]

The plays made no attempt to conceal, and took care to exploit, the fact that they were shot in a studio. Medium and close-up shots were used heavily, the props were basic, the set sparse – their retention throughout the serial providing a strong sense of unification. Most importantly the aesthetic mirrored more closely that of the theatre, a fact which Dews readily acknowledged. 'No film will be used. When the author has apologized for the absence of horses, who am I to put them back?'[28] Dews believed the small acting space influenced

the actor's delivery: 'the intimacy of the action and the absence of a large auditorium allow the actor to use the time he normally spends in projecting his voice in assuming a more rapid and urgent delivery'.[29] Some years later actor Robert Hardy interviewed in *The Times* confirmed the strengths of anti-naturalism: 'There was an audience still hungry for the classics, and willing to accept a heightened language; now all they want is naturalism.'[30]

As early as the 1960s producers and schedulers were seeing and exploiting the benefits of presenting plays under a series or serial banner, a format which has closer associations with late eighteenth- and nineteenth-century fiction than it does sixteenth-century drama. Audiences, it was hoped, would come to identify with the characters (helped by employing a repertory cast), become involved in sad stories of the death of kings, and want to know what happened next. The ploy worked. The serial was watched by 9 per cent of the viewing population commanding a RI in the high seventies or eighties for each episode, viewers' reactions making it clear that what they most valued was that the actors spoke clearly and told a story, one viewer commenting, in an interesting choice of words, that *An Age of Kings* was 'one of the finest entertainments ever arranged for television'.[31]

Publicity for the series in the *Radio Times* treated the drama as it would any other, no special case being made for Shakespeare, no suggestion (in sharp contrast to the marketing of *ShakespeaRe-Told* over forty years later) that this is Shakespeare but we will do our best to disguise it. Half a page was devoted to listing the full cast and a full page given to a feature article. The article did not dwell on the

---

[26] Dennis Potter cited in Joan Bakewell and Nicholas Gainham, *British Television Today* (London, 1970), p. 80.

[27] Undated memo from Peter Dews in *An Age of Kings* production files. BBC Written Archives Centre, Caversham.

[28] Dews, *An Age of Kings*.

[29] Dews, *An Age of Kings*.

[30] Robert Hardy interviewed by Sheridan Morley, *The Times*, 26 April 1982, p. 11.

[31] Audience Panel Viewing Report, *The Boar Hunt* (17/11/60). BBC Written Archives Centre, Caversham.

careers and personality of the actors but empha-sized the fact that what audiences would be seeing was a part of England's history presented as drama; the fact that Shakespeare was the dramatist seemed neither here nor there.

The television critics were enthusiastic but typ-ically assessments rarely confronted the medium of television, regarding it as an unwelcome (if inevitable) substitute for the cinema or theatre, an instrument of viewing convenience rather than an inherent art form. Live theatre was still regarded as the final measure of what was authentically Shake-spearian and evaluations were directed to an audi-ence who, they assumed, would obviously prefer to see the show on stage if they could. An excep-tion was Irving Wardle, reviewing *Henry IV Part 1* in *The Listener*. In a piece headed 'Exciting Shake-speare', he wrote, 'It had plenty of invention, but no superfluous decoration, no "business", every excursion into novelty was an expression of the underlying dynamics, proportioned strictly in rela-tionship to the whole. The effect was quite extraor-dinary'.[32] What Wardle saw was that Peter Dews and his team understood Shakespeare, understood dramatic structure, understood the strengths and weaknesses of television as a medium, and under-stood audiences. It was an unbeatable combination. *An Age of Kings* commanded an average viewing figure of 3 million each episode, making Dews the most influential interpreter of Shakespeare in the English-speaking world.[33]

Three years later, banking on the goodwill engendered by those remembering *An Age of Kings*, Dews produced *The Spread of the Eagle*, a nine-part series comprising Shakespeare's Roman plays: *Coriolanus*, *Julius Caesar* and *Antony and Cleopa-tra*. Again he employed an ensemble cast and a permanent set. This time the strategy was far less successful, familiarity not engendering the antici-pated respect. Audiences were not responsive – 'noisy and confusing', 'so much shouting' said two viewers in the panel viewing reports on *Coriolanus*. Despite the fact that the *Radio Times* outlined the plot, viewers were bewildered. The RI remained in the sixties. Perhaps the real failing was that the serial structure which had served *An Age of Kings* so

well here appeared contrived, the climaxes seem-ing forcibly separated from the development which led up to them. The connection between the plays is tenuous: Mark Antony appearing in both *Julius Caesar* and *Antony and Cleopatra* does not make for dramatic unity, and the fact that the three plays were influenced by Sir Thomas North's transla-tion of Plutarch, and there are textual similarities between *Coriolanus* and *Antony and Cleopatra* influ-enced audience appreciation not a jot.

If Robert Hardy is correct in his belief that all audiences wanted was realism, then their desires would be gratified in the style of television drama that developed in the 1960s, a style which did not serve Shakespeare's text and dramatic struc-ture well. An influential manifesto 'Nats Go Home' by television writer Troy Kennedy Martin heav-ily criticized theatrical naturalism, the reliance on the literary tradition which 'made tv drama a makeshift bastard born of the theatre'.[34] Martin argued that drama which told stories by means of dialogue should be 'OUT'. He addressed televi-sion camerawork style, challenging the belief that the close-up of the actor's face acts subjectively on the viewer – 'we, therefore, get the spectacle of the writer, actor and director all combining to some-how involve the viewer emotionally in a character's predicament by close-up writing, acting and shoot-ing'. Acting styles became less 'stagey', more nat-ural and invisible. Filmmakers were experimenting with *cinéma-vérité* techniques in their dramas and

[32] Irving Wardle, *The Listener*, 5 May 1960, p. 815.

[33] *An Age of Kings*, and many other productions (for example the RSC's *Wars of the Roses* (1965) and John Barton's *All's Well That Ends Well* (1968)), have never been released on VHS/DVD and are available for viewing only in archives. For an account of the commercial distribution history of the *BBC Television Shakespeare* series see Olwen Terris, 'BBC Television Shakespeare DVDs', *Viewfinder*, 62 (March 2006), p. 17. A high proportion of BBC and ITV productions pro-duced before the mid 1970s have been lost or wiped. Televi-sion plays made before the War were transmitted live; there was no means by which to record them and none has sur-vived. For details of archival holdings and current distribution information visit www.bufvc.ac.uk/shakespeare.

[34] Troy Kennedy Martin, 'Nats Go Home', *Encore 48* (March/April 1964), p. 21–33.

casting little known or untrained actors often with strong regional accents. The new screen heroes were Albert Finney and Tom Courtenay, leaving little room for the grander, gestural acting styles and trained voice projection of Shakespearian actors in the mould of Gielgud and Olivier. What television required was intensity of voice but without vocal projection, the small screen rarely sympathetic to rhetoric and heightened language. It is interesting to note that Olivier stayed away from performing Shakespeare on television. *The Merchant of Venice* (1974) was not conceived for television (of his own admission the only concession made to his small screen performance was to install a smaller set of false teeth), and *King Lear* (1983) for Granada Television was his Shakespearian swan-song, but that is all. Olivier himself gives no clues, reflecting in his autobiography, 'I'm just sorry I stood aloof from television for so long', but offers no explanation as to why this was so.[35] Perhaps he sensed that television often militates against performance, preferring to display 'types' of character rather than the finely textured unique individuals which Shakespeare creates.

Drama began to move out of the studio which, in its restricted space, and the tendency to film faces talking and reacting, supported a style of production very much closer to theatre. As cameras became lighter, location shooting on 16 mm was prevalent, and montage sequences, freeing narratives from natural time, provided a different kind of visual storytelling. It is a truism to observe that Shakespeare did not write shooting scripts; the fluid shooting style, edited into short segments, does not always serve the blank verse well, often seeming as if the impatient, ever-changing images can't wait for the dialogue to catch up. Television plays were now becoming films in all but name.

THE BBC AND CONSERVATISM
1970–1990

There are many reasons why television executives have produced Shakespeare on television, few of them related to a strong commitment to communicate the unique beauty of his dramatic verse. They are made to further personal ambition, as showcases for specific performances, to gain ascendancy in franchise rivalries over cultural output, or as a filmed record of a stage production; almost all are made as an act of faith over the realities of economic projections.

In the case of the *BBC Television Shakespeare* series, which dominated British screens from 1979–1985, the origins were less concrete. 'One fine summer day in Scotland the BBC Shakespeare series was conceived out of whimsy' – so Susan Willis begins her definitive book on the televised canon.[36] Strolling round Glamis Castle in 1975, while directing James Barrie's *The Little Minister* on location, BBC producer Cedric Messina believed that this was the perfect setting for *As You Like It* – and so the series was born.

The BBC series, led by Messina, conflated the superiority of Shakespeare with its own tradition and created the canon in its own image – conservative, culturally authoritative, durable and necessary. More damaging still was the stated desire to meet perceived audience expectations of how Shakespeare's dramas should look and sound – that expectation being voiced and shared by both the BBC and the series's corporate funders, thus forming a dominant circle of intent from which the wider audience was effectively excluded. Lacking the will or imagination to challenge audiences by offering them what they never knew they wanted, the productions that emerged were generally innocuous and unimaginative – no cutting or re-arranging of text, no modern costumes, no foreign or regional accents, no radical interpretations.

At the close of the series Shaun Sutton (the third and final producer for the series) commented cheerfully and unquestioningly on the project, 'It's all been enormous fun . . . never solemn, full of giggles, not too immersed in intellectual content, it's the end of a great era, a great incident in the life of television.'[37] Viewing figures in Britain were

---

[35] Laurence Olivier, *On Acting* (London, 1986), p. 228.
[36] Susan Willis, *The BBC Shakespeare Plays: Making the Televised Canon* (Chapel Hill, 1991), p. 3.
[37] Shaun Sutton cited in Willis, p. 32.

modest (between one and three million for each play); the lure of Shakespeare might be considered against the fact that the opening play *Romeo and Juliet* attracted 1.9 million viewers while ten years earlier *The Forsyte Saga* had commanded seventeen million and, three weeks after *Romeo and Juliet*, the first television showing of the musical *The Sound of Music* (1965) reached an audience of 26 million. But by 1982 the series had paid for itself and was making a handsome profit from foreign sale, Brian Wenham, Controller of BBC2, claiming that 'Shakespeare is the *only* series of programmes whose sales have completely covered their costs in this way.'[38]

Ironically, the perception that the *BBC Television Shakespeare* series should offer a definitive permanent canon may have been another nail in the coffin for Shakespeare on television, relieving the BBC of the obligation to produce any more. Viewers had to wait nine years before the BBC televised another Shakespeare play, *Measure for Measure* (1994) directed by David Thacker, the only play to be screened in the two-month *Bard on the Box* season. Some critics argued that the *BBC Television Shakespeare* series was so dull that it would effectively kill any viewer's potential interest in Shakespeare at the first stroke. Director Michael Bogdanov, commissioned by Jonathan Miller to direct *Timon of Athens*, left when his oriental modern-dress interpretation was vetoed at an early stage, declaring that the series was 'the greatest disservice to Shakespeare in the last twenty five years'.[39]

THE SINGLE PLAY

In the 1950s audiences (children and adults) were privileged to be offered over thirty 'straight' productions of Shakespeare plays on British television (i.e. productions which used Shakespeare's text and a conventional five-act structure). In the twenty years following the close of the *BBC Television Shakespeare* series in 1985 only eleven such productions have been broadcast. The majority of these plays in the late 1980s and 1990s were not conceived for television but took their impetus and aesthetic from successful stage productions – Richard Eyre's National Theatre 1997 produc-

tion of *King Lear* with Ian Holm for example, or plays filmed live from Shakespeare's Globe Theatre. Only David Thacker's modern-dress *Measure for Measure* (1994) was made specifically for television and commanded a very modest viewing figure of 734,000, 4 per cent of the available BBC2 audience.

The demise of the single, authored play (even the word 'play' seeming now quaint having been largely replaced by the more cinematic word 'drama') also accounts for dwindling productions of Shakespeare or indeed any other single drama. From the 1960s producers and schedulers were becoming increasingly aware that presenting single plays gave them problems and larger audiences could be obtained by scheduling plays in a named series. Scheduling drama at the same time each week would, it was supposed, encourage audience familiarity and create both a continuing style and a set of expectations which the broadcasters would aim to exploit, build up and maintain.

The single play is expensive to produce and when drama has to deliver an economic as well as a cultural return (i.e. high viewing figures and strong international sales) such programmes are a high-risk investment, especially as Shakespeare's plays command two to three hours of broadcasting time. The introduction in 1982 of Channel 4 was also significant in the part it played in the fall of the single play. The number of plays shown in the BBC's *Play for Today* slot noticeably declined after this date, falling from fifteen productions in the 1979–80 season to three in the final 1984–5 run when it was replaced by the films screened under the *Screen 2* and *Screenplay* banners. Film production from the start was an important part of C4's remit; television budgets could not compete and new writers penned their dramatic work with the aim of a cinematic release. C4, as did other channels, looked for co-producers to help fund these expensive productions and willing assistance came more often than not from America. When

---

[38] Brian Wenham, cited in Willis, p. 9.
[39] Michael Bogdanov, cited in Willis, p. 26.

producers are beholden to funders, and pro-grammes are tailored to the requirements of the prospective buyer and not the indigenous audience, this in turn strongly influences the drama that is made, the *BBC Television Shakespeare* series with its 'straightforward' productions where the brief was no monkey tricks being a good example. Receding rapidly were the days when television directors could produce Shakespeare plays (or any drama) in innovative and provocative ways free from thoughts of ratings; now creativity had to be tailored to conform to a product which would offer maximum acceptance to the widest audience.

The single play has been largely replaced since the early 1970s by the serial or mini-series, usually scheduled over four or six weeks, each episode ending on a narrative or emotional cliff-hanger. Serialization serves the structure of novels far better than it does the single drama, reflecting the way they are read in several sittings. Shakespeare's plays, even those written in five acts, are intended to be seen and assimilated in a single experience. Watching *Othello*, for example, develop over several weeks holds few charms, the Shakespeare fan feeling instinctively that such an extenuation would lower tension, slacken the pace, diffuse the emotions and be, in short, bad drama.

In the 1980s, under the leadership of the Conservative Prime Minister Margaret Thatcher, the British government increasingly applied its belief in free-market economies to broadcasting. In 1990 the White Paper *Broadcasting in the Nineties: Competition, First Choice and Quality*[40] (the ordering of priorities was felt to be significant) entered the statute books as the *Broadcasting Act*. Renewal of ITV franchises was put to competitive tender, cable and satellite channels increased, a new terrestrial channel, Channel 5, was introduced and in the early 1990s the new BBC Director-General, John Birt, brought in the widely despised policy 'producer choice' designed to bring a more cost-effective management to BBC programme making. These profound changes in both the production and delivery of television made the 1990s the most significant decade for change in British television since the arrival of commercial television in 1955.

1990s – LITERARY ADAPTATIONS AND COSTUME DRAMA

The 1990s saw many television adaptations of classic novels, and the trend continues – three adaptations of Jane Austen's work alone being screened in the UK in 2007. Such productions (Andrew Davies's screenplay for *Pride and Prejudice* to take an obvious example) are popular and critical successes, expensive to produce but an investment yielding rich dividends, securing audiences in their millions, and selling to broadcasters worldwide.

Shakespeare fits awkwardly in this popular genre of costume drama (or its close relative, heritage drama), many surveys of the genre failing to mention his plays at all in their analyses. The intricacies of Shakespeare's plots and themes, his dramatic structure and language, resist the surface levelling of the costume drama where ironies and social nuances implicit in the text are frequently smoothed away, the past 'de-historicized', and emotional and political complexities reduced to a concentration on romantic relationships and simple narrative. Dressing actors in ruffs and doublets may reinforce a twenty-first century audience's notion of its past, but it can conflict with the vision of many directors who are uneasy with that history, preferring modern costume or costuming deliberately resisting evocations of a particular period and seeking contemporary relevance rather than historical accuracy. Such thinking is often directly opposed to the wishes of television viewers looking for a strong correlation between costume and language; Elizabethan verse spoken by actors sporting jeans and trainers adding an unwelcome layer of confusion for viewers already struggling with unfamiliar sights and sounds. Frequently Shakespeare set his plays in single locations, or foreign countries, or no place at all, portraying a metaphorical abstract space far removed from cinematic 'realism'. The various periods and geographical locations in which Shakespeare chose to place his dramas, and the uncertainties of life on which he dwells, deny audiences the

---

40 *Broadcasting in the Nineties: Competition, First Choice, Quality*, Cmd 517 (London, 1989).

comforting reassurance of some golden age of stable, imperialist Britain which heritage drama celebrates.

In 2001 London Weekend Television, mindful of the fact that no Shakespeare had been broadcast on ITV for almost twenty years, and wanting to up the stakes in 'quality drama', approached Andrew Davies asking him if he would write a modern adaptation of Shakespeare. Davies, a highly articulate and engaging self-publicist, is a television executive's dream, celebrated by the public and critics alike for his successes in adapting classic novels, casting intelligently, upping the sex quotient and commanding impressive viewing figures while eliciting good critical reviews. Davies readily agreed and proposed a modern adaptation of *Othello* placing John Othello as the first black Chief Commissioner of London's Metropolitan Police against a background of racial violence. The broadcasters accepted the proposition with alacrity. *Othello* was screened in the Christmas week on ITV1 on 21 December 2001 in primetime and commanded an audience of over three million, 17 per cent of the audience share; although this success can be measured against an episode of *Heartbeat* (a heritage drama series set in 1960s North Yorkshire) which it followed, which was watched by 10 million.

Throwing out Shakespeare's lines and setting the story in contemporary times is the favourite method of attempting 'relevance' to secure younger audiences and those unacquainted with the work who might be deterred by the word 'Shakespeare' and the learning associated with Elizabethan verse. The debate continues as to whether, if the language goes and all that remains is the mechanics of plot together with the emotions which the narrative generates (jealousy, ambition, love etc), is this still Shakespeare? The answer is 'no', but the discussion continues. When Davies's *Othello* was shown in the United States as part of the PBS's 'Masterpiece Theatre' series, Russell Baker (the host) could barely disguise his contempt: 'First of all, he's thrown out all of Shakespeare's beautiful blank verse. Not a line of iambic pentameter remains. Instead the characters speak the modern English of tv cop shows.'[41] Along with the verse went most

of the subtleties of interpretation; audiences were given Davies's firm view of what the play was about – Ben Jago/Iago (Christopher Eccleston) explains the play for us: 'It was about love, that's what you've gotta understand. Don't talk to me about racism, don't talk to me about politics. It was love. Simple as that.' One should perhaps remember that Davies in his appropriation of good stories had the best role model; Shakespeare himself was not a great constructor of original plots, taking stories penned by other writers, fashioning them for dramatic effect and writing in his own idiom. This was quite acceptable; it is difficult to imagine Elizabethan audiences filing out of the theatre after seeing a performance of *Othello* murmuring 'Well it was OK I suppose, but Cinthio's *Hecatommithi* it ain't.' Sold as being simultaneously Shakespeare and not Shakespeare, Davies's *Othello* is an excellent drama in its own right with fine insights into Shakespeare's characters and motivations; the dangers of the casual easiness of the relationship between Desdemona and Cassio, for example, have rarely been better realized and played.

In 2003 the BBC transmitted *The Canterbury Tales*, a six-part series which told Chaucer's stories in modern idiom and contemporary settings. In 2005, building on the favourable reception of the endeavour, and mindful of the fact that its charter was up for renewal and the licence fee might have to be re-negotiated, the BBC once again looked to classic literature to fulfil a cultural remit and commissioned the *ShakespeaRe-told* series. These dramas, written by writers of popular television series, took four of Shakespeare's best known plays (*A Midsummer Night's Dream*, *Macbeth*, *The Taming of the Shrew* and *Much Ado About Nothing*) and re-wrote them as contemporary dramas with only the odd Shakespeare quotation or naming of characters to remind you of their origins. To those who knew the plays there was some fun to be gained picking up the Shakespeare allusion; to other observers this was the worst example of dumbing down. Former BBC Director-General Alasdair Milne (who

---

41 www.pbs.org/wgbh/masterpiece/othello/baker.html.

had presided over the *BBC Television Shakespeare* series) was quoted as saying 'I think it's preposterous and perverse and foolish to reject the greatest dramatist that has ever lived and have him rewritten. Some clown was quoted as saying the other day he was making Shakespeare more accessible. He's been accessible, for Christ's sake for 400 years and they don't need to do that.'[42]

The dramas were strongly marketed in the *Radio Times*[43] which promoted the series on its front cover with photographs of the female protagonists lined up, Billie Piper as Hero, fresh from her success in *Dr Who*, prominent in her wedding dress. Girl power was the angle; over the photograph of Jaime Murray with one arm raised was the caption 'Bianca – the model'. And the strapline posed the rhetorical question 'Shakespeare's SISTERS – would the Bard have ever believed that his plays would look like this'. The feature article entitled 'William's Women' in the same issue blamed Shakespeare for not making things clear enough, but did recognize that television drama doesn't always respond well to uncertainty and particularly the open-ended nature of Shakespeare's plays. Peter Moffatt, writer of *Macbeth*, was all for closure, observing 'You have to fill in gaps for a twenty-first century audience . . . Shakespeare very often leaves things unresolved, whereas the rule of television says you have to finish what you've begun.'[44]

The writers' belief, or what they were instructed to believe, was that twenty-first century audiences are unable to engage imaginatively with the past and consider Shakespeare's concerns within the context of Elizabethan society. The strategy in current Shakespeare film and television production is always to bring Shakespeare to us, not take us back to Shakespeare. Any awkwardness in Shakespeare's assessment of life is smoothed away. The plot of *Much Ado About Nothing* caused particular problems, featuring as it does a father who appears to choose death before dishonour for his daughter Hero, and a heroine, Beatrice, who, outraged when Hero is shamed at the altar by Claudio, orders Benedick to prove his love by killing him. 'There's no way in a twenty-first century screenplay, that you can have the loss of virginity making someone want to drop dead of shame, or want their daughter dead', observed author David Nicholls. And then we hit *The Taming of the Shrew*, the author, Sally Wainwright, believed 'The whole forced marriage thing just wouldn't wash with a contemporary audience, unless you went outside our own culture, which I didn't want to do.' Broadcasting the dramas at 9 pm on the supposedly more popular BBC1 channel meant that they inherited the audience from the soap *EastEnders*. The shrewd scheduling paid off, and attracted a respectable viewing figure of around 4.6 million for each episode. What became clear was that investment in the series could only make a profit by finding a new audience, an audience that has little or no interest in Shakespeare on the stage, or at all.

CONCLUSION

Many factors – economic, political, technical – contributed and continue to contribute to the present dearth of Shakespearian drama on British television. If the viewer were to ask why the landscape for Shakespeare plays is so desolate, there is a straightforward if unconsoling answer: not enough people watch them to make them a cost-effective product and, as channels proliferate, free-market economics flourish and value for money is demonstrable only through high ratings, it is essential that they should.

In a post-colonial culture the BBC finds it no longer needs to cling to Shakespeare to remind itself, and the nation, of Britain's greatness. David Attenborough, the world's most famous broadcaster and naturalist, is the new Shakespeare, the cultural signifier, a dazzling demonstration to the world of British broadcasting (and Britain) at its best – civilizing, educational and entertaining. His wildlife programmes, unlike Shakespeare's plays on television, are watched by many millions. Whether we now see Shakespeare on our screens rests largely

[42] Raymond Snoddy, 'BBC: Knives are out for the BBC bosses', *The Independent* (London), 9 January 2006, p. 8.

[43] *Radio Times*, 5–11 November 2005.

[44] *Radio Times*, 5–11 November 2005, p. 14.

on the decisions of commissioning editors. In 2006 *Televisual* asked the senior commissioning editors from the drama departments at the BBC, ITV and C4 what they were looking for. Jane Tranter, BBC Controller of Drama Commissioning, replied 'comedy drama, big impactful returning drama series, slightly more high octane with more testosterone. Romantic drama. Event pieces that capture the Zeitgeist of a twenty-something generation.'[45] It is hard to see how a production of *King Lear* could have a place in this vision. In a poll of critics and broadcasters conducted by Channel 4 in 2007 to name the '50 Greatest Television Dramas' Shakespeare didn't feature at all: *The Sopranos* – an American series – won. Will the viewing public, or British broadcasting, be the poorer as Shakespeare on television dwindles? The consistent pattern of modest viewing figures for his dramas over sixty years strongly suggests that the answer is 'no'; the nation's appetite for televised Shakespeare has never been strong. The future for Shakespeare on British television is bleak, but television will survive without Shakespeare and Shakespeare will certainly survive without television.

---

45 Jane Tranter, cited in 'The Dramatic Question', *Televisual*, April 2006, p. 33.

A LOCAL HABITATION AND A NAME: TELEVISION AND SHAKESPEARE

LAURIE E. OSBORNE

In a world where feature film production has increasingly become an international enterprise, television Shakespeare is often positioned as more local than global. Feature filmmakers and producers must now take into account the foreign market that will generate important global earnings; they frequently extend their imaginative reach into different lands and incorporate filming on location in different countries. By contrast, television production is more embedded in national or regional contexts because those performances must appeal to viewers and sponsors who inhabit the same cultural and geographical space as the TV producers. As a result, television writers and producers embrace situations and settings of immediate local relevance, a tendency that has significant implications for televised Shakespeare.

Although some Shakespearian television productions like the *BBC Shakespeare* and *Shakespeare: The Animated Tales* are presented as international in intended audiences and, in the case of *The Animated Tales*, in collaborative production, television nonetheless still retains the potential for 'local' programming.[1] *ShakespeaRe-told* makes this trait of television explicit by transposing *Much Ado about Nothing* into the office politics of a local British news show, *Wessex Tonight*. The topical immediacy of local news as well as the eavesdropping potential of the TV station audio equipment re-contextualize the slandered maiden and quarrelling lovers.[2] US, UK and Canadian television localize Shakespeare by positioning the plots within national political, historical and artistic contexts. In fact, a wide range of recent Shakespearian TV

performances address national, sometimes even regional audiences through connotations of places with specific histories or accents. Just as important, particularized relationships to Shakespeare and to adaptation enhance what televised Shakespeare offers to a local audience. Ultimately, both local specificity and Shakespeare in these productions enable their claims to relevance beyond their national audience.

Both the origins and the destinations of these recent productions are important; however, whether the market for these televised Shakespeares is envisioned as national or international, the conceptual and directorial work often remains nationally focused. The emplacement of Shakespeare in American, British and Canadian contexts responds to national concerns with artistic value and domestic media expertise, with race and class structures, and with the commercialization of Shakespeare within and beyond national borders. Moreover, national self-definition in these productions relies on 'our' Shakespeare, at times imagined in contrast and conjunction with the Shakespeares of others. Occasionally these productions originate in specific domestic contexts and then promote those particularities in performance to other national audiences through relationship or analogy. Their local particularity derives from a complex blend of

---

[1] BBC/Time-Life *Shakespeare Series* (1978–85), BBC DVD (2005) and *Shakespeare: The Animated Tales* (Ambrose Video, 2004).

[2] 'Much Ado about Nothing' in *ShakespeaRe-Told* (BBC Warner, 2007).

topical references to current events, communally identified audiences and casts, and details of local performance production; their extended influence depends on the marketing, quality and relevance of local Shakespeares beyond their immediate contexts.

As Michael Bristol and others have argued, Shakespeare is claimed by different English-speaking countries as 'their own' in distinctive ways.[3] The textual and performance histories of Shakespearian plays in England have supported strong arguments about the production of Shakespeare as a national poet and the precursor/creator of bourgeois subjectivity.[4] These readings of Shakespeare's contributions to nationalist humanism suggest strong allegiances between British self-definition and their investment in adapting Shakespeare in the eighteenth and nineteenth centuries. At the same time, British empire-building in North America produced complex uses and claims on Shakespeare in the US and Canada. In *Shakespeare's America, America's Shakespeare*, Michael Bristol makes a significant case for the ways in which America's negotiations with Shakespeare throughout its history involve US self-definition as well as Shakespearian appropriation. Canadian appropriations and productions of Shakespearian plays are doubly complicated: by their complex relationship to Britain as the least self-differentiated of the post-colonial heirs to British cultural authority and by their uniquely strong artistic, economic and social interactions with the US.[5] Their most recent televised Shakespeare, the three seasons of *Slings & Arrows*, thus proves especially significant and interesting: it not only embraces an important and uniquely televisual genre, the series, but its Shakespearian performances also encompass issues in adaptation as well as self-reflection on the various media Shakespeare currently inhabits.[6]

Complex networks of alliance, affirmations of superiority and cultural/financial insecurities characterize the relationships between these three nations; these relationships, as well as their relative resources, contribute to some notable similarities and differences in adapting and televising Shakespeare. For example, televised Shakespeare in the US and Britain generally includes three major categories: televised theatrical productions, made-for-TV films and Shakespearian adaptations. However, among the US productions, both televised stage performances, like the Kirk Browning/Kevin Kline *Hamlet* (1990) and Nicholas Hytner's *Twelfth Night: Live at Lincoln Center* (1998), and the Shakespearian adaptations, like the much maligned TNT adaptation of *King Lear*, *The King of Texas* (2002), invoke a peculiarly American Shakespeare.[7] British TV also offers filmed Shakespearian stage performances, often drawn from the Royal Shakespeare Company. Their made-for-TV movies include productions that adhere to Shakespearian language, like Tim Supple's *Twelfth Night* (2003), full-fledged adaptations, like Andrew Davies's *Othello* (2001) and the BBC's *ShakespeaRe-told*, and thoroughly local productions like the documentaries that Susanne Greenhalgh has explored.[8] In contrast to this goldmine of recent TV Shakespeare in the US and Britain, Canada's contribution may seem slight, but Rhombus Media's *Slings & Arrows* (2004–7) offers the most continuous TV engagement with Shakespeare – eighteen hour-long episodes – as well as the greatest self-awareness in its exploration of Shakespearian performances across different media and contexts.

---

3 Michael Bristol, *Shakespeare's America, America's Shakespeare*, (New York, 1990).

4 Michael Dobson, *The Making of a National Poet: Shakespeare, Adaptation, and Authorship, 1660–1769* (Oxford, 1992) and Margreta De Grazia, *Shakespeare Verbatim: The Reproduction of Authenticity and the 1790 Apparatus* (Oxford, 1991).

5 Diana Brydon, *Shakespeare in Canada: 'A World Elsewhere'?* (Toronto, 2002), p. 395.

6 *Slings & Arrows*, Seasons 1–3 (Toronto, 2004–7).

7 *Hamlet*, Dir. Kevin Kline (Broadway Theatre Archive, 2001; first aired 1990), *King of Texas*, Dir. Uli Edel (TNT/Hallmark production; May 2002 airdate) and *Twelfth Night*, Dir. Nicholas Hytner (PBS: Live at Lincoln Center, 1998).

8 *Othello*, Dir. Geoffrey Sax (Acorn Media, 2002, first aired in 2001), *Twelfth Night*, Dir. Tim Supple (Homevision Video, 2005; first aired in 2003) and *ShakespeaRe-Told* (BBC Warner, 2007). Susanne Greenhalgh, '"Alas, poor country!": Documenting the Politics of Performance in Two British Television *Macbeths* Since the 1980s', in Pascale Aebischer *et al.*, eds., *Remaking Shakespeare: Performance across Media, Genres, and Cultures* (New York, 2003).

My opening analyses emphasize a handful of US and UK TV Shakespeares: Kevin Kline's *Hamlet* (1990), Uli Edel's *King of Texas* (2002), the Andrew Davies/Geoffrey Sax British adaptation *Othello* (2001) and Tim Supple's British Channel 4 *Twelfth Night* (2003). However, I will concentrate most closely on Canada's *Slings & Arrows* (three seasons, 2004–7). While each of these productions adds to our understanding of Shakespearian television, *Slings & Arrows'* distinctive television format, sustained representation and complex national origins most fully reveal how local Shakespearian programming enters international exchange.

Televised theatrical productions self-evidently incorporate the original theatrical context and, in theory, celebrate a national theatre. When Kirk Browning produced the televised performance of Nicholas Hytner's *Twelfth Night: Live at Lincoln Center*, he employed the conventional minimalism of televised stage productions, its literal location – onstage in New York's Lincoln Center – as well as the cast of American actors including Helen Hunt, Paul Rudd and Kyra Sedgwick. The production announced its Americanness through its venue at the same time that it insisted on the live quality of simulcast performance. For that production, the simultaneous validation of US actors and of television as an American medium is at the heart of its appeal.

More explicitly, Mary Z. Maher hails Kevin Kline's 1990 television production of *Hamlet* as 'At Last, an American *Hamlet* for Television.'[9] Maher carefully identifies the differences in process and place that situate the Kline *Hamlet* as particularly American television: 'Located near Union Square, the hallways were alive with aspirant dancers and daytime "soap" actors. This was truly the American system of creating television, not the monolithic Eurostyle institutionalized studios, complete with immobile equipment and many levels of bureaucracy, but a company on the move, now in downtown Manhattan, renting lights and shipping in catering services further out in Queens.'[10] According to Maher, 'this brave new Elsinore' is both Shakespearian and quintessentially American.[11]

However, Maher's argument about this American Shakespeare closes with both celebration and veiled defensiveness. For her own part, she claims that 'at last, an American actor, in his stage and television debut as a director, had made a Hamlet for posterity'.[12] However, she also cites the *Washington Post* review of Kline's production that recalls long-held cultural insecurities in US–UK relations with Shakespeare: 'Public television's production of "Hamlet", with Kevin Kline as the gloomy prince, shows how elegant and riveting the medium can be when it is intelligently and expertly employed. Even those who have seen the play umpteen times will hear some lines for the first time, and the uniformly excellent performances should set to rest the scurrilous canard that Americans can't talk Shakespeare.'[13] Excellence in American TV as a medium helps confer permanent stature on Kline's *Hamlet* and offers a wide audience his televisual proof of Americans 'talking Shakespeare'. In contrast the televised British productions of stage performances directed by Trevor Nunn, Adrian Noble, Kenneth Branagh and others do not, and need not, aspire to be, 'at last', the British *Merchant* or *Dream* or *Twelfth Night*.

Televising Shakespearian stage productions involves adapting those stage productions in technical and sometimes substantive ways to the dictates of television – television filming strategies, sound stage dynamics, screen size, audience attention span. However, the made-for-TV movies that both employ these strategies and freely adapt the language of Shakespeare often become productions where particular British, American or Canadian social realities or events prove crucial to the effects and effectiveness of performance. While critics like H. R. Coursen and James Welsh have denounced Uli Edel's *King of Texas* (2002) and director Geoffrey Sax's *Othello* (2001) as Shakespearian failures,

---

[9] Mary Z. Maher, 'At Last, an American *Hamlet* for Television', *Literature/Film Quarterly*, 20 (1992), 301–7.

[10] Maher, 'At Last', p. 303.

[11] Maher, 'At Last', p. 304.

[12] Maher, 'At Last', p. 307.

[13] Quoted in Maher, 'At Last', p. 307.

the motives and local concerns which made those projects so viable for television are important as is their role in establishing Shakespeare as a subject for television.[14]

The King of Texas (2002) translates *Lear* into the well-established American genre of the Western. Director Uli Edel invokes director Antony Mann's longstanding desire to do a Western *Lear* and notes that 'Even Howard Hawkes said that Shakespeare's *King Lear* could become a wonderful western.'[15] TNT reinforced this move into the popular American film genre by premiering the film at the pinnacle of their 'Western week' on 3 June 2002. This aggressively American context for Shakespeare clearly had immediate production appeal since Patrick Stewart describes the conversation with Robert Halmi as a near instant 'sell': 'I very briefly pitched him the idea of a Western *King Lear*. Before he had finished his glass of wine, he said we'd do it.'[16] Ultimately, *The King of Texas* was 'branded' in three ways: as Shakespeare, as a Western in a TNT stable of television films, and as a Hallmark Hall of Fame production. Constructing the film as a Western yoked Shakespeare both to American regional history and to a quintessential American film genre. At the same time, the Hallmark Hall of Fame is a particularly American version of 'quality television'.[17] Whereas Tise Vahimagi notes that '[t]hough, curiously enough, Hallmark Hall of Fame hasn't presented a Shakespearian adaptations since the 1970s the series remains a "cultural landmark" in American television history', *The King of Texas*, in fact, tries to revive and rely upon this television heritage.[18]

The King of Texas presskit repeatedly attests to the suitability of its distinctively American context for Shakespeare. Marcia Gay Harden (Susannah/Goneril) avers that 'egos, racism and a lust for life, land and power were all prominent themes in the story of King Lear. Hence, it is actually hard for me to remember now that *King Lear* was not set in Texas.'[19] Despite the very scripted quality of the presskit 'interviews', their dual emphasis on both the Western and Shakespeare treats the double investment as if it were a natural pairing. At the same time, Lauren Holly (Rebecca/Regan) insists that the female characters are the central focus, very much in the mode that Jane Smiley adopted in her novelistic adaptation of *Lear*, *A Thousand Acres*: 'This is a story of a dysfunctional family and the drama between the sisters, as well as the competition between the sisters for their father's attention.'[20] In *The King of Texas*, the tragedy lies in Lear's pride and his misunderstanding of his daughters rather than his kingship and misjudgement of the way to control inheritance and maintain his kingdom.

In turn, Patrick Stewart, who produced and performed as Lear, emphasizes 'the racial dramas of the Mexicans, Tejanos, and the Texans' as well as the 'interfamily relationship'. His suggestions about the importance of racial tensions and interactions resonate with the directorial choice to identify Lear's fool as the black character, Rip, 'based on a character that was actually at the Alamo . . . he was one of the two or three surviving people there. The Mexicans refused to fire on him, so he survived. Rip comes into this . . . having faced the worst massacre he's ever seen in his life, so he's fearless.'[21] Through David Alan Grier's

[14] H. R. Coursen, 'Shakespeare on Television', in Stephani Brusberg-Kiermeier and Jorg Helbig, eds., *Sh@kespeare in the Media: From the Globe Theatre to the World Wide Web* (New York, 2002) and James M. Welsh, 'Classic Demolition: Why Shakespeare Is not Exactly "Our Contemporary", or "Dude, where's my hankie?"', *Literature/Film Quarterly*, 30 (2002), 223–7.

[15] Uli Edel, 'A Conversation with Uli Edel', *King of Texas*. TNT, 2002, Presskit.

[16] Patrick Stewart, 'A Conversation with Patrick Stewart', *King of Texas*. TNT, 2002. Presskit.

[17] Tise Vahimagi, '"When you care enough to send the very best": Televised Shakespeare and the Hallmark Hall of Fame', in *Walking Shadows: Shakespeare in the National Film and Television Archives*, eds. Luke McKernan and Owen Ferris (London, 1994), pp. 207–18.

[18] Vahimagi, '"When you care enough"', p. 216.

[19] Marcia Gay Harden, 'A Conversation with Marcia Gay Harden', *King of Texas*. TNT, 2002. Presskit.

[20] Lauren Holly, 'A Conversation with Lauren Holly', *King of Texas*. TNT, 2002. Presskit. Jane Smiley, *A Thousand Acres* (New York, 1991).

[21] Stewart, 'A Conversation with Patrick Stewart'.

outspoken fool and the aggressive characterizations of Lear's daughters, *The King of Texas* embeds *Lear* within current social struggles over US white male authority through relatively distant American geographical conflict and the even more distant lens of Shakespeare.

By re-locating *Lear* in this milieu, *King of Texas* exploits fully the freedom of adaptations which are not linguistically faithful to Shakespeare's text. The production taps into US concerns about the political powers and ongoing immigration issues currently associated with Texas, while also registering the power of the women's movement. These issues collide in an adaptation of Shakespeare's play that represents local concerns through plot resemblance rather than language. *The King of Texas* suggests that the more adapted the production, the more locally focused can be the performance.

Andrew Davies's *Othello* bears out this principle. This full adaptation of Shakespeare's play pursues its modern language production in response to recent British issues: '*Othello*, a 2001 ITV production, uses Shakespeare's plot to interrogate the explosively racialized politics surrounding the history of Stephen Lawrence, a black teenager brutally beaten and murdered by racist thugs at a bus stop in Eltham, southeast London in 1993.' Barbara Hodgdon also links the Lawrence case and Davies's *Othello* with US racial scandals, describing the British event as 'an ongoing national scandal reminiscent of that following America's equally infamous Rodney King case'.[22] The British television film, however, is much more closely linked to its own national context: Eamonn Walker (John Othello) argues that the screenwriter, Andrew Davies, 'was dealing with a London problem: the Metropolitan Police and death within custody'.[23]

Davies's own description of pitching the project suggests that ITV required a national resonance in the adapted Shakespearian plot. Davies originally envisioned and proposed an adaptation of *The Tempest* 'with Prospero as a New Age guru on a Caribbean island'.[24] Despite his keen enthusiasm for the project, ITV rejected his proposal, presumably in favour of opening the series with a famous tragedy. However, the instant success of Davies's second pitch is suggestive. As Davies describes it, 'I went away from the meeting feeling disappointed, but it suddenly flashed into my head – Othello – the first black commissioner of the Metropolitan Police. In the end it was the easiest deal I've ever made . . . it only needed one sentence.'[25] The eerie echo of how readily Stewart obtained approval and funding for the Western *Lear* suggests that nationally based TV production companies in the US and Britain find Shakespeare relocated into national genres and/or linked to recent events practically irresistible. Shakespeare made local, it seems, will sell, at least to those who produce made-for-TV movies.[26]

However, these TV Shakespeares sometimes do more than represent immediate community concerns: the performance is intended to affect as well as reflect current social conditions, at least in the case of Davies's *Othello*. In fact, Davies acknowledges that his film invokes the Lawrence case and notes that 'ever since then the police have been making huge efforts to clean up their image, but it still hasn't shown up in terms of notable numbers of black and Asian-origin policemen being

---

22 Barbara Hodgdon, 'Race-ing Othello, Re-engendering White-Out II', in Richard Burt and Lynda Boose, eds., *Shakespeare the Movie II* (New York, 2003), p. 94.
23 'An Interview with Eamonn Walker', PBS Corporation. www.pbs.org/wgbh/masterpiece/othello/ei_walker.html, 15/1/06.
24 'An Interview with Andrew Davies', PBS Corporation. www.pbs.org/wgbh/masterpiece/othello/ei_davies.html, 15/1/06.
25 As quoted in Marion McMullen, 'Othello's thoroughly modern shake-up', *Coventry Evening Telegraph*, 15 December 2001, 27.
26 It is worth noting that the ITV *Othello* did have outside financing, as Daniel Rosenthal notes, 'LWT [London Weekend Television] could only make Othello with co-production finance from WGBH Boston and the Canadian Broadcasting Corporation, and Wright acknowledges that ITV's commercial obligation to secure a mass audience means she could never have raised the requisite seven-figure budget for a Shakespeare which used the original language' ('Inspector Moor: Othello as the first black Metropolitan Police chief? If you think ITV has lost the plot, then what about Macbeth as a fight between rival fast-food joints?', *The Observer*, 25 November 2001, 7).

promoted into high positions'. Davies argues that his Othello scenario

is something that you would imagine that Tony Blair and his team of advisors would do. They would think of a bold political gesture, taking a risk on promoting a guy like Othello, who's made a stir. He's a black man in the right position at just the right time. And they think, let's do it. It might be a good idea for its own sake. But perhaps they're more concerned with how it will play in the media. I suppose I'm having a little dig at the way not just the British government but most governments work these days.[27]

He characterizes his production as an intervention as well as a commentary on current racial conflicts in England. This dual engagement with local British racial politics reveals the complex position of topical adaptation. Obviously the film invokes a recent, volatile racial scandal and critiques the British government and police force for its weak record in promoting ethnic candidates to high positions. However, Davies simultaneously suggests that John Othello's promotion to 'the first black commissioner of the London Metropolitan Police' represents a 'media response' to resolving police racism.

The film thus participates in and reflects a double bind within British racial politics: the government should diversify the police force, but, if/when they do, their decision almost inevitably reads as a media gesture. Arguably, the Davies/Sax *Othello* itself is also a media response to local issues; certainly the film represents John Othello's speech to an angry crowd as an authentic engagement that rapidly becomes a media event. Moreover, such gestures have potential power. Eamonn Walker speaks directly to the effects of the film on its immediate audience:

I don't know if you can hope that something can be changed by this particular production, but what you can hope for is that you plant a seed in somebody's brain – maybe a person of power who is able to do something about it. You can hope that they can turn around and make a difference in the society that we are living in. That's basically what we do as playwrights, as directors, as actors: We shine a mirror on to society for them to

look into. If they see something they don't like, then it's up to them to change it.[28]

With its intriguing variation of the 'mirror up to nature', this comment suggests that the made-for-TV movie not only reflects the pressing turmoil of race relations in London but could also, in true New Historicist fashion, influence the specific culture that it reflects. By 'having a little dig at the way not just the British government but most governments work these days', Davies also implies that these British problems are generalizable to 'most governments'.[29] Both Davies and Hodgdon expect the very specificity of these adaptations and their influence on viewers to extend into the vexed racial politics of other nations by 'shining a mirror on society'.

These interviews appeared on the PBS website after the film's successful British debut. Moreover, PBS, a US channel known for its quality television imports, took pains to present Davies's *Othello* in connection with a documentary on the Lawrence case, *The Murder of Stephen Lawrence*, which aired one week before the film's US television debut. Including the British context to establish both relevance and interest in the film undermines rhetorical positioning of the film's broader, international significance voiced by PBS, by Davies and Walker in interviews and later by Hodgdon. Davies's film thus foregrounds the issue of translating Shakespeare's exploration of Othello as a cultural outsider into new national as well as historical contexts where racial tensions have different political and historical implications. The transfer of the film to a new context, the US audience, raises questions about whether nationally specific new contexts for Shakespeare are generalizable to other cultures and whether one government's implication in media representation truly extends to other governments similarly. Both the social circumstances and the media culture vary distinctively.

27 'An Interview with Andrew Davies'.
28 'An Interview with Eamonn Walker'.
29 'An Interview with Andrew Davies'.

Edel's *King of Texas* in the US was not quite as successful with TV audiences as it was with its production company and seems not to have garnered an international audience. Although David Alan Grier's Rip is one of the most effective and interesting characters in the Texan *Lear*, the racial politics introduced into the production by his wise folly seems to overload a plot that already has been at some pains to validate the importance of Lear's daughters. Davies's *Othello* was considerably more successful: Daniel Rosenthal of *The Times* credits it with 3.57 million viewers, and the production garnered the best single drama award from the British Press Guild.[30] In Davies's made-for-TV Shakespeare, Christopher Eccleston's Jago is chillingly effective as the man betraying Othello, but this Iago's survival and success in getting John Othello's job conflicts with his voice-over insistence at the end that 'it was love, simple as that. Don't talk to me about race, don't talk to me about politics'. This turn to romance may echo the self-sacrifice at the end of Shakespeare's *Othello*, but the unpunished Jago's expression of this view argues that such closure does not work for the contemporary, local *Othello*.[31] Perhaps, as Welsh suggests, 'the Davies *Othello* features strong performances but has difficulty emerging from the shadow of Shakespeare'.[32] Arguably, the very topical issues and situations that assure local interest and relevance in these films outweigh and sometimes capsize the political and social critiques within Shakespeare's plays.

I read the relationship between Shakespeare and adaptation in these two productions as conflicts that neither side fully wins. Although the resulting mutual critique could be radical in the sense Graham Holderness has articulated, these productions do not achieve that result because they do not fully engage the complexities of their own projects.[33] Eliminating Shakespeare's language implicitly raises the stakes in national topicality: Shakespeare's text loses its poetic purchase while the plot is transferred. This shift may be the tipping point that leads critics to dismiss these productions as insignificant. In a more positive reading, such productions could be considered 'tradaptations' in the sense that Denis Salter uses the term: adaptations whose meaning is immediate and used up once the specific context has passed, making way for new adaptations responsive to immediate local circumstances.[34] As one critic praising the ITV *Othello* put it, 'By being so specific, Davies has produced a superb dramatization for today that might not be of much interest decades from now – not to mention centuries and millennia.'[35] Nonetheless, the producers often envision the relevance of their adaptations extending beyond the local by virtue of analogy or artistry.

British and Canadian television that maintains Shakespeare's language while relocating and specifying contemporary social contexts has yielded productions that more thoroughly engage both the medium and the message. On the British side, Tim Supple's 2003 *Twelfth Night* transports Shakespeare's play into twenty-first century, multicultural England. Producer Rachel Gensua clearly states that 'we'd all known from the very beginning that we wanted it to be a multicultural, multi-racial cast that reflected the Britain that we live in today and would make it more accessible to people who sort of think of Shakespeare as something for white, middle class, middle-aged audiences'.[36] Although Michael Maloney asserts that the US is 'thirty to fifty years ahead' in 'color blind casting', Supple's

---

30 Daniel Rosenthal, 'There's a Will, but no way', *The Times, London* (23 Aug. 2004), 18 and 'Office comedy a double winner in showbiz awards; BROADCASTING: BBC takes most titles', *Western Mail* (12 April 2002), 7.

31 Linda Charnes has dissected similar uses of the romance narrative in productions of *Antony and Cleopatra* in '"What's love got to do with it?": Reading the liberal humanist romance in Shakespeare's *Antony and Cleopatra*', *Textual Practice*, 6 (1992), 1–16.

32 Welsh, 'Classic Demolition', p. 225.

33 Graham Holderness, 'Radical Potentiality and Institutional Closure: Shakespeare in Film and Television', in Jonathan Dollimore and Alan Sinfield, eds., *Political Shakespeare* (New York, 1985).

34 Denis Salter, 'Acting Shakespeare in Postcolonial Space', in James Bulman, ed., *Shakespeare, Theory and Performance* (New York, 1996), pp. 113–32.

35 Ed Siegel, 'Modern "Othello" Shows that Shakespeare Still Endures', *Boston Globe* (28 January 2002), B8.

36 Rachel Gensua, 'The Business of Film', in *21st Century Bard: The Making of Twelfth Night* (Princeton, NJ, 2004), 4 disks, DVD.

Twelfth Night uses its ethnic differences more deliberately and thematically than the phrase suggests.[37] The film contrasts a black Orsino with a white Olivia and yokes the Indian twins still more closely to each other by presenting some of their lines in Hindi. Even the physically affectionate relationship between Sebastian and Antonio draws on Indian culture and the public, physical friendliness of homosocial male friendships between Indian men.

As a result, Supple's film differs from Edel's *King of Texas* and Sax's *Othello* in key ways. Supple simultaneously uses the Shakespearian text, albeit some of it translated or rearranged, and alludes to contemporary events and communities. For example, the death of Olivia's brother in a fiery automobile crash as well as Olivia's black lace dress, modelled on a dress Princess Diana wore to the Vatican in the 1980s, yokes the production to British royal contexts and tragedies.[38] Arguably the film's proposed romance between Olivia and Orsino could also allude to Diana's life, but close adherence to the Shakespearian plot maintains Olivia as an independent, powerful virgin, rather than a divorced wife, and produces a comic union at the end. At the same time, because multicultural casting reflects general culture rather than specific events in Britain, Supple's *Twelfth Night* offers a located contemporary Shakespeare that is not tied, as Sax's *Othello* is, to immediate, topical trauma but to ongoing social conditions: London's multicultural mix. Although the film had a much smaller audience (as well as a much smaller budget), its less topically driven plot and greater use of the Shakespearian text may ensure it a more sustained market in the long run.[39]

Twelfth Night, like these other television productions, finds its international venue through the marketing of high culture television. The Kline *Hamlet* and Hytner's *Twelfth Night: Live at Lincoln Center* are PBS productions, and Sax's *Othello*, which is partially funded by WGBH Boston and the Canadian Broadcasting Corporation, becomes one.[40] *The King of Texas* draws on a tradition of quality television designated by the Hallmark Hall of Fame and was marketed heavily to teachers. Supple's *Twelfth Night* participates in a comparable academic venue through the Films for the Humanities and Sciences. Although they did not release the film for international DVD sales, they did produce and market a four-DVD collection on the making of Supple's *Twelfth Night*.[41]

While the DVD set focuses on the television production of *Twelfth Night*, the separate sequences take on the business, art, language and technology of film with Shakespeare's play as the example which showcases how television production actually works in the British system. These DVDs, available only in the US and Canada, present television film production as the adaptation's most important context, local by virtue of the collaborative work of an immediate community of British TV professionals. The production internally emphasizes television in the use of video surveillance in Act 3, scene 4 where Malvolio is tricked with the letter and elsewhere. While the relationship fostered between the film and Britain's multicultural audience is clearly important, Films for the Humanities and Sciences identifies TV filmmaking as the international draw: its extensive collaborations, its balancing act between directorial vision and budget, and the details of physical and cinematic creation. In the case of Supple's *Twelfth Night*, a different kind of specificity positions the film for the international market: the details of television production itself.

In contrast to these TV films, the Canadian mini-series, *Slings & Arrows*, engages with several dimensions of televising and adapting Shakespeare

---

37 Michael Maloney, 'The Business of Film' in *21st Century Bard: The Making of Twelfth Night*.

38 'The Art of Film' in *21st Century Bard: The Making of Twelfth Night*.

39 As Rosenthal notes, '[Antony Sher]'s *Macbeth* and [Tim Supple]'s *Twelfth Night* both drew 600,000 viewers – a minority compared with 3.57 million viewers for Davies's *Othello*, let alone the 10 million fans of *Holby City*. Yet 600,000 is still higher than the audience for the BBC's *Richard III* 20 years ago and, more importantly, exceeds the 570,000 admissions for the RSC's entire 2002–03 British season' ('There's a Will', p. 8).

40 See Daniel Rosenthal, 'Inspector Moor'.

41 *21st Century Bard: The Making of Twelfth Night*.

explicitly within a popular television genre. The most overtly local and fully televisual of these adaptations, *Slings & Arrows* is also both a popular and an artistic success, lauded internationally, often in nationalist terms. The three-year series explores the back-stage world of the New Burbage Theatre Festival and interrogates Shakespeare's ongoing relevance and national status in Canada. Each of its seasons centres on a Shakespearian play: 'the first season, youth (*Hamlet*), the second, mid-life (*Macbeth*), and the third, old age (*Lear*)'.[42]

Throughout all three seasons, *Slings & Arrows* offers paradoxical and striking conjunctions. It both adapts Shakespeare and retains the original language for the onstage performance segments and often within stray conversations; it reflects upon theatrical production and its vicissitudes while itself embracing the recently favoured hour-length cable TV drama series. Although *Slings & Arrows* in some ways resembles theatrical films like Kenneth Branagh's *In the Bleak Midwinter* or Al Pacino's *Looking for Richard*, its 'TV à clef' setting invokes the very specific Shakespeare industry in Stratford, Ontario. Moreover, its concerns with the encounter between Shakespeare and commercialization take place within the dual contexts of Shakespeare's plays and the television mini-series. From its overdetermined position as a Canadian production, this TV Shakespeare reflects directly and self-consciously on the different consequences of local (Canadian) and international (most often American) influences on TV Shakespeare.

The development of the Canadian television production met with more obstacles than either Stewart or Davies reportedly encountered with their national television production giants. After problems getting funding from CBC, the screenwriters ultimately worked with Rhombus Media, a Toronto-based production company, and Showcase, a Canadian pay-TV channel along the lines of HBO or Showtime. These difficulties are surprising because, as Matthew Hays puts it, 'In a country with as rich a theatre history as Canada's, you would think an ongoing TV series about a struggling theatre festival company would be a no-brainer.'[43] Moreover, because of its strong local Canadian

appeal, the project should be a 'no-brainer' in the strictly controlled Canadian television market, where 60 per cent of all programming must originate in Canada to protect local programming from US television dominance. The ongoing anxieties about the response of the Stratford Shakespeare Festival throughout the series' run suggest that *Slings & Arrows* offers a direct challenge to local control over Shakespearian performance, local competition over Shakespeare that does not figure as significantly in the US or UK television productions.[44]

Both the cast and writers of the series have strong connections to the Stratford Shakespeare festival which the series tacitly invokes from the start. As Richard Paul Knowles observes of the key moments of the Stratford Shakespeare Festival history, 'the Festival was eventually (if temporarily) to assume the mantle of Canada's national theatre, and it has served throughout its history as a site of recurring disputes about Canadian nationhood, theatrical and otherwise'.[45] Daniel Fischlin goes further to argue that 'adaptation is a genre, if one takes the significant increase in adaptations produced in Canada over the last thirty years as any indication, that suits the aesthetics of Canadian self-representation'.[46] Though Fischlin points out that neither Shakespeare nor Canadian national identity is necessarily coherent, his point is that

---

[42] Matthew Hays, 'Sex and Shakespeare', *Canadian Screenwriter* (Summer 2005), 11.

[43] Hays, 'Sex and Shakespeare', p. 10.

[44] The ITV *Othello* and Channel4 *Twelfth Night* do face competition and comparison with BBC1 and BBC2 in the British market, but that competition thrives in a range of programming, not focused explicitly on Shakespeare, even though the recent BBC productions of *ShakespeaRe-told* could be responding to the critical and popular success of the ITV *Othello* on British TV. See also Daniel Fischlin's arguments about Shakespeare's centrality to Canadian national self-image (see n.46).

[45] Richard Paul Knowles, 'From Nationalist to Multinational: The Stratford Festival, Free Trade, and the Discourses of Intercultural Tourism', *Theatre Journal*, 47 (1995), 20.

[46] Daniel Fischlin, 'Nation and/as Adaptation: Shakespeare, Canada, and Authenticity', in *Shakespeare in Canada: 'A World Elsewhere'*, eds. Diana Brydon, Diana and Irena Makaryk (Toronto, 2002), p. 315.

Canada's involvement in adaptation, particularly in Shakespearian adaptation, speaks to and negotiates with that nation's unusual post-colonial status and efforts at self-definition.

However, the tense relationship between Canadian and British Shakespeare that Fischlin identifies and Knowles so persuasively delineates in Stratford's long history only occasionally surfaces in *Slings & Arrows*. Most directly, American movie star Jack Crew (Luke Kirby) is ruffling through New Burbage stores in search of 'accent tapes, you know, in English, for the play'. His Canadian co-star, bemused by his explanation of what he is doing, suggests that *Hamlet* is set in Denmark, so perhaps he should be looking for Danish accent tapes, neatly turning aside the issue of British Shakespeare. Any threat from British theatre (or television) is all but invisible compared to the challenges posed by the newly Americanized corporate sponsor, 'Cosmopolitan Lenstrex', and the American movie star brought in, as many of the actors initially think, to ruin *Hamlet*. The first season identifies the threat to Shakespeare and, by implication, threats to Canadian culture, as American entrepreneurship. Overall, the series explores intra-national struggles over Shakespeare and theatre within Canada while wrestling itself with international, specifically American, artistic ascendancy in television production.

The series taps into an important site of Canadian nationalist and cultural discourse with its pseudo-Stratford setting of the 'Swan Theatre' of 'New Burbage'; however, on the surface level of the plot, the first season of *Slings & Arrows* satirizes how American corporate and artistic challenges threaten an overly commercialized Canadian theatre festival already in danger of collapsing from its own self-importance. Geoffrey Tennant (Paul Gross) first appears as the possibly insane director of *The Tempest* at the aptly named Theatre Sans Argent (Theatre without Money). Committed to the theatrical arts and struggling with faulty toilets, missing rent and exploding lights, Tennant represents the antithesis of his former friend Oliver Welles (Stephen Ouimette), the artistic director of the New Burbage Shakespeare Festival who opens

the series (and his season) by directing *A Midsummer Night's Dream*, complete with sheep noises as humour. As Geoffrey later puts it, 'this festival likes its theatre overdone, fry the life out of it and smother it in sauce'.[47] When Oliver dies at the end of the first episode, Geoffrey becomes the interim artistic director. Not only does he ultimately have to direct *Hamlet*, the play which drove him crazy, but he also converses with Oliver's ghost, which makes him look as mad as he is reported to be.

The iconoclastic, still idealistic Geoffrey Tennant initially exemplifies the vigorous, small-budget Canadian theatre scene which has freely adapted Shakespeare, in opposition to Oliver Welles, the artistic director and self-proclaimed 'King of New Burbage', whose productions, both pre- and post-mortem, specialize in spectacle and self-aggrandizing bombast. If Geoffrey pushes Canadian theatrical idealism to the point of insanity, Oliver embodies the more reverent approach of the Stratford festival, taken to stultifying extremes. His entirely appropriate death, falling underneath wheels of a Canadian Ham truck, initiates the three-season collaboration. The artistic struggle between Oliver and Geoffrey recalls the conflicts between Stratford and the independent Canadian adaptations of Shakespeare in the '80s and '90s which, as Knowles describes, 'in their different ways (re)appropriated Shakespeare for their particular(ist) communities in ways that are unavailable to directors at Stratford, given the material conditions, institutional discourse, and construction of the audience that obtain there'. *Slings & Arrows* also incorporates the theatrical rivalries facing Stratford, which 'during this period put most of its efforts into competing with the new and burgeoning commercial theatre scene in Toronto, which consists primarily of so-called megamusicals'.[48] The first season of *Slings & Arrows* draws gleefully on this history and includes that conflict in the plotline that runs parallel to Geoffrey's struggles with incompetent

---

47 'Playing the Swan' (*Slings & Arrows*, Season 1).
48 Knowles, 'From Nationalist to Multinational', p. 36.

Ophelias, importunate ghosts, and an intransigent lead actress who happens to be his former lover.

Behind the scenes of the behind-the-scenes theatrical problems, American entrepreneur Holly Day (Jennifer Irwin) pursues both profitability and the festival's general manager, Richard Smith-Jones (Mark McKinney). Her plan for the Disneyfication of New Burbage and the revamping of the theatrical schedule to include more musicals not only directly invokes the rivalry between Stratford and the commercially popular Toronto theatre scene but also prompts Smith-Jones to confess that he doesn't like Shakespeare.[49] 'No one does, Richard. That's the thing. You put on plays nobody wants to see', responds Holly.[50] In the first season, the displacement of theatrical rivalries within Canada onto the obnoxious American entrepreneur seems to rewrite a local artistic conflict as an international threat; however, this strategy also foregrounds the challenge that ubiquitous US television poses to the Canadian TV production.

The series even takes careful aim at Canadian business involvement with the New Burbage Shakespeare Festival. Geoffrey has refused to direct *Hamlet* and instead agreed to take on the corporate workshop. He opens the first session by asking the assembled corporate participants from Allied Acrylic why they are there. One responds by reading – hesitantly – from the brochure: 'We're here [reading] to improve management strategies and interpersonal communication skills through an examination of key works by the great English playwright William Shakespeare.' Once the workshop attendees agree that they will not learn to sell more acrylics from 'the crisis management techniques of Claudius', Geoffrey jettisons the curriculum and suggests 'we should just fuck around with some texts'.[51] What he teaches them – and Terry, the accountant, in particular – are the pleasures and the social recognition associated with acting and Shakespeare. His skilful usurpation of the Shakespeare workshop for business people foreshadows the ultimate defeat of Holly Day.

As this analysis of Season 1 suggests, *Slings & Arrows* draws together several threads of conflict and local interest from the Canadian theatre scene

in complex and unexpected ways. The satire of American commercial intrusion may be over the top – Holly Day is the kind of character who listens to self-empowerment tapes with such dedication that she recites along with 'I am god' right up to 'please turn tape'.[52] However, truly no corner of local Canadian theatrical lore is safe from ironic juxtapositions with its New Burbage counterparts. As Hays puts it, 'The constant poking fun at theatre in general pleases fans of live performance, but the specific jabs at the Canadian theatre scene leave those in the know howling. Hollywood star Jack Crew (Luke Kirby), for example, shows up in season one to sell tickets as a luminous choice to play Hamlet – an obvious reference to Keanu Reeves' 1995 Winnipeg gig in the role.'[53] In fact, the script is so locally relevant that some allusions are even regional – for example, Oliver's death by ham truck is even more hilarious for those who know that Ontario is the home of the Pork Congress of Canada.

David Fischlin's website, the *Canadian Adaptations of Shakespeare Project*, explores the reception of the series, in particular responses that identify its 'Canadianness'. The initial reviews of *Slings & Arrows* from US critics consistently celebrate its Canadian specificity as part of their perception of its high quality as a television production. Canadian reviewers, on the other hand, more frequently register surprise about great Canadian TV. Like the British and American productions, *Slings & Arrows* reached international audiences first on a premium arts network, Sundance in the US and the ArtsNetwork in the UK. The reassuring success of Season 1 in exploring idiosyncratically Canadian preoccupations for the larger international and especially American audiences allowed *Slings & Arrows* to

---

49 See Daniel Fischlin's website, *Canadian Adaptations of Shakespeare Project* (University of Guelph, 2004) www.canadianshakespeares.ca for this scene: www.canadianshakespeares.ca/multimedia/video/slings_9.mov.

50 'Madness in Great Ones', *Slings & Arrows*, Season 1.

51 'Madness'.

52 'Mirror up to Nature', *Slings & Arrows*, Season 1.

53 Hays, 'Sex and Shakespeare', p. 11.

focus still more closely on local negotiations with Shakespearian theatre in later seasons.

Season 2 abandons the easy US scapegoats of the first season in favour of directing its satiric eye at Canadian bureaucracies and national arts funding. While Ellen Fanshaw (Martha Burns) faces a tax audit because of her feckless, artistic approach to her finances, the New Burbage Shakespeare Festival, in the figure of Richard Smith-Jones, seeks funding from the Canadian Minister of Culture, who neatly punctures his appeal for support by caustically noting how much more good the money could do in the beleaguered Canadian health care system. The Canadian government ultimately demands $27,867.53 in back taxes from Ellen; at the same time, it loans New Burbage $2.2 million for 'rebranding'. While the central plot follows Geoffrey Tennant's difficulties directing the production of *Macbeth* that Oliver Welles planned for years and plans to control from beyond the grave, the personal artistic negotiations with Shakespeare in Season 2 coincide with governmental participation in the arts, Richard Smith-Jones's inept negotiations with advertisers, and the festival's mandate to foster Canadian playwriting.

Most locally of all, this 'season' at the Swan theatre includes a reading of a new Canadian play, part of the festival's support for a national artistic identity. However, Lionel Train, the temperamental playwright whose new work they are reading, writes from his own life and freely includes conversations and life stories that he has acquired by seducing the New Burbage executive assistant, Anna Conroy (Susan Coyne). The result is a vivid representation of how playwrights – and presumably TV writers – exploit and often diminish the real, local people and events that they import into their art. There is a subtle irony in putting Anna's life and words into Train's play in ways that both misrepresent her and violate her privacy. As one of the writers of the series, Susan Coyne, who plays Anna, is well aware that she and her fellow writers are using Stratford as well as real Canadian theatrical events and people to produce *Slings & Arrows* as televisual art.[54] Arguably, the second season responds to the persistent queries about the relationship between the New Burbage Shakespeare Festival and the real Canadian theatre.

The audience's series-long knowledge of Anna underscores how much more complex she is than Train's 'Annette'. This strategy creates a layering of televisual realities and greater empathy with the comparatively 'real' television character. In this way, the series reflects upon the distinctions between the representation of Canadian theatre in *Slings & Arrows* and its reality on the stages of Stratford, the Shaw Festival and others. The more nuanced experiences of the real 'Anna' become cautionary moments in the series's exploration of TV Shakespeare as a local production. Television's representation of the local will necessarily be partial, in both senses of the word – not only biased but also incomplete.

In parallel to the ambition and theft of authority displayed in the *Macbeth* production, the second season's exploration of its own successful usurpation of the Canadian theatre scene acknowledges explicitly that such artistry exploits and inevitably misrepresents the concrete events and people which enable its specificity. At the same time, Anna's responses – both her horrified chagrin and her ongoing attraction to the playwright – are more complex and important reactions than Train's Annette from Winnepeg conveys. In part, her more sustained and developed presence throughout the television series gives the TV character greater power than the characters created on stage or in the rehearsal hall. The playwright's complacency about his artistic theft underscores the pain Anna experiences.

Comparable issues of complacency and theft recur in the lead actor of Geoffrey's *Macbeth*. Convinced of his own excellence since he has played the role several times, Henry Breedlove upstages his director and fellow actors at every opportunity and practically scuttles the production with his unwillingness to take risks or perform Macbeth as human

---

[54] See 'An Interview with Susan Coyne' (www.canadianshakespeares.ca/multimedia/video/susancoyne_interview.mov).

and afraid. By re-blocking the performance at the last moment to produce the necessary fearfulness in his lead actor, Geoffrey re-animates the sense of risk and anxiety in Macbeth's usurpation of the crown while affirming theatrical spontaneity and risk as a source of artistic value. This satisfyingly dense representation underscores how the series' treatment of Shakespeare as an on- and offstage property enriches its depiction of Shakespeare in TV form. Both television's multi-season scope and its multi-level parallel plot collude in establishing Shakespeare's appropriateness for television.

In Season 3, the triumph of the New Burbage *Macbeth* has made the festival a financial winner and catapulted the cast to Broadway, reinstating the US as a measure of success for the theatre. The return to American intervention surfaces concretely in the *Lear* season with the inclusion of Barbara Gordon, a character who takes on the role of Goneril as a break from her career as an American TV actress. Work on an American TV series has transformed Ellen's old friend into an ageing narcissist who bedecks the walls of her Manhattan condo with oversized stills of her TV persona. Alternating between self-absorption and brutal criticism of others, Barbara insinuates herself into Ellen's home and rivals New Burbage's own diva for sheer bitchiness. Her interventions as Goneril in rehearsal bleed over into the *Lear* production and wreck Geoffrey and Ellen's home life. She even almost lures Ellen into a similar US television series at the end of the season. In Season 3, Broadway recognition, Barbara's television career, and the identification of the US with commercial success and television exploitation contribute to a portrait of Canadian theatre as an undervalued, even moribund local phenomenon.

The very public and international attention that Geoffrey's *Macbeth* has garnered proves his undoing and debilitates the festival: impotent in his home life, he also bursts into weeping fits whenever he appears on stage. As his production reaches the US audience and thus acquires international recognition, so *Slings & Arrows* itself now bears the burdens of global as well as local attention. Television enables easy distribution that transports the series

to the American Sundance Channel, the British ArtsNetwork and DVD boxed sets of the series that are widely available beyond Canada. The television success proves bittersweet since it seems to threaten the very qualities of Shakespearian theatre that the series celebrates.

In keeping with the planned end of the series and with *King Lear* itself, the third season of *Slings & Arrows* also explores the possible demise of theatre in the inevitable death that each individual actor faces. Oliver's death in the opening episode of Season 1 first raises this issue and establishes from the start a pseudo-elegiac tone in the TV show's approach to theatrical Shakespeare. However, parallels between Charles Kingman's deterioration on cancer drugs and the stripping of his powers and role as Lear create a powerful image of Shakespeare's tragedy as the theatre itself.

In Season 3, a return to the local represents the only hope. Whereas Season 2 only celebrates local theatre in the grade school production *Macbeth*, Season 3 uses community-based performances to concentrate on the strong links between immediate communal concerns and theatre. The second episode of Season 3 includes a brief reprise of *A Midsummer Night's Dream*, a nursing home rehearsal of the comedy that is, in effect, the antithesis of Oliver Welles's overdecorated *Dream* of Season 1. Moreover, although Geoffrey's production of *Lear* is hobbled by his lead actor, Charles Kingman (William Hutt), who is dying of cancer and fails in every preview and many rehearsals, the Kingman *Lear* succeeds spectacularly in a single, final production that the actors clandestinely put on in a church basement for a minimal local audience.

Slings & Arrows's final season, planned from the start to offer closure, deliberately returns theatre to dominance as the preferable form of Shakespearian performance, validating the community and private experience of the theatre in its local venue over the extended reach and considerable temptations of television that Season 3 also represents. Although the venerable professional representative of classic Canadian theatre dies at the end of his performance of *Lear*, Geoffrey Tennant and Ellen Fanshaw move to Montreal to revive the *Theatre Sans*

Argent. The final episode, which seems set to close with the funeral for Charles Kingman, actually concludes with Geoffrey and Ellen's wedding and their proposed return to the most locally intense and idiosyncratic of Canada's theatrical locales, Quebec. As Fischlin, Knowles and others have noted, Montreal is Canada's major source of Shakespearian adaptations, most of which are inflected through the intense local self-fashioning of a province distinguished by its bilingualism, deeply implicated in its unusual status as Canada's only French-speaking province, and always on the verge of secession.

Throughout its run *Slings & Arrows* illuminates the local qualities of television in all modes: topical allusiveness, community frames of reference and settings, and idiosyncratic local conditions of production. The series' successes beyond national borders as well as its preoccupations with local theatrical performances lead the writers to reflect upon the strengths, limitations and ambiguous successes of television itself in representing the local. The issues of adaptation that Supple's *Twelfth Night*, Sax's *Othello* and Edel's *King of Texas* encounter in the condensed format of TV film, *Slings & Arrows* explores over three years and in the context of ongoing critical responses in Canada and beyond.

These examples of televised Shakespeare are suggestive rather than definitive. Most broadly, they indicate the varied ways that television can offer local Shakespeare: through topicality, community or production practice. The TV Shakespeares I have explored here blend these modes of localization, and, for some, the balance determines the adaptation's success. National, even regional, specificity is necessary to the financial viability of Shakespearian productions on TV; however, the fullest commercial success now requires an appeal to international markets, especially in Western and Anglophile countries. The relative effectiveness of these productions implies that a high degree of topicality, in references and settings, only thrives when balanced out by more general invocations of community and self-aware explorations of production itself.

Beyond the obvious fact that fully adapted Shakespearian productions can use more local references and contexts, television adaptations, locally pitched and produced, have extraordinary opportunities to explore the stakes involved in transforming Shakespeare's plays within contemporary contexts. Television Shakespeare clearly serves as a crucial site where negotiations between local concerns and self-representation interact with international markets and social pressures. Most notably, in *Slings & Arrows*, the tensions between Shakespearian theatrical performances and series television, between local Canadian concerns and American cultural clout, lead a sustained exploration of the relationship between television and Shakespeare. Even though television's global reach through repackaging on arts channels and on DVD ultimately conflicts with its claim to present and immediate representation, the remediations of TV Shakespeare are one of our richest resources for examining the increasingly complex negotiations between local and international Shakespeare.

PAYING ATTENTION IN SHAKESPEARE PARODY: FROM TOM STOPPARD TO YOUTUBE

CHRISTY DESMET

Within Anglo-American criticism, the phenomenon of Shakespearian appropriation has been framed largely as an encounter between 'mighty opposites'. Harold Bloom's competitive model from *The Anxiety of Influence* (1973) offers the best-known version of this critical narrative.[1] Mikhail Bakhtin's dialogism is sometimes offered as an alternative to the dominance/submission dynamic of Bloom; in this model, Bard and appropriator engage in a serious, dignified conversation between equals.[2] Either construction entails critical costs. Bloom's model is exclusionary; you cannot have true anxiety of influence unless you are Shakespeare or Milton and have already gained admittance to the canon. The Bakhtinian model, which can elide the distance between 'dialogism' and 'dialogue', assumes a similarity of voice, as well as an (often unexamined) equality between two writers who may have vastly different backgrounds and goals.

APPROPRIATION AS THRIFT AND THEFT

My own approach to appropriation posits a more equitable (although not necessarily equal) exchange between texts and writers by considering appropriation as a form of imaginative 'donation' as well as a potential theft of intellectual property or cultural capital.[3] Graham Holderness reminds us that my translation of the term works better in American than in British English.[4] But even more broadly, from a rhetorical perspective some of the persistent theoretical barriers to imagining appropriation as a two-way exchange, or a process of give-and-take, are inherent to the theoretical frameworks that inform appropriation studies: first, the economic metaphors that govern Foucault's concept of authorship; and second, an insistently textual bias in post-Derridean notions of performativity. Both have tended to equate Shakespearian appropriation with the norms of print culture. In a study of the relation between intertextuality and an older concept of literary 'influence', Jay Clayton and Eric Rothstein note the 'normative implications' of the 'economic metaphors in which influence is expressed, *owing* and *indebtedness*'[5] (italics in original), citing Foucault's recognition that authorship

---

[1] Harold Bloom, *The Anxiety of Influence* (New Haven, 1973).

[2] M. M. Bakhtin, *The Dialogic Imagination: Four Essays*, ed. Michael Holquist and trans. Caryl Emerson and Michael Holquist (Austin, Texas, 1981), pp. 259–422.

[3] See the discussion in Christy Desmet, 'Introduction' to *Shakespeare and Appropriation* (London, 1999), pp. 1–12. A recent essay that details a two-way process of appropriation involving Shakespeare and the Beijing Opera is Faye Chunfang Fei and William Huizhu Sun, '*Othello* and Beijing Opera: Appropriation as a Two-Way Street', *TDR, The Drama Review: A Journal of Performance Studies*, 50 (2006), 120–33. In this case, the 'two-way street' involves very specific performance conditions and a narrative of explicit cultural exchange.

[4] Graham Holderness, '"Dressing Old Words New": Science, Shakespeare and Appropriation', *Borrowers and Lenders: The Journal of Shakespeare and Appropriation*, 1.2 (Fall/Winter 2005), 22 pp. in PDF, available online at www.borrowers.uga.edu/ (cited 7 February 2007).

[5] Jay Clayton and Eric Rothstein, 'Figures in the Corpus: Theories of Influence and Intertextuality', in *Influence and Intertextuality in Literary History*, ed. Jay Clayton and Eric Rothstein (Madison, 1991), p. 13. They are referencing here the work of Göran Hermerén.

operates as 'the principle of thrift in the proliferation of meaning'.[6] This principle of 'thrift' suggests that with a finite amount of cultural capital to go around, appropriating Shakespeare is a form of theft. As Jean Marsden puts it:

Associated with abduction, adoption and theft, appropriation's central tenet is the desire for possession. It comprehends both the commandeering of the desired object and the process of making this object one's own, controlling it by possessing it. Appropriation is neither dispassionate nor disinterested; it has connotations of usurpation, of seizure for one's own uses.[7]

Thrift and theft go together in criticism as well as in literature. For instance, spending energy on tracing prior ownership of a later text to Shakespeare-as-source is not merely wasteful, but a form of symbolic robbery. Thus, treating African American writer Gloria Naylor as an appropriator of Shakespearian texts, despite the writer's denial of Shakespearian influence, could devalue the kinship of her novels to those by African American writers (one kind of critical thrift that works by circumscribing intertextual relations); it also runs the risk of denying Naylor an authorial voice, the right to articulate her own influences (another form of thrift, the circumscribing of literary contexts). Authorship, within this culture of thrift, is intimately bound up with censorship and canonization. While in Marsden's definition of 1991, the marauding appropriator was a daring artistic thief, more recently, work based in cultural studies has extended the critique of cross-cultural appropriations of styles and subject matter by Western artists from non-Western cultures to Shakespearian criticism.[8] In response, we have seen an emerging set of critical anthologies that work to sort out the politics of local Shakespeares in a worldwide context and a concomitant effort to come up with new terms (remaking, re-imagining, collaboration) or to return to older terms (adaptation).[9]

A second critical trend that works against efforts to see Shakespearian appropriation as a two-way street is the continuum that links Kristevan intertextuality to performativity by way of the concept of citation. The notion of performativity has been put forward as a theoretical escape mechanism from anxiety of influence. A line of argument that stretches from Jacques Derrida to Judith Butler has resisted the despotism of authorial influence by redefining identity (or subjectivity) as a performance built from the iterated citation of conventional behaviours and ideologies. These iterations are normative, tending to censorship and social conservatism, but the citational

---

[6] Michel Foucault, 'What is an Author?', revised version, trans. Josué V. Harari, in *Textual Strategies: Perspectives in Post-Structuralist Criticism*, ed. Josué V. Harari (Ithaca, NY, 1979), p. 159; cited by Clayton and Rothstein, p. 4.

[7] Jean I. Marsden, ed., *The Appropriation of Shakespeare: The Works and the Myth* (Hemel Hempstead, 1991), p. 1.

[8] For a critique of the appropriation of non-Western cultures by the West, see, for instance, Rustom Bharucha, 'Somebody's Other: Disorientations in the Cultural Politics of Our Times', in *The Intercultural Performance Reader*, ed. Patrice Pavis (London, 1996), pp. 196–212; and 'Foreign Asia/Foreign Shakespeare: Dissenting Notes on New Asian Interculturality, Postcoloniality and Recolonization', *Theatre Journal*, 56 (2004), p. 7. For the critique of critical appropriation in Shakespeare studies, see Thomas Cartelli, *Repositioning Shakespeare: National Formations, Postcolonial Appropriations* (London, 1999); Ania Loomba and Martin Orkin, eds., *Post-colonial Shakespeares* (London, 1999); and Martin Orkin, *Local Shakespeares: Proximations and Power* (London, 2005).

[9] On local Shakespeares in a world-wide context, see, among others, Sonia Massai, ed., *World-Wide Shakespeares: Local Appropriations in Film and Performance* (London, 2005). For contributions to conversation about names for the practice I have been calling appropriation, see Pascale Aebischer, Edward J. Esche and Nigel Wheale, eds., *Remaking Shakespeare: Performance Across Media, Genres and Cultures* (Houndsmills, 2003); Naomi J. Miller, ed., *Reimagining Shakespeare for Children and Young Adults* (New York, 2003); Diana E. Henderson, *Collaborations with the Past: Reshaping Shakespeare across Time and Media* (Ithaca, NY, 2003); Norbert Schaffald, *Shakespeare's Legacy: The Appropriation of the Plays in Post-Colonial Drama* (Trier, 2005); Catherine O'Neil, *With Shakespeare's Eyes: Pushkin's Creative Appropriation of Shakespeare* (Newark, Del., 2003); Alexander Shurbanov and Boika Sokolova, *Painting Shakespeare Red: An East-European Appropriation* (Newark, 2001); Lemuel A. Johnson, *Shakespeare in Africa (and Other Venues): Import and the Appropriation of Culture* (Trenton, NJ, 1998); Ton Hoenselaars, ed., *Shakespeare's History Plays: Performance, Translation and Adaptation in Britain and Abroad* (Cambridge, 2004); and Courtney Lehmann, *Shakespeare Remains: Theatre to Film, Early Modern to Postmodern* (Ithaca, NY, 2002).

mechanism offers, as well, opportunities for subversive (e.g., feminist or queer) performances of identity.[10] Nevertheless, the genealogy of performativity, which traces back from Judith Butler through Derrida to J. L. Austin (whose speech-act theory is specifically anti-theatrical) makes the idea of performance through citation almost exclusively textual. The dialectic between citation and a more radical form of signification is still recognizably Derrida's *écriture*, mixed with the print-based context of Foucauldian authorship. Appropriation may be performative, but it is still conducted through the written word. Linda Hutcheon makes a similar point in her *Theory of Adaptation* (2006). Debunking a series of clichés about the genre, Hutcheon discovers a similar privileging of adaptations that 'tell' through discursive language, most notably in the genres of prose fiction.[11] Hutcheon's book aims to rehabilitate those adaptations that are not merely performative, but involve media linked more closely to drama than the novel – that is, adaptations that are *performances*, and, to some extent, that is my goal in this paper: not only to bring dramatic appropriations of Shakespeare back into the critical conversation, where in Anglo-American studies, I think, they have been overshadowed by studies of novelistic revisions; but also to recuperate 'performance' as an alternative metaphor for the artistic, ethical and political act of appropriating Shakespeare.

APPROPRIATION AS PERFORMANCE

As a metaphor for Shakespearian appropriation, 'performance' offers an alternative to 'intertextuality' and 'performativity', both of which maintain connections with the Foucauldian economics of authorship. Separately, Jill Dolan and Janelle Reinelt have discussed the transfer of theatrical metaphors to other enterprises in cultural theory; by documenting the parallel growth of studies of 'performativity' and 'theatricality' in different, nationally based strains of literary theory and by promoting the usefulness of bringing the metaphor of performance 'back home' to the discipline of theatre studies, these writers remind us that pre-

vailing metaphors are not only conditioned by local circumstances, but also can be confining.[12] As Kenneth Burke said, 'Every way of seeing is a way of not seeing.'[13] The wonderful anthology *Adaptations of Shakespeare* (2000), edited by Daniel Fischlin and Mark Fortier, reminds us as well that despite the Anglo-American preoccupation with novelistic Shakespeares, dramatic adaptations of Shakespeare go back at least to John Fletcher's *The Woman's Prize, or The Tamer Tamed*.[14] The genre is alive and well today in the US popular culture phenomenon, YouTube. In the remainder of this article, I will suggest a dramatic genealogy for YouTube parodies of Shakespeare, discuss their educational/cultural context, and, I hope, make a start towards defining a rhetoric of give-and-take in these amateur productions. My hope is not to offer these videos as Urtexts of appropriation's 'savage mind', but simply to shift the metaphor and slip the yoke.

SHAKESPEARE IN BRIEF: *THE FIFTEEN-MINUTE HAMLET*

Perhaps the most innovative dramatic appropriation of Shakespeare produced in the English language is Tom Stoppard's *The Fifteen Minute*

---

[10] The ethical valence of the term 'performativity' has its own philology and local histories according to national literature and discipline, and I know personally the work that the term has done in only a few of these venues. This definition is just a synecdoche.

[11] Linda Hutcheon, *A Theory of Adaptation* (London, 2006), pp. 52–77.

[12] Janelle Reinelt, 'The Politics of Discourse: Performativity Meets Theatricality', *SubStance*, 31 (2002), 201–15; and Jill Dolan, 'Geographies of Learning: Theatre Studies, Performance and the "Performative"', *Theatre Journal*, 45 (1993), 417–41.

[13] Kenneth Burke, *Permanence and Change: An Anatomy of Purpose*, Second Edition (Indianapolis, 1965), p. 49.

[14] Two important works on novelistic appropriations of Shakespeare, particularly by women writers, in the Anglo-American literary tradition are Julie Sanders, *Novel Shakespeares: Twentieth-Century Women Novelists and Appropriation* (New York, 2002) and *Transforming Shakespeare*, ed. Marianne Novy, New Edition (New York, 2001); for dramatic appropriations, see Daniel Fischlin and Mark Fortier, eds., *Adaptations of Shakespeare: A Critical Anthology of Plays from the Seventeenth Century to the Present* (London, 2000).

Hamlet (first performed at the National Theatre in 1976), a hilarious transformation of Shakespeare's famously expansive tragedy that works its rhetorical magic by simple condensation.[15] Stoppard's play neither rearranges *Hamlet*'s (conflated) text, nor adds language of its own. (Only Shakespeare, as the Prologue, even gets his lines out of order.) It achieves comedy simply by pruning Shakespearian lines to create amusing juxtapositions of culturally familiar statements and events. Thus, Hamlet's decision to launch the Mousetrap is followed immediately by a three-line condensation of the Nunnery scene and then by Claudius's determination to send Hamlet to England:

> The play's the thing,
> Wherein I'll catch the conscience of the King.
> > *Pause.*
> To be, or not to be (*he puts a dagger to his heart*)
> > *Claudius and Ophelia enter.*
> > > > that is the question.
>
> OPHELIA
> My lord –
> HAMLET
> Get thee to a nunnery!
> > *Ophelia and Hamlet exit.*
> CLAUDIUS
> Love? His affections do not that way tend
> There is something in his soul
> O'er which his melancholy sits on brood.
> He shall with speed to England.
> > *Claudius exits.*
> > > > (Scene 4, p. 9)

A knowing audience – and Stoppard's parody requires such an audience – acknowledges not only the comic effects that follow when such an emotionally fraught exchange is reduced to a curt shorthand, but also the condensation's ironic deflation of all the critical ink spilled over this scene. In Stoppard's version, there is no complex motivation behind Hamlet's cutting words to Ophelia; here, the man who famously could not make up his mind, just acts, and by acting – that is, by moving forward relentlessly from event to

event – the characters of *Hamlet* also manage to act up.[16]

The Fifteen Minute Hamlet works in counterpoint with Stoppard's earlier rewriting of *Hamlet* in *Rosencrantz and Guildenstern Are Dead* (1966). On the one hand, we have a comically condensed ventriloquism of Shakespeare's words; on the other, an imaginative rhapsody that alters both plot and dialogue of this most familiar of Shakespeare's plays. For the kinds of popular appropriation that interest me here, what Stoppard's paired plays enact is a tension between textual fidelity (an 'exact' mimesis of a Shakespearian text) and artistic freedom (new plots, new dialogues, newly foregrounded characters, new ideas and new registers of colloquial language). A comparable tension between textual constraint and creative freedom – perhaps learned directly from Stoppard, himself a staple of high-school literature curricula, but refracted as well through other sources – shapes the Shakespeare parodies found on YouTube.

---

[15] Tom Stoppard, *The Fifteen Minute Hamlet* (London and New York, 1976).

[16] Throughout this article, I will refer to the YouTube appropriations as parodies, following the authors' own designation of them and also the definitions and discussion of that term offered by Linda Hutcheon, *A Theory of Parody: The Teachings of Twentieth-Century Art Forms* (New York and London, 1985). Hutcheon sees parody as embracing a range of motives, from homage to purely ludic play to artistic competition with the parent text, and I see these same qualities in the YouTube productions. The parodies do share some qualities with the genre studied by Richard W. Schoch in *Not Shakespeare: Bardolatry and Burlesque in the Nineteenth Century* (Cambridge, 2002). By virtue of their medium, YouTube parodies are, like burlesques, disposable (Schoch, *Not Shakespeare*, p. 16), and like burlesques, they aim to deflate 'highbrow' Shakespeare. But while the YouTube parodies approach the phenomenon of Bardolatry with tongues firmly in cheek, the examples I discuss lack the focused hostility to canonical literature that Schoch identifies in nineteenth-century Shakespeare burlesques (p. 7), and they are less relentlessly topical than burlesques (p. 33). Finally, my chosen examples acknowledge and keep their eye firmly on the language of the Shakespearian 'parent' text, a feature that is characteristic of parody rather than burlesque.

18 Guinea Pig Theater, *Romeo and Juliet*.

SCHOOL SHAKESPEARE AND
YOUTH CULTURE ON THE WEB

YouTube dramatists do not operate in a vacuum, of course. They engage with the 'Shakespeare' put forth in the US educational system, the ethos of YouTube itself and appropriations of Shakespeare offered through popular and consumer culture.[17] Sheila Cavanagh has argued that the US educational system is overly invested in making Shakespeare not only 'fun', but also 'relevant'.[18] Thus, *Romeo and Juliet* provides an opportunity for discussing topics ranging from cardio-vascular resuscitation to the dangers of illicit drugs. Students are also invited to rework Shakespearian plots with more *heimlich* content: one classroom assignment, for instance, asks that students 'make your own adaptation of *Romeo and Juliet*. Romeo and Juliet can be anything from rival figure skaters (as my friend did) to pigs on a farm. Just be creative!'[19] A charming reductio ad absurdum of this kind of appropriation is provided online by the Guinea Pig Theater's *Romeo and Juliet*, which not only reduces Shakespeare's text

---

[17] The line separating amateur from professional theatre and consumer culture can be particularly porous. Douglas Lanier reminds us, for instance, that *The Bomb-itty of Errors*, which had a successful run as an off-Broadway show, began as a project for a New York University film class (*Shakespeare and Modern Popular Culture* [Oxford, 2002], p. 78).

[18] Sheila Cavanagh, 'Crushing on a Capulet: Culture, Cognition and Simplification in *Romeo and Juliet* for Young People', *Borrowers and Lenders: The Journal of Shakespeare and Appropriation*, 2.1 (Spring/Summer 2006), 21 pp. in PDF, available online at www.borrowers.uga.edu (cited 7 February 2007). See also Derek Longhurst, '"You base football player": Shakespeare in Contemporary Popular Culture', in *The Shakespeare Myth*, ed. Graham Holderness (Manchester, 1988), 59–73.

[19] '*Romeo and Juliet*, Choose Your Fate', available online at http://library.thinkquest.org/19539/randj.htm (cited 3 February 2007).

to brute grunts, but also offers a truncated pantomime of the play's action, a Guinea Pig equivalent of *A Midsummer Night Dream*'s 'Pyramus and
Thisbe'.[20] Teachers can also purchase from Theatrefolk Original Playscripts such dramas as Lindsay
Price's two-act play *Football Romeo*, which uses a
school production of Shakespeare's play as a backdrop for teenage angst. (There is also a ten-minute
version for shorter classes and attention spans.)[21]
Other formats from popular culture are evident in
such events as 'The Oprah Donahue Show Talks
about Fatal Attractions with Special Guests: Juliet,
the Shrew, Hamlet's Mother, and Lady M.'[22] From
here, it is only a small step to Gil Junger's *10 Things
I Hate About You* (1999).[23]

Still another type of school assignment – not
unlike the exercises in imitation performed by early
modern schoolboys – involves a more concentrated
and painstaking transformation of Shakespearian
plots and speeches into another cultural idiom. One
of my favourite examples posted on the internet
comes from a teacher in Anchorage, Alaska, who
writes on his website that 'the story of Romeo and
Juliet wasn't too far removed from the Yup'ik stories based upon the ancient wars on the tundra'.
The result is *The Tragic Story of Kenke & Atsaq: A
Yup'ik Adaptation of Shakespeare's Romeo & Juliet*.[24]
As a student work sample, the teacher offers a nicely
turned translation of the Queen Mab speech that
begins:

O, then I see Raven has been with you. He is the
dreamer's giver, and he comes in shape of a shadow bird,
as black as night. Pulled [by] a group of wolves, his sled
ropes [are] made of caribou's hair; he leaves behind the
smallest eggshells. His musher [is] a small gray-coated
gnat, not half so big as a round little worm pricked from
the lazy finger of a slave; his toboggan is an abandoned
nest.

Some of the exercises, instead of replacing the
content of Shakespearian speeches, involve a line-
for-line translation of Shakespeare's poetry into a
more colloquial register, combined with a pugnacious revision of the Shakespearian plot, particularly when the conclusion is not palatable. We
see an optimistic (and perhaps didactic) rewriting of Shakespeare in '*ROMEO AND JULIET*:
A Sock Puppet Adaptation' (2004), a product of
the young author's literary/political blog that features plain-language translations of Shakespearian
poetry in conjunction with plot alterations. Here,
for instance, is the sock-puppet version of the balcony scene:

NARRATOR

And so, Romeo and Juliet parted. But that's
not the end of the story; It would be a pretty
lame story if it was. The very next night,
Romeo appeared outside Juliet's castle.

SCENE 3 – The Ubiquitous Castle Scene
[ROMEO appears, with a ladder, outside
JULIET's tower window. She's inside.]

ROMEO

'Sup, homegirl?

JULIET

Oh, it's you. What are you doing here? I
thought you were going to go away.

ROMEO

Shhh! I've come to see you.

JULIET

No kidding. Why else would you be here?

ROMEO

(with a Shakespearian British accent) But,

---

[20] Not the fruits of a school assignment, but a digital sandbox
for professional web developers, the Guinea Pig Theater is
an elaborate and witty piece of amateur culture (Guinea Pig
Theater, *Romeo and Juliet*, Musearts Cartoons, 2001, available
online at www.musearts.com/cartoons/pigs/romeo.html
(cited 7 February 2007)).

[21] Lindsay Price, 'Football Romeo', Theatrefolk Original Playscripts, available online at www.theatrefolk.com/
products/play/53 (cited 16 November 2007).

[22] Mark Leiren-Young and Kate Johnston, 'The Oprah Donahue Show Talks About Fatal Attractions with Special Guests:
Juliet, the Shrew, Hamlet's Mother, and Lady M'; I found
this reference on the Routledge site for the Fischlin and
Fortier anthology, available online at www.routledge.com/
shakespeare/adaptations.html.

[23] *10 Things I Hate About You*, Director Gil Junger, Performers Heath Ledger, Julia Stiles, Joseph Gordon-Levitt, Larisa
Oleynik, USA, Mad Chance, 1999.

[24] Don Reardon, 'Cultural Adaptation of a Classic Play',
LitSite Alaska, available online at http://litsite.alaska.edu/
workbooks/adapt.html (cited 9 February 2007).

soft! What light through yonder window breaks? It is the east, and Juliet is the sun.

JULIET

What the heck is that supposed to mean?

ROMEO

I don't know, I just thought it sounded distinguished-like.

JULIET

You know, I have a confession to make. I really like you, and I don't care if our families hate each other. Now, what were you going to say?[25]

The author adheres to the general shape of Shakespeare's dialogue, but transposes the lovers' flights of poetic fancy into a series of colloquial registers, ranging from 'Sup, homegirl?' to Juliet's artless declaration of love: 'You know, I have a confession to make.' There is the obligatory mock-confusion caused by the one famous line that Romeo quotes directly. As often happens in such adaptations, the abandonment of Shakespearian language serves as the couple's *bona fides*, ensuring their happy ending. In the style of Disney films, they also manage to correct the faults of their feuding parents, the Joneses and Smiths, who according to the narrator, finally abandon their 'sensless [*sic*] fighting'.

Although only two genres within the vast range of Shakespearian appropriation available on the web, both the humorous condensation (in the tradition of Stoppard's *The Fifteen Minute Hamlet*) and the colloquial rewriting (in the style of *Rosencrantz and Guildenstern Are Dead*) are part of the cultural genealogy for YouTube Shakespeare parodies. As performance-driven appropriations, they can also hearken back directly to Stoppard's parody and to its descendants, such as the Reduced Shakespeare Company's *The Complete Works of William Shakespeare (Abridged)*.[26] Finally, as a growing archive of digitized video snatched from commercial film and popular culture, YouTube also provides aspiring actors and directors with clips from such popular, and previously often difficult to locate, episodes as the *Moonlighting Taming of the Shrew* (1986) or *Hamlet, the Musical*, from the *Gilligan's Island* episode, 'The Producer' (1964).[27]

SHAKESPEARE PARODY ON YOUTUBE

The YouTube ethos is congenial to parody.[28] Prior to legal action demanding their removal, among the most frequently reproduced Shakespeare items on the site were the Beatles' not terribly funny enactment of 'Pyramus and Thisbe' and the Rowan Atkinson and Hugh Laurie skit that dramatizes the ruthless editing process by which 'To be or not to be' ('it's gibberish!') becomes immortalized. (A few copies still continue to be posted.) School-sponsored and amateur parodies are also ubiquitous, their number increasing exponentially every month and showing some signs of internal influence and cross-referencing.

In compliance with YouTube conventions, the Shakespeare parodies are brief; the longest by far that I have watched was about thirty-four minutes. They generally work by translation (largely a shift in rhetorical register that puts high-falutin' Shakespearian statements into the plain style) and the related operation of excision (eliminating words and entire lines in the service of parody). The emphasis on Shakespeare's verse is perhaps less pronounced today than it was a year ago. The growing

---

[25] Jordon Kalilich, '*Romeo and Juliet*: A Sock-Puppet Adaptation', available online at www.theworldofstuff.com/other/rj.txt (cited 7 February 2007).

[26] Reduced Shakespeare Company, *The Complete Works of William Shakespeare (Abridged)*, Performers Adam Long, Reed Martin, Austin Tichenor, DVD, USA, Acorn Media.

[27] *Moonlighting*, Director Will McKenzie, Perfomers Bruce Willis, Cybil Sheppard, USA, ABC, 1986; 'The Producer', *Gilligan's Island*, Directors Ida Lupino and George M. Cahan, USA, 1964. Shakespeare parody in popular culture has been profitably studied by Shakespeare critics, most notably Richard Burt, *Unspeakable ShaXXXspeares: Queer Theory and American Kiddie Culture* (New York, 1998); and Douglas Lanier, *Shakespeare and Modern Popular Culture* (Oxford, 2002).

[28] Although by no means all YouTube videos derive from youth culture, the Shakespeare parodies generally do; as the 'Introduction' to *Shakespeare and Youth Culture* reminds us, youth culture is highly appropriative and mediated, which would make both parody and YouTube congenial to its members (Jennifer Hulbert, Kevin J. Wetmore, Jr and Robert L. York, *Shakespeare and Youth Culture* (New York, 2006), p. 6).

popularity of invented movie trailers (original videotaped action set to pre-recorded music and framed by movie titles and scrolling cast lists) and of video-mashups (the ironic juxtaposition of video from one film and music from elsewhere) have given rise to Shakespeare appropriations that have few or even no words. We see, as well, a rise in single-scene parodies (probably influenced by class assignments), especially of the final swordfight between Hamlet and Laertes. One well-done version that uses *Star Wars* sabres in place of swords, for instance, distorts the characters' speech through a Darth Vader filter and adds clever tag lines from other popular culture venues; as Gertrude dies, she cries 'Oh, my god!' in honour of *South Park*'s Kenny and then rises to quip, 'I'm not quite dead. Actually, I'm feeling better' (a homage to *Monty Python and the Holy Grail*). While setting the duel cleverly to the *Star Wars* soundtrack, the clip is also attentive to Shakespearian stage directions – for instance, making sure that Hamlet and Laertes exchange light sabres and making Gertrude fall down from poisoning at the right moment – but the action is performed almost entirely in pantomime.[29]

At their worst, appropriations that do focus on Shakespeare's language can involve nothing more than two giggly 'actors' reading from printed scripts in front of the camera. But some are much better. The collective that calls itself futurebrien has posted a series of amateur videos, probably produced with iMovie, that are variously called adaptations or parodies. They demonstrate the dialectic between textual condensation and exfoliation and the play with Shakespearian language that characterizes Stoppard's parodic rhetoric, and as a result offer a suggestive picture of Shakespearian appropriation taking place in a space located somewhere between education as an institution, amateur culture on the World Wide Web and both popular and literary Shakespeare.

Hamlet Out-Takes (2007), a light-hearted romp from futurebrien that, apart from the ghost's appearance at a softball park, has no particular relation to its Shakespearian predecessor, in fact seems to be a kind of director's cut for *Hamlet, Prince of Denmark, a Parody* (2007), which comes in at thirty-four minutes.[30] Filmed over a space of five days, this abbreviated *Hamlet* exhibits the full range of parodic motives identified by Linda Hutcheon in her study of the subject.[31] The video pays homage to Shakespeare, playfully mocks both his iconic status and the youth culture that does the mocking, and finally, uses this act of sustained attention to *Hamlet* and its language to assert the young filmmakers' claim to artistic and intellectual merit. Some of the dialogue falls flat ('It looks like King Hamlet, but King Hamlet wasn't dead'). Some of it works pretty well (as when Claudius gloats, 'I'm your poppa'). And some of the dialogue, in conjunction with the video's manipulations of Shakespearian plot, arguably achieves the aims of Stoppard's comedy.

Hamlet, Prince of Denmark expresses youth culture's general disdain for the older generation, an impulse that certainly is justified by Shakespeare's play; but in a more Bakhtinian style, it also pokes fun in both directions, avoiding the impulse towards satire and bitter mockery. The 'older' generation – a cherubic Claudius and his cross-dressed Gertrude – are clearly enjoying themselves. And the younger generation can be insufferable. When the King and Queen counsel Hamlet against excessive grief, the Prince's wrenching, colloquial reply, 'My father died. And now, one week later . . . How do you expect me to feel?' is then undermined by an adolescent outburst of temper as Hamlet, his faced screwed up in self-pity, stomps up the stairs to his suburban bedroom. There follows an extended – indeed, grotesque – display of princely anguish as Hamlet writhes on the floor for a good ten seconds before the door opens and Horatio initiates this deadpan exchange:

29 'Star Wars Hamlet Parody Hilarious', available online at www.youtube.com/watch?v=WPxjYF5niik.

30 futurebrien, *Hamlet Out-Takes*, Director Brien Henry, Performers Brien Henry, Jason Wells, YouTube, available online at www.youtube.com/watch?v=A7qzH6Xf_K0&mode= related&search= (cited 9 February 2007); futurebrien, *Hamlet, Prince of Denmark*, YouTube, available online at www.youtube.com/watch?v=bm1_zwUDOSE&mode=related& search= (cited 9 February 2007).

31 Hutcheon, *A Theory of Parody*, pp. 61–4.

19 The Nunnery scene, from futurebrien, *Hamlet, Prince of Denmark*.

HORATIO

So, I was in the graveyard and saw your dad.
Dead. Want to see him?

HAMLET

Yeah.

HORATIO

How about tomorrow night?

HAMLET

Sounds good.

The balance of sympathy then shifts once again. When Hamlet and his father's spirit meet, Hamlet asks, 'You want me to kill him?' and the apparition merely says, 'Yeah, whatever. See you around.' Hamlet replies, 'Byeeeee . . .' Righteous elder and cool youth speak the same laconic idiom; they are 'deep' but, in the final analysis, also rather silly. Throughout *Hamlet, Prince of Denmark*, the filmmakers not only deflate the pretensions of both old and young, but – a much more difficult achievement – also transform moments of comedy into pathos. Ophelia's death offers a good example. As she lies inert by the swimming pool (perhaps recalling the swimming-pool balcony scene of Baz Lurhmann's *Romeo + Juliet*), the family dog – which had been heard yapping incessantly behind closed doors throughout the duration of Rosencrantz and Guildenstern's first appearance – snuffles slowly around the body in a way that is eerie and surprisingly affecting.

Probably the most powerful moment in the futurebrien *Hamlet* is the Nunnery scene. Inter-

estingly, the 'To be or not to be' speech is excised completely, eliminating any metaphysical distractions from Ophelia's and Hamlet's confrontation. After a brief bit of business, during which Claudius and Polonius hide behind a door representing a two-way mirror (an obvious reference to Kenneth Branagh's *Hamlet*), the camera focuses on a closeup of the two lovers' faces. 'I never gave you gifts', says Hamlet. 'Yes, you did', insists Ophelia, 'Take them'. Dressed in understated drag and sporting a clipped beard, Ophelia faces off impassively against the clean-shaven, long-haired and tightly wound Hamlet. When Hamlet screams, 'I never loved you', the outburst has a real homoerotic edge.[32] The video's energy is centripetal, focusing attention on the two players with whom we have shared not two hours' traffic of the stage, but in YouTube time, a relatively long acquaintance. In the following scene, as Ophelia races through the kitchen, chanting 'Hey nonny nonny' to a relentless techno beat, she grates on our nerves, but is also an object of genuine pity. This parody, like that of Stoppard, walks a fine line between comedy and tragedy; to a large extent, its subject is the doomed, unclearly gendered love between Hamlet and Ophelia. The conclusion of *Hamlet, Prince of Denmark* fits more easily into the genre of YouTube video. The final swordfight is recast as a home-run derby; as Claudius sneers, 'Hamlet is an all-star pitcher. And he thinks he can bat.' In a typical translation from one cultural register to another, the fencing court is changed to a softball field and the poisoned cup replaced by a doctored Macdonald's burger, giving us one final motive for Hamlet's revenge: transfats. And so the production careens energetically to its conclusion.

futurebrien's *Action Macbeth* is shorter and sweeter than *Hamlet, Prince of Denmark* and plays more with Shakespearian language in a

---

[32] This filmic composition can be found in commercially distributed Shakespeare films, where the thematization of homoerotic cross-dressing is also growing. Richard Burt, for instance, discusses such closeups in Henry V's relation to the traitor Scroop in the Kenneth Branagh *Henry V* (UK, Samuel Goldwyn, 1989), in *Unspeakable ShaXXXspeares*, pp. 31–2.

20 Birnam Wood Comes to Dunsinane, from futurebrien, *Action Macbeth*.

sophisticated, almost academic way. (It was also identified explicitly as an earlier school project when posted to YouTube on 14 January 2007.)[33] There is also a more self-conscious quotation of cinematic styles. The play opens on a Fisher-Price model of Castle Dunsinane, while a Baz Lurhmann-type TV announcer brings the audience up to speed. Much of the video is taken up with Macbeth's extended battles, which are set to the raucous punk/Irish music of L.A. band Flogging Molly and are indebted for their choreography to action films and perhaps the Jeremy Freeston *Macbeth*.[34]

Action Macbeth's best feature, however, is an increased ability not just to translate Shakespeare's idiom, but to interact meta-dramatically with it. The part of Young Siward is beefed up and is granted the following exchange with Macbeth:

YOUNG SIWARD

My name is more fearful than any in hell.

MACBETH

Who are you?

YOUNG SIWARD

Young Siward.

What teacher at any level would fail to appreciate a student who could remember who Young Siward was? What Shakespearian would fail to get this sly jibe at the notion of Shakespeare's 'authoritative' text? There are also improvisational riffs on Shakespeare's most portentous lines. At their final meeting, for instance, Macbeth tells Macduff, 'Out of everyone in the world I have avoided you, Macduff', and then expatiates, 'Killing Macduffs has grown stale . . . You're a bachelor now. Go have fun . . . I'm not killing any more Macduffs today.' 'Turn, hell hound, turn', is Macduff's textbook reply. This dialogue may not be Stoppard, but it is good, moving athletically between quotation and low-style paraphrase of the Shakespearian text.

---

33 *Action Macbeth*, by futurebrien, Director Brien Henry, Performers Brien Henry, Jason Wells, YouTube, available online at www.youtube.com/watch?v=zwrHNZsgkh8&mode=related&search= (cited 7 February 2007).

34 *Macbeth*, Director Jeremy Freeston, Performers Jason Connery, Helen Baxendale, Graham McTavish, Kenneth Bryans, UK, Cromwell Productions, 1997.

PAYING ATTENTION IN PARODY

The joke behind Stoppard's *Fifteen Minute Hamlet* is that simply by trimming the source text, the playwright at once plagiarizes Shakespeare (theft by thrift) and makes a wholly new dramatic artefact (appropriation as performance). This is rhetorical discipline pitted against the regimes of authorship. The futurebrien videos are more workmanlike in selecting and then translating Shakespearian verse into a contemporary idiom, but author and performers keep their eye on the source text and, just as important, interact productively with it. In subjecting such light-hearted efforts as the *Action Macbeth* to a traditional literary analysis, I admittedly run the risk of appropriating these amateur productions to the highbrow/lowbrow dynamic of academic Shakespeare. Douglas Lanier, agreeing with Richard Burt, suggests that much of Shakespop is what Burt calls 'post-hermeneutic'. 'Refusing the academic imperative to "read closely"', as I have done here to these videos, 'is often the point, a source of anarchic pleasure'.[35] I am arguing, by contrast, that what gives the amateur productions that I discuss their particular character is their focused *attention* on specific moments of action and, more important, specific speech acts from the parent text. The engagement between Shakespeare and appropriator is thoroughly rhetorical, a matter of textual give-and-take rather than a wholesale usurpation of the Bard's words and authority.

In Renaissance rhetoric, the name for adopting a fictional persona and speaking in that person's voice is prosopopoeia. In these exercises, which are part of the drama's rhetorical genealogy, young (male) speakers are asked to place themselves in the circumstances of a fictional, mythic or historical person – interestingly, given the parodic propensity for cross-dressing on YouTube, often a woman – and to give a hypothetical speech suitable to the character's circumstances: detailing, for instance, what Niobe might have said after discovering the slaughter of her children; what Juliet might say when discovering that her new love is a Montague; or what Cassio might (rather than did) say in his sleep. Based frequently on literary examples, the prosopopoeia therefore becomes in part a rhetorical translation of set texts, in part a dramatic improvisation. One way of identifying this dynamic in terms useful for appropriation studies is provided by Derek Attridge, who describes the 'singularity' of literature as 'reading for the event'. This kind of reading involves both alterity (confrontation with otherness) and invention.[36] Reading, in Attridge's view, is also by nature dramatic performance; to respond to a work of art, 'we must *perform* it; or more accurately, and preserving the undecidability between act and event, when we read a literary work as a literary work *we find ourselves performing it*' (italics in original).[37] In extremis, reading for the event can therefore produce the emotional power that forces tears for Hecuba into the Player's eyes in *Hamlet*. In humbler venues such as YouTube, it is more likely to elicit an approving 'Awesome dude. lol' on the message board. But in either case, the appropriation-as-performance is not just an agon, but also a declaration of affiliation through performance; and perhaps more important, it demands an exertion of attention to the rhetoric of both source text and appropriation.

THRIFT, THEFT AND RHETORIC IN AMATEUR CULTURE

The artistic world to which YouTube parodies of Shakespeare belong has been called, by both fans and detractors, amateur culture. For Lawrence Lessig, who uses the term approvingly, amateur culture is a digital space 'where amateur doesn't mean inferior or without talent, but instead culture created by people who produce not for the money, but for the love of what they do'.[38] William Gibson, the intellectual father of cyberspace, celebrates the

---

[35] Burt, *Unspeakable ShaXXXpeares*, p. 243, discussed by Lanier, *Shakespeare and Modern Popular Culture*, p. 52.

[36] Derek Attridge, 'Performing Metaphors: The Singularity of Literary Figuration', *Paragraph: A Journal of Modern Critical Theory*, 28 (2005), 18–34.

[37] Attridge, 'Performing Metaphors', p. 20.

[38] Lawrence Lessig, *Code: Version 2.0* (New York, 2006), p. 193.

power of amateur culture in terms that are familiar to students of Shakespearian drama and adaptation: 'Our culture no longer bothers to use words like *appropriation* or *borrowing* to describe those very activities. Today's audience isn't listening at all – it's participating.'[39] But not all critics of the web celebrate the rise of this 'participatory' culture. As Andrew Keen writes, 'In a world in which audience and author are increasingly indistinguishable, and where authenticity is almost impossible to verify, the idea of original authorship and intellectual property has been seriously compromised.'[40] So while Gibson depicts appropriation positively as a form of creative performance, for Keen amateur culture both dumbs down high art and authorizes the theft of intellectual property when audiences download, reproduce and disseminate copyrighted material and remix those digital properties in any number of genres.

To protect and restore the economics of authorship, Keen promotes regulation of the web, a return to a politics of thrift. Richard A. Lanham suggests, by contrast, that quarrels about property in the world of electronic media are, to a great extent, beside the point. The real currency, he argues, is not information-as-property, but *attention*: '[W]e live in an "information economy". But information is not in short supply in the new information economy. We're drowning in it. What we lack is the human attention needed to make sense of it all.'[41] Lanham's economics of attention, as it turns out, is synonymous with the 'art of persuasion' – that is, with rhetoric. In this article I have suggested that YouTube Shakespeare parodies engage in the art of persuasion through a rhetorical dynamic of giving attention (to Shakespeare) and attracting attention (to the artist's appropriation).

Meditating on the problem of how to 'accommodate a viable sense of give and take in theatrical communication to the unending silence, the absence of human voices in the postmodern mode of information', Robert Weimann argues: 'This, then, is finally the question of a participatory mode of reception: how to project and realize a cultural potential of communicative action in a theatre that, in its obsession with the materiality of dramatic action, tends to end up speechless.'[42] As the YouTube parodies of Shakespeare suggest, however, in this performance medium the speechless theatre of postmodernity has been succeeded by an amateur culture in which participation in parody involves not so much the dialectic between speech and silence – the endpoints of Derridean *écriture* – as a careful cultivation of attention structures amid the copia of available Shakespeare videos. A criticism of YouTube Shakespeare that is responsive to its particular mode of appropriation would, arguably, need to be equally rhetorical, not exactly an encomium for popular culture, but not aloof from it, either; such criticism is itself an act of attention, 'reading for the event' rather than against the grain. To pay attention to *how* YouTube parodies pay attention to Shakespeare is to participate in that community neither as an (academic) fan nor as a (cultural/political) advocate, but as a fellow student of rhetoric.

---

[39] Quoted in Andrew Keen, *The Cult of the Amateur: How Today's Internet is Killing Our Culture* (New York, 2007), p. 24.
[40] Keen, *The Cult of the Amateur*, p. 23.
[41] Richard Lanham, *The Economics of Attention* (Chicago, 2002), p. xi.
[42] Robert Weimann, '(Post)Modernity and Representation: Issues of Authority, Power, Performativity', *New Literary History*, 23 (1992), p. 960.

MADAGASCAN WILL: CINEMATIC SHAKESPEARES / TRANSNATIONAL EXCHANGES

MARK THORNTON BURNETT

Conventionally understood as the movement of *émigrés* across national borders, transnationalism has been described as affecting 'groups . . . no longer occupying discrete spaces or . . . cultures', as prompting individuals to forge 'relations that link together their societies of origin and settlement' and as encouraging the creation of 'geographically dispersed . . . *migrant communities*'.[1] The reverberations accompanying transnationalism are most easily identified in the flows of capital that traverse state parameters, in deterritorialized constructions of space, in the development of hybridized identities, in the determining power of technology and in the simultaneous collapse and reinforcement of local–global associations. Complementary interpretations of transnationalism pursue the phenomenon's ideological meanings and implications. Commentators are interested in the ways in which transnationalism licenses exchanges and interactions that contribute to the 'intermingling of cultures'; as Aihwa Ong writes, 'transnationality . . . alludes to the *trans*versal . . . the *trans*lational, and the *trans*gressive aspects of contemporary . . . imagination . . . the multiplicity of . . . conceptions of culture'.[2] Such transactions are not bound by the physicality of place, since, as a number of observers have pointed up, 'we attempt' more and more to comprehend 'our . . . transnational world' via '*symbolic and imaginary geographies*'.[3] Transnationalism is a historically specific and economically determined product of the late twentieth and early twenty-first centuries; at the same time, it is indissoluble from a unique

aesthetic that might function as a register of collaborative and cross-fertilizing cultural processes.

Two recent films, *Makibefo* (2000) and *Souli* (2004), lend themselves with a particularized urgency to the concerns that transnationalism announces. Both are versions of Shakespearian tragedies: *Makibefo* declares itself, through the use of an opening on-screen parenthetical translation of the title, as a recasting of *Macbeth*, while *Souli* is advertised in the end credits as 'librement inspiré d'*Othello* de William Shakespeare'. Director Alexander Abela, born in Britain and now based in France, takes *Macbeth* to the Antandroy people of Faux Cap in the south-east corner of Madagascar. *Othello* he transposes to the fishing village of Ambola on Madagascar's western shoreline. The

---

[1] Hastings Donnan and Thomas M. Wilson, *Borders: Frontiers of Identity, Nation and State* (Oxford and New York, 1999), p. 10; Linda Basch, Nina Glick Schiller and Cristina Szanton Blanc, 'Transnational Projects: A New Perspective', *Nations Unbound: Transnational Projects, Postcolonial Predicaments, and Deterritorialized Nation-States*, ed. Linda Basch, Nina Glick Schiller and Cristina Szanton Blanc (Langhorne, 1994), p. 7; Peter Dicken, *Global Shifts: Mapping the Changing Contours of the World Economy*, 5th edn (London, 2007), p. 449.

[2] David Held and Anthony McGrew, 'The Great Globalization Debate', *The Global Transformations Reader: An Introduction to the Globalization Debate*, ed. David Held and Anthony McGrew (Cambridge, 2000), p. 35; Aihwa Ong, *Flexible Citizenship: The Cultural Logics of Transnationality* (Durham and London, 1999), p. 4.

[3] Peter Jackson, Philip Crang and Claire Dwyer, 'Introduction', *Transnational Spaces*, ed. Peter Jackson, Philip Crang and Claire Dwyer (London and New York, 2004), p. 3.

aim, in Abela's words, was to engender a communal and intercultural reading of Shakespeare (*Makibefo* was enacted by fishermen and herdsmen, while *Souli* combined a professional, non-native cast with local performers), one which is invigorated by the participation of 'individuals isolated from the rest of the world'.[4] The idealizing tendencies of the aspiration notwithstanding, it is certainly the case that the conjunction of a number of interpretive constituencies facilitates the emergence of fresh Shakespearian readings and creations, with a particular emphasis being given to the position of the written word in this transnational era. Transnationally – and textually – relocating Shakespeare, the director and his collaborators find themes centring upon the flow of individuals inside and beyond national perimeters, the constitution of identity, the status (even in its absence) of technology and the economic underpinnings of political allegiance. Such is the facility with which these preoccupations are aired, moreover, that an interrogative dimension is afforded. Through processes of adjustment and appropriation, Shakespeare comes to speak to the histories of possession and dispossession that have dictated both the fortunes of Madagascar and other colonially governed countries. By acknowledging the pressures of the past on the present, *Makibefo* and *Souli* are able to contemplate the ways in which a transnational configuration of material geographies may yet allow for the formation of alternative imaginative landscapes that can challenge current inequities of space and place.

Transnationalism also informs, this article argues, the modalities of reception through which the films have been appreciated. Due in large part to the vagaries of global exhibition and distribution, *Makibefo* and *Souli* have slipped beneath the radar of the impetus that has made Shakespeare on film – and not least so-called 'spin-offs' and 'derivatives' – an established discipline.[5] Tracing the individual release careers of both works, and recovering the contexts of their fleeting visibility, offers an individualized test-case for assessing the means whereby Shakespeare continues to signify in the cinema in particular and in mass media more generally. What does the relative anonymity of *Makibefo* and *Souli*

in popular terms tell us about the universal cultural imprimatur with which Shakespeare is invariably associated? How does the Bard's symbolic capital differ and fluctuate according to localized circumstances of production and dissemination? And in what ways might 'Shakespeare', and his historic association with language, be transformed and revivified via filmic interpretations that place under scrutiny the transmission and commodification of words in the global marketplace? Hazarding answers to such questions invites us to reflect upon the ethical dimensions of the film's transnational subject matter and, in so doing, to think about the political potential of our own critical practice. For, in the same way that *Makibefo* and *Souli* highlight issues of voice and authority (the question of who benefits from the multiple exchanges of which transnationalism consists), so are we enjoined to recognize the roles we play as public commentators in the increasingly diversified – and yet perhaps still insufficiently global – world of Shakespeare studies.

I

It is clear from *Makibefo* that the re-imagining of the play derived from a non-textual encounter with Shakespeare, and this is confirmed in the director's observation that a 'comic strip . . . and photographs' were initially used in local explanations of the Bardic narrative.[6] Hence, Makibefo's name is pronounced in different ways through the film, suggesting a varying index of a heard English signifier and encoding a glimpse into the ways which

---

[4] *'Makibefo': An Alexander Abela Film based on William Shakespeare's 'Macbeth'*, press booklet (London, 2000), p. 4.

[5] Douglas Lanier acknowledges the signal achievement of *Makibefo* (but not *Souli*) in 'Film Spin-offs and Citations', *Shakespeares after Shakespeare: An Encyclopedia of the Bard in Mass Media and Popular Culture*, ed. Richard Burt, 2 vols. (Westport and London, 2007), vol. 1, p. 213, while both films are briefly applauded in Daniel Rosenthal's *100 Shakespeare Films: BFI Screen Guides* (London, 2007), pp. 114–17, 184–5.

[6] Interview between Alexander Abela and Mark Thornton Burnett, 15 August 2006. Unless otherwise stated, all further Abela quotations are taken from this interview and appear in the text.

unfamiliar cultural alignments prompt additions to an already mediated Shakespearian script. Names in *Souli* are equally inconsistent: the fiction concerns the attempts of Carlos/Cassio (Eduardo Noriega), a doctoral student, to recover the story of Thiossane: to this end, he seeks out the guardian of the tale, Souli/Othello (Makena Diop), an African writer. Primarily discovered as an ethnographer, Carlos functions in the film as a figurative manifestation of the west's cultivation of the indigenous: 'I've travelled over twelve thousand kilometres to meet you!' he announces, his indignant boast testifying to a process one critic describes as the 'mystification and reification of [the] . . . other's seemingly authentic experiences'.[7]

Ethnography in *Souli* belongs with the film's thematic content; in *Makibefo*, by contrast, an ethnographic component is apparent at the level of sound and image. 'People . . . think it's an anthropological film!', notes a surprised Abela in interview, yet the reaction is understandable given *Makibefo*'s representation of Malagasy villagers dressed in loin-cloths as well as the traditional *lamba* or wrap-around printed sheets: the clothing decision encourages an illusion of a society at a pre-modern stage of development. Certainly, the gaze of the ethnographer might be detected in those scenes in which a Shakespearian sequence is remodelled to suit Antandroy *mores* and beliefs. Thus, at the moment where the (male) witch (Victor Raobelina) draws charms (*ody*) from a pouch in order to trace Makibefo/Macbeth's (Martin Zia) fate on the sand, the film makes a virtue of gesturing towards the cultural prominence of the healer or *ombiasy* who, as John Mack states, is 'also a diviner . . . skilled at foretelling the future'.[8] The conjuration of an ethnographic perspective is most powerfully felt in the suggestions of documentary realism with which the film is suffused. A construction of an undiluted cultural encounter is communicated in *Makibefo*'s reliance upon a representational mode that is not so much linguistic as sensory in orientation: that is, the ear is exercised (heavy breathing is overlaid with the crash of waves in a syncopated, rhythmical fashion) at the same time as the eye is appealed to (an opening shot of funerary sculptures gives way to the image of tribesmen picking their way across the dunes). At times, this diegesis operates in a particularly transformative narrative capacity, as when the new king, Makibefo, is realized sacrificing an ox in a scene intercut with the murder of Bakoua/Banquo (Randina Arthur). In the protagonist's lifting to the sky of the decapitated, horned head of the *zebu* is communicated both a diabolical association (Makibefo metaphorically crowns himself with the sign of his evil) and a totemic suggestion (because the frequently seen totems are also horned, a manipulation of the local cult is implied). Once again, the whole is animated by sublimated ethnographic associations, for, as one commentator remarks, 'sacrifice' in Madagascar 'has as its overt purpose the seeking of ancestral blessing'.[9] In its reworking of tribal practices and the Shakespearian plot, *Makibefo* here hints at a parodic deployment of tradition: the bloody protagonist is figured as impersonating the authority of the previous royal incumbent. It is not until the end of the film, however, that the veil imperfectly concealing the ethnographer is properly lifted. An on-screen announcement informs us that the 'ox . . . was sacrificed in our honour according to the customs of the Antandroy people and was distributed to the families involved in the making of *Makibefo*'. The *apologia* is provided for the benefit of Western audiences at the same time as an authorial voice enters the narrative in order to stress an experience defined by mutual respect. The statement raises the prospect of a 'making of' documentary but fails to provide it: the transnational exchanges that helped to shape the film are recognized but not elaborated upon, and a mixed sense of unmanageable distance, shared endeavours and different agendas is momentarily suggested.

Ethnography depends upon dialogue and, at the level of the individual narratives of *Makibefo* and *Souli*, one effect of a variety of off-screen

---

7 Sarah Brouillette, *Postcolonial Writers in the Global Literary Marketplace* (Basingstoke, 2007), p. 16.

8 John Mack, *Madagascar: Island of the Ancestors* (London, 1986), p. 62.

9 Mack, *Madagascar*, p. 66.

conversations is the generation of felicitous Shake-spearian parallels and translations. The substitution of the windswept Faux Cap dunes for the barren heath of Scotland is obvious, as is the way in which the coming of a flotilla of pirogues stands in for the movement of 'Great Birnam Wood to high Dunsinane Hill'.[10] Given the general stripping of language from the films, a related series of alter-ations and expansions is introduced to explain and encapsulate. The familial claim of Bakoua/Banquo to the throne is not predicted; rather, the char-acter is represented as an expert wrestler whose local reputation precipitates Makibefo's motivation to murder. In other translations lurk the ghosts of the Shakespearian word. For example, shortly before Danikany/Duncan (Jean-Felix) arrives in a progress at Makibefo's hut to be royally enter-tained, we are granted a shot of the protagonist sitting on the beach next to a boat looking out to sea. The composition suggests both Makibefo's passage by water to a type of Hades (he is, of course, shortly to dispatch his guest) and a version of the infamous, ocean-inspired deliberation, 'But here upon this bank and shoal of time, / We'd jump the life to come' (1.7.6–7). *Souli* is no less eco-nomic in the means whereby it references the word of the 'original'. In this connection, the role of Yann/Iago (Aurélien Recoing), the unsympathetic French trader who dominates the coastal commu-nity, is relevant. Commanding his black girlfriend, Abi/Emilia (Fatou d'Diaye), to bestow herself in the back of the landrover when he drives, Yann is discovered as subscribing to a particularly violent brand of ghettoization, one that both inverts the 'black ram . . . tupping your white ewe' construc-tion of *Othello* and brings to mind the continuing manifestations of colonial policy.[11] More gener-ally in *Souli*, the elaboration of a Yann who feels overlooked accords with the play's realization of an 'ensign' (1.1.32) unsuccessful in his bid to become 'lieutenant' (1.1.9). Hence, the film details the ways in which the protagonist's companion is neglected as a possible disciple who may inherit the story of Thiossane. Matching Iago's social dissatisfaction is, of course, Othello's cultural unease: *Souli*'s trans-lation of the 'Moor' (1.1.128) as 'extravagant and

wheeling stranger' (1.1.138) makes itself felt in the filmic idea of a writer who, as the director states, is 'not at home . . . he's called the Senegalese . . . [he's] an African immigrant. In African films we tend to see the white man as immigrant. It's very rarely the Africans who get displaced.' Abela here gestures through the film to a larger transnational theme, finding in the peregrinations of modernity a con-ceptual equivalent for the dramatic character's sense of isolation and alienation.

Hastings Donnan and Thomas M. Wilson remark that 'border crossings . . . can be both enabling and disabling . . . [they] implicate the twin narratives of inclusion and incorporation on the one hand, and of exclusion and dispossession on the other'; as a result, the commentators con-tinue, 'people who cross international borders must . . . re-evaluate many of their own notions of culture and identity'.[12] Certainly, such a sce-nario is glimpsed in the conjuration in *Souli* of a writer-protagonist who, in the wake of mov-ing in and between nation states, is constructed as inhabiting a condition of psychic divisiveness. At once, it is implied that the character's literary reputation and village status are mutually reinforc-ing. The most palatial residence – complete with well-positioned desk – is occupied by Souli, and it is he who leads the community's fishermen. Simultaneously, however, the film makes clear that Souli is as much disempowered as he is empow-ered by his relocating experiences: Souli fishes for Yann and is in his employ. Caught between communities and professions, and cast adrift inside polarized positions of inferiority and superior-ity, Souli is envisioned as an exile paradoxically robbed of a sustaining and meaningful relation to his world. At first sight, *Makibefo* would appear to trade in no such clear conceptions of a split

[10] Quotations from *Macbeth* are taken from William Shake-speare, *The Complete Works*, ed. Stanley Wells, Gary Tay-lor, John Jowett and William Montgomery (Oxford, 1986), 4.1.109.

[11] Quotations from *Othello* are taken from Shakespeare, *Com-plete Works*, 1.1.88–9.

[12] Donnan and Wilson, *Borders*, pp. 107, 108.

or disunited self. A seeming manifestation of the 'milk of human kindness' (1.5.16) feared by his wife, Makibefo is initially drawn as exemplifying compassion, tending the wounds of his captives, resisting his wife's blandishments and, because the speech is excised, rather than reflecting unfeelingly that 'She should have died hereafter' (5.5.16), actively grieving her passing. His probity distinguishes him from the ruthless Malikomy/Malcolm (Bien Rasoanan Tenaina) who is seen dispatching the traitor, Kidoure/Cawdor (Boniface), in a fit of anger. The episode, in its compromising of other claimants, seems to legitimate Makibefo's own bid for power. However, a parallel tendency throughout points up Makibefo's potential for moral deterioration (illustration 21). He sports a talisman comprising a crocodile's tooth in a cloth surround, a superstitious adornment which associates him both with the diabolic and with the 'insignia worn by high-ranking Merina', the dynastic class of rulers who dominated Madagascan society in the eighteenth and nineteenth centuries.[13] Otherwise identified as an 'ordinary man', in the director's words, and merely as a 'good and true' common soldier, according to the voice-over, this individualized Makibefo is seen as revealing in the cultivations of his appearance his predilection for aristocratic dominion. As a preface to its representation of larger transnational developments, *Makibefo* draws the central player as transgressing the systems of categorization designed to keep his loyalty – and subordination – intact.

The representation of Valy Makibefo's (Noeliny Dety) more obvious agitation for greatness carries in its wake the cultural specificities of the histories of Madagascar and the place of women in the transnational economy. Electing to live outside the village, Valy Makibefo, it is implied, entertains an alternative perspective on the world to that of the other villagers. Her alacrity in painting the local symbol of royalty on her husband's forehead, and the emblematic devices displayed on her toga-like shawl, announce her will to betterment. Printed with images of a coliseum, crowns and the *fleur-de-lis*, the *lamba* advertises both enduring

21 Makibefo/Macbeth (Martin Zia) ponders the implications of his actions.

monarchical ciphers and the attractions of empire, systems of rule that are simultaneously temporally anterior (classical civilization) and nationally distant (the *fleur-de-lis* is traditionally associated with the French royal family). Identified through migrant signs from other topographies, Valy Makibefo is consistently discovered as displaying a need to be something other than what she is: here, it is notable that she wears no traditional jewellery around her neck as if in rejection of an indigenous affiliation. Her suicide by drowning accords with the Malagasy belief that, as Aidan Southall states, 'submergence [underwater] signifies failure or expulsion', yet it is also thematically resonant in view of the character's disconnection from community and

---

[13] Mack, *Madagascar*, p. 52.

suggested projection of self onto cultures not her own.[14]

The filmic attention dedicated to Valy Makibefo accords with the ways in which women in *Makibefo* are granted more prominent roles. Typical, for instance, is the invention of Valy Kidoure (Dety) and Valy Danikany (Todia), wives respectively for the Cawdor and Duncan equivalents. Yet, despite inclusion, and notwithstanding Valy Kidoure's public lamentation for her husband's murder, such women make little difference to broader narrative outcomes or dispensations of authority. In Valy Makibefo's social stasis, and in scenes that show her, in common with other women in the film, waiting or immobile, Aihwa Ong's comments that 'across transnational space . . . the reproduction of gendered inequalities' is consistent are powerfully registered.[15] A scene from *Souli* encapsulates a comparable logic. Abi/Emilia enters the women's co-operative that manufactures toy animals for tourist export only to find that she is mocked and castigated as a 'city girl' who will not 'dirty her hands'. Here, an idea of honest and productive women's 'work' is set alongside the suggestion that Abi's 'work' with Yann is degrading and dishonest. Also a type of Bianca, with her European style of dress and carefully managed braids, Abi functions as a potent signifier of prospective mobility: hers is a 'black . . . gendered . . body' primarily imagined, to adopt a formulation of Katherine McKittrick, as 'an indicator of spatial options and the ways in which geography can indicate racialized habitation patterns'.[16] For Abi, however, the film insists, the choices are restricted once she has been sexually distinguished, with *Souli* spotlighting the exclusion of the character from male trajectories of movement and underlining the limited spaces within which she operates. Border crossings may permeate the fabric of the narrative, but they do so in socially ostracizing ways and in relation to larger shifts in the distribution of power and privilege.

II

The distinctive conjuration of an absorption in other cultural environments is epitomized in the ways in which both films allow their audiences to glimpse what lies outside the local worlds upon which they are so seemingly centred. With *Makibefo*, the suggestion of a different viewpoint is summoned via the figure of the narrator who delivers speeches from *Macbeth* on the beach. In *Souli* (in the latest cut), an impression of an additional interpretation is introduced through the periodic appearances of the fluteplayer who provides a melodic accompaniment to the action from a busy port location. Each framing commentator looks to camera, suggesting an overseeing omnipotence, and each enjoys a choric, authoritative importance. In contemporary approximations of the Shakespearian language, *Makibefo*'s narrator summarizes and explains, substituting for the actors and becoming, in the process, a participant. Thus, at the point where the 'Tomorrow, and tomorrow, and tomorrow' soliloquy is sounded, the narrator's face is blank: his own voice overlays his impassive countenance, suggesting emotional identification and subjective involvement. The fluteplayer in *Souli* is less obviously implicated in the narrative, but here, too, revealing connections are made, as when the film pauses at those moments concerned with the story of Thiossane – Carlos rhapsodizes about 'a coming of age story . . . it's never been written down' – only to cut to the musician plying his lonely trade on a windswept jetty. The fluteplayer, too, tells a story, and the effect is to reinforce the filmic preoccupation with questions about discipleship and inheritance.

Whatever power inheres in these alternative tellers of *Souli* and *Makibefo*, however, is ultimately compromised. The metal grille against which the fluteplayer leans points up a construction of imprisonment, and, while narrator and fluteplayer

---

[14] Aidan Southall, 'Common Themes in Malagasy Culture', *Madagascar: Society and History*, ed. Conrad Phillip Kottack, Jean-Aimé Rakotoarisoa, Aidan Southall and Pierre Vérin (Durham, 1986), p. 415.

[15] Ong, *Flexible*, p. 11.

[16] Katherine McKittrick, *Demonic Grounds: Black Women and the Cartographies of Struggle* (Minneapolis and London, 2006), p. 7.

may shape and determine audience response, they labour, it is suggested, beneath the burdens of lent representational credentials. Held together with tape that mimics the colours of the French flag, the *peule* flute in *Souli* stands as a metaphor for a damaged African musical tradition beholden to other national priorities. A parallel idea is pursued in *Makibefo*. Because the narrator speaks a language (English) different from that of the Malagasy filmic drama, the implication is that he inhabits an exilic condition. Attired in an orange manual worker outfit, the fluteplayer similarly brings to mind the typical *émigré* and his menial employment. Extra filmic contexts are supportive here. Ali Wagué, who takes the part of the fluteplayer, hails from the Republic of Guinea, formerly French Guinea; Gilbert Laumord, a dancer and actor who plays the narrator's role, was born in Guadeloupe, an overseas department of France and an island scarred with struggles for black independence. The film's account of displacement and dispossession in *Souli* is also, it might be argued, the fictional musician's autobiographical trajectory, while *Makibefo*'s tale of tyranny, deepened via the narrator's delivery, awakens memories of the agitations of European colonial practice. Touched with the energy of their real-life histories, narrator and fluteplayer appear as destabilized types who, in the same moment as they circulate their stories, are locked in cycles of narrative compulsion and repetition. On the one hand, the suggestion is that these Shakespearian tellers have left their homelands behind; on the other, it is implied that such a movement has resulted only in the endless rehearsal of the pasts which they unwittingly incarnate.

Such histories are glimpsed again in *Souli* and *Makibefo* in the ways in which both films imagine quasi-colonial processes, and accompanying transnational developments, as part of their narrative content. Part of the effect of *Souli*, in particular, hinges upon the representation of a variety of protocapitalist themes. A common denominator is the predilection for profit, as when, for example, Buba (Ravelo), who stands in as local commentator and clown, tricks Carlos into buying some warm beer: at once a replay of the gulling of Cassio by

Iago and the 'Put money in thy purse' (1.3.339) refrain, the episode illuminates, too, the villager's projected insertion of himself into a Western economic modality. In the reverberations set up by the incident, the film goes on to chart the extent to which all of its players are in some senses exploitatively enmeshed. Hence, Abi is discovered as seeing both Yann and Carlos as passports to an alternative existence, and, while Carlos is adamant that he seeks the story of Thiossane purely for academic reasons ('It's for my thesis', he states), a parallel suggestion is that its acquisition would indissolubly involve him in wider networks of consumption. 'Our friend is eager to sign the preface of a best-selling tale', observes Souli, a judgement that underscores some of the means whereby narrative operates as another form of commodity. Tales connote trade, the argument runs, and are inextricably entangled in related functions of a global market mentality. What is played out in miniature is mirrored in the film's more obviously enunciated contests and conflicts. So it is that Yann is imagined as having lost Mona/Desdemona (Jeanne Antebi) to Souli and, hence, as having been sexually supplanted. The suggestion works, first, as a reanimation of the 'it is thought abroad that 'twixt my sheets / [Othello] has done my office' (1.3.379–80) imputation and, secondly, as an explanation for the compensatory energy with which Yann throws himself into his unscrupulous lobster export business. 'I won't give up my place so easily . . . not a second time', reveals a Yann who chafes at the prospect of other economic competitors. Mona's introduction of an ice-making machine to her fair trade collective spells an end to the trader's monopoly and, in the interplay of characters that the film details, the figures of Yann and Mona are consistently pitched against each other as overarching signifiers of a drive to deploy natural resources and perceived opportunity.

The protocapitalist and transnational meanings of these forms of enterprise are borne out by the film's emphasis upon motifs of transport and concepts of place. *Souli* abounds in scenes that concern movement between one location and another, whether enabled either by Yann's landrover or

Mona's ox-cart. Ironically, of course, the ox-cart proves more dramatic in terms of an effect on the local economy, but the more pressing point is that both means of conveyance analogize larger displacements and transactions between communities, cultures and even nations. In a discussion of the despatialization of global relations, Ulrich Beck argues that 'social communities, and political action based upon them, can no longer be understood from the point of view of a single location'.[17] *Souli* refracts this reading in hinting at the filaments that bind situation and mobility. The port where the fluteplayer pursues his musical story, for example, is Dunkirk, a maritime conurbation that, even as it substitutes for Shakespeare's Venice, connotes *par excellence* a history of global conflict, the excesses of industrial production and a place of embarkation and transit for human cargo. 'Shakespeare' is not too far removed here, with the associations of the port bringing to mind the film's suggestion that small-scale operations (such as ice manufacture) can precipitate the evolution of larger-scale corporations, inequitable distributions of wealth and political privilege/protest. Such a sense of transformation is implied in the cinematography's concentration on Dunkirk's foundries, complexes, of course, primarily organized around making, moulding and fusing processes. Quasi-colonial endeavours (even ethical and salutary ones) are tied in *Souli* to their post-industrial incarnations and consequences. Neither Yann nor Mona, the film maintains, are satisfactory symbolic ciphers: both are at odds, both leave desecration in their wake. At base, *Souli* suggests, there is little difference between a women's co-operative that makes toy giraffes (instructions on the hut wall betray that this is an imposed, rather than an indigenous, cultural practice) and the ways in which Yann arranges showings of generator-powered action movies to entertain his workers. Each species of activity is ensnared in the capitalist logic that spells dispossession and despoliation; each interchange is premised upon a system that divides and organizes in the ultimate interests of the dominant majority. The 'characters are mythical', states the director, 'of the ways in which the West

and Africa interact with each other' and, as *Souli* demonstrates, such interactions are apprehended both in the representation of outward locations and in the glimpses into an isolated society's internal operations.

Souli rehearses its transnational preoccupations as part of an explicit narrative engagement; by contrast, *Makibefo* approaches transnationalism by way of a more suggestive and muted representational procedure. This is seen nowhere more obviously than in the film's realization of episodes of flight and return. With Kidoure/Cawdor, for instance, the attempted usurpation of Danikany/Duncan is granted far less attention than the condition the rebel inhabits as a fugitive. The society of *Makibefo* is portrayed primarily as one anxious about its borders, concerned with its own self-sufficiency and threatened by the possibilities of depopulation and development. It is entirely in keeping with this perspective, therefore, that Danikany is filmed always seated and that Kidoure is branded a 'traitor' because he defects. Maureen Covell's description of traditional Malagasy systems of rule emphasizes '*fokonolona* [or] . . . self-policing and self-defence': this resembles what Anthony Giddens describes as a version of 'the kinship system . . . organized in terms of *place*, where place has not yet become transformed by distanciated time–place relations'.[18] Yet that effort to insist upon and institute the laws and practices of the local community might also be seen as a globally aware response to wider change. Ulf Hannerz notes that 'countries may pursue policies of cutting themselves off . . . a kind of active anti-globalization which is in a dialectical relationship with globalization itself', while Stephen Castles identifies 'reactive moments' in the global economy that 'try to rescue myths of autonomous national communities and unitary identity'.[19] By

[17] Ulrich Beck, *The Brave New World of Work* (Oxford, 2000), p. 155.

[18] Maureen Covell, *Madagascar: Politics, Economics and Society* (London and New York, 1987), p. 15; Anthony Giddens, *The Consequences of Modernity* (Oxford, 1990), p. 101.

[19] Ulf Hannerz, *Transnational Connections: Culture, People, Places* (London and New York, 1996), p. 18; Stephen Castles,

extension, it might be argued, *Makibefo*'s ultimate concern is with forms of organization that cannot offer a sustaining programme. With contacts and relations fractured and distributed, the society upon which the narrative centres is imagined as afflicted by a disjunction between territory, subjectivity and social intercourse: no longer do these constituents of community productively coalesce. In Makibefo and Valy Makibefo's assumption of Danikany and Valy Danikany's royal places these suggestions find a particularly succinct statement: the newly crowned couple are pictured presiding over a village that has lost its inhabitants. The image of an abandoned ox-cart implies a hurried removal, while an accompanying shot of empty houses points up a sense of desolation and deprivation. By the close of the action, it is suggested, the fugitive experience has become a collective theme: Makidofy/Macduff (Jean-Noël) leaves the landmass altogether; Makibefo evolves from a fugitive-catcher to a fugitive-maker and a politics of terror holds sway over a shrunken and dwindling populace. 'Ours', Dennis Kennedy writes, 'has been the century of global disruption, the century of the refugee', and what *Makibefo* moves towards underscoring in its final stages is just such a scenario, a state of affairs in which the individual is, in Anthony M. Messina and Gallya Lahav's words, obliged to leave 'his or her country due to fear of persecution'.[20] If Madagascar, in the director's conceiving of his subject, can also conjure Africa, then the representation of the society of *Makibefo* might be seen as suggesting some of the demographic crises of non-Western regions and the transnational particularities of enforced unsettlement.

On the one hand, both *Makibefo* and *Souli* would appear to respond to the realities of global movements by subscribing in their respective conclusions to the *mores* and belief systems of traditional communities. A typical instance is the way in which Makibefo, after some initial resistance, is pictured bowing before Malikomy/Malcolm as a prequel to his sacrificial death. The episode highlights a filmic rendition of the cult of *fomban-drazana* or ancestral practice; as John Mack explains, 'the foundation of Malagasy ideas is the notion that everyone

by virtue of the date and time of their birth inherits a particular destiny (*vintana*)'.[21] In submitting to his own death, Makibefo, it is suggested, finds that a pre-ordained system has run its natural and institutionalized course. Cast in a similar mould is the scene in which Souli, after he has murdered Mona in a fit of jealous rage (the key property that triggers the *dénouement* is not the handkerchief but a bracelet that ends up on Carlos's arm), is knifed to death by Yann in a bloody embrace (illustration 22). The episode links directly to the film's opening and to a sequence intended for the re-release of the film: in the director's words, 'Souli slowly walks towards the camera through a "mystical" passage of tall cactuses. As he advances we hear his voice-over. We understand he's doing the dance of the passage – the transition from earth to heaven.' This constitutes, then, a self-consciously anticipatory moment in which Souli is primarily identified through nation and culture-specific discourses and conventions. To adopt a formulation of Seán McLoughlin, there is, in this separation of the *ambiroa* (soul) from the body, a 'nostalgic emphasis on the particular "chains of memory" . . . associated with "tradition" and "community"' as a means of restoring 'certainty in the face of cultural "translation"'.[22] On the other hand, the films' endings are shot through with traces of the very non-traditional developments that they have paradoxically both resisted and entertained. The return of Malikomy in *Makibefo*, for example, might be seen as a pertinent illustration

---

'Migration', *A Companion to Racial and Ethnic Studies*, ed. David Theo Goldberg and John Solomos (Oxford, 2002), p. 577.

[20] Dennis Kennedy, 'Afterword: Shakespearian Orientalism', *Foreign Shakespeare*, ed. Dennis Kennedy (Cambridge, 1993), p. 294; Anthony M. Messina and Gallya Lahav, 'Concepts and Trends', *The Migration Reader: Exploring Politics and Policies*, ed. Anthony M. Messina and Gallya Lahav (London and Boulder, 2006), p. 10.

[21] Mack, *Madagascar*, p. 39.

[22] Seán McLoughlin, 'Migration, Diaspora and Transnationalism: Transformations of Religion and Culture in a Globalizing Age', *The Routledge Companion to the Study of Religion*, ed. John R. Hinnels (London and New York, 2005), p. 534.

22 Yann/Iago (Aurelien Recoing) and Souli/Othello (Makena Diop) contemplate each other.

of what Roger Rouse has termed 'transnational migrant circuits' – the movement of individuals or communities away from and back to their place of origin.[23] What Makibefo destroys, the film maintains, can be renewed, but only in the context of cultural cross-pollination and the importation of energy from elsewhere. Souli, too, is not unilaterally imagined: the peace that he asks for in a voice-over at the start is in shocking contrast to the violence of his demise, while the slow prelude to the death itself hints, as in *Makibefo*, at a knowing personal decision and a suicidal will. Yet this is not necessarily to argue that the films' engagement with conflicts precipitated by an experience of other environments is wholly disabling. Here, the envisioned 'passage' episode in *Souli* is once again central, since it simultaneously demonstrates that, according to the director, the 'ancestors are welcoming' the protagonist: before he joins them, however, he 'must tell his story'. In a discussion of 'incommensurable differences', Homi Bhabha writes that 'interstitial' and 'disjunctive' spaces are 'crucial for the emergence of new historical subjects of the transnational phase of late capitalism': with this statement in mind, *Souli*, it might be suggested, aspires to establish the eman-

cipatory personal and representational possibilities that the encounter with borders facilitates, even if at this precise moment that aspiration is not fully realized.[24] Despite his lived cultural confusions, Souli in death, it is implied, enters a communicative third space which, because immortalized, may have the potential to involve other audiences beyond a strictly limited national and cultural purchase.

III

No doubt linked to the will to move from the local to something broader is the way in which Abela conceives of his work as possessing a universal relevance. In interview he agitates for a filmic modality that 'can be understood anywhere', while, in press releases for *Makibefo*, the 'universal reach

[23] Roger Rouse, 'Making Sense of Settlement: Class Transformation, Cultural Struggle, and Transnationalism among Mexican Migrants in the United States', *Towards a Transnational Perspective on Migration: Race, Class, Ethnicity and Nationalism Reconsidered*, ed. Nina Glick Schiller, Linda Basch and Cristina Blanc-Szanton (New York, 1992), p. 45.

[24] Homi K. Bhabha, *The Location of Culture* (London and New York, 1994), pp. 217, 218.

of . . . *Macbeth*' is highlighted as a prime Shake-spearian characteristic.[25] A similar take on *Macbeth* is offered in the narrator's opening presentation of 'a land washed by the waves' where 'a tribe of people lived in sight of sands'. The lack of geo-graphical reference, coupled with the evocation of eternal values, work to guide the Bard towards a realm defined by generality, trans-historicity and semi-mythical familiarity. Yet, as Dennis Kennedy argues, 'universality . . . derives not from . . . transcendence but from . . . malleability', and such is the way in which Shakespeare is shaped and adapted in *Makibefo* and *Souli* that the local and the indigenous, ghost-like, keep coming back.[26] When a French vocable occasionally strays into the Malagasy flow of *Makibefo*, or when the hired murderer is seen puffing at a temporally incongru-ous cigar, for instance, an eruption of the particular becomes strikingly apparent. The particular is specifically identified in one of the concluding on-screen announcements to *Makibefo*, which runs: 'The Antandroy people of Madagascar who played the characters and helped in the making of this film are an ancient tribe with a truly great sense of pride, honour and tradition. A poor people in what is already a poor country, they have few possessions and little knowledge of the outside world . . . The majority of the actors have never seen a television, let alone a film, and have never acted before in their lives.' The statement demonstrates a discrete trajectory of exclusion and ostracization. Behind the overarching longings of the filmic endeavour lies a fractured and still evolving narrative of deter-ritorialization and disequilibrium: the universal in *Makibefo* and *Souli* is inevitably confronted by the particular, and in such a way as to illuminate the continuing resonances of the nation-state's pursuit of independence.

Madagascar in the late twentieth and early twenty-first centuries, as one historian remarks, can be characterized as a 'disarticulated economy' with 'a non-articulated communications system.'[27] In part this is a by-product of an earlier history of con-version and conquest: in the seventeenth and eight-eenth centuries, French slave traders attempted settlement; over the course of the nineteenth cen-tury, Christian missionaries arrived; and in 1896, the Malagasy National Movement, the Menalamba, was founded and the state finally ceded place to institutionalized French control and dominion.[28] An armed rebellion of 1947 in which over 100,000 died had as its stated aim the achievement of an independent state, while the violent response that came in its wake engendered a traumatic legacy.[29] Full independence was only granted in 1960, but that event in turn was the prelude to a series of internecine contests and widespread social unrest.[30] In the contours of the Madagascar of modernity are these and other conflicts adumbrated: the nation is host to two main linguistic systems; it exhibits a belief system split between Christian and 'tradi-tional' paradigms; and it consistently makes visible social and geographical economic polarities.

Previous sections of this article have suggested some of the passing ways in which the histo-ries of Madagascar are encoded in *Makibefo* and *Souli*; a more general sense of the films' preoc-cupation with the country's past is evidenced in a repeated emphasis upon the previous existences of individuals or artifacts. Not only is *Makibefo*, for example, framed by images of totems that, as John Mack states, declare 'the wealth and status of the dead'; the film is at the same time phrased in the anterior tense and concerned with what is via a contemplation of what was.[31] *Souli*, too, centres upon how the present is played upon by the past, not least in the representation of the search for a story that, although 'ancient', is res-olutely of the moment. Such an attention is made

[25] '*Makibefo*', press booklet, p. 4.
[26] Kennedy, 'Afterword', p. 301.
[27] Covell, *Madagascar*, p. 9.
[28] Covell, *Madagascar*, pp. 14, 16; Bill Freund, *The Making of Contemporary Africa: The Development of African Society since 1800*, 2nd edn (Basingstoke, 1998), p. 62.
[29] Frederick Cooper, *Africa since 1940: The Past of the Present* (Cambridge, 2002), p. 64; Covell, *Madagascar*, pp. 17, 28; Freund, *Making*, p. 179.
[30] Robert Cabanes, 'Madagascar and Mozambique: The Global–Local Dialectic', *Science, Technology and Society*, 8 (2003), 345–61, p. 346.
[31] Mack, *Madagascar*, p. 84.

all the more obvious in the light of the films' corresponding concern with the future. Whatever is anticipated, however, is tinged with a muted sense of reservation. Typical is Buba's prediction in *Souli* that Abi will enjoy 'a good life, but [that she will also] pay the price'. Characteristic, too, is *Makibefo*'s incarnation of Malikomy who at the close is flanked by warriors and a small fleet of ocean-confident boats, pointing up both the Malagasy idea that 'emergence [from water] signifies success' and the contemporary notion that 'new communities . . . are likely to be increasingly transnational in scope and power'.[32] That this is simultaneously a state of play that evokes Madagascar's past is made clear in the paired images of an erect, mobile and technologically superior Malikomy and a crouched, reduced and still Makibefo who, metaphorically trapped by nets and a beach-bound boat, seems to have reverted to a species of 'primitivism'.

The second major way in which Madagascan history seeps into the films is at the level of language. Typical of art-house films targeted at international audiences, *Makibefo* and *Souli* subtitle the dialogue. *Souli* is particularly dense in this respect, stacking on top of each other both French translations of Malagasy and English translations of French in a visible rendering of the film's linguistically hybridized setting and subject. Such a procedure, it might be suggested, bears out Homi K. Bhabha's claim that 'in the act of translation the content . . . is . . . overwhelmed and alienated by the form of signification'; one might also argue, as does Naoki Sakai, that, in view of the supplanting of one set of linguistic systems for another, the films' subtitles constitute a 'political manoeuvre' that is 'always complicit with the building [and] transforming . . . of power relations'.[33] Certainly, the hypothesis might be reinforced by the director's admission, in interview, that, in *Makibefo*, the 'subtitles are not the exact words they say in Malagasy . . . It's closer to what I was asking them to say. It's in between.' To hold this against the film would, I think, be a mistake, for, as Dirk Delabastita in a study of the ethics of translation also asserts, 'the scholar has to direct his/her attention to the

conditions and constraints in the receptor culture that create the terms in which this reconstitution of the foreign text takes place'.[34] As the director explains, '[we wanted] to do a talking film in a foreign language without subtitles. It was to be a film where dialogue would become noise, not to transport emotion or explain an action.' Of course, the film in its current manifestation is not cast in this mould, yet a trace of the utopian project remains in the ways in which *Makibefo* resists subtitling the opening and closing score, the chant at the meal to welcome Danikany and the song that accompanies the wrestling competition. In presumed resistance to the distancing effect of translation, and via a move that plays down the discriminations that subtitles potentially generate, Abela elects here to dispense with the recasting of language altogether, favouring a filmic method that speaks for itself. If the subtitle, in Amresh Sinha's words, is a 'superimposition' that 'tears' the audience away from the 'visual and acoustic matrix', in *Makibefo*, at least, it is disallowed from exercising a totalizing control.[35]

Inconsistency in subtitling creates interest in those voices which are not affected. 'Who speaks? Where do they speak from? And for whom?' asks Robert Carr in a discussion of transnational feminisms, and his questions are particularly germane to films which, because made in Madagascar, implicitly concern themselves with linguistic hierarchies.[36] The preoccupation is held in play in the

---

32 Southall, 'Common Themes', p. 415; Paul Kennedy and Victor Roudometof, 'Transnationalism in a Global Age', *Communities across Borders: New Immigrants and Transnational Cultures*, ed. Paul Kennedy and Victor Roudometof (London and New York, 2002), p. 7.

33 Bhabha, *Location*, p. 227; Naoki Sakai, 'Translation', *Theory, Culture and Society*, 23 (2006), 71–86, p. 72.

34 Dirk Delabastita, 'More Alternative Shakespeares', *Four Hundred Years of Shakespeare in Europe*, ed. A. Luis Pujante and Ton Hoenselaars (Newark and London, 2003), p. 117.

35 Amresh Sinha, 'The Use and Abuse of Subtitles', *Subtitles: On the Foreignness of Film*, ed. Atom Egoyan and Ian Balfour (Cambridge, MA and London, 2004), p. 173.

36 Robert Carr, 'Crossing the First World/Third World Divides: Testimonial, Transnational Feminisms, and the Postmodern Condition', *Scattered Hegemonies: Postmodernity and*

questions surrounding the narrator's voice in *Makibefo* and is extended into a constituent narrative component in *Souli*: Carlos, for instance, regrets that his hero chooses not to be 'edited anymore' in a statement that makes unwittingly visible the white frames of reference that determine the reception of post-colonial utterances. Via Souli, who notes that he 'only writes for myself now: it's a way of protecting myself', the film points up the process whereby the non-Anglophonic voice is both commodified – what Rustom Bharucha has labelled elsewhere a form of 'cultural tourism' – and manipulated and misused.[37] Powerfully implied is the bruising of Souli at the hands of the Western literary establishment, and it is perhaps not accidental that several scenes show Mona anointing or massaging her lover: his body, it seems, is in pain. 'If we are to understand the social figure of a globalization of personal life', writes Ulrich Beck, 'we must focus on the oppositions involved in stretching between different places'.[38] An insistent element of Souli's fame is a sense of linguistic splitting or stretching: the world, we are led to understand, has welcomed him, but in such a way as to damage and ultimately oppose continuing modes of public articulation.

Such global forms of reception and distribution may also lie behind the fortunes of the films themselves. In a filmic world dominated by Hollywoodized versions of Shakespeare, *Makibefo* and *Souli* slipped off the compass of mainstream attention, falling into the category of productions that, as Ramona Wray notes, because 'global conversation inhibits the knowledge transfer', run the risk of remaining relatively anonymous.[39] The 'strong regulatory framework with a well-established support system' that French cinema enjoys meant that both films enjoyed theatrical runs in France and festival exposure, but neither film subsequently went on to that vital world-wide commercial release.[40] In addition, even within France, and despite the award of the 'Golden Triangle', *Makibefo* intially played only in one theatre for a three-week period. Similarly, although *Souli* toured festivals, distribution was problematic.[41] 'The production company went bankrupt', comments the director, '*Souli* got stuck . . . I ended up getting the film back, having

the opportunity to re-edit.' At the time of writing, however, even that re-edited version is bedevilled, caught, as it is, between the competing demands of local theatres, broadcasters and television networks. *Makibefo* and *Souli* highlight, in fact, in their trajectories of (in)visibility the demise of the independents, the vagaries of corporate decision-making, the global face of cinema's afterlife and the inherent unpredictabilities of the Shakespearian filmmaking initiative.

'From the point of view of . . . modern societies,' writes Zygmunt Bauman, 'all . . . "exchange" is unequal and must remain unequal.'[42] It is perhaps too great an argumentative leap to suggest that Abela also re-enacts in his exchanges with Madagascar the postcolonial and global themes that are his subject; nevertheless, in part because of the films' ethnographic subtexts, questions about his role may legitimately be pursued. Part of 'the Antandroys' . . . initial motivation [in *Makibefo*]', notes the director, 'was the prospect of earning some money', an admission that prompts

Transnational Feminist Practices, ed. Inderpal Grewal and Caren Kaplan (Minneapolis and London, 1994), p. 156.

37 Rustom Bharucha, *The Politics of Cultural Practice: Thinking Through Theatre in an Age of Globalization* (London, 2000), p. 53.

38 Ulrich Beck, *What is Globalization?* (Cambridge, 2000), p. 75.

39 Ramona Wray, 'Shakespeare on Film in the New Millennium', *Shakespeare*, 3.2 (2007), 270–82, p. 279.

40 Laurent Creton and Anne Jäckel, 'A Certain Idea of the Film Industry', *The French Cinema Book*, ed. Michael Temple and Michael Wit (London, 2004), p. 209. *Makibefo* has been shown at the following festivals: Festival d'Amiens (France), Rencontres Internationales de Cinéma à Paris (France), Rencontres Cinéma de Manosque (France), Festival Cinéma de Alès (France), Rencontre du Cinéma Britannique d'Abbeville (France), Regard sur le Cinéma d'Afrique du Sud (France), Festival de la Rochelle (France), Festival de Lama, Corse (Corsica), BFM International Film Festival (Great Britain), Inspired by Shakespeare Season, BFI Southbank (Great Britain), Taormina Film Festival (Italy), Pesaro Film Festival (Italy), Vues d'Afrique, Montréal (Canada) and Pan-African Film Festival (US).

41 *Souli* was shown at the following festivals: 21st International Festival du Film Francophone de Namur (France), Festival de Saint Denis (France) and Montréal World Film Festival: Cinema of Africa (Canada).

42 Zygmunt Bauman, *Postmodern Ethics* (Oxford, 1993), p. 213.

speculation about the implications of the economic transaction and a potential disruption to the systems of the community – the effects of a Shakespearian baptism.[43] Certainly, at one point during the production of *Makibefo*, conflict was in the air: 'the film needed another two weeks of shooting, which I had to cut short', states the director, continuing, 'there was a group who . . . were suspicious . . . jealousy started to come . . . people . . . said "Can we be in the film now?", and we said "Sorry, it's too late, you can't be in the film", and they couldn't understand why . . . I felt we had come to a danger point, and we had to go, it was . . . very sudden.' The details are not elaborated upon, but the implication is clear: a construction of Shakespeare's timeless pertinence provokes a historically specific dispute over meaning, interpretation and authority. From another perspective, however, the ultimate effect of both *Makibefo* and *Souli* is less confrontational, and more inclusive, than this reading suggests. 'The transnational', write Françoise Lionnet and Shu-mei Shih, 'can be conceived as a space of exchange and participation', and it is just such a working model of creative collaboration that is summoned in the film's final on-screen announcement.[44] 'We would like to thank the Antandroy people for their co-operation, their enthusiasm and their hospitality', the statement runs, 'Without them *Makibefo* would never have lived.' Although it is Abela's mediating voice which dominates, there is nevertheless an implicit approval of a type of cultural polysemy, with the encounter between the filmmaker and the Antandroy people appearing to operate in a back-and-forth fashion that bespeaks a shared acknowledgement. As the director states, commenting upon his method, 'we devised a script together, and *Macbeth* soon became *Makibefo*, a work of two cultures united by Shakespeare'.[45] And, arguably in a move that bypassed the influence of the global movie machine, Abela took the finished film of *Makibefo* back to Madagascar for a week-long tour which was inaugurated by an on-the-beach 'world première'. The activities suggest a nexus of mutual ties and demonstrate that the reworking of Shakespeare can forge unexpected forms of global connectivity.

At least at first sight, a narrative stress upon comparable networks of collaboration would seem to be missing from *Souli*, if only because the central characters appear unable to agree as to the essential mode through which the story of Thiossane might be communicated. Fiercely protective of his mother's 'lineage', Souli contemplates transcribing his precious burden, but then resists, concluding, 'without an initiation into the oral tradition, how do you decipher the blanks between the words?' By contrast, Carlos is as passionately persuaded that 'Thiossane' exists in written form and searches for it at every opportunity. The difference in viewpoint betrays a larger cultural collision, yet the prospect of interaction is not dismissed; rather, it is conjured in the film's melding of techno-music and the traditional piped score and in seemingly innocuous scenes, as when Buba laughingly aids Carlos in the erection of his tent. Not so much, in Luis Eduardo Guarnizo and Michael Peter Smith's words, a 'subversive' or 'counter-hegemonic' expression of 'transnationalism from below', this episode establishes that efforts at exploitation can be superseded by gestures towards reciprocity.[46] As the film demonstrates, however, Carlos is ultimately excluded from any suggestion of collaborative relations, for the *dénouement* reveals that it is Abi who comes to occupy the disciple role. Dying in Abi's arms, Souli is represented, Harry Lime-like, as nodding to convey the tale. For her part, Abi is discovered as shuddering at the point of what amounts to a psychic transmission of her inheritance. The sequence is instrumental in finally taking Carlos out of the picture, and it is striking that, while he is again rummaging for a script, the story is being communicated just beyond him on the beach. But the privileging of Abi is not without its

---

[43] '*Makibefo*', press booklet, p. 5.

[44] Françoise Lionnet and Shu-mei Shih, 'Introduction', *Minor Transnationalism*, ed. Françoise Lionnet and Shu-mei Shih (Durham and London, 2005), p. 5.

[45] '*Makibefo*', press booklet, p. 5.

[46] Luis Eduardo Guarnizo and Michael Peter Smith, 'The Locations of Transnationalism', *Transnationalism from Below*, ed. Michael Peter Smith and Luis Eduardo Guarnizo (New Brunswick and London, 1998), p. 5.

difficulties. It is premised upon the suggestion of a reformation in character and it would seem to suggest that only Africa can speak for Africa: only women, the argument runs, might figure as oral guardians. Transmission, finally, must take place within a physical/magical realm, and other cultural and national actors are disallowed from playing a part. If the narrative end leaves questions unanswered, the music that accompanies the closing credits brings them into better resolution. *Souli* re-edited replaces the score earlier written by Deborah Mollison with a new theme composed by Ali Wagué and David Aubaile: a male and female voice join in a traditional African song, and the tale that is told concerns Abi's travel and work abroad. Now, it is asserted, she is on the point of another journey: 'we who have immigrated', the lyrics announce, 'are ready to return to our homeland'. Immediately noticeable is that the conjunction of perspectives underwrites the idea of male–female collaboration; vital, too, is the fact that the song comprises a performance of a narrative. In these additional imaginings, Abi remains peripatetic: her status functions so as to recall and celebrate Souli's soul in passage, to assert a powerful equation between rest and mobility, and to declare the virtues of what Rosi Braidotti terms a 'nomadic subjectivity'.[47] The transnational commerce enunciated here traverses a number of levels: the point of origin defines but does not confine communication, a sense of independent purpose has been arrived at, and a plural construction of possibility is afforded.

IV

Given his multiple associations, it is highly appropriate that the questions introduced by *Makibefo* and *Souli* are conducted around the body of Shakespeare. Both the idea of an ancient tale and the cultivation of ancestry are energized by being enfolded in a figure that, in the popular imagination, is indelibly tied to issues centred upon writing, lineage, symbolism and iconicity. In the late twentieth and early twenty-first centuries, of course, the Bard is also a local/global phenomenon and even (from some perspectives at least) himself a transna-

tional migrant and exilic author. Interestingly, these more recent journeys undertaken by Shakespeare are also refracted in the films. The leather tome (a weathered edition of Shakespeare) from which the narrator reads in *Makibefo*, for instance, served as a chief property in occasional theatrical realizations of the filmic narrative. That is, the same film, stripped of the on-screen narrator, was presented in individual nation-states by an indigenous, 'live' storyteller.[48] Each time a performance took place, the resident storyteller would add to the book his or her 'translation' of the text, creating another Bardic representation and an increasingly polyphonic corpus of material. At once, the procedure recalls the moment, during the shooting of Kenneth Branagh's *Hamlet* (1997), when the director/filmmaker was presented, as Russell Jackson notes, with a 'small red-bound copy of the play that successive actors have passed on to each other with the condition that the recipient should give it in turn to the finest Hamlet of the next generation'.[49] Where *Makibefo* leaves company with this tradition, however, is in its non-Anglophonic emphases: its *Hamlet* is not only a product of multiple transnational readings but also constitutes a still evolving, as opposed to culturally fixed, 'Shakespeare'. The likelihood of other Shakespeares emerging from a process of reorganization might also be inferred from the intertextual resonances with which *Makibefo* appears to play. In his garb, appearance and vernacular departures from his volume, the narrator brings to mind Caliban (Michael Clark) in *Prospero's Books* (dir. Peter Greenaway, 1991): the apparent reference back to this earlier island-bound Shakespeare raises the prospect of further Bardic endeavours that, spanning classes and nations, press

---

[47] Rosi Braidotti, *Transpositions: On Nomadic Ethics* (Oxford, 2006), p. 60.

[48] Such a version of the film was shown with a Caribbean actor as the narrator at the Festival Off in Avignon and with a Czech actor in the role at the International Theatre Festival, Hrade Králové.

[49] Kenneth Branagh, *'Hamlet' by William Shakespeare: Screenplay and Introduction* (London, 1996), p. 211.

at, while expanding upon, existing representational boundaries.

These must, however, be posited as readings that the wider interpretive community brings to the productions themselves. In interview, Abela confesses to a lack of awareness of more obvious counterparts to his own initiative, including *Shakespeare on the Estate* (dir. Penny Woolcock, 1994) and *The Children's Midsummer Night's Dream* (dir. Christine Edzard, 2001), works also distinguished by their efforts to bring Shakespeare to an untried cast. Instead, Abela's achievement is closer in spirit to fieldwork instances of anthropologists rehearsing Shakespeare to the subjects of their studies and closer in execution to quasi-ethnographic cinematic versions of mythic and international stories, such as *It's all True* (dir. Orson Welles, 1942), *Medea* (dir. Pier-Paolo Pasolini, 1969) and *Tabu* (dir. F. W. Murnau and Robert Flaherty, 1931).[50] Thomas Healey reminds us that 'anthropological inquiry into the meaning of cultures . . . has been especially influential on New Historicist thought', and it may well be the case that the resistant tendencies of the director's approach to his materials owe at least some of their inspiration to the critical orientation that Shakespearian commentators have detected in other disciplines.[51] One might also wish to suggest, taking note of Richard Wilson's identification of an 'elective affinity' between 'the France of *liberté*, *égalité* and *fraternité*' and an 'author who looks forward, in so many of his works, to an age of freedom, peace and justice', that Shakespeare, for Abela, proved an enabling provider of critique in the light of one nation's revolutionary appropriation of his writings.[52] Yet the nation-specific parallel is not as easy to sustain when placed alongside the director's reflections on his biographical lineage: on his father's side hailing from the Lebanon and Malta, and on his mother's side hailing from Greece, Italy and Syria, Abela, in his own (joking rather than plaintive) words, 'belong[s] nowhere. I feel English but in England I'm not accepted as an Englishman . . . [the] Lebanese . . . don't really accept me, and in Greece or Italy I don't feel at home.' To bring discussion back to the author or *auteur* is not to reinscribe the values of an earlier phase of film criticism, but it is to suggest that *Makibefo* and *Souli* are animated by a peculiar personal veracity and it is to recognize the increasingly transnational subject that lies behind twentieth- and twenty-first-century acts of representation. At a time when Shakespeare on film studies begins to take stock of where it is, and to reflect upon what constitutes a Shakespeare film *per se*, it is perhaps salutary to remember the producers as well as the products, the creative forces as well as the final statements.

To return to the subject is also to begin the process of acknowledging our own critical responsibilities. Reflecting upon the afterlife of *Makibefo*, the director states: 'The deal was we would . . . come back to Madagascar on a regular basis . . . the second time we came back, we [brought] a lot of nets and hooks . . . we were supposed to bring back eight pirogues . . . [but] haven't done [that] yet. I've brought [only] three . . . the idea was that if ever the film made money . . . a proportion would go back to [the] . . . fishermen.' The failure of the scheme, I suggest, has less to do with the execution of the aim as the contexts of distribution and exhibition within which the film is identified. In a powerful sense, the fates of *Makibefo* and *Souli* rest with us or, at least, with the global circuit that both defines and determines reception. For films such as these to be entered and appreciated requires a shift in the conception and canon of Shakespeare in his film, television, radio and other media manifestations. Urgently needed is a move away from the separate bracketing of the 'foreign Shakespeare' and a reversal of the unidirectional 'cultural flow' that, as Inderpal Grewal and Caren Kaplan state,

---

[50] See Laura Bohannon, 'Shakespeare in the Bush', *Natural History*, 75.8–9 (1966), 29–33; Robert Koehler, '*Makibefo*', *Variety*, 18 February 2003; Lanier, 'Film Spin-offs and Citations', I, p. 213; Annick Peigné-Giuly, 'Shakespeare sur mer', *Libération*, 17 October 2001.

[51] Thomas Healey, *New Latitudes: Theory and English Renaissance Literature* (London, Melbourne and Auckland, 1992), p. 63.

[52] Richard Wilson, *Shakespeare in French Theory: King of Shadows* (London and New York, 2007), p. 21.

invariably travels 'from the "west" to the "rest"'.[53] As Ramona Wray argues, there is surely possible in the discipline of Shakespeare on film 'integration ... a prioritizing of the "inclusive", and ... a critical method that is as particular as it is comprehensive'.[54] But what such a change in sensibility necessitates, in turn, is a reassessment of cinematic exchanges as ethical repositories and a new political bedrock of interpretation which would allow us to continue to challenge the 'channels through which we have access to' Shakespearian production and which would insist upon a re-engagement with plurality.[55] It is here, I think, that a working application of transnationalism may be useful. Contrary to commentators who have argued that the phenomenon is empty conceptually and hegemonic politically, this article has sought to demonstrate that, because it urges us to reconsider, in Nina Glick Schiller, Linda Basch and Cristina Blanc-Szanton's words, 'categories of nationalism, ethnicity and race', and formulations of 'culture, class and society', transnationalism carries an ethical charge.[56] Global and local questions can be debated inside a transnational framework; alternative models for a more productive sense of belonging might be proposed; and a properly reciprocal sense of collaboration may yet arise. Within the exchanges that an 'ethical transnational relationality' facilitates the virtues and valences of a global Shakespearian citizenship are potentially something to celebrate.[57]

---

53 Inderpal Grewal and Caren Kaplan, 'Introduction: Transnational Feminist Practices', *Scattered Hegemonies*, p. 12.
54 Wray, 'Shakespeare on Film in the New Millennium', p. 279.
55 Aijaz Ahmad, *In Theory: Classes, Nations, Literatures* (London and New York, 1992), p. 45.
56 Nina Glick Schiller, Linda Basch and Cristina Blanc-Szanton, 'Transnationalism: A New Analytic Framework for Understanding Migration', *Towards a Transnational Perspective on Migration*, p. 5.
57 Shu-mei Shih, 'Towards an Ethics of Transnational Encounters, or, "When" does a "Chinese" Woman become a "Feminist"?', *Minor Transnationalism*, p. 76. My thanks to Adrian Streete and Adam Hansen for productive and energizing conversations about the films and to Alexander Abela for extending many courtesies to me and for facilitating the writing of this article. *Makibefo* is available on DVD from Scoville Film (www.scovillefilm.com).

STILL LIFE? ANTHROPOCENTRISM AND THE FLY IN *TITUS ANDRONICUS* AND *VOLPONE*

CHARLOTTE SCOTT

They say yet againe; But why should a good God take pleasure in so many néedlesse things? For to what purpose serveth the Fly, and such other things? Tell me, wouldest thou like well that thine owne Children should speake such reproach of thy workes? Nay rather wherein doth the Flye anoye thee? . . . And this serueth to conuict thee of blockishness, thee (I say) which haddest rather to finde fault with God and with the Flye, then to wonder at the excellencie of him who hath inclosed so liuely a life, so quick a moouing, and so great an excellencie in so little a thing . . . Hereby therefore we perceiue, that of all the things which they can alledge, there is none which is not good and behofefull in it self; and that the euilnesse thereof commeth onely through vs, and therefore that the thing hath but onely one Beginner thereof, who is good.[1]

When *Titus Andronicus* appeared in the first folio of Shakespeare's plays in 1623 it included a 'new' scene, not present in the 1597 quarto and possibly not performed in Shakespeare's lifetime. This scene comprises eighty-six lines and runs to approximately five minutes' performance time; its inclusion bears little impact on the textual or performative length of the play, and yet it remains one of the most powerful scenes of the drama. This extraordinary scene, known as the fly-scene, or mad scene, not only poses a significant problem to directors, actors and audiences of the theatre – how do you make a fly audible let alone visible? – but most importantly, 'What purpose serveth the Fly'? Some six years later at the Globe, Jonson turns this iniquitous insect into a consummate actor: the brilliant and vital force of Mosca.[2] Despite the difference between Titus's organic mat- ter and the more complex symbolic construction of Mosca, the fly, it seems, can be a theatrical prop, a pre-Cartesian anthropomorphic device, a metaphor and a symbol; whether it is riddled with 'pretty buzzings', 'coal-black' like the Moor or 'but a poor observer' like Mosca, the stage imports the fly to prey on the mind, incite petty violence, defy the madness of mutilation or turn the sin- ner upon himself.[3] If 'the euilnesse . . . cometh onely through vs' when 'there is none which is not good and behofefull in it self', what is the dra- matic significance of the space – human or animal – between the image and idea of the fly?[4]

---

[1] William Patten, *The Calendar of Scripture. Wherein the Hebru, Challdian, Arabian, Phenician, Syrian, Persian, Greek and Latin names of nations, cuntreys, men, weemen, idols, cities, hils, riuers, [and] of oother places in the holly Byble mentioned, by order of letters ar set, and turned into oour English toong* (1575), pp. 25–6.

[2] Although the fly scene was not published until its inclusion in the 1623 Folio, most scholars date its composition between 1597 and 1600.

[3] I have particularly chosen *Titus Andronicus* and *Volpone* since they import the fly into their theatres with significant and dra- matic consequences. Whilst insects are often the vehicles for metaphor or analogy, these two plays make use of the organic or emblematic fly to push the boundaries of the represen- tation of the human and the mutability of what constitutes humanness.

[4] Insects are not, of course, unusual in literature. From the Old Testament to Aesop, through the allegorical battle of the insects to Milton's Lord of the Flies, these small creatures fre- quently crop up in literature to perform allegorical, spiritual or tropological tasks. Insects often creep into Shakespeare's plays to express a moral, psychological, political or comedic point in the relative responses of man and nature: from Iago's entrapment of Desdemona: 'He takes her by the palm. Ay,

Unlike almost any other insect the fly attends on man, his food, body and house, travelling between the organic and inorganic worlds with apparently equal ease. Both Shakespeare and Jonson choose to represent this insect on stage and in doing so confront the traditional binaries between man and (his) nature. The fly is both mysterious and mundane, appearing everywhere, manifesting from nowhere, lying in the margins of exquisite illuminations and still lifes and supporting the commonplaces of much proverbial wisdom.[5] This is part of the fly's mythology: to hang about life's aesthetics and to lie among the ruins of allegorical absolutes. Yet Shakespeare and Jonson go beyond proverbial tales of pride, ruination, patience and forethought to dramatize the insect, and set their stage for the fly to perform.[6] This article will explore the point of the fly, its performative role at Titus's dinner, the shift from prop to emblem, and type to character, and the way in which the insect dynamically imports social and evolutionary binaries that find no relief in either the pre- or post-Cartesian ontological soul. The dramatic space between the human and the animal is constantly in crisis, finding neither humanity nor bestiality a stable resource for behavioural psychology. Yet, in Cartesian terms, we find the soul as the province of the human self: 'The (solely human) soul exists during life in the pineal gland, and on death leaves the body to rise to the afterlife. To discover, to see the soul is out of the question, because it would entail opening up, vivisecting the human – a moral impossibility.'[7] The animal can, of course, be vivisected and an examination of the pineal gland reveals nothing, literally.[8] But the idea of the ontological soul is problematic. *Titus* conceptually asserts itself through dismemberment and the body, 'lopped', 'hewed', traded, raped, suffocated, starved and consumed. But the body is also the site of radical consciousness; the body can be pulled apart in front of us precisely because it is more, troublingly more, than the sum of its parts. The play may visually reduce the status of the human body but it leaves its potential, its soul, intact. If trying to discover the soul in vivisection is a 'moral impossibility', what moral boundaries, human or animal, does *Titus* preserve?

Much of the scholarship that explores the relations between man and animal seeks to interrogate the complex value system that not only defines the human but also suspends it on the flux of definition. Famously, Donna Haraway isolated three categories in the state of the human – animal, machine and non-physical – as she also interrogated the ways in which the boundaries between such categories have shifted.[9] Through the idea of the hybrid competing visions of danger and disorder and metamorphosis and transformation emerge. The boundaries between the human, animal and machine are not

---

5 well said – whisper. With as little a web as this will I ensnare as great a fly in Cassio' (2.1.170–2), or Isabella's 'poor beetle', Leontes's poisoned steeped spider, Coriolanus's butterfly or Falstaff's gnat – these winged and leggy things crawl about the plays, but perhaps none so compellingly and ubiquitously as the fly.

5 The fly frequently appears as decoration in illuminated manuscripts and Books of Hours. Proverbially, the fly supports such wisdom as: 'The fly (moth) that plays too long in the candle singes its wings at last' (F394), 'He capers like a Fly in a tarbox' (F395), 'Not worth a Fly' (F396), 'You must lose a Fly to catch a trout' (F399), 'Dead Flies corrupt the most precious ointment' (F400), see Morris Palmer Tilley, *A Dictionary of the Proverbs in England in the Sixteenth and Seventeenth Centuries* (Ann Arbor, 1950); and the more familiar, 'A fly in the ointment', stems from the Bible: 'Dead flies cause the ointment of the apothecary to send forth a stinking savour: so doth a little folly in him that is in reputation for wisdom and honour', Ecclesiastes 10:1. *Esops Fables* include a cautionary tale about an ant and a fly, the moral of which is 'Hee that proceeds to say what hee will, shall heare what he will not. If the fly had spoken well, she had heard well. But I consent to the ant. For an obscure life with security, seemeth to be more to be wished, than a glorious life with peril', John Brinsley, trans., *Esops Fables* (London, 1624), p. 23.

6 Certain animal relations, behaviours or types appear to carry more specific or readable discourses; apes, cats, dogs and bears, for example, or, in the insect world, bees are particularly responsive to theories of social grouping and authority.

7 Erica Fudge, Susan Wiseman, Ruth Gilbert, eds., *At the Borders of the Human: Beast, Bodies and Natural Philosophy in the Early Modern Period* (Basingstoke, 2002), p. 3.

8 See Erica Fudge, *Animal* (London, 2004), pp. 100–5 for a comprehensive discussion of the philosophy of science and, particularly, vivisection.

9 Donna Haraway, 'A Manifesto for Cyborgs: Science, Technology, and Socialist Feminism in the 1980s' in *Feminism/Postmodernism*, ed. Linda J. Nicholson (London, 1990), pp. 190–223.

secure. This insecurity is grounded in the definition and the idea of the human itself. The human 'produces' or throws into relief the 'non-human' and through the tensions and productions of this dynamic we are forced to constantly reassess what humanness is, and in what ways we are entitled to make such distinctions. The production of the human is 'often violent' and the need for 'border-figures' illuminates our need for the constant resurrection of human values and images. As Erica Fudge, Sue Wiseman and Ruth Gilbert explain:

A central category in the early modern period, the 'human' . . . has no sharp or evident frontier and is for its existence in constant need of contrasting border-figures, partly human – or, rather, intermittently human and inhuman according to their context.[10]

If, then, the human seeks definition at the borders of the animal, and 'there is none which is not good and behofefull in itself; and that the euilnesse thereof commeth onely through vs', who (or what) authorizes the moral sites of good and evil? If humans reflect and delegate the corruption of values what role does the animal have in the assertion or representation of moral decline? The complex relations between man and the animal world can in part be understood in terms of early modern anthropocentrism.[11] Bruce Boehrer's *Shakespeare among the Animals* explains two types of anthropocentrism, relative and absolute, which seek to define and celebrate humankind as both separate from and in harmony with the animal world.[12] Crucial to these distinctions is humankind itself. Whilst humankind may remain different from the animal world in anthropocentric terms – at its lowest it may become nearer to animal as an 'impaired group' (women, idiots, ethnic and racial minorities), and at its highest it may represent the right social order (based on superiority and subordination) – anthropomorphism challenges the human to deny animal nature and resist a potential degeneracy. The animal reminds man of his essential superiority at the same time as threatening it. The debate around the human and the animal continues to emerge in many forms; through science, gender, natural philosophy, the body and faith, and the ever-shifting conversations on the human/animal divide are a testimony to the ways in which we seek to understand, mystify and control our anthropological visions through difference.

When Titus buries his sons he bids 'farewell' to their souls, relegating their bodies to the ceremony of destruction but maintaining their selves in the metaphysics of belief. Yet Aaron has a 'soul' of which Tamora is the 'empress':

> Hark, Tamora, the empress of my soul,
> Which never hopes more heaven than rests in thee,
> This is the day of doom for Bassianus,
> His Philomel must lose her tongue today.
>
> (2.2.40–3; TLN 776–9)[13]

If the heaven to which Aaron's soul ascends is Tamora's body, the human self is navigated through the living body of desire, out of which Aaron's tongue will swiftly declare the loss of Lavinia's. Lavinia is, Titus tells us, 'dearer' than his soul:

> dear Lavinia, dearer than my soul.
> Had I but seen thy picture in this plight
> It would have madded me; what shall I do
> Now I behold thy lively body so?
>
> (3.1.103–6; TLN 1245–8)

Titus urges his soul into confrontation with both the image and actuality of his brutalized daughter, finding her 'lively' yet 'martyred'. Re-humanizing her in empathy Titus sees Lavinia's body with his soul. But the idea of the soul as the humanizing mechanism is in contention throughout the

---

[10] Fudge, Wiseman, and Gilbert, *At the Borders of the Human*, pp. 2–3. See also Erica Fudge, *Animal*.

[11] Within the context of this article, I use the term 'animal' to refer to all non-human living creatures.

[12] Bruce Boehrer, *Shakespeare Among the Animals: Nature and Society in the Drama of Early Modern England* (Basingstoke, 2002), see especially, pp. 14–27.

[13] Folio references are from the Norton Facsimile of *Mr. William Shakespeares Comedies, Histories, and Tragedies* (*The First Folio*), prepared by Charlton Hinman (New York, 1968); references are to the through-line-numbers (TLN). William Shakespeare, *Titus Andronicus*, ed. Jonathan Bate, The Arden Shakespeare, third series (London, 2000). All further references, unless otherwise stated, are to this edition.

play – it is manifest in the most inhuman human, Aaron, and as a site of both lust and destruction. Aaron's willingness to commit evil and repent good as willingly as he would kill a fly, centralizes his soul as the repository of random brutality. What soul he has brings him nearer the animal, but also his human self.

In *Titus* and *Volpone* the fly challenges that self; whether it is taking Titus's eye to the corners of his humanity, or pushing the parasite to the limits of its behavioural psychology this grubby little insect enters the playing space neither to displace nor represent man, but to contaminate him. Semantically the parasite had yet to acquire its specific etymology, for until the eighteenth century the term 'parasite' could be applied to anyone or thing displaying obsequious or fawning behaviour; it was particularly associated with flattery and patronage. Thomas Thomas's hard-word dictionary of 1587 describes a parasite as 'A smell feast, a flatterer, a parasite, a trencher or belly friend: one that saith and doth all things to please the humour of another, and agreeth vnto him in all things, to haue his repast scotfree. In olde time this worde was vsed in the good parte for them that . . . attended vpon, accompanied, or were assistants to high priests or chiefe magistrates', and John Florio defines 'Parasitare' as 'to play the parasite, to sooth one vp in all things, to hold one vp with yea and nay, to faune and flatter, to cogge and foist with one for a meales meate'.[14] The parasite thus stands in the limbo of living, near enough to human life to reflect on it, yet not near enough to claim it as its own. On the stages of Jonson and Shakespeare, the fly, in challenging art with the vulgarisms of living, moves beyond a colloquy with the natural world to man's inhumanity to man and the ethics of the imagination. Equally, the problems of the soul as the site of the human are amplified. Where Aaron, the play's 'beast', fly and formidable operator, traces his own soul in lust from body to body, or tongue from dismemberment to delight in evil, he compromises the very boundaries of the body that the play tries to maintain (the distinction between dismemberment and vivisection); in *Volpone* the nature of the human as animal and the transmigration of souls finds an alternative image in Androgyno, the human who is both everything and nothing.

Nano, a dwarf, talking about the great game of the human that is also the animal declares,

> For know, here [*Pointing to* Androgyno] is enclosed the
>   soul of Pythagoras,
> That juggler divine, as hereafter shall follow;
> Which soul (fast and loose, sir) came first from Apollo.[15]
>   (1.2.6–8)

That which appears to hold fast is actually loose; the soul can move and, as it does, it destabilizes not only what it means to be human but also what it means to be animal. The soul is part of the cheating game, the trickery of the human which disengages from stable binaries even as it tries to hold onto them. But this, too, is part of Jonson's drama, presenting animals or insects with human qualities, offering up the notion of the human as animal yet blurring any sense of form on which such definitions may exist. As *Volpone* stages the limits and illusions of trickery, we are told of the game of the moving soul in the body of a man who is also a woman.[16] Perfectly human and impossibly 'other', the hermaphrodite can simultaneously celebrate and condemn relations between the human and animal world. If the soul distinguishes us from the animal, when the soul is in transit or, worse, appearing to be stable but actually in motion, there can be no such thing as 'moral impossibilities', since there is no essential limit to the human or animal condition.

When, in *King Lear*, Gloucester chillingly laments that 'as flies to wanton boys are we to the gods, they kill us for their sport', we are reminded of the 'wanton', reckless, even malicious pleasure that lay between Aaron and the fly; but in terms of Gloucester's metaphor, of course, Aaron is the god

---

[14] See Early Modern English Dictionary Database at www.chass.utoronto.ca/english/emed.

[15] *The workes of Benjamin Ionson* (London, 1616), p. 478. See also *The Merchant of Venice*, 4.1.127, when Graziano invokes Pythagoras for the construction of Shylock's 'currish' nature.

[16] See Ruth Gilbert, *Early Modern Hermaphrodites: Sex and Other Stories* (Basingstoke, 2002), for a discussion of the hermaphrodite in both art and literature.

and the human the fly. At the end of *Titus*, when Aaron faces his nemesis and his 'heinous deeds', he wishes that he 'had done a thousand more' rather than repent those he did. Cataloguing the missed opportunities of tyranny and evil, 'Wherein I did not some serious ill', he concludes

> Tut, I have done a thousand dreadful things
> As willingly as one would kill a fly,
> And nothing grieves me heartily indeed
> But that I cannot do ten thousand more.
>
> (TLN 2257–60; 5.1.141–4)

The most recent Arden editor proposes that Aaron's recklessly murderous use of the fly is a possible inspiration for the interpolation of the fly-killing scene: 'Aaron's willingness to do dreadful things as readily as he would kill a fly is flipped around so that he becomes the fly.'[17] The metaphor of fly-killing jostles the human's capacity for power amidst careless tyranny and potential mercy. Yet if Aaron becomes the objectification of his own careless horror, how are we to understand the dramatic relationship between casualty and causality, between a voluntary act and the order of nature? The fly easily translates, it seems, from cause to effect, at once both victim and perpetrator of moral atrophy. The relationship between the fly and iniquity is perhaps most explicit in *King Lear* when Lear turns to the abused Gloucester and declares:

> Adultery? Thou shalt not die. Die for adultery!
> No, the wren goes to't, and the small gilded fly
> Does lecher in my sight. Let copulation thrive,
> For Gloucester's bastard son
> Was kinder to his father than my daughters
> Got 'tween the lawful sheets.
>
> (TLN 2557–61; 4.5.107–12)

Here the fly is bound into the great teeming world of lawless nature, which thrives on the absence of social codes. The brutal irony is of course Lear's ignorance of the reality of 'Gloucester's bastard son', and the lecherous fly is no more exemplary than the faithful Lear. Yet there is something lawless about the fly: unlike the wren it is not bound to its own fragile order of survival; the fly feeds on

carrion, it is a parasite and thrives everywhere and always. This is Jonson's fly, the indomitable Mosca, who claims to:

> be here,
> And there, and here, and yonder, all at once;
> Present to any humour, all occasion.
>
> (3.1.26–9)

The mercurial, even metamorphic, capacity of the fly to 'change a visor swifter than a thought!' seems to emerge from its ubiquity, but unlike Menenius's grub it has no evolutionary potential: 'There is a difference between a grub and a butterfly; yet your butterfly was a grub. This Martius is grown from man to dragon: he has wings: he's more than a creeping thing' (*Coriolanus*, 5.4.11–14). Coriolanus overleaps himself, metamorphosing from a grub to a dragon, beyond the fragility of the butterfly's wings. Yet Menenius's description evokes a stark grandeur in the synthesis of the natural and mytho-logical worlds that is denied to the grubby domes-ticity of the fly. Jonson's Mosca, however, surfaces with all the seedy appetites of a fly and the splen-dour of a dragon. But Titus's fly is neither a charac-ter nor a metaphor, but a moving picture of random injustice and careless violence. Despite the obvious differences between the 'real' fly that intrudes upon the family meal of the Andronici and the more complex symbolic construction of Jonson's Mosca, both flies emerge as products of anthropocentrism and the constantly shifting notion of humankind. Mosca's symbolic construction is predicated upon those qualities of the fly that we are meant, perhaps most strongly, to abhor – its potential anarchy, its casual disregard for both the animal and human world. Travelling without compromise between these two worlds, the fly attends to man as it does to faeces or blood, food or carrion. Titus's

---

17 In his Arden edition, Jonathan Bate ties this line into the question of authorship, suggesting that, contrary to the claim that the play bears the hand of George Peele, the fly-scene is stylistically very similar to the rest of the play and 'Line 5.1.142 perhaps gave him [Shakespeare] the germ of it . . . the added scene thus gives Titus an occasion to express his vindictiveness against Aaron, whereas elsewhere he always identifies Tamora as his chief antagonist', p. 118.

personification of the fly, however, moves from empathy to malice, from Lavinia to Aaron, retaining a human imperative in an animal world. Despite his dramatic construction, Mosca is, in many ways, more 'animal'; his behaviour stems from a pathological imperative realized in human cunning but projected as 'nature'. Mosca, it seems, cannot escape his fly-self, Titus's fly can. In the terms of absolute anthropocentrism, where Mosca's 'humanization' makes him the superior animal, it is Aaron's dehumanization that makes him the insect. Yet Aaron plays with his own inhumanity, revealing his soul as a place of temporal desire – neither ineffable nor invisible – Aaron's soul is visceral and finite, it moves as his lust does, from body to body, seeking no other 'heaven' than the consummation of desire. Aaron presents his potential humanness through the transmigration of souls, from extremity to extremities, sex to sex. This is the carnality of the beast; yet it expresses itself through the metaphysics of the soul.

When the Andronici sit down to face the grim horror of their reality, Titus turns to his mutilated daughter and declares,

> Thou map of woe, that dost talk in signs,
> When thy poor heart beats with outrageous beating,
> Thou canst not strike it thus to make it still.
> Wound it with sighing, girl, kill it with groans,
> Or get some little knife between thy teeth
> And just against thy heart make thou a hole,
> That all the tears that thy poor eyes let fall
> May run into that sink and, soaking in,
> Drown the lamenting fool in sea-salt tears.
>
> (TLN 1464–72; 3.2.12–20)

The construction of the body is, of course, central to the play's exploration of humanity. If Descartes will leave the soul intact through the 'moral impossibility' of vivisection, how does the play distinguish between dissection and dismemberment? At what point does it leave the site of the human intact? Reclaiming Lavinia's body in violence, Titus may look to his table for 'some little knife' to offer his 'lamenting fool'. As they go on to notice and name, reject and despise their suffering bodies, unexpectedly '*Marcus strikes the dish with a knife*'

(SD Folio). Using the everyday objects of eating, Marcus strikes the scene with a noise that must sound loudly and crassly next to the 'speechless complainer':

TITUS:
> What dost thou strike at, Marcus, with thy knife?

MARCUS:
> At that that I have killed, my lord – a fly.

TITUS:
> Out on thee, murderer. Thou killest my heart.
> Mine eyes are cloyed with the view of tyranny;
> A deed of death done on the innocent
> Becomes not Titus' brother. Get thee gone;
> I see thou art not for my company.
>
> (TLN 1505–11; 3.2.52–8)

Suddenly, in Marcus's simple action, Titus sees too much; the view of tyranny that he faces in the loss of his own hand and his daughter's mutilation is replayed in the petty destruction of a life. Titus's empathy with the natural world and his anthropomorphic application of human values to the fly seek to amplify rather than compromise his own humanity. Titus aligns himself with nature as a refuge from man, who has become so separated from himself in violence that he no longer values his god-given right to life. Like Aaron's later comment – and Gloucester's famous indictment of life's reckless justice in *Lear* – the fly is recognition of man's potentially wanton attitude towards the value of human life and the fragility of the body. The fly often accompanies punishment: in Exodus the Lord tells Moses to confront Pharaoh and ask him to let his people go; if he does not, 'I will send swarms of flies on you and your officials, on your people and into your houses. The houses of the Egyptians will be full of flies, and even the ground where they are.' The Lord uses this punishment to signify the safety of his followers: 'But on that day I will deal differently with the land of Goshen, where my people live; no swarms of flies will be there, so that you will know that I, the LORD, am in this land. I will make a distinction between my people and your people. This miraculous sign will occur tomorrow' (8:20–2). Those with flies are condemned, those without are saved. Despite the intensely visceral idea of these swarms, the role of the fly is spiritual; it is a symbol to distinguish between the faithless and the faithful. Yet the vivid horror of the fly lies in its proximity to decay, carrying disease and spreading infection as it moves from flesh to matter. The fleshy substance of the body becomes grossly apparent in the manifestation of the fly. Blood, food and wounds attract the fly and it is the insect's arrival at the dinner table of the mutilated Titus and Lavinia that reminds us of what it feeds on. John Foxe, in his *Book of Martyrs*, narrating the punishment of Marcus Arethusius, to whom 'Great cruelty [was] Shewed', sets his pages alight with the bodily spectacle of punishment:

Lastly, they put him into a basket, and being annoynted with hony and brothe, they hoong hym abroad in the heate of the sonne, as meate for waspes and flies to feede vpon. And all this extremitie they shewed vnto him, for that they would enforce him to do one of these thinges (that is) eyther to builde vp agayne the temple, which he had destroyed, or els to geue so much mony as should pay for the building of the same . . . But he hāging in the basket, woūded pitifully with the sharpened sticks of boyes and children, & all to be bitten with wasps and flyes, did not onely conceale his payne and griefe, but also derided those wicked ones, and called them, base, low and terrene people, and he himselfe to be exalted and set on high.[18]

Travelling between the two worlds of nature and humankind, the fly often attends both cruelty and rectitude. Yet to 'not harm a fly' is to be merciful, kind and gentle; it is to show resistance in the face of opportunity.

In John Heywood's epically dull poem *The Spider and the Flie*, the Fly, Buz, delivers a speech on the nature of justice, mercy and tyranny:

Mercy: joined with justice doth either remit
Or qualifie peines, that dewe by justice seme.
Tiranie not with justice, but against it:

Not weiyng deserte, awardth peines most extreme.
Tyranie, and mercy, thus maie we here deme

Tyrany: not with but againste justice showth,
Mercy with: and not against justice growth.[19]

The Fly takes possession of Mercy, telling the Spider: 'I wish that we: eche as our callings asine, / Maie leane to that hande with mete strength, or vigor, / That mercie leanth unto: rather than rygor'.[20] The sensitivity of the Fly to the 'rygor' of injustice makes it a fitting subject for victimization. The primal dynamic between the spider and the fly supports an everlasting war of absolutes – right and wrong, victim and aggressor, tyranny and justice. Heywood's projection of faith and tolerance onto the insects imagines Protestantism as the irritant to the right Christian commonwealth. But Buz is essentially weak and permanently under threat, holding onto his zeal, not through physical strength, but through moral righteousness. Treating the fly as a victim of an apparently random and thoughtless act of brutality, Titus extrapolates a sympathetic network of loss:

MARCUS: Alas, my lord, I have killed but a fly.
TITUS: 'But'?
How if that fly had a father and a
mother?[21]
How would he hang his slender gilded
wings
And buzz lamenting doings in the air.
Poor harmless fly,

---

[18] John Foxe, *Acts and Monuments of the Church* (London, 1570), p. 127.

[19] John Heywood, *The Spider and the Flie*, reprinted from the edition of 1556, printed for the Spenser Society (Manchester, 1894), M2v, p. 116.

[20] Heywood, *The Spider and the Flie*, p. 116.

[21] The Oxford Complete Works and single edition have 'brother' instead of 'mother': this follows an ingenious conjecture first made by Ritson over two hundred years ago: 'one has to suppose that Shakespeare intended 'brother' as an address to Marcus and that the printer changed it to 'mother' because 'father and mother' is a more natural combination.' I have, however, retained the Folio's 'mother'.

That with his pretty buzzing melody
Came here to make us merry, and
thou hast killed him.

(TLN 1512–19; 3.2.59–66)

Titus focuses on three aspects of the fly – its family, sound and wings, which emotively replicate the vision of Lavinia. As Titus turns from his 'poor lamenting fool' to the 'poor harmless fly', he notices that it is now incapable, like his daughter, of making its melody. If, as Cicero says in *De Oratore*, 'the one point in which we have our very greatest advantage over the brute creation is that we hold converse one with another, and can reproduce our thought in words' (*De Oratore*, I.8; 32),[22] what happens to the idea of the human when it is wrenched from its voice? Titus's response to the fly does not condemn Lavinia but supports her. Since language can no longer operate as a value system for the admission of the human, consensual compassion takes its place, and morality gives way to empathy. Yet, at the same time, it is Lavinia's difference, *her* 'slender gilded wings', *her* 'lamenting doings in the air', that reaffirms her humanity. Her human body deprived of speech remains humane, her body is deformed but her soul is intact.

The relationship between the fly, the flesh and the soul, however, appears ambiguous; whilst, on the one hand, its carrion feeding draws the insect to blood, food and the body (man or beast) in decay, on the other it often comes to represent mortality and ephemera. In many early seventeenth-century still life paintings the fly is frequently manifest in elaborate and exquisite compositions of flowers, insects and shells.[23] The fly is often hidden, nestling in petals, shadowed by stems or hanging by the glimmer of its wing in a darkened corner beneath the sumptuous display. In paintings such as these, the fly's emblematic role is to suspend the distance between man and nature, to capture the transient life and the perennial earth. The unquantifiable distance between life and death is acutely dramatized in Titus's reaction to Marcus's action; and yet if the purpose of this scene is to highlight Titus's madness, his raving grief, then are we to observe the absurdity, even irrationality, of his response?

Marcus deftly notices Titus's anthropomorphic engagement with the fly and chooses to turn this to all their advantages:

MARCUS: Pardon me, sir, it was a black ill-
                 favoured fly,
             Like to the empress' Moor. Therefore
             I killed him.

(TLN 1520–2; 3.2.67–8)

The fly mutates from a semblance of Lavinia to a vision of Aaron. The insect is dead, a prop that is now an emblem, and it forces the Andronici to move beyond the misery of their meal. With this metamorphosis Titus swiftly turns too much tyranny into charity:

TITUS: Oh, Oh, Oh!
           Then pardon me for reprehending thee,
           For thou hast done a charitable deed.
           Give me the knife; I will insult on him,
           Flattering myself as if it were the Moor
           Come hither purposely to poison me
           There's for thyself, and that's for Tamora.
           Ah, sirrah!
           Yet I think we are not brought so low
           But that between us we can kill a fly
           That comes in likeness of a coal-black
           Moor.

(TLN 1523–32; 32.69–79)

Titus willingly enters into a performative pact with the insect; he knows he 'flatters' himself into creating its part, from which he extrapolates a story of presence and poison and which gives the fly a sense of purpose, as one who came dressed 'in likeness of a coal-black Moor'. Yet Marcus, the author of this show, fails to observe Titus's acknowledged commitment to make-believe:

---

[22] As noted by Terence Hawkes, *Shakespeare's Talking Animals: Language and Drama in Society* (London, 1973), p. 9.

[23] Although the fly became a frequent inclusion in the emerging genre of still life, perhaps the most famous artists to involve this insect were George Hoefnagel and Ambrosius Bosschaert. Hoefnagel's etching, 'Archetypa Studiaque Patris' (1592), and Bosschaert's 'Flower Vase in a Window Niche' (1620) are exquisite examples.

Alas, poor man! Grief has so wrought on him
He takes false shadows for true substances.

(TLN 1533–4; 3.2.80–1)

This scene uses shadow to find its way to substance; from the *Aeneid*, the diversion of 'some pleasing tale' or 'Sad stories chanced in the times of old', the shadow or flattery of distraction leads Titus into action. As Titus will later show in his response to Tamora's pageant of Revenge, Rape and Murder, he is profoundly aware of the difference between substance and shadow, and more than this he is perspicacious enough to turn it to his advantage. Although Jonathan Bate suggests that this scene allows the play to perform Titus's hatred towards Aaron, rather than only Tamora, it is the acutely domestic, even mundane, appearance of the fly that charges the moment with its full theatrical weight. Titus's bathetic comment that 'I think we are not brought so low / But that between us we can kill a fly' affirms the insignificance of the insect he was once so quick to defend; it marks his movement back into the consensual violence of the play. Like the cruelty of Gloucester's 'wanton boys' and the random injustice of the gods, Titus returns – though with a degree of humour – to the horror of their reality. In Titus's irrational rationale the fly is an abstract embodiment that supports his relative anthropocentrism, predicated on neither speech nor reason, but image and idea. Yet, rather than the 'coal-black' colour of the fly, it is in fact Titus's ability to recognize constructions of humanity that supports his translation of the fly from insect to idea, companion to symbol. That the fly is an outsider and an intruder makes this journey possible. Titus's madness is not in making the fly Aaron but in making the action significant. Constructions of 'humanity' abound and bounce through the air: at first in the fly's pretty buzzings, which engage Titus in a sympathetic network of socialization, then in the fly's unintelligibility and fragility, making it closer to the re-humanization of Lavinia, but ultimately the humanity of the fly finds its apotheosis in death and evil; at the far corners of what we call 'humanity', the fly becomes a personification.

The fly begins by performing as itself, reminding us that there is food on the Andronici's table and that there is blood on their hands. The terrible sound of the knife hitting the dish or the merry buzz of everyday things resounds loudly through the dull silence of trauma. Real or not real, staged or imagined, the fly is always symbolic as it jostles with the human in an attempt to articulate what humankind can or has come to mean. In accordance with the shift from absolute to relative anthropocentrism, the fly represents at first the potential and then the canker of structured social relations. In relative anthropocentrism, the 'impaired' human is nearer to the animal in its greater distance from the ideal human (as Bruce Boehrer notes, the white, male protestant).[24] Human, in these terms, evinces completeness in the realization of superior potential and 'perfect' form. Where Aaron plumbs the depths of his humanness in the personification of a fly, Mosca reaches his height. The implication is that Mosca, by way of anthropocentrism, moves from the animal to the possible human, but Aaron falls from the possible human to the animal, still clutching his soul.

In *Volpone* the characters' names leave us in no doubt as to their dramatic function. The prevailing images of carrion and parasite immediately set the substance of the play within the realms of deceit, hypocrisy, avarice and iniquity. Despite the determining narrative of the eponymous hero, it is Mosca who drives *Volpone*, who, delighting in his own nimble brilliance, declares:

> This is the creature had the art born with him;
> Toils not to learn it, but doth practise it
> Out of most excellent nature: and such sparks
> Are the parasites, others but their zanies.
>
> (3.1.30–3)

The 'zanies', or imitators, litter the play, the carrion feeders of Voltore, Corvino and Corbaccio who, as they 'Echo my-lord, and lick away a moth', fail to reach the nimble heights of the 'true parasite' Mosca. It is he, the 'flesh-fly', not the vulture, crow, raven or even fox, who succeeds, above all

---

[24] Boehrer, *Shakespeare among the Animals*, p. 18.

else, in cheating the cheaters, in feeding on the sub-parasites: 'Almost /All the wise world is little else, in nature, / But parasites, or sub-parasites'. The scene in which Mosca announces his own parasitic brilliance in this pest-ridden world lies between perhaps two of the most sinister scenes of the play: just before Mosca holds the stage to soliloquize, he cajoles Corvino into prostituting his wife for Volpone's dying pleasure; just after, he persuades Bonario that his father is to disinherit him, announcing: 'for the pure love, which I bear all right, / And hatred of the wrong, I must reveal it' (3.2.41–2). Between Mosca's attempts to bring forth rape and annihilation, he takes the stage to declare the machinations of his species, proclaiming self-love for his 'prosperous parts' which 'do so spring and burgeon':

> Oh! Your parasite
> Is a most precious thing, dropped from above,
> Not bred 'mongst clods and clot-poles, here on earth.
> I muse, the mystery was not made a science,
> It is so liberally professed! Almost
> All the wise world is little else, in nature,
> But parasites, or sub-parasites. And yet,
> I mean not those that have your bare town-art,
> To know who's fit to feed 'em; have no house,
> No family, no care, and therefore mould
> Tales for men's ears, to bait that sense; or get
> Kitchen-invention, and some stale receipts
> To please the belly and the groin; nor those,
> With their court-dog-tricks, that can fawn and fleer,
> Make their revenue out of legs and faces,
> Echo my-Lord, and lick away a moth.
>
> (3.1.7–22)

Ironically translating the fly's air-born existence into something heavenly, Mosca synthesizes the natural and urban worlds, making a skill or trade (mystery) – even a field of learning (science) – of this prevalent type. Yet the sort of parasite we might imagine, who lurks for 'kitchen-invention' and 'stale receipts', who has 'no house, / No family, no care' and hangs about to flatter, 'to bait that sense', to fawn and grimace (fleer) in obsequy, has no place in Mosca's evolutionary tale. He is not the insect that lies about our peripheral vision, feeding

and consuming the orders of the depraved and the deprived,

> But your fine, elegant rascal, that can rise
> And stoop (almost together) like an arrow;
> Shoot through the air, as nimbly as a star;
> Turn short, as doth a swallow; and be here,
> And there, and here, and yonder, all at once;
> Present to any humour, all occasion;
> And change visor swifter than a thought!.
>
> (23–9)

This elegant rascal has all the gossamer beauty of a star, the aim of an arrow and the summer's ease of the swallow. Mosca represents the fly as the ultimate parasite, metamorphosing from irritating and grubby pest to the finest creation of the celestial, natural and man-made worlds:

> This is the creature had the art born with him;
> Toils not to learn it, but doth practise it
> Out of most excellent nature: and such sparks
> Are the true parasites, others but their zanies
>
> (30–3)

The true parasite is not an imitation or an actor; it is authentic nature, and authentic nature stands outside the remit of the humane. This fly cannot be taught and cannot be changed; this is Aaron, who under guard and facing death, still declares

> Some devil whisper curses in my ear,
> And prompt me that my tongue may utter forth
> The venomous malice of my swelling heart.
>
> (TLN 2507–9; 5.3.11–13)

Although much of the comedy of *Volpone* springs from our delight in Mosca's role as the double-agent, the 'flesh-fly', feeding the sinners with their own sin, he is the greatest villain of the play. The parasite's fawning nature is particularly associated with money and the rich man; Bullokar, in 1616, offered this definition: 'A Flatterer, a trencher friend. One that is still hanging on some rich man, and flatteringlie feedeth his humor because he would bee partaker of his good cheere.' Erasmus, however, a century earlier in his *Education of a Christian Prince* (1516), very particularly notices the danger of avarice and the parasite:

But be it inn case there were one special frende amonge a thousande that loued a ryche man hertely without any maner of faynynge / yet can not the ryche man but haue in suspicion & mistrust euery man. He iudgeth all men to be vultures & rauenous vyrdes gaping for careyn: he thinketh all men to be flyes flyng to him / to sucke out some profit of him for themselues. What so euer commoditie therefore ryches semeth to brynge / it for ye apperyng otherwise than it is in very dede. But they bryng very many thingis which are euyll in dede / & taketh away very many of these thynges which are good in very dede.[25]

Erasmus's attention to 'careyn', 'rauenous vyrdes', 'vultures' and 'flyes' strikes an obvious chord in relation to *Volpone*. 'Ryches' have the potential to bring evil and expel the good, and the creatures of *Volpone* import threat and disorder in their very being, and it is the point at which the human world meets the animal that corruption thrives. This uncanny 'border', however, operates less as a place in which the human defines his/her humanness but more as a shoreline, a shifting boundary between learned and essential values. The nature of the fly-man 'flyng' to the rich man breeds distrust and destabilizes any semblance of essential value. Jonson plays out Erasmus's warning and, as Voltore predicted, Mosca's summer is over and his winter does come (5.9.1–2) as he is sentenced to 'live perpetual prisoner in our galleys'. Ultimately, however, it is Volpone, 'by blood and rank a gentleman' who is mortified with his own iniquity:

> To the hospital of the *Incurabili*:
> And, since the most was gotten by imposture,
> By feigning lame, gout, palsy, and such diseases,
> Thou art to lie in prison, cramped with irons,
> Till thou be sick and lame indeed.
>
> (5.7.120–4)

It is the human that condemns Volpone and Mosca's 'most excellent nature', which protects him; as the parasite, Mosca has neither the blood nor rank of a gentleman and has outwitted those who have. The fly does not quite seem to die on the stage of Shakespeare and Jonson; whilst Marcus has 'but killed a fly', the real fly of the scene, Aaron, leaves the stage to be starved and buried alive. Unlike Chiron and Demetrius we do not see his death, and Mosca remains in 'our perpetual galleys'. It is tempting to read 'galleys' as a play on 'galleries', as the fly remains always above the stage as the 'poor observer' with the 'bare town-art' or the 'most excellent nature'. What becomes increasingly harder to discern, and more subtle, is whether the animal has the potential to condemn or transcend the human condition. But is there a composite image of the fly or does its power lie in the unstable distance between inhumanity and nature? As man hands on inhumanity to man, the insect focuses our attention on the arbitrary nature of both cruelty and mercy, and we find no relief in logic or causality. In Aaron's willingness to kill a fly as to commit many heinous deeds we recognize the sign of cruelty, yet in the fly itself we recognize the potential for mercy. Daniel Leeds, in 'Fair Virtue the Shepherd's Mistress', describes gentleness and virtue, which culminate in the compassion for the fly:

> Cruelty her Soul detests,
> For within her Bosom rests
> Noble Pity, usher'd by
> An unequal Courtesie,
> And is griev'd at good men's mean,
> As the grief were all her own.
> Just she is, so just, that I
> Know she will not wrong a Fly,
> Or oppress the meanest thing,
> To be a Mistress to a King.[26]

The smallness of the fly supposes that the easiest acts of violence are the most nobly refused. Here pity reproduces an idealized anthropocentric order of social hierarchy that, rather than exclude the shepherd's mistress from society, makes her fit for a King. Universal compassion sustains pity and nobleness

---

[25] Desiderius Erasmus, *A booke called in latyn Enchiridion militis christani, and in englysshe the manuell of the christen knight replenysshed with most holsome precepts, made by the famous clerk Erasmus of Roterdame, to whiche is added a newe and meruaylous profitable preface.* (London, 1533), p. 160.

[26] Daniel Leeds, *The Temple of Wisdom for the Little World in Two Parts*, 'Fair Virtue the Shepherd's Mistress' (Philadelphia, 1688).

through an equal relationship to both the human and animal world.

Yet rather than reproduce a conventional dialectic between the natural and human world, both playwrights insist upon the proximity between them. The space to which these plays constantly allude, between the humane and the tropological, between the image and the action, is a space which is constantly in crisis. Boehrer, talking of 'absolute' and 'relative' anthropocentrism, makes the distinction between nature as the cultural pattern which endorses a hierarchical, indeed exploitative, model of society, and nature as the point at which man digresses, sharing some qualities with the natural world but ultimately finding his humanity in perfect difference. This latter notion of relative anthropocentrism organizes itself against marginal groups of 'impaired humanity', which include racial, social, intellectual and physical 'others'. Just as for Erica Fudge or Ruth Gilbert, it is the space – social, visceral, spiritual or linguistic – between the human and the animal that is constantly in a crisis of definition, seeking to both expose and expunge difference. In *Volpone* Jonson's nature reflects humanity itself as 'impaired groups' wherein 'All the wise world is little else, in nature, / But parasites, or sub-parasites.' The fly, however, demonstrates the potential of its own apotheosis, achieving its fullest state in the art of its nature: 'This is the creature had the art born with him.' Yet if, as Boehrer suggests, 'the only difference is that relative anthropocentrism adopts a much narrower definition of humankind', [27] where is Jonson's humankind? There can be no difference between humanity and nature in a world where the true parasite serves a lighter punishment than 'the blood and rank of a gentleman'. When man preys upon himself, and the worst of nature supports the best of men, only the value of life remains to narrow the definition of humankind. Titus's rejection of Marcus in support of life seeks to affirm the commitment to absolute anthropocentrism, and yet the imaginative link between Aaron and the fly translates the fate of impaired nature from relative anthropocentrism to anthropomorphism. Salvaging man from the animal becomes

increasingly compromised by his amoral proximity to the natural world, and conventional idealism turns to organic contamination.

Paradoxically, however, the animal world often confirms rather than challenges processes of dehumanization. Initially the relationship between Lavinia and the fly is Titus's way of rescuing his daughter's humanness. The proximity between Lavinia and the fly, rather than interrogating their shared status as 'impaired groups', seeks to celebrate empathy and socialization as the core aspect of humanity. Imbuing the fly with such qualities and notions recovers Lavinia as an essential human, despite her mutilation. In Titus's reaction to the fly he restores Lavinia's humanity but betrays Aaron's. The fly, dramatic, symbolic or organic, provides a transitional passage for the evolution of human values. Titus's shift from empathy to aggression registers a shift from anthropocentrism to anthropomorphism, wherein being human is no longer enough to sustain the distinction between man and beast – since the body of Lavinia challenges these binaries – so that humankind itself must be subject to the ever-shifting tide of social and emotional differences. The personification of Aaron as the fly is not a symptom of Titus's madness but an expression of his attempt to recover his daughter and articulate the soul. Making Aaron an expendable part of nature and a symbol of careless violence simultaneously resurrects Lavinia and reduces Aaron. The interrelationships between man and animal associated with anthropomorphism endow the human with the inherent potential to degenerate. The presence of the animal means that humankind is constantly at risk. The bestial qualities of the characters in *Volpone*, however, are somewhat complicated by their non-bestial counterparts, suggesting that the idea of the human is always in contention. Nano, the dwarf, talks to Androgyno, the hermaphrodite, as the body of a soul in transit. Speaking through the limits of the human body, as it is both all and nothing, he tells us of the migration of souls. Neither the body nor the soul

---

[27] Boehrer, *Shakespeare among the Animals*, p. 17.

can, it seems, locate the human as an ontological condition in the theatre of animals. Androgyno is deformed and perfect, a symbol of the essential body and the lucid soul, but neither the body nor the soul can salvage an idea of the human. Lavinia's body is dismembered. Aaron's soul is in league with his parts; moving from lust to torture to the fly, it neither recognizes nor recovers his humanity.

The proximity of the fly to man and the insect's history, steeped alike in punishment, horror, art and faith, makes the journey from symbol to matter a constantly changing one. The early modern fly is an irritant to notions of anthropocentrism, as it is simultaneously able to contaminate and celebrate humankind. The fly is mysterious and ignomin-

ious, it cohabits with man yet remains out of his reach; neither beautiful nor useful, edible nor aesthetic, mastered nor masterful, the fly surrounds man's mortality as the base remembrance of his body and the imaginative link to his mercy. Like Boehrer's description of Caliban (p. 27), Aaron's wilful malice is a testimony to the human animal dynamic that haunts our evolutionary potential. The fly theatrically and symbolically recognizes both the potential for and the absence of a value system.

Vulnerable and disgusting, lively and pointless, the fly asks us to travel to the far side of what humanity and nature have come to mean: 'Alas, my lord, I have but killed a fly.' '"But?"'

RIDDLING Q1: HAMLET'S MILL AND THE TRICKSTER

IAN FELCE

ENTER Q1

When the First Quarto of Shakespeare's *Hamlet* was rediscovered in Henry Bunbury's closet two hundred years after the publication of the First Folio, it came in such a questionable shape that it has haunted critics ever since. The First Quarto of *Hamlet* (Q1) was printed in 1603, a year or so before the Second Quarto (Q2) of 1604–5 and twenty years before the First Folio (F) version of 1623. Though they contain notable differences, Q2 and F are close, sharing some of Shakespeare's most celebrated verse, characters who behave similarly and a comparable chronology of scenes. However, Q1, or the 'bad' quarto, is an oddity. Barely more than half the length of the other two variants, it comprises characters who differ in name and action from their Q2 and F counterparts, a radically divergent chronology of scenes and verse that is often patchy, 'To die, to sleep: is that all? Ay all. / No, to sleep, to dream; ay marry, there it goes.'[1] Indeed, the first quarto is so erratic that it seems doubtful that Shakespeare could possibly have written it as it stands. Thomas Clayton's opinion that the printed text is a memorial reconstruction recalled by a player who had been in a version of *Hamlet* is widely held: 'In my view, much of the dialogue of Q1 is very much inferior to that of Q2 and F, and memorial reconstruction seems the most eligible explanation for it as such.'[2] The question then arises, what lies behind the text of Q1? Almost invariably critics have sought the answer by textual comparison, particularly concentrating on the order in which the plays behind the published texts of Q1, Q2 and F

may have been conceived. The most popular explanation currently appears to be that of Kathleen O. Irace, who accounts for Q1's short length and different chronology of scenes with the theory that it represents a 'skillful theatrical abridgement of *Hamlet*, a fast-paced popular version especially designed for a tour outside London' (p. 107).[3] Irace agrees with Clayton that Q2 and F were not revised from the play behind Q1 but that the play behind Q2 was written first, then the play behind F and lastly that behind Q1. She proposes that Q1 derives from a reconstructed abridgement of the play behind F, and that F derives from Q2, which was printed from Shakespeare's 'foul copies'. This theory disregards the order of printing, and presumes that Q2 represents Shakespeare's earliest conception of the play and that, since the abridged play behind Q1 was supposedly created last, it is the furthest from Shakespeare's original intention. It is a convincing and now pervasive theory but, as Alan C. Dessen emphasizes, it is only a supposition: 'Indeed, the formulation that Q1 dimly reflects a version of the play seen more clearly in Q2 and F has become so

---

I would like to thank Helen Cooper, Judy Quinn, Anne Barton and Emily Lethbridge for their support during the writing of this article.

[1] William Shakespeare, *The First Quarto of Hamlet*, ed. Kathleen O. Irace (Cambridge, 1998), 7.115–16 (Hereafter 'Q1').

[2] Thomas Clayton, Introduction to *The Hamlet First Published (Q1, 1603): Origins, Form, Intertextualities*, ed. Thomas Clayton (London, 1992), p. 29.

[3] Kathleen O. Irace, 'Origins and Agents of Q1 Hamlet', in Clayton, ed., *The Hamlet First Published*, pp. 90–122, p. 107.

familiar that hypothesis has hardened into fact.'[4] However, the theory that Q1 is a hazy version of the longer texts ignores one of its most transparent characteristics: namely, that it, in many ways, appears closer to the Hamlet tradition that came before Shakespeare than either Q2 or F. If, instead of comparing Q1 only to Q2 and F, one compares it to the Hamlet stories that pre-date Shakespeare, not only to the extant texts by Saxo Grammaticus and François de Belleforest, but to the clues that survive of the lost legend before Saxo and the elusive *Ur-Hamlet* of 1589, Q1 ceases to look like an anomaly and begins to look like a stepping-stone between those stories and Shakespeare's longer versions of the play.

LIÐMELDR AMLÓÐA AND THE PATTERN OF THE TRICKSTER

The textual record of the Hamlet story is a thing of shreds and patches. There are several texts and more than one gap. Hamlet emerges only to disappear again before reappearing in a later text. To try to understand the history that led to the appearance of Q1 in 1603 is to try to get inside these gaps: to sift the earlier texts through the perforations in the record and to see what remains. Hamlet makes his earliest entrance in extant literature in a short verse attributed to the poet Snæbjörn, contained in Snorri Sturluson's catalogue of Norse poetry known as his *Edda* (circa 1220):

Sem Snæbjörn kvað:

> Hvatt kveða hrœra Grotta
> hermgrimmistan skerja
> út fyrir jarða\<r\> skauti
> eylúðrs níu brúðir,
> þær er – lungs – fyrir löngu
> liðmeldr – skipa hlíðar
> baugskerðir rístr barði
> ból – Amlóða mólu.

Hér er kallat hafit Amlóða kvern.[5]

It is only a fleeting appearance. Hamlet (Amlóði) appears in the kenning *liðmeldr Amlóða* (Hamlet's *liðmeldr* or the *liðmeldr* of Hamlet). The kenning is difficult to interpret because of the elusive sense of *liðmeldr*. It is a compound word made from *meldr* 'meal' and *lið* 'ship/vessel', 'ale', 'a host of people/army' or as *liðr* 'a bone-joint'. This has led to a number of translations, among them: 'ship-meal', 'drink-meal' and Faulkes's choice 'meal-ship' (Faulkes, *Skáldskaparmál* p. 346). Leaving aside exactly what the kenning refers to for the moment, what is perhaps more significant to the history of the Hamlet stories is its very existence in the stanza. Since kennings work by alluding to myths or legends that are external to the poems in which they stand, *liðmeldr Amlóða* requires an external Icelandic Hamlet story upon which an audience could draw in order to interpret its meaning. Any aspect of the kenning could have been part of the legend. What's more, when Snæbjörn wrote his verse, the Hamlet story must have been immediate enough to his audience for them to be able to interpret the kenning and its relation to the poem. Since Snorri was collating fragments of poetry that he used in his *Edda* around 1230, Snæbjörn must have lived sufficiently early for Snorri to have considered him an established poet. The lost Hamlet legend must, therefore, have been very old indeed. Unfortunately, Snæbjörn's verse does not refer directly to the content of the legend. Hamlet is only a passing allusion in the stanza. The central figure is the *baugskerðir* 'ring-damager [prince]' cutting his ship across the waves. However, a puzzle in the verse's imagery may shed a tiny shard of light back to the

---

[4] Alan C. Dessen, 'Weighing the Options in Hamlet Q1', in Clayton, ed., *The Hamlet First Published*, pp. 65–78, p. 66.

[5] Snorri Sturluson, *Edda: Skáldskaparmál*, ed., Anthony Faulkes, 2 vols. (London, 1998), 1, p. 38. Prose word order (my own): *Sem Snæbjörn kvað: kveða níu brúðir skerja hrœra hvatt hermgrimmistan Grotta eylúðrs út fyrir jarðar skauti þær er fyrir löngu mólu liðmeldr Amlóða. Baugskerðir rístr barði skipa ból hlíðar lungs.*

'As Snæbiorn said: They say the nine skerry-brides [Ægir's daughters, waves] turn fast the most hostile island-box-mill [churning sea] out beyond the land's edge, they who long ago ground Hamlet's meal-ship [Hamlet's mill = sea]. The ring damager [generous ruler] cuts with the ship's prow the dwelling [sea] of the ship's slopes [waves]. Here the sea is called Hamlet's mill', from Snorri Sturluson, *Edda*, ed. and trans., Anthony Faulkes, pp. 92–3.

lost legend as well as sideways to the Danish Hamlet story found in Saxo Grammaticus's *Gesta Danorum* (*c.* 1200).

Snorri cites the Snæbjörn fragment in answer to the question *Hvernig skal sæ kenna?* 'How shall sea be referred to?' because it contains repeated periphrastic descriptions of the ocean. The nine brides of the skerries [waves] are qualified with the clause that contains the Hamlet kenning: *þær er mólu fyrir löngu liðmeldr Amlóða* 'they who long ago ground Hamlet's *liðmeldr*'. Snorri himself seems to provide an interpretation of the Hamlet kenning in his gloss on the verse: *Hér er kallat hafit Amlóða kvern* 'Here the sea is called Hamlet's mill'. On the face of it, it seems that Snorri considers *liðmeldr* [?meal ship] to be synonymous with *kvern* 'quern/mill' and that both *liðmeldr Amlóða* and *Amlóða kvern* are kennings for the sea. If, however, *liðmeldr Amlóða* is indeed a kenning for the sea, a fully extrapolated version of the stanza's initial lines might read: 'they say the waves move/turn [*hrœra*] the sea out beyond the land's edge, they who long ago ground [*mólu*] the sea'. This interpretation is curious for two reasons. Firstly, it appears odd to define the waves that are presently churning the sea with the same action in the past. Secondly, it seems peculiar that the waves should grind water. The possibility, therefore, arises that *liðmeldr Amlóða* is not, in fact, a kenning for the sea and that Snorri either did not mean it was synonymous with *Amlóða kvern* or, somewhat characteristically, he was guessing. In his essay 'Hamlet in Iceland' Israel Gollancz offers an alternative interpretation of the kenning: 'There seems, therefore, no reason why "meldr-lið" should not be preferred to "lið-meldr," which might well stand for "ship-meal" (? "sea-meal," to be compared with the Eddaic phrase "grædis meldr," *i.e.*, sea-flour, a poetical periphrasis for the sand of the shore)' (p. xv; see n.22 below). If, as Snorri says, the sea is *Amlóða kvern* 'Hamlet's mill', it seems appropriate that the meal which it grinds should be the sand. Thus, the lost legend may, at the least, have associated Hamlet with flour, mills, sand or the sea and, at the most, related him to the sea milling the sand. To whatever degree the legend uses this imagery, there seems to be a cor-relation between Hamlet's mill and a moment on the seashore in Saxo's *Gesta Danorum*.

Saxo's Amleth is the only one to deduce that his uncle Fengo has killed his father, so he feigns madness in order to win time to plan his revenge. The courtiers become suspicious, however, and plan to test the authenticity of his madness by setting him challenges of interpretation. It is at this point that the intriguing link to Snæbjörn occurs:

Idem littus praeteriens cum comites invento periclitatae navis gubernaculo cultrum a se eximiae granditatis repertum dixissent: eo inquit praegrandem pernam secari convenit: profecto mare signficans, cujus immensitati gubernaculi magnitude congrueret. Harenarum quoque praeteritis clivis, sabulum perinde as farra aspicere jussus eadem albicantibus maris procellis permolita esse respondit.[6]

The imagery of both the riddles of the rudder and of the sand are strongly connected to the sea. Hansen points out that the ham metaphor is an Old Danish pun on *laar* 'thigh' and 'coastal waters' (Hansen, p. 128), which he cites as an indication that the Saxo story was at the very least an oral Danish tale before it was written down in Latin. As his companions test Hamlet's discernment by referring to the sand as flour, Hamlet takes up the allusion and reckons the flour to have been ground by the sea storms. The potential correlation to Snæbjörn is evident. Both early Scandinavian texts conceive of the sea as a mill, and while the *meldr* 'meal' is only implicitly ground as sand in Snæbjörn, it is explicitly so in Saxo. Neither is the sand riddle

---

[6] Saxo Grammaticus, *Gesta Danorum*, from *Hamlet from the Historia Danica of Saxo Grammaticus*, in *The Sources of Hamlet*, ed. Israel Gollancz (London 1967; first published 1926), pp. 94–162, pp. 107–8 [hereafter, 'Saxo']. 'As he was passing along a beach and came upon the rudder of a wrecked ship, his companions said that he had found a huge knife. "Yes," he said, "it is suitable for cutting a huge ham" by which he really meant the sea, since its vastness matched the size of the rudder. They also came by some sand dunes and told him to look at the flour, meaning the sand. He replied that it had been ground fine and bleached by the storms of the sea. His companions praised his retort, and said that he had put it rather well', from William F. Hansen, *Saxo Grammaticus and the Life of Hamlet* (Nebraska, 1983), pp. 99–100 (hereafter, 'Hansen').

incidental to the Saxo story. When, in the second half of Saxo's story, Hamlet becomes king, a shield is made on which are illustrated all the details of his life:

Istic depingi videres Horwendilli jugulum: Fengonis cum incestu parricidium . . . adhibitam insidiis foeminam . . . inventum gubernaculum: praeteritum subulum . . . elusis comitibus rem seorsum cum virgine habitam.[7]

(p. 142)

The passing of the sand is mentioned as an integral part of Hamlet's history. Inscribed on the shield, the sand puzzle stands shoulder to shoulder with other major episodes in the story. Hamlet's ability to use words with a mixture of trickery and insight to express his situation and to interpret the riddles that are dealt him while keeping ahead of the game is emphasized as a fundamental aspect of Saxo's narrative. The early Icelandic legend may have included such riddling: Hamlet's mill as the sea or the waves grinding the sand, or even a passage in which the cunning Amlóði alluded to the sand as flour in order to outwit his opponents.

In her essay 'Loki and Saxo's Hamlet' H. R. Ellis Davidson posits a Norse tradition of the wily hero: 'The character of the cunning trickster is a favourite one in the Icelandic Sagas; he is devious, plausible and ruthless, and better men than he meet their deaths through his strange skills and elaborate strategies' (p. 3). Ellis Davidson argues that with characters such as Ofeigr in *Bandamanna Saga* and Snorri the Goði in *Eyrbyggja Saga* 'the Saga writers have developed a vague tradition of skill and duplicity into a definite pattern, the pattern of the Trickster' (p. 3). The character of the trickster lies at the heart of Norse mythology. Both the gods Loki and Oðinn are renowned for their capacity to dissemble. While the figure of Loki as a trickster is ultimately humorous, mischievously tying his testicles to the beard of a goat to make the goddess Skaði laugh and, in the poem *Lokasenna*, alluding to his sexual trysts with her, Oðinn is a more ominous presence, always one step ahead, assuming disguises to pursue his undisclosed ends. Ellis Davidson considers Saxo's Amleth to fall within the tradition of this darker trickster:

Yet Amleth is hardly a true parallel to Loki; he is in a desperate and not a comic situation; he only seems a fool to those who lack the discernment to appreciate his true wit; and he has a ruthless savagery in obtaining his ends which is more characteristic of Odin. Like Odin he knows precisely what he is about, and perseveres with apparently pointless schemes until they reach fruition, causing terrible suffering; like Odin again he can see what is hidden, and has the gift of verbal dexterity which enables him to excel in riddles.[8]

The gift of verbal dexterity is, indeed, fundamental to Saxo's Amleth. He is a trickster who dissembles and riddles his way to vanquishing his enemies. What the Snæbjörn kenning, the Danish story and potentially the saga tradition have in common is their interest in this verbal dexterity.

THE TRICKSTER AND Q1

Q1 picks up strongly on the idea of Hamlet as a trickster. If in no other way, his hero came to Shakespeare via the Hamlet story in François de Belleforest's *Histoires Tragiques*, which follows the shape of Saxo, translating and augmenting it, but keeping as its basic premise (in the first half, at least) the account of the series of trials of the trickster. In the words of Geoffrey Bullough:

The source story involved a period of waiting between the perpetration of the old king's murder and the accomplishment of his son's revenge. This was punctuated rather than filled by the various tests of Amleth, the sexual encounter in the forest, the closet scene with the Queen . . . and the journey towards England . . . These incidents are almost all initiated by Amleth's enemies; he is lurking, avoiding all appearance of rational behaviour or vengeful planning, yet mingling shy mocking and disturbing *double entendres* with apparent imbecility.[9]

---

[7] On the shield you could see painted the murdering of Ørvendil, Fengi's fratricide and incest . . . the woman who was to seduce him . . . the rudder they came upon, the sand they passed . . . and his secretly having sexual relations with the maiden (Hansen, p. 111).

[8] 'Loki and Saxo's Hamlet' in Poul V. A. William, ed., *The Fool and the Trickster* (Cambridge, 1979), p. 15.

[9] See Geoffrey Bullough, ed., *Narrative and Dramatic Sources of Shakespeare*, 8 vols. (London, 1957–75) vol. 7, p. 50.

Q1 clearly follows this outline. Hamlet adopts his disguise and the period of preparing his revenge is punctuated by three tests, each of which he overcomes with guile. First, he is tested with Ofelia in the nunnery scene (the equivalent of the sexual encounter in the forest). Next, he is sent to his mother in her closet (a plan which, unlike in Q2 and F, is made sometime before the play within the play,[10] so that it is not a spontaneous reaction to the king's displeasure but an anticipated episode in the plot's overall structure). Finally, Hamlet is sent to England where he escapes 'the danger / And subtle treason that the king had plotted' (Q1, 14.3–4, p. 82).

In terms of Hamlet as a trickster, the position of the nunnery scene is an important aspect of Q1. As in the sources, as soon as Hamlet puts on his antic disposition the plan is hatched to put Ofelia before him as bait to test the nature of his madness. Corambis is keen to plant Ofelia in a specific place where, like Belleforest's girl in the woods, Hamlet will come across her, 'The prince's walk is here in the gallery / There let Ofelia walk until he comes' (Q1, 7.103–4, p. 58). He soon gets the opportunity since Hamlet enters unexpectedly:

KING   See where he comes poring upon a book.

Enter HAMLET.

CORAMBIS   Madam, will it please your grace to leave us here?

GERTRED   With all my heart.

CORAMBIS   And here, Ofelia, read you on this book
And walk aloof; the king shall be unseen.

[*Exeunt King and Corambis*]

HAMLET   To be, or not to be; ay, there's the point.

(Q1, 109–14)

It is entirely plausible that when Q1 Hamlet enters in scene 7, appearing for the first time after he has adopted his disguise, he is aware of the trap. The Hamlet of Belleforest is always one step ahead of his assailants and it would seem quite out of character with the sources for Q1 Hamlet to adopt

the habit of the trickster only to be immediately tricked himself. Hamlet's entrance is marked four lines before he begins to speak. With Corambis already established as loud-mouthed, it is possible that Hamlet overhears the instructions to Gertred and Ofelia. 'To be or not to be', therefore, becomes a performance of trickery with Hamlet pretending he is suicidal in order to demonstrate to the king that he is harmless: a prime motivation for Belleforest's Hamlet in choosing to counterfeit 'le fol.'[11]

Q1 also picks up strongly on the idea of Hamlet as a sexual trickster in the nunnery scene. The premise of the episode with the girl in both Belleforest and Saxo is primarily sexual. Hamlet is only truly mad if he does not attempt to seduce the girl, 'D'autant que le naturel de tout jeune home, mesmement estant nourry a son aise, est si transporté aux plaisirs de la chair, et se lance avec telle impetuosité à la jouyssance, qui lui est octroyee, de ce qui est excellemment beau, qu'il est presque impossible de couvrir telle affection.'[12] It is never clear whether or not Belleforest's Hamlet seduces her although he later affirms that he has. The Q1 nunnery scene highlights this ambiguity and plays on it more explicitly than Q2 and F:

HAMLET   I never gave you nothing.

OFELIA   My lord, you know right well you did.

(Q1, 7.150–1)

The pun on 'nothing' sexualizes the dialogue. In denying that he and Ofelia have slept together, the trickster creates the possibility that they have. This ambiguity is taken up again later when Ofelia sings

---

[10] Q1, 8.31–6, p. 67.

[11] François de Belleforest, *Le Cinquiesme Tome des Histoires Tragiques*, (Paris, 1582), in *The Sources of Hamlet*, ed. Israel Gollancz (London 1967; first published 1926), pp. 164–310, p. 192 (hereafter 'Belleforest'); 'the madman' from *The Hystorie of Hamblet* (London, 1608) in *The Sources of Hamlet*, ed. Israel Gollancz (London 1967; first published 1926), pp. 165–311, p. 193 (hereafter 'Hystorie').

[12] 'for the nature of all young men (especially such as are brought up wantonlie) is so transported with the desires of the flesh and entreth so greedily into the pleasures thereof that it is impossible to cover the foul affection' (*Hystorie*, p. 199).

about the sexual trickery of men once she has gone mad. If Corambis is suggested behind her song about the dead man, Hamlet is surely suggested behind the song about the seducer:

> By Gis and by Saint Charity
> Away and fie for shame!
> Young men will do't when they come to't
> By cock they are to blame.

> Quoth she, 'Before you tumbled me,
> You promised me to wed'
> 'So would I 'a done, by yonder sun,
> If thou hadst not come to my bed'
> (Q I, 13.97–104)

The young man in the song has misled the girl, tricking her into bed by promising to marry her. Although in the Q I nunnery scene it is Hamlet's 'love' that Ofelia has been tricked by, she shares the feeling with the girl of having been misled:

HAMLET   I never loved you.
OFELIA   You made me believe you did.
(Q I, 7.156–7, p. 59)

Whereas Q2 and F's Hamlet claims to have loved Ophelia once and then later denies it, Q I's Hamlet was apparently always deceiving her. His disposition as a deceiver is starker than the Hamlet of the longer versions, the 'crimes' (Q I, 7.160, p. 59) of which he could accuse himself (including Ofelia's possible defloration) darker. Since the nunnery scene comes earlier in Q I than in Q2 and F, before Hamlet has begun to think about his plan for the players, his exchange with Ofelia comes on the heels of the back-story about the precise nature of their relationship. It is clearer in Q I that the recent intensifying of their relationship, to which Laertes refers in his warnings to his sister, has been suddenly cut short by Hamlet's adoption of his antic disposition. Ofelia's shock at his alteration seems fresher because of this than in Q2 and F, and Hamlet's trickery, and the question of whether or not he has behaved inappropriately towards her, closer to the surface of the scene. Since the scene comes before Hamlet has hatched his plan for revenge, the nature of their relationship carries a significance to

the plot that makes Ofelia's plight less marginal to Q I than it appears in the longer versions. In Q I, her descent into madness potentially springs as much from Hamlet's humiliation, rejection and possible ruination of her, as it does from her father's death.

Q I Hamlet's riddling continues immediately after the nunnery scene in the fishmonger episode so that the initial introduction of him as a trickster is concentrated. Irace thinks that this order elucidates the episode: 'The juxtaposition of Nunnery Scene and the Fishmonger episode makes the reasons for Hamlet's bitter remarks even clearer in Q I than they are in Q2/F: Hamlet has perhaps seen Polonius (and the King) behind the arras; he certainly heard Ophelia's lie about where Polonius is, and may suspect that he is the cause of her altered behaviour.'[13] It is certainly true that, if Hamlet is aware that his confrontation with Ofelia was a trap, his interaction with Corambis is all the more pointed. Hamlet's pregnant replies appear, in Q I, like a final flurry of sword strokes after the combat of the nunnery scene, to ensure absolutely that he has outfoxed his opponents. Having overcome the first test by baffling the king and Corambis, Q I Hamlet has the space to entertain Rossencraft and Gilderstone, welcome the players and resolve upon the plan that he makes in the 'dunghill idiot slave' soliloquy (Q I, 7.355, p. 65) to 'catch the conscience of the king' (Q I, 7.387, p. 66). The trickster Hamlet, unfettered by delay, is then able to put his plan of revenge into action almost immediately, re-entering after an absence of only forty lines to rehearse the players.

As in Belleforest, Q I Hamlet only entirely drops the demeanour of the trickster when, in his second major test, he is sent to his mother in her closet. Privacy is essential to him if he is to reveal his true nature to his mother without others overhearing and ruining his chances of revenge, so he resolves to 'make all safe' (Q I, 11.6, p. 74), presumably securing the chamber before he feels he can speak honestly to his mother. Once he has secured the

---

13 Irace, 'Origins and Agents of Q I Hamlet', in Clayton, ed., *The Hamlet First Published*, pp. 90–122, p. 104.

room, killing Corambis in the process, Q1 Hamlet unmasks his lucidity, revealing to Gertred the full extent of her crime, 'A! have you eyes and can you look on him / That slew my father, and your dear husband, / To live in the incestuous pleasure of his bed?' (Q1, 11.39–41, p. 75), and demonstrating his own sanity, 'my pulse doth beat like yours. / It is not madness that possesseth Hamlet' (Q1, 11.88, p. 76). As Belleforest's Geruthe quickly resolves to help her son as soon as she sees that he has been tricking them, 'puis que l'esprit estant sain, je voy les moyens plus aysez de la vengeance de ton pere'[14] (Belleforest, p. 220), so Q1 Gertred gives her full support to Hamlet's plan for revenge, once she sees that he has been playing the trickster:

HAMLET   And mother, but assist me in my revenge,
         And in his death your infamy shall die.
GERTRED   Hamlet, I vow by that majesty
         That knows our thoughts and looks into our hearts,
         I will conceal, consent, and do my best,
         What stratagem soe'er thou shalt devise.
                (Q1, 11.93–8, p. 77)

Gertred trusts Hamlet. The trickster Hamlet's phases of madness and lucidity are clearly polarized; so it is more evident to Gertred that her son has definitely been dissembling than it is to her Q2 and F counterparts. She puts his perceived hallucination of his father down to his 'heart's grief' (Q1, 11.82, p. 76) rather than madness and tells the king that Hamlet is 'raging' (Q1, 11.103, p. 77) without using the word 'mad'. True to her word, Gertred sides with Hamlet, sending him advice via Horatio, 'Bid him a while be wary of his presence, / Lest that he fail in that he goes about' (Q1, 14.19–20, p. 83). Meanwhile, Q1 Hamlet re-adopts his trickster disguise, and, ever riddling, 'My mother, I say . . . and so my mother, farewell. For England, ho' (Q1, 11.150–1, p. 78), is shipped towards England during which time he will outwit the king's plan to have him dispatched.

Q2 AND F: THE TRICKSTER TRANSFORMED?

Although there are significant differences between Hamlet's words in the Second Quarto and the First Folio, the character is fundamentally recognizable as the same man. He seems differently conceived from the Q1 trickster Hamlet. The play moves away from the cunning planner to a figure who ultimately becomes the scholar, the introspective, the melancholic, the Romantic. The ruthless determination that the trickster employs to succeed in his long-term clandestine goal of revenge means that there is little access into the inner workings of his mind. In fact, the purpose of his riddling is to obstruct this access. By contrast, Q2 and F's Hamlet ruminates rather than plans. His scenes with Horatio and the soliloquies provide a degree of access to his interior that is denied in the sources and Q1. Indeed, the longer versions supply such access to his mind and thoughts that they become plays about the very nature of interiority and perception. If anything, it is Hamlet's enemies who are the tricksters in Q2 and F, not him. Polonius is all too alert to the judiciousness of psychological privacy, advising Laertes, 'give thy thoughts no tongue, / Nor any unproportion'd thought his act'[15] before schooling Reynaldo in the arts of deception and surveillance, 'And thus doe we of wisedome, and of reach, / With windlesses, and with assaies of bias / By indirections find directions out' (Q2, 2.1.61–3, p. 72). Claudius is equally a master of manoeuvre and manipulation, conditioning the entire court from the beginning of the play to think of him as reasonable and even-handed: 'Yet so farre hath discretion fought with nature, / That we with wisest sorrowe thinke on him / Together with remembrance of our selves' (Q2, 1.2.5–7, p. 25). His disguise is almost impenetrable. Far more so than the

---

[14] 'For seeing that thy sences are whole and sound, I am hope to see an easie means invented for the revenging of thy father's death' (*Hystorie*, p. 221).

[15] William Shakespeare, *The Three-Text Hamlet: Parallel Texts of the First and Second Quartos and First Folio*, ed. Paul Bertram and Bernice W. Kliman (New York, 1991), Q2 (1604–5), 1.3.59–60, p. 44 (hereafter 'Q2').

king of Q1, Claudius is a shrewd and treacherous force whom Hamlet cannot afford to underestimate.

Unlike the trickster, the Hamlets of Q2 and F seem disabled by their inner lives, rather than spurred on by them, 'And thus the Native hew of Resolution / Is sicklied o're, with the pale cast of Thought',[16] with Q2 Hamlet in particular becoming a procrastinator:

> now whether it be
> Bestiall oblivion, or some craven scruple
> Of thinking too precisely on th'euent,
> A thought which quartered hath but one part wisedom,
> And ever three parts coward, I doe not know
> Why yet I live to say this thing's to doe,
> Sith I have cause, and will, and strength, and meanes
> To doo't
>
> (Q2, 4.4.41–8)

The idea of the Hamlet of Q1, Saxo or Belleforest deliberating his self-determination is laughable. Rather than the trickster, Shakespeare makes Q2 Hamlet the thinker. Yet, his transformation into an intellectual is not without its problems. The re-casting of Hamlet strains the fundamental plot of the Hamlet tradition. The simple chronology of Hamlet feigning madness and then being tested becomes fuzzy in the chronology of Q2 and F. The 'tested' no longer, Hamlet is reconceived as the tester, assessing everyone around him. His delay in pursuing revenge is insufficiently accounted for and, as the thinker, it seems strange that his capacity for self-scrutiny is not more successful at generating resolute conclusions and action. The further Shakespeare moves away from the underlying story of the trickster, the less the plot makes straightforward sense. As Lukas Erne writes,

For the order in which the long texts dramatise events seems in some ways rather odd. Polonius suggests spying on Hamlet with the help of Ophelia, but rather than putting this plan into practice, Polonius and the King wait until the next day. The succession of Hamlet's moods is perhaps more surprising. After the arrival of the actors, he forges a plan: 'I'll have these players / Play something like the murder of my father / Before mine uncle. I'll observe his looks, / I'll tent him to the quick. If a but

blench, / I know my course'. At the end of the second act, Hamlet is finally ready to take action. Yet, when he re-enters some fifty lines later, he muses on suicide and seems to have forgotten about his project.[17]

The chronology of scenes in Q2 and F between the arrival of the players and the performance of *The Mousetrap* does indeed seem rather odd. Hamlet oscillates between the euphoria of 'The Play's the thing, /Wherein Ile catch the Conscience of the King' (Q2, 2.2.604–5, p. 118) to the paralysis of 'To be or not to be' (Q2, 3.1.55, p. 122), only to re-enter vigorously with 'Speak the speech' (Q2, 3.2.1, p. 130) thirty lines after his exit at the end of the nunnery scene. Hamlet's oscillation makes little sense and bears no resemblance to the Hamlets of Q1, Saxo or Belleforest, who always have one eye on the long-term goal of revenge. The degree of complexity in the Q2 and F soliloquy, coupled with its fame, make it difficult to write off as a ruse to trick the hidden listeners into thinking that Hamlet is suicidal and, therefore, of no threat. However, Shakespeare's magnification of the idea of Hamlet as a melancholic, which Belleforest introduced somewhat incidentally to the Hamlet tradition, does not sit well with his persona as a revenge hero. The entire sequence of the second half of Act 3, scene 1 from 'To be or not to be' appears to sit outside of the development of the play as a whole in Q2 and F, with the nunnery scene in particular having something altogether vestigial about it. The back-story concerning Hamlet and Ophelia is a distant memory to the audience, now that Hamlet has hatched his plan to test Claudius. Since Q2 and F's Hamlets are not necessarily aware of the trap, it is not clear why they wish to humiliate their respective Ophelias. The scene is no longer the overt sex-test that it is in the sources, nor the trial of Hamlet's mettle and desire that it is in Q1, but an opaque melange of anger and bitterness, strewn with vague allusions to Ophelia's virginity,

---

[16] Shakespeare, *The Three-Text Hamlet*, F1 (1623), 3.1.83–4, p. 125 (hereafter 'F').

[17] See Lukas Erne, *Shakespeare as Literary Dramatist* (Cambridge, 2003), p 235.

'Are you honest? . . . Are you faire?' (Q2, 3.1.102–4). The indistinct sexual material seems to be a residue of the sources but it is not clear what significance it holds to Q2 and F any more. Hamlet the melancholic no longer seems to have the drive to be a seducer.

The nunnery scene is not the only relic. Though Q2 and F's Hamlets no longer have the conviction of the trickster, they remain riddlers. Shakespeare may recast Hamlet as an intellectual but his inclination to riddle permeates his speech even from before the time that he puts his antic disposition on. From his first utterance, 'A little more then kin, and lesse then kind' (Q2, 1.2.65, p. 28), Hamlet tricks his way through the play: on the battlements, 'There's never a villain dwelling in all Denmark / But he's an arrant knave' (Q2, 1.5.123–4, p. 62); with Polonius, 'For yourself, sir, shall grow old as I am – if like a crab you could go backward' (Q2, 2.2.202–4, p. 94); at the play-within-the-play, 'Excellent, i'faith, of the chameleon's dish. I eat the air, promise crammed' (Q2, 3.2.94–5, p. 136); with Rosencrantz and Guildenstern, 'You would play upon me, you would seem to know my stops' (Q2, 3.2.364, p. 154); again with Polonius, 'Do you see yonder cloud that's almost in shape of a Camel?' (Q2, 3.2.377, p. 154); again with Rosencrantz and Guildenstern, 'The body is with the King but the King is not with the body' (Q2, 4.3.27–8, p. 182); with Claudius, 'A man may fish with the worme that hath eate of a king, and eate of the fish that hath fed of that worme' (Q2, 4.3.27–8, p. 184); and with Osric, 'But yet me thinkes it is very sully and hot for my complection' (Q2, 5.2.99, p. 248). It seems that Shakespeare considered riddling a fundamental requirement of the Hamlet story and the primary characteristic of his antic disposition. Yet, his antic disposition no longer appears entirely necessary to Q2 and F. Whereas the Hamlets of Saxo and Belleforest instinctively sense the king's guilt from the beginning and are in danger of being seen as too perceptive, Shakespeare's Hamlet does not really need to adopt an antic disposition disguise because Claudius has already professed friendship to him. In fact, Claudius only becomes suspicious when Hamlet begins to act strangely. Neither does

Hamlet's riddling serve to conceal his plan for revenge since, to begin with at least, he does not have one. Yet, Shakespeare considers the riddles important enough to the story to include them in his conception of Q2 and F. Curiously, though Shakespeare is not known to have read Saxo, the riddles appear to be residual of the Scandinavian tradition, rather than Belleforest (who merely says of Hamlet, 'toutes ses actions, et gestes, n'estoyent que les contenances d'un home qui est privé de toute raison et entendement, de sorte qui ne servoit plus que de passetemps aux pages et courtesans'[18] (Belleforest, p. 194)). There is a visually memorable quality in the riddles of the rudder and the sand, and in Shakespeare's backward moving crab and camel, weasel or whale-shaped cloud that is suggestive of an oral tradition that reaches back as far as Snæbjörn's mill churning the sea or further. The riddles serve Amleth in diverting attention away from his purpose while still enabling him to hold on to his honesty:

Qui cum illo prudenti response usum astruerent: ipse quoque se de industria locutum asseverabat, ne aliqua ex parte mendacio indulgere videretur. Falsitatis enim alienus haberi cupiens ita astutiam veriloquio permiscebat: ut nec dictis veracitas deesset, nec acuminis modus verorum iudicio proderetur.[19] (Saxo, p. 106)

Q2 and F's Hamlet retains the basic desire for integrity of his ancestor in Saxo. Indeed, the Hamlet of the longer versions' incessant impulse towards contemplation seems to spring from this search for integrity. There are other similarities with Saxo. Just as the riddles are left out of the story by Belleforest, so are the companions who test

---

[18] 'all his actions and jestures being no other than the right countenances of a man wholly deprived of all reason and understanding in such a sort, that as then he seemed fitte for nothing but to make sport to the pages and ruffling courtiers' (*Hystorie*, p. 195).

[19] They said that he had given a clever answer, and he declared that he had meant to do so, since he did not want people to think that he ever indulged in lying. Amleth desired to be held an honest man, but he mixed truth and cleverness in such a way that you could not call his words false, although they did not betray their real meaning (Hansen, p. 99).

Hamlet's perception with the rudder and the sand. Yet, these companions look mysteriously like the Rosencrantz and Guildenstern figures that survive into Shakespeare.

It is uncertain how these traces of the earlier Hamlet tradition, which are not picked up firmly by Belleforest, made their way into Shakespeare's conception of Q2 and F. It may be that the missing *Ur-Hamlet* was somehow a bridge between the two traditions. This late sixteenth-century play, probably staged before 1589 when Thomas Nashe mentioned 'whole Hamlets' in his introduction to Robert Greene's *Menaphon*,[20] was performed in London in the early 1590s when Philip Henslowe recorded a performance in his diary and Thomas Lodge wrote of 'the ghost which cried so miserably at the theatre, like an oyster-wife, Hamlet, revenge!'[21] Unless he was the author himself, Shakespeare certainly borrowed from the *Ur-Hamlet* to some degree, using the device of the ghost to spur on his son to revenge. If he borrowed these details he may well have borrowed others that had somehow made their way into the *Ur-Hamlet*, possibly from Saxo, which was published in Paris in 1514, in Strasbourg in 1547 and in Basel in 1548,[22] and possibly via an unknown route. Unfortunately, like the Icelandic legend, the play is simply lost to time and any discussion of it is little more than speculation. Nonetheless, it is evident that somehow the longer tradition survives into Shakespeare. Bullough postulates a reason for the unevenness of the unabsorbed relics in Q2 and F by suggesting that they were already patchy in the *Ur-Hamlet* and that Shakespeare was attracted to the dramatic potential of its scenes rather than the consistency of its plot:

It may well be that in taking over the old *Hamlet* and preserving its outlines Shakespeare was much less interested in explaining the delay inherent in the story than in the many interesting scenes to be presented during it . . . The Icelandic saga-hero, regarded as a pagan by Belleforest, is Christianized and put into a Renaissance setting, with allusions to Christmas, Wittenberg, Paris as a finishing-school for young courtiers, the latest in fencing-fashions etc. He becomes a modern, sophisticated University man faced with a task almost as likely to befall a prince in the sixteenth century as in the Dark Ages. It seems that Shakespeare was not greatly interested in filling the gaps in Kyd's motivation of the delay. He sketched a partial explanation and left his audiences to fill it out, and they have been doing so ever since.

(Bullough, *Narrative and Dramatic Sources*, p. 52)

It may well be that Shakespeare was not particularly interested in filling the gaps in Q2 and F. His interest was in the creation of an icon of thought, his most scholarly character, an epitome of insight, wit and sensitivity. Yet, however much he attempted to re-conceive Hamlet into a thinker, the trickster endured. The power of the trickster is so strong, in fact, that it opens the gaps that Shakespeare left in his conception of the Hamlet of Q2 and F. In the vestiges of the nunnery scene, in Hamlet's instinct for riddles, in his altercations with Rosencrantz and Guildenstern, in the killing of Polonius, in his mocking of Claudius before he is sent to England, it is not the intellectual but the cunning trickster who is glimpsed.

AFTER Q2 AND F: RE-ENTER THE TRICKSTER

The Hamlet tradition did not stop at Shakespeare. As *Ambales Saga* it continued in Iceland, independently from the English theatre, into the seventeenth century and beyond. While it is heavily influenced by medieval romance with dwarfs and pirates, prophetic witches, neighbouring kingdoms and distant lands, the saga is fundamentally an elaboration of the trickster story. Ambales feigns madness and gradually whittles sticks that are later used in his revenge (an activity shared by Saxo and Belleforest's heroes). The fact that he attains safety by adopting a foolish demeanour is emphasized particularly strongly in the saga. Ambales and his older brother are taken to see their father being hanged, and while his brother re-acts bitterly and

---

[20] George Duthie, *'Bad' Quarto of Hamlet* (Cambridge, 1941), p. 55.
[21] Duthie, *'Bad Quarto'*, p. 76.
[22] Hansen, p. 66.

is hanged too, Ambales saves himself from execution by behaving like a fool:

tók hann á ad er finna kunni og grítti sinn bródur med í andarslitrunum. Sögdu á allir ad slíkt grei væri; Sprurdi á hyrdinn Fástínus ad hvört deida skildi Fól etta? Enn han qvad ar eingan mun til draga, og sagdi hann til Skémtunar lifa mætti sér og höfdíngjunum.[23]

Once he has won safety a great period of time elapses. He acts like an idiot and hangs around the castle's kitchens where the servants give him the nickname 'Amlódi' which has come to mean 'fool' in modern Icelandic (*Hamlet in Iceland*, p. 70), indicating that the characteristic which he is most renowned for is his act of dissembling. He is not subjected to tests but takes refuge in his mother's chamber and eventually wreaks his revenge on the court by pinning them to their chairs and burning them to death where they sit.

The Hamlet tradition also survived well into the eighteenth century in the play *Der Bestrafte Brudermord*, 'Fratricide Punished', which is another text in the Hamlet tradition that takes this trickster quality for granted. The history of the play is surrounded by mystery. It appears to have some connection to Q1, or even the *Ur*-Hamlet, using the name Corambus and putting the nunnery scene immediately after it is planned. It is unclear how it came to be adapted from Shakespeare or translated into German but it was probably performed, in some version or other, in Germany and Scandinavia at various times between 1626 and 1690.[24] Even compared to the text of Q1 the play is a muddle: 'The original *Hamlet* is seen through a glass darkly' (Isaacs, p. xvii). All the battlement scenes are grouped together at the beginning so that, as in Saxo and Belleforest, Hamlet already knows of his uncle's guilt when he is first seen in court and the audience first meets the king. It is just possible that the *Ur-Hamlet* grouped the battlement scenes together like this and Shakespeare heightened the effect of suspense by delaying the conclusion of the battlement scenes to the end of the first act. There is almost no contemplation in *Der Bestrafte Brudermord*. Hamlet is said to be melancholy but, since there are no soliloquies, there is little insight

into it, and he moves quickly towards revenge. He is shrewd in adopting his disguise, aware that the king is particularly well defended, telling Horatio that 'through this assumed *madness* I hope to get the opportunity of *revenging* my father's death. But as my step-father is always surrounded by many guards it may miscarry.'[25] Having adopted his disguise, the *BB* Hamlet, who is something of a comic, riddles through the equivalent of the nunnery scene, 'stay girl – no, go to a nunnery, but not to a nunnery where two pairs of slippers lie at the side of the bedside' (*FP*, p. 16) before out-witting the England ploy with the aid of the pirates by tricking the equivalents of Rosencrantz and Guildenstern into shooting one another:

2ND PIRATE Well, we'll easily grant him this favour.

1ST PIRATE Go ahead!

HAMLET (*Spreading his hands.*) Shoot! (*Throwing himself forward on his face between the two, who shoot each other.*)

(*FP*, p. 28)

The play as a whole is closer to burlesque than tragedy, with mad Ophelia inviting the Osric-character, Phantasmo, to bed while he offers to 'soap' her and 'wash [her] out' (*FP*, p. 25). Though it is extremely slight and lacks the revenge momentum of Q1 or the complexity of Q2 and F, *Der Bestrafte Brudermord* is an entertaining play. It draws on the tradition of the trickster to fuel this romping entertainment. If the *BB* author did know Shakespeare it is an example of the trickster breaking back

---

[23] *Ambales Saga*, in Israel Gollancz, *Hamlet in Iceland* (London, 1898), p. 40.

'He seized whatever he might lay his hands on, and pelted his brother therewith while the life was passing from him. All said that such a dog as he could not be found. Then the court asked Faustinus whether this fool should be killed, but he said it mattered little, he might as well live and be sport for him and for his lords' (*Ambales Saga*, Gollancz, *Hamlet in Iceland*, p. 41).

[24] Bullough, *Narrative and Dramatic Sources*, p. 20.

[25] *Fratricide Punished*, in *William Poel's Prompt-Book of Fratricide Punished*, ed. J. Isaacs (London, 1956), p. 16 (hereafter '*FP*').

through; if he did not, then Shakespeare's conception is not strong enough to overwhelm it.

The trickster Hamlet is resilient. From the riddle of *liðmeldr Amlóða* to the burlesque bravura of *Der Bestrafte Brudermord* he persists. In sieving the textual record as a whole it becomes clear that the protagonists of Q 2 and F are not the platonic ideals of Hamlet but rather the versions of the character who least resemble the others. Out of Shakespeare's versions of the play, it is Q 1 that is the closest to the Hamlet tradition. It seems logical to me, therefore, that the play behind the memorial reconstruction of Q 1 was written between the earlier tradition and Shakespeare's reconceived vision

of the play: Shakespeare adapted the *Ur-Hamlet* into a conventional version of the Hamlet story (Q 1) and later transformed it into his masterwork (Q 2 and F). But this is a contentious view. If, as most Shakespearians believe, it came after the longer versions (a view that protects Q 2 from the iconoclastic insinuation that it does not represent Shakespeare's vision of the play as conceived in a single moment of quasi-divine creation), then Shakespeare or an unknown abridger must have felt the need to bring the play back closer to the tradition. While Shakespearians look at *Hamlet* and see the intellectual, the Elizabethans, it would seem, saw the trickster.

'SPEAK, THAT I MAY SEE THEE': SHAKESPEARE CHARACTERS AND COMMON WORDS

HUGH CRAIG

Recording the number of times a particular word or phrase is used in a passage, or the relative frequency of a metrical feature or of a rhetorical figure, has been a familiar practice in Shakespeare studies for at least a century. This sort of measurement and comparison is a staple of authorship studies. Along the way these practices have suffered some swingeing blows, such as Sir E. K. Chambers's attack of 1924 on the 'disintegrators',[1] Samuel Schoenbaum's ridicule of the 'parallelographic school' in the 1960s,[2] and Brian Vickers's recent demolition of the case for Shakespeare's authorship of *A Funerall Elegie*.[3] Nevertheless, they have proved indispensable (when soundly practised) as a complement to documentary evidence and to subjective estimates of what is, or is not, the authentic style of a particular writer. Statistical work plays a large part in Gary Taylor's *Textual Companion* to the Oxford Shakespeare (Oxford, 1980), and in important recent books by Vickers himself and by MacDonald P. Jackson.[4] It is sympathetically assessed in Harold Love's *Attributing Authorship: An Introduction* (Cambridge, 2002).

Much less use has been made of these methods in describing Shakespeare's style, or that of his peers, more generally, even in the age of effortless counting and calculation by the computer. Two exceptions are Barron Brainerd's work on pronouns and other common words in relation to genre and period in Shakespeare's works,[5] and Jonathan Hope's book on the sociolinguistics of Shakespeare's idiolect in contrast with Fletcher's.[6] (Hope and Michael Whitmore have recently presented the results from a more ambitious computational-

stylistics venture using a complete set of Shakespeare plays.[7]) Meanwhile there are promising precedents in other areas of English studies. John Burrows's book *Computation into Criticism: A Study of Jane Austen and an Experiment in Method* (Oxford, 1987) offers remarkable insights into the patterning of Jane Austen's language, and the subtly varied idiolects of her characters. Franco Moretti has applied quantitative analysis to a wide sweep of literary history, with fascinating results, in his *Graphs, Maps, Trees: Abstract Models for a Literary History* (London, 2005). David L. Hoover has demonstrated the extraordinary consistency of the progressive changes in the style of Henry James's novels through computational stylistics.[8]

[1] *The Disintegration of Shakespeare* (London, 1924).

[2] *Internal Evidence and Elizabethan Dramatic Authorship: An Essay in Literary History and Method* (London, 1966).

[3] *'Counterfeiting Shakespeare': Evidence, Authorship, and John Ford's Funerall Elegie* (Cambridge, 2002).

[4] Vickers, *Shakespeare, Co-Author: A Historical Study of the Five Collaborative Plays* (Oxford, 2003) and *Shakespeare, A Lover's Complaint, and John Davies of Hereford* (Cambridge, 2007); Jackson, *Defining Shakespeare: Pericles as Test Case* (Oxford, 2003).

[5] 'The Chronology of Shakespeare's Plays: A Statistical Study', *Computers and the Humanities* 14 (1980), 221–30, and 'Pronouns and Genre in Shakespeare's Drama', *Computers and the Humanities* 13 (1990), 3–16.

[6] *The Authorship of Shakespeare's Plays: A Sociolinguistic Study* (Cambridge, 1994).

[7] 'The Very Large Textual Object: A Prosthetic Reading of Shakespeare', *Early Modern Literary Studies*, 9 (2004), 6.1–36 (http://purl.oclc.org/emls/09-3/hopewhit.htm).

[8] 'Corpus stylistics, stylometry, and the styles of Henry James', *Style* 41 (2007), 160–89.

Part of the hesitation of Shakespearians in adopting the new methods must arise from doubts about the validity and value of assessing dramatic language like Shakespeare's through computation, and from uncertainty about how to interpret the constructs which the calculations produce. Can a statistical method be properly sympathetic to the richness and subtlety of literary language? Assuming that the data collection, and the procedures, are sound, can the results escape banality, and can any commentary on them be anything other than tautology, or wild speculation? While most would accept the usefulness of statistics in epidemiology, or market research, its application to literature still seems a barbarous practice. Stanley Fish's two articles on stylistics deny that the quantitative study of style can have any usefulness at all.[9] Even more sympathetic scholars like Willie van Peer have argued that the trade-off between what is countable, and what is of interest to literary scholars, must always result in a loss of all specifically literary aspects of textuality.[10] For a humanist like George Steiner computational techniques compromise the ineffable essence of literary works.[11] The post-structuralist, on the other hand, might see literary statistics as a display of extreme bad faith, insofar as it claims an application of the patterns of language to anything outside itself, and one free of ideology at that.[12]

My own view is that the computer has indeed made a difference. Given the abundance of machine-readable text now available, and the speed of processing now possible, literary statistics finally does have some particular things to offer which we can get in no other way. There is a bargain to be made. To count something, and thus secure the data on which the procedures can work, one must apportion linguistic features to a finite number of discrete categories. To do this, a thousand subtle distinctions obvious to every reader have to be ignored; but having done this, the computer can deploy a superhuman capacity to remember and to process systematically. The computer can make a representation of the textual world which is nothing like an interpretation, but is certainly directly and objectively related to that world. It offers a scientific instrument, as it were: a spectrometer, say,

which could never replace human vision in understanding an object, but can yield information not available to the naked eye.

Computation is in fact in sympathy with some aspects of language. Language is inherently repetitive and works by variation against a pattern of predictability. In its written form, at least, it works as an assembly of base-level items, words, which are necessarily limited in number because they must be shared by writer and reader. A finite set of items is repeated in different combinations to produce meaning. In this sense a language like English is not only susceptible to counting – each string of characters between spaces or punctuation is a recognizable item – but works in part by sheer frequency. An abundance of the words *I* and *me* relative to the established pattern for that kind of discourse conveys important information to the hearer; consistently writing *upon* where the reader expects *on* does the same.

The present article describes an experiment in which a group of Shakespeare characters are compared on the basis of their recourse to a small group of common words. At its heart is a statistical process drawing out some key patterns in contrast and likeness in the language of the characters. These calculations are performed though an open access website at the Centre for Literary and Linguistic Computing at Newcastle (Australia) and so can be replicated, or re-run with different stipulations, by anyone with an internet connection. A reader

---

9 'What Is Stylistics and Why Are They Saying Such Terrible Things About It?', *Approaches to Poetics: Selected Papers from the English Institute*, ed. Seymour Chatman (New York, 1973), pp. 109–52, and 'What Is Stylistics and Why Are They Saying Such Terrible Things About It? Part ii', *Boundary 2*, 8.1 (1979), 129–45.
10 'Quantitative Studies of Literature: A Critique and an Outlook', *Computers and the Humanities*, 23 (1989), 301–7.
11 *Real Presences: Is There Anything in What We Say?* (London, 1989), pp. 82–3.
12 No critique of this kind has in fact been mounted. Thomas Merriam does relate some of the postulates of post-structuralism to computational methods in 'Linguistic Computing in the Shadow of Postmodernism', *Literary and Linguistic Computing* 17 (2002), 181–92.

can thus check the results by reproducing them, or test some of the conclusions by running a similar experiment with (say) whole texts instead of characters. The website also allows users to launch an experiment of their own with a quite different set of words, and directed to a different aspect, like chronology, instead of character, genre or gender.[13]

The study begins with the commonest words, and the dialogue of the characters who speak most words overall. In this way the predilections of the researcher are allowed minimum play, since a simple principle of frequency is followed in selections. The commonest words tend to be function words like the pronouns, articles and conjunctions, and this has other advantages. It would seem on the face of it that they take less of their colour from their context, and thus are better candidates for counting, than lexical words. One instance of *you* is interchangeable with another, whereas (one might argue) one instance of *blood* is not. Examining only characters with larger spoken parts has the advantage that local variations, arising from particular settings or situations, tend to be ironed out by a balance with a variety of other settings and situations. Larger samples like these, we can hope, allow core tendencies, which might otherwise be masked, to be revealed. Smaller characters, though of course interesting in their own different ways, will tend to the idiosyncratic; if included, their extreme departures from the norm would tend to overwhelm the steadier patterning of the larger characters.

I have chosen as samples characters who speak more than 3,000 words in all (there are fifty of these), and as variables the fifty commonest words in this collection of dialogue. At the beginning, then, is a table fifty columns wide, one for each character, and fifty rows deep, one for each word. In each of the 2,500 cells of the table is a count for that word in that character's dialogue. The first step is to divide the counts by the total number of words for the character, so that (say) Hamlet's use of *you* is expressed as a fraction of his eleven and a half thousand spoken words, and can be compared with Isabella's, once her count has been divided by her total of just over 3,000 words.

To make some sense of the table we can call on a statistical procedure named Principal Component Analysis. This works to find a line of differentiation through the counts which accounts for the greatest amount of variation in it, as a process of 'data reduction'. It is as if, in a two-variable situation, one had counts for people's weights and counts for their height, and could simplify this to a single new variable, 'size', combining the two original ones. PCA looks for the new composite variable which accounts for most of the variation, then a second which accounts for the second largest amount, and so on. The new variables combine the counts from all the original variables, giving each of these contributory variables a different weighting. In a slightly more complicated case, one might take a series of counts of daily average temperature, rainfall, humidity and barometric pressure. The first principal component that emerged from this, the factor which accounts best for the various individual fluctuations of the measures, might well be related to the contrast between summer and winter, and the second to the difference between maritime and continental locations. In the case of the Shakespeare characters and the common-words data, one might expect a difference between comedy and tragedy, or perhaps early and late dates of composition, to be the strongest lines of difference. What we get is shown in illustration 23.

Here the horizontal axis is the first Principal Component, a mathematically derived 'factor' which accounts for sixteen per cent of all the variation in the table.[14] (If there were no patterns in the table, if all the variables fluctuated independently

---

[13] *PCA Online: The Shakespeare Computational Stylistics Facility,* www.newcastle.edu.au/cllc/pcaonline.

[14] The illustrations to the article use results from the Newcastle *PCA Online* website. This is also the source for the statistics for word-variables given here. *PCA Online* draws on the Moby Shakespeare text, a derivative of the Globe edition of the 1860s, obviously not all one would hope for in a Shakespeare text, but unambiguously in the public domain and so suitable for use in an open-access website like *PCA Online.* The Moby Shakespeare excludes *The Two Noble Kinsmen;* there would, of course, be arguments for including parts of this in a complete Shakespeare, and for excluding all

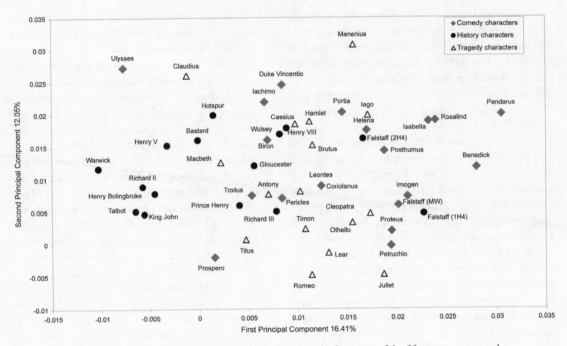

23 PCA plot of the fifty largest Shakespeare characters based on the frequency of the fifty commonest words.

of each other, we would expect a figure of two per cent for each Component.) The vertical axis is the second Principal Component, accounting for twelve per cent.

The graph maps characters according to their use of the fifty words, weighted so as to find two lines of best fit. Pandarus from *Troilus and Cressida* and Warwick from *The True Tragedy of Richard Duke of York* are the extremes along the continuum of the First Component, the horizontal axis. We can check a cognate map of the words to see which words are most significant in forming the continuum (illustration 24).

These are the same components, this time expressed in terms of the weightings of the word-variables. At the left-hand or Warwick end the words are *and, our, we, from, with* and *of.* At the right-hand, Pandarus end the words are *I, not* and *is.* First-person plural pronouns are opposed to first-person singular ones. Markers of complexity and precision in description and argument are set against markers of contradiction and immediacy. In

Douglas Biber's study of a range of modern writing and speech, he found that 'high informational density and exact informational content versus affective, interactional, and generalized content' was the primary factor of differentiation.[15] This contrast shares characteristics with the First Principal Component in this characters study, which pits markers of informational density (to the left-hand end of illustration 24) against words common in intensive interactions (to the right-hand end). It may be that this contrast between disquisitory and dialogic styles is a general feature which emerges in most large mixed language samples, rather than a peculiarly Shakespearian one. The words suggest impersonal, collective authority to the left, and individual assertion and contradiction to the right.

or parts of a number of plays that are represented, such as the *Henry VI* plays, *Macbeth* and *Pericles.*

[15] *Variation across Speech and Writing* (Cambridge, 1988), p. 107.

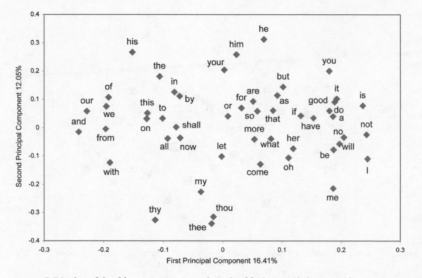

24 PCA plot of the fifty commonest words in the fifty largest Shakespeare characters.

Pandarus (to the right in illustration 23) is a character formed of negation, querulously undercutting and anxiously re-directing.

Nay, that shall not serve your turn; that shall it not, in truth, la. Nay, I care not for such words. No, no. – And, my lord, he desires you that, if the King call for him at supper, you will make his excuse.

(*Troilus and Cressida*, 3.1.72–5)

If he mouths the word 'truth' we can be sure the word 'not' is close by. He works upon others by qualifying and prevaricating: 'Faith, to say truth, brown and not brown', he says to Cressida of Troilus's colouring (1.2.92), trying, unnecessarily as it proves, to talk this blemish on Troilus's beauty out of existence.

Ulysses in the same play is at the other end of this spectrum. He has half as many *not*s as Pandarus, and a quarter the *I*s. At the extreme opposite to Pandarus is Warwick, notable for his use of *and*, with more than four instances in a hundred in his total dialogue. Warwick uses the conjunction to join events with a minatory inevitability: 'to London we will march, / And once again

bestride our foaming steeds, / And once again cry "Charge!" upon our foes' (*3 Henry VI*, 2.1.182–4).

Looking at the disposition of the characters by way of the genre symbols in illustration 23 gives further insight into the differentiae that the method has identified as the strongest in this analysis of the commonest words in the largest Shakespeare characters. Characters from history plays (with black circles as markers) tend to be towards the left, characters from comedies (marked by shaded diamonds) towards the right. Nobles and kings cluster at the choric end, go-betweens and wisecrackers at the interlocutory one, and going along with these more extreme tendencies are the more mainstream characters of history plays and comedies. The Hal of *The History of Henry the Fourth* (labelled 'Prince Henry' in illustration 23[16]) is to the left, and Petruccio from *The Taming of a Shrew* to the right. Going against the trend is one of the three Falstaff characters, the Falstaff of *The History of Henry the Fourth* – the black disk to the lower right – a character from a history play in territory occupied mainly by characters from comedy. (The fact that

---

[16] His part in *2 Henry IV* is not long enough to qualify.

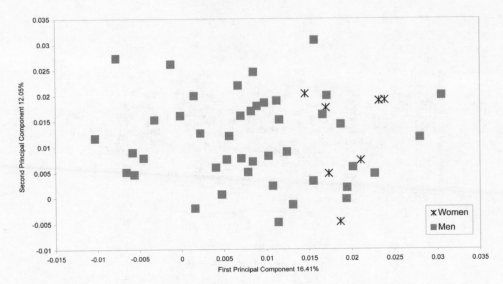

25 Characters identified by gender.

the three Falstaff parts constitute three of the fifty largest Shakespeare characters is itself of interest, a reminder that Shakespeare spent quite a large fraction of his total output in writing through this one vehicle.)

Ulysses from *Troilus and Cressida* (the shaded diamond to the top left) is the comedy character farthest to what we can call the history-play end. It is easy to see that this is because his is a choric role. He speaks for a collective rather than for himself, and about others rather than about himself. He makes well-developed pronouncements rather than involving himself in banter or altercation. There is not usually such a large role of this kind in Shakespearian comedy. Its presence is one of the many aspects that make this play unusual as a comedy.

Characters from tragedies (marked by hollow triangles) are in middling positions. Clearly the dialogue of tragedy overall is not sufficiently distinctive to make this one of the poles of Shakespeare's style in these terms. The graphs suggest that Shakespeare's generic range is better thought of as comedy versus history, rather than as comedy versus tragedy. This notion is supported by Hope and Whitmore's study of Shakespeare's writ-

ing as a 'Very Large Textual Object', based, like the present one, on computational methods, but with a much more mixed set of variables. Hope and Whitmore conclude that the contrast between history plays and comedies is the primary one to emerge from a linguistic study of the canon.[17]

To get a broad overview of the place of women characters as a group in this analysis, we can present the same results as in illustration 23, with labels this time reflecting gender instead of genre (illustration 25). The women characters are all in the right-hand half of the graph.

These characters do not often call on the grand coalitions implied by *we* and *our*; they speak more often of *I* and *me*; they respond to others' conversational gambits with *no* and *not*. There are seven women characters in all who speak more than three thousand words. The range in terms of the choric-reactive axis is from Portia (most choric) to Rosalind (most reactive), though this is in all not such a great range, only a little over a quarter of the span between Warwick and Pandarus.

---

[17] 'The Very Large Textual Object: A Prosthetic Reading of Shakespeare', paragraphs 21–33.

The vertical dimension of illustration 24 contrasts especially the masculine third person singular forms, and to a lesser extent the *you* forms, with *thou*. The users of *thou* and its partners are an interesting group: Romeo and Juliet, and then Prospero, King Lear, Petruccio and Titus Andronicus. There is no doubt that Shakespeare, along with the rest of his fellow-dramatists, and indeed his fellow speakers of English, used fewer of these forms as time went on. The replacement of *thou* forms with *you* ones is one of the most marked developments through the period of Early Modern English. The presence in the lower part of illustration 23 of Lear and Prospero, characters from the latter part of Shakespeare's career, goes against this trend. In his dialogue Prospero uses three instances of *thou* and *thee* to one of *you*. He addresses Miranda, Ariel and Caliban in this way, to an extravagant degree, one might say; this form is a handy shorthand for his miniature patriarchy, a tiny kingdom more or less willingly bound to its father-ruler. The circle inscribed by the pronoun is later extended to Ferdinand, and then to the rest of the Milanese court.

Lear's court is also a blend of family and kingdom, if more feudal in character. His use of *thou* is not quite as insistent as Prospero's, but it is still his dominant second-person form, with instances of *thou* and *thee* together outnumbering those of *you*. He bestows 'thou' on Cordelia, in his curses, and also in their reconciliation ('Thou art a soul in bliss' [4.6.39]). He calls Kent 'thou', as imagined recreant, and again as the masterless retainer Caius. The 'all-shaking thunder' (3.2.6) is addressed as 'thou', and so are most of the participants in the mock trial in scene 13 of the Quarto.

Illustration 23 shows Romeo exactly on a par on the vertical dimension with Juliet – their abundance of *thou*, *thee* and *thy* is a measure of the focus of their spoken parts on each other – but he is to the left of her on the horizontal dimension, slightly more authoritative and less reactive than she is.

At the top of the graph is Menenius from *Coriolanus*. He uses *he*, *his* and *him* frequently. Together they are more than three in a hundred of all the words he speaks. The main explanation for this is his focus on Coriolanus, whether as returning hero

('Is he not wounded? He was wont to come home wounded', 2.1.116–17), aspirant politician or treasonous exile. He turns only rarely to the *thou* forms, using *you* eight times as often as the corresponding *thou* and *thee*. Similarly, Claudius says 'he' often, 'thou' rarely; like Menenius, most of his instances of *he* refer to one person, in his case the absent and dangerous Hamlet ('he which hath your noble father slain', 4.7.4).

The displacement of the Falstaff of *The Second Part of Henry the Fourth* towards the northern border of illustration 23 and away from the southern one can be traced through his changed use of *thou* and *he*. To an extent this is a direct swap. In the first part Hal is most often present, and Falstaff's resilient hold over him is reinforced by addressing him as 'thou'. '[W]hen thou art king', he says, twice, within a few lines (1.2.16, 23). In the second part the Prince is more often absent, and becomes 'he'. This takes on a poignant quality in the final instance of the pronoun, in a speech to Shallow.

That can hardly be, Master Shallow. Do not you grieve at this. I shall be sent for in private to him. Look you, he must seem thus to the world. Fear not your advancements. I will be the man that shall make you great.

(*2 Henry IV* 5.4.75–9)

Overall Falstaff uses *thou* twice as often in the first part of *Henry IV* as the second, proportional to all the words he speaks, and *he* half as often. He is more an observer and commentator in the second part, losing his favoured position in the alternative royal court of Eastcheap, and being brought more into the daylight world of legal and military affairs.

Certainly it is an unfamiliar brand of characterization that we have been discussing here. One is led to talk not of imaginative or emotional life, or complex cognitive modes, but of vectors of interaction between characters, especially traced through pronouns, and the tricks of style with which they work on each other. This is a sociolinguistics of character. Roger Brown and Albert Gilman's classic study of *thou* and *you* forms is relevant here, with its commentary on instances in Shakespeare and their reflection of local questions of status and relationship.[18] This work leads to a sense of the drama as a play of types, stock parts, defined this time not as villains, braggarts, wily servants and doting lovers, but more broadly by their place in a network of relationships. Among other things, Shakespearian characters speak for social purposes, to inform, persuade, control, seduce and sometimes to entertain. These purposes are reflected in their syntax and deixis and thus in frequencies of the very common words in their dialogue.

There are of course unending layers of complexity beyond this simple account. There are fifty characters in the analysis, but Shakespeare wrote more like a thousand parts in all. Characters change, and here they have been represented as a single static point. Shakespeare's original audiences heard the plays against a background of a repertoire of rival talents, and this is an important context for patterns of characters' dialogue, but here we have compared them only to other Shakespeare characters. The fifty words we have been considering represent a surprisingly large proportion of the total number of words these speak, around forty-five per cent, but only a tiny fraction of the total number of different words they use, more like two in a thousand. And of course, beyond the purely linguistic components are all the elements of action, setting, casting, acting and direction that make up a full picture of what it is to be Falstaff or Pandarus.

A study like this, then, starts with a drastic subtraction of all but a very few of the created and perceived materials that make for meaning in drama. It defines rigidly a small set of features to count and chooses one limited context in which to make comparisons among the results. The compensation is that this narrow set of variables is remarkably rich in information, since it offers access to patterns of syntax, of the structuring of language. Once the terms of the statistical analysis are defined, it misses nothing, and gives every item equal play. Its processes can be checked and replicated.

Most important, it presents us with some challenging propositions. Comedies and history plays are the generic poles of Shakespearian drama. It is the Falstaff of *The Second Part of Henry IV* who is the odd man out. Pandarus is defined by his *not*, Prospero by his *thou*, and Warwick by his *and*. In certain strictly defined terms, these observations are incontrovertible. They are discoveries, waiting to be made, recalling Falstaff's joking explanation for Worcester's taking to rebellion: it 'lay in his way, and he found it' (*1 Henry IV* 5.1.28). What bearing, if any, they have on anyone's understanding of Shakespeare is another matter. This is the province of readers or auditors, who are (mercifully) free to deploy in response to these propositions about the plays those many rich resources of interpretation of which the computer knows nothing.

---

[18] 'The Pronouns of Power and Solidarity', *Style in Language*, ed. Thomas A. Sebeok (New York, 1960), pp. 253–76.

WHO DO THE PEOPLE LOVE?

RICHARD LEVIN

Not so long ago, within the memory of some professors emeriti yet living, a number of Shakespearian critics spent considerable time and energy in attempts to determine 'what Shakespeare believed' about some subject, which usually meant what they wanted him to believe, which always meant what they themselves believed. They had no trouble in demonstrating, by a judicious selection of supporting evidence from the plays, and a judicious avoidance of any evidence to the contrary, that he shared their views on art, family, friendship, honour, justice, love, marriage, nature, religion, revenge, sex, war and many other subjects. But they had a great deal of trouble with his view of politics, because they wanted him to believe in democracy but he obviously did not.[1] He only gives us three extended treatments of 'the people' as a separate political entity and agency in the action – Jack Cade's rebels in Act 4 of *2 Henry VI*, and the Roman plebeians in the first three acts of *Julius Caesar* and of *Coriolanus* – and in all three plays they are presented as a 'rabble' who are mindless, fickle, easily swayed and murderous.[2] Moreover, they are always shown to be wrong. Cade's rebels set out to exterminate the middle and upper classes (hence their notorious proposal to 'kill all the lawyers') and establish an egalitarian utopia where food and claret wine are free and 'all things shall be in common', including wives, but finally, in one brief scene (4.8), they are persuaded by Clifford to yield to the King, and then by Cade to continue their rebellion, and then by Clifford to abandon Cade and go off to fight the French. The plebeians in *Julius Caesar* cheer Caesar at the Lupercalia, but after his assassination they are persuaded by Brutus to approve of the conspirators responsible for it, and then they are persuaded by Mark Antony to go on a violent rampage against them (during which they kill the wrong Cinna), and this results in civil war and the destruction of the Roman republic. In *Coriolanus* the plebians begin with a legitimate grievance, the refusal of the patricians to distribute the surplus grain, but they vote to give the consulship to Coriolanus, even though he supports this policy and is their sworn enemy, and then they are persuaded by the two tribunes (with some unintended help from Coriolanus himself) to revoke their votes and to banish him, which almost leads to the destruction of Rome itelf.

My title, including the nominative form of 'who', is adapted from Stanley Cavell, '"Who Does the Wolf Love?": Reading *Coriolanus*', in *Representing the English Renaissance*, ed. Stephen Greenblatt (Berkeley, 1988), pp. 197–216; his title quotes Menenius's question in 2.1.7.

[1] Some of the earlier Marxist and feminist critics tried to make Shakespeare a proto-Marxist or proto-feminist – see, for example, Juliet Dusinberre, *Shakespeare and the Nature of Women* (London, 1975), Kiernan Ryan, *Shakespeare* (London, 1989), and most of the essays assembled in *Shakespeare in a Changing World*, ed. Arnold Kettle (London, 1964), and in *The Woman's Part: Feminist Criticism of Shakespeare*, ed. Carolyn Ruth Swift Lenz, Gayle Greene and Carol Thomas Neely (Urbana, 1980). But this enterprise has largely been abandoned.

[2] They are called the 'rabble' or 'rabblement' in *Julius Caesar* 1.2.244, *Coriolanus* 1.1.218, and the stage directions at *2 Henry VI* 4.8.1, and *Coriolanus* 3.1.262. My reference text is *The Riverside Shakespeare*, ed. G. Blakemore Evans *et al.* (Boston, 1974).

It is important to recognize that in these three plays 'the people' are limited to the lower classes or 'the common people', and therefore that they do not include – in fact, they are sharply distinguished from – the higher orders of society or what in early modern England were called 'the better sort'. This is obvious in both Roman plays because of the crucial division between plebeians and patricians: thus in *Coriolanus* the plebeians complain that Caius Martius (not yet Coriolanus) is 'chief enemy to the people' and 'a very dog to the commonalty' (1.1.7–8, 28–9), and the two 'tribunes for the people' are attacked by Menenius as 'the herdsmen of the beastly plebeians' (1.1.254, 2.1.95); and in *Julius Caesar* the tribunes address their plebeian constituents, who include a carpenter and a cobbler, as 'mechanical' and 'the poor men of your sort' (1.1.3, 57), while Casca refers to them as 'the rag-tag people' and 'the common herd' (1.2.258, 264), and the conspirators plan to deliver the funeral oration for Caesar to 'the people' or 'the multitude', who are, again, the 'plebeians' (3.1.180, 234, 3.2.1.SD). Although Cade's rebels are not labelled plebeians, they are defined immediately by their mechanical vocations, such as 'Best's son the tanner', 'Dick the butcher' and 'Smith the weaver' (4.2.21–8), and they are later described by the Messenger as 'a ragged multitude / Of hinds and peasants' (4.4.32–3). These, then, are 'the people' who are presented to us in these three plays, and in all three it is made painfully clear that they are not fit to govern the state or even to engage in political action, which led his latest biographer (as of this writing) to conclude that 'Shakespeare seems to have been averse to any kind of popular movement' and to 'the common people . . . in the mass'.[3]

It is true that all three of these plays are based on history, and that Shakespeare found these portrayals of 'the people' in his historical sources, mainly Hall, Holinshed and North's Plutarch. Of course, he made some changes in these sources, the most obvious one being his invention of individuals (really just individual voices) to represent 'the people', which was a dramatic necessity if he wanted to present the crowd on stage for any extended period.[4] And in inventing them he obviously relied on and exploited absurd caricatures, which presumably owe something to the tradition of 'low' comedy that goes back to the mystery cycles and morality plays, as well as to a stereotype of 'low' rebellions. But he did not significantly change the negative attitude towards 'the people' that he found in his sources,[5] which he certainly could have done if he wished, since he was not bound by them (in *Antony and Cleopatra*, for example, his treatment of the titular characters is quite different from Plutarch's). Moreover, this negative view of 'the people' is not merely the opinion of some particular characters, which therefore could not be ascribed to Shakespeare; it is, in each case, the judgement rendered by the play as a whole, so it seems reasonable to infer that it was also his own view. It also seems to have been the view held by most of 'the better sort' in his own day, which we can infer from the existence of that stereotype.[6]

---

[3] Peter Ackroyd, *Shakespeare: The Biography* (New York, 2005), pp. 176, 294 (see also pp. 468–9).

[4] He does not do this in the crowd episodes in *Hamlet* 4.5, *2 Henry VI* 3.2 and the end of *Titus Andronicus*, because these episodes are brief and the crowds are only given a few short lines in which they literally 'speak as one voice', sometimes from off stage. (The last two scenes will be examined below as apparent exceptions to my argument.)

[5] Ackroyd claims that Shakespeare 'describes the followers of Jack Cade as a "rabblement", quite different from the presentation of them in the chronicles', and that 'Cade himself is vilified by Shakespeare in a manner wholly at odds with his immediate sources' (*Shakespeare*, p. 176). Presumably he is thinking of this comic elaboration, which is not found in Hall or Holinshed, but their judgement of the uprising is just as negative as Shakespeare's. They call Cade a 'cruel tyrant', 'outrageous losel', 'villainous rebel', 'mischievous catiff' and 'bloody wretch', among other things, and call his followers 'idle and vagabond persons', 'evil rude and rustical persons', and so on – see Geoffrey Bullough, ed., *Narrative and Dramatic Sources of Shakespeare*, 8 vols. (London, 1957–75), vol. 3, pp. 113–18, and Richard Hosley, ed., *Shakespeare's Holinshed* (New York, 1968), pp. 179–83.

[6] Compare the portrayal of 'the people' in the anonymous *Life and Death of Jack Straw*, which is also based on historical sources. They are called a 'rowt' rather than a 'rabble', but are very similar to Cade's rebels – they want to 'make diuision equally, / Of each mans goods' (1.1.106–7), to kill every 'man of lawe' (2.1.519), and so on (ed. Kenneth Muir and F. P. Wilson, Malone Society (Oxford, 1957)). Bullough says that this

There are, however, some very different portrayals of 'the people' – or, more precisely, statements about them – in a number of Shakespeare's plays, although they have not attracted much critical attention. In *The Tempest*, when Miranda asks Prospero why Alonso and Antonio did not kill them after conquering Milan, he explains that 'they durst not, / So dear the love my people bore me' (1.2.140–1). In *Hamlet*, Claudius says that he cannot arrest Hamlet for the murder of Polonius because 'He's lov'd of the distracted multitude' (4.3.4), and later, when Laertes asks him why he did not proceed publicly against Hamlet, he explains that he did not dare to because of Gertrude's attachment to Hamlet and 'the great love the general gender bear him' (4.7.18), which is just a more elevated term for 'the people'.[7] In *Antony and Cleopatra* we are told by Antony that 'Our slippery people' bestow their 'love' on Pompey (1.2.185–6), and by Caesar that he is 'lov'd' by the 'common body' (1.4.43–4), and Pompey himself asserts that 'The people love me' (2.1.9). In *Titus Andronicus* one of the tribunes, Marcus Andronicus, announces to the quarrelling patricians that 'the people of Rome [i.e., the plebeians], for whom we stand / A special party, have by common voice' chosen his brother Titus to be emperor (1.1.20–1). In *Troilus and Cressida*, as the Trojan heroes pass by after the day's fighting, Pandarus asks Cressida, 'Hark, do you not hear the people cry "Troilus"?' (1.2.224–5). In *Pericles* Cleon assures Pericles that 'the people's prayers still fall upon you' in Tharsus, defining these 'people' as 'the common body' (3.3.19–21), and Gower informs us that later in Tharsus Marina has become 'both th' heart and place / Of general wonder' and 'gets / All praises' (4.Chorus.10–1, 33–4), which arouses the jealousy of Dionyza. In *Othello* Iago tells Othello that Brabantio 'is much belov'd' in Venice (1.2.12), and Othello tells Desdemona that 'I have found great love amongst' the people of Cyprus (2.1.205). In *Romeo and Juliet*, when Capulet discovers that Romeo is one of his guests, he acknowledges that 'Verona brags of him / To be a virtuous and well-govern'd youth' (1.5.67–8). In *Henry V* the Chorus tells us that when Henry landed in England, after his victory over the French, he was greeted by 'men, wives, and boys, / Whose shouts and claps out-voice the deep-mouth'd sea', and when he entered London the city 'pour[ed] out her citizens' from 'The Mayor and all his brethren in best sort' down to 'the plebeians swarming at their heels' to applaud him (5.Chorus.10–1, 24–7). In *All's Well That Ends Well*, when the King of France complains that he has grown old and is now useless to his subjects, the Second Lord replies, 'You're loved, sir' (1.2.67). In *Cymbeline* the First Gentleman tells the Second Gentleman that Posthumus is 'most prais'd, most lov'd' by 'the youngest', 'th' more mature', and 'the graver' (1.1.47–9), and later in the dream sequence his father asserts that Posthumus 'deserv'd the praise o' th' world' (5.4.50). In *The Two Noble Kinsmen* the suppliant First Queen tells Theseus that, because of his 'boundless goodness', his 'fame / Knolls in the ear o' th' world', and when he agrees to help her, she says, 'Thus dost thou still make good / The tongue o' th' world' (1.1.51, 133–4, 226–7); Palamon recalls the happy times when he and Arcite 'Outstripp'd the people's praises' (2.2.16); and in the final act, when he is being led to the scaffold, he takes comfort in the fact that he has not 'outliv'd / The love o' th' people' and will die 'not without men's pity' (5.4.1–5). The largest number of these statements appear in *As You Like It*: Oliver resents the fact that Orlando is 'of all sorts enchantingly belov'd, and indeed so much in the heart of the world, and especially of my own people . . . that I am altogether mispris'd' (1.1.167–71); Adam asks Orlando, 'Why are you virtuous? Why do the people love you?' (2.3.5); LeBeau reports that Duke Frederick dislikes Rosalind because 'the people praise her for her virtues, / And pity her for her good father's sake' (1.2.280–1), where the affections of 'the people' proceed from Duke Senior to his daughter; Duke Frederick warns his own daughter Celia that Rosalind's

---

play may have influenced Shakespeare's Jack Cade scenes, but he prints it as an analogue (*Narrative*, vol. 3, pp. 91, 138–50).

[7] Thus Hamlet refers to a play that 'pleas'd not the million, 'twas caviary to the general' (2.2.436–7); but in Gower's statement from *Pericles*, quoted below, 'general' is not confined to 'the general'.

silence and patience 'Speak to the people, and they pity her' (1.3.79); he also acknowledges to Orlando that 'The world esteem'd thy father [Sir Rowland] honorable' (1.2.225); and Rosalind tells Orlando that 'My father lov'd Sir Rowland as his soul, / And all the world was of my father's mind' (1.2.235–6).

We cannot assume that in these statements the conception of 'the people' is always limited to the common people or the lower classes, as we found in *2 Henry VI, Julius Caesar* and *Coriolanus*. It clearly is limited to them in the first nine statements, while in the remaining ones it seems to extend to the entire population. This is evident, for example, in Oliver's complaint that Orlando is loved by 'all sorts' and is 'in the heart of the world, and especially of my own people' (where the 'people' are even more narrowly limited to the servants and tenants on his estate), and we can infer that Rosalind's comment that 'all the world' loved Sir Rowland also covers 'all sorts', like the references to 'the world' in the statements of Oliver, Duke Frederick, Posthumus's father and the First Queen. My point is simply that all these statements include the common people, even though they do not all refer exclusively to them.

While they differ in this one respect, these statements share some significant features. According to them, the individual loved or admired by 'the people' is always a member of the upper class, often a ruler or close relative of one. Except in *Pericles* and *Henry V*, this affection is part of the situation that existed prior to the beginning of the action, which is why so many of the statements are placed in the expository opening scenes of the plays, whose purpose is to inform the audience about that prior situation. But these plays never actually show 'the people' expressing this affection – in fact, they never even show us 'the people', except for a brief appearance of the Roman populace at the end of *Titus Andronicus*, who give no sign of the admiration for Titus (killed earlier in the scene) that Marcus spoke of, and an even briefer appearance of the mob led by Laertes in *Hamlet*, 4.5, who give no sign of the love for Hamlet that Claudius spoke of.[8] Moreover, this reported love or admiration felt by 'the people' is not affected by the

ensuing action, but seems, rather, to be presented as a constant or donnée. And, even though it serves to restrain Alonso's and Antonio's treatment of Prospero and Claudius's treatment of Hamlet, and to motivate Dionyza's attempt to murder Marina, and Oliver's abuse of Orlando, and Duke Frederick's banishment of Rosalind,[9] it has no further effect on the ensuing action, which can be seen as a consequence of the fact that 'the people' are not represented in these plays and therefore cannot figure as agents in them, and may help to explain why these statements about their love have received so little critical attention. Finally, and most important for my purposes, in these statements 'the people' are always right, because the characters who win their affections (Prospero, Hamlet, Pompey, Titus Andronicus, Troilus, Pericles, Marina, Brabantio, Othello, Romeo, Henry V, the King of France, Posthumus, Theseus, Palamon, Arcite, Orlando, Rosalind, Duke Senior and Sir Rowland de Boys) are all basically good individuals who are worthy of this. No Shakespearian villain is ever loved or admired by 'the people'.

This also applies to the pity felt by 'the people', which is closely related to their love and admiration. Aristotle observed that pity is evoked in us by the spectacle of 'undeserved misfortune',[10] which means that the more we love or admire the person who suffers the misfortune, the more undeserved and therefore the more pitiful it will seem to us. We have already encountered this connection between the love or admiration of 'the people' and their pity in *The Two Noble Kinsmen*, where Palamon says that he has 'The love o' th' people' and will die 'not without men's pity' (5.4.1–5), and in *As You Like It*, where LeBeau says that

---

[8] They are called 'the rabble' (4.5.103). The stage direction in Q2 has them enter with Laertes, but in F1 it only has Laertes enter, so they may speak their few lines from off stage.

[9] Duke Frederick banishes Rosalind because 'the people' praise her more than his own daughter Celia; Dionyza tries to kill Marina because they praise her more than her own daughter Philoten; and Oliver is enraged because Orlando is so beloved by them that he himself is 'altogether mispris'd'.

[10] Aristotle, *Poetics*, 13.1453^{a}5, trans. Ingram Bywater (London, 1942).

'the people praise' Rosalind 'for her virtues, / And pity her for her good father's sake' (1.2.280–1), and Duke Frederick admits that her silence and patience 'Speak to the people, and they pity her' (1.3.79). There are a number of other examples. In *Antony and Cleopatra* Maecenas tells Octavia, after Antony deserts her, that 'Each heart in Rome does love and pity you' (3.6.92), and in *Henry VIII* the Lord Chamberlain says that 'every true heart weeps for' Queen Katherine because Henry is divorcing her (2.2.39). In *King Lear* Regan tells Oswald that it was a mistake to let the blinded Gloucester live because 'where he arrives he moves / All hearts against us' (4.5.10–1), and later Edmund tells Albany that he sent Lear to prison because the sight of 'the old and miserable King' would 'pluck the common bosom on his side' (5.3.46–9). Macbeth realizes that Duncan is so beloved for his 'virtues' that, if he were killed, 'pity . . . Shall blow the horrid deed in every eye, / That tears shall drown the wind' (1.7.18–25). And at the end of *Richard III* the negative corollary of this connection between the love and the pity of 'the people' is acknowledged by Richard himself, who laments that 'there is no creature loves me, / And if I die no soul will pity me' (5.3.200–1).

These statements about the pity felt by 'the people', unlike those about their love, do not describe a situation that exists before the beginning of the play, because this pity is the result of some event (i.e., the misfortune) that occurs during the course of the action. But they share all of the other features that we found in the statements about the love of 'the people'. There is the same definition of 'the people', since the phrases 'each heart', 'every true heart', 'all hearts' and 'every eye', like Oliver's reference to 'all sorts' and the many references to 'the world' in the statements quoted earlier, are meant to cover the entire social spectrum, while Edmund's 'the common bosom', like the 'common body' alluded to by Octavius Caesar and Cleon, focuses on the lower part of this spectrum, so that these statements always include the common people but are not always limited to them. The person who is pitied always belongs to the upper class, usually to the ruling family. Moreover, this pity is never shown because we never see 'the people',

who do not figure as agents in the action, and therefore their pity is not affected by the ensuing action and has no effect on it.[11] And, once again, 'the people' are always right, since they only bestow their pity on admirable individuals who deserve it. Indeed the recipients of this pity – Octavia, Queen Katherine, Gloucester, Lear and Duncan – could be added to our earlier list of basically good individuals who receive their love. As Richard III tells us, in Shakespeare no villain is ever pitied by 'the people'.

We should go on, then, to ask what is the dramatic function served in the plays by these statements about the love or pity felt by 'the people' for some individual. It obviously cannot be to advance the plot, since we found that the feelings of 'the people' have no effect on the later action. Nor can it be to influence our response to 'the people', who are not even seen. Therefore it must be to influence our response to the individual who is the recipient of these feelings, and this influence has already been suggested – the statements serve as testimonials that help to define this individual as someone who is basically good and worthy of our sympathies, and therefore help to shape our positive attitude towards him or her. They are not, of course, as important in shaping our attitude as the individual's own words and actions, but they can have a significant role here, especially when they appear, as many of them do, early in the play and thus contribute to our crucial first impressions of this individual. In fact, a number of these statements are presented before we even see the individuals in question, and so predispose us to sympathize with them. And this testimony about the affection of 'the people' for this individual is especially impressive when it comes from, or is acknowledged by, what

---

[11] There is a striking exception in *King Lear*, 3.7, where a servant (whose class status is emphasized by their calling him 'dog', 'peasant' and 'slave') tries to stop Cornwall and Regan from blinding Gloucester and two other servants treat Gloucester's wounds, and in 4.1, where the Old Man, who is Gloucester's tenant, helps him. The servants and Old Man seem to represent the common people and prepare us for Regan's report, just quoted, that 'All hearts' pity Gloucester.

lawyers call hostile witnesses, such as Alonso and Antonio on Prospero, Claudius on Hamlet, Antony and Caesar on Pompey, Dionyza on Marina, Capulet on Romeo, Oliver on Orlando, Duke Frederick on Rosalind and Sir Rowland, Regan on Gloucester, Edmund on Lear, and Macbeth on Duncan, who wish that 'the people' did *not* feel this way. Perhaps it is necessary to add that, while the love or pity of 'the people' functions as a kind of guarantee that the individuals are basically good and sympathetic, this does not mean that they are faultless. Some of them, notably Hamlet, Titus, Othello, Posthumus, Gloucester and Lear, make very serious mistakes that result in the suffering (and often the death) of innocent victims, but these are always mistakes, made without full knowledge of the circumstances, and never are deliberate crimes, like those of Richard III, Claudius, Iago and Edmund, and therefore they can be forgiven or expiated in the resolution. Indeed there is no indication that their mistakes diminish the love or the pity of 'the people' for them, which, we saw, figure as constants, and so continue to function in helping to shape and maintain our sympathetic attitude towards them.

This explanation of the dramatic function of the affection felt by 'the people' receives a kind of confirmation in *Macbeth*, which is a special case because it is the only Shakespearian play where a major character begins as the recipient of this affection but then loses it during the course of the action. Before he agrees to kill Duncan, Macbeth says to his wife, 'I have bought / Golden opinions from all sorts of people' (1.7.32–3), where 'all sorts of people' clearly includes but is not limited to the common people, as we also saw in Oliver's statement that Orlando is 'of all sorts enchantingly belov'd'. Indeed, Macbeth's statement follows the same pattern as those we examined earlier, up to a point: the love of 'the people' is bestowed on a member of the nobility; it was bestowed by them before the beginning of the play (although not long before, since it is the result of Macbeth's great victories recounted by the bleeding Sergeant and Ross in the expository second scene); we are never shown this love or shown 'the people' themselves; and it has no effect on the ensuing action. But there are some obvious and crucial differences. This love is radically affected by the ensuing action, which causes Macbeth to lose it. Moreover, Macbeth is not a sympathetic character, because he is guilty of deliberate crimes, like Shakespeare's villains, rather than of the mistakes that we found in Hamlet, Titus, Othello, Posthumus, Gloucester and Lear. More precisely, he begins as a sympathetic character, which is when and why he earns those 'Golden opinions from all sorts of people', but then he becomes a villain, which is when and why he loses them.

There is another major difference. Not only is the love of 'the people' lost as an effect of the subsequent action, but that loss itself has an effect on this action, since it causes them to reject Macbeth. As we would expect, the emphasis of the play is on the abandonment of Macbeth by the nobles, the 'false thanes' who, he says, 'fly from me' (5.3.7, 49); but he has also lost the loyalty of 'the people' who made up, or should have made up, the ranks of his army. The only ones who remain in it are held there under coercion and no longer feel any affection for him – thus we are told by Malcolm that 'Both more and less [i.e., the upper and lower classes] have given him the revolt, / And none serve with him but constrained things, / Whose hearts are absent too' (5.4.12–14), and by Angus that 'Those he commands move only in command, / Nothing in love' (5.2.19–20). Many of them must have deserted, because in the final attack on Macbeth's castle, Macduff only encounters 'wretched kerns, whose arms / Are hir'd to bear their staves' (5.7.17–8).[12] And many went over to the attacking army, which has been reinforced, as Macbeth acknowledges, 'with those that should be ours' (5.5.5), where he functions as what I have called a hostile witness who guarantees the truth of the statement. Therefore this loss of the love of 'the people' is not only an effect of Macbeth's criminal career, but is also a significant cause of his military defeat that ends this career, and the play makes

---

[12] Many critics have noted the similarity between his situation here and that of the rebel Macdonwald, whose army was supplied with 'kerns and gallowglasses' (1.2.13), and whose defeat earned Macbeth those 'Golden opinions'.

us aware of their role in this causal sequence even though it never actually shows them to us. It also makes us aware that the loss of their love is a significant aspect of Macbeth's internal punishment, which is separate from his military defeat and centres on his despair when he realizes what he has given up and what it has been replaced with:

And that which should accompany old age,
As honor, love, obedience, troops of friends,
I must not look to have; but in their stead,
Curses, not loud but deep, mouth-honor, breath,
Which the poor heart would fain deny, but dare not.
(5.3.24–8)

I think we can conclude, therefore, that the role played by the love of 'the people' in *Macbeth* confirms my account of the dramatic function of this love in the other statements we considered, and that this function necessarily involves a very positive view of 'the people', since they are always right in giving their love (or pity) to upper-class characters who are worthy of it, and also in withholding or withdrawing it from those who are or become unworthy. Yet this seems to be inconsistent with the very negative view of them presented in the popular uprisings in *2 Henry VI*, *Julius Caesar* and *Coriolanus*, where we saw that they are always wrong. The explanation, which has already been suggested, is that the negative view of 'the people' always appears in plays where they try to operate as an independent entity and to intervene in the action, while the positive view of them always appears in plays where they do not try to do this. And that also applies to *Macbeth*, even though here 'the people' have a significant effect on the plot, because we found that they produce this effect, not by acting independently (in fact, they are not even seen on the stage), but simply by transferring their allegiance from one nobleman to another. It would seem, therefore, that within this political sphere 'the people' can be right only on the condition that they do not engage in their own political activity.

We can test this explanation by seeing if it applies to two apparent exceptions – the only two plays of Shakespeare in which 'the people' are right, since they give their love to a good nobleman who is worthy of it, and yet are represented on stage, very briefly, as a separate body and engage in a very brief political action based on their love. We have already noted that in the opening scene of *Titus Andronicus* Marcus Andronicus announces that the plebeians ('the people of Rome') have 'by a common voice' chosen his brother Titus as their emperor (1.1.20–1), but we never see these 'people' and their choice does not result in any action because Titus refuses the crown and insists that it be given to Saturninus instead, so Marcus's announcement fits the pattern that we found in the other statements about the love of 'the people' that has no effect on the dramatic situation.

Later in the play, however, Titus's son Lucius, who was banished by Saturninus, leads an army of Goths against him, and Saturninus therefore functions as a hostile witness to inform us that

'Tis he the common people love so much;
Myself hath often heard them say,
When I have walked like a private man,
That Lucius' banishment was wrongfully,
And they have wish'd that Lucius were their emperor.
. . . the citizens favor Lucius
And will revolt from me to succor him.
(4.4.73–80)

But 'the common people' never revolt or do anything to succour Lucius. The resolution is brought about entirely by lethal interactions among the patricians themselves: Titus and Lavinia kill Tamora's sons, Chiron and Demetrius, and cook them in a Thyestean banquet for Saturninus and Tamora, then Titus kills Lavinia and Tamora, Saturninus kills Titus, and Lucius kills Saturninus. Only after this slaughter is completed do the 'people and sons of Rome' appear (5.3.67), to hear Lucius and Marcus explain the past events to them, and to hear Aemilius tell them that Lucius is the new emperor, 'for well I know / The common voice do cry, it shall be so' (139–40), just as Marcus invoked the 'common voice' to choose Titus as emperor in the first scene, whereupon they are given exactly two lines to hail Lucius as 'Rome's royal Emperor' and 'Rome's gracious governor'

(141, 146).[13] Thus their only action here is to ratify the decision of the surviving patricians, although the fact that it coincides with their own love of Lucius serves as a guarantee that it is the right decision and so makes the resolution even more satisfactory.

The other apparent exception is the love of 'the people' for Humphrey, Duke of Gloucester, in *2 Henry VI*, which is a little more complicated. In the opening scene we are informed of this love by Cardinal Beauford, who is one of Humphrey's enemies and therefore qualifies as yet another hostile witness:

> the common people favor him,
> Calling him 'Humphrey, the good Duke of Gloucester',
> Clapping their hands, and crying with loud voice,
> 'Jesu maintain your royal Excellence!'
> With 'God preserve the good Duke Humphrey!'
>
> (1.1.158–62)

Later Queen Margaret tries to turn King Henry against Humphrey by complaining that 'By flattery hath he won the commons' hearts' (3.1.28);[14] and when she plots with his enemies to get rid of him, the Duke of Suffolk, who is her secret lover and a leader of this conspiracy, warns them that 'The commons haply [will] rise, to save his life' (3.1.240).

The conspirators have him murdered, and at 3.2.122 'many Commons' do rise up in protest and break in on the King, but it is a remarkably decorous uprising. They allow themselves to be ushered out of the royal presence very quickly by the Earl of Salisbury, and then allow him to present their demand to the King, while they remain offstage and limit their participation to two short sentences from 'within' (270, 278).[15] Moreover, their demand, as reported by Salisbury, is simply that Suffolk should be banished because he is responsible for Humphrey's death and also poses a serious threat to the King, whom they want to protect, so the King responds, again through Salisbury, by thanking them 'for their tender loving care' (280) and assuring them that he has already decided to banish Suffolk, after which they disappear from the play. Therefore on the emotional level 'the people' are doubly right – not only do they love the right nobleman, 'the good Duke Humphrey', who is the most admirable person in the play, but they also hate the right one, since Suffolk is very reprehensible and very dangerous.[16] And while they operate briefly as an independent entity and undertake a political action on their own, it turns out to be nothing more than a kind of ratification of the correct decision already made by their 'betters', as we also saw in the conclusion of *Titus Andronicus*. Therefore this apparent exception to Shakespeare's presentation of 'the people', like the one in *Titus Andronicus*, does not really contradict my explanation of the conditions governing his positive treatment of them and their love in the statements quoted earlier, and stands in sharp contrast to his very negative treatment of Cade's 'rabble' in the next act of this play,[17] so our survey of his portrayals of 'the people' has come full circle in *2 Henry VI*, which presents both aspects of what I think is a single basic attitude towards them and their role in the state.

---

[13] In Q1–3 and F1 these two lines are part of Marcus's speech, but modern editors give them to the plebeians, and after the second Lucius says, 'Thanks, gentle Romans' (5.3.147). Compare the 'common voice' to the 'common bosom' and 'common body' in the statements quoted earlier, and compare this ending to that of *The Rape of Lucrece*, where Brutus 'acquainted the people' with past events, and 'the people were so moved, that they with one consent and a general acclamation' ratified the patricians' political decision (Arg.40–4). In *Julius Caesar* a later Brutus expects a similar response from 'the people' to his funeral oration (3.1.234–42).

[14] In *Richard II* we hear of Bullingbrook's 'courtship to the common people' (1.4.24), which is presumably related to the later report of their enthusiastic reception when he enters London in triumph (5.2.7–21), but we never see them and they never take any action.

[15] The F1 stage directions do not indicate when (or if) they exit, but most modern editors have them speak these two sentences from off stage. There is a similar problem with the crowd's speeches in *Hamlet*, 4.5 (see note 8).

[16] It is significant that the most disparaging comments on them come from Suffolk himself, who calls them 'rude unpolish'd hinds' and 'a sort of tinkers' (3.2.271, 277).

[17] Annabel Patterson discusses this contrast in *Shakespeare and the Popular Voice* (Cambridge, MA, 1989), pp. 48–51.

The resolution of these apparently conflicting aspects of that basic attitude can be found, I believe, in a conception of society, or what we would now call an ideology, that has come to be associated with feudalism (with the feudal ideal, that is, and not with the actual practice), although it also appears in some of Shakespeare's plays set in prefeudal times, as we saw, and can be traced back at least as far as Plato. In this conception society was viewed as a hierarchical, organic whole constructed around a system of mutual but asymmetrical obligations between kings and their subjects, landowners and their tenants, masters and their servants, and parents and their children, in which those above were required to take care of those below them, and those below were required to obey those above them. (The idea survives in the military slogan of 'loyalty up and loyalty down'.) Moreover, this entire system was regarded as 'natural', which meant that in sociopolitical relationships the common people were supposed to have a kind of instinctive sense of how to be a good subject (i.e., one who 'knows his place' and stays in it) and how to recognize and cherish a good ruler (i.e., one who promotes the welfare of his subjects). That is why they are always right when they bestow their love on some of their 'betters', and always wrong when they allow themselves to be misled by evil demagogues or tribunes and act against their 'betters' and the natural order of the state.[18]

There are brief statements of this political concept in Menenius's 'pretty tale' of the 'time when all the body's members / Rebell'd against the belly' in the opening scene of *Coriolanus* and in Ulysses's speech on 'Degree' in *Troilus and Cressida*, 1.3.75–137; but it is more fully developed and plays a more important role in *King Lear*, where it is clearly expressed and endorsed in some of the speeches of Gloucester, Lear and Albany. Gloucester extends the concept to the heavenly bodies, so that a disorder in their natural motions causes disorders in the natural social relations on earth:

These late eclipses in the sun and moon portend no good to us . . . nature finds itself scourg'd by the sequent effects. Love cools, friendship falls off, brothers divide: in cities,

mutinies; in countries, discord; in palaces, treason; and the bond crack'd 'twixt son and father . . . We have seen the best of our time. Machinations, hollowness, treachery, and all ruinous disorders follow us disquietly to our graves. (1.2.103–14)

Lear swears 'by the sacred radiance of the sun' and 'By all the operation of the orbs, / From which we do exist and cease to be' when he disowns Cordelia for cracking the natural bond between child and parent (1.1.109–12); and later he prays to 'Nature', his 'dear goddess', to punish Goneril for her unnatural treatment of him by making her sterile (another violation of nature) or having her give birth to a 'disnatur'd' child (1.4.275–89). And Albany compares her cruelty towards Lear to the severing of the natural relationship of the parts of a tree:

That nature which contemns its origin
Cannot be bordered certain in itself.
She that herself will sliver and disbranch
From her material sap, perforce must wither,
And come to deadly use.

(4.2.32–6)[19]

Shakespeare even emphasizes this concept of the natural basis of society by setting up a contrast between it and the concept espoused by Edmund in his prayer at the beginning of 1.2, where he addresses 'Nature' as 'my goddess' (the counterpart of Lear's prayer to 'Nature' as his 'dear goddess' in 1.4.275–89), and insists that it is natural for each individual to try to 'prosper' at the expense of others, and unnatural to be constrained by social bonds, which he dismisses as 'the plague of custom'. And all the major characters in the play define themselves in terms of these two opposing views of nature, since Cordelia, Edgar, Albany and

---

[18] Compare the alleged role of 'outside agitators' blamed by many American conservatives for the labour unrest in the 1930s and the civil rights movement in the 1960s, the assumption being that if it were not for them the workers and blacks would accept their natural subordination.

[19] Both Lear and Gloucester call Goneril and Regan 'unnatural' daughters (2.4.278, 3.3.1–2), Edmund (deceptively) calls Edgar an 'unnatural' son, and Gloucester (mistakenly) calls Edmund a 'natural' one (2.1.50, 84).

Kent consistently respect, in both their words and actions, the natural bonds between child and parent and subject and ruler, while Goneril, Regan, Edmund, Cornwall and Oswald just as consistently disparage and violate them.

Indeed, several critics have associated Lear's and Gloucester's organic conception of nature with the feudal ideal, which was declining in early modern England, and Edmund's atomistic conception with an emerging individualism that would evolve into capitalism, and some of them have gone on to argue that the play expresses a nostalgic yearning for the good old days of the feudal system (Gloucester's 'We have seen the best of our time') and a distrust and fear of the new system ('all ruinous disorders').[20] I think this is plausible, although it is far from certain, because nostalgia for the 'good old days', which I call Edenism,[21] is a very common emotion and can be found in many cultures and periods that were not undergoing this socioeconomic change – it is embodied, for example, in the pagan myth of the Golden Age. In fact, Northrop Frye points out in his analysis of literary genres that this myth underlies some of the basic patterns of comedy which, again, appear in many different cultures and epochs.[22] And the archives are full of laments by members of the older generation (usually grumpy men) that they have seen the best of their time and that the younger generation is rapidly going to ruinous disorder in a handbasket. (Even the King of France voices this complaint in *All's Well That Ends Well*, 1.2.24–48, where he accuses the young men today of 'levity', which can scarcely be considered a capitalist trait.) So perhaps in trying to connect these two conceptions of nature in *King Lear* to the decay of feudalism and rise of capitalism we may be guilty of overhistoricizing, which is one of the dangers of several of the new critical approaches that came into prominence in the 1980s.

This nostalgia for the good old days is often accompanied by the hope of bringing them back or of going back to them, which might be called the dream of restoration.[23] This is not a significant aspect of *King Lear*, because the world ruled by Lear and Gloucester at the outset is very far from

a Golden Age – it is deeply flawed by the serious mistakes made by both men as fathers in their relationships with their children, as I noted earlier, and Lear himself admits that he was also deficient as a king when, after thinking of the poor, naked, houseless and unfed wretches out in the pitiless storm, he exclaims, 'O, I have ta'en / Too little care of this!' (3.4.32–3), which means that he has failed to show 'loyalty down'. Moreover, the painful ending certainly does not suggest the return to a happier time. The best that the survivors are able to hope for is that they can 'the gor'd state sustain', and they conclude that 'The oldest hath borne most, we that are young / Shall never see so much, nor live so long', which would make the past even worse than the present, and that, of course, is the exact opposite of Edenism and the dream of restoration.

The restoration of a lost Golden Age has a much more prominent role in several of Shakespeare's comedies, which is just what Northrop Frye's study of genres would lead us to expect. It is most

---

[20] This is the argument of Paul Delany, '*King Lear* and the Decline of Feudalism', in *Materialist Shakespeare: A History*, ed. Ivo Kamps (London, 1995), pp. 20–38, which I think is still one of our best Marxist readings of Shakespeare. Compare Ryan (*Shakespeare*), who finds in the play a plea for socialism.

[21] See 'Bashing the Bourgeois Subject', in *Looking for an Argument: Critical Encounters with the New Approaches to the Criticism of Shakespeare and His Contemporaries* (Madison, 2003), pp. 114–22; pp. 118–21.

[22] See Northrop Frye, *Anatomy of Criticism: Four Essays* (Princeton, 1957), pp. 163–86; pp. 171, 181–4.

[23] Stephen Greenblatt, in the next-to-latest biography of Shakespeare, says that his plays reveal a 'fascination' with 'the dream of restoration', but this is limited to individuals who regain their lost status, such as Egeon, Viola, Sebastian and Prospero, which he explains as Shakespeare's reaction to his father's social and economic decline (*Will in the World: How Shakespeare Became Shakespeare* (New York, 2004), pp. 81–6). But Ackroyd invokes this same paternal decline to explain why Shakespeare 'sympathizes' with 'authoritative rulers who have failed' and to 'elucidate' his 'unprecedented interest in the figure of the king' (*Shakespeare*, pp. 68–9). Thus the comparison of these two biographies demonstrates the dangers of overbiographicalized interpretation.

prominent, I believe, in *As You Like It*,[24] where we are given an idealized picture of a kind of Eden that existed not long before the beginning of the play, when Sir Rowland de Boys was alive and Duke Senior ruled the land. In the opening scenes we learn that Sir Rowland was a benevolent father to his sons as well as a benevolent master to his servants, and that Duke Senior was a worthy ruler. Moreover, we are told three times that these two very good men were also very good friends (1.2.235, 1.3.29–30, 2.7.195–6). All this changed, however, in the recent past because of the actions of the two villains of the play, who serve the same basic function here as the serpent in the garden of Eden. Oliver, the oldest son of Sir Rowland, rejects his father's example – and even his father's expressed wishes – by abusing his younger brother, Orlando (thus Orlando complains that Oliver 'bars me the place of a brother', 1.1.19–20), and also by abusing his servants (thus when he calls Adam 'you old dog', Adam replies that 'my old master, he would not have spoke such a word', 1.1.81–4). And Duke Frederick is a usurper who has exiled his older brother, Duke Senior, threatens Orlando, and then banishes his niece, Rosalind. Thus Orlando can equate these two men and sum them up when he says that he must go 'From tyrant Duke unto a tyrant brother' (1.2.288). To complete this striking contrast between the good old order and the bad new one, we are informed that Duke Frederick, unlike Duke Senior, was the enemy of Sir Rowland (1.2.226, 1.3.33),[25] and later he even becomes the enemy of Oliver, his fellow villain (3.1.15–18).

In this play, however, the idealized world of the recent past has not completely disappeared after the two villains come to power and establish their new order. It has been transported instead by the exiled Duke Senior to the forest of Arden, and Charles the wrestler invokes two Edenic images to describe the life there:

They say he is already in the forest of Arden, and a many merry men with him; and there they live like the old Robin Hood of England. They say many young gentlemen flock to him every day, and fleet the time carelessly, as they did in the golden world. (1.1.114–19)

Moreover, this 'golden world' preserved in Arden seems to emanate a kind of benign magical power, because the two villains who were responsible for creating the fallen world we saw at the outset are both converted there. Oliver comes to the forest to bring Orlando to Duke Frederick 'dead or living' (as he was commanded in 3.1.4–7), but when Orlando rescues him from a hungry lioness, he changes completely, admits that his treatment of Orlando was 'unnatural' (4.3.122–4), and later offers to bequeath Sir Rowland's entire estate to his brother (5.2.10–12); and Duke Frederick comes to the forest with an army to kill Duke Senior, but when he encounters 'an old religious man' on 'the skirts of this wild wood', he changes completely, abandons 'the world', and bequeathes the dukedom to his brother (5.4.159–63).[26] Thus the forest to which Duke Senior, Orlando and Rosalind fled to escape from Duke Frederick and Oliver, and to which Duke Frederick and Oliver come to capture or kill Duke Senior and Orlando, defeats the designs of both of these villains and enables the innocent victims to return in triumph, along with their fellow exiles, and resume their former lives. The result, therefore, is that we experience a very powerful feeling of restoration, not only of Duke Senior to his original status, but also of the entire prelapsarian world that he presided over and that was lost before the beginning of the play.

I do not think it is a coincidence that this play, which produces the strongest sense of restoration in the Shakespeare canon, also produces the largest number of statements about the love and pity of 'the people' that were examined earlier. For in these

---

[24] Greenblatt does not mention this play in his comments on 'the dream of restoration' (see note 23), presumably because the emphasis of the ending is on the restoration, not of an individual (who could be connected to Shakespeare's father), but of the entire society.

[25] References to Duke Senior's love of Sir Rowland and Duke Frederick's hatred of him are juxtaposed for special emphasis in 1.3.29–34.

[26] These two conversions are not shown to us but only reported (in 4.3 and 5.4), presumably because they would be difficult to stage and also, I think, because Shakespeare is much less interested in them than in their consequences.

statements the recipients of the affections of 'the people' are Duke Senior, Sir Rowland, Rosalind and Orlando – the first two being, as we saw, the model ruler and the model father and master in the Edenic world that is destroyed and then restored, while the other two are their children, who preserve the memory of their fathers and the values of this world,[27] and whose marriage at the end embodies the restoration of those values and the promise that they will be passed on to the next generation. Indeed, this love and pity felt by 'the people' for Orlando and Rosalind arouse the envy of the two villains and thus drive Oliver to persecute Orlando (1.1.167–71, 2.3.5–24) and Duke Frederick to exile Rosalind (1.2.280–1, 1.3.79). It is also significant that, shortly before the conclusion, Duke Frederick decides to attack and kill Duke Senior in Arden because he has heard 'that every day / Men of great worth resorted to this forest' to join his exiled brother (5.4.154–5). Even though these 'Men of great worth' are clearly not 'the people' in the sense in which I am using this term, they too must be motivated by their love of Duke Senior and their nostalgic longing for the Golden Age that they all enjoyed when he was in power and that they all would like to bring back.

The play also confirms the relationship that I suggested earlier connecting this love of 'the people' to what I called the feudal ideal of 'loyalty up and loyalty down', which would explain why 'the people' love Duke Senior, Sir Rowland, Orlando and Rosalind, who represent this ideal. In fact, the ideal seems to be epitomized in the special bond that develops between Orlando and the aged servant Adam. In 2.3 Adam saves Orlando's life by warning him of Oliver's plot to kill him, and offers to help him escape by going with him (still as a servant, of course, because the feudal ideal is asymmetrical) and even to support him afterwards by giving him all the wages 'I sav'd under your father' (2.3.38–45), which must be the ultimate expression of 'loyalty up'. When we next see them they have reached the forest of Arden, where Orlando carries the weak and starving Adam to a shelter and even

offers to risk his own life to feed him by hunting for some wild animal ('I will either be food for it, or bring it for food to thee', 2.6.7–8), which must be the ultimate expression of 'loyalty down'. And after Orlando joins Duke Senior's little society, he refuses to eat any of the food that they share with him until he has first brought some of it to Adam (2.7.127–33).[28]

When Adam offers Orlando his lifetime savings, Orlando's response establishes a contrast between two kinds of servants that corresponds to the opposition of the prelapsarian and postlapsarian worlds that we have been tracing in this play:

> O good old man, how well in thee appears
> The constant service of the antique world,
> When service sweat for duty, not for meed!
> Thou art not for the fashion of these times,
> Where none will sweat but for promotion,
> And having that do choke their service up
> Even with the having. It is not so with thee.
> (2.3.56–62)

The 'antique world' is clearly supposed to be the Edenic society that existed before the beginning of the play, when servants worked for their masters out of a sense of 'duty', which is just another name for the feudal ideal of 'loyalty up' and for the love felt by 'the people' for their betters. (Thus Orlando later tells Duke Senior that Adam has followed and served him 'in pure love', 2.7.131.) And their service was 'constant' because it was based on this ideal, which was regarded as natural. But in 'these times', which refers to the fallen world shown to us in the early scenes of the play, servants only work for their masters for a reward ('meed' or 'promotion'), and therefore when they have received their

---

[27] LeBeau says that 'the people' pity Rosalind 'for her good father's sake' (1.2.280–1), and Adam addresses Orlando as 'you memory / Of old Sir Rowland!' (2.3.3–4).

[28] This is the last we see of Adam, who has no further function in the play, but it should be noted that in the society established in Arden by Duke Senior and his fellow nobles, which Orlando joins, there do not seem to be any servants.

reward they terminate their service.[29] And this distinction also applies to 'loyalty down', since we have already seen that Adam, speaking from a servant's perspective, establishes the same kind of contrast between the good master of the past, represented by Sir Rowland, and the bad master of the present, represented by Oliver (1.1.181–4). Thus in the relationship of Orlando and Adam we can see a concrete example of how the concept of the love of 'the people' and the larger concept of an organic society operate in *As You Like It*.

I am not claiming, of course, that my brief comments on this play constitute a 'reading' of it, or even of its most important components, which are developed in the central episodes set in the forest of Arden. I have not touched on the other two groups who inhabit this forest – the Latin-named shepherds, Silvius, Phebe and Corin, and the English-named peasants, Audrey and William – who seem to live in separate worlds of their own that never make contact with the world of Duke Senior and his French-named nobles, so that they cannot be considered part of 'the people' in my sense of the term. Nor have I discussed the complex treatment of the contrasting romantic relationships that lead to the four marriages at the end, or the complex critiques of these romantic relationships and of pastoralism voiced by Jaques and Touchstone, or many other matters, because I have focused on the dramatic function of the love of 'the people' and of the feudal ideal on which it is based. And I certainly do not want to suggest that this love and this ideal are what the play is 'about', which would involve the kind of overthematized interpretation that was one of the dangers of the old New Criticism. I am only arguing that they establish the moral framework of the play (especially, as I indicated earlier, in the opening scenes) in terms of which we are supposed to judge the characters and their actions, and also that they operate in this same basic way in other plays of Shakespeare where he makes a point of telling us who 'the people' love.

---

29 Compare the opposition set up in *King Lear* between the disguised Kent, who serves Lear because he still loves him and because, he says, Lear has 'that in your countenance which I would fain call master', so that serving him is natural (1.4.6, 27–8), and Oswald, who is attacked by Kent as a social climber who will undertake any dishonourable action to please his master and thus advance himself (2.2.72–80).

A PARTIAL THEORY OF ORIGINAL PRACTICE

JEREMY LOPEZ

How do we account for the rise of the 'original practices' movement in the production of early modern drama over the past twenty years? How do we account for the increasingly energetic collaboration, and indeed collusion, of theatre historians and other kinds of scholars working in a sceptical and relativistic academic climate with a form of theatrical practice that is based on highly dubious, manifestly problematic notions of authenticity and the uses of history? The range of possible answers to these questions is as complex as the questions themselves are stark. In this article I provide one partial and very specific kind of answer. My purpose is to situate the original-practices movement firmly in the world of literary discourse and, consequently, to destabilize some of the powerful claims to authority it currently makes with reference to material process and embodied action. In the pages that follow, I discuss the development of the original-practices movement of the past twenty or so years – since the groundbreaking for the new Globe and the founding of the Shenandoah Shakespeare Express, in 1987 and 1988 respectively – among and alongside one of the key developments in literary criticism during that same period, the reaction against new historicism. I argue that the original-practices movement seems in part to be both a critique of and an attempt to co-opt 'new historicism' broadly considered as both a critical and an ethical practice. In making this argument, I hope to identify with precision and with sympathy some of the impulses (beyond the quest for authority and authenticity) that drive the original-practices movement – to identify how it responds to a need, or a variety of needs, in the academic community, and to begin to suggest some ways in which these needs might be met without recourse to the dubious theoretical and methodological assumptions and practices upon which the movement currently relies.

Critics of new historicism have been careful to point out that 'new historicism' does not define a single methodology or a single set of theoretical assumptions. In 'After the New Historicism',[1] Steven Mullaney provides a survey of the variegated theoretical and critical camps with which the label 'new historicism' has been associated (p. 20), and arrives at a usefully broad interpretation of the label that conceives it less as a single methodology than an ethical perspective underlying a range of evidently related critical practices:

From its early focus on the relationship between cultural forms and structures of state and institutional authority, new historicism has been an enquiry, or rather a series of not always harmonious enquiries, into the power such forms and structures have to determine ideas and ideologies, historical subjects and their actions, cultural practices and their potential for either reinforcing or contesting that power and those structures.

(p. 21)

I am very grateful (in alphabetical order) to Ralph Alan Cohen, Andrew Hartley, Peter Holland, Russ McDonald, Paul Menzer, Peter J. Smith, Holger Syme and Sarah Werner for reading and criticizing drafts and earlier versions of this article.

[1] In Terence Hawkes, ed., *Alternative Shakespeares, Volume II* (London, 1996), pp. 17–37.

'Original practices' is similarly a label that cannot be said to define a single set, but rather a range of (sometimes inharmonious) methodologies and critical practices. In part because of its grounding in the theatre and in part because of its resistance to self-theorization (which is related to its grounding in the theatre), 'original practices' is an even more difficult range of methodologies to define and critique than 'new historicism'. No manifesto of original practices has been written; in print, it has no Greenblatt-style champion or scapegoat;[2] its 'manifestos' might be said to be buildings like Shakespeare's Globe or the Staunton, Virginia Blackfriars, but the things that happen in these buildings are complexly, divergently mediated by the exigencies of the Shakespeare-driven tourism industry (and/or the tourism-driven Shakespeare industry).

The project this article embarks upon, then, to analyse the rise of a diffusely defined amalgam of critical and theatrical practices among and alongside critiques of a diffusely defined theoretical perspective, is a difficult one. I want to acknowledge at the outset that the theoretical history I give to the original-practices movement is, as my title insists, only partial; the question of the relationship between original practices and twentieth-century theatre history is of equal if not greater importance to the movement's identity, but requires fuller exposition than the limited space of this article will allow. I also want to acknowledge that there is no real overlap – as far as published positions go – between practitioners and critics of new historicism on the one hand and practitioners of original practices on the other; what I seek to do in this article is not to outline a causal relationship between the two, but instead to illustrate the way in which critiques of new historicism through the late 1980s and the 1990s helped create a critical climate in which original practices could begin to flourish. In order to do this, I must assume that 'new historicism' broadly considered – let us take Mullaney's summary as a working definition – was and to a certain extent continues to be the normative perspective from which literary criticism of Shakespeare has been undertaken over the past two decades. I

understand that this is not an entirely safe assumption, but I feel it is just safe enough to function as a productive interpretive convenience.

With these caveats firmly in mind, I begin by identifying some of the tenets of the original-practices movement in almost the only way it is possible to do so: by means of the websites that articulate the practices and goals of theatre companies operating wholly or in part under the rubric of 'original practices'. Readers of drafts of this article have understandably been somewhat surprised at my reliance on what amounts mainly to marketing materials in giving voice to the original-practices 'methodology'. Doing so has to a large extent been a necessity because there is no scholarly treatise that amounts to a systematic statement of original-practices principles. There are, of course, Andrew Gurr's *Rebuilding Shakespeare's Globe*[3] (written with John Orrell, author of the standard reference on the sixteenth and seventeenth-century Globes, *The Quest for Shakespeare's Globe*[4]), and J. R. Mulryne and Margaret Shewring's *Shakespeare's Globe Rebuilt*,[5] published in advance of the new Globe's opening to explain its scholarly history and

---

[2] Mark Rylance is, of course, the major representative figure for original practices, but his printed work, some of which I discuss below (see note 6), is much less influential in this regard than his theatrical work; the same might be said of Ralph Alan Cohen, also discussed below. William Poel's *Shakespeare in the Theatre* (London, 1913), especially chapter 1, can be seen as a statement of original-practices principles, and much of the work done at Shakespeare's Globe and the Staunton Blackfriars is in a direct line of descent from Poel; but the combination of Poel's antiquarianism (notably contrasted to the demands of the modern theatre in J. L. Styan's *The Shakespeare Revolution*) and his distance from our present moment prevents him from being used as a figurehead for the contemporary original practices movement. The American Shakespeare Center's biennial Blackfriars conference has resulted in one published and one forthcoming collection of essays (the first, published by Susquehanna University Press, appeared in 2006), but the essays in these volumes are only loosely centred on the idea of 'original practices'. See my review of this book in *Review of English Studies* 58 (2007), 237.

[3] (London, 1989).

[4] (Cambridge, 1983).

[5] (Cambridge, 1997).

purposes. But while these books are highly detailed in their description of the practice of theatrical *reconstruction*, they are cagily and necessarily vague with respect to the practice of theatrical *production*. Thus the keynote for Gurr's book is that 'We lose or distort much of what is valuable in [Shakespeare's] plays so long as we remain ignorant of the precise shape of [the] playhouse . . . the precise shape of the stage and the auditorium, the quality of the light' (pp. 18–19), and the work of the subsequent chapters is to explain precisely how and to what degree such information was obtained and applied. But he is surprisingly candid when it comes to imagining how these precisely reconstructed physical elements will affect theatrical performance: 'A *new* tradition of ensemble playing will have to develop to cope with the complex, novel, and probably unforeseeable demands on acting in the Globe repertory' (p. 46, emphasis added).[6]

The websites of theatres and theatre projects that advertise themselves as making use of original practices are not primarily concerned with the methodology of reconstruction, but rather with making claims for and selling that reconstruction's definite effects. The selling that these theatres do, largely in the interest of creating and cultivating student audiences, is enabled and legitimized by the original-practices scholarship of reconstruction, and is the primary means by which that scholarship can continue to justify and seek funding for its existence. Focusing on the rhetoric of original-practices theatre websites is a vivid means by which to emphasize the fact that the language used to describe 'original practices' at all systematically as a methodology is, and in the current academic climate probably can be nothing other than, the language of advertising. One of my chief concerns in the first section here is to demonstrate the way in which the language of advertising overlaps with the language of pedagogy.

After providing a basic outline of original practice and some of the crucial assumptions that underlie it, I will proceed to a highly selective survey of critiques of and reactions against new historicism. My purpose in this survey is not to discuss the validity of each critique, but to construe its view of one or more of new historicism's shortcomings as importantly representative – and to argue that each perceived lack is something that the original-practices movement has sought to compensate for. As well, I want to be careful not to suggest that the early or latterly advocates of 'original practices', scholars or theatrical practitioners, have drawn, consciously and directly, on the criticism I survey. Rather, I use a range of theoretically and historically sophisticated critiques of new historicism, some of them not primarily concerned with the theatre or theatrical performance, as representative evidence in support of my hypothesis that the critical ferment of the late 1980s and the 1990s was one important factor in allowing reconstructed theatrical spaces to become the field on which a kind of proxy war can be fought against a powerful form of professional and ever more self-professionalizing literary criticism. The fighters in

---

[6] See also Mulryne and Shewring's collection, in which the majority of the chapters have to do with highly technical elements of physical reconstruction. The final chapter, a statement of 'Artistic Policy and Practice' by Mark Rylance, is highly (and realistically) vague in its understanding of the effect these elements have upon theatrical practice. On the subject of whether or not to use directors, for example, he says: 'My experience . . . has confirmed my understanding of the need for directors and the difficulty of that role. We do not, however, want tyrants. Fortunately in the theatre climate of the nineties it feels as if there has been a swing in the conception of the director's role. Many more directors are now interested in freedom of communication between actors and audience. For a director to control this communication at the Globe will be, in any case, impossible. There is minimal scenery, no lights, and so many random variables . . . all of which demand constant adjustment from the actor outside the director's control' (p. 170). Here, the design components of the Globe only help facilitate something (the 'swing' in directorial attitude) already in process. Some sense of what Gurr's 'new tradition' involves is given by Pauline Kiernan's *Staging Shakespeare at the New Globe* (New York, 1999). This book is decidedly more of a record of what the Globe *has done* than an analysis of what it should be able to do, and an examination of this record – see, for example, section II, on the day-to-day process of getting *Henry V* onto the stage – demonstrates that rehearsing at the Globe can be very much like rehearsing in any other theatre, only more difficult and annoying due to, say, the obstructing pillars or the noisy rushes.

this proxy war have for the most part been actors, whose familiarity with new historicism might be casual at best. But they have been led into battle by academics – perhaps most directly by academics like Andrew Gurr, John Orrell, J. R. Mulryne, Margaret Shewring and Ralph Alan Cohen, but also by or alongside the army of university teachers and scholars who have taken their students to reconstructed theatrical spaces such as the London Globe and Staunton Blackfriars. Original practices lives in the theatre, but it was born in, and continues to take much of its nourishment from, the academy.

The picture of the original-practices movement that will emerge from my analytical method is particularly appropriate, considering the theatrical medium and processes in which the movement resides: it is the picture of a historical-political-theatrical-scholarly movement in motley, improvising expediently, brilliantly and apparently self-sufficiently, but always aware of its spectators' approbation or opprobrium – unable to break free entirely from the reality for which it claims to provide the antidote.

Although the term 'original practices' was apparently coined by the Globe's Mark Rylance,[7] most of the dissemination of the original-practices ideology now originates in Staunton, Virginia, site of Ralph Alan Cohen's magnificent reconstruction of the Blackfriars theatre, home of the American Shakespeare Center (formerly the Shenandoah Shakespeare Express); Staunton is also the home of Mary Baldwin College, whose M.Litt./MFA programme offering degree concentrations in acting, directing and teaching, was founded by Cohen. The first semester of the Mary Baldwin graduate programme was Fall 2001, precisely coincident with the 21 September 2001 opening of the reconstructed Blackfriars. A recent graduate of Cohen's programme at Mary Baldwin, Megan McDonough, runs the website www.originalpractices.com, which features a page loosely defining 'original practices' as well as links to eight theatre companies operating under an original-practices rubric. One of these companies is, of course, the American Shakespeare Center; another is the Maryland Shakespeare Festival (MSF). McDonough is currently the associate director of education at the MSF, where she was responsible, in 2007, for booking that company's Shakespeare Alive! Tour, bringing Hamlet and a medley of scenes and speeches to over 40 middle schools, high schools and colleges in Maryland.[8] The artistic director of MSF, Becky Kemper, is currently enrolled in the M.Litt./MFA programme at Mary Baldwin College where, according to the MSF website, she is working on a thesis that will be 'put to practical use' when she directs Hamlet.[9]

Ralph Alan Cohen is an extraordinarily influential teacher, himself moulded by an extraordinarily influential teacher, the great textual scholar and bibliographer George Walton Williams. Profiled in the September–October issue of Duke Magazine, Cohen said that Williams was 'one of those teachers who seem to embody his subject'. And, 'When Williams took me on as his advisee, he did so – as I've learned in the last thirty-three years – on a permanent basis . . . and I never write or direct

---

7 See The Times, 14 August 1998. In this article, which is a response to Benedict Nightingale's feeling that the Globe was 'coarsening' Shakespeare by pandering to its audiences (The Times, 3 August 1998), Rylance uses the simultaneously more specific and more vague term 'original playing practices'. In the context of Nightingale's critique, this phrase implicitly refers to actors deliberately engaging and encouraging responses from the audience. (Nightingale worried that the resultant audience behaviour might be too 'authentic'.) Rylance lists 'original playing practices' alongside a number of other Globe practices, some of which could be called 'original' and some not: 'daily class in movement, speech and verse-speaking during the rehearsal period for the actors, live music which becomes a powerful tool in the absence of lighting and sets, and beautiful, hand-crafted Elizabethan clothing'. In the absence of anything like material evidence for 'playing practices' of the early modern period, the term 'original practices' has simultaneously narrowed and broadened to refer largely to things that can be slightly more easily recovered, such as lighting, stage construction, rehearsal practice, doubling and music.

8 See the Mary Baldwin M.Litt./MFA Folio for Winter 2007: www.mbc.edu/docs/publications/FolioFall2006.pdf.

9 www.mdshakes.org/research.html#current.

anything without first assuring myself that I can justify my choices to George.'[10] This kind of deep continuity between teacher and student is everywhere evident on McDonough's original-practices website, whose home page features a photograph from the Blackfriars stage and whose links include papers given by other Mary Baldwin students in classes and at Cohen's Blackfriars conferences. The first tenet of original-practices dramaturgy given on the site's homepage is 'Universal lighting' and, underneath this, '(doing it with the lights on)', a paraphrase of the well-known Staunton Blackfriars slogan, 'We do it with the lights on.' Megan McDonough and Becky Kemper collaborate with the MSF (whose 'original practices' page incorporates and elaborates slightly upon McDonough's own homepage) to embody forth the principles of Ralph Cohen's Blackfriars dramaturgy to the theatregoers and scholars of the future. And because Cohen's dramaturgy is very much a product of his work with George Walton Williams, a textual scholar who inspired Cohen with his 'utter belief in the critical importance of every word [of Shakespeare]',[11] it is a text-based dramaturgy that is genuinely, literally conservative.[12]

I begin my discussion of original practices this way in order to emphasize how closely their dissemination and rhetoricization are bound up with teaching. The deeply personal way in which Ralph Cohen conceives and carries out his theatre's mission makes him a particularly vivid, perhaps even exaggerated, example of the phenomenon I want to discuss in this section. But the similarities between the pedagogical structure and rhetoric of the Blackfriars and that of other high profile original-practices projects are fundamental and important. The Globe depends heavily, as I have noted, upon student audiences, and the 'Education' section of its website makes this boast about the educational programmes it offers:

Words do not lie lifeless on the page in Globe Education workshops. Playful and play-filled approaches are shared year round with over 70,000 students and teachers at the Globe. From October to March they can experience the relationship between play and playground for themselves as they take to the Globe stage.[13]

The Shakespeare and the Queen's Men project, a theatre-history conference accompanied by original-practices productions presented at the University of Toronto in the fall of 2006, was put together by a tightly knit group of faculty and graduate students at the University of

---

[10] www.dukemagazine.duke.edu/dukemag/issues/091002/depmini-cohen.html.

[11] This quotation is also from the *Duke Magazine*.

[12] I borrow the formulation 'genuinely, literally conservative' from the closing sentence of Stephen Booth's essay on Sonnet 146 in his edition of the *Sonnets* (New Haven, 1977). Booth is another of Cohen's mentors and close friends, and is, like Williams, a scholar who inspires students with his belief in the 'utter importance of every word'. (Just to be clear about the levels of influence at work here: I am both a former and lifelong student of Booth, happily but complexly unable to formulate any idea without mentally running it past him first.) For Booth, 'conservative' criticism is, somewhat paradoxically, a criticism that admits the full range of possible meanings in a poem by refusing to take a single (in Booth's case, this frequently means ideologically coloured) interpretive position on it. The cornerstone of this criticism is a meticulous attention to detail, the goal being 'to insure that a reader's experience of the sonnets will as far as possible approximate that of the first readers of the 1609 Quarto' (*Sonnets*, p. xii); the parallels between this form of criticism and the kind of experiential reconstruction sought at the Blackfriars – one that deliberately eschews an ideological bias – are clear and suggestive. After reading a draft of this article, Ralph Cohen, in email correspondence, emphasized the importance of Booth's 'as far as possible': '[W]e have no illusions . . . that we can replicate the experience as a whole. What we aim to do is to show audiences the efficacy of choices that have been obscured by theatrical innovations – darkened auditoria, curtains, black outs, cast of thousands, revolves. We (I at least) have found that there is a remarkable correlation between recovering older conventions and recovering linguistic meaning.' Drawing an important distinction between the scholarly apparatus that frames original-practices advertising and what spectators can be expected to take away from original-practices theatres, Cohen went on to say that 'If our audiences think about [recovered or reconstructed effects such as doubling or universal lighting] at all they don't think about it in terms of original practices, but the accumulated record of the ease with which we do it makes it possible for others to think about it, to factor it in without hesitancy in understanding the plays. Again, our work hasn't so much discovered anything as simply remove the obstacle to thinking about those things.'

[13] www.shakespeares-globe.org/globeeducation/.

Toronto and McMaster University; its website announces that 'in the third year of the project, 2007–8, Shakespeare and the Queen's Men's documentary film, interactive DVD, internet production records, and print publications will make this Toronto area experience available to students, scholars, and theatre artists throughout Canada and around the world'.[14] In its somewhat charming optimism about achieving a benign form of world-domination, the self-promoting language of these websites provides a totalizing rhetoric of pedagogical empowerment that on one level serves, I suggest, as an alternative to the totalizing rhetoric of disempowerment that new historicism has been said to have effected.

The foregoing claim ultimately cannot be more than hypothetical, and the degree to which the hypothesis is or is not convincing will depend on my reader's assessment of the final part of my argument. For the moment, I want to elaborate my claim about the totalizing rhetoric of original practice by looking at Megan McDonough's website and the network of rhetorical relationships that branches out from it. McDonough's website is both comprehensive and modest in its claims for the scope of the movement. 'Original Practices is a term used as short-hand for the recreation of one or more aspects of Elizabethan staging techniques by modern day theatre practitioners, based on the discoveries and deductions of historians and textual scholars.' The slight tentativeness of 'one or more', in contrast to the scholarly confidence of 'discoveries and deductions', is brought out further in the next, highly unpretentious sentence: 'It basically means doing theatre like Shakespeare and his fellows did, at least in some ways.' McDonough goes on to list some of the ways in which an original-practices company might do theatre like Shakespeare and his fellows did: universal lighting; thrust stage or 'in the round'; doubling; minimal set; live music and sound effects; Elizabethan rehearsal techniques (chiefly as they have been elaborated by the research of Tiffany Stern); and 'driving pace'. These are dramaturgical conventions that are common, singly or collectively, to all the original-practices companies linked from the site.

But the most fascinating thing about this web-page is the self-interrogating question that follows this list of dramaturgical conventions: 'Is that it?' It is as though McDonough feels that her reader will wonder if the energy and excitement of theatrical experience can be simply the sum of so many component mechanical parts. She then proceeds to answer her own question:

The individual staging conventions open for recreation are numerous, and many have yet to be explored . . . [T]he most basic requirement lies not in any of these individual components, but rather in the desire for discovery. The single factor uniting scholars and practitioners under the heading of the modern original practice movement is an understanding that there is much left to discover. Whether a company decides to explore one component or many; to produce Shakespeare, Marlowe, or to write new works for the original practice playhouse; the desire for discovery . . . unites them all in a growing and innovative movement, changing the way theatre is made.

Original practice, it turns out, is not really about nailing down the specificity of actual historical practice, but simply the quest itself for this kind of information – and the infinitude of the quest as it is presented here suggests that finishing it, actually *finding* what you're looking for, is neither necessary nor desirable. The rhetoric here is emphatically that of the pedagogue, the enthusiastic teacher convincing her students of the literally boundless pleasures (pleasurable because boundless) of scholarly work. One of the most remarkable things about the original-practices movement is the way adherent theatre companies, whether or not they have an academic affiliation, willingly and vehemently adopt this pedagogical rhetoric.

Megan McDonough's website shows a savvy awareness that if 'original practices' is going to flourish not only as a form of scholarly inquiry but also as a commercial phenomenon it cannot be too narrowly construed. The companies linked to her website (and to one another through their websites) indicate the selective manner in

---

[14] www.reed.utoronto.ca/QueensMen/about.html.

which theatre companies use the term. Thus the American Shakespeare Center uses a reconstructed theatrical space, universal lighting and 'costumes that speak to our audiences in the most familiar language possible', but eschews all-male casts;[15] the Pigeon Creek Shakespeare Company (Grand Haven, Michigan) uses universal lighting and minimal sets but, lacking a purpose-built theatrical home, construes its use of space as a loose version of Elizabethan touring practice, where plays might have been performed in 'non-traditional theatrical spaces';[16] Shakespeare & Co. (Lennox, Massachusetts) claims to be a company that 'performs as the Elizabethans did – in love with poetry, physical prowess, and the mysteries of the universe',[17] and is in the process of building a replica of Henslowe's Rose. Its current main-house playing space is, however, an 'air-conditioned scaffold-and-canvas theatre' that seats 406 in 'box seats and in comfortable, armless, cushion-backed benches'.[18] This list of exceptions to or variations from the original-practices 'rules' could be continued through an examination of the websites of the New American Shakespeare Tavern (Atlanta, Georgia),[19] the Excellent Motion Shakespeare company (San Diego, California),[20] Shakespeare's Globe in London and the Shakespeare and the Queen's Men project. There are, however, two important consistencies that give structure to this variation: an explicit, vehement concern with audience interaction, and a focus on the importance of the physical performance space.

'Never seen a Shakespeare play?' asks the New American Shakespeare Tavern's 'Experiencing Shakespeare' webpage.[21] 'Or maybe it's been a while and you're afraid you won't understand what's going on?' Construing original practice as the 'communion of audience, actor, and playwright through poetry', the company's discussion of your impending experience is positively shrill in insisting that you won't be able to avoid understanding what Shakespeare is saying: 'in true Elizabethan fashion, you will always be included in the joke'; 'Our job is to make the words of the playwright come alive and to explore that message *with* you rather than merely reciting it "at" you.' 'YOU are PART of the conver-

sation, and in our experience that goes a long way towards making Shakespeare's language accessible and clear'; 'you'll *understand*'; 'We promise you'll get the jokes.' All emphasis is original here. This is not only enthusiastic pedagogical rhetoric, it is a version of the rhetoric of student evaluations: an audience understands most when it is being most entertained, when the material presented to it is presented spontaneously (not 'recited') and when it is made highly accessible; communication is most effective when someone is looking right at *you*.

The New American Shakespeare Tavern is only the most extreme example of the pervasive pedagogical language used by original-practices companies. The three 'central and inter-dependent activities' that constitute the purpose of the Shakespeare's Globe Trust yoke the 'faithfully reconstructed Globe' with 'performance conditions reproducing those of Shakespeare's time', and both with 'educational programmes . . . for students at all levels'.[22] Excellent Motion's 'About Us' webpage features a statement of their particular form of original practice – 'audiences will have actors directly addressing them and sometimes might be pulled right onto the stage! One way or another . . . audiences become part of the action' – and follows this with a more general mission statement:

---

[15] www.americanshakespearecenter.com/about/whatWeDo.html.

[16] www.pcshakespeare.com/originalpractices.html. Pigeon Creek Shakespeare was founded in 1998; one of its founding members, Katherine Mayberry, is a recent graduate of Mary Baldwin College's MA programme. I am grateful to Ralph Cohen for pointing this out to me.

[17] www.shakespeare.org/sandco.php?pg=about&category=about%20the%20company&subCat=Mission%2c+Vision%2c+%26+ Values+Statement.

[18] www.shakespeare.org/sandco.php?pg=performance&theatre=Founders'%20Theatre&file= theatres.php.

[19] www.shakespearetavern.com/.

[20] www.excellentmotion.com/main.html. Excellent Motion was founded in 2006 by Dennis Henry; before this, Henry worked with the American Shakespeare Center for three years. I am grateful to Ralph Cohen for pointing this out to me.

[21] www.shakespearetavern.com/experiencing.htm.

[22] www.shakespeares-globe.org/information/introduction./

The Excellent Motion Shakespeare Company exists for the purpose of making life on earth just a little bit better by seeking to integrate theatre arts into the everyday lives of the people of the US and the world by means of exhilarating educational programs and passionate productions of the plays of Shakespeare and other playwrights who share his (and our) love of life and belief in humanity.

Like an inspiring teacher, original-practices theatre companies conflate the forms of art with the structures of education; they refuse to let their audiences be intimidated by the esoteric, the anachronistic, the arcane; and they explain their own immersion in these things by allegorizing them, representing them as essential tools for self-understanding.

Of course, the notion of Shakespeare as the great teacher, and Shakespearian theatre as the ultimate humanistic education, has been around for a long time and is certainly not the exclusive province of original-practices theatre. The particularity of original-practices pedagogical rhetoric has to do with its conception of the physical space from which Shakespeare's plays speak as being essential to their ability to communicate.[23] *Thrust stage*; *non-traditional theatrical spaces*; *a place to eat, drink, and nourish the soul*; *minimal sets*; *the southern shore of the Thames river*; *plasterwork and thatching*; *the world's only recreation of Shakespeare's original indoor theatre*: these are the terms original-practices companies use, independently and jointly, to establish the location where the unique experiences they provide and recreate occur and have occurred. The kind of theatre produced in these spaces is and was *shamelessly entertaining*; it allows audiences to feel *that anything could happen*; it allows actors to *wow you with the immediacy of their performances and the clarity of their communication*; it is *fast paced and exciting*; it facilitated *an explosion of creativity not seen before or since*; it is part of a *lasting memorial to one of the greatest playwrights in the world*; it is *changing the way theatre is made*. The simultaneous immediacy and timelessness to which original-practices productions lay particular, and particularly vehement, claim is a function of the space in which they occur – a function of understanding those spaces as absolutely distinct from any other extant space, and absolutely contiguous (or analogous) with spaces that have been lost to the

ravages of time. The novelty of this kind of space, so conceived, makes it possible to court an audience that is, in its generality, the inverse of the particularity of the experiences that occur therein. The sense of immediacy original-practices companies strive for in these experiences is enabled by the fact that their spaces are simultaneously everyplace and noplace, infinitely capacious and thus incapable of conceiving something beyond their walls: the stage is all the world.

The critiques of and reactions against new historicism which I will now connect to the rise of original practices have two different but related concerns: one is with empirical or documentary evidence and the rhetorical force of the new historical anecdote; the other involves seeing theatrical events as having access to meanings that transcend or are distinct from the rhetorical (and political) paradoxes and impasses that drive new historical literary critical practice. I want to stress again that I am not arguing for a causal relationship between critiques of new historicism and the rise of original practices; the former provides one important means by which to understand the latter. Neither

---

[23] The importance of locality is something with which Ralph Cohen has been concerned since the beginning of his career. See 'The Importance of Setting in the Revision of *Every Man In His Humour*' (*English Literary Renaissance* 8.2 (1978), pp. 183–96), where he argues that the 'effect of a London background on the play's action is a sense of real movement in the play . . . Jonson clearly wants to take advantage of this effect and throughout the revision he gives to airy nothing a local habitation and a name' (p. 189). Although 'the improvement Jonson made on his original play may seem minor, . . . a Jacobean Londoner would have found that Jonson's efforts produced a more satiric, more unified, and more profound play' (p. 196). See also 'Looking for Cousin Ferdinand: The Value of F1 Stage Directions for a Production of *The Taming of the Shrew*' in *Textual Formations and Reformations*, ed. Laurie E. Maguire and Thomas L. Berger (Newark, Delaware, 1998), an essay whose first paragraph links the enterprise of teaching with that of directing, and sees both as compromised by the editorial tradition that has led readers away from the stage directions in the Folio text. The first example Cohen gives of the dangers of this tradition is Dover Wilson's detailed imagination of 'Petruccio's house in the country' superimposed upon the Folio's simple direction 'Enter Grumio' (p. 264).

movement, however broadly or narrowly construed, obviously implies the other; the relationship they share is surprising and vexed, and it has a great deal to tell us about the identity and status of Shakespearian performance and pedagogy in the late twentieth and early twenty-first centuries.

I begin with Jean Howard's 1986 'The New Historicism in Renaissance Studies',[24] a now classic advocation of the new historicist methodology and far-sighted critique of its potential limitations. In predictable new historicist-influenced fashion, I want to focus on what seemed to me – in rereading this essay for the first time in many years, and from this particular point of view – a surprising aspect of the critique, namely its concern with empirical evidence. Discussing Greenblatt's 'use of the illustrative example', Howard presents what would become a standard objection to new historicist methodology: 'he does not really question whether his perception of the centrality of these figures is an effect of the critical attention they have historically received or if it stems from some essential quality they inherently possess'. The next part of the sentence is somewhat arresting in its *difference* from the kind of critiques of new historicism made by subsequent authors, especially authors who, like Howard, write from a perspective that is more within than without the methodology: 'nor does he make any serious attempt to prove their representativeness in the statistical terms likely to satisfy the empiricist'. The long sentence then immediately takes another turn, as Howard withdraws the objection she's just made in favour of the kind of critique that she, and others both before and after her, is more interested to make – and one to which Greenblatt would become more and more concerned to respond in his work: 'nor [does he] argue for the irrelevance of [empirical data] in ways likely to satisfy those who see the "facts" of history largely produced by the operations of a particular discourse or act of theoretical intervention' (p. 38).

Similar to most critiques of new historicism before and since, Howard's concern is with the authority of the critic, with understanding the relationship of a charismatic and powerful subject like Stephen Greenblatt to the influential arguments for the containment of the subject enabled by his methodology. Raising the empiricist objection, gesturing towards 'statistical' proof as another possible locus of interpretive authority, Howard gives brief voice to a mode of critique that has, I would suggest, come into its own with the resurgence of highly archival theatre history we have seen in the past decade or so – and especially, for my purposes, the use of this theatre history for large scale academic-theatrical projects such as the Globe and Blackfriars reconstructions, and the Shakespeare and the Queen's Men productions.

Three related and more detailed expressions of the empiricist objection, more or less contemporary with Howard's article, might be seen to have laid some of the groundwork for the theatre-historical movement as a reaction to new historicism's location of interpretive authority in the figure of the critic. Perhaps the most influential of these is Leeds Barroll's 'A New History for Shakespeare and His Time',[25] a dense and rigorous interrogation of new historicism's intertwining of *Richard II* and the Essex conspiracy, and of Stuart power and Shakespeare's theatrical politics. Barroll is concerned to work through the implications of Howard's question about choice of evidence, using new historicism's 'continual adduction and uniform interpretation of the Essex locus' as a representative case in which are evident 'important reasons why any historical method must first deal with its own theoretical premises' (p. 443). The method by means of which Barroll addresses the question is a 'systematic study of the texts detailing *the entire episode* in which the Earl of Essex attempted to seize control of Queen Elizabeth's person and of her closest advisors' (p. 444, emphasis added). Although he is at pains to indicate sympathy for the new-historical project (see p. 442) and although he is well-versed in the theoretical assumptions that underlie (or do not underlie) it, Barroll also fashions himself (justifiably) as a critic who understands better than almost anyone else

[24] *English Literary Renaissance* 16 (1986), 13–43.
[25] *Shakespeare Quarterly* 39 (1988), 441–64.

how things worked in the late sixteenth and early seventeenth centuries. The language of his warning against a new historical method built upon 'an unquestioning acceptance of an extremely narrow set of documents . . . ensconced in traditional narratives and premised upon elementary concepts of political process' is stern, authoritative and echoed elsewhere in his published work.[26] Somewhat ironically, Barroll's archive-centred criticism serves to create a politically neutralized Shakespeare very much like the 'contained' Shakespeare of new historicism; the difference between the two lies in Barroll's unwillingness to rhetoricize the seductive possibility of subversion.

Writing in the 1991 issue of *Medieval and Renaissance Drama in England*, a journal edited by Leeds Barroll at the time, Alan Somerset invoked Barroll's language as he set forth his own critique of new historicism's subversion-and-containment model: for Somerset, the 'ideological positions' discussed and analysed by new historicists, when 'applied historically, are theories of society and historical process, and are dependent upon discoverable evidence'. Like Jean Howard, Somerset wonders how one decides 'what facts are "typical," and hence what is trustworthy evidence?' (p. 246). And, like Barroll, Somerset's method in addressing the question is to examine a wider range of documents – in this case documents pertaining to a legal case surrounding some festivities gone awry in Shrewsbury, collected by the researchers working on the *Records of Early English Drama* (REED) project. In using REED documents to complicate new-historical reliance upon and use of the rhetoric of subversion and containment as a model for the relationship between theatre and state (see, especially, p. 254), Somerset was heeding the call for a more rigorous historicism in Clifford Davidson's 1988 review of Steven Mullaney's *The Place of the Stage*.[27] In his analysis of Mullaney's claim that the early modern theatre emerged 'from a participatory phase when the drama was integrated with the city's understanding of itself and performed within the city's walls rather than on its fringes', Davidson takes Mullaney to task for 'failing to take note of the topography of London drama detailed more fully and accurately in

Ian Lancashire's magisterial *Dramatic Texts and Records of Britain: A Chronological Topography to 1558*', and thus failing 'to establish the requisite contrast between the public stage and the vigorous tradition of civic pageantry in London' (p. 361). The idea here is to neutralize the ideological force of the separation Mullaney sees between the early modern theatre and civic government by arguing that a fuller examination of the documentary evidence will reveal a similar separation in an earlier period.

Ian Lancashire's book, in which Davidson anchors his critique of Mullaney, was published by the University of Toronto Press in 1984 as the first volume in its *Studies in Early English Drama* (SEED) series – a series founded as an adjunct to REED, to which latter project Lancashire is a principal adviser. As an archival, primarily medieval theatre historian, Clifford Davidson is methodologically very closely aligned with the REED contributors – whose work he regularly reviewed in *Comparative Drama* (a journal he co-edited). Alan Somerset not only edited the REED volume on Shropshire (1994), but is also the General Editor of the SEED series and the co-director, with Sally-Beth MacLean, of the REED 'Patrons and Performances Website'.[28] MacLean was co-author, with Scott McMillin, of *The Queen's Men and their Plays*,[29] a book that provided the basis for the Shakespeare and the Queen's Men (SQM) conference at the University of Toronto. What I am suggesting here is not a systematic or programmatic response to new historicism, culminating in an original-practices project; rather, I am attempting to outline the way in which the Toronto school of theatre history has over two decades provided a very general locality for a variety of related methodological reactions against new historicism suggested briefly by Jean Howard and in great detail by Leeds Barroll in the late 1980s. One goal and effect of these reactions has been to locate the criteria for

---

[26] See the first two chapters of *Politics, Plague, and Shakespeare's Theater* (Ithaca, 1991), especially pp. 1–7 and 23–5.

[27] *Comparative Drama* 22 (1988–9), pp. 359–69.

[28] http://link.library.utoronto.ca/reed/.

[29] (Cambridge, 1998).

evidentiary selection and the authority for evidentiary interpretation not in the person of the critic but in the topography and physical spaces of early modern history.[30]

At the end of his review of Mullaney's *The Place of the Stage*, Clifford Davidson makes 'a few general comments' on new historicism, arguing that

This methodology potentially will have much more to offer to drama criticism if it will attempt to come to terms with the literature as scripts for the actual stage, which requires to be understood in terms of its visual dimension, its position *vis-à-vis* its audience, and its phenomenological context. (p. 369)

Davidson's emphasis on the materiality of the theatre ('scripts for the actual stage', 'visual dimension') becomes a persistent refrain in criticisms of new historicism, a critical methodology whose potential for rhetorical elegance seems always in danger of effacing the reality of the phenomena it is discussing. Such a concern with the materiality of location is the basis of Mullaney's own critique, some years later, of Greenblatt (see n.1 above):

[Greenblatt] tends to aestheticize the sites occupied by the popular playhouses – areas outside the city walls known as the Liberties – describing them as 'carefully demarcated playgrounds' . . . Rather than neutral zones, however, the Liberties were complexly inscribed domains of cultural contradiction, ambivalence and license; the emergence of popular drama in them was not the escape of an artform to a sheltered retreat . . . but rather a forceful, and forcefully felt, appropriation of a highly volatile zone in the city's spatial economy . . . (p. 29)

For Mullaney, Greenblatt tends anachronistically to understand early modern popular theatre as 'literature' rather than *as theatre*, and is thus too easily able to ignore its chaotic materiality and locality, and to subject it to the formulations of a literary criticism.

Mullaney's 1996 essay overlaps incidentally with work such as that done by Somerset and the REED school in that both are concerned to provide a highly historicized location for theatrical phenomena. And it overlaps specifically with other theoretical work arising in the late 1980s and the 1990s

and in search of the 'agency' that new historicism's subversion-containment model seems to preclude. Anthony B. Dawson, in his 1988 '*Measure for Measure*, New Historicism, and Theatrical Power',[31] found new historicism 'as a mode of interpretation' to be 'antithetical . . . to current theatrical practice' (p. 329). And he argued that those moments in new historicist discourse

when 'nostalgia' for the subject and his/her freedom, however inconsistently, breaks through . . . reveal a hidden desire or lack in the theory itself, one that should, I think, be given some theoretical weight (especially since one way of appeasing such desire would be to go to the theatre). (p. 340)

Dawson's turn to the agency of the actor, and the highly physicalized, temporized act of going to the theatre as a way beyond new historicism's power paradigm was echoed in M. D. Jardine's 'New Historicism for Old: New Conservatism for Old? The Politics of Patronage in the Renaissance'.[32] The work of this essay is to critique new historicism's use of an overly conservative patronage paradigm to frame its arguments about the circulation of power; the essay concludes by suggesting that a 'way forward' out of the paralysing containment model provided by new historicism is to begin looking at 'areas of agency' in early modern drama, and one direction in which Jardine sends a reader is to

---

[30] While SQM's ideology of original practices was, as I discussed in the first section of this article, contiguous with that of the Globe and Blackfriars, it also worked to distinguish itself by means of a REED-inspired interest in touring and variable venues: 'Thanks to award-winning research from our own team members, the experiment included: using locations representative of those used in Elizabethan companies [and thereby] encountering difficulties they must have met . . .' (www.reed.utoronto.ca/QueensMen/performance.html). Not at all coincidentally, in 2007 REED established a base in the United States, at Mary Baldwin College and the American Shakespeare Center: see http://reed-usa.org/mission.html. The purpose of this partnership is to 'complement the educational mission of "original practices" (O.P.) early modern drama study by supporting the documentation which underlies pedagogy and performance.'

[31] *Shakespeare Quarterly* 39 (1988), 328–41.

[32] *Yearbook of English Studies* 21 (1991), 286–304.

Isobel Armstrong's 'Thatcher's Shakespeare?'[33] In that piece, Armstrong finds that Michael Bogdanov's English Shakespeare Company's 'radical' readings of Shakespeare's plays, 'productions with a sense of theatre, clarity of diction and intellectual control . . . actually [made] Greenblatt's thesis look questionable, even when there was an uncanny convergence of interpretation' (p. 9). For Armstrong, the ESC 'worked systematically against the patriotic readings of the texts in a way which had to be bolder than Greenblatt's new historical provisos in order to achieve a radical production in the theatre' (p. 9).

Two years later, in 'The Impasse over the Stage',[34] Anthony B. Dawson backed away somewhat from the claims for potential textual and political subversiveness he attributed to modern performance (see, especially, pp. 318–19), but he continued to construe 'going to the theatre' as an activity that 'operates at a level distinct from writing and the meanings that writing generates' (p. 326); and he seemed, like Armstrong, to be looking for a way of retheorizing 'the cultural importance of pleasure' (Armstrong, p. 14) as a way of complicating or re-energizing discursive literary analysis. Paul Yachnin was working with similar questions during this period. His 1996 'Personations: *The Taming of the Shrew* and the Limits of Theoretical Criticism'[35] outlined the limitations of materialist, rationalist, and new-historicist approaches to a play like *Shrew*, in order to arrive at the conclusion that 'the contradictions in the characterization and story of Katherine are not difficult to grasp in the theatre where they are always rooted in the persons of the actors' (p. 31). Yachnin and Dawson would go on to collaborate, in 2001, on *The Culture of Playgoing in Shakespeare's England*, in which their two disparate ideas about the nature of theatrical phenomenology and reception ('personation' for Yachnin, 'participation' for Dawson) converged in a vision of 'the theatre as a kind of way-station, a place where different cultural avenues cross'. For these authors, theatrical pleasure arises out of 'mixed affiliations . . . its location at the intersections of various elements of culture – visuality, the market, the production of material goods

and theatrical props, memory, news', and this view puts them 'at a certain distance from the view that the Elizabethan theatre was located at the margins of Elizabethan society' which had been promulgated by new historicism (p. 5).

One thing Yachnin and Dawson are doing is attempting to ground discussion of theatrical power *in the theatre*, and to offset the literary critic's power to subjugate the power of the theatre to the rhetorical or stylistic imperatives of a literary critical methodology. In this way, they are working within a critical context perhaps most vividly delineated by Edward Pechter's 'New Historicism and its Discontents',[36] which rather unexpectedly whittles down its detailed critique of new historicism's Marxian inflections to an issue that has not appeared anywhere else in the essay:

[New historicism] is criticism that systematically deprives *the theatre* of its capacity to surprise, and who wants to go to *a theatre* where there are no surprises? To the extent that new historicism takes the surprise out of *the theatre*, it seems to me a bad thing.   (p. 302, emphasis added)

At a point in his argument where he admits to the difficulty of imagining a clear alternative to the power-centred ethics of interpretation typical of new historicism, Pechter seizes upon a notion of theatre that provides a feeling of productive immediacy and capacity for personal agency that seems to be precluded by the rhetorical and analytical formulae of new historicism.

Pechter's 1996 edited collection, *Textual and Theatrical Shakespeare*,[37] continues in the same vein. This volume was given impetus by the 'widespread adoption' of the new-historicist perspective, which has created 'a problem determining on what bases to organize and regulate interpretive activity' (p. 2). Pechter's introduction quotes a passage from an earlier essay of one of his contributors, Kathleen

---

[33] *Textual Practice* 3 (1989), 1–14.
[34] *English Literary Renaissance* 21 (1991), 309–27.
[35] *Early Modern Literary Studies* 2 (1996), 1–31.
[36] *Publications of the Modern Language Association* 102 (1987), 293–303.
[37] (Iowa City, 1996).

McLuskie, which might be seen as both a rigorous complication of new-historicist goals and a statement of purpose for an original-practices movement; it might be seen as the combination of the phenomenological concerns of Yachnin and Dawson with the space-based historicism of Mullaney or the REED school:

In our excitement at the discovery that Shakespearian drama was implicated in the real social relations of early modern England, we have perhaps neglected the formal and material circumstances of its operation; the way in which . . . dramatic material is differently inflected according to the rhetorical and dramatic requirements of different stages and audiences . . .[38]   (p. 8)

Of course, neither Pechter nor his contributors nor Yachnin and Dawson are simply signposts on the road to original-practices drama as a coherent school of thought conceived in opposition to new historicism. Rather, the work I have drawn together in the preceding pages can be seen to have been symptomatic of a widespread desire to resist new historicism's apparent ability to systematize something like lived experience within critical formulations of disempowerment; and I suggest that it is not coincidental that, gaining momentum at approximately the same time, was the movement towards original practice – a movement that would enable the bodies of persons to communicate with other persons, that would allow scholars to be 'surprised' by, and in, the theatre again, and that could operate at least partly under legitimizing claims to quasi-empirical historicity that allowed it to remain within the purview of the academic community.

The diffuse debate between new historicism and some of its discontents which I have been sketching in these pages is as much about pedagogy as it is about the 'power of the theatre'. The rhetoric of pedagogy and outreach characteristic of original practices, which is consistent across companies even where the practices are not, indicates that what is perhaps more at stake than anything else is the mode by which we, experts in the field, communicate about the material we love and study to our students and to the theatre-going public. New historicism helped to give us, in the theatre, what Alan

Sinfield has called 'Shakespeare plus relevance',[39] as well as, in the classroom, a new kind of rigidly conventional student essay purporting to address questions of political repression 'in Shakespeare's time'. A pedagogy that combines the theatre's passion for communication and sense of personal agency with the theatre historian's understanding of physical, historical space might give students a vocabulary with which to do something other than contain the past within predetermined critical paradigms. Thus Ralph Alan Cohen advocates an original-practices pedagogy:

a classroom, rightly configured, can show students how the Elizabethan stage unlocks an understanding of Shakespeare's words. One reason is that the Elizabethan stage worked like a classroom in which the audience simultaneously experienced the subject and learned lessons about it. For that reason, teachers who stage their classrooms as Elizabethan theatres will not only find a place from which to view Shakespeare's language more clearly, they will also re-create a venue that teaches as it moves its audience.[40]

For Cohen and, by extension, I would argue, for all original-practices practitioners, the classroom and the theatre become a single location where Yachnin's 'personation' and Dawson's 'participation' occur simultaneously, where embodiment and communication are co-extensive – what you experience when you move, and when you are moved.

It should be obvious that my interpretation of original practice's ultimate goals puts it ironically back into alignment with new historicism, at least as it has been construed by critics such as those I have cited in this article: in both cases,

---

[38] The quoted passage is from McLuskie, 'Lawless Desires Well Tempered', in *Erotic Politics: Desire on the Renaissance Stage*, ed. Susan Zimmerman (London, 1992), pp. 103–26.

[39] In *Political Shakespeare*, ed. Jonathan Dollimore and Alan Sinfield, 2nd edn (Manchester, 1994). The phrase occurs a number of times in Sinfield's essay 'Royal Shakespeare: Theatre and the Making of Ideology' (pp. 182–205).

[40] 'Original Staging and the Shakespeare Classroom', in *Teaching Shakespeare Through Performance*, ed. Mila Riggio (New York, 1999), pp. 78–101. The quotation is from p. 99.

the specificity of location is abstracted and aestheticized for the sake of academic paradigms that might be said to serve 'talking about the theatre' more than 'the theatre itself'. And indeed, for as much antagonism as there has been and continues to be between discourses (like new historicism) that locate theatrical meaning in the person of the critic and discourses (like original practices) that locate it in the activity of the theatre, the delight each takes in mystifying the past has always kept them on the verge of surprising conflation. Thus, although Edward Pechter's 1992 anthology contains the seeds of an authentic-theatre revival that might help relocate early modern plays in their material theatrical context, it also contains W. B. Worthen's 'Actors Reading Shakespeare', which identifies the actorly discourse of authenticity with new-historicist strategies for constructing a symbiotic relationship between present and past. Focusing mainly on the Cambridge *Players of Shakespeare* series, Worthen incisively problematizes what would become one of the central tenets of original-practices theatre – seeing the practice of acting, imagined essentially and transhistorically, as a source of authoritative and authentic interpretation: 'To seize on an eccentric yet dramatic detail drawn from the character's period and make it signify in an apparently remote discourse has more in common with the practices of contemporary new historicism than with traditional "historical" representation in the theatre' (p. 217). He goes on to argue that

Much as new historicism is often criticized for removing 'facts', events, or texts from their original context to make them signify in other, surprising (or eccentric) registers, so it might be argued that that *Players of Shakespeare* actors develop history in a similarly anecdotal fashion, deploying details in ways that register the contingency of terms like 'past' and 'present'. (p. 217)

What Worthen says of the *Players of Shakespeare* actors is even more the case with original-practices actors, who generally lack expertise in early modern history or theatre history, but who work in a context in which they are called upon to deploy, by means of their decidedly modern training and skills, a wealth of academically sanctioned details for a similarly inexpert audience, under the pretense that 'discoveries' about historical performing conditions and audience response are being made.

Because of the role it affords the critic in choosing evidence and in foregrounding his or her own critical perspective, new historicism is an incredibly flexible, powerful critical paradigm; I would not identify myself as a new-historicist critic, but many or most of that methodology's fundamental structures underlie the contextualizing analysis I have done here, sometimes deliberately and sometimes just inevitably. As long as the ideology of 'original practice' is underwritten by the academic community and put indirectly (in the form of conferences and teaching) in service of the dissemination of theatre-historical or literary-interpretive information, it will be unable to avoid reproducing the critical paradigms it most pointedly resists, unable to avoid effacing or rendering irrelevant the embodiment it is meant to make central. Original-practices theatre fulfils some widespread needs, or at least desires, in our academic community: the need or desire for embodied (rather than abstract, mental) experience; for the application of theory to practice; for a broad (even popular), receptive audience; for imaginative, creative engagement with artistic material that ordinarily must, of professional necessity, be dealt with coldly or at a distance. The energy that goes into original-practices productions is, like the value that comes from them, personal and emotional, and always has the potential to become powerfully, beneficially communal. This energy also, like all forms of euphoria, does not necessarily have a rigorous intellectual component; and it can be dangerously misleading if mistaken for or enforced upon scholarly inquiry.

The more we work to conflate (rather than understand and practice as separate) the energy of embodied performance and response with the rigors of scholarly inquiry; the more we work to mystify the craft of modern actors in order to make them the media through which we conjure an embodied and authentic past; then the more we become a loose, communal version of the figure of the critic Paul Stevens identifies in his critique of Stephen Greenblatt, 'Pretending to be Real'.[41] Beginning with an article in the *Harvard College Gazette* about Greenblatt's appointment at Harvard, Stevens argues that Greenblatt's tendency to self-dramatize by means of anecdotes about near misses with fame (he performed at Cambridge with the troupe that would go on to become Monty Python's Flying Circus; as a camp counsellor he played guitar and sang folk songs with the young Art Garfunkel, who wanted to introduce him to a musician friend – Paul Simon) 'cuts right to the heart of his work and ultimately has much to do with explaining its extraordinary influence' (p. 492). For Stevens, Greenblatt's preoccupation with the inseparability of self-fashioning and being fashioned by cultural institutions does not free him from the traditions of modernist existentialism and aesthetic humanism against which new historicism explicitly positioned itself; rather, it is a continuation of these traditions 'in a different key' (p. 494):

> [In *Renaissance Self-Fashioning*, Greenblatt's] assumption . . . is that *being* is a matter of pretending in order to be real, that is, acting not only in the sense of doing but of playing. It is a matter of art, of being both artistic and artful – only through art can the answering voice of an informed audience vouchsafe the authentic experience of selfhood. It is in this sense that the aesthetic may be understood as the key to being, both personal and political, and, as *Marvelous Possessions* attempts to show, that pleasure may be reconciled to virtue.   (p. 509)

The *art* and *artfulness* to which Stevens refers are Greenblatt's noted abilities as a storyteller. The theatrical metaphor implicit in Stevens's 'playing' and 'informed audiences' (referring in his argument to new historicism's large and responsive following) suggests the analogy I am trying to make here: original-practices theatre, in its use of a vivid anecdotal historical method to cultivate a revelatory sense of self in performer and audience alike, and in its dogged insistence that theatrical experience is not only fun but also educational, can in one way be seen as striving for a full embodiment of the Greenblattian project, its continuation in a different key.[42] Both projects are deeply modernist, in spite of (and/or in fact *because of*) the promise they hold

out for an escape to early modern experience;[43] and each project's conception of theatrical power depends upon the fantasy of the theatre as an ideologically neutral or neutralized space.

Thus, the development of the original-practices movement out of and alongside resistance to new historicism has been a vexed struggle characterized by the anxiety of influence, and this is why the scholarly membership of the original-practices movement is generally so fluid and hard to define – why being a part of that movement involves so much fundamental intellectual contradiction.[44] To

---

[41] *New Literary History* 33 (2002), 491–519.

[42] It is certainly worth noting at this point that Stephen Greenblatt was one of the featured keynote speakers at the 2007 Blackfriars Conference at the American Shakespeare Center.

[43] For a differently focused critique of new historicism's recapitulation of particularly modernist problematics, see Richard Halpern, 'Shakespeare in the Tropics: from High Modernism to New Historicism', *Representations* 45 (1994), 1–25. Halpern's discussion of the way in which new historicism reconceives modernism's figuration of Shakespeare as a 'primitive' is suggestively related to the analysis I have been doing in this article. See, for example, page 21: 'For Eliot, Lewis, and Welles, the juxtaposition of Shakespeare and "primitive" cultures served as a kind of alienation effect, estranging the experience of a dramatist who for the Victorians had come to seem all too comfortably a national possession. Their Shakespeare, like the jaguar, eyes us savagely through the dense foliage of time. Our Shakespeare, more ambiguously, is both guide and quarry, leading us through a cultural landscape which, as in a dream, seems both alien and our own.'

[44] It is perhaps only partially a coincidence that so many of the scholars – Yachnin, Dawson, Pechter, Stevens, the REED contributors – on whose work I have drawn for this analysis are Canadian or have worked (as I currently do) at or in affiliation with Canadian institutions. It is certainly not surprising, at least in the conventional terms used to frame Canadian identity, that Canadian scholars like Yachnin and Dawson (or an American scholar working in Canada, such as Pechter) have fallen somewhere between the 'American' new historicism and 'British' cultural materialism; or that the recent Shakespeare and the Queen's Men project was spearheaded by a Toronto medievalist (Alexandra Johnston), organized by a committee that included Helen Ostovich (whose PhD is from the University of Toronto), Holger Syme (a former Greenblatt student) and myself (a performance-studies contrarian), was heavily influenced in its costumes and

borrow a formulation Stevens makes in a different but not unrelated context: what seems to be an argument about evidence, or the uses of evidence, is in fact an argument about identity.[45] Seeking new forms of discursive authority, original practice adapts new historicism's experiential theory of historical fact to a rigorous theatre-historical vocabulary and inflects it with the essentialist language of the actor and the proselytizing rhetoric of the pedagogue; as the material we read and teach seems daily to become more foreign to our students and the world they inhabit, *original*-practice theatre becomes a proving ground for *academic* practice,

where whether or not you applaud is a matter of the kind of scholar and teacher you imagine yourself to be: one who critiques the past, or one who could have lived there.

---

dramaturgy by Globe aesthetics, and attracted a membership that overlapped closely with that of Ralph Cohen's Blackfriars conferences.

[45] Stevens is referring to John Lee's 1995 attack on what he perceived (incorrectly) as Greenblatt's non-response to Anne Barton's critique of a crucial misreading in *Learning to Curse*. See pp. 494f.

SHAKESPEARE PERFORMANCES
IN ENGLAND, 2007

MICHAEL DOBSON

Whatever other side-effects it may have had, the impending collapse of the British economy caused by the fetchingly titled Great Credit Squeeze of 2007 had still, by December, failed to discourage the nation's theatre companies from continuing to mount an impressive and expensive range of productions of Shakespeare. In fact in one instance the poor financial outlook may even have brought one Shakespeare play more onto the boards: with the autumn news bulletins full of predictions about rising numbers of bankruptcies and repossessions, the Globe were moved to announce that their 2008 season would include their first-ever production of *Timon of Athens*, a play which by the time it opens is likely to look very topical indeed. What ought to have been the most conspicuous tranche of productions in 2007, however, the last four months of the RSC's Complete Works Festival, in the event concluded with what in terms of publicity at least was a whimper rather than a bang. The year-long project to stage or host productions of each of Shakespeare's plays between April 2006 and April 2007 had been scheduled to culminate with the opening of Trevor Nunn's *King Lear* at the Court-yard Theatre on 3 April, with Sir Ian McKellen in the title role, but when Frances Barber, cast as Goneril, damaged her ankle in a cycling accident late in rehearsals the company, although they cancelled no performances, decided to postpone the press night. The result was that several thousand people had already seen the show before anyone in the media was allowed to say what it was like, some weeks of excellent work by Barber's under-study Melanie Jessop went compulsorily unsung, and any number of projected features in the Sunday newspapers and on the BBC's arts programmes that had planned to combine an account of McKellen's Lear with a retrospective look at the entire festival were never published or broadcast. The imagined final great public discussion about what the Festival had actually added up to or proved never really happened; it was more a case of people gradually noticing that it had finished, and realizing that the RST had now closed for its internal remodelling and that the Swan was about to go dark too, and that once it did there was nothing worth coming up to see in Stratford for months apart from a poor *Twelfth Night* and yet more Michael Boyd productions of the English histories.

Since I charted the first eight months of the Festival in chronological fashion in the last issue of *Survey* I shall narrate its closing weeks in the same way, but I will then revert to this section's customary generic classification when describing the year's other productions. These included strong contributions, sometimes more impressive than their Complete Works Festival counterparts, under all three of the Folio's headings: among the comedies, a lively *Tempest* by Northern Broadsides, and an intricate *Cymbeline* from Cheek by Jowl (which I will deal with as a comedy with due deference to the Folio's placing of it among the tragedies); of the histories, a fine *Henry V* at the Royal Exchange in Manchester; and in an unusually rich year for tragedy a spectacular *Coriolanus* by Yukio Ninagawa at the Barbican and a dazzling *Macbeth* by Rupert

Goold at the Minerva in Chichester, which amply deserved its subsequent sell-out, prize-winning run in the West End.

THE RSC COMPLETE WORKS FESTIVAL, CONTINUED

4 January 2007. At the Swan is Dominic Cooke's production of *Pericles*, which, along with his *Winter's Tale* cast from the same company, opened in December 2006 and will soon be closing. Both are billed as promenade productions, but the layout of this auditorium – with at least half of the seating capacity located in the two upstairs galleries – militates against the sorts of complete interpenetration of cast and audience possible in more flexible spaces like the National's Cottesloe. The building is, however, much altered by the decking-over of all the downstairs seating at the same height as what is usually the thrust stage, and by the construction of a horseshoe-shaped sloping ramp by which actors can move up from this newly lifted ground level and parade themselves under the noses of everyone seated around the front row of the first balcony. The area behind the proscenium arch, meanwhile, has been built up, and along with the ramps remains one acting area into which no audience member can stray. As a result, in practice Cooke's *Pericles* is not so much a promenade production as one which alternates between being played in the round down on the ground floor, played along the ramp at balcony level, and played on the conventional stage, with the standees in what are usually the stalls shuffling themselves into better viewing positions accordingly.

Most promenade productions have a conceit by which the unseated spectators are to understand their roles as followers of the action – implicitly casting them as honorary witnesses or bystanders, having them led here and there or held back behind cordons by supernumerary soldiers or security personnel – but this one leaves the promenaders downstairs visibly uncertain, at first, as to what they are supposed to be for the evening, except the audience to a more or less genial exercise in village storytelling. This is an African *Pericles*, called into being by Joseph Mydell's smiling tribal elder of a Gower, and like the Globe's production of 2005 (see *Survey 59*) it has put considerable effort into distinguishing geographically between the different communities which Pericles encounters. Antioch is a military dictatorship, from which the standees are cleared at gunpoint by combat-fatigue-clad soldiers while Clarence Smith's Antiochus barks paranoid orders in the manner of Idi Amin; Tyre is an altogether more relaxed and ceremonial place, all coloured robes and pyjamas, like a tourist's fantasy of Ghana; Ephesus is some sort of spiritual retreat, largely populated by white ex-hippies who have gone elaborately native; and, while the brothels of Mytilene offer black African girls for sale to a white (colonial?) governor, their owners and administrators are (expatriate?) Cockneys. The one destination which looks explicitly Mediterranean, and which has a white indigenous population, is Pentapolis, which Michael Britton has designed as comedy modern-dress ancient Greek; here the tournament for Thaisa's hand becomes an extravagant dumb-show parody of the Olympics, in which Lucian Msamati's Pericles, despite looking older and tubbier than any of his rivals, wins every event of a mock-slow-motion Pentapolis pentathlon. (In keeping with the festive light-heartedness of this sequence, some of the audience get to dine with the contestants and their hosts at a long trestle table in the middle of the stalls area afterwards.) In general, the nastier the locale, the more this production places it on the proscenium-arch stage, where Antiochus parades the severed heads of the unsuccessful suitors, and where the seedy pimps of Mytilene make their successive thwarted attempts on Marina's chastity. Gower is much happier speaking from the ramp or from the centre of the downstairs floor, where the revival of Thaisa and the reunion with Marina take place on a small raised platform covered in cushions while the onlookers sit cross-legged around it in a circle like participants in a junior-school drama exercise.

As this may suggest, the production, already vulnerable to accusations of exploiting glib notions about Africa for merely decorative exotic effect, also risks infantilizing the continent by identifying it with theatrical languages which most Stratford habituées are likely to associate with children's theatre. To some extent, this is latent in the faux-naive mock-medievalism of this play's script anyway, but the most successful productions of *Pericles* are able to exploit the magnificent obviousness of its dramaturgy as a short-cut to an intense engagement with the story's emotional content from which any greater level of self-consciousness or psychological detail would only be a distraction. In Cooke's *Pericles* the novelty of the settings, the audience's uncertainty as to where the action will be taking place next (both spatially and culturally) and the oddity of some of the casting (it is hard to believe that Msamati looks any more like an African idea of the unproblematically handsome quest-hero than he does a European one, and his singing a song at Simonides's court in a language no one else either on the stage or off it can understand only distances him from us still further) tend to disrupt the emotional trajectory of the plot rather than to strengthen it. The hints at an interpretation offered by some of the doubling, meanwhile, seem merely incidental and distracting. Ony Uhiara plays both Antiochus's daughter and a Marina who spends too much time looking bashfully at the floor to connect much with either the audience or the other characters; academic critics of the play convinced that all its secrets are to be found in the incest riddle in the first scene can tick their boxes in satisfaction, but otherwise neither performance registers very memorably at all. Linda Bassett, more controversially, gets to be both a bad mother as the Bawd and a good mother as a re-gendered Cerimon, who takes an unconscionable time bringing Kate Fleetwood's Thaisa back to life using a nonsensical New Age healing ritual which deserves to be far less medically effective than it is. The show remains inventive, good-hearted, well-acted, colourful and far from tedious, but when applied to this intensely simple play its methods are in danger of looking at once childish and over-elaborate.

6 January 2007. Back at the Swan the following evening I see some of the same architectural

and directorial novelties applied to a much fussier play, *The Winter's Tale*, for which the proscenium-arch stage area has in the first instance been converted into a bandstand on which musicians in dinner suits are already playing early 1950s dance-band music as I take my seat upstairs. A mirror ball and a clock, awaiting the stroke of twelve, are suspended above the stalls floor; elegant couples are dancing among the spectators, and occasionally separating to invite individual audience members to dance with them; and soon Archidamus and Camillo are surveying the scene from the ramp and exchanging their diplomatic pleasantries about the rival levels of hospitality available in Sicilia and in Bohemia. Cooke, it appears, has made a virtue of having his *Winter's Tale* squeezed into a short time slot over December and early January by setting its opening at a New Year's Eve ball; this turns out to be a much cannier way of previewing time's role in the action than Nicholas Hytner's interpolated sonnet at the National in 2001 (see *Survey 55*), and one which motivates an unusual and effective collaboration between England's national poet and Scotland's when the tableau of the unbroken amity between the triangle of Leontes, Hermione and Polixenes which will eventually be recreated at the close of the statue scene is here established with hand-clasps at midnight to the strains of *Auld Lang Syne*.

This choice of setting for the opening – with Polixenes playing 1.2.1–8 as a public speech from the balcony announcing his impending departure to the revellers and making formal thanks, and much by-play with a Mamillius who is clearly up well past his usual bedtime – is something of a coup. It is true that 'We two will walk, my lord, / And leave you to your graver steps' (1.2.173–5) seems an odd way for Leontes to say he will sit the next dance out with his son while his friend waltzes with his wife, but the opening of the aside which ensues works beautifully as the utterance of a man obsessively watching just such a dance: 'How she holds up the neb, the bill to him, / And arms her with the boldness of a wife / To her allowing husband!' (184–6). It has long seemed to me that the fourth act of *The Winter's Tale* would lend itself very well to promenade production (in the manner, perhaps,

26 *The Winter's Tale*, RSC, Swan Theatre, directed by Dominic Cooke. Linda Bassett as Paulina, Anton Lesser as Leontes.
Malcolm Davies Collection.

of Keith Dewhurst's *Lark Rise*), but the first and last movements of the play look much less obviously promising for this treatment, and Cooke does well to invent a setting in which Leontes's first outbreaks of jealousy can be plausibly voiced as he wanders distractedly among a crowd. What rather undercuts this bright directorial idea, however, is the fact that as Leontes he has cast Anton Lesser, a highly accomplished performer with more than enough experience, intelligence and verbal finesse to cope with the intricacies of the king's neurosis and his syntax alike, but about the last actor on earth to place in situations requiring him to interact face-to-face with an audience at point-blank range. Twitchy and introverted, already shut away from direct engagement with others during the first three acts of the play behind heavy 1930s spectacles of the design once favoured by laboratory technicians and Harold Pinter, Lesser moves among the promenaders as if he is having to invest at least half of his mental energy in the task of pretending that they aren't there, his body language giving every sign that he will scream if anyone so much as brushes against him. As a result, precisely those moments which ought to be most electric in a setting where actor and spectator can meet eyeball to

eyeball – such as 'And many a man there is, even at this present, / Now, while I speak this, holds his wife by th'arm' (1.2.193–4) – go for nothing, flung nervously away as if addressed to no one in particular at all. Lesser is visibly more at ease when safely out of the crowd's reach on the ramp, from which he conducts most of the trial scene, and where he collapses penitently to his knees at its conclusion as thunder sounds and spectacular quantities of rain are hosed down upon him. If Paulina didn't lead him away to penitence, it appears, he would stay there and drown rather than go back down among the audience.

Paulina is played (to great effect, as ever; this remains one of the few roles in Shakespeare in which I have yet to see anyone fail) by Linda Bassett, and it becomes retrospectively clear that her less obvious casting as Cerimon in *Pericles* was part of a general AS-level sort of exercise in pointing out that some of the characters in *The Winter's Tale* perform analogous roles to some of the characters in the earlier romance. Hence Kate Fleetwood – an endearingly playful and desirous Thaisa before her maritime obstetric adventures put her into cold storage – here plays the corresponding miraculously restored wife, Hermione; her superb playing in the trial scene, confined on a podium in the centre of the stalls area, climaxes with a traumatic fit of shrieking as she hears the news of Mamillius's death and is carried out at 3.2.145–52. Similarly, Amanda Daniels plays both Lychorida and Emilia, the nearest things to adequate midwives that either unfortunate queen gets; and Richard Katz, in clear danger of being typecast in sleazy underworld roles after his superb Pompey in the Complicité/NT *Measure for Measure* in 2004 and 2006 (see *Survey 58*), plays Boult and Autolycus. The pattern, however, does not hold throughout. Msamati and Lesser appear in only one play each as the principals, for example; Nigel Cooke, a worryingly mature roué of a Lysimachus in *Pericles*, returns not as Florizel but as Polixenes; and Perdita is played not by Ony Uhiara (Marina) but by Michelle Terry (who in *Pericles* plays Cerimon's customarily male sidekick Philemon).

This latter piece of casting, even if it does contribute to Cooke missing this moderately pointless opportunity to prove consistently that *Pericles* and *The Winter's Tale* are really the same play, produces some of the most original touches in the second half of his *The Winter's Tale*, which otherwise looks dangerously like a composite of ideas drawn from every other revival of the play Cooke has ever seen. Instead of being the usual standard-issue petite RADA ingenue speaking pretty and docile audition speeches with or without a cosmetically rustic accent, Terry's big-boned, toothily attractive country wench is on the edge of being positively hoydenish, so much so that one begins to wonder whether had Florizel's falcon taken a different flight he might not have been just as happy to be more conveniently and impermanently partnered by Mopsa or Dorcas. Distributing flowers to Polixenes and Camillo (4.4.70–108), Terry's Perdita really does sound as much above herself in her borrowed flaunts as she says she feels: she sassily drops the word 'ancient' into the conversation at line 79 with a sly grin at Florizel, and then euphemistically presents her two guests with flowers appropriate 'To men of middle age' with a smiling curtsy (before she slips hastily away back to Florizel on a pert 'You're very welcome', line 108), a smirking

gesture which is half embarrassed but half positively insolent. At 4.4.442–4 she comes a lot nearer to telling Polixenes plainly that the self-same sun that shines upon his court hides not his visage from her cottage than does any other Perdita I have ever seen. In this reading her fairytale genetic royalty shines through less because she displays incongruously maidenly manners than because she has inherited an absolute underlying determination, for all her strategic protestations to the contrary, to get exactly what she wants.

Terry deserves the more credit for establishing this simultaneously touching, alarming and funny performance at the heart of Act 4 in that it not only runs against the mainstream tradition of playing this role but here has a great deal of distracting extraneous material to contend with. Blatantly following Hytner, Cooke treats the sheep-shearing as a parody of a rock festival, and while Katz makes a comical and energetic early 1970s con-man-come-busker, and while the area beyond the proscenium makes a convenient Glastonbury side-show stage (a splendidly awful sub-Cropredy folk-rock act turns up to supply the backing for 'Get you hence', with which Mopsa and Dorcas bravely and incompetently sing along at a microphone stand), this incongruously satirical comic gambit, as in 2001, risks upstaging the central narrative altogether. Back in Sicilia, Cooke switches from copying from Hytner to copying from Matthew Warchus's 2002 production at the Roundhouse (see *Survey 56*), having Florizel and Perdita arrive by air and involving the broadcast media in the offstage recognition scene (though he sensibly replaces Warchus's disembodied wireless broadcast of the three gentlemen's dialogue in 5.2 with a colloquy between Autolycus and a clutch of eager onstage 1930s reporters, one interviewing another with a microphone as if on live radio). Lesser's Leontes has by now settled convincingly into a desolate middle age (a condition which, miraculously, has improved his eyesight to the extent that he no longer needs the glasses that concealed some of his wrinkles during the first three acts), and he gives the rather moving impression that he has spent much of the sixteen years since we last saw him on his knees at exactly

27 *Henry V*, Compagnia Pippo Delbono, Swan Theatre, directed by Pippo Delbono. Pippo Delbono as the King.

the spot on the ramp where he heard the news of Hermione's death. His relationship with the widowed Paulina, and the careful, tender relinquishing of it which still manages to occupy part of his astonished mind during the statue scene, are immensely touching, and although the final scene itself (played down below the proscenium arch, as in any conventional production) seems slightly rushed, perhaps it needs to be for this predominantly happy reading of the play's ending to be sustained. With much of the action after the first scene, with the exception of the sheep-shearing, played in single parts of the auditorium so that the downstairs audience can settle and even sit down for substantial periods of time, this isn't really the promenade *Winter's Tale* it claims to be, but it is a consistently engaging and worthwhile production, which might have developed into something richer if it had been allowed a longer run.

On **1 February** it is the Compagnia Pippo Delbono, with a version of the *Henry V* which they first performed in Cremona as long ago as 1993. The cast of this enterprise is so small that I can for once name all the principal performers. Pippo Delbono himself directs and plays the king; Pepe Roblado is a composite 'Friend of the King'; Gustavo Giacosa is 'the French' (in effect, the Dauphin); and Lucia Della Ferrera and Margharita Clemente have marshalled some 25 local non-

professional supernumeraries to be the armies. This is an odd but strangely affecting little show, barely more than an hour long, which uses very little of Shakespeare's dialogue and often owes as much to the structure and affect of Branagh's film as to the original play. Delbono, whose stage persona is perhaps best described as that of a noble yob, a sort of half-comprehending, stocky, inarticulate and insecure Everyman in dirty jeans and a bomber jacket, is persuaded by his friend to wage war; works himself up with football-fan-like gestures of bravado against the affected French; goes to battle in the face of their contempt; and, victorious, is abruptly struck with pity and horror at what he has done, the Swan's stage now a carpet of inert amateur corpses and his friend now lacking one leg. Both light relief and further pathos are provided along the way by the Dauphin's horse, half-acted and half-danced by an actor in a white mask, which is another of the battle's casualties. It is all slightly like watching an abbreviated, cartoonish impression of what *Henry V* might be like if its protagonist were an Italian equivalent of Andy Capp. There clearly hasn't been time to rehearse the local extras into as many stage pictures or scenarios as must have been included in earlier Italian performances of this show, and in some ways there is hardly anything to it, but I suspect I may remember its vigorous tragicomic tableaux more vividly than some much more substantive and faithful productions of this play. (But then they have all been obliged to leave the horse off stage.)

24 February 2007. The next visiting troupe in the Swan, who have brought a show offering an equally abbreviated and unfamiliar version of a Shakespearian text, make the potential contradictions of playing international Shakespeare in Stratford particularly visible. This is Grzegorz Bral's Polish-based company Teatr Piesn Kozla – Song of the Goat Theatre – and in keeping with the probably false etymology that gives them their name they have brought a version of one of the tragedies, a show currently billed as *Macbeth: work-in-progress*. Bral himself compères the hour-long event, and a programme note explains that his fourteen-strong company have been working together on *Macbeth* since April 2006, and that their evolving production is destined to appear at various different international festivals before achieving its final form in April 2008. Although this perpetually out-of-context show will thus play to a disparate set of audiences around the world, and although it draws its actors variously from Poland, Scotland, England, Siberia, Slovenia, Norway, Wales, Spain and Australia, this band of miscellaneous exiles nonetheless runs something called an annual 'Brave Festival – Against Cultural Exile', 'presenting art of vanishing cultures and traditions from all over the world'. In fact so far from celebrating Shakespeare as a writer whose work can serve as a *lingua franca* for postmodern trans-global hybridity, Bral's *Macbeth* turns out to be committed to a notion of the local every bit as naive and romantic as the impulse which first led the English, more than two centuries ago, to consecrate this very spot of earth beside the Avon (the site of David Garrick's Jubilee rotunda) to the memory of the national poet whose works were supposed to have given that native soil a voice.

Twelve chairs are placed in a circle on the stage, with three more at its centre; two drums are brought to a spot downstage left; and the company sit in the chairs, and start solemnly to hum. Accompanied by the drums, this humming takes shape as a low minor third with occasional unexpected grace notes, a sort of choric keening, and

after a surtitle board lights up with the sub-heading 'Crown', one of the actors eventually recites part of the bleeding captain's narrative, 'Doubtful it stood' (1.2.7–42). The ensemble singing continues, denser and more complex now, as one performer, Anna Zubrzycki, stands and recites 'They met me in the day of success' (1.5.1–29), with a curious priestess-like wavering on 'Hie thee hither' (24); then she sits, and Gabriel Paul Gawin rises to incant 'If it were done when 'tis done' (1.7.1–28). Now the whole company rises and sings 'Alas poor country' (4.3.165–74). I had at first imagined that all this choral singing was simply an overture to something more like an orthodox theatrical production of the play, but by now fifteen minutes have passed without a word of unaccompanied dialogue, and it is clear that this is to be a *Macbeth* closer to oratorio than to conventional tragedy, in fact closer in performance style to a folk-dancing-and-singing revue called *Siamsa* which I once saw at the National Folk Theatre of Eire in Tralee in the late 1960s than to anything I have previously seen in Stratford. I have been trying to place the style of the music for some time now: among its harmonies, the thirds and fifths are if anything less numerous than the eerie, dissonant seconds, and the women in particular give their voices a hard, nasal edge. At first I provisionally identify it as Moldavian or Bulgarian – it is particularly reminiscent of that *La mystère des voix bulgares* record that was such a hit across Europe at around the time of the fall of the Berlin Wall – but now Bral arrives on the stage and speaks a few words of explanation. What we have been listening to, apparently, is adapted Siberian folk song. 'I first heard music like this on a visit to Siberia,' he says, 'and it spoke to me immediately and profoundly. I had no idea, in fact, why it moved me so viscerally. But then I found out, soon afterwards, that I have Siberian ancestors, that I am myself part-Siberian.'

I have to confess that I spent much of the remainder of the show – as the company/choir offered a series of similar movements, surtitled 'Cauldron', 'Come, you spirits', 'Dagger', 'Thou hast it now', 'Horse and rider', 'Full of scorpions is my mind', and so on, some variegated with gymnastic movements, some with banners, some with dance – pondering the implications of this remark rather than concentrating fully on the performance. Does Bral really think he only responds to Siberian music because of his Siberian forebears, and if so, what does he expect us non-Siberians to get out of it? Isn't his implicit romantic nationalist notion that culture springs directly from the genes of the indigenous folk exactly the same one that Dr Goebbels used to peddle? Perhaps Bral feels that his goat-singers are only entitled to superimpose Shakespeare's untranslated words onto this determinedly ethnic soundtrack because his company includes some members of the Anglo-Saxon diaspora carrying at least a few strands of olde English DNA, but if so, what was the Bard of Avon doing with all this Scottish material in the first place? It's very odd, in any event, to be watching a part-Siberian adaptation of *Macbeth*, performed by an international company from Poland within yards of the site where Garrick claimed Shakespeare had been inspired by the native fairies, and to be told that it represents an act of resistance to cultural exile. This is surely the equally tautologous artistic equivalent of the International Alliance Against Globalization; a cosmopolitan theatre company drawing audiences around the world with a work by the most internationally translated and reinterpreted playwright of all time in support of what sounds worryingly like repatriation to the tribal homelands.

6 March 2007. There could be no greater contrast to this Eastern European chamber *Macbeth* than that offered by the tragedy which has its press night in the RST a fortnight later, Gregory Doran's *Coriolanus*. This will be the last production ever mounted in this auditorium as originally designed, proscenium and all, which for seventy-five years has been resisting successive attempts to make it feel less like an Odeon cinema while nonetheless playing host to some intermittently glorious theatre. As if in salute to the venue's illustrious past, Doran has managed to ornament his cast with a couple of well-loved veterans, Janet Suzman (Volumnia) and Timothy West (Menenius), and he has dressed everyone in old-style shiny Elizabethan-classical

clothes (including a lamentable lurex breastplate and ra-ra kilt for Tullus Aufidius which look like a cruel joke about the actor's unfortunate name, Guy Burgess). His designer, Richard Hudson, has even cluttered the stage with a big, old-fashioned set, a claustrophobic affair of multiple receding pinkish marble archways which looks more like a stone portcullis or a set of expensive cloisters than anywhere the poor could muster a useful riot.

Sadly, in this production they never really threaten to do so anyway; arriving down the aisles through the stalls and climbing faux-marble steps onto the stage, the plebeians look woefully clean and polite throughout, dwarfed by the set and unable to make up in energy or menace what they lack in numbers. (There will only be just enough soldiers in the Roman army to make a minimal human pyramid to support Coriolanus as he cries 'Make you a sword of me' at 1.7.76, and later Aufidius's porters in 4.5 will be rendered even more ineffectual by being played as would-be comic camp Northerners.) Despite this unworthy collective adversary, West makes an impressive Menenius, able to stiffen his backbone like a war veteran when it is rhetorically useful for him to do so, but as his protégé Caius Martius, William Houston gets into a shouting, grinning rut very early in the evening, his voice monotonously sibilant through clenched teeth ('Have I had children's voissus?', 3.1.32). This is a performance varied only by an interestingly unconvincing death, possibly influenced by Simon Russell Beale's as Macbeth in 2005 (see *Survey 59*), whereby, instead of being instinctively provoked into thoughtless rage by the taunt of 'boy' and murdered by all the Volscian guards at once, Coriolanus abruptly acquires a perverse out-of-character cunning, starting a duel with Aufidius and then ingeniously insisting on impaling himself deliberately on his adversary's sword (why?).

But this is a show whose strongest moments belong throughout to the older generation. Suzman makes a formidable Volumnia: it is clear in 1.3, for example, that she is not just visiting Virgilia's house but allowing her daughter-in-law to live at hers during Martius's absence, on sufferance, and that she has already completely alienated the filial devotion of Young Martius, who sits at her feet throughout the scene and joins her in her impersonation of his absent father, 'Come on, you cowards . . .!' (1.3.35–6), as though this is a customary game of theirs. Virgilia is subordinated in the embassy scene too, when Coriolanus's 'O, a kiss / Long as my exile, sweet as my revenge!' (5.3.44–5) is played as an aside describing what he is denying himself rather than what he will take, a passing idea which flits through his mind before he turns his attention to the woman who will actually demand and hold it for the remainder of the scene, Volumnia. The two missions from Rome to Coriolanus provide easily the most moving sequences of this production, much assisted by the removal, before West's Menenius arrives at the Volscian camp, of the set: at last there is a huge, deep, empty space through which the spurned old man can wander, the very weight of his own body suddenly almost unsustainable, and into which Virgilia, Valeria, Young Martius and Volumnia can process forwards out of the darkness. Suzman's Volumnia is wonderfully outraged by the sheer rudeness of her son's silence in the face of her entreaties – 'yet here he lets me prate / Like one i'th' stocks' (5.3.160–1), where will people think he was brought up? – but she seems as inwardly dismayed by his eventual capitulation as she would have been by continued defiance. Even if this production as a whole is profoundly disappointing after Doran's previous revivals of Roman plays – especially his 2005 *Sejanus*, with Houston in the title role – it should be recorded that its most affecting moment is a directorial invention. In 5.5, the short, often cut scene depicting the women's triumphal return to Rome, Doran has the crowd fall expectantly silent (after shouting not only 'Welcome, ladies, welcome' but 'Vivat mater!') just as Suzman reaches the centre of the stage. She pauses, and looks up, and takes a breath, about to make a speech in response; but suddenly, already too keenly aware that the effect of her intercession can only be to condemn her son to death, she cannot utter a word, almost cries, looks at the floor, hurries away. After all the fierce eloquence of the last five acts, it is like seeing Violetta no longer able to sing at the end of *La Traviata*, and every bit as affecting.

The remainder of March is given over to the last two comedies to be seen in the Festival, two more visiting productions, both of them more consistently stimulating than this slightly lumbering and under-cast attempt on *Coriolanus*. On **7 March** I am in the Swan to see Sam West's production of *As You Like It*, which after a short run at the Crucible in Sheffield is playing in Stratford for just a week. I should probably declare an interest at this point, since I wrote a programme note for this show in early January after discussing it extensively with its director before that, but like all good directors West has had the sense and the open-mindedness to abandon a lot of his initial ideas in the light of the cast he has in practice assembled, and then to replace a lot more of them during rehearsal, so that tonight the piece is no less delightfully surprising to me than to anyone else in the audience, and the programme note, in the great tradition of such things, bears at best a peripheral relationship to the production it purports to introduce.

As the audience take their places, the brightly lit whitewashed stage and rear wall are immediately reminiscent of the white-box sets in which West himself appeared in Stratford as Richard II and Hamlet (see *Survey* 54 and 55), but Katrina Lindsay's design for *As You Like It* is altogether less austere than this first impression might suggest. At the sides of the acting area we can already see a number of objects which look as though they are waiting to be arranged as part of a Selfridge's window display – the silver life-sized stylized silhouette of a tree, sheets on what look like towel rails, a chair, some intensely clean white rope – and as it turns out this entire production, taking the play's interest in dressing-up to heart in what will sometimes look like a consumerist utopia of voluntary identity-formation, is probably best described as a boutique *As You Like It*. First, though, an introductory meta-theatrical gag. An elegantly dressed, slim young man is having trouble finding his seat in the front row of the stalls – all these places seem to be filled already. He looks at once frustrated and cocky; abruptly he climbs onto the stage and

28 *As You Like It*, Crucible Theatre, Sheffield, directed by Sam West. Harry Peacock as Touchstone, Lisa Dillon as Celia and Eve Best as Rosalind.

grins defiantly around the auditorium. Is he drunk, or just a complete show-off? The Swan audience almost freezes in embarrassment as he stretches out his arms, evidently about to say something. 'All the world's a stage!' he shouts, rather badly, and there is a tiny, ghastly pause before we see that he is now leaving not back into the stalls but into the wings; this *is* part of the show, and the house-lights are now dimming to a ripple of relieved laughter.

A surprise whole-cast tableau swiftly convenes, with this briefly centre-stage Jaques now subdued and inconspicuous in a military cap (which he subsequently discards and drops) among a group of mourners bearing a coffin. Much as many *Twelfth Nights* nowadays like to start with an unscripted glimpse of Olivia's brother's funeral, this *As You Like It* has apparently started at that of Sir Rowland de Boys, which as swiftly as it assembled now dissolves, some fleeing, presumably to the woods, and some, more soldierly, filing ominously off towards, presumably, Duke Frederick's court. A tall dark-haired girl picks up the military cap as she leaves, reluctantly caught up in the latter group; apples roll across the stage and artificial leaves fall; one young mourner has stripped his funeral suit to a vest and, along with a much older man who has donned an apron over his, is left behind on the stage, laboriously and unwillingly gathering the scattered fruit. Here we are in 1.1's orchard with Orlando and Adam, in short, and before a word of dialogue has been spoken we have already watched three different costume changes. It is already clear that it doesn't do to take your eye off the clothes in this highly nuanced modern-dress *As You Like It* for a minute: when Christopher Brandon's Oliver arrives, for instance, he is wearing expensive, suave, gentleman's country casuals that give the impression that he would like to be a decade older than he is, his lordly manner with his younger brother just one symptom of an affected desire to pose as Gerald Harper before his time. (He is appropriately young-fogeyish and awkward later in the scene when given a parting Continental kiss on the cheek by Michael Taibi's international star of a Charles.)

Eve Best's Rosalind, similarly – the tall girl who picked up the cap, the first of several items of headgear with which she will experiment over the course of the evening – first expresses her intimacy with Lisa Dillon's wry and delicate Celia by another minor costume change. At the start of 1.2 the two women have retreated to talk together in one corner of a dreary drinks reception at Duke Frederick's court (a court marked already by a longstanding interest in hunting, indicated by several sinister sets of trophy antlers that have descended into view above their heads), and, after clinking her glass against her cousin's to formalize an agreement that they should not fall in love in earnest (at 1.2.28), Rosalind indicates part of what she means in remarking that Fortune 'doth most mistake in her gifts to women' (35) by slipping off her uncomfortable high-heeled shoes, at which Celia immediately follows suit. The friendship between the two is exquisitely played throughout, whether in formal day-wear or in lingerie: at the start of 1.3, for instance, Celia has come downstairs in a dressing gown to find a sleepless Rosalind waltzing in a nightdress and cardigan with an imaginary Orlando, so that the subsequent irruption of the angry Duke Frederick (a wheelchair-bound, thug-escorted tyrant who turns out not to remove his sadistic mirrored Ray-Ban sunglasses even at night) comes like the proverbial knock on the door at three in the morning. The violent banishment of Rosalind and the girls' resolve to go into exile together, however, does nothing to dent their shared sense of humour: Rosalind, for instance, makes no secret of her low opinion of her cousin's choice of alias for the occasion, mouthing the word 'Aliena!' repeatedly in amused despair at a number of points well after 1.3.127. The great thing about this plot development, though, is that it motivates another costume change, and before 2.4 we are treated to a little dumb-show of the girls' disguised escape from the court with the fool. Harry Peacock's tough, cheeky-chappie Touchstone (a vigorous, saturnine end-of-the-pier type who with enough discouragement might yet turn into Archie Rice) has abandoned the comedy jacket with the arrow-stuck target on the back which he wore in 1.2 in favour of a furtively buttoned-up blazer and scarf, and has crammed a ludicrously unconvincing white curly wig under his bowler hat; Celia, previewing the elegantly Chelsea-supermodel-style shepherdess outfit she will wear in Arden, has donned an expensive Edwardian motoring outfit complete with chiffon scarf around floppy-brimmed hat, as if trying to pass herself off not as Aliena but as Truly Scrumptious from *Chitty Chitty Bang Bang*; and Rosalind, adding a uniform greatcoat to the cap we saw her pick up after the opening funeral, looks like the guard who is checking their papers at an imaginary gate, only much more nervous. But despite the transparency of the three disguises, he lets them out of the court and away towards the Forest of Arden.

Our first glimpse of Arden, in this production, is provided by 2.5, as Amiens sings 'Under the greenwood tree' (and the lords silently welcome Le Beau, who has fled after bravely letting himself be seen by one of Frederick's guards while encouraging Orlando at the end of 1.2); the second act is here reshuffled so that 1.3 (the banishment of the princesses) is directly followed by 2.3 (Adam and Orlando set out for Arden), then 2.5 ('Under the greenwood tree', with Jaques's satire here pointedly addressed to the latest fugitive, Le Beau), 2.2 (Frederick sends for Oliver to seek the missing Celia), 2.4 (Celia, Rosalind and Touchstone arrive in Arden) and only then a conflation of 2.1 ('Now, my co-mates and brothers in exile') with 2.7 (the picnic, here of Purdey-bearing lords, interrupted by Orlando's demand for food, backed up on this occasion by the brandishing of a comically large random sword). This transposition of scenes, characteristically, is partly designed to enable another two costume changes, one off stage (as Christopher Ravenscroft metamorphoses from crippled Duke Frederick to gracious, gardening-hat and sandal-clad Duke Senior) and one on, as Jaques, attempting to conceal his identity from the Duke by turning up his collar, speaks what is usually the First Lord's account of his encounter with the wounded stag (2.1.25–63), and then adjusts his jacket and feigns to enter afresh for 'A fool, a fool' (2.7.12ff), rather spoiling this latter speech's claims to spontaneity. (John Philip Kemble used to steal the First Lord's lines in 2.1 when he played Jaques too, but he rewrote them so that Jaques was speaking in the first person rather than in unconvincing disguise, and I suspect it worked better that way.) In whatever order we encounter it, however, this Arden is a chic, toy-theatre sort of place rather than the graphically muddy or snowy representation of rural life which it can be, where birds are indicated not only by sound effects but by a sheep-sized plain-blue plastic robin, like some giant postmodern Christmas ornament, placed inertly at one back edge of the stage, and where the local country people, instead of simulating subsistence agriculture, carefully position a flat designer tree, hoist a Habitat-like four-foot inflated plastic sphere into position to be lit from within as a pretend sun or moon, or tend a small flock of upholstery woolly goats on castors. After the interval (here nicely placed at the end of 3.1, the interrogation of Oliver; brutally questioned with a sack over his head, Oliver, left alone, tentatively removes the bag, and finds himself in Arden, and then the house-lights come up), the forest has been still further ornamented. The tree is now a mass of colour-co-ordinated ribbons, from which already dangle some of Orlando's poems, and downstage there is a little clump of ten sticks on which a selection of different hats are perched, for use in further experiments in posing and in being during the remainder of the action. (Eve Best, though she probably missed the old children's television series to which this prop seems to allude, *Mr Ben*, whose bowler-clad protagonist was forever visiting a milliner and having a different adventure with each successive hat he tried on, may just be old enough to have seen Juliet Stevenson as Rosalind in 1984; in any event, in preparation for speaking to Orlando like a saucy lackey in 3.2 she chooses a bowler.)

This knowingly artificial, dressing-up-box *mise-en-scène* may sound trivial or even irritatingly arch, but in practice it is neither of these things, held in its proper place by some superbly detailed and serious ensemble acting. The plot of *As You Like It* is hardly a rigorous, kitchen-sink realist exercise in cause and effect in any case but a pretext for more important things, and West's cast never lose sight of them, playing the danger and the excite-ment of mutual self-discovery not only with wit and charm but with a real sense that important things are at stake. Duke Frederick's court may be decorated with arbitrary antlers but it is also a gen-uinely disturbing place, where Orlando's jubilant self-announcement when questioned after his vic-tory in the wrestling match – 'the youngest son of Sir Rowland de Boys!' (1.2.212) – is imme-diately greeted by one of the Duke's henchmen pulling a gun on him; and love too offers unex-pected perils. Rosalind, talking briefly with Jaques at 4.1.25, sounds genuinely frightened that experi-ence might make her sad too, touchingly anxious that her exploratory games with Orlando might all go wrong; Celia, after watching her friend's love-prate in the ensuing scene while sitting prepar-ing runner beans, is later genuinely shocked at being asked to conduct the betrothal, outraged that her friendship is being exploited even in the act of being superseded. (Dillon's minutely responsive cousin pleasingly gets her own back later on; after delightedly appraising Oliver while giving comi-cally distracted and incompetent directions to the cottage at 4.3.79–81, she gently corrects him for asking Ganymede whether he is the owner of the house: 'It is no boast, being asked, to say *we* are', 91, here not only asserts women's right to hold property, but tells Oliver to redirect his attention towards her, which he then does for the remain-der of the play, ultimately promoting Celia from being Rosalind's cousin to being her sister-in-law.) Above all, Sam Troughton's wide-eyed Orlando, instead of being the stolid, stooge-like figure who sometimes merely feeds cues to a Rosalind with whom he has nothing in common apart from ban-ishment, is achingly vulnerable throughout, and just as eager for a world of larger possibilities as she is. Suddenly raised from torpor by Rosalind's interest at the wrestling match (the thrill that passes through both of them as their hands touch while she is giving him the necklace at 1.2.234, here a little string of pearls, is beautifully registered), he arrives in Arden as the very personification of youth and hope, adopting the endearingly silly posture of a card-carrying Lover by wearing eye-liner along with the necklace itself and experimenting with a

29 *As You Like It*, Crucible Theatre, Sheffield, directed by Sam West. Patrick Godfrey as Adam.

latently camp swagger borrowed from Captain Jack Sparrow.

The script's own games with gender are hardly confined to Rosalind's thinly motivated disguise as Ganymede, and in this particular Arden bisexuality is in the air well before Phoebe enters the picture; Daniel Weyman's strangely young and uncertain Jaques, for example, totters around the forest in high heels and a little plumed hat, with a silk camisole under his jacket. Not so much melancholy as not quite gay, he stalks off in a sulk at the end of 'All the world's a stage', so that he doesn't see Patrick Godfrey's hungry but cheerful Adam contradicting his bleak vision of old age. It's a pity that Jaques's delicate pale blue-greys don't give place to more black; in this production, the important task of being sarcastic at the expense of the rest of the show falls much more heavily onto Touchstone, who at least manages to deliver 'Ay, now am I in Arden; the more fool I', 2.4.14, as a withering comment about the set. Before the love plots' normative resolutions can be achieved or enforced, all sorts of alternative options are acknowledged and briefly explored in Shakespeare's script, and, delightfully, in this production Olivia Darnley's pretty, poised Phoebe takes more persuading than usual that she doesn't really want Ganymede even if he does turn out to be a woman. At the re-entry of Celia and Rosalind in 5.4, Hymen (Patrick Godfrey again, who also plays Sir Oliver Martext) at first recites 'Then is there mirth in heaven' (5.4.106–12) from off-stage as an amplified, resonating voice-over, but after Rosalind has come tenderly down to Phoebe for 'Nor e'er wed woman, if you be not she' (122) the shepherdess seizes her and kisses her on the mouth, and a few delirious moments of complete sexual free-for-all break out across the whole stage before Hymen rushes anxiously on from the wings with a hand-held microphone ('Peace, ho, I bar confusion!') and sorts out the lovers into their socially approved pairings more or less by force. (This Hymen has strong convictions, turning out, when indicated by the hilariously convenient Jacques de Boys at 5.4.158, to double as 'the old religious man' who has converted Duke Frederick.) During the Greek dance to which 'Wedding is great Juno's crown' is set, Rosalind and Orlando appropriately celebrate their union by swapping clothes – she wears his jacket, he her wedding veil, and they both look very fetching too, and absurdly, contagiously happy. It's a mark of Best's commitment to this compelling, intent performance that during the epilogue, after 'If I were a woman, I would kiss as many of you as had beards that pleased me, complexions that liked me, and breaths that I defied not,' she, like Phoebe, decides to have a kiss anyway, and kisses one surprised spectator in the front row, and then another. I was myself, alas, sitting in the second row; but then you can't have everything, not even from the most enjoyable production you are ever likely to see of your favourite play.

On **24 March** I am back at the Swan to see another visiting exercise in modern dress, albeit a rather more conventional one, the Brooklyn-based Theatre For A New Audience performing *The Merchant of Venice*, directed by Darko Tresnjak. The time of this production, we are told by the programme, is 'the near future', but although the place is listed as 'Venice and Belmont' the production really treats the play's principal locales as New York City and the Berkshires. John Lee Beatty's designs are elegant and expensive-looking, even before the show proper begins: there are three plasma screens above the shiny-floored acting area (elegantly chequered in gold, silver and lead), screens which will later serve as the video-monitors of computerized caskets, and they bear respective warnings in English, Italian and Hebrew that mobile telephones should be switched off. All three instead turn to showing graphs of the NASDAQ share-price index as the house-lights fade and we find a besuited Salerio and Solanio bringing their older business colleague Antonio a small espresso at a perspex table downstage. This staging of the Venetian scenes in a reasonable facsimile of the milieu of Wall Street is throughout reminiscent of David Thacker's Square Mile, *Serious Money* production at the RST in 1991, and is in general nicely observed – Saxon Palmer's Bassanio, for instance, in a dark blue shirt instead of a white one and initially in hangover-mitigating sunglasses, looks plausibly spivvier and sexier than Tom Nelis's self-consciously greying Antonio (who may well have monopolized the attentions of the person intriguingly listed in the programme as the company's 'Hair Consultant'), while John Lavelle's Gratiano is clearly an old fraternity pal, and every bit as embarrassing as that description implies.

It is perhaps troubling that none of the extras who occasionally pass along this lower Manhattan Rialto are women (I'm still not sure whether to read this as a piece of documentary realism about the homosocial world of American finance, or simply as a bid to keep Portia's masculine disguise in countenance regardless of the present-day setting), but what becomes a more intrusive mannerism of this production is its growing obsession, as the evening progresses, with the mobile telephone and

30 *The Merchant of Venice*, Theatre for a New Audience, Swan Theatre, directed by Darko Tresnjak. F. Murray Abraham as Shylock.

electronic technology in general, whatever trilingual prohibitions it may seek to impose on its audience. In Belmont, for instance, where the keys to the caskets are memory-sticks plugged into the respective laptops which appear to be generating the gold, silver and lead displays on the three plasma screens, Arnie Burton's shamelessly part-building performance as a camp Balthasar comes with a running gag whereby he has to move fastidiously around the stage to try to find the best reception for the bluetooth gadget behind his ear through which he receives news of each suitor's approach. Even some of the play's most famous and moving exchanges are robbed of their drama by being recast as electronic communication rather than personal. In 3.1, for instance, Shylock's terrible interview with Tubal, during which he receives the news of all that Jessica has been squandering since her elopement, is played, for no obvious reason, as a

mobile telephone conversation between a downstage Shylock and a Tubal standing up on the musicians' gallery behind him, the climax of which is laboriously muffled while Tubal transmits a digital photograph of the ring Jessica sold for a monkey to Shylock's handset so that he can verifiably recognize it as the turquoise Leah gave him when he was a bachelor. 3.1.110–12 consequently runs as follows:

TUBAL, *above, into handset*: One of them showed me a ring that he had of your daughter for a monkey. *Takes handset from mouth, fiddles with keys, presses another button, waits.*
SHYLOCK, *below, takes handset from ear, waits, hears a small bleep; presses a button, looks aghast at screen, fiddles with another key as Tubal lifts his own handset back to his ear, then lifts handset back to mouth*: Out upon her! Thou torturest me, Tubal . . .

If Tubal were really in Genoa and Shylock really in Venice, the telephones would of course be wonderfully useful, but actually they are both in the theatre, within a few feet of one another, and the things merely ruin the flow, momentum and immediacy of their dialogue. If we can accept for the purposes of the play that Manhattan dealers sometimes speak in blank verse (and even that some of them have scruples about taking interest!), we can surely pretend too that they occasionally speak to one another in person as well as via cellphone.

This distracting piece of business is the more regrettable, since F. Murray Abraham's straight-down-the-line performance as Shylock deserves to be as uninterrupted as possible; this is in all other respects a splendidly uncluttered portrayal, an impersonation of a man whose feelings run so implacably deep that even his immediate animosity towards Antonio seems like a pretext, the tip of a whole unarticulated iceberg of violated dignity. Around this often frightening performance, the production adopts what have become standard approaches towards the play's depictions of anti-Semitism. Apparently anxious that its audience might otherwise sympathize with them, Tresnjak has Salerio and Solanio behave so grossly and violently towards Shylock on his entrance in 3.1 that it is incredible that he should confide in them to the extent that he does, although their behaviour here does usefully enable Shylock to look more potentially sympathetic in the trial scene, when he is at the very point of yielding to Portia's persuasions at 4.1.202 and only reverts to demanding his pound of flesh after recognizing these two bigots in the public gallery. The prejudice at work in the courtroom is otherwise largely attributed to Antonio, whose stipulation that Shylock should convert visibly horrifies Portia (as it usually does nowadays, despite her undisguised racism towards Morocco earlier), and who vindictively snatches off Shylock's skullcap as a trophy while he is kneeling and sobbing in grief after the verdict. At the end of Act 5, in another standard directorial move, Jessica is made to look sorry for having betrayed her father and her faith, here when, as Lorenzo eagerly and obliviously reads her father's deed of gift, she finds the skullcap on

the stage where Antonio has dropped it while producing the document. She doesn't actually repeat the interpolated Jewish song which she and her father sang, as per Trevor Nunn's National Theatre production of 1999–2000, in 2.5, but you can see that she is thinking about it.

The glossiness and confidence of this production, and the obvious strength of most of its cast, make its occasional weaknesses and self-indulgences stand out the more clearly. Lorenzo and Jessica (Vince Nappo and Nicole Lowrance), for instance, never quite seem to understand their lines, although Jessica's monotonous tremolo, it is true, may be trying to indicate the complicated feelings of guilt suggested above, to which the text as written unfortunately offers no clues. (It is in any event very difficult to understand why she sounds so harsh with Launcelot Gobbo in 3.5, or why she flounces angrily away from Lorenzo after telling him she is never merry when she hears sweet music at 5.1.69.) As far as the show's lighter touches are concerned, Morocco's entrance in 2.1 is certainly a comic tour-de-force: to the sound effect of a passing aircraft, Balthasar, Nerissa and Portia appear disbelievingly to watch something descending to the ground offstage right, and then Morocco and his servant enter up the right-hand aisle of the stalls in outrageous jumpsuits, trailing parachutes, and the latter produces a huge silver scimitar from a case with which Morocco poses, kneeling, at Portia's feet, while the servant takes a (digital) photograph. It is quite funny, too, to follow this up at the end of 2.7 by indicating that Arnie Burton's Balthasar has enjoyed a quick offstage fling with Morocco's corresponding aide and visibly regrets his departure with his defeated master, signing as they leave that he will telephone later. But allowing Balthasar to accompany Portia and Nerissa to the trial scene in a fake moustache, even if Burton did have a regular part in *Frasier*, is too much, and then to have him visibly Googling on a laptop behind Portia at its crisis – evidently looking up 'pound of flesh as debt penalty – loopholes?' – and whispering the crucial solution to the legal problem in Portia's ear at 4.1.301 is completely fatal to her importance in the play. If she isn't even the clever one, in this account of *Merchant*, what is she? Kate Forbes's Portia – given to breaking up her sentences into short, non-connecting units, and always on the back foot when dealing with Palmer's unfazedly puppyish Bassanio, even when the resolution of the ring plot should put her on top forever – could have done with a clear field at this point rather than this shocking piece of upstaging. This is often a powerful show, as well as a handsome one (the gold ingots with which Bassanio tries to pay off Shylock in court are a typically opulent touch), but despite the haunting force of some of its images it doesn't quite find anything new to say about the play.

From a production influenced by Trevor Nunn to one directed by the man himself. I would have been in Stratford again for the press night of his contribution to the Complete Works Festival as originally scheduled little more than a week after this, but in the event I do not arrive at the Courtyard and find myself sitting down to watch *King Lear* once again until 6 June. Directed and staged back-to-back with Chekhov's *The Seagull* and, as if rather needlessly advertising its sister production, given a Russian nineteenth-century setting to match it, this is a typically assured and highly finished specimen of Nunn's directorial manner, determined to re-imagine the play as fully as possible within the terms of its chosen design. From the stalls, as the capacity crowd take their seats, the set resembles part of a different, less public kind of auditorium somewhere within the Hermitage: behind an acting area currently bearing a large heavy desk, a matching chair and, downstage, an ecclesiastical-looking lectern, Christopher Oram has built an immense structure which, receding into the gloom at a slight angle, looks like the tiered boxes of half a Victorian opera house, all hung with swags of heavy crimson fabric and matching long gathered vertical curtains. During the course of the play this palace-come-theatre will be progressively desecrated, the fabric stripped away to reveal shattered lathe and plaster, the great chandeliers smashed and removed, the vertical curtains torn down to reveal rickety wooden scaffolding, and the high suspended ceiling splintered and destroyed.

I use the word 'desecrated' advisedly, since we are told very insistently from the very opening of this production that Lear's regime, despite the text's theologically inconsistent gestures towards various pagan deities, is very much an Orthodox theocracy, understood not just as sovereign but as holy. Before the dialogue between Gloucester, Kent and Edmund which usually opens the play, Nunn, to great Gothic surges of organ music, choreographs a ceremonial entry for the entire court, who, splendid in Tsarist uniforms and dark court dresses, kneel in unison as McKellen's Lear, a patriarch of the Church as well as of the state, ritually dons a sort of cope and mitre amidst clouds of incense and processes slowly across the space, wafting a blessing on his subjects. It is only as they rise and disperse after his departure that Gloucester and Kent quietly greet one another downstage and nervously compare what here sound like slightly conspiratorial notes about the King's preferences among his sons-in-law, and at 'The King is coming' (1.1.33) they hurry swiftly back to their places like choirboys almost caught gossiping in church. What is here the King's second entrance is almost as formal as the first, but is now more military than ecclesiastical; white-bearded, and wearing a small crown instead of a mitre, he looks small and slightly frail, and would be almost dwarfed behind the great desk where he takes his seat did its candles not reflect such a mass of gold braid and frogging on his scarlet tunic. The King is clearly becoming genuinely conscious that his powers are fading – he has to produce a little set of cue-cards to prompt his crisp, dry-toned announcement of the love-test, as attendants spread a map across the desk – though even Frances Barber's severe-looking Goneril and Monica Dolan's feline Regan register a moment of surprise that he is handing over power so completely, and so soon, and in this manner: they meet one another's apprehensive glances before taking it in turns to cross to the lectern and make their protestations to the whole court. As Cordelia, however, Romola Garai is not just surprised but in a state of complete and at first amused disbelief. As if convinced that this is all another of her father's eccentric practical jokes at her sisters' expense, she

31 *King Lear*, RSC, Courtyard Theatre, directed by Trevor Nunn. Romola Garai as Cordelia, Ian McKellen as King Lear.

laughs openly at their declarations of abject filial loyalty, says her first 'Nothing, my lord' from the lectern with a wry, indulgent smile, and asks Lear why her sisters have husbands if they say they love him all as if expecting him at any moment to stop pretending to be so cross and laugh uproariously with her at the way in which the two of them have caught the two more censorious grown-up girls out once again. By playing Cordelia as more spoiled than righteous, Garai paradoxically makes her much more sympathetic than she can often be; her mounting panic as she realizes that her father never is going to dismiss the court and revert to his playful nursery-games self, and her sudden confusion as to where she should stand on the stage as he pronounces her banishment, are extremely touching, and the little involuntary shriek of despair she utters as Lear removes his crown and passes it to Albany and Cornwall on 'This crownet part between you' (1.1.139) beautifully marks the point

at which she abandons all hope of regaining his favour.

Lear, meanwhile, seems to be deliberately working himself up into a rage with Kent, punching him at 'O vassal! Miscreant!' (1.1.160) as if afraid that his ranting threats to date (from which McKellen so far withholds some of his vocal force, husbanding it for later in the play) will not otherwise be taken seriously. The sense of humour of which his youngest daughter seemed so confident returns only in twisted, aggressive form, when on the arrival of Cordelia's two suitors he at first takes Cordelia and Burgundy in either hand and asks what dowry the latter will require in a soothing, unctuous voice, as if about to bless their union, and then sneeringly springs his real attitude on Burgundy when, on the words 'with our displeasure pieced, / And nothing more' (1.1.198–9), he drops their hands, snatches up the crown where his anxious and awkward sons-in-law have placed it on the desk and shouts the word 'nothing' through it, parrotting the offending term back at Cordelia once again. Cordelia herself is still too dazed to respond to Burgundy's defection with much more than a sort of constrained pity, or to France's suddenly revived courtship with much of anything; all her thoughts of the future are still centred on her father, and on her siblings, who in this reading embrace her with what may be genuine compassion at parting even while telling her not to prescribe them their duty. I have never seen Cordelia's story in 1.1 told more carefully or more effectively.

This is a closely reasoned, highly wrought account of the play's opening, anything but a swift, expository piece of fairytale just to start things off, and it strikes me that one reason this Russian setting may have seemed so congenial to Nunn is that it brings with it generic expectations drawn not from the early modern stage but from the nineteenth-century novel. This is one of the most elaborately explained productions of *King Lear* I have ever seen, not only in terms of psychological motivation but in terms of logistics. In 2.1, for example, we see that Edmond's strategic betrayal of his father is enabled by his corruption of the servant Curran, who slips him the key to Gloucester's bureau of compromising letters at the end of an exchange which less fastidious productions tend to cut; Kent is given food by the Gentleman who brings him news of the French powers in the quarto's scene 17, and then observes the disposition of Cornwall's army through a telescope; and in the last scene of all Nunn is so keen to add novelistic circumstantial plausibility to Goneril's poisoning of Regan that he has the doctor from the reunion scene brought on under arrest with Lear and Cordelia and then separated, as all three are led off to prison, from his Victorian medicine chest, from which Goneril can then opportunistically abstract something lethal with which to spike Regan's post-battle drink. The reunion scene itself is beautifully played around another period prop, the immense bath chair, looking like a relic from some Black Sea sanatorium, in which Lear is wheeled on asleep under a blanket at 4.6.20. At first mainly annoyed that he cannot recognize his fresh garments, he is already becoming

properly aware of his surroundings when he feigns, in a dim reminiscence of their jokes together, to think that Cordelia is a spirit at line 42, but once he has pricked himself at line 49 to see if he is dreaming, using a dog-rose left over from his crown of weeds in his previous scene, he is sure of her. Very slowly and weakly he begins to slide himself forward out of the chair, so that both she and the audience only gradually realize that he is trying to kneel; but at the end of the scene, wet with her tears as he is, he is still proud enough not to let her help him up, slowly rising on one knee and making 'You must bear with me' (76) an instruction not to intervene. Drawing himself to his full height, he appears inwardly to shoulder his responsibility for all that has happened; 'Pray now', he says, but then, faltering, he looks down at his child, and though he tries to confine himself to primly adjusting the shawl on her shoulders he suddenly embraces her, eyes closed, with a desperate sigh of 'forget / And forgive'. Then he holds her at arm's length, and manages a quick, self-deprecating smile as he musters his determination once more, leading her off with 'I am old and foolish.' It is fiddly, and intricate, and more than adequately heartbreaking.

Less successful, perhaps, is Nunn's correspondingly novelistic decision to tie up one famous loose end in the text, this time lethally. (Despite the publication in April of a dogmatically Folio-based *Complete RSC Shakespeare*, incidentally, Nunn's production mixes, matches and transposes material from the quarto and folio texts *ad lib*.) Sylvester McCoy's touching, ragdoll-wigged, carpet-bag-bearing Fool is not allowed to disappear enigmatically from the play but is hanged on stage, as a grand finale to the first half, by the idle and vicious soldiers who arrive, at the end of a conflation of the mock-trial scene of the quarto with the folio's 3.6 (designed to restrict the use of a slightly clumsy flown-in wooden hovel to a single period of the action), to arrest Gloucester, who has himself compassionately returned to fetch him after Lear and the disguised Edgar have already set off towards Dover. It's true that the Fool's recitation of the prophecy from the end of 3.2 while this impromptu execution is in progress looks unlikely (I'd have

32 *King Lear*, RSC, Courtyard Theatre, directed by Trevor Nunn. William Gaunt as Gloucester, Ian McKellen as King Lear, Seymour Matthews as Curran, Jonathan Hyde as Kent and Sylvester McCoy as the Fool.

recommended 'Help, please don't hang me!', personally, rather than 'When priests are more in word than matter', which doesn't seem to deter them at all), but the incident does save the play from including an unexplained absence which no exponent of classic realist fiction would have tolerated, and in case we haven't got the point that Lear, released into madness, no longer needs this externalized comedy conscience hereafter, the King turns out to have retained his jester's coxcomb (a little stick bearing a doll-like portrait-head of the fool at its tip) to use in his dialogue with the blinded Gloucester later on, and to have adopted one of his signature mannerisms, the little music-hall cuckoo-cadenced whistle by which the Fool used to punctuate his more phallic innuendoes.

It's all tremendously clear, and tremendously effective, and is put over by a strong cast: McKellen comes gloriously into his own from the mad scenes onwards, Frances Barber's Goneril dwindles interestingly into a dominatrix after being literally laid low by her father's curse in 1.4, lying retching and sobbing in horror, and William Gaunt makes a fine, soldierly Gloucester, and if among the younger players Ben Meyjes isn't quite an intellectual enough actor to make the maximum sense of Edgar's metamorphoses, he and Philip Winchester's Edmund put on one of the best sword-duels I've seen for years. But at the end of the performance, even though quite adequately tear-stained, I still have a nagging sense of disappointment about the whole production, as if it has been holding something back about the play to which less lavishly supported and exquisitely cast *Lear*s have done fuller justice. I eventually decide that the whole affair has somehow been too polite with us, inadequately extreme. One old man insists on visiting his eldest child with a gang of unruly knights (who here, unequivocally confirming Goneril's account of the situation, even seem

337

to drag off one of the maidservants to rape her); another gets put in the stocks after a brawl; the first old man goes mad in a storm and exposes himself at us (to say 'strips naked' would be inaccurate, since McKellen never removes his boots and can thus only lower his breeches); yet another old man has his eyes gouged out; and there is a savage civil war with all sorts of gunfire effects, after which one sister poisons another and then stabs herself while a third is hung off stage, then carried dead onto the stage by her dying father; and yet in Nunn's rendition it is all somehow in the best possible taste, kept at a slight remove from us by the handsome *War and Peace* way in which the court's gorgeous reds gradually give place to black and white, and the stirring *Boris Godunov* way in which Steven Edis's incidental orchestral music sweeps forebodingly between the scenes. With that opera-house wall perpetually before our eyes, even in designer ruin, the production always seems safely contained under a Victorian proscenium, never matching the broken, ugly, no-holds-barred vehemence of either the play's language or its structure. Meanwhile *Lear*'s deep, terrifying uncertainty about the gods – who in the script's account would be as much of a problem whether absent or present – is in Nunn's interpretation reduced to a simple diagnosis of the God delusion. In the last scene, recapitulating his interpolated opening benediction, Nunn has everyone on stage kneel in collective prayer for the successful reprieve of Lear and Cordelia at Albany's 'The gods defend her!' (5.3.231), so that the sound which eventually comes in answer to that prayer – Lear's 'Howl, howl, howl' – becomes in context a simple apparent demonstration of the impotent misguidedness of religious faith. Moving as it is, the death of Lear in Nunn's production seems to be mainly there to tell us that the Russian Orthodox Church does not have the answer, which seems rather to underestimate the question. To revert to a term I tried to coin in this column years ago, the RSC's Complete Works Festival thus ended with a *King Lear* which provided both a magnificent textbook example of the Perfectly Composed Production and a fine demonstration of why, of all Shakespeare's plays, this one is the least suited to this treatment. And thus came the promised end of the Festival – perhaps ominously, with a production that offered a gratifying reunion of the RSC of the 1970s rather than a vision of the company's future – and here ends, too, this *de-facto* blog.

COMEDIES

Outside the Complete Works Festival, 2007 may well be remembered as a year in which *Twelfth Night* could have done with a rest. In May, Edward Hall's Propeller company brought theirs to the Oxford Playhouse, in conjunction with the *Taming of the Shrew* which they played in Stratford in November 2006 as part of the Festival and took to the Old Vic thereafter. Hall's *Shrew* adapted the Induction so as to start with a present-day wedding party waiting around the foyer of the theatre, and eventually on the stage, amongst whom the drunken bridegroom (Dugald Bruce-Lockhart) turned out to be Christopher Sly; when the bride arrived she promptly left in angry disgust, leaving him to lapse into a drunken stupor and fall prey to a practical joke here played by the rest of the morning-suited guests, with the Lord possibly the bride's father. In the play-within-the-play, Lockhart reappeared as an equally coarse and brutish Petruccio, sadistically and unmutually breaking-in Simon Scardifield's sorrowful Katherina, but the spectacle's claims to offer an outraged comment on the marital abuse of women were rather undercut by the company's customary and still under-explained exclusion of any women from its cast. It turned out to be a mistake to see a matinee of this *Shrew* immediately before an evening show of the *Twelfth Night*, which was similarly dominated by laddish drunkenness in the person of Jason Baughan's retching, unfunny Sir Toby, so much so that leaving the theatre after these two consecutive all-male shows felt like escaping with relief from someone else's stag party. The *Twelfth Night* was one of Hall's busier efforts, with Miss Havisham-like cobwebs for Olivia's house and a marked reluctance to let any of the cast leave the stage for very long, so that Dugald Bruce Lockhart here played not only

Olivia but a statue of her in the garden scene (cueing the usual predictable sight gags, here rendered slightly confusing by the deployment of that other implausible old favourite by which Sir Toby, Sir Andrew and Fabian miraculously escape detection by posing as garden ornaments themselves, here statues of the three wise monkeys). The costumes were vaguely Edwardian, as they also were for Neil Bartlett's undistinguished RSC production in the Courtyard in the late summer (which, to confusing and slightly flattening effect, cast Marjorie Yates, Annabel Leventon and Joanne Howarth as Belch, Aguecheek and Fabian, and Chris New as Viola, but had a passable Malvolio in John Lithgow), and for Philip Franks's equally undistinguished production in the main house at Chichester.

In Franks's over-designed, unsexy affair – with a set which perpetually kept one guessing as to whether we were supposed to be on a beach or in a conservatory, and why we should want to be in either – only two performances stood out, Scott Handy as the perfect, whey-faced, tragicomic Sir Andrew, and Patrick Stewart as an ageing, Morningside Malvolio, complete with Bobby Charlton comb-over and, after his gulling, the expected kilt by which to display his yellow stockings to Olivia in 3.4. What was less expected was Stewart's handling of his subsequent dialogue with Sir Toby, Fabian and Maria. Having sat on a chair for his soliloquy of self-congratulation after Olivia's departure and unfastened the uncomfortably tight Highland-dancing ribbons by which he was cross-gartered, he remained seated when his unsuspected tormentors arrived, deliberately and with scrupulous dignity re-tying his garters as he dismissed their efforts to diagnose him as mad. It was only when he decided to leave at 3.4.122, 'I am not of your element', and stood up, that he realized that he had accidentally tied his knees together. Refusing to acknowledge this mistake, he could just about walk stiffly, pigeon-steppingly away from the chair, but unfortunately his exit route lay down the stairs from the front of the stage; at which, mustering what remaining dignity he could, he paused, and then departed in a series of prim little jumps, feet

together. This incident, at least, was very funny, and it is always a pleasure to hear this play's lines spoken, even ineffectually, but someone is going to have to have a better idea about *Twelfth Night* than evening dress and a Toad Hall-ish subplot and the possibility of yet another male Viola to lure me to another revival any time soon.

The two comedies in the Globe's 2007 season, mercifully free of dinner suits, offered contrasting takes on that theatre's house style. Dominic Dromgoole's *Love's Labour's Lost*, a huge improvement on his contributions to the previous season, was a nicely paced, rather charming example of the Globe's established recreated-clothing-of-the-period manner, a duel of wits between russet-and-green silk lords and rustling taffeta green ladies, embellished with some occasional interpolated amorous bunraku deer between scenes which stayed just on the amusing side of cute. Michelle Terry, proving that she can play the regally sportive sort of princess as well as the accidentally rustic, was a fine Princess, and Timothy Walker an impressive, uncaricatured Don Armado; Trystan Gravelle made a lively, funny, Welsh Berowne who, at the matinee I attended, coped extremely well after the interval with a series of upstaging incursions by pigeons during his rhetorical set-pieces. These birds, it proved, knew what they were about; Dromgoole had arranged that the picnic of baguettes which the aristocrats were enjoying during the Pageant of the Nine Worthies in Act 5 should break up into a food-fight when the performance itself foundered, and at this point in the action half of the pigeons in Southwark, including the ones who had been trying to stake their places in the queue during the preceding act, descended onto the stage to claim their shares of the crumbs. It was no small achievement for Terry to shift the mood so chillingly from this accidental quotation from *Mary Poppins* to her response to the news of her father's death. The text seemed to be almost entirely uncut, even during Moth's scenes – so that we even heard the gag about the dancing horse, which surely can't have got a laugh once since the 1590s – but then it is a very short play.

Rebecca Gatward's *The Merchant of Venice*, perhaps more ambitiously, attempted a compromise between the simulated Elizabethan and modern dress; the cast wore what were sometimes Renaissance garments made up in modern fabrics (pinstriped gowns on some of the businessmen, for instance), and sometimes Elizabethan outfits finished with modern accessories (such as doublet and hose with white shoes and a pork-pie hat). A complicated opening tableau before Antonio's first entrance as a result offered a busy picture of a Venice that never was, with a little part-early-modern, part-present-day Catholic procession, offstage Jewish singing, and a band of ice-cream advert Italian street musicians in silly hats; later, the masquers arrived through the yard in a pretend cardboard gondola. Despite some potentially interesting performances – Philip Cumbus, for instance, made a splendidly unreliable Bassanio, disingenuously flippant about his debts and at first unable to remember Portia's name when trying to borrow yet more from Antonio in 1.1 – the unreality of the setting gave the impression that none of these events could really matter, not even to Peter McEnery's Shylock, who, spiteful, small-minded and uncharismatic, seemed less interesting and less central to the play than any other Shylock I can remember.

As in Stratford, the late comedies attracted more inventive treatments in 2007. Northern Broadsides followed their usual trans-Pennine touring circuit in the spring and early summer with a fine *Tempest*, directed as ever by Barrie Rutter, which I saw in the round at the Stephen Joseph Theatre in Scarborough in May. As ever, many of the cast remained around the edges of the action playing incidental music when not on stage in character – in this as in other respects this company's house style closely resembles that of Propeller, except that Northern Broadsides somehow manage to get away with not hiring Southerners instead of not hiring women – and their resident composer and associate director Conrad Nelson had scored this highly musical play so thoroughly that the whole of the opening scene, the tempest proper, verged on being as much operatic as theatrical, with even those pieces of dialogue which weren't actually sung played as a sort of rough recitative. Nelson himself played an explicitly gay Trinculo, given to mingling ad-libbingly among the audience in the manner of a pantomime Dame (predictably, the clothes he stole from the line in Act 4 were female), and speaking throughout in the whining Scouse accent patented by Lily Savage. (It's quite striking, I think, that this Yorkshire-based company, founded to resist the regional and class stereotyping by which Northern accents were once only heard in Shakespeare when spoken by comic peasants, now habitually casts its clowns and villains as Liverpudlians instead.) Nelson's music, though always simple enough for a non-expert company to play, achieves ever greater range: that range was expanded here by the very effective casting of three athletic and graceful young women, Nicola Gardner, Simone Saunders and Belinda Everett, as a composite Ariel, so that the play's best songs could be sung in three soulful parts, over plangent vibraphone and drums. As well as directing, Rutter played a variously gruff and twinkling Prospero, and as usual both his direction and his performance gave the slight impression that he was anxious above all else lest someone hard of hearing and short-sighted at the back might be unable to follow the plot; but there are many worse priorities to have when staging Shakespeare, and his rendition of Prospero's epilogue struck a nice balance between asking for personal applause (which Rutter always does with great aplomb) and genuinely looking beyond the theatre for an unforced, humble, confessional register of speech and behaviour (which I have never seen him do before, and by which the audience at this particular Thursday matinee were clearly moved).

One worse priority to have than Northern Broadside's energetic, extroverted emphasis on the narrative may just be a willingness to be seduced by the incidentally clever, at least on the evidence of Cheek by Jowl's at once beguiling and unsatisfying *Cymbeline*, which appeared at the Barbican Theatre in June as part of the Barbican International Theatre Event. If ever there were a play which demands a steady tiller-hand on the

33 *Cymbeline*, Cheek by Jowl, Barbican Theatre, directed by Nick Ormerod and Declan Donnellan. Tom Hiddleston as Posthumus.

storytelling, this is it, but – to mix the metaphor, as late Shakespeare itself often does – *Cymbeline* is also a script whose gargoyles are every bit as captivating as its architecture, and here by focusing too much of their company's energy on the intriguing details Declan Donnellan and Nick Ormerod risked letting the roof fall down. As ever with this company, the keynote of the production's style was a non-naturalistic, complicatedly advertised simplicity. With the stage floor extended outwards to cover the first few rows of the stalls, the play took place in a large, flat, dimly lit area traversed by two large green curtains, and otherwise punctuated only by two chairs facing one another at a distance, one beside a small table of drinks. In early twentieth-century clothes, the whole cast gathered to recite by turns a rewritten version of the two courtiers' opening exposition, each actor speaking sufficient lines or phrases relating to the character he or she would subsequently play for the sequence to function like an animated cast-list as well as a plot-summary. In evening dress, Posthumus and Imogen spoke the first part of their yearning, parting dialogue at 1.1.108 ff while facing each other from the two distant chairs (as if in directorial homage to the late Stephen Pimlott, who regularly used

this device of playing intimate conversation perpendicularly across a vast space), and then, after they had finally met more literally to exchange tokens, Cymbeline's arrival cued most of the cast to gather in two opposing groups, one pulling Imogen back towards stage right, one Posthumus towards stage left. It was all very smoothly and impressively choreographed, but an uncluttered way into the lovers' story it wasn't, and their situation was only distanced from us further by the behaviour of Pisanio when he returned to narrate Posthumus's embarkation later in the scene. Richard Cant had clearly been encouraged during rehearsals to think extremely hard about the fact that his character was a servant, and perhaps had been all his life, so much so that throughout the production it was difficult to concentrate on the content of the lines he actually spoke because his perpetually cringing, obsequious body-language was so busy telling the audience about his rank.

Two further directorial choices conspired to well-nigh sabotage the play's mainspring, the audience's involvement in the central adventures of Imogen. One was a comparable encouragement of Jodie McNee to play her as early twentieth-century upper-crust first and a romance heroine a poor second, so that she emerged as a woman devoid of warmth or spontaneity from whom even 'O for a horse with wings!' (3.2.48) sounded as though it were being spoken, after a calculating pause, in embarrassed inverted commas. The other was the more commonplace decision to double Posthumus with Cloten, and while Tom Hiddleston was undeniably delightful as both it was something of a problem that, distinguishing the beloved commoner from the loathed royal stepson by adopting bookish round spectacles as the former (usually in full view of the audience), he was more obviously attractive as the latter. It's a pity that his Cloten – who in this Ruritanian court seemed refreshingly uninhibited rather than just half-knowingly brutal – looked more obviously eligible, too, than Guy Flanagan's slick-haired, French-sounding Iachimo, and that his death at the hands of Guiderius in 4.2 looked practically unprovoked.

The result was a *Cymbeline* from which Imogen almost disappeared, left awkwardly to one side while the directors concentrated on the interesting things happening between and within the men. Cloten's serenade, for instance, instead of being performed by hired musicians, was a glorious, microphone-wielding set-piece pop parody sung by Hiddleston himself centre stage, which was nicely pitched somewhere between Freddie Mercury and Robbie Williams, and which made Imogen's irritated and preoccupied response seem at once ungenerous and beside the point. Rescued from her constricting crimson ball-gown for the flight to Wales, McNee managed to get a bit more attention once disguised as a boy, but her soliloquy over the headless corpse of Cloten, 4.2.293–333, was cut to little more than its first ten lines. Even the dirge over her own presumed corpse was in danger of being upstaged, recited to the accompaniment of a nagging period waltz tune (a paraphrase of 'I'm Forever Blowing Bubbles') played on an 'ingenious instrument' which was here a surprisingly loud wind-up gramophone. The evisceration of Imogen's most challenging and extreme speech was only one of many deep cuts, especially in the latter half of the play, which suffered some officious simplifying of both plot and phraseology throughout. (Caius Lucius was somehow Posthumus's host in Italy as well as Roman ambassador to Britain, for example, while Iachimo's 'the wide difference / 'Twixt amorous and villainous', 5.6.194–5, characteristically became 'the difference between love and villainy', which isn't the same thing at all). The longed-for stillness of the prison scene, 5.5, with Hiddleston's Posthumus a penitent, handcuffed PoW, was drastically reduced; no dead brothers appeared in Posthumus's vision, nor any eagle, and the invisible voice-over Jupiter left no tablet, so that the final scene could do without any soothsayer. Equally, we never heard the princely brothers' false Welsh names, Polydore and Cadwal; Imogen never incorrectly deduced that Pisanio must have been trying to poison her when he passed on the queen's medicine; and the Romans never got their tribute. What everyone did get, however, was much more of the nagging waltz tune, which was repeated endlessly under the whole of what remained of 5.6's multiple *éclaircissements*, including a nice final VE Day sort of view, during the remnants of 5.6.476–86, of Cymbeline and the restored princes waving regally from a hitherto unused Buckingham Palace-like balcony at the back of the stage while Posthumus and Imogen embraced, unnoticed, behind them. This was a persistently clever and stimulating *Cymbeline*, but on reflection I would rather have seen either Hiddleston's Posthumus or his Cloten, together with Jake Harders's fine, acerbic Cornelius and David Collings's firm Cymbeline, in a much more naive production of the play.

HISTORIES

In Stratford, Michael Boyd responded to the impending closure of the main house and the Swan, as RSC directors always do at moments of perceived crisis, by scheduling some more revivals of histories, gradually appending, over the summer and autumn, *Richard II*, *Henry IV Parts 1 and 2* and *Henry V* to the Courtyard productions of the first tetralogy by the ensemble company-within-a-company which had represented the earlier plays as part of the Complete Works Festival. This rendition of the second tetralogy will be described in the next *Survey*, when it briefly takes its place in the 2008 repertory alongside the first so that hard-core RSC fans will for the first time be able to see all eight plays performed in sequence by the same team of actors. Meanwhile, in the face of all this chronicle-play activity in Stratford, most producers elsewhere steered clear of the histories in 2007, with the exception of the Royal Exchange in Manchester, who in the autumn mounted a clear, forceful *Henry V* under the direction of Jonathan Munby.

This was an impressive piece of work throughout, but it is a sign either of my having seen the *Henriad* too often over too many years or of a general shortage of new ideas about how to play it that it was liable to look like an efficient composite of ideas already developed in earlier productions. The Chorus, for example, was a bull-necked, overweight Ulster veteran wearing his bemedalled old greatcoat and a poppy, retelling the tale of Agincourt once more as an act of Armistice Day remembrance much as did Matthew Warchus's D-Day anniversary production at the RST in 1994. (In the scenes of the play proper the same actor, Gerard Murphy, took off his coat and donned a Commando beret to reappear as a presumably younger Exeter.) The costumes were predominantly Second World War (with ceremonial red tunics on the English nobles for formal occasions), with the French army as ever looking dangerously like the underdogs, despite their reported numerical superiority, because dressed in over-foppish breastplates and epaulettes as compared to the workaday camouflage gear of their English adversaries. (This unfortunate impression was furthered, as on previous occasions, by the irresponsible cutting of the gratuitously wheelchair-bound French king's speech calling his massive military forces into play at 3.5.36–55.) The round metallic acting area was almost unadorned, but a central strip could be hydraulically lifted up to first balcony level at one or both ends, producing a ramp up which the English could attempt to storm Harfleur, or a gantry along which the French could strut before Agincourt (as per Adrian Noble's RSC production of 1984),

and under which the English army could occasionally trudge along the trench-like channel of water exposed by its raising. A blue pavilion-like roof decorated with silver fleurs-de-lys opened above the French nobles before Agincourt, as in Terry Hands's RSC production of 1975; Claire Cox's French princess was discovered listening to a repeat radio broadcast of Henry's threatening speech to the citizens of Harfleur before her English lesson in 3.4, much as Felicité du Jeu watched it on television in Nicholas Hytner's National Theatre production of 2003; and as in most modern productions before, during and after Branagh, much was made both of Bardolph's offstage hanging (here, as usual, carried out on stage at Henry's nod, but this time with the added surprise touch of the king abruptly shooting his old comrade with a service revolver to shorten his agony), and of the equally offstage killing of the Boy (here carried out on stage by the Dauphin as the lad defiantly tried to raise an English flag like the G.I.s immortalized at Iwo Jima).

In the centre of all this, it wasn't always clear what we were to make of Henry as impersonated by Elliot Cowan, an actor who resembles a stiffer version of a young Richard Harris. He seemed usually to be playing for straightforward British war-film heroics despite a felt lack of Olivier's vocal edge; his rendition of 'Once more unto the breach', for example, benefited very much from the use of a megaphone. Overall triumphalism notwithstanding, Munby had him not only give the instruction to kill the French prisoners at 4.6.37 (two nameless captives, with bags over their heads which looked like a single gesture towards Hytner's post-Iraq topicality, were butchered onstage at once), but cut the throat of the unfortunate Monsieur le Fer himself. Before Agincourt he was utterly bested in argument by Fred Ridgeway's superb, West Country Williams, and his game with Fluellen and the gloves looked especially petty and unfair as a result, so that Williams emerged with dignity as the moral victor even from their post-battle encounter. Cowan's sole moment of visible self-consciousness or regret, however, came just before this, in 4.7, when in response to Fluellen's 'I need not be ashamed of your majesty, praised be God, so long as your

34 *Henry V*, Royal Exchange Theatre, Manchester, directed by Jonathan Munby. Elliot Cowan as Henry V.

majesty is an honest man' (4.7.111–12) the king paused and looked away with a terrible gulp before saying 'God keep me so' in a low near-whisper. But the structure of the whole play wants us to want both the king and the actor to succeed, however inconsistent both may be, and here once again we did. The wooing scene was disappointingly glib, with Henry's unflinching demand that the French king should disinherit his own children in his favour cut, but the capacity audience in that glorious aluminium O that is the Royal Exchange didn't seem to mind at all. Gerard Murphy's hulking Exeter/Chorus came to attention and saluted at the end of his final sonnet, left alone as the lights dimmed like the final survivor of his battalion listening to the Last Post on the last Sunday in November once again. I applauded as much in memory of his own doomed youth as in homage to this particular performance, fine though

it was: it seems only yesterday that he was playing a lithe slip of a Prince Hal for Trevor Nunn at the newly opened Barbican Theatre. As I say, I have been watching revivals of the *Henriad* for too long.

TRAGEDIES

Let me record as briefly as possible the fact that after the Complete Works Festival finished in Stratford the RSC occupied the Swan with back-to-back productions of *Macbeth* and of Ionesco's *Macbett*. One of these was directed by a major European interpreter of Shakespeare, Emil Purcarete, but all-too typically of RSC policy with really interesting guest directors he was only allowed the lesser play. *Macbeth* was instead entrusted to Conall Morrison from the Abbey in Dublin, who made the most noisy, incoherent and dishonourable hash of it that I have ever seen in the professional theatre. With a part Irish and English and part Anglo-Caribbean cast, Morrison set the play in a mysteriously kilted, leather-jacketed and brogue-shouting version of Africa, where to pounding drums we at first witnessed Macbeth, Banquo and their fellow soldiers besieging some civilian women and children in what appeared to be a schoolroom and then massacring the lot. After the soldiers' departure, unfortunately, three of the murdered women rose zombie-like from the dead, but even more unfortunately and puzzlingly their infant children didn't, so they set out to avenge them by becoming the Three Witches and leading Macbeth, very, very slowly, to his destruction. Never mind that the path to that destruction runs via Macbeth carrying out some more murders on the way, about which you'd think these bereaved mothers might have more scruples; never mind that the whole trajectory of the play depends on its depiction of a man who, to our and his horror, *becomes* an infanticide over the course of the action, rather than being a callous career child-killer from the start . . . It looked like the sort of idea that a student company might have during the first rehearsal and throw out five minutes later, and only use thereafter in extreme panic if something else had mysteriously become impossible at the last minute. In fairness to this show,

35 *Coriolanus*, The Ninagawa Company, Barbican Theatre, directed by Yukio Ninagawa. Kayoko Shiraishi as Volumnia and Toshiaki Karasawa as Coriolanus.

I quite enjoyed seeing David Troughton in a kilt and leathers and long grey greasy hair as Duncan, looking like a cross between a Glaswegian biker and a pillage-weary pirate finally overtaken by mildew, but otherwise this was a production to file under 'unresisting imbecility' and leave well alone. This wasn't the only weak production of a tragedy competing for the summer tourist audience, mind: Wilson Milam's *Othello* opened at the Globe at around the same time, with Eamonn Walker as a handsome but verse-mumbling Moor and Tim McInnerny looking too saggy and tired to be still chasing a lieutenancy as Iago, and sounding far too hoarse to be doing so in such an unforgiving acoustic.

Far more satisfying, indeed genuinely exhilarating, was the *Coriolanus* brought to the Barbican

soon afterwards by Yukio Ninagawa (or Ninagawa Yukio, depending on whether you think of him as an expert director of Western plays who happens to be Japanese or a Japanese director who happens to like using Western scripts). Perhaps surprisingly, this late, verbally complex play turned out to suit Ninagawa's highly visual style rather better than did *Titus Andronicus* in 2006, perhaps because its action is so much more thoroughly externalized (its longer speeches usually purposefully directed at an onstage group rather than seeking to evoke individual states of feeling), and because it is so much more concerned with an early Republican warrior code which suits Ninagawa's favoured Samurai *mise-en-scène* more readily than did the complicated decadence of the earlier Roman tragedy. A wonderfully mis-translated glossy Anglo-Japanese programme full of advertisements for Japanese breakfast cereals included a note stating enigmatically that 'It is said that rehearsals make Ninagawa bark', and if by this it meant that he finds himself issuing curt military orders to his cast and crew, one could see why he might have to do so even from just observing the size of the set and the length of the cast list. The Barbican stage, behind a narrow apron, resembled an Oriental ziggurat, a flight of twenty broad stairs, mirrored down the sides, leading up to a platform area that could be closed off behind lacquered doors bearing stylized images of silver fir trees. As the house lights faded, this immense, precipitous structure was suddenly populated by an entire brown-clad plebeian riot, twenty strong and redoubled and redoubled again by the side mirrors, converging down the centre of the stairs, almost covering them from view with their brandished clubs and tools, and all shouting at a volume which only the fiercest directorial bark could hope to interrupt.

I have no idea how Ninagawa and his producer Thelma Holt can have afforded a cast this size – presumably the breakfast cereal adverts helped – but to this play it made all the difference. For one thing, it made the battle scenes thrilling as I have never seen them before: half-stylized in the manner of manga comics, they took place between genuinely army-sized detachments of athletic Samurai

Romans and Volscians, their spears and halberds clashing with visible sparks to digitized clangs over the sound system, and while when William Houston ran off alone through the gates of Corioli in Doran's production in Stratford one half-wondered how he would find any of the three-strong defending army to fight while he was in there, after Ninagawa's high-energy, high-risk skirmish up the stairs, when the lacquered doors slid violently shut behind Toshiaki Karasawa's Caius Martius, the audience had an almost physical sense of the awful butchery of the lone warrior by the massed infantry that ought by rights to have followed behind them. Directed this lucidly and with these numerical resources, it transpires, *Coriolanus* will work beautifully, even if one ignores the surtitles and thus follows the dialogue only in terms of its levels of anger, as a sort of massed martial arts ballet of the many against the one. Disabled by my non-existent Japanese from savouring the different inflections given to individual lines, what dazzled me about this production was its perfect revelation of this play's structural rhythm, its alternation between a few crucial scenes in privacy or some simulacrum of it (climaxing in Volumnia's embassy) and great public conflicts between Caius Martius and a crowd: first the rioting citizens, then the defenders of Corioli, then his banishers (twice), and at last the Volscian army which hacks him to pieces in the final scene. Each of these was magnificently articulated, and even in the quieter scenes Ninagawa physicalized the play's events with tremendous clarity: in the scene between Volumnia and Virgilia in Martius's absence, for instance, both women were at work on an epic-sized silken tapestry which spread over much of the stairs, with Volumnia, bustling and fierce, very much in control of the design, while Menenius returned from his rejected embassy casting off his briefly resumed armour in despair, as if now ready to die as a failed soldier. Karasawa's response to Volumnia at the climax of the embassy scene was equally shown through an almost dance-like body language: from standing tremblingly erect, eyes forward, throughout her oration, it was if something in his spine finally snapped during the final killer pause on

which, though not backing away an inch, she feigned to give up, and very slowly he dropped shapelessly forward onto his knees to hug her, sobbing, about the waist – a complete collapse from his patrician, warrior self which, painfully, even though she had begged for it she could not help but find shameful, constrainedly failing to return his embrace. Above all, this is the only *Coriolanus* I have seen which properly treated Coriolanus's death scene among the Volscian guards as the last nightmarish re-run of every one of his previous battles against the crowd, a battle he is pre-programmed to fight even though this time he can only lose. Reduced by Aufidius's taunt not just to being a boy but to being some sort of toy, an action figure in every sense, Karasawa fought off group after group of attackers from a position in the very centre of the steps, until gradually he began to acquire wounds which even he could no longer ignore; he fell first to one knee, still fighting, still killing, his left arm disabled but his right still despatching Volscian after Volscian; then at last he was lying broken across the steps, but with his right arm still mechanically making awful vertical slashing movements with his sword, which he never dropped, long after the rest of his body was motionless. Only when the arm had stopped hacking and then stopped twitching altogether did Aufidius dare to speak his perfunctory epitaph. I doubt I will ever see a stage embodiment of Coriolanus who more fully matches Cominius's description of him as 'a thing / Made by some other deity than nature' (4.6.94–5): this production achieved a near perfect fit between the imagination of the play and that of its director.

The other really outstanding production of a tragedy in 2007 was Rupert Goold's *Macbeth*, which so quickly sold out in the 400-seat Minerva theatre in Chichester over the summer that I was unable to see it until it transferred to the Gielgud in the West End for an equally sold-out run during the autumn. This show's success at the box-office can in part be attributed to the appearance of a cross-media star in its title role, Patrick Stewart, but, as with the *Tempest* in which Goold directed Stewart in 2006 (see *Survey 60*), the presence in the cast of someone who is a senior embodiment of RSC

36 *Macbeth*, Chichester Festival Theatre Company, Gielgud Theatre, directed by Rupert Goold. Patrick Stewart as Macbeth and Kate Fleetwood as Lady Macbeth.

tradition as well as a name in Hollywood did nothing to inhibit Goold's characteristic directorial dash. The production worked primarily by taking tropes and techniques which have almost become clichés in large-budget horror movies and then translating them in deadly earnest into claustrophobic live theatre, with Goold prepared to cut and transpose speeches and indeed whole scenes in the service of visual and dramatic effects to ensure that they would shock even those long inured to the play's horrors by over-familiarity with its text. The set remained unchanged throughout, a large, gloomy white-tiled utility room, equipped with a large sink downstage left and a big old-fashioned refrigerator with a television set perched on it upstage right, with a centre-stage rear entrance in the form of a grille-doored industrial lift. This lift always descended into view from

above rather than ascending from below: the effect was that we were in some sort of unloved institutional basement kitchen, which might just also have been an annexe of Hell. This space served perfectly as a castle kitchen, and as a waiting area for the Porter (who horrified Macduff, on this occasion arriving not alone but with his wife and three children, by urinating in the sink in their presence), and later as a morgue, but at first, to distant gunfire and in a panicked emergency rush of face-masked nurses and wires and trollies, it was a field hospital. Here, as the production abruptly burst into light and noise, the bleeding captain was bravely struggling to narrate the events of the battle (including those reported in the script by Ross) to Paul Shelley's Cossack-uniformed Duncan and Scott Handy's Malcolm, as he lay on a trolley undergoing a blood transfusion. Reassured, Duncan and Malcolm began to depart on 'Go, get him surgeons' (1.2.44), here an instruction that the attendant nurses should take him through into the operating theatre, and one of the nurses injected the captain with what one assumed to be a general anaesthetic as the generals left. It was only when the prostrate soldier, horribly, went into spasms of agony, the heart-monitor machine behind him bleeping wildly and then uttering a monotonous drone as his body finally stiffened, that one noticed that the nurses around the trolley, who were now the only other characters on the stage, numbered exactly three. The one who had administered the injection pulled the mask from over her mouth with a gratified smile as of a job well done. 'When shall we three meet again?' she inquired pleasantly, and, casually removing the dead soldier and the medical equipment, they were off into a composite of 1.1 and 1.3, waiting for Stewart's Macbeth and Martin Turner's Banquo to descend in the lift (wearing black leather greatcoats that might have been the same ones Ian McKellen and John Woodvine wore in the Other Place thirty years earlier) to wash themselves at the sink after the day's fighting and, accosted, hear their prophecies.

The production somehow managed to maintain this level of ghastly, high-energy black humour throughout, without ever trivializing the human cost of the atrocities it depicted. Without their face-masks, the witches ceased to be nurses and, having arrived alarmingly from the refrigerator, blended among the domestic staff in the kitchen at Dunsinane, where in 1.6 Kate Fleetwood's elegant Lady Macbeth, with characteristic directorial wit, was caught unexpectedly by Duncan's back-door arrival supervising and taking part in the preparation of his evening meal and, having just been chopping some meat, had to wash her hands prophetically at the sink before greeting him. During 1.7 – into which Stewart arrived as from a just-upstairs feast to seek and uncork a dusty bottle of claret, looking at the knife by which he was removing its foil on 'If it were done when 'tis done', and then being prompted to the image of the poisoned chalice at 1.7.10–12 as he decanted its contents – Lady Macbeth arrived not only to find her absent husband but to fetch her prized chocolate gateau from the refrigerator, a confection which she was clearly on the point of thrusting into Macbeth's face in angry frustration before holding herself back and resorting to reminding him of their dead child instead at 'I have given suck' (1.7.54). This cake was ingeniously used again in a particularly chilling version of the next scene, in which Fleance had crept downstairs in his pyjamas to steal some of the leftovers and was caught out by his father; 'How goes the night, boy?' (2.1.1) translated as '*Do* you know what time it is, young man?', but Fleance was then made indulgently welcome by a creepily avuncular Macbeth. Father and son ended up eating cake together, but Macbeth, pointedly, refused it, broaching the subject of the witches when Banquo offered him the plate.

The detailed opening-up of the script's interest in the perversion of hospitality made possible by this confinement of much of the action to a kitchen continued after Macbeth's coronation, when, briefing the two murderers in 3.1, Stewart first made himself a ham and mustard sandwich and then made one for them too, which they were visibly and appropriately afraid to accept. The play's greatest image of broken hospitality, however, is provided by the banquet scene, and Goold rose beautifully to its challenges, with as cunning an

37 *Macbeth*, Chichester Festival Theatre Company, Gielgud Theatre, directed by Rupert Goold. Martin Turner as the ghost of Banquo.

example of directorial having your cake and eating it as I have ever seen. For more than a century, interpreters have wondered whether it is more effective to have the ghost of Banquo visible to the audience, or visible only to Macbeth. Goold simply had it both ways in turn. With the banquet laid out on a long central table running straight upstage and down, and Macbeth's place at its downstage end with his back to the audience, the scene was running quietly enough through the hasty, muttered conversations with the First Murderer until after Macbeth resumed his seat. Suddenly, over the sounds of constrained conversation we heard the sound of the lift mechanism engaging; the lights in the room dimmed; awful music began to build towards a screaming crescendo; brilliantly lit within, the lift descended into view, and stopped, and a bloodstained Banquo pushed back the grille and strode straight forwards and up onto the table, staring straight at Macbeth as he came pacing inexorably down its length – until just as he was surely about to trample over him and fall into the stalls, there was a complete blackout. And the house-lights came up, and it was the interval. After which, the production having told us exactly what Macbeth was about to see, the scene re-started from the beginning, this time with Macbeth's dialogue with the murderers inaudible, and this time with the ghost appearing solely to Macbeth.

All these effects – not to mention the setting of Macbeth's interview with the witches in 4.1 in a morgue, where corpses laid out in three body-bags sat horribly up into life when touched by the enchantresses in order to speak the prophecies, nor the way in which the sink briefly ran blood when Lady Macbeth tried to wash her hands at it during the sleepwalking scene – may sound merely clever-clever, but they were always in the service of lifting what might otherwise have been a conventional, if brilliantly acted, Perfectly Composed Production into something far more exciting. With Russian-looking early twentieth-century costumes, Stewart seemed to have decided that he was not just going to become a tyrant as Macbeth but would become one tyrant in particular, Joseph Stalin, sporting a fur hat and a shotgun after his coronation, cultivating a sort of self-congratulatory peasant wiliness for his dealings with his underlings, and employing a security apparatus, visibly modelled on the KGB, who were given to interrogating Tim Treloar's hapless intellectual of a Ross, and who carried out the murder of Banquo (in the one sequence that looked a bit too elaborate for its own good) by lethal injection during a tram journey. This was a virtuoso performance (even at the lowest, most technical level; not many actors could tie a bow tie that expertly during 'We have scorched the snake, not killed it', 3.2.15 ff), but it was one which had Macbeth withdraw from the audience as quickly and as thoroughly as he withdrew from his wife. Characteristically, Stewart played even his response to his wife's death as a demonstration to Seyton of his achieved macho immunity to human feeling, rather than as a dismayed confidence in the audience: Lady Macbeth's body was wheeled onto the stage, and Stewart dispassionately uncovered her face as he began 'Tomorrow, and tomorrow, and tomorrow' (5.5.18 ff), but at the end of the speech he dismissively pushed the trolley away, and ignored it thereafter. Goold counterpoised this steely, remote piece of work not only by waking up the play's horrors as never before (and I am deliberately refraining from describing the scene of Lady Macduff's murder) but by allowing Kate Fleetwood to make the most of Lady Macbeth's sufferings – her pathetic groping for an industrial-sized bottle of detergent in the sleepwalking scene, and her final screams before her exit, were unforgettable – and by giving plenty of space and actorial leeway to those playing the Macbeths' victims, particularly Michael Feast's Macduff. Feast's long risky pause as he tried to assimilate the news of the killing of his family, playing painfully at trying to break one of his own fingers by pressing it obsessively down on the back of a chair as he stood, made one feel so much more that one were watching a real bereavement than as if one were just watching a play about one that it came close to being unbearable. In the play's final sequence, he finally got his revenge with a knife, after Macbeth, having failed to shoot himself with an exhausted revolver, threw away his own blade and was wrestled into the ascending lift: the last of the many nasty things which descended in it was Macduff carrying Macbeth's savagely severed head (a prop which many productions shirk), over which a nauseated Malcolm took a long time drawing breath before eventually managing to give the whole of his final speech while holding it aloft. Both Stewart and Goold won a number of awards for their work in this production, and they well deserved them: rarely can the scalp of *Macbeth* have been so convincingly won. It is extraordinary to remember how unimpressive most of this same cast were in its companion-piece in the Chichester season, Franks's *Twelfth Night*: it almost restores one's faith in the figure of the director.

There remains one very last, anticlimactic production of a tragedy to record from 2007, the last

I shall ever attend on behalf of this journal. In December Michael Grandage directed an *Othello* for the Donmar Warehouse, with Chiwetel Ejiofor in the title role and Ewan McGregor as Iago. This was a tasteful, non-committal affair in nondescript Jacobean clothes, in which the only distinctive directorial touches one noticed were mistakes (suddenly bringing on a carpet and cushions at 3.3 and leaving them in place for the whole of the ensuing act and a half, for example, so that the temptation scene took place on Desdemona's territory rather than Iago's and Cassio and Bianca appeared in 3.4 to irrupt straight into her drawing room, and letting McGregor paddle pointlessly in the little gutter of water at the back in his best leather boots as no real soldier ever would). Ejiofor's physically under-weight Moor was too busy being dignified and exotic to appear remotely dangerous, while McGregor, who somehow managed to speak all his words in the right order without giving anything quite recognizable as a performance, clearly has no gift for intimacy with a live audience at all. (His eyes moved so restlessly during his soliloquies that he never seemed to be addressing anyone in particular at all.) The production didn't get anything drastically wrong, but only because it never risked getting anything drastically right; watching *Othello* under these circumstances was rather like watching a long and pointless corrida between a tame bull and a colourless matador, and the production was enlivened only by Tom Hiddleston's able Cassio. (But when one sees all of *Othello* and the best piece of acting in it is a convincing simulation of someone only just managing not to vomit, at 2.3.256 . . .) Nonetheless, such is the power of cinematic fame that this show was the hottest ticket in town throughout its run, and had I been less scrupulous, I learned, I might have sold my press seat on Ebay or to the hopeful touts outside for the suitably Shakespearian sum of a thousand pounds. On my way home afterwards, I seriously wondered whether perhaps I should have done; but then I thought, well, but supposing that I could have had a thousand pounds for every single one of the 250-odd tickets I have had in the service of *Shakespeare Survey* over the last eight years, but on condition that I missed all the good productions as well as the bad, would I have accepted it? What, and have missed forever Simon Russell Beale's Malvolio, and Daniel Evans's Ariel, and Harriet Walter's Lady Macbeth and Cleopatra, and David Tennant's Edgar, and Anthony Sher's Iago, and Stephen Pimlott's *Richard II* and *Hamlet* and *King Lear*, and Lucy Bailey's *A Midsummer Night's Dream*, not to mention Ninagawa's *Coriolanus* and West's *As You Like It*? No. Not for the world. Even Michael Grandage may preside over the occasional dud, but the first decade of the twenty-first century hasn't been the worst time in which to be watching Shakespeare in England.

PROFESSIONAL SHAKESPEARE PRODUCTIONS IN THE BRITISH ISLES, JANUARY–DECEMBER 2006

JAMES SHAW

Most of the productions listed are by professional companies, but some amateur productions are included. The information is taken from *Touchstone* (www.touchstone.bham.ac.uk), a Shakespeare website maintained by the Shakespeare Institute Library. *Touchstone* includes a monthly list of current and forthcoming UK Shakespeare productions from listings information. The websites provided for theatre companies were accurate at the time of going to press.

ANTONY AND CLEOPATRA

Royal Shakespeare Company. Swan Theatre, 19 April–14 October.
www.rsc.org.uk
Director: Gregory Doran
Antony: Patrick Stewart
Cleopatra: Harriet Walter

AS YOU LIKE IT

Royal Shakespeare Company. Novello Theatre, London, 7–25 March.
www.rsc.org.uk
Director: Dominic Cooke
Rosalind: Lia Williams
Celia: Amanda Harris

THE COMEDY OF ERRORS

Royal Shakespeare Company. Novello Theatre, 10–28 January. Transfer from Stratford-upon-Avon.
www.rsc.org.uk
Director: Nancy Meckler

Bell Shakespeare Company (Australia). Theatre Royal, Bath, 7–11 March.
www.bellshakespeare.com.au
Director: John Bell
Part of Bath Shakespeare Festival.

Bard in the Botanics. Botanical Gardens, Glasgow, 21 June–8 July.
www.bardinthebotanics.org
Director: Gordon Barr

Shakespeare's Globe, London, 1 August–7 October.
www.shakespeares-globe.org
Director: Christopher Luscombe

CORIOLANUS

Stamford Shakespeare Festival. Rutland Open Air Theatre, Tolethorpe Hall, Tolethorpe, June–September.
www.stamfordshakespeare.co.uk

Shakespeare's Globe, London, 10 May–13 August.
www.shakespeares-globe.org
Director: Dominic Dromgoole
Coriolanus: Jonathan Cake
Dromgoole's inaugural production as Artistic Director of Shakespeare's Globe.

CYMBELINE

Kneehigh Theatre. Swan Theatre, Stratford-upon-Avon, 21–30 September.
www.kneehigh.co.uk

Adaptors: Emma Rice and Carl Grose
Director: Emma Rice
Cast of five. Freely adapted text.

HAMLET

English Touring Theatre. New Ambassadors
 Theatre, London, 20 February–22 April.
www.ett.org.uk
Director: Stephen Unwin
Hamlet: Ed Stoppard
Gertrude: Anita Dobson

Baxter Theatre Centre (Cape Town). Swan
 Theatre, Stratford-upon-Avon, 3–6 May.
Director: Janet Suzman
Hamlet: Vaneshran Arumugam

ADAPTATION

Hamlet, the Outsider
New Fortune Theatre. Southwark Playhouse,
 London, 24 May–9 June and tour.
Director: John Russell Brown
In rep. with *Malvolio and his Masters*.

Hamlet – the Actor's Cut
Pitlochry Festival Theatre, 23 August–19 October.
www.pitlochry.org.uk
Director: John Durnin
First Quarto.

Shamlet
King's Head, London, 31 August–24 September.
www.kingsheadtheatre.org
Playwright: Andrew Doyle
Director: James Robert Carson

HENRY IV PARTS 1 AND 2

Chicago Shakespeare Theatre. Swan Theatre,
 Stratford-upon-Avon, 6–15 July.
www.chicagoshakes.com
Director: Barbara Gaines

HENRY V

The National Youth Theatre. Hackney Empire,
 19–23 September.
www.nyt.org.uk
Director: Paul Roseby
Abridged: Arnold Wesker
Part of the Shakespeare Schools Festival. Abridged
 to 50 minutes and played with a similarly abbreviated *Much Ado About Nothing*.

HENRY VI PARTS 1–3

Royal Shakespeare Company. Courtyard Theatre,
 London, 9 August–21 October.
www.rsc.org.uk
Director: Michael Boyd
Henry VI: Chuk Iwuji
Margaret: Kay Stephens
Richard Plantagenet: Clive Wood
Inaugural production at the Courtyard Theatre.

HENRY VIII

AandBC Theatre Company. Holy Trinity Church,
 Stratford-upon-Avon, 24 August–2 September.
Director: Gregory Thompson

JULIUS CAESAR

Royal Shakespeare Company. Royal Shake-
 speare Theatre, Stratford-upon-Avon, 16 May–
 10 October.
www.rsc.org.uk
Director: Sean Holmes
Caesar: James Hayes
Antony: Ariyon Bakare
Brutus: John Light

KING JOHN

Royal Shakespeare Company. Swan Theatre,
 Stratford-upon-Avon, 3 August–10 October.
www.rsc.org.uk
Director: Josie Rourke
King John: Richard McCabe
Constance: Tamsin Greig

KING LEAR

Creation Theatre Company. BMW Group Plant Oxford, 10 February–1 April.
www.creationtheatre.co.uk
Director: Douglas Rintoul

Maly Drama Theatre of St Petersburg. Barbican Theatre, London, 10–14 October.
Director: Lev Dodin
Lear: Petr Semak
Translated into Russian.

Yellow Earth Theatre Company with Shanghai Dramatic Arts Centre. Tour November–9 December.
www.yellowearth.org
Director/Adaptor: David Tse Ka-Shing
Cast of 8 speaking Mandarin and English with surtitles.

LOVE'S LABOUR'S LOST

Shakespeare at the Tobacco Factory. Tobacco Factory, Bristol, 23 March–29 April.
www.sattf.org.uk
Director: Andrew Hilton
Critically well received.

Shakespeare Theatre Company (Washington, DC). Swan Theatre, Stratford-upon-Avon, 17–26 August.
www.shakespearedc.org
Director: Michael Kahn

MACBETH

Southwark Playhouse, 24 January–11 February.
Director: Andy Brereton
Shakespeare for Schools project.

Community 20 Theatre Company. Theatro Technis, London, 22 February–18 March.
Director: Tarek Iskander
The witches played by one actor, on stage throughout.

Queen's Theatre, Hornchurch, 17 March–8 April.
www.queens-theatre.co.uk
Director: Bob Carlton

Creation Theatre Company. Headington Hill Park, Oxford, 2 June–9 September.
www.creationtheatre.co.uk
Director: Gareth Machin

Oxford Shakespeare Company. Great Hall, Hampton Court Palace, 7 August.
www.oxfordshakespearecompany.co.uk
Director: Chris Pickles
Macbeth: Max Digby
Billed to commemorate the 400th anniversary of a performance for King James at Hampton Court.

Long Overdue Theatre Company. UK tour September–November.
www.longoverdue.co.uk
Director: Euan Manson

ADAPTATION

Project Macbeth
National Theatre of Scotland. Brunton Theatre, Musselburgh, 6 October–11 November.
www.bruntontheatre.co.uk
Adaptor/Director: Simon Sharkey
A production framed by a discussion on the historical accuracy of Shakespeare's play.

OPERA

Macbeth
Royal Opera House, London, 18 February–9 March.
Composer: Giuseppe Verdi
Director: Phyllida Lloyd

MEASURE FOR MEASURE

National Theatre and Theatre de Compliciteé. Lyttelton Theatre, London, 15 February–18 March.
www.nationaltheatre.org.uk
Director/Vincentio: Simon McBurney
Revival of 2004 Olivier production.

Peter Hall Company/Theatre Royal Bath. Theatre Royal, Bath July–August; Courtyard Theatre, Stratford-upon-Avon 13–16 September and tour.
Director: Peter Hall
The Duke: James Laurenson
Angelo: Richard Dormer
Isabella: Andrea Riseborough

THE MERCHANT OF VENICE

Creation Theatre Company. Oxford Castle, Oxford, 30 June–19 August.
www.creationtheatre.co.uk
Director: Gari Jones

Royal Lyceum Theatre, Edinburgh, 23 September–21 October.
Director: Mark Thomson
Shylock: Jimmy Chisholm

THE MERRY WIVES OF WINDSOR

ADAPTATION

Merry Wives: The Musical
Royal Shakespeare Company. Royal Shakespeare Theatre, 12 December 2006–10 February 2007.
www.rsc.org.uk
Adaptor/Director: Gregory Doran
Lyrics: Ranjit Bolt
Music: Paul Englishby
Falstaff: Simon Callow
Mistress Quickly: Judi Dench

OPERA

Sir John in Love
English National Opera. London Coliseum, 12 March–1 April.
www.eno.org
Composer: Ralph Vaughan Williams
Director: Ian Judge

A MIDSUMMER NIGHT'S DREAM

Royal Shakespeare Company. Novello Theatre, London, 7–25 February.
www.rsc.org.uk
Director: Gregory Doran

Royal Shakespeare Company. Swan Theatre, Stratford-upon-Avon, 8–17 June and tour.
www.rsc.org.uk
Director: Tim Supple
Bottom: Joy Fernandes
Set in India, using seven different languages.

New Shakespeare Company. Regent's Park Open Air Theatre, London, 9 June–30 August.
www.openairtheatre.org
Director: Ian Talbot

Ludlow Shakespeare Festival. Ludlow Castle, 26 June–8 July.
www.ludlowfestival.co.uk
Director: Glen Walford

Yohangza Theatre Company. Barbican, London, 28 June–1 July.
Director: Jung Ung Yang
In Korean with English surtitles.

Stamford Shakespeare Festival. Rutland Open Air Theatre, Tolethorpe Hall, Tolethorpe, June–September.
www.stamfordshakespeare.co.uk

Chapterhouse Theatre Company. UK tour June–September.
www.chapterhouse.org

The Lord Chamberlain's Men. UK tour June–July.
www.lordchamberlainsmen.co.uk
Director: Lucy Pitman-Wallace

British Shakespeare Company. UK tour July–September.
www.britishshakespearecompany.co.uk
Director: Robert J. Williamson
Robin Goodfellow: Wayne Sleep

Dundee Repertory Theatre, 28 August–16 September.
www.dundeerep.co.uk
Director: Dominic Hill

ADAPTATION

Susurrus
Bard in the Botanics. Botanical Gardens, Glasgow, 21 June–22 July.
www.bardinthebotanics.org
Playwright: David Leddy
Promenade production in the form of an audio tour through Glasgow's Botanical Gardens. Interweaves themes from Shakespeare's plot and Benjamin Britten's *A Midsummer Night's Dream*.

OPERA

A Midsummer Night's Dream
Glyndebourne, East Sussex, 14 July–7 August.
Opera: Benjamin Britten
Revival of Peter Hall's 1981 production.

MUCH ADO ABOUT NOTHING

Royal Shakespeare Company. Swan Theatre, Stratford-upon-Avon, 18 May–12 October; Novello Theatre, London, 13 December–6 January 2007.
www.rsc.org.uk
Director: Marianne Elliott
Benedick: Joseph Millson
Beatrice: Tamsin Greig
Set in 1950s Cuba.

The National Youth Theatre. Hackney Empire, London, 19–23 September.
www.nyt.org.uk
Director: John Hoggarth
Abridged: Arnold Wester
Part of the Shakespeare Schools Festival. Abridged to 50 minutes and played with a similarly abbreviated *Henry V*.

Manchester Library Theatre Company. Library Theatre, Manchester, 23 February–18 March.
www.librarytheatre.com
Director: Chris Honer
Beatrice: Lucy Tregear
Benedick: Peter Lindford

OTHELLO

Tight Fit Theatre. Broadway Theatre, London, 7 February–4 March.
www.tightfittheatre.co.uk
Director: Mark Oldknow

Münchner Kammerspiele Theatre, Royal Shakespeare Theatre, Stratford-upon-Avon, 27–29 April.
Director: Luk Perceval
Othello: Thomas Thieme
Iago: Wolfgang Pregler
In German with English surtitles.

ADAPTATION

Black and White Sextet
Rosemary Branch Theatre, London, 31 January–26 February.
Adaptor and Director: Robert Pennant-Jones
Condensed to six characters: Othello, Iago, Cassio, Rodrigo, Desdemona, Emilia.

PERICLES

Royal Shakespeare Company. Swan Theatre, Stratford-upon-Avon, 15 November 2006–6 January 2007.
www.rsc.org.uk
Director: Dominic Cooke
Pericles: Lucian Msamati
Promenade production.

RICHARD II

Berliner Ensemble. Courtyard Theatre, Stratford-upon-Avon, 16–18 November.
Director: Claus Peymann
Performed in German.

ROMEO AND JULIET

Birmingham Repertory Company. UK tour January–April.
www.birmingham-rep.co.uk
Director: Bill Bryden
Romeo: Jamie Doyle
Juliet: Anjali Jay

Citizens' Theatre, Glasgow, 9 February–4 March.
www.citz.co.uk
Director: Gregory Thompson
Set in contemporary Glasgow.

Royal Shakespeare Company. Royal Shakespeare Theatre, Stratford-upon-Avon, 18 April–14 October.
www.rsc.org.uk
Director: Nancy Meckler
Romeo: Rupert Evans
Juliet: Morven Christie

Chapterhouse Theatre Company. UK tour June–September.
www.chapterhouse.org

British Shakespeare Company. UK tour July–September.
www.britishshakespearecompany.co.uk
Director: Robert J. Williamson

Mokhwa Repertory Company. The Pit, Barbican, London, 23 November–9 December.
Director: Oh Tae-Suk
In Korean. The actors addressed their lines directly to the audience.

ADAPTATION

Shakespeare's R&J
Glasgow Repertory Company. Cumbernauld Theatre, 2–3 February and touring.
Playwright: Joe Calarco
Director: Gordon Barr

BALLET

Romeo and Juliet
The Royal Ballet. Royal Opera House, London, 3 March–10 April.
Composer: Sergei Prokofiev
Choreographer: Kenneth MacMillan

THE TAMING OF THE SHREW

Bristol Old Vic, 3–27 May.
www.oldvic.ac.uk
Director: Ann Tipton
Petruccio: Richard Dillane
Katherina: Flora Montgomery

New Shakespeare Company. Regent's Park Open Air Theatre, London, 5 June–10 September.
www.openairtheatre.org
Director: Rachel Kavanaugh
Petruccio: John Hodgkinson
Katherina: Sirine Saba

Propeller in assoc. with Young Vic. Newbury, Watermill, 18–28 September and tour.
www.propeller.org.uk; *www.youngvic.org*
Director: Edward Hall
Sly/Petruccio: Dugald Bruce-Lockhart
Katherine: Simon Scardifield
All-male production.

THE TEMPEST

Zecora Ura Theatre. Greenwich Playhouse, London, 9 March–2 April.
www.zecoraura.com
Director: Gabriel Gawin
Cast of three.

Royal Shakespeare Company. Royal Shakespeare Theatre, Stratford-upon-Avon, 8 August–12 October.
www.rsc.org.uk
Director: Rupert Goold
Prospero: Patrick Stewart

Tron Theatre, Glasgow, 17–28 October.
www.tron.co.uk
Director: Paddy Cunneen
Prospero: Paul Higgins

ADAPTATION

Tempus Fugit: Prospero's Will
Greenwich Playhouse, London, 11 May–4 June.
Playwright: Frank Bramwell
Director: Marcus Fernando
Set seven years after the end of Shakespeare's play.

TIMON OF ATHENS

Cardboard Citizens. Shakespeare Centre, Stratford-
upon-Avon, 26–28 October.
www.cardboardcitizens.org.uk
Adaptors: Adrian Jackson and Sarah Woods
Director: Adrian Jackson
Homeless people's professional theatre company.

TITUS ANDRONICUS

Shakespeare at the Tobacco Factory. Tobacco
Factory, Bristol, 10 February–18 March.
www.sattf.org.uk
Director: Andrew Hilton
Titus: Bill Wallis

Wildcard Theatre Company. Courtyard Theatre,
London, 2–26 February.
www.wildcardtheatre.org.uk
Adaptor/Director: Andrew Potter
Cast of six, including puppetry.

Shakespeare's Globe, London, 30 May–6 October.
www.shakespeares-globe.org
Director: Lucy Bailey
Titus: Douglas Hodge

The Ninagawa Company. Royal Shakespeare
Theatre, Stratford-upon-Avon, 15–24 June.
Director: Yukio Ninagawa
Stylized violence. In Japanese with English surtitles.

TROILUS AND CRESSIDA

Edinburgh International Festival in association
with the Royal Shakespeare Company. King's
Theatre, Edinburgh, 14–26 August; Royal
Shakespeare Theatre, Stratford-upon-Avon, 5–
9 September.
www.rsc.org.uk
Director: Peter Stein
First English language production from Peter Stein.

TWELFTH NIGHT

National Theatre Marin Sorescu (Romania).
Theatre Royal, Bath, 14–18 March.
Director: Silviu Purcarete
In Romanian with English surtitles.

Cheek by Jowl. Barbican Theatre, London, 13–
17 June and tour.
www.cheekbyjowl.com
Director: Declan Donnellan
All-male production in Russian with English
surtitles.

Clockhouse Theatre Company. Greenwich Playhouse, London, 5–29 October.
www.clockhousetheatre.com
Director: Maggie Edwards

Chapterhouse Theatre Company. UK tour June–
September.
www.chapterhouse.org

Heartbreak Productions. UK tour July–August.
www.heartbreakproductions.co.uk
Director: Peter Mimmack

ADAPTATION

Malvolio and his Masters. New Fortune Theatre.
Southwark Playhouse, London, 24 May–10 June
and tour.
Director: John Russell Brown
In rep. with *Hamlet, the Outsider*.

THE TWO GENTLEMEN OF VERONA

Nos Do Morro/Gallery 37. Courtyard Theatre, Stratford-upon-Avon, 27 August.
Director: Guti Fraga
Performed in Portuguese.

THE WARS OF THE ROSES

West Yorkshire Playhouse and Northern Broad-sides. West Yorkshire Playhouse Quarry, Leeds, 1–22 April.
www.northern-broadsides.co.uk
Director: Barrie Rutter
Richard: Dave Newman
Margaret: Helen Sheals
Tetralogy adapted into three plays *Henry VI*, *Edward IV* and *Richard III*.

THE WINTER'S TALE

Theatre Set-Up. Tour June–August.
www.ts-u.co.uk

Bard in the Botanics. Botanical Gardens, Glasgow, 21 June–22 July.
www.bardinthebotanics.org
Director: Gordon Barr

Royal Shakespeare Company. Swan Theatre, Stratford-upon-Avon, 15 November 2006–6 January 2007.
www.rsc.org.uk
Director: Dominic Cooke
Leontes: Anton Lesser
Hermione: Kate Fleetwood
Promenade production.

POEMS AND APOCRYPHA

Sir Thomas More
Royal Shakespeare Theatre. Trafalgar Studio 1, London, 5–14 January. Transfer from Stratford-upon-Avon.
Director: Robert Delamare

The Rape of Lucrece
Royal Shakespeare Company. Swan Theatre, Stratford-upon-Avon, 10 September.
www.rsc.org.uk
Director: Gregory Doran

MISCELLANEOUS

Fairy Monster Ghost
News from Nowhere. Unicorn, Weston, 13 September–8 October.
www.newsfromnowhere.net
One man show. Three short plays for children: *I, Banquo*; *I, Caliban*; *I, Peaseblossom*.

Rough Magyck
Forkbeard Fantasy. The Cube, Royal Shakespeare Theatre, Stratford-upon-Avon, 25–28 October.
An exploration of the supernatural in Shakespeare.

The Shakespeare Revue
Antic Disposition Theatre Company. New End Theatre, 12–31 December 2006.
www.anticdisposition.co.uk
Devisers: Christopher Luscombe and Malcolm McKee

THE YEAR'S CONTRIBUTIONS TO
SHAKESPEARE STUDIES

1. CRITICAL STUDIES
reviewed by MICHAEL TAYLOR

BEFORE SHAKESPEARE

Janette Dillon's *Cambridge Introduction to Early English Theatre* is a nicely judged, sensibly structured, lucidly written introduction to medieval and early Renaissance drama, complete with a variety of illustrations and quotations from all kinds of relevant documents helpfully set off in shaded boxes. Every now and then Dillon judiciously breaks away from her main narrative to focus for a couple of pages on an exemplary piece of representative dramatic entertainment: *Mankind* (1465–70), *The Death of Herod* (1450–75), *Tamburlaine Parts One and Two* (1587–8), *The Masque of Blackness* (1605). These case studies are supplemented by shorter considerations of other plays: for example, *The Lady of May* (1578–9), *King Lear* (1605–6) and *A Game at Chess* (1624). The chronological arc of the book is only just noticeable as Dillon prefers to deal with her subject-matter under a number of mutually illuminating thematic links: genre and tradition, instruction and spectacle, actors and audiences, and the like. Overall it's a lively, entertaining and stimulating mix, modelled, one might say, on the very material under consideration.

For we learn that this material is not easily pegged or sharply demarcated. It's slippery stuff. There is an essential blurring of boundaries, categories, binaries and chronologies. The indispensable term here is the sixteenth-century *mot juste*, 'mingle-mangle'. The history of early English

theatre, Dillon claims, is far more mingled (and much less mangled) than we have up to now been led to believe. For one thing, the dramatic past continued into the dramatic present in all manner of ways. Continuities abounded. Indoor theatres, for instance, were mainly conversions of halls originally designed for other purposes. (It's instructive to learn, by the way, that in 1525 there were more active playhouses than at any time in Elizabeth's reign.) Acting styles, while moving, by and large, towards a greater naturalism, towards the interiority of 'personation', continued to employ 'various kinds of formal, patterned and excessive performance' based on half-remembered images in stained-glass windows and devotional books. Acting was still 'demonstrative, gestural, explicit and focused on stage picture'. The notion of 'mingling', Dillon suggests, is useful in contemplating phenomena such as the soliloquy, which was 'the dominant mode of many of the most fully rounded characters of early theatre' and at the same time 'one of its least realistic modes of operation'.

'Mingle-mangle' ruled, then. In the case of genre, for example, where we may look for 'clarity and fixity, what we find, often, is overlap and blurring of boundaries'. Non-dramatic material, revel, interlude, play – all were mingled together; there are difficulties in establishing clear distinctions between 'mystery' plays, 'miracle' plays and 'morality' plays, not to mention 'interludes'. Under analysis, boundaries collapse between biblical history and moral allegory, between interlude and religious-moral-allegorical plays, and so on. Dillon suggests that we use the word confluence rather than influence in talking of this process. The binaries religious/secular or ritual/drama were unsteady in the extreme. The tastes of varieties of audiences were unexpectedly catholic; the notion, for instance, 'that clerics would only accept serious matter, or that farm labourers would only appreciate low comedy is both misconceived and patronizing; and the play in any case functions via the interaction of the two modes, not by presenting them as episodic only or conceptually separate'. Learned dramatists writing in the classical tradition 'imitated vernacular tradition in the same way as more popular dramatists imitated some elements of classicism'. Acting companies themselves co-operated (and mingled). Instruction fruitfully mingled with (surrendered to, even) spectacle; the images instruction came in were always 'excessive in themselves . . . more exciting, more powerful, more risky, than they need to be in the interests of piety'. Excess, plenitude, abundance are key terms. The growth of theatrical sophistication was provocatively erratic, a question of 'the crammed and complex ways in which theatre really does develop, exceeding, modifying, extending and discarding in a rich and uneven swivelling between the radical and the familiar'.

What this book does so well is to introduce students to early English drama at a proper level of sophistication in response to the perhaps unexpected complexity and sophistication of the material itself. In the process the gap between this early material and (say) the maturer drama of Shakespeare – himself a master of the mingle-mangle – is respectfully narrowed.

Such is the gospel also of *REED in Review: Essays in Celebration of the First Twenty-Five Years*. It's a heavily polemical compilation of essays written by contributors to the Toronto-based Records of Early English Drama celebrating the first quarter-century of a precarious existence. It is polemical on its own behalf, convinced of a history of underestimation by mainstream scholars, and on behalf of the material it so avidly researches. Arguably

the most powerful essay in the collection, Gervase Rosser's 'Roles in Life: The Drama of the Medieval Guilds', is particularly eloquent in its advocacy of 'both the historical importance and the aesthetic value of the earlier drama in its own right'. Medieval drama of all kinds, Rosser argues, with an enthusiasm and a focus that no doubt Janette Dillon would appreciate, 'was unpredictable, surprising, and at times disconcerting' – at times, indeed, incendiary (he notes, for example, that the Peasants' Revolt of 1381 was precipitated by the feast of Corpus Christi). And in a move that would, I suspect, be prized by the author of *Early Responses to Renaissance Drama* (to be reviewed below) it lays claim to a performative function for the drama in the way it helped forge the medieval individual's social and moral relationships. We should, in other words, abandon the dismissive habit of interpreting medieval drama only through the sclerotic category of ritual. Rosser makes it clear that for medieval audiences this 'drama of everyday life', with its 'moments of disturbing moral ambiguity', was provoking, provocative, disturbing, transforming and dangerous. Just as resolutely, he urges, must we reject the patronizing evolutionary argument of an E. K. Chambers for whom all these medieval rough roads are important only for the way they lead to the high civilization of the drama of Shakespeare and his contemporaries.

Some of the essays in this collection voice their irritation with the way REED itself has been patronized by many in the scholarly community over the years. In 'Everything's Back in Play: The Impact of REED Research on Elizabethan Theatre History' Roslyn L. Knutson sums up the impact of REED research in this area as profound in the sense of what it has actually achieved, and much less so in the awareness of that achievement by other scholars in the field. From its inception the Records were dogged by an unwillingness on the part of funding authorities to fund the enterprise adequately, so it isn't all that surprising, given this history of parsimony and indifference, that many of the essays in this collection justifiably blow REED's horn. This is especially the case in the book's second part, 'REED's "Performance": Impact and Response', where we find, for instance, Suzanne Westfall's impassioned essay, 'What Hath REED Wrought? REED and Patronage', which she begins by itemizing some of the many disciplines REED has profoundly affected: art history, music history, social history, performance studies, cultural studies and literary history. The 'grunt work of collecting', she goes on to demonstrate, has unearthed treasure after treasure, 'more patrons, more troupes, more touring patterns'.

Most importantly she, and other essayists, emphasize the way in which REED over the years has expanded its horizons (and ambitions), moving from what Audrey Douglas and Sally-Beth MacLean describe in their 'Introduction' as an early emphasis on 'the smallest details of performance practice, such as acting styles, the payment scale for actors, and the determination of their status as professional or amateur' ('the anorexic approach' in MacLean's words from a later essay), to a bolder interest in contexts rather than (or at least as well as) texts. (This obviously has to be the case with patronage studies.) Westfall deserves to be quoted at some length here for the justice of her summary of REED's expansionist achievements. REED volumes, she writes, 'have inspired and enabled us to broaden our temporal and theoretical horizons, to unseat the dramatic text as the principal document of inquiry, to recover marginalized entertainers, to blur the division between medieval and Renaissance, to appreciate forms of entertainment that twenty-first century viewers might not even comprehend as entertainment, in short to contextualize early modern theatre and to speculate anew about how these patterns affected aesthetics, political power, and ideological state apparatuses in the past'.

In the nature of things, Shakespeare is not even a subsidiary target for this book, though his sometimes baleful influence is occasionally acknowledged. (The Introduction also notes the inclusion of a number of Shakespeare scholars on REED's board in the 1990s.) One essay, however, has him partially in its sights, Paul Werstine's 'Margins to the Centre: REED and Shakespeare'. Here Werstine, in praise of REED's 'methodicalness', notes

that REED research has demonstrated that touring for early theatrical companies was important, regular and above all money-making. Indeed, 'the players may have preferred provincial playing places to those of London'. If this were the case, it seems unlikely that Greg's notion that the 'bad' Shakespeare quartos were slap-dash memorial reconstructions of provincial performances is justified. What we now realize, Werstine argues, is that we know less than we thought we did about the relation of the quartos to other printed versions of Shakespeare's plays. Indeed, 'London playgoing needs to be recognised as part of a much larger, highly mobile communication network.' It's REED's painstaking exploration of this larger network that this book of essays essentially celebrates.

The first part of Katherine Goodland's *Female Mourning and Tragedy in Medieval and Renaissance English Drama: From the* Raising of Lazarus *to* King Lear examines medieval English drama in the light of the mourning rituals of its female characters. The background to this drama's mourning women are Mary Magdalene's (and to a lesser extent the Virgin Mary's) mourning over Christ. Laments by one or other of them are included in every medieval cycle play; in each of them she wails and rages. Behind Mary and the mourning women in medieval drama is a fraught social practice of great antiquity through which a small group of keening women assumes the symbolic role of mourners for the larger society. There has always been, so Goodland argues, great power in women's tears. But the title to the second part of her book, 'Deranging Female Lament in Renaissance Tragedy', has equal application to the first part, for it is the 'deranging' power of women's tears that is the book's primary focus. In medieval English religious drama 'mourning women both threaten and sustain the Christian eschatology of the plays' – their tears are 'deranging' and 'resistant' (and in secular romance 'deceptive and sinister').

And so in, for instance, the Townley Lazarus play, Mary Magdalene's grief is 'a sign of weakness bordering on sinful despair', and in all the Lazarus plays female sorrow is 'excessive, contrary to faith, and offensive to God'. However, in the Nativity and Passion plays the maternal mourning is also 'the primary agent against evil'. And the Resurrection plays 'interpret the drama of the Resurrection as a process of grieving and healing, assimilating the action of female mourning to Christian teleology'. Throughout these medieval religious plays female mourning is regarded as something suspect, both necessary and dubious, only to be welcomed if it is 'expressed within the ritual structure of Christianity'. Medieval religious plays seem aimed to turn 'the grief-stricken away from the practice of lament led by women towards the rituals of the church controlled by men'. Such an antagonistic attitude towards mourning women, and excessive mourning in general, increased with the Reformation. Protestant preachers asked the question: why should you grieve when the dead are with God? Women's tears 'that had once spoken eloquently to communities, and God and the dead, were now coded as slavishly feminine, hypocritical, and wasteful'. Mourning for the dead was 'effeminate, heathen, popish, and contrary to reason'.

Part Two of *Female Mourning* shifts the focus to Renaissance tragedy of the sixteenth and seventeenth centuries where the stages are 'stalked by berserk, anguished, and violent men' obsessed by and fearful of 'monstrous, mad, and dangerous grieving women whose excesses elicit a complex mixture of loathing and wonder'. Mourning women in these plays are seen to be 'threatening and elusive, feared and desired, excessive and insufficient': they are the marks of 'a culturally vexed ritual'. While this may be true, Part Two seems to me less convincing than Part One, primarily because the connections Goodland wants to establish between the mourning women in these later plays and those in the earlier medieval ones are unspecific, generalized, tenuous and vague. 'In this final chapter,' Goodland writes, 'I focus on how Lear's mourning over Cordelia . . . resonates with the Virgin Mary's laments for Jesus as depicted in the medieval English Passion plays.' 'Resonates' tells us nothing very much, and flies in the face of the large-scale effect of the large body of differences between what and how the Virgin Mary mourns in the medieval cycles and Lear's mourn-

ing for his daughter. Goodland herself admits that in this play 'we have come a long way from the passionate laments of Constance [in *King John*] and even further from the women's laments of mediaeval drama'. But one may say that Constance has also come a long way from her medieval forebears, and Goodland is equally unspecific about the connections between them, seeing Constance unremarkably and uninformatively as the 'descendant of the mourning Virgin Mary of medieval English drama'. Likewise with Ophelia's laments for Hamlet which 'echo those of her medieval foremothers', or Hecuba's for Priam which 'evokes the lamenting Virgin of medieval drama who witnesses the slaughter of Christ'. We're told again that Ophelia's mad voice 'resonates with the voices of her medieval and ancient foremothers', or that 'the fragmented, lyric sorrow of Hecuba, Ophelia and Gertrude resonates with the mourning customs of England's recent past'. Words like 'echo', 'evoke', 'resonate' have simply too much to do and too little to say.

A final note. There are too many errors in this book: 'principle' for 'principal'; misspellings; typographical errors; a phantom **B** that separates words instead of a space; *The Road to Calgary* (instead of *The Road to Calvary*); inconsistent treatment of verse lineation; superfluous prepositions; incorrect quotations; missing words.

Charles Whitney's *Early Responses to Renaissance Drama* – is 'English' deliberately omitted from this title? – begins with a consideration of early responses to Marlowe's plays. The book might have begun with earlier plays and playwrights as much of it is inferential and speculative in the manner of Jannette Dillon's and Katherine Goodland's, but for Whitney things really heat up with Marlowe, whose plays were the first to inspire, so he believes, 'a deeper emotional involvement and more imaginative interpretation' on the part of their audiences than had up till then been the case. Indeed Marlowe's work empowered those audiences, and 'seems to have played a significant if unobtrusive role in the emergence of modern attitudes, sensibilities, and institutions'. The *Tamburlaine* plays were particularly arousing for their early audiences (especially for those among them with aspiring minds – or who loved the military), and Whitney traces allusion to and comment on them from Simon Eyre in *The Shoemaker's Holiday* (who was, as a character, a comic version of Tamburlaine) through John Davies of Hereford's sonnet ('one of the most illuminating of all responses to early modern drama') and John Donne's view of Tamburlaine as 'an emblem of the popular theatre's power to tyrannise the emotions' to positive, historically informed responses to Tamburlaine in the early 1620s and then to disdain for him during the Civil War when he was 'recruited for partisan political ends'.

Being able to adduce 'commentary' by Eyre, Davies and Donne should not mislead the reader into thinking that there were all kinds of early witnesses and critics of the drama available for quotation. There weren't. Hence the importance for this book of allusions to Marlowe (and others) in plays and works of literature. And the importance too of inference and speculation. Take the case, for example, of Richard Norwood's autobiography *The Journal* which 'provides no responses to individual plays, mentions no play by title, and adopts an anti-theatrical point of view'. Nonetheless, so Whitney believes, his work is of 'the first importance for the study of early modern audiences and their responses'. Elsewhere, too, evidence of early responses is 'fragmentary in the extreme' and necessitates the use of much speculative phrasing of the 'may have seen' and 'it seems plausible that' variety. Evidence is even more fragmentary, pared to a sliver, when it comes to those whom Whitney describes as the common theatregoers, the meaner sort, apprentices, fishwives and the like – I. M., for instance, a household servant, or Robert Cox, a good example of a young, playgoing 'vagrant'. The better sort fare almost as meanly in terms of providing evidence as is illustrated by Whitney's chapter on gentlewomen's responses to plays; he has to acknowledge that '[a]side from queens there is still not a single unimpeachable example of an individual, identifiable woman's response to particular dramatic material before the Restoration', but that doesn't prevent him from talking about the putative responses to the theatre from the likes of Amelia Lanyer, Joan Drake, Anne Murray Halkett and Dorothy Osborne.

Whitney's thesis hinges on the notion of the power of the drama to produce among its early audiences what he calls 'unpredictable actualisations'. Tamburlaine, for instance, strides into their lives as a 'monstrous ambivalence' – both an unlikely mentor for self-actualization and a warning against overweening ambition – offering, on the one hand, a blissful 'amoral allure' and, on the other, the sober second thoughts of the new Protestant aesthetic: 'self-identity through a triumph over the affections'. The most referenced playwright along these lines was Shakespeare, the target of reflections by, among others, John Manningham, Robert Tofte, John Davies of Hereford, John Milton and especially Simon Forman. A character such as Falstaff had a Tamburlaine-like double appeal: his catechism on honour helped some members of his early audiences to mobilize 'pragmatic, patient citizen values against extravagant and intemperate nobility', or acted, for others, as a warning, the 'carnival body [that] has become an emblem of sin'. The to-and-fro pattern of these early responses culminates with Milton, whose reading of Shakespeare provided 'the pattern of bliss and comparatively free interpretation enabled by a liberated Protestant aesthetic', but who then turned 'decisively away' from a complete 'autonomous aesthetics' in a move that 'may be symptomatic of the crucial failure in English Republican culture'.

Before Shakespeare there were the Protestant Bible and Roman Catholicism. How these seep into Shakespeare's plays in the years between 1592 and 1604 is the main concern of Beatrice Groves's book, *Texts and Traditions: Religion in Shakespeare 1592–1604*. I'm happy to report that it's a book that attempts to 'engage with the religious nuances in Shakespeare's plays in a less sectarian manner' than is usually the case. For Groves, what Shakespeare believed is of much less interest than how his plays assimilate and employ religious traditions. Assimilation is the word: on the one hand, the Protestant English Bible and its linguistic wealth; on the other, 'the theatrical splendour of liturgy, images, and mystery plays from England's recent Catholic past'. These mesh and mingle in that mingle-mangle tradition so evocatively conveyed by Janette Dillon's book. Between 1592 and 1604 the Bible in its various forms was everywhere. Fifty editions of it were printed in this period: two Bishops' Bibles, five Bishops' New Testaments, twenty-two Geneva Bibles (Shakespeare's Bible of choice), twelve Tomson New Testaments and nineteen composite Geneva–Tomson Bibles. The Catholic tradition was equally ubiquitous. By the 1590s, despite the ongoing recusancy threat, it had 'a nostalgic appeal for the older generation, and novelty value for the younger'. In Shakespeare's plays, so many of them set in the Catholic past, their Catholic imagery was subordinated to the 'vagaries' of his plots.

The book then goes on to explore in competent fashion the seamless assimilation of the two traditions, primarily in the first and second quartos of *Romeo and Juliet*, *King John*, *Henry V* and *Measure for Measure*. In the case of the *Romeo* quartos, Shakespeare may well have revised his play in Q2, Groves infers, 'to give prominence to the comedic side of the plot and the latent Easter narrative which is integral to the promise of a happy resolution' as well as to use religious allusion to 'increase the tragic shock of its catastrophe'. More sharply, Groves makes much of Shakespeare's identification in *King John* of Arthur with the 'archetypal suffering victim, Christ' rather than of John himself (as was the case in Shakespeare's source *The Troublesome Raigne of King John*). Shakespeare's attachment to Arthur of the 'signifiers of divinely sanctioned rule' gives the play 'a subversive political edge'. In the case of both *Henry V* and *Measure for Measure* the 'illusion of divinity' (Henry's and the Duke's) is a precarious business, morally speaking. To conclude the book on such a sceptical note is in keeping with its emphasis throughout on the subordination of religion to art.

Before Shakespeare (after 1440 at any rate) were books galore and notions about them. Charlotte Scott writes her book not so much about the book itself (or books themselves) but the *idea* of the book ('the plays' representations of the book') as gleaned from a reading of seven plays by Shakespeare, stretching from *Titus Andronicus* to *The Tempest*. It is, I suppose, only to be expected that the book (often referred to as the 'book' in this book) should be more of an ideational concept than a material object, as only two of Shakespeare's plays, *Titus Andronicus* and *Cymbeline*, give it a local habitation and a name, in both cases Shakespeare's favourite book, Ovid's *Metamorphoses*, which 'enters the playing space with the dramatic impact of a fugitive'. We should not be surprised that Ovid's book sounds here more like a flesh and blood actor than an inanimate object as Scott clearly thinks of the book as a kind of actor and subject to interpretations of its performances. She talks about them typically as difficult to pin down: they are 'ambiguous and elliptical', inscrutable and recondite, unstable and protean; they constitute 'a dynamic challenge to both thinking and seeing'. These books are 'volatile companions'. On the other hand, Scott often thinks of the plays' characters as a kind of book: Lavinia in *Titus* is a book to be read; in *The Taming of the Shrew* the idea of the book is a metaphor for Bianca's body. (Scott notices how often the book appears in Shakespeare in the hands of women.)

Books not only frequently appear within quotation marks but are often expanded into metaphor by interpretative prepositional phrases: the precious book of love, the book of life, the book of the heart, the book of heaven, the book of fate. Such phrases stress the metaphorical application of the word: the metaphorical book of the mind, memory and soul, let's say, or the generic book of education. Of all Shakespeare's plays, *Richard II* complicates the term most thoroughly and, as elsewhere in Shakespeare, its image 'often appears at critical moments of powerlessness'. In *Hamlet* there is 'a dreadful complexity in the book, which the play chooses never to ignore'. By the time we get to *The Tempest* the idea of the book has become so profoundly saturated in the imagery and semantics of the idea of this book that we're not particularly startled to be reminded that no book is named in this play, nor does one appear on stage. Prospero's books and reading, for example, remain 'in the metaphysical hinterland of the play'. What we see of the book is 'the chaos of its absence'.

Scott's book is a challenging one, often written, it seems to me, in a rhapsodic prose that verges on a kind of prose poetry. It's a volatile companion of a book, and like Shakespeare's idea of the book constitutes 'a dynamic challenge to both thinking and seeing'.

LATE SHAKESPEARE

'Work' in Raphael Lyne's title *Shakespeare's Late Work* alerts us to this short book's larger territorial ambitions. We're not just dealing with late Shakespeare here but with early Fletcher and one-off Wilkins as well as Shakespeare the reviser, and a missing Shakespeare (the lost play *Cardenio*). And if we include under 'late' the publication of Shakespeare's Sonnets in 1609 then at least a number of poems might also be considered late work (though precisely which ones is not easy to determine). Even more provocatively, if we include in our remit, as Lyne does, the 1623 Folio edition of *King Lear* (thought to be Shakespeare's revision in 1610 of the 1606 quarto) then it makes sense, let's say, to think of Cordelia as one of those 'late' daughters around whom the late plays gravitate. We shouldn't stop here though. Lyne links the romances with earlier plays – with the early comedies, for instance, when he talks of the 'shared feelings and gestures' of *The Two Gentlemen of Verona* and its quizzical descendant *The Two Noble Kinsmen*; with the tragedies as *The Winter's Tale* reworks the jealousy tragicomically of *Othello* (and *A Midsummer Night's Dream*); with the histories as *Henry VIII* looks back to *Richard III*. Such examples could be multiplied.

Lyne strenuously argues that there's a connection too with all of Shakespeare's previous plays in the late work's hospitality to irony and subversive sexual desire. The romances may indulge the therapeutic romance of the family to be sure, but in the pursuit of their conservative endings even their exemplary daughters are caught in a net of innuendo or 'innuendo about innuendo' – 'a faint indication that something is faintly implied' – as the plays release their 'incestuous energy'. There is

a persistent 'erotic undertow', 'a sexual undertone'. Something murky 'lurks within' for whose accommodation 'the text makes some edgy gestures'. (It's not only the daughters who are jostled by 'problematic subtexts'.) All of this edginess works within the framework of an irony that Lyne insists is ubiquitous in the romances and which acts as 'a self-conscious defence against excessive sincerity'. Hence, for example, that alternative title to *Henry VIII*, *All Is True*, 'the obviousness of which hints at its own deception'. Wonder throughout these plays is enmeshed in irony and even cynicism (Cleopatra's death for instance). The wonderful vision that concludes *The Winter's Tale* competes with 'the sense of intellectual anxiety caused by improbability and machination'. For all the romances the audience's interpretation is based in 'liberated irony'.

The book's final chapters valuably if briefly explore the differences between Shakespeare's treatment of romance and Middleton's and Fletcher's. Middleton, Lyne believes, travesties Shakespeare who uses a 'gentler irony'. Fletcher is more genial and co-operative and writes plays that are 'creative commentaries' on Shakespeare. This book is a useful, balanced introduction to some of the larger issues involved in Shakespeare's late work and might be read as an introductory companion-piece, a first course to the banquet that Russ McDonald dishes up in the book next in line for review.

Anyone who thinks formalist criticism is somehow *passé* and *jejune* should take a look at Russ McDonald's *Shakespeare's Late Style* which examines Shakespeare's late work mainly in terms of its 'microscopic units': phrases, words, letters as they occur in or make up 'syntax, metre, diction, repetition, [and] figurative language'. The overall configuration of these units constitutes style, and Shakespeare's late style is 'audacious, irregular, ostentatious, playful, and difficult'. Perhaps above all difficult, McDonald concedes: 'difficult to listen to, difficult to read, difficult to understand, and difficult to talk about'. But this promiscuous difficulty is not something to abjure (as used to be the case, and sometimes still is) but something to luxuriate in. It's the major delight of this book that

McDonald's painstaking analyses of his micro-scopic units are performed in order to increase our pleasure in Shakespeare's poetry (and his prose). McDonald talks time and again of the way in which the plays' style, their 'managed complexity', 'gen-erates a feeling of pleasurable uncertainty'. He calls Shakespeare's exercises in pleonasm 'the delights of not arriving'; audiences (and readers) are 'diverted by being diverted'. He quotes Cecily's wonderful remark from *The Importance of Being Earnest*: 'The suspense is terrible. I hope it will last.'

McDonald's own style is diverting without being difficult, full of picturesque phrasing: he talks, for instance, of 'rhythmic adventurism', 'architectural grammar', 'poetic tantalization'. It's true that he uses a fair number of technical terms such as polyp-toton, hypotaxis and ecphonesis, but these are in fact useful aids and in their oddity pleasurable bits of language (my favourite is parenthomania which McDonald defines as 'the alarming out-break of brackets'). Most of the time, however, he talks a language we can all understand, concentrat-ing on Shakespeare's late use of ellipsis, pleonasm, repetition, elision, alliteration (including cross-alliteration and concealed alliteration), assonance – all contributing to what he calls an 'enchanted aural atmosphere'. If you notice that this list con-tains contradictory elements, pulling and tugging at each other, then you notice something that is essential, in McDonald's view, to Shakespeare's late style which oscillates between 'radical compres-sion' and 'narrative amplitude and structural loose-ness', between 'superfluity and omission', between 'elimination and supplementation'. These clashes in themselves manifest a 'stylistic recklessness' and are taxing on the reader (let alone playgoer): we are battered by a barrage of 'convolutions, reversals, ellipses, delayed metrical units, repetitions, addi-tives'. And we should simply sit back and enjoy it.

After having pursued the various early manifes-tations of this style through the late tragedies – *Mac-beth*, the laconic, asyndetonic *Coriolanus*, *Antony and Cleopatra* – McDonald concentrates on the romances, which he believes exhibit, *pace* Lytton Strachey, a 'refreshed view of language'. And in a provocative move McDonald links language with romance plot, treating 'the sentence as a plot and the plot as a sentence'. In its most difficult passages, he suggests, 'the sentence itself becomes a kind of miniature romance narrative'. And the amaz-ing conclusions to these plays are 'as the last clause is to an extravagant periodic sentence'. To think in terms of the imbrication of plot and language leads to the book's last chapter – the one we've all been waiting for (the last clause, we might also say, of an extravagant periodic sentence) – as it tack-les the why of it all. Why does Shakespeare write like this in what turns out to be his final period? We have to move on from what McDonald calls modestly (and inaccurately) 'a dry accounting of poetic devices'. His conclusion is that the style is new because 'the way of thinking is new'; there is a renewed faith in the beneficent power of fic-tion, the 'compensatory value of the word', and, above all, in the restorative power of woman (more symbol than character perhaps). We've moved from mimesis to poesis. And yet, although these last plays embrace and express the value of illusion, fantasy, magic and women, the book's roller-coaster ride doesn't then come gently to a halt. These last plays are also full of doubt (as Lyne has also argued) and in *Henry VIII* and *The Two Noble Kinsmen* – the last last plays – Shakespeare 'seems to be changing his mind again'. This is a book that may change a number of minds up to now unconvinced of the supreme artistry of Shakespeare's late work, and is certainly one that the reader will wish didn't have to come to a halt, gently or otherwise.

Robert L. Montgomery's *The Perfect Cere-mony of Love's Rite: Shakespeare's 'Sonnets' and 'A Lover's Complaint'* illuminates the notion that Shakespeare's Sonnets are little rooms full of everywheres. His little book stresses the poems' provisionality, their elusive inter-connectedness battling what seems to be 'no arrangement, no obvious starting point and no destination', in con-trast to sequences with which Shakespeare was familiar 'such as Sydney's *Astrophil and Stella* or more obviously Spenser's *Amoretti*'. The dark lady Sonnets, in particular, 'appear random and plot-less'. Throughout the sequence, then, we have to be on our toes as readers, for the Sonnets 'keep inventing and reinventing selves', their speaker is 'a wavering, shifting character', his moods 'variable and alternative'; he is full of contradictions, deprecating self-judgements as well as self-assertiveness, intent on 'claiming a territory' then abandoning it, then reclaiming it in yet another ironic reversal. The poems' difficult language constitutes a 'rhetorical Mardi Gras'.

The Sonnets' randomness and plotlessness, for Montgomery, are offset by their thematic interrelations and the tradition in which they operate. He doesn't miss an opportunity to remind us that Shakespeare's Sonnets are often 'flagrantly conventional'; they may be full of genius, but they have a secure home 'within the broad borders of the Petrarchan lyric sequence'. Although Montgomery concedes the heavy-handedness, prolixity and excessiveness of *A Lover's Complaint* (comparable, he believes, to Shakespeare's Ovidian narrative poems), he nonetheless thinks the poem to be the 'child of Shakespeare's pen' and the Sonnets and linked narrative poem children of a literary tradition exemplified by Daniel's sonnet sequence *Delia* and its complaint, *The Complaint of Rosamond*.

Montgomery's book has some wise and just observations but I think its sinews could have been stiffened had it ventured more often into McDonald's territory. It needs to linger more than it does on just how the poems work to do what Montgomery says they do. Their rhetorical Mardi Gras could benefit from a more searching post-festivities analysis.

Such a searching analysis of the Sonnets, or series of analyses, is provided by *A Companion to Shakespeare's Sonnets* which stretches for 521 pages, has nine sections, and some twenty-six contributors (not to mention their numerous advisers and affiliates). In no uncertain terms then it manifests in itself Schoenfeldt's conviction in his Introduction that now is the time to be reading the Sonnets, equipped as we are with new understandings of their hitherto unexamined motifs: their implicit racism, for instance, their obsession with social class, their subjugation of women 'in an economy of erotic energy'. To encourage further reading many of the essays append lists of references and

suggestions for further reading. And to help us see why all this is necessary and timely, the 1609 text of the Sonnets and *A Lover's Complaint* rounds off the book though it's noticeable that a majority of the contributors refer to other editions, perhaps because the 1609 text is 'a copy-text of tantalizing irresolution'. All of the essays with the exceptions of famous ones by Stephen Booth, Helen Vendler and Stephen Orgel have been written especially for the occasion and it's a pleasure to be able to say that there isn't a dud among them.

Tantalizing irresolution, often brought about by a conflict of beliefs in tantalizing certainties, marks both poems and essays. James Schiffer's essay, 'The Incomplete Narrative of Shakespeare's Sonnets', manages to be light-hearted about the difficulties of reading the poems. An immersion in them, he says, can't help but be deranging and may be Shakespeare's 'revenge against critics yet unborn'. He follows Stephen Booth in 'The Value of the Sonnets' who talks of a verse form 'crowded with coherences' and Helen Vendler in 'Formal Pleasure in the Sonnets' who marvels at Shakespeare's 'wonderful fertility in structural complexity'. Because they are so crowded with coherences (which tends in the end to incoherence) the poems are and probably always will be open to startling reversals of judgement and interpretation. And so, for instance, Ilona Bell can more than get away with 'Rethinking Shakespeare's Dark Lady' as someone who is 'made of truth' with the young man 'black as hell, unscrupulous, dishonest, and fiendishly alluring'. Perhaps, she alluringly suggests, these Sonnets in particular are 'murky and messy, fraught with unexplained complications, unforeseen conflicts, and unresolved contradictions' simply because Shakespeare is dealing with real people in them (including himself). On the other hand, Margaret Healy in ' "Making the quadrangle round": Alchemy's Protean Forms in Shakespeare's Sonnets and *A Lover's Complaint*' almost gets away with 'something strenuously rejected by most modern editors', namely that spiritual improvement is a 'key feature' of the sonnet sequence and that *A Lover's Complaint* is an allegory of the Resurrection. Such a position flies in the face of conventional and unconventional wisdom, the latter exemplified in Douglas Trevor's 'Shakespeare's Love Objects' which claims the Sonnets to be 'defiantly anti-Platonic', anti-Christian, with the love objects as the Sonnets themselves. The principals are, Trevor resolutely maintains, 'literary creations, not real people'.

And so it goes. The difficulties, complexities and enigmas of the Sonnets often engender a complementary opaqueness in the writings on them – productively so sometimes as in the case, say, of William Empson (see Lars Engle's essay 'William Empson and the Sonnets') or as in Rayna Kalas's 'Fickle Glass', an imaginative reading of Sonnet 126 responding to 'the conventions of courtly love literature with its complexities of word play and profusion of figurative language', or in William Flesch's 'Personal Identity and Vicarious Experience in Shakespeare's Sonnets'. Less productively in other cases as in Bradin Cormack's 'Tender distance: Latinity and Desire in Shakespeare's Sonnets' whose thesis that the poems 'seem unusually alive to the Latin roots and prefixes that inhabit English' seems to me open negatively to Stephen Greenblatt's admiring charge (quoted by Cormack) that Shakespeare 'heard things in the sounds of words that others did not hear, and made connections that others did not make'. There are good essays on the sonnet tradition. Richard Strier, for example, in 'The Refusal to be Judged in Petrarch and Shakespeare' argues that Shakespeare is most Petrarchan when his Sonnets are 'most complex and modulated' and Heather Dubrow's ' "Dressing old words new"? Re-evaluating the "Delian Structure" ' asks us to think in terms of sonnet cycles rather than sonnet sequences. Mention might be made here of Margreta de Grazia's intriguing 'Revolution in *Shake-speares Sonnets*' which is very cyclically minded in examining 'desire's perennial inflammability' in the Sonnets.

Constraints of space preclude discussions of more of these exemplary essays, but I should draw the reader's attention to the last essay in the book, Catherine Bates's 'The Enigma of *A Lover's Complaint*', which takes up a poem that has been 'slighted, sidelined, passed over, ignored' but which 'nags, troubles, and complains – piques and irri-

tates [and] clearly refuses to go away'. Publications on the Sonnets outnumber those on this poem by hundreds to one. But Bates not only thinks the poem Shakespeare's but admires it and believes that it 'looks ahead to recent developments in psychoanalytic theory', parading a heroine whose subjectivity is 'wilfully self-destructive and masochistic'. It's no wonder, then, as Bates points out, that the Old Man in the poem turns away from her, taking with him, as it so happens, a great number of those as yet unborn literary critics mentioned by James Schiffer.

One such critic turns away not just from the complaining heroine but from the *Complaint* itself. I wonder what Catherine Bates will make or has made of Brian Vickers's *Shakespeare, A Lover's Complaint, and John Davies of Hereford*, which describes *A Lover's Complaint* as 'an extremely mediocre poem' unworthy of Shakespeare and on a par only with those equally mediocre poems – equally unworthy of him – 'Shall I die?' and *A Funerall Elegye* for William Peter. None of this fustian stuff is by Shakespeare, according to Vickers, who then, in what must have been for him a time of heroic self-sacrifice given his conviction of its mediocrity, writes a long book about *A Lover's Complaint* attempting to prove that it couldn't have been by Shakespeare for all kinds of reasons, not just its inherent worthlessness. (He made a similar sacrifice for those unworthy shorter poems in *Counterfeiting Shakespeare: Evidence, Authorship, and John Ford's 'Funerall Elegye'* (2002).)

The book is divided into two parts: Background and Foreground. The former helpfully delineates the life of John Davies with an account of the literary background of *A Lover's Complaint*. The latter, the meat of the book, is a devastatingly painstaking rundown and analysis of all the poem's blemishes: its vaguenesses, its 'ambiguities of grammar and syntax', its 'paucity of invention', its 'flaccid repetitions and tautologies', as well as its literalness, strained syntax and general opaqueness. Everything about it, diction, rhetoric, metaphor (all vehicle and no tenor), *compositio*, verse form is, so Vickers fervently believes, profoundly un-Shakespearian. On the other hand, having steeped himself painfully in Davies's twelve volumes of verse (written between 1602 and 1617), Vickers is convinced that he's found the perfect match for the mediocrity of the poem in the writing of that 'keen moralizer and mediocre poet from Hereford'. Every blemish in a poem stuffed with them has numerous parallels in Davies's other poetry. Vickers shows us just how derivative a poet Davies is, his 'magpie mentality' making him virtually a plagiarist of Fletcher, Beaumont, Shakespeare (in *The Rape of Lucrece* as well as the Sonnets) and, above all, Spenser. An invaluable section of the book demonstrates the degree to which Shakespeare's alleged linguistic innovations can be found all over the place in that 'remarkably fruitful period of linguistic expansion' in the late sixteenth and early seventeenth centuries. (Vickers suggests that for this we consult Charles Barber's *Early Modern English* (1976, rev. 1997).)

It's hardly possible not to be convinced (swept away even) by the thoroughness and passion of Vickers's argument. I'm happy to acknowledge myself a convert. One strange omission though. Nowhere in the book does Vickers talk about the possible justice of the argument that *A Lover's Complaint* is the envoy of Shakespeare's Sonnets (as complaints were for other sonnets sequences). Obvious connections can be made between the poems: among them, of course, the characters of the Sonnets' dark lady and duplicitous lover, and the maid and seducer of the *Complaint*. When the maid admits at the poem's end that she'd fall again to the blandishments of her unscrupulous lover, she is reworking the conclusion of Sonnet 129 (although the sex has changed): 'All this the world well knows, yet none knows well / To shun the heaven that leads men to this hell.' I don't think any of this would do much to trouble Vickers's conclusions, but I'm surprised he doesn't talk about these narrative links if only to lay bare with his usual trenchancy their (presumably) nugatory value as evidence of Shakespeare's authorship.

SHAKESPEARE AND OTHERS

Tom MacFaul's *Male Friendship in Shakespeare and his Contemporaries* works best in those chapters in which the contemporaries and their iconic colleague tread the boards together in a succession of mutually illuminating analyses. In the chapter 'Servants', for instance, the restricted and fraught friendship between servants and masters in Shakespeare's plays (e.g. in *The Tempest*, *Timon of Athens*, *The Comedy of Errors*) is illuminated by MacFaul's discussion of its counterpart in, among other plays, *Damon and Pythias*, *Every Man in his Humour* and *The Jew of Malta*. The necessary restrictiveness of any friendship between men of different ranks in the Renaissance (as in the 'friends' of the Sonnets) is only the most straightforward example of the tendency of pretty well all of the friendships discussed in this book. Not for nothing does MacFaul begin it with a quotation from Amiens in *As You Like It*: 'Most friendship is feigning' (2.7.182). The Ciceronian, ultra-humanist notion of a friendship between consenting equals – what Cicero in *De Amicitia* (1481) describes as a friendship of virtue – is hard to find in the drama, not just because it is hard to find anywhere (especially in real life) but because it is inherently undramatic. Things become interesting in the drama when you have someone like Iago as your friend.

If most friendships in early modern England, if not exactly feigned, were riddled with ulterior motives, expressed more often than not in 'a rhetoric of social aspiration', there was nonetheless an overall slow movement away from feudal modes of allegiance to the 'modern friendship of affection', but one that was a 'self-assertive, imperfect friendship, driven by peculiar affinities and oddities of personal taste'. MacFaul makes an interesting distinction between fellowship and friendship noticing that in Shakespeare's plays 'true friendship struggles to emerge from friendly groupings' – those, for example, that enmesh the likes of Berowne, Romeo and Hal. He draws interesting contrasts between friends from different Shakespeare plays: Mercutio as opposed to Horatio, or Poins as opposed to Benvolio, for instance.

Every judgement in the book is based upon a psychological reading of the friends' characters. Although MacFaul quotes liberally from the plays (and the Sonnets) I can't remember an occasion where he investigates the way these friends say what they say except in the vaguest of terms. It's rather like reading a book that might have been written by an imaginative theatre director. It's true, for instance, that an actor could rewardingly have Hamlet speak to Rosencrantz and Guildenstern of 'the beaten way of friendship' with 'unconcealed boredom'. There's no way of telling from the text of the play, however, whether or not this manner of speaking is the case despite MacFaul's certainty that it is. Nor can we be so certain as MacFaul is that Rosencrantz and Guildenstern are 'two false and treacherous friends', undeniably sycophantic. When Hal as Henry talks of being Harry not Amurath it is, according to MacFaul, with 'a certain menace' (despite that friendly 'Harry'); or when Banquo agrees to speak later with Macbeth 'some words upon that business' it is in a 'clotted language' (though it doesn't seem at all clotted to me). Then there's the 'self-conceit of Benvolio' in *Romeo*, the 'disarming' Parolles in *All's Well*, or the 'reproachful' Antonio in *Twelfth Night* when he says, 'How have you made division of yourself?' on seeing the disguised Viola and her brother Sebastian together. Such old-fashioned impressionistic readings of the spoken word stem from certainties on the part of the critic about the psychology of the character who speaks them (cf. A. D. Nuttall's book). How far such an elaborately fragile construction infects the larger points about friendship made in the book is an open question.

The others in Fiona McNeill's book *Poor Women in Shakespeare* are the Marian and Cicely Hackets of Shakespeare's world whose household, according to Christopher Sly, is 'crosscut by drinking, sexual activity outside of marriage, overnight lodgers, arguments over bar bills, and criminal enterprise'. They represent (if only by hearsay) a disorderly mass of poor women out there in Shakespeare's society, largely invisible to us up to now, who suffered under the tyrannies of early capitalism, but who were nonetheless vital to the burgeoning economy (especially the cloth trade). Such is the thesis of this book. Although invisible because unrecorded, poor women were in fact everywhere,

including, of course, the playhouses (except as actors on the stage): as workers, patrons, prostitutes. What we need to winkle them out from these and other social places is a 'kind of new *old* historicism', a combination of old historicism and a post-structuralist approach to language, because it is in the language that was spoken or written about these ubiquitous poor women that we can find their painful traces.

The book is misleadingly titled, however. True, McNeill talks about the shadowy presence of poor women in *The Taming of the Shrew*, *Twelfth Night* and *Measure for Measure*, but far more attention is paid by her – rightly so – to their more considerable manifestation in plays such as Dekker's *The Shoemaker's Holiday*, Nathan Field's *A Woman's a Weather-Cock*, John Lyly's *Galathea* and above all *The Roaring Girl* (1611). McNeill's is an interesting and enjoyable book to read, but it should have been called *Poor Women in the Drama of Shakespeare's Time* (if Shakespeare has to be in the title at all).

The others in Cary DiPietro's *Shakespeare and Modernism* are a world removed from the poor women of Shakespeare's time. They are a conglomeration of modernists in the worlds of literature, the theatre and the arts generally in the first quarter or so of the twentieth century. Names such as George Bernard Shaw, T. S. Eliot, James Joyce, Frank Harris, Virginia Woolf, Harley Granville-Barker and Edward Gordon Craig come and go with a rather bewildering absence as far as I can see of any pivotal moorings to the Shakespeare of the book's title (except in the cases of Granville-Barker and Gordon Craig). In this the book resembles McNeill's *Poor Women*: it's much more about the modernists and modernism as a twentieth-century phenomenon than it is about Shakespeare and modernism. It's also something of a rag-bag of a book, full of dates, places and incident, telling us interesting stories in a bustling manner about a variety of literary people but leaving us (me anyway) bemused as to its inter-relatedness, its over-all purpose, often its connection to Shakespeare.

Why this should be the case is perhaps especially odd given that this book is prefaced by an

Introduction which takes pains to point out exactly what is going on in what comes after it. We all know that Introductions are the last chapters to be written, and are usually a précis of the book's argument. But they can also be temptations for the writer, as we know equally well, to put something of a gloss on what we are about to experience, give it a sheen which it may not deserve, tell us perhaps how the book should be read (when the how isn't entirely clear just from reading it). There may well be an element of wishful thinking in such an endeavour, and in this book there is a strange disconnect, it seems to me, between the tone, manner and assumptions of the Introduction, with its heavily theoretical leanings, and the rest of the book which seems happy to forget its connections to, say, the 'emancipatory potential of Marxism', or to that 'collective expression of angst and futility precipitated by the disenfranchising, dehumanizing forward-movement of modernisation'. The clue lies perhaps in the Introduction's last sentence where DiPietro tells us that his book is 'happily committed to that modernism' understood as 'a system of narratives' which 'provides a valuable, necessary and satisfying framework for reading aesthetic practice in this period'. What follows indeed are narratives but their systemic framework doesn't seem to me to be valuable or satisfying enough to give them the coherence they deserve.

The others in Catherine Belsey's enchanting book *Why Shakespeare?* are spirits, witches, urchins, elves, hags, fairies, giants, enchanters and changelings. These and their stories subtend Shakespeare's plays (particularly the seven Belsey investigates) and in large part help to provide the answer to the book's title. We return to Shakespeare time and again because his stories touch a primal narrative nerve in us; when we read him we re-experience a childhood delight in versions of the hypnotic stories of the Golden Goose, or Cinderella, or Tom Thumb, or the Sleeping Beauty, or Snow White, or Tattercoats or, most likely, an elusive yet resonant mingling of bits and pieces of them. Belsey urges us therefore to acknowledge the important debt Shakespeare owed to 'the unwritten stories that

must have been in circulation among the country people in Warwickshire and the old wives of London'. But in the history of appropriation (so fashionable a subject these days) Shakespeare himself can be considered the greatest appropriator of them all, and Belsey is rightly concerned to stress that what he does to these old wives' tales is to modernize and gentrify them: in his hands they grow up and glitter with adult sophistication, so that there's no contradiction, as Belsey says in her discussion of *As You Like It*, between the 'fairytale structure of the plot and the play's artistic and literary elegance'.

Belsey's book also glitters with sophistication, and yet seems more relaxed and straightforward than is usually the case with her work, as though she too had come under the narrative spell of the fairytales she is considering. (Even Lacan and Derrida, in her analysis, come through with a clarity they themselves seldom attain.) And there is a winning autobiographical element in the book when she talks of her parents, her schooldays, and admits that her favourite character in Shakespeare is William in *As You Like It*. Her treatment of her chosen seven plays is full of insight and nicely culled particulars: in *King Lear*, the folktale pattern counteracts the possible perversity of Cordelia's 'reticence'; *The Winter's Tale*'s sequestration of Hermione for sixteen years should be pondered bearing in mind that 'the Sleeping Beauty passes a hundred years of oblivion in the blink of the textual eye'; *A Midsummer Night's Dream*'s fairies – anarchic, non-human, agents of love – are really 'desire, a force outside conventional morality, unconstrained by the obligations, prohibitions, and restrictions of human society'; Shakespeare's presentation of *Hamlet*'s Ghost justifies Hamlet's fear and suspicion of it/him, and so on. And Belsey doesn't allow Shakespeare's work the cover of historical darkness. Her final sentences on *The Merchant of Venice*, for instance, thrust us into our own moral confusion: the play 'constructs, on the basis of two folktale motifs, a riddle that it does not answer: can a society preserve cultural difference and at the same time do away with social antagonism?' Belsey leaves us with the same agonizing riddle: can *we*?

NEW SHAKESPEARES

In the Introduction to each volume of the Routledge series of essays on individual plays by Shakespeare, the General Editor commends the sprightly cutting-edge quality of the collection's criticism: these are self-consciously, head-turning *new* critical essays. In the substantial opening essay of this collection of New Critical Essays on *All's Well That Ends Well* by its editor, Gary Waller, that claim is reiterated and enlarged. (See his 'From "the Unfortunate Comedy" to "this Infinitely Fascinating Play": the Critical and Theatrical Emergence of *All's Well, That Ends Well*'.) We're dealing here, Waller claims, with a play that has been unjustly neglected; indeed, it's only in the last twenty years that its 'radical achievement' has received 'an adequate critical vocabulary' or, even, any performances that do justice to its brilliance, usually by 'non-mainstream theatre companies'. While I found the majority of the essays in this book to be engaging and thought-provoking, I have to say that they didn't strike me as being particularly new, either in terms of their critical vocabulary or in the conclusions they come to about the play's meaning or significance (though they often lay claim to a revolutionary newness). Where they sometimes are provokingly new they are so unconvincingly. To take a minor instance (but one that Don Weingust might have enjoyed – see the following review): in Waller's essay he makes quite an interpretative fuss about the necessity – the *new* necessity – of inserting F1's comma after *All's Well* in the title of the play (as this collection of essays does throughout, *All's Well, That Ends Well*). That comma is an important one for (new) interpretation, so it is claimed. But the First Folio itself doesn't appear to think so as the comma can only be found on eight of its twenty-four pages of running titles which would suggest statistically that the title without the comma is the more important. (We might, say, contrast *Twelfth Night* whose RT in F1 has throughout an interpretation-laden dou-

ble comma and capitalization: *Twelfe Night, or, What you will*. I imagine that this is a title Weingust would love to get his hands on.)

Not unexpectedly, many of these essays on *All's Well* find the new in 'discovering' the play's kinky sexuality. In order of intensification, Kent R. Lehnhof's essay, 'Performing Woman: Female Theatricality in *All's Well, That Ends Well*', finds that Helena as Doctor She, the 'Quacking Dalilah' or female mountebank, heals the King with an 'implicitly sexualized' procedure ('When women "mount," he writes, 'they tend to dismount the structures of patriarchy'). In ' "'Twas mine, 'twas Helen's": Rings of Desire in *All's Well, That Ends Well*', Nicholas Ray argues that Shakespeare's text labours to speak indirectly about the unspeakable (i.e. anal eroticism) – at least he acknowledges its indirectness. While some of the essays are, like his, appropriately uncertain (indirect you might say) about the location of the King's fistula (as in fact notoriously is *All's Well* itself – in Shakespeare's source, William Painter's *Palace of Pleasure*, it is clearly on the King's chest), others brook no argument as to its provocative position. What may in fact be new here is the essayists' wilful certainty of its unspeakable locality, climaxing in Catherine Field's essay, ' "Sweet Practicer, thy Physic I will try": Helena and Her "Good Receipt" in *All's Well, That Ends Well*', where the anality of the fistula is taken for granted, a textual given. Even more outrageously 'new' along these lines is the sort of musing we find in Terry Reilly's article '*All's Well, That Ends Well* and the 1604 Controversy Concerning the Court of Wards and Liveries': did Helena have sex with a possibly syphilitic King? (Not in this play, I'd say.)

More substantially, despite Waller's fashionable disdain for 'our residual essentialist critical vocabulary and the recurring positivistic nostalgia for certainty', most of these essays seem to me to be in headlong pursuit of a comfortable interpretative haven. And so Catherine Field argues that *All's Well* is caught between two systems of understanding the world: the newly emerging scientific episteme, and the medieval religious. But all's well, for the story of Helena demonstrates without a doubt that 'scientific proof is valued more than shifty excuses and astrological superstition'. In ' "As Sweet as Sharp": Helena and the Fairy Bride Tradition' Regina Buccola is convinced that the folk tales lying behind *All's Well* 'point the way to at least one way of resolving [Helena's] seeming contradictions', while in similar vein Paul Gleed in 'Tying the (K)not: The Marriage of Tragedy and Comedy in *All's Well, That Ends Well*' (85–97) believes that the mythic tradition clarifies 'the play's notoriously intractable generic elements'. Michele Osherow is a little more indirect in 'She is in the Right: Biblical Maternity and *All's Well, That Ends Well*' maintaining that to see Helena's behaviour in the light of the biblical matriarchs 'does not remove the troublesome quality of Helena's behavior, but it does authorize it'.

Authority, clarity, certainty: these are the nostalgic concerns of this book of critical essays on *All's Well*, with one or two interesting exceptions such as Ellen Belton's ' "To make the 'not' eternal": Female Eloquence and Patriarchal Authority in *All's Well, That Ends Well*' which ends with a somewhat plaintive rhetorical question, 'has anyone in this play really learned anything?' Or Helen Wilcox's 'Shakespeare's Miracle Play? Religion in *All's Well, That Ends Well*' which, while noting how *All's Well*'s wit 'keeps touching religion like a sore tooth', believes the play's ending to be 'the least conclusive of all Shakespeare's happy endings'. Perhaps the 'newest' thought, though, about the play is a disinterment of one of the oldest. In 'Playing it Accordingly: Parolles and Shakespeare's Knee-crooking Knaves' Craig Dionne dusts off the cobwebs of universal opprobrium and boldly re-asserts the sentimentalist's belief that at the play's end Bertram does indeed love Helena dearly. Nothing could be more nostalgic perhaps than this renewed confidence in that particular certainty.

Don Weingust's *Acting From Shakespeare's First Folio: Theory, Text and Performance* also asserts its controversial newness through a re-working of the past. In this case, it's the 1623 Folio that Weingust dusts off, claiming for it, through its orthography and punctuation (and various other paralinguistic phenomena), a special status as the conduit to Shakespeare's will-o'-the-wisp real and final intentions. There's a juicy irony here in that the second part of this three-part book, 'First Folio techniques and the death of the bibliographer', is happy to join in the strident repudiation of the New Bibliographers' vain hope of arriving scientifically at Shakespeare's real and final intentions. And it also just as gleefully joins an alarming scepticism in general about the editing of Shakespeare's plays: Weingust talks for instance of the 'reverent monotony' and 'the heavy hand of modernizing editors'.

But there is an authority to turn to – bearer of a nostalgic certainty – namely the Gospel of the First Folio (even though we have to acknowledge the heavy hand of what Weingust himself describes, to mix metaphors, as 'that alphabet soup of typesetters'). This claim for the Folio's authority is based on the original investigations of Richard Flatter's largely forgotten book *Shakespeare's Producing Hand: A Study of His Marks of Expression to Be Found in the First Folio*, first published in 1948. It was Flatter's notion of the producing hand, as Weingust tells us, that inspired Neil Freeman and Patrick Tucker, teachers and professional men of the theatre, to regard the First Folio as a kind of coded actors' manual, responding to Flatter's belief that the Folio texts 'represent documents rooted in theatricality'. While Weingust acknowledges that the work of Freeman and Tucker could be seen as 'a patchwork of critical naivete', his experience in watching and working with Tucker's Original Shakespeare Company persuaded him that Flatter, Freeman and Tucker were on to something revolutionary. He became convinced that the 'openness of the early texts', their 'specifically elocutionary sensibilities', as conveyed by F1's accidentals, offer exciting possibilities for an acting company to produce performances more authentically Shakespearian.

Apart from the occasional odd locution ('lacrimal simulacra', 'characterlogic emotionality', and the like) the book is jauntily written and enjoyable to read. It's a moot point, though, as to how seriously we should take the claims made for the First Folio's biblical status. Weingust more than once tussles with the unignorable fact of the layers of intermediaries between Shakespeare and the 1623 end product, and is reduced to that fashionable evasion, 'Shakespeare', in response. (As well as such doubtful analogies as that between author/scribe, and secretary/boss, where scribe and secretary may have such a symbiotic relationship with their employer that what they write down amounts to his/her real and final intentions.) Weingust claims that FI has important things to say about entries, pauses and metrical gaps, 'O' and 'oh', irregular stresses, simultaneousness ('acoustic counterpoint'), line division, and other markings. FI's capitalization, italicization and speech prefixes need to be examined. Its punctuation and spelling demand special consideration. He asks us to think about the importance of the line-ending comma, as in, say, Ophelia's 'My Lord, he hath emportun'd me with loue, / In honourable fashion' where the comma at the end of the line offers the actor(s) opportunities for significant business. Or he wants us to respond to the aural significance of the spelling, 'warre', in Constance's line from *King John*, 'War, war, no peace, peace is to me a warre'. The obvious objection that such examples are highly selective is never really answered.

But, in any case, it's the book's third and last section that carries the day. It conveys the modern professional actor's delight in working for a company, the Original Shakespeare Company, that eschews the necessity of a director, takes its direction from the (moral) authority of the First Folio, and explores the 'rougher possibilities of original Shakespearian production methods' in which 'there is no blocking, no acting coaching, no movement or business specified, and no running of lines with other actors'. What we get as a result of this radical divestiture, so Weingust believes, is 'interactive spontaneity', 'vitality' and increased audience involvement, the very things that the restored Globe on London's Bankside should most assiduously encourage.

John Russell Brown (whose 1974 *Free Shakespeare* would have welcomed the idea of the Original Shakespeare Company) doesn't go back as far as 1623 to find the new in the old, but his *A. C. Bradley on Shakespeare's Tragedies: A Concise Edi-*

tion and Reassessment returns to a text written in 1904 which, he thinks, is desperately in need of fresh critical eyes, not to mention a new readership. It may seem odd that the one book on Shakespeare that can be found in all academic and most non-academic libraries, often in multiple copies, by the one Shakespeare critic who is almost a household name, should need to have his work reprinted and reassessed, as though he were someone like Richard Flatter, obscure and unappreciated. Especially as Russell Brown himself talks of a fruitful collaboration with Robert Shaughnessy, the editor of the fourth edition, no less, of Bradley's *Shakespearian Tragedy*, published as recently as 2006. Indeed, Bradley is in Russell Brown's own words 'this apparently unsinkable critic'.

Unsinkable maybe, but also misread, misunderstood, patronized and comprehensively devalued. Or so Russell Brown believes – and he may be right. Certainly, the chunks of Bradley that occupy most of the pages of this book have been judiciously chosen by Russell Brown and represent Bradley at his most 'durable'. Russell Brown's experience as a director of Shakespeare's plays enables him to pick out the Bradleyan criticism that is most alive to the playability of the drama, and he connects Bradley provocatively with Stanislavski (and Freud). Above all he asks us to respond to and appreciate the vitality, emotion and sincerity of Bradley's personal engagement with Shakespeare's tragedies: 'he wrote as he instinctively felt . . . his judgements are based on his own personal sentiment'. Yet that instinctiveness included a deep-seated scepticism which Russell Brown finds provocatively 'in keeping with the present times'; Bradley's *Shakespearian Tragedy* is 'consonant with contemporary scepticism and the relativity of all understanding'. In a word, it's new.

Equally consonant with contemporary scepticism and the relativity of all understanding is a book of essays edited by Stephen Cohen, *Shakespeare and Historical Formalism*. In his Introduction, Cohen argues that the New Historicism hasn't lived up to its alleged concern for literary form. What we need now, he believes, is a reinvigoration of New Historicism, a *new* New Historicism willing to explore the complexity of the 'mutual implication' of history and form – we need to study 'the literary text in its full historical specificity'. (We might compare Fiona McNeill's appeal for a new *Old Historicism* in *Poor Women in Shakespeare*. I hope that neither appeal falls on deaf ears.) Only two of the essays have been previously published (compare the three in the book of essays on Shakespeare's Sonnets), Jean E. Howard's incisive 'Shakespeare, Geography, and the Work of Genre on the Early Modern Stage' with its emphasis on the Renaissance stage as 'a veritable factory of experimentation' and Heather Dubrow's meditation, ' "I would I were at home": Representations of Dwelling Places and Havens in *Cymbeline*', which entertains us with instructive parallels with the Coen brothers, *Star Trek* and James Bond. Both of these essays appear in the first section, *Historicizing Form*, along with Douglas Bruster's 'The Materiality of Shakespearian Form' with its plea for a more capacious understanding of materiality.

The second section *Re-Forming History* is perhaps the more provocative. In an 'admittedly partial view', Nicholas Moschovakis has another fling at soldering a heuristic context onto the ever-mercurial *Hamlet* in 'Partial Views: Literary Allusion, Teleological Form, and Contingent Readings in *Hamlet*'. Maybe, he argues, early audiences identified the form of *Hamlet*'s revenge plot with that of Virgil's *Aeneid*, that 'providentialist epic', and were thus able to experience more acutely the play's 'epic teleology' in contrast to Horatio's emphasis on a story full of 'accidental judgements' and 'casual slaughters'. The book's final essay by Mary Janell Metzger is an unexpectedly moving defence of the importance of literary form in the classroom to help ward off some students' determination to manipulate the strategies of New Historicism to affirm unpleasant fundamentalist ideologies. Metzger believes that the power of form in Shakespeare, rightly taught, will awaken her students' 'capacity for and hope in the imaginative construction of meaning'. Amen to that, but I suspect that any liberal strategy will have a hard time denting the mindsets of the 'Nathans' of this world.

A new old historicism or a new New Historicism have their counterpart in Andy Mousley's conception of a new humanism in *Re-Humanising Shakespeare: Literary Humanism, Wisdom and Modernity*. His new humanism is what he calls literary humanism as opposed to 'mainstream humanism', which fosters 'the image of humanism as a conceited, bourgeois ideology founded upon an inflated concept of "man" '. (On another occasion he calls this simplistic humanism an 'unbridled humanism'.) This is the humanism that has been the target of so much postmodern scepticism. Opposed to it, Mousley offers what might be called a bridled humanism, or a sceptical humanism: a 'cautious humanism', a 'vigilant humanism'. It is the kind, for example, that animates the socialist wisdom of a Terry Eagleton. But this new humanism turns out to be, not unexpectedly, not so new. For literary humanism has a more than familial connection with Renaissance humanism (itself a form of bridled humanism): 'the "how to live" question of literary humanism is so appropriate to Renaissance humanism as to be blindingly obvious'.

So the book is really an investigation of the plurality of the humanisms we find in Shakespeare (in particular): humanism isn't just one thing. (In *As You Like It*, for instance, we need to attend to the 'subaltern humanism' we find in the forest.) The book is full of like-minded pluralities. The scepticism that is the hall-mark of the anti-humanist can also be broken down into a variety of scepticisms including, of course, a scepticism about scepticism which contrasts with an 'empty scepticism' and, for that matter, with various other fuller ones. Similarly, there are different understandings of individualism, ranging from the hubristic kind to a more saintly community-minded variety. Ditto historicisms, the most important of which for Mousley is the literary humanist kind; and fear also comes in different packages ('the fear *of* transgression and fear *as* transgressive' in *Macbeth*, for instance), as does folly, which can be 'wise, foolish and sophisticated'. All these splinter groups are pursued by Mousley through nine Shakespeare plays in order to reassure us that Shakespeare is still eminently worth reading for the advice he can offer us as to how to live a fuller, more human life. I don't think what Mousley says is untrue; but it's a bit of an oddity to read a book so up-to-date theoretically that has such a ringing nineteenth-century moral.

For the brand spankingly new we have to turn to a recent Accents on Shakespeare essay collection, *Presentist Shakespeares*, edited by Hugh Grady and Terence Hawkes. It's very difficult to imagine a Shakespeare criticism that hasn't at least one foot planted in the present, but presentism, as it's unattractively known, has a tendency to gobble up the whole body. Only a tendency though, as the book's editors insist. On the one hand, as the 'Introduction: Presenting presentism' evenhandedly puts it, it's absurd 'to deal with the plays in blissful ignorance of their historical context'; on the other, it's equally absurd to think that the present can be 'drained out of our experience'. It must be a question of emphasis, then, of priority, of today's 'material present' as opposed to yesterday's, of talking with the living rather than with the dead, of having 'a committed engagement with the developments in critical and cultural theory that have taken place since the 1980s' and of responding to the now of the plays' aesthetic power, their 'paradoxical presentness'.

There's certainly no blissful ignorance of history in Terence Hawkes's essay 'Band of Brothers', and he has the footnotes to prove it (twice as many as his nearest rival in this collection). Clever and provocative as always, Hawkes, a storyteller *manqué*, threads a hectic narrative line that links George W. Childs's gift of a drinking fountain to Stratford-upon-Avon with *Timon of Athens* with the blood brotherhood between the United States and the United Kingdom with Bram Stoker with Karl Marx with *Timon of Athens* again with Allardyce Nicoll and the Yale Dramatic Society's production of *Timon of Athens* with the fledgling CIA with 'the ambiguity-obsessed, boundary-blurring, duplicitous concerns of New Criticism' with the Shakespeare Institute and with the annual International Shakespeare Conferences in Stratford. Whew! *Timon* at nodal points along this line takes the temperature of the culture in which it is read and performed; an appropriate choice, for instance, for the 1946–7 season at the Birmingham Repertory Theatre where it reflected life in a postwar Britain, 'wretchedly unpleasant, shamingly drab'.

The essay ends on a sour (or sourer) note. Now, it seems, Shakespeare is the 'International Superstar' of the British–American alliance. But he is so in the wake of Allardyce Nicoll's (largely forgotten) 1952 *Shakespeare*, 'a serene ahistorical, apolitical wonder', and will be found floating 'in all his gaseous glory' in 2006 in Stratford's presentation of the Complete Works. But from the sound of what Hawkes describes as the 'chilling details' of the celebration it doesn't seem to me inevitable that it will jettison 'overt political issues'. Is a Saddam Hussein *Richard III*, for instance, above politics? Isn't this theatrical presentism (as was the case in 1947) at its indefatigable work? There's a 'shape-shifting' manoeuvre in the last paragraphs of this essay that I found unexpected and not particularly convincing.

Catherine Belsey's essay 'Historicizing new historicism' is of course historical to its bootstraps. It's written in the main in generous and discerning praise of Stephen Greenblatt, especially for his famous 1980 book, *Renaissance Self-Fashioning*. Belsey convincingly shows us that the roots of Greenblatt's pessimistic view of the irresistibility of power can be found in American culture (not in Foucault where power 'is always threatened, perpetually precarious'). Greenblatt, Belsey maintains, writes in the tradition of the functionalism of Talcott Parsons, Francis Fukuyama and Clifford Geertz. Sounding still the historical note, historicizing *Hamlet* criticism from the early nineteenth century to the advent of postmodernism is the burden of Hugh Grady's '*Hamlet* and the present: Notes on the moving aesthetic "now"'. But he does it in the name of presentism, as his 'now' insists, as *Hamlet* like any work of art appears 'in constantly regenerated and re-organized forms as history develops'. An essay that treads a well-beaten path, it's notable for its emphasis – not to be found all that often in presentist criticism – on the 'resistance to certain interpretive schema' of all texts (that of *Hamlet* most notably) for they are 'aesthetic objects . . . cultural creations that surpass linear, cognitive rationality'.

Interpretative schema, you might say, take over Linda Charnes's 'Shakespeare, and belief, in the future' which channels current American politics through the experience of *Othello*. But there's a strange disregard for what happens or doesn't happen in the play (often the case I find in recent discussions of *Othello*). Instead Charnes substitutes that old question-begging favourite, the life and times of the European times: 'By any measure of Venetian, or Shakespearian culture, the elopement of Othello and Desdemona is an outrage.' By any measure, that is, except the play's, which doesn't support Charnes's claim that the Duke imposes a 'suspension of normal laws and values' to allow for the lovers' elopement. Nor does it support Charnes's confident accusation that it judges Othello as 'the very perpetrator of the domestic insurrection'. Where does it talk in however camouflaged a way of an *FISA* (Forbid Interracial Sexuality Act)? Where does it suggest that Othello 'clearly parks his person in a place where it does not belong'? The answer is that it does so only in the mouths of Iago and Brabantio, the one the real but mysterious 'perpetrator of the domestic insurrection', the other Desdemona's hidebound father. Perhaps we may say, to return to the book's Introduction, that Charnes is simply too heavily in thrall to today's 'material present' as opposed to yesterday's to allow the play to talk back to her.

A humane and convincing essay that allows for all kinds of talking back can be found in Michael Bristol's '. . . And I'm the King of France' where he parses the valuable intuitive responses to Cordelia's 'Nothing' of some twenty-five students who 'speak what they feel because they don't know what they ought to say'. In the process of teaching them what they ought to say (and learning from what they feel), Bristol delves into the moral and philosophical intricacies of the stand-off between Cordelia and her father. And why is Bristol the King of France? Presumably because he married the daughter of a father-in-law who 'is just like King Lear'. Equally humane, if not quite as convincing, Ewan Fernie's 'Action! *Henry V*' attempts to answer an important question: 'What is the professional Shakespeare criticism of recent years failing to confront when it holds the play in sceptical regard?' Fernie contrasts the play's 'absorbingly complex' advocacy of 'fierce agency' with 'our own aesthetic leisure', with our 'ethically fastidious denial of . . . power to act', just at a time when we most need to 'build stronger, more objective international institutions and – let it be said – a fairer world'. In an unexpectedly fruitful application of Fluellen's 'There is figure in all things', Fernie suggests that the fairer world in *Henry V* can be found in Henry's and Katherine's mutual kiss, the climax of Henry's new-found role as the coaxing wooer soliciting 'female will and agency'.

Surpassing (but not abandoning) linear, cognitive rationality, and arguably the strongest essay in the book, Kiernan Ryan's '*Troilus and Cressida*: the perils of presentism' offers the collection's most passionate advocacy of presentist criticism. In a language of persuasive excess, the essay denounces historicism's 'trance of retrospection' and argues that the 'eccentric hybridity' of *Troilus* 'begs to be read as a scathing parable on our modern plight' as much as, in all its 'delinquency', it was determined to 'vex' its original audiences. We're talking here about 'the precocious modernity of *Troilus and Cressida*', its 'awesome prognostic power', its 'grim prevision of life under late capitalism at its most predatory, alienating and destructive'. Piling on the paradoxes, Ryan maintains that our postmodern readings of the play are '*more truly historical*' (his emphasis) than previous ones, for Shakespeare's dramatic imagination is anachronistic, the play has been waiting on the future and the future has arrived: we are able to articulate 'for the first time . . . matters that were always on its mind, but that could not be apprehended until now'. This essay is seductively bold, provocatively extreme and iconoclastic, yet, in what might be seen as its richest paradox, Ryan insists that our modern approaches must be 'close and consistently confirmed by the text'. Indeed, in his view, what presentism must avoid at all costs, what is in fact its chief peril, is its tendency to 'omnivorous assimilation'. In a word, Shakespeare's plays must be allowed to talk back, an injunction that all isms, not just presentism, would be wise always to heed.

The 'new' in another Accents on Shakespeare book, Alan Sinfield's *Shakespeare, Authority, Sexuality*, stretches into the future as its subtitle tells us, *Unfinished Business in Cultural Materialism*. Like Ryan's essay, this book not only encourages Shakespeare's plays and poems to talk back to their readers (though they sometimes also get a talking to from Sinfield) but could plausibly make a similar claim to Ryan's that what were always on their minds has here (at last) been given articulation (with a little bit of help from other like-minded critics). As Sinfield reminds us on more than one occasion, he isn't just any old cultural materialist but a gay cultural materialist, and one of the consequences of this combination is a rewarding openness to, for instance, the homosexual implications of Antonio's love for Bassanio in *The Merchant of Venice*. Why, Sinfield asks, is Antonio so conspicuously and 'motivelessly' sad at the beginning of the play? His answer is that Antonio is hopelessly in love with a male friend who is in love with a woman. But, given Shakespeare's notorious hospitality to theatrical improvisation, Sinfield also suggests that Antonio's love need not be forever sad. At the play's end an enterprising director could have Antonio leave the stage arm in arm with Portia and Bassanio 'delighted with his boyfriend's lucky break'. (A much less outlandish theatrical intervention than, say, the one that has some productions of *Twelfth Night* showing Antonio and Sebastian in bed together.) Such an ending would be in keeping with Sinfield's emphasis throughout the book on Renaissance writers' unthreatened, casual treatment of 'boy-love'.

Sinfield's last chapter, 'Unfinished Business II', lays his cultural materialist cards on the table. He claims that cultural materialism is a 'rational and principled endeavor, connecting textuality, history and politics, in a world where people have purposes and culture has consequences'. His purpose as a cultural materialist is to uncover 'the political potential of the text', but, he also claims, it isn't a question of subduing the text 'to a political project' but of allowing us to see 'that critics have always done that' whether they knew it or not. (Sounds like a political project to me.) Despite this didactic political intent Sinfield is often a playful critic, flexible, aware that a play might be radical from one point of view and conservative from another, happy to read against the grain (even if this means reading with the grain in some instances as in the case of *Troilus and Cressida*), committed 'to the recovery of subordinated voices'. He's especially thought-provoking on *As You Like It* (Raymond Williams's *Country and the City* (1975) looms large here), Jonson's *Poetaster*, and *Measure for Measure*. I particularly liked the chapter in which he reads *The Two Noble Kinsmen* in order to throw light on *A Midsummer Night's Dream* (and vice versa), but is aware all the time that these two plays 'are actualizing different ranges of ideological potential'. It's stimulating stuff, this, and expressed with an admirable frankness.

A new series of short books on Shakespeare asserts its newness with a pugnacious authority. The streakily black *Now!* of the series' title, *Shakespeare Now!*, takes up over a third of the bottom half of each of the books' covers and fairly bristles with menace. We're told in the Preface by the General Editors, Simon Palfrey and Ewan Fernie, that the *Now* 'minigraphs' turn their backs on an 'ascendant and detached' academic criticism replacing it with an 'intellectual adventure story', accessible, to be sure, but often discomfortingly and unpredictably so. Eric S. Mallin's *Godless Shakespeare* certainly lives up to this billing. Each of this short book's short chapters is a sharp jab in the solar plexus of conventional wisdom about Shakespeare, as Mallin wittily and slangily pursues his Blakeian notion that Hell is Heaven, Heaven Hell, in Shakespeare, with the likes of Aaron and, supremely, Cleopatra as the only gods fit to be worshipped. And so, from this viewpoint, Isabella's religion in *Measure for Measure* is a species of 'terrified sadism', *Titus Andronicus* 'a rebuke against the Eucharist ritual', Paulina's punishment of Leontes in *The Winter's Tale* is revenge of an 'almost unimaginable, sustained viciousness'. Mallin doesn't hold anything back as in this visceral (and persuasive) judgement of the behaviour of Hamlet and Laertes in Ophelia's grave: 'Do they really think that the construction of a super-hill on the body of Ophelia will bring them closer to heaven? It is a marvellous vignette of shame, self-justification, and rampant bullshit.' I have to say that Mallin's demotic enthusiasm tumbles at times into absurdity, as in his breathless chapter on *Macbeth* as the 'funniest' of Shakespeare's plays with Seyton as the murderer of Lady Macbeth. Nonetheless, overall, I found the notion of a secret godless Shakespeare more intriguing than that of the secret Catholic Shakespeare so fashionable nowadays in some influential quarters.

We zoom in from the stratosphere of a godless universe to the minutiae of the most famous 34 lines Shakespeare ever wrote. Douglas Bruster's *Now!* contribution takes Hamlet's 'To be or not to be' soliloquy and subjects it to a merciless set of dissections, re-dissections and counter-dissections. Even in the short space of a *Now!* book this means that there are about four pages of *Now!* text for every line of the soliloquy (though 'Remember me' repeats of the soliloquy itself take up a fair number of pages). Bruster does Shakespeare proud (as did Russ McDonald) in his slow passes over this 'quite messy' and hence mysterious speech in which Hamlet's compulsive restatements of what he has within that passes show tend, if anything, to muddy even more *Hamlet*'s notoriously muddy waters. Slow motion readings of this kind have their dangers and occasionally Bruster falls into what Philip Davis in *Shakespeare Thinking* calls a 'picky minuteness', but by and large his dogged analyses make a fine contribution to our understanding of Shakespeare as artist nonpareil. I was particularly taken with Bruster's insight into the way this 'most resonant presentation of the personal in all of literature' achieves a surprising impersonality by eschewing the use of the first person, making the speech 'float above the rest of the play'. And in the compelling section that deals with the soliloquy's context Bruster makes a convincing case for the speech as 'a miniature version of the play itself' (cf. McDonald). It is a measure of Shakespeare's genius (among other things) that even this exhaustive analysis of so few lines fails to mention a plausible reading. When Hamlet says 'to sleep – / No

more' the absence of any punctuation after 'sleep' in the quartos and Folio supports the interpretation that Hamlet may be saying that to die is nothing but to sleep.

Philip Davis's *Now!* contribution, *Shakespeare Thinking*, is indeed discomforting and unpredictable, but is not as accessible, it seems to me, as the other two. It's one of a number of critical works lately obsessed with Shakespeare as the thinking man's literary thinker. It might be of some interest then to compare Davis's foray into the workings of Shakespeare's intellect with the much longer, compulsively accessible book by the late A. D. Nuttall, *Shakespeare the Thinker*. (Shakespeare *the* thinker, in fact, to emphasize his Einsteinian status.) *Thinking* as opposed to *Thinker* catches something of the difference between the two books: Davis's extraordinary attempt to catch Shakespeare as a thinker on the wing, as opposed to Nuttall's more sedate and comprehensive account of a writer who manages not to repeat himself intellectually speaking while repeating himself in most other ways. And yet there is a meeting of obsessions in these two writers, who are on the surface so different. Here, for instance, is Nuttall sounding like Davis in his insistence on the importance of 'the notion of process to any understanding of Shakespeare as a creative intellect'. He sounds like Davis even more when he gets excited about the something 'glancingly wild' in Shakespeare whose literary genius takes him (and us) on visits to 'the wilder shores of thought'. These are where Davis parks his book, though he, unlike Nuttall, matches wildness with wildness in the way in which his rhapsodic yet precise prose attempts to burrow beneath Shakespeare's astonishing 'symbols of tacitly connected thought' to a 'life-force' which is 'anterior to character as it is prior to explicit theme or conceptualized agenda, which is entrusted to work itself out'. We're dealing here not just with an 'endlessly inventive' writer, but one whose language is 'locked into the very structures of creation', taking us down into 'the brain's deep in-between formative places'.

There is much more of this kind of thing. But what I really liked about Davis's difficult squib of a book was the way in which the proof of its thinking lay in the reading – the reading, that is, of Shakespeare's lines. (For all its length, Nuttall's book rarely demonstrates Davis's (or McDonald's) flair in the art of reading poetry.) On numerous occasions, Davis validates the large claims he makes for Shakespeare's preternatural powers of thinking, his extraordinary 'mental leaps', his 'visceral meanings', by catching it at work in, for instance, his 'sheer power of lineation' (numerous persuasive examples are supplied) or, especially, in the section that occupies the last third of the book 'A Shakespearian Grammar' (wherein Davis explores the genius of E. A. Abbott), in his masterful exploitation of the 'functional shift', particularly from noun to verb. The *activity* of Shakespeare's thinking, in all its neural and linguistic coruscation, is the subject of Davis's book, Shakespeare as verb, you might say. Nuttall is more concerned with Shakespeare as noun, a thinker in the history of thinking, and the best parts of his book, it seems to me, are those which place Shakespeare's capacious mind in various philosophical traditions: Realism and Nominalism, Utilitarian ethics, empiricism and immaterialist idealism, Gnosticism (especially in *Measure for Measure* and *King Lear*). Nuttall is a master of the enlightening analogy from Martin Scorsese to *Gawain and the Green Knight*, from *Tom Jones* to Waugh's *Decline and Fall* or Forster's *A Room with a View*. He contrasts Shakespeare's over-determination with Ockham's principle, 'the law of parsimony'; he cleverly imagines Hippolyta in *A Midsummer Night's Dream* as addressing David Hume across the centuries; there is much fruitful exploration of Shakespeare in relation to Greek and Roman writers. His chapters on *Hamlet* and *Troilus and Cressida* are particularly valuable: Shakespeare's task in *Hamlet*, Nuttall writes, 'was to enlarge uncertainty'; when the play is over, 'we can still ask, "Who was there?"'

I don't think Nuttall would have had much truck with Davis's life-force anterior to character; he might well have expostulated that character is the life-force in Shakespeare, and he is unapologetically in Bradley's camp rather than L. C. Knights's.

Indeed, he ups the ante by speculating about the *future* lives of Shakespeare's characters as well as their pasts. There is, though, a curious resemblance, I would argue, between Nuttall and Davis in the extraordinary value they place on their own insights into what makes Shakespeare tick. No false modesty here. In Nuttall's case, it sometimes produces judgements on Shakespeare's characters that seem to require such admonitions as 'this must be taken seriously' or even more brow-beatingly, 'It will be said that I read too much into "simple". Not so. It is all there.' I for one often found myself worrying about the all there that Nuttall finds there, either because his *ex cathedra* pronouncements simply cut off the possibility of adding to (or subtracting from) that all there, or, more culpably, because they seem to me to be simply wrong-headed in their insistence on the undeniability of their truth. This is the danger of character criticism, or one of the dangers. You frequently can't prove what you're saying about someone (just as in real life), so you may be tempted to replace reliance on chapter and verse with the magisterialness that comes from a lifetime of critical thinking and teaching.

It's hard to imagine a lengthy book on *Hamlet* able, in 2007, to come up with something arrestingly new to say about a play that seems to have had everything said about it many times over. But Margreta de Grazia's Hamlet *without Hamlet* has accomplished this difficult feat mainly because she's managed, as her title informs us, to resist the siren-song of Hamlet's 'intransitive inwardness' that has so dominated criticism since the end of the eighteenth century. Instead, she sets out to restore the play's plot to the position it may once have held before the discovery of the black hole of Hamlet's mind (a discovery intensified by Kant's and Hegel's espousal of the 'freedom of absolute consciousness', and by Freud's discovery of 'subinwardness'). For de Grazia the plot of *Hamlet* should no longer be the play's 'inert backdrop', nor should its premise continue to be ignored. It is important for an understanding of the play as a whole, she urges, to acknowledge the reverberating fact that Hamlet has been legitimately dispossessed of the

Danish throne in a murky electoral process tacitly or actively approved by Hamlet's father (his 'inertia in his final days') and Claudius's imperial jointress, Hamlet's mother. What Hamlet has within which passes show, then, might well have been an open secret to the Danish court and to early modern English theatre audiences.

Hamlet's unvoiced predicament gains resonance from the play's obsession with history as it circles round 'the fall of states, kingdoms, and empires'. Troy, Carthage, Rome, Britain, Wittenberg and Vienna have their rhetorical moments – through 'scattered allusions, tropes and puns' – in what de Grazia calls the play's 'temporal jumble'. In all their cases, as with Hamlet's, the obsession bears down on 'the centrality of land' – who owns it, who goes to war for it, who inherits it (even Hamlet's name suggests it): 'the plot of the play is driven by the desire for a plot'. Hamlet himself throughout (notoriously in the graveyard scene) is obsessed with the earth, and things of the earth, and this obsession helps to explain Shakespeare's treatment of him (and Laertes) in the scene of Ophelia's hugger-mugger burial. What these fatherless courtiers indulge in is 'a wild territorial battle over a flower-strewn plot of earth'. Here we have, in de Grazia's memorable words, 'two desperately disenfranchised men' who 'invoke piles over a sexualised pit, clutching at the chimera of estate and lineage, while themselves on the brink of extinction' (cf. Mallin's chapter on *Hamlet* in *Godless Shakespeare*). Allusions, tropes and puns, taken from 'the play's surrealistic semantics', are what de Grazia unearths as important evidence for her argument: 'mole', 'mould', 'hide' (a unit of land measurement), 'man' are portentously linked, for instance.

De Grazia's book is rich and powerful and a pleasure to read. We can't agree therefore with the opening sentence of her Acknowledgements: 'If writing were not for me such a hard act of self-absorption, this book would have come out better, and earlier'. We may not agree either though with that friend of hers who assured her 'again and again that there really was nothing left to be understood'. Of course he didn't mean that there was nothing left to know about *Hamlet*; what he meant was that de Grazia had exhausted the potential of her argument. Without being ungrateful, I hope, for what we do get, I have to admit that my mounting excitement with the book's climactically constructed argument didn't get the revelation we seemed to be heading for. I was hoping, I suppose, for a novelistic ending that linked together the main themes of the book in a satisfying explanation of the last chapter's subject, Hamlet's delay. Instead, the book takes off in a new, Stollian and Empsonian direction explaining the delay tautologically in dramaturgical terms. There's delay on Hamlet's part, that is, because his audiences expected it. There's truth in this argument, of course, but by no means the whole truth, nor, I would think, the most interesting truth. Fine though de Grazia's book is, its original contribution to *Hamlet* criticism is clearly an adjunct to the obsession with Hamlet's intransitive inwardness not a replacement for it.

José Manuel González's collection of essays, *Spanish Studies in Shakespeare and His Contemporaries*, could not have been written and published before 1975, so González tells us in the Introduction – before, that is, the date of General Franco's death, and the beginning of the relaxation of political and artistic censorship. It was not until Spain's entry into the European Community in 1986, however, that the 'new' criticism began to emerge, and this book concentrates on the years between 1986 and 2006, years in which Spanish Shakespeare criticism explored 'a democratic Shakespeare' and his 'reception and acculturation in Spain'. One might expect from such an Introduction a collection of essays self-consciously political, pointedly 'democratic' (perhaps, say, in the manner of an Alan Sinfield), but few essays oddly enough have this kind of ambition. One that does is Keith Gregor's '*Julius Caesar* and the Spanish Transition' written, we're told, as part of the Research Project BFF2002-02019, financed by the Spanish Ministry of Science and Technology and FEDER. (I quote this in full to give you an idea of the political reality behind the politics of the essay.) Gregor traces the political ambitions of the productions of *Julius Caesar* appearing in the transitional period from Francoist feudalism to uncertain democracy. Unsurprisingly, *Julius Caesar* continues to function in Spain as everywhere else as a remarkably manipulable theatrical work, open to a range of often competing political interpretation.

The book's chief interest is for students of comparative literature: Shakespeare or one of his contemporaries linked to a Spanish writer or two. Shakespeare and Cervantes, for example, in Jesús Tronch Pérez's 'Editing (and Revering) National Authors' where the editing of Shakespeare is 'emendatory, more speculative, more suspicious of the witnesses'; or 'The Court of Ben Jonson and Calderón' by José Manuel González; or (more ambitiously) María J. Pando Cantelli's, 'John Donne, Francisco de Quevedo, and the Construction of Subjectivity in Early Modern Poetry' where the self that emerges in both poets is 'halfway between an Augustinian inner awareness and a Cartesian supreme expression of individuality'. Where the essays deal with Shakespeare by himself the level of critical sophistication is not very high and the English expression sometimes bizarre (as in the case, for instance, of Luis García Mainar's 'Shakespeare's *Romeo and Juliet*, and Male Melodrama'). An unusual contribution (by Brian Crews) to the interpretation of Sonnet 18 – 'Shall I compare thee to a summer's day' – posits the poem's addressee as the sonneteer's penis.

It may not be inappropriate to end this year's round-up of Shakespeare criticism on such a note of cheeky irreverence. One of the characteristics of this year's crop of studies on Shakespeare – a welcome one as far as I'm concerned – was the more frequent than usual injection in them of light-heartedness, banter even, of the sort that we can imagine someone like Benedick enjoying. There seems to me no reason why the seriousness of the pursuit of Shakespeare criticism shouldn't be leavened in this way. One can only hope that the examples in this respect of Russ McDonald, Margreta de Grazia, Terence Hawkes, Alan Sinfield,

Eric Mallin, Catherine Belsey, Michael Bristol, James Schiffer and others will inspire Shakespeare critics to make next year's studies an entertaining as well as an educational read for the reviewer weighed down by the fardels of scholarship and ingenuity.

WORKS REVIEWED

Belsey, Catherine, *Why Shakespeare?* (Houndmills, Basingstoke, 2007)

Brown, John Russell, *A. C. Bradley on Shakespeare's Tragedies: A Concise Edition and Reassessment* (Basingstoke, Hampshire, 2007)

Bruster, Douglas, *To Be Or Not To Be*. Shakespeare Now Series (London and New York, 2007)

Cohen, Stephen, ed., *Shakespeare and Historical Formalism* (Aldershot, Hampshire, 2007)

Davis, Philip, *Shakespeare Thinking*. Shakespeare Now Series (London and New York, 2007)

de Grazia, Margreta, Hamlet *without Hamlet* (Cambridge, 2007)

Dillon, Janette, *The Cambridge Introduction to Early English Theatre* (Cambridge, 2006)

DiPietro, Cary, *Shakespeare and Modernism* (Cambridge, 2006)

Douglas, Audrey and Sally-Beth MacLean, eds., *REED in Review: Essays in Celebration of the First Twenty-Five Years* (Toronto, 2006)

González, José Manuel, *Spanish Studies in Shakespeare and his Contemporaries* (Newark, NJ, 2006)

Goodland, Katherine, *Female Mourning and Tragedy in Medieval and Renaissance English Drama: From the Raising of Lazarus to King Lear*. Studies in Performance and Early Modern Drama (Aldershot, Hampshire, 2005)

Grady, Hugh and Terence Hawkes, eds., *Presentist Shakespeares* (Abingdon, Oxon., 2007)

Groves, Beatrice, *Texts and Traditions: Religion in Shakespeare 1592–1604*. Oxford English Monographs (Oxford, 2007)

Lyne, Raphael, *Shakespeare's Late Work*. Oxford Shakespeare Topics (Oxford, 2007)

MacFaul, Tom, *Male Friendship in Shakespeare and his Contemporaries* (Cambridge, 2007)

Mallin, Eric S., *Godless Shakespeare*. Shakespeare Now Series (London and New York, 2007)

McDonald, Russ, *Shakespeare's Late Style* (Cambridge, 2006)

McNeill, Fiona, *Poor Women in Shakespeare* (Cambridge, 2007)

Montgomery Robert L., *The Perfect Ceremony of Love's Rite: Shakespeare's* Sonnets *and* A Lover's Complaint. Medieval and Renaissance Texts and Studies, volume 305 (Tempe, Arizona, 2006)

Mousley, Andy, *Re-Humanising Shakespeare: Literary Humanism, Wisdom and Modernity* (Edinburgh, 2007)

Nuttall, A. D., *Shakespeare the Thinker* (New Haven and London, 2007)

Schoenfeldt, Michael, ed., *A Companion to Shakespeare's Sonnets* (Oxford, 2007).

Scott, Charlotte, *Shakespeare and the Idea of the Book* (Oxford, 2007)

Sinfield, Alan, *Shakespeare, Authority, Sexuality: Unfinished Business in Cultural Materialism.* Accents on Shakespeare (Oxford, 2006)

Vickers, Brian, *Shakespeare,* A Lover's Complaint, *and John Davies of Hereford* (Cambridge, 2007)

Waller, Gary, ed., *All's Well, That Ends Well: New Critical Essays* (New York and London, 2007)

Weingust, Don, *Acting From Shakespeare's First Folio: Theory, Text and Performance* (New York and London, 2006)

Whitney, Charles, *Early Responses to Renaissance Drama* (Cambridge, 2006)

2. SHAKESPEARE IN PERFORMANCE

reviewed by EMMA SMITH

Reviewing a big doorstep of a book such as the first volume of John O'Connor and Katharine Goodland's *A Directory of Shakespeare in Performance 1970–2005*, it's tempting to stress quantitative vital statistics in a sort of academic publishing version of Top Trumps. Length: 1756 pages: I win. Weight: I win again. Number of entries: 'almost 1200': me again. Price: yes, you got it. Or, to spar with other kinds of data. Did you know there are more index entries for the *Guardian*'s veteran theatre critic Michael Billington than for Trevor Nunn, Peter Hall and Simon Russell Beale combined? Or that productions of *Timon of Athens* come round once every four years, while if you miss a *Hamlet* there'll be another along ere those shoes are old? Or that Laurence Olivier spoke a prologue written by Christopher Fry before a 1973 National Theatre touring production of *Twelfth Night* to celebrate Britain's entry into the EEC? What country, friends, *is* this? So what, avoiding the clichés of both 'did you ever?' and 'phew, what a whopper', does this *Directory* have to offer? A good deal. It's an immense standalone resource which, caveats about its coverage aside, gives a substantial snapshot of performance trends for particular plays, enables a preliminary trace of the careers of Shakespearian theatre professionals, and samples some pithy, informative newspaper reviewing. It will be an indispensable first point of call for anyone reading up the recent stage history of a particular play: neither overwhelming with detail like the *Shakespeare in Production* series nor over-interpreted as the *Shakespeare in Performance* series can be. Each entry has the details of cast and crew, of place and date, and then two or three gobbets from reviews in major newspapers and periodicals. Of course these records are not neutral: they weren't when they were initially printed and are not when they are excerpted here, and of course the volume therefore implicitly, and patchily, constructs the history of performance as that of reception rather than intention. Validating the views of drama critics over those of directors or actors skews the project of theatrical history, and perhaps the *Directory* is vague about its own processes of selection. But it is still a substantial and highly recommended volume of reference.

One slight niggle about the *Directory* is that the films included feel out of place. Filmed Shakespeare has developed its own critical protocols and these have been reiterated and modestly extended by a crop of recent books. Thomas Cartelli and Katherine Rowe's *New Wave Shakespeare on Screen* constructs its chapters around a primary Shakespearian text and one or two filmic iterations. Some of these are familiar – Taymor's *Titus*, Luhrmann's *Romeo + Juliet* – but others less so – Kristian Levring's *The King is Alive* offers a version of *Lear* reconstructed from memory by a group of tourists stranded in the Namibian desert, Geoffrey Sax's racially topical television *Othello* is set in London's Metropolitan police force. Cartelli and Rowe are adept at interweaving what they identify as 'Shakespeare-centric' concerns – questions placing the host Shakespearian play at the centre of the analysis – and those constructed as 'Shakespeare-eccentric' – generated by non-Shakespearian contexts and interests. On *Hamlet* as an intertext for Godard's *Bande à Parte*, the argument is exemplary. Referencing theories of postmodernity and technologies of storage and retrieval, Cartelli and Rowe work back to the play's own multimedia arts of memory via early modern mnemonic culture and forward to the cinematic evocation of a past within and of the play. Almereyda's Hamlet's Mousetrap functions as the epitome of the composite mode of cinematic retrieval and pastiche. The chapter on *Scotland, PA* enjoys the campy aesthetic of one branch of Shakespearian cinema, seeing the film's Mac-Duff as a version of television detective Columbo and deftly implicating its fast food setting into a parody of corporate America. Self-consciously, the film is concerned to assesss 'the costs and benefits of a recycling process that it sees as an essential feature of culture'; intriguingly, Cartelli and Rowe suggest this reworking registers as ultimately tragicomic, even as a nostalgic lament for the possibility of tragedy in the past. This is a clever, engaged book that sent me back to, and in some cases to, the film-texts with new eyes.

Mark Thornton Burnett's *Filming Shakespeare in the Global Marketplace* makes a strong case for a Shakespeare relevant to, and co-optable for, debates about the local and the global, about identity and difference. Burnett's approach is at once radically modern – giving careful scholarly consideration to teen movies like *Get Over It*, never quoting a line of Shakespeare – and nicely old-fashioned – Shakespeare, much redacted, is ultimately a vehicle for the dissection of pressing, but humane, values and concerns. Burnett is properly alert to context, as all scholars of Shakespearian film must be, but he is also an adept formalist, and uses this technique extremely fruitfully. Discussing Michael Hoffman's *William Shakespeare's 'A Midsummer Night's Dream'* as a sort of post-hoc collaboration with Branagh's earlier *Much Ado About Nothing* makes an undervalued and insecure film much more interesting, as if what is missing can be supplied by a careful reconstruction of a filmic dialogue. So everything about Hoffman's film is seen as a particularly postmodern form of sequelization, in which it is not narrative but connotation that is extended: Italian settings multiply, classical motifs are corralled to suggest timelessness, Anglophilic casting extended. The result is a cinema of worry – about live performance, about the legacy of Shakespearian authority, about cultural heritage and about filmic comedy. Burnett can't make a fairly woeful film any better (like the other writers on film discussed here, these evaluative terms aren't his preferred currency), but he does make thinking about it more rewarding. An interesting epilogue on Branagh's *As You Like It* prompts a moot dialectic: 'does Shakespeare sponsor the possibility of film or does the process work in the opposite direction?'

Filming Shakespeare in the Global Marketplace is attentive to questions of economics. Burnett reports that Branagh's *Love's Labour's Lost* recouped less than 5 per cent of its costs, compared with Luhrmann's *Romeo + Juliet* (over $30 million profit) and Madden's *Shakespeare in Love* (over $100 million profit). Shakespeare scholars' attentiveness to, even fascination with the market, means that Emma French's timely *Selling Shakespeare to Hollywood* is an inevitable development. French resoundingly reconstructs the cinema industry as commercial rather than aesthetic, turning away from the literary bias of 'Shakespeare on film' and towards the industrial. If Stratford-upon-Avon cannot produce commercially viable Shakespeare, how can Hollywood? Basically, French argues that 'faithful' adaptations tend not to be successful at the box office whereas hybrid or irreverent versions can be: Branagh's *Hamlet* versus Luhrmann's *Romeo + Juliet*. So, the recipe for success is to bridge high and low culture. Her historical focus is narrow: arguing that the Shakespeare film began as an offshoot of the heritage film of the 1980s sacrifices the tantalizing prospect of earlier encounters, including any analysis of Olivier in Hollywood, where an ingenious campaign mass-marketed his *Hamlet* as a ghostly thriller. French's sustained analysis of advertising posters and trailers is informative, particularly as she traces attempts to mobilize both highbrow and popular associations, usually by disguising commercial as erotic desire (or perhaps *vice versa*). French's prose sometimes creaks under the weight of Gramscian cultural analysis or the ubiquitous term 'postmodern', but is energetic and poised when quoting from a wide range of reviews and marketing material – Max Factor *Midsummer Night's Dream* cosmetics, anyone? – or trawling the web for perfectly parodic litcrit demotic, as this, from the Luhrmann film website: 'the Bard's group was bad. They kicked ass so bad his competitors used . . . to try to make their own bootlegged copies of his plays. The unauthorised "boots" were known as "The Bad Quartos". (Weird but true.)'

'Bad quartos' are one of the shibboleths of twentieth-century bibliography recently exposed to rigorous reconceptualization, particularly in considering anew the playtexts' relation to the practices of the early modern theatre. Many recent critics have also been newly interested in the prospect of Shakespeare as a collaborator, but it may be that the absence of explicitly collaborative patterns of academic inquiry make it (doubly) hard for us to imagine that joint creative process. In writing together a book about the fragmented playtext, *Shakespeare in Parts*, Simon Palfrey and Tiffany Stern offer a challengingly disintegrationist view of the early modern playtext even as they reassure us that their own process has been a dialogue in which each has been in full possession of the other's speeches. Arguing that the 'part' is the first, and perhaps the only, unit of text explicitly designed by Shakespeare for study and interpretation, this book reconstructs those cue-scripts as the building block of Shakespeare's aesthetics and stagecraft. Of all the works reviewed this year, it is Palfrey and Stern's that radically shifts the field, bringing carefully materialist and thematic interpretive energies to bear on a text at once disaggregated and fundamentally unified by their

analysis. Reconstructing sandwiches of cue and text, and imaginatively entering into the experience of the plays' first actors, Palfrey and Stern read the part as an interplay between anonymous cue and actor's role, to great literary and practical insight. Macduff's role, for example, is aptly characterized by belatedness, entering after a richly dilated cue, the play's response to his knocking that resonates through the Macbeths' guilt and the porter's equivocation. Tracing Macduff's speeches and cues reveals an appositional quality, a sense of alienation from a play already half over at his first entrance, and one which is characterized by delayed action, speech and recognition. There are so many insights in the book that it's difficult to pick out indicative ones, but I relished their analysis of how repeated, empty cues in *King Lear* prompt replies which signal failures of communication and the abrogation of dialogue, or how Richard III's loss of control of the interstice, the half-line cue, dramatizes his inevitable downfall and the shifting patterns of allegiance and betrayal in the play. Thinking about the ways actors would have read and understood their own parts, and how those understandings might mutate or become provisional during rehearsal and performance, gives a real imaginative scope to a book at once minutely detailed and cleverly inventive.

Film and other modes of performance feature prominently in Robert Shaughnessy's *Cambridge Companion to Popular Culture*. Sometimes performance is unproblematically figured as 'popular': my own essay on the BBC's *Age of Kings* sequence of history plays televised in 1960 rather falls into this trap, comparing this elite Reithian product with contemporaneous forms of serial production and consumption, particularly the soap opera *Coronation Street*. Diana E. Henderson is more properly reflexive in tracing the move away from the popular in the early reception of Shakespeare; Peter Holland writes on abbreviated Shakespeares performed in different amateur, professional and historical contexts; Barbara Hodgdon moves with her usual wit from the star phenomenon that was Richard Burbage, to Edmund Kean and Ian McKellen's carefully self-promoting website; W. B. Worthen considers the specific materiality of DVDs as Shakespearian texts.

Judith Buchanan's *Shakespeare on Film* is the most readable of this year's interest in media, and the one most likely to make it onto student reading lists. Both descriptive and analytical, Buchanan moves away from the focus on the most recent wave of Shakespearian film, reminding us of the aesthetic and interpretive contribution of silent cinema in impressive early chapters. Buchanan takes her vocabulary of adaptation from Dryden's *Preface to Ovid's Epistles*, thinking about the translation onto film in terms of 'metaphrase', 'paraphrase' and 'imitation': imitation has the highest cultural status even as it may be literally furthest from the Shakespearian text, and it is aspects of this mode in even apparently metaphrased or paraphrased films to which Buchanan directs us. Elsewhere the choice of texts is familiar but accessible – comparative studies on *The Tempest* and *A Midsummer Night's Dream* are flanked by chapters on Branagh's films and on American offshoots. Throughout there is a refreshing tone of enjoyment: the prose is accessible and practical, the volume is well-illustrated with stills, a select filmography gives locations for the copies of the major films discussed (I think she wants us to watch them, not just read about them) and modest 'Further Reading' sections after each chapter are helpful rather than exhaustive. Both a history and a model of interpretive enquiry, then, Buchanan's book is strongly recommended.

Buchanan writes engagingly about Asta Nielsen's *Hamlet* of 1920. In this film, an extraordinarily implausible central premise – that Hamlet is really a woman – is supported and given a curious credibility by cuts and emendations elsewhere to generate verisimilitude. Fortinbras is working with Claudius, whose guilt is manifest in a discovered dagger rather than an ambiguous response to a performed play and the testimony of a compromised Ghost. Tony Howard's *Women as Hamlet: Performance and Interpretation in Theatre, Film and Fiction* elaborates on this tendency towards feminizing the brooding Prince. A surprising number of Hamlets turn out to have been women, or vice versa, from Sarah Bernhardt to Frances de la Tour, and Howard traces a culture of reshaping Hamlet's gender via the novelist Mary Braddon and the painter Eugène Delacroix. Beginning with Angela Winkler's androgynous performance in *Hamlet 2000* directed by Peter Zadek at the Hanover Schauspielhaus, in which Hamlet emerged as an arrested, pre-pubertal child, Howard describes female Hamlets as 'a walking, speaking alienation effect', a way to denaturalize empathic Romantic sentiment at the play and reactivate its political and psychic strangeness. When Hazlitt announced 'It is we who are Hamlet', I don't think the first person pronoun was exactly inclusive, and it's not clear on reading about these female Hamlets that recasting the central role can ever quite counter that weight of gendered history. Often Howard's female Hamlets seem to draw on, and even corroborate surprisingly essentialized notions of gender norms: sensitivity, melancholia, unwillingness to commit violence, rather than challenging them. Director Richard Eyre anatomizes *Hamlet* as 'a war between the female, the feminine, within a man and the masculine within a man; and the story is effectively how you drive out the woman from the man': this gender *agon* still privileges the male, and indeed, constructs that slippage between 'female' and 'feminine' as merely a pathologized obstacle to secure male identity. It's not clear in this model that a female Hamlet would be any more subversive than the female Ophelia or Gertrude. There are radical moments though, too: the interest around the Irish singer Sinéad O'Connor's rumoured involvement in the Dublin *Hamlet's Nightmare*, for example, or another abortive casting of Fiona Shaw, who described the role in terms not explicitly, but troublingly, gendered: 'He's a sort of car crash between aspiration and self-hatred, and no other character represents the twentieth century and its anxieties so completely.'

A group of men discuss the ending of *Hamlet* in the Secured Housing Unit at Wabash Valley Correctional Facility in Indiana. This Denmark really is a prison. Cell E's inhabitant, 'a deep, rich, bass voice', criticizes Shakespeare for failing to offer an alternative to the retaliatory violence of the final scene, and proposes instead an additional speech by Hamlet: 'He needs to say to Laertes, "I don't want to become what my father was. I don't want to become what your father was. We've got to break this cycle, man, the two of us, right here and right now".' Moving, yes. Ethically preferable, yes. But Shakespeare? The idea that literature makes us better people is uncomfortable; most of us can't readily take on that moral role as educators; we're probably more at ease with the prisonhouse of language salted with Foucault's panopticon than with our own institutions of literal incarceration and their inmates. One disturbing effect of Amy Scott-Douglass's *Shakespeare Inside: The Bard behind Bars* is to rehabilitate precisely those humanist paradigms scorned by the recent generations of critics, and to make it seem churlish and ivory-towerish to resist the heartfelt reappropriation of Shylock's 'Hath not a Jew eyes' substituting 'prisoner' for 'Jew'. When Mike Smith, working in a dry cleaners having served his sentence for threatening his girlfriend and mother with a knife, says that his life was turned around by playing Desdemona in the Shakespeare behind Bars programme in prison, that is a statement about Shakespeare which is – shamefully? I'm not sure – unamenable to the kinds of academic debate we are used to. Scott-Douglass is a sensitive witness to the educational and theatrical programmes she observes; sometimes, inevitably, a little self-conscious in the expression of that sensitivity, but frustratingly unwilling to engage the differences between her day job as literature professor and this strange alternative world of penal Shakespeare as therapy, as transformation, as personal odyssey.

Alternative Shakespeares now seems a sort of oxymoronic title, and with the third volume, edited by Diana E. Henderson, we might feel that both the adjective and the plural have outlived any connotative shock. Of course, Henderson is acute about this, tackling the scepticism head on in her introduction, citing performance as one of the major new alternatives and further arguing that 'alternativity in and beyond Shakespeare studies has produced meaningful effects in our classrooms by enlarging the range of perspectives and readings allowed, and has contributed to more social inclusiveness in higher education'. I am unfairly reminded here by a dispiriting, if not surprising, report about the demography of English Studies students in the UK, finding that they/we are still whiter and richer and studded with X chromosomes, bluntly, than students in comparator humanities subjects, let alone the population at large (www.english.heacademy.ac.uk/explore/publications/newsletters/newsissue13/gawthrope.htm). In locating the sphere of influence as the classroom rather than the monograph, Henderson indirectly introduces her contributors' reflections on their own practice. Some seem more preoccupied with the profession of scholar than teacher – Mary Ellen Crane's smart dissection of acknowledgements and the networks of patronage and authority constructed by and through scholarly publication is a nice example – but there is throughout an abiding awareness and investigation of audience, in both a pedagogic and a dramatic sense. Robert Shaughnessy writes on silence and performativity in *Henry IV*, establishing his alternative credentials in a subheading 'Taking the piss'; Katherine Rowe sees screen and media Shakespeare as 'an arena for counter-Shakespearian practice'; W. B. Worthen returns, with characteristic deftness and insight, to the encounter between text and performance in the digital age. Interestingly, Henderson gives the afterword to a theatrical practitioner, Michael Boyd, artistic director of the Royal Shakespeare Company, who urges scholars to do more work on the 'Kremlinology' of Shakespeare's cryptic language, and identifies, in the book's final sentences, how easy it is for the most radical of Shakespearian intentions to be co-opted and neutralized by 'a conservative yearning' for an unalternative Shakespeare.

Perhaps a really alternative Shakespeare would not be Shakespeare at all. In addressing *The Early Stuart Masque: Dance, Costume and Music*, Barbara Ravelhofer sidesteps, elegantly, perhaps rather like Justinian Pagitt, a noted dancer who advised writing dance steps under the notes of the tune. No one performs masques in prison or suggests they should transform the possibilities of higher education. Ravelhofer offers a detailed, nuanced account which transforms the masque from a verbal to a visual semiotic, which is attentive to choreography, colour and aural chromatics. Jonson's contempt of the actors' bodies in his preface to *Hymenaei*, Ravelhofer suggests, has been inherited by scholarly writing on the genre which has previously followed poetry rather than performance as the masque's primary axis of interpretation. Her book instead re-imagines the visual, gestural difference between anti-masque and masque, and intriguingly relates the *mise-en-page* of masque texts to the tricks of perspective practised by Inigo Jones and his collaborators. I don't at all suggest that non-Shakespearian drama is an uncomplicated space in which neutral inquiry can be undertaken untroubled by the presentism always pressing on Shakespeare himself, but there is a scholarly ease in Ravelhofer's analysis which is genuinely, perhaps yearningly, alternative.

WORKS REVIEWED

Buchanan, Judith, *Shakespeare on Film* (Harlow, 2005)

Cartelli, Thomas and Katherine Rowe, *New Wave Shakespeare on Screen* (Cambridge, 2007)

French, Emma, *Selling Shakespeare to Hollywood: The Marketing of Filmed Shakespeare Adaptations from 1989 into the New Millennium* (Hatfield, 2006)

Henderson, Diana E., ed., *Alternative Shakespeares 3* (London and New York, 2008)

Howard, Tony, *Women as Hamlet: Performance and Interpretation in Theatre, Film and Fiction* (Cambridge, 2007)

O'Connor, John and Katharine Goodland, *A Directory of Shakespeare in Performance: 1970–2005. Volume 1: Great Britain* (Basingstoke, 2007)

Palfrey, Simon and Tiffany Stern, *Shakespeare in Parts* (Oxford, 2007)

Ravelhofer, Barbara, *The Early Stuart Masque: Dance, Costume, and Music* (Oxford 2006).

Scott-Douglass, Amy, *Shakespeare Inside: The Bard behind Bars* (London 2007)

Shaughnessy, Robert, ed., *The Cambridge Companion to Shakespeare and Popular Culture* (Cambridge 2007)

Thornton Burnett, Mark, *Filming Shakespeare in the Global Marketplace* (Basingstoke 2007)

3a. EDITIONS AND TEXTUAL STUDIES
reviewed by ERIC RASMUSSEN

Few new editions of Shakespeare can deservedly be called 'magisterial', but *The Winter's Tale* in the New Variorum Shakespeare is one of those happy few. Robert Kean Turner and Virginia Westling Haas have produced a great and glorious piece of scholarship, representing a lifetime or two of detailed research and careful synthesis. After going through its 974 pages with fairly fine combs, a graduate assistant and I found only a paltry number of trivial errors.[1] Although variorums are generally used as research tools rather than reading texts – and the searchable PDF file that comes on a disk bundled with this book will certainly make the vast amounts of data therein more readily accessible – the subtle brilliance of Turner's work also rewards sustained reading.

A New Variorum commentary note standardly provides the most salient remarks of previous critics, interspersed with sometimes lengthy responses by the editor. (In Marvin Spevack's variorum edition of *Antony and Cleopatra*, for instance, the fairly typical note on TLN 3305 includes forty lines of quotation from critics and an additional twenty-five lines of commentary from Spevack.)

With thanks to Arthur Evenchik.

[1] In the transcript of the Folio text, for 'Thornes,' read 'Thornes' (TLN 428); for '*King of*' read '*King / of*' (1187) with '*of*' beginning line 1188; for '*Pol.*' Read '*Po.*' (1975); for 'beene,' read 'beene.' (2850). The lone typographic error is 'Farmer(n' for 'Farmer (in' on p. 385. I am indebted to Trey Jansen for his assistance in checking the text and collations of this enormous work.

Turner's approach, on the other hand, is a model of elegant concision. He tends to preface each critical quotation with a single adverb or, at most, an adverbial phrase. Turner's adverbs are comparative, evaluative, perspicacious and playful. Moreover, the use of adverbs rather than adjectives signals that the focus is (unapologetically) on the *act* of criticism, as the voices of commentators through the centuries are introduced with such modifiers as 'more gently', 'less exactly', 'oddly', 'questionably', 'wrongly', 'more accurately', 'fruitlessly' and 'too delicately'. In the rare instances in which he ventures more than a single-word critique, Turner is nonetheless incisive, and often withering: 'Parry alleges that few people worry about such things, though it is evident that Sh. did.'

The only disappointment in this volume lies in the appendices. Although there is, to be sure, a wealth of material here on critical assessments, genre, theme, technique and the like, some of the essays are pedestrian: the one on the character of Antigonus runs to two paragraphs, the first beginning 'Not all critics treat Antigonus kindly', and the second, 'Other critics view Antigonus favorably.' And there is no remedy for the inherent problems of the variorum format: though 'Browes' (TLN 222) appears in the text on page 72, the note discussing it is not found until page 79. But in the presence of intellectual history on so grand a scale, such considerations are of no account. You may not call yourself a Shakespearian if you do not own this book.

Given the yin and yang of the review essay, this year's also features a somewhat less careful edition of *The Winter's Tale*, one that misspells *than* as *then* throughout. The New Cambridge Shakespeare edition of the play, edited by the late Susan Snyder and Deborah T. Curren-Aquino, explicitly states that 'since F spells both "then" and "than" as "then", we have silently emended the spelling to "than" when the modern sense requires it'. Never mind that this is modernization rather than emendation; the promised change does not occur, leaving the reader to confront 'More then the common blocks' (1.2.222), 'thicker then a cuckold's horn' (1.2.266), 'Whose sting is sharper then the

sword's' (2.3.86), 'faster then you'll tell money' (4.4.185) and 'I shall have more then you can dream of' (4.4.368). These absurd errors are complemented by a host of others in the text: the '*Enter*' has dropped out of the opening stage direction at 1.2; there's a stray apostrophe at the beginning of 1.2.420; spelling repeatedly shifts between American and British, sometimes within the space of a few lines (e.g., 'honor' at 1.2.307 but 'honour' at 1.2.437, 'honour' at 3.2.108 but 'honors' at 3.2.112); for 'Beside' read 'Besides' (3.3.11); for 'ere' read 'e'er' (5.1.11). The formatting is a mess,[2] as are the collations.[3] Like Elvis Costello, I used to be disgusted, but now I try to be amused.

An eloquent critic and a formidable textual scholar have joined forces to produce an impeccable *Shakespeare's Poems* for the Arden 3 series. To a reader (or reviewer) accustomed to finding at least a few errors in any new edition, Katherine Duncan-Jones and H. R. Woudhuysen will seem to have achieved the impossible: with two minor rule-proving exceptions, their text and collations are perfect.[4]

---

[2] The act/scene number is centred rather than flush left at 2.2.0; characters' names are in italic rather than in small caps at 2.2.0 SD, 2.2.2 SD, 2.2.4 SD, 2.2.14 SD, 2.2.15.1, and 2.2.17.1; 'Servants, Antigonus, and Lords' is not italicized in the SD at 2.3.26; 'Servant' is in roman rather than small caps at 2.3.192 SD and the entrance direction is flush left rather than centred; prose is indented as verse at 4.4.164.

[3] The apostrophes are reversed in the F readings at 1.1.9 and 1.1.16; lemmas are in all caps instead of small caps at 1.2.0 in the commentary, and again at 5.1.12 in the collations; there's an unneeded ellipsis at 2.1.0 SD; 2.1.71 for 'petty' read 'Petty' in F reading; 2.1.112, 116 for 'Beseech' read 'beseech' in F reading; 4.1.41 for '*Prethe*' read 'Prethe'; 4.3.7 for 'an' read '*an*'; 4.3.10 for 'with heigh' read '*with heigh*' in F reading; 4.3.15 for 'my deere' read '*my deere*'; 4.3.17 for 'here, and there' read '*here, and there*' in F reading; 4.4.222 for 'heele:' read '*heele:*' in F reading; 4.4.300 for 'Crpe' read '*Crpe*' in F reading; for 'undone' read 'vndone' in F reading; 4.4.474 for 'me as' read 'me, as' in F reading; 5.1.114 for 'upon us' read 'vpon vs' in F reading.

[4] There is a missing comma in line 1464 of *Lucrece*; the collation of *Lucrece* 50 gives 'ariued' as the Q1 reading, but should note that this is a variant reading that only appears in some copies of Q1 whereas other copies read 'arriued'.

In an innovative introductory essay that discusses *Venus and Adonis* and *The Rape of Lucrece* in tandem, instead of treating them sequentially, the editors suggest that these works were key to Shakespeare's financial success. As an actor-playwright, he could easily have been ruined by the closing of the theatres during the plague in 1592–4. Yet only two years after the playhouses reopened, Shakespeare purchased both a grant of arms and a mansion – an indication that 'the poems made him rich'. The Elizabethans, write Duncan-Jones and Woudhuysen, appreciated the 'immediate delight' provided by 'the decorative and harmonious qualities of Shakespeare's poetic rhetoric'; hence the frequency with which his contemporaries called him 'sweet'. To these early readers, *Venus and Adonis* was 'a kind of rhetorical manual for wooers' and 'almost a piece of soft porn'. *Lucrece*, in contrast, was seen as the more serious poem, which may explain why the miscellanies of 1600 include considerably more extracts from *Lucrece* than from *Venus*.

Duncan-Jones and Woudhuysen argue that in turning to non-dramatic verse, Shakespeare was 'liberated to explore aspects of female behaviour that were beyond the reach of even the most brilliant boy actor' and to indulge in 'copious soliloquizing [that] would not be tolerable in the playhouse'. The previous Arden editor, F. T. Prince, asserted that, 'after her violation, Lucrece loses our sympathy exactly in proportion as she gives tongue'. The present editors, detecting more than a hint of misogyny in this judgement, remind us that there was very little critical interest in *Lucrece* before the emergence of feminist criticism in the 1980s and that many of the poem's 'most powerful contemporary critics and analysts have been women'.

This edition highlights the often overlooked changes that Shakespeare made in his sources. Venus's traditional companion, her child Cupid, is wholly excluded from Shakespeare's poem. More crucially, although the classical sources present the story of Venus and Adonis as a 'fully consummated love affair', Shakespeare makes Adonis 'resolutely unresponsive to Venus's wooing'. Noting that *Venus* is composed of 199 stanzas, Duncan-Jones and Woudhuysen suggest that this number may imply 'incompleteness and unfulfillment'. They also see a connection between Shakespeare's Adonis, whom they view as 'still a child', and the poem's dedicatee, Southampton, 'who was legally, and perhaps physically, a youth rather than an adult'.

Among the many fresh contributions that the editors make to literary scholarship is a previously unnoted allusion in *Westward Ho!* to the black blood of Shakespeare's Lucrece. They are also the first to observe that two of the Sonnets in *The Passionate Pilgrim* (*PP* 4 and *PP* 11) are included in a manuscript collection of song settings and lute music by the distinguished composer John Wilson, who was apprenticed to Shakespeare's colleague John Heminges and almost certainly provided musical settings for the King's Men. Duncan-Jones and Woudhuysen suggest that early audiences of *Cymbeline*, hearing Iachimo's explicit identification with Tarquin as a fellow Roman ('Our Tarquin'), would have been shocked by his decision not to rape Innogen but simply to take notes of her body. And they point to the 'extremely arresting' use of 'Deuoring time' in Robert Parry's 1597 dedication to *Sinetes' Passions upon His Fortunes*, twelve years before the publication of Shakespeare's Sonnets (in which Sonnet 19 opens with 'Devouring Time, blunt thou the lion's paws'). The phrase may add to the evidence that the Sonnets circulated in manuscript before they were published.

The narrative poems are probably the only printed works that Shakespeare authorized, yet, as the editors point out, these texts 'have received surprisingly little close attention'. Woudhuysen's comprehensive discussion brings an end to this history of neglect, and includes at least one invitation to future research ('an investigation of watermark evidence might help to confirm' whether sheets A and N of *Lucrece* were printed on the same sheet). The Arden 3 text of *Lucrece* adopts the 'uncorrected' readings from the inner forms of sheets B and C (in lines 24, 31, 125 and 126), dismissing the 'corrected' readings as 'unnecessary' changes. Since there is, however, no way firmly to establish which press variants necessarily represent the uncorrected and which the corrected state, it is at least possible that those preferred by the editors actually represent the second state of the printed text. In other words, the 'uncorrected' readings may actually be corrections supplied by someone with an aesthetic sensibility equal to Duncan-Jones's and Woudhuysen's – such as the author himself.

The major textual innovation in this edition is the retention, throughout *Lucrece*, of Q1's small caps for proper names. Woudhuysen argues that 'the capitals contribute to the poem's gravity and take on a neo-classical inscriptional form'. He realizes that retaining the small caps is a 'bold and probably controversial' choice, but it is a reasoned decision, and one that reflects the growing awareness among textual critics of typography's importance as a means of articulating meaning. Since proper names in small caps are unheard of in modernized editions, readers may respond haltingly at first, like the misguided actors who give special emphasis to the capitalized words in the First Folio. But once the initial strangeness subsides, these same readers may appreciate the chance to encounter the text as it was, in all probability, intended by its author.

The few errors of omission in this edition are trivial: the commentary for the *Passionate Pilgrim* 9.12 should signal that 'showed' requires a syllabic 'è'; Gary Taylor's emendation of 'her stained excuse' to 'her stain's excuse' in *Lucrece* 1316 probably deserved comment; the assertion on page 74 that lines 386–95 of *Lucrece* 'were also printed in Sir John Suckling's *Fragmenta Aurea* (1646)' is imprecise, and ignores the tantalizing implications of Suckling's variant version of the lines, which are set in the six-line stanza used for *Venus* rather than the seven-line rhyme royal of *Lucrece* and may thus provide evidence of a lost version. I also think it would have been wise to omit the entire blank page that the editors devote to the present absence of the 'lost motto' for the Earl of Rutland's impresa, for which Shakespeare was paid 44 shillings.

In his excellent new edition of Q1 *Romeo and Juliet* in the Cambridge Early Quartos series, Lukas Erne says that he 'does not advocate study of the first quarto for its own sake'. Rather, his edition is intended to complement the Q2 edition in the New Cambridge Shakespeare series, and thus 'invites

comparative study of the different versions'. Erne's trenchant introduction explores and dismisses various theories about the origins of Q1: 'adaptation for touring in the provinces is an unconvincing hypothesis about what would have been an uneconomic theatrical practice'; 'the memorial reconstruction theory failed to produce a believable narrative'. Though his exacting analysis appears contemptuous in places ('the figures resulting from Irace's painstaking research arguably belie the conclusions she draws from them'), it is never unfair. Like many recent editors, myself included, Erne concludes that the practice Humphrey Mosley describes of actors preparing transcripts of plays from memory to give to friends 'accounts rather better for the evidence than the theories proposed by most twentieth-century scholars'.

Erne has contended for several years that abridgement of Shakespeare's lengthy 'literary' dramatic texts 'must have been a standard feature of the preparation for performance in London', an argument he now applies specifically to Q1 *Romeo and Juliet*. If Q1 represents such an abridgement, or an actor's transcription of such an abridgement, then it 'probably takes us as close as we can get to the play as it would have been performed by Shakespeare and his fellow players'. The rehabilitation of Q1 is significantly advanced by a listing of the Q1 readings that were adopted in the edited texts prepared by Pope, Theobald, Capell and Malone. As Erne observes, 'before the New Bibliography introduced the label "bad quarto" [these early editors] found that many of Q1's readings were remarkably good, so much so that they preferred them to those in Q2'. All of this leaves open the question of why Erne declines to advocate study of Q1 for its own sake.

There are a few slips in Erne's text: for 'lye' read 'lie' (10.139); for 'pray thee' read 'prithee' (7.80); 'palmer's kiss' (4.167) is usually rendered as 'palmers' kiss'. Printers' devils seem to have inserted rogue blank lines at 9.19, 13.20 and 20.35; similarly, there are blank lines above and below '*She kneels down*' at 14.120 but not surrounding the identical stage direction at 16.20. Prose lines are wrongly indented at 2.53 and 16.5; verse lines are wrongly indented at 14.98, 15.16 and 20.95. The illustrations are rather poor throughout – the one of a double-page opening of Q1 on page 38 is so dark as to be unreadable.

In a strikingly original new book, *Shakespeare and the Rise of the Editor*, Sonia Massai focuses on the long-neglected editorial activities that took place during the seventeenth century, beginning with manuscript annotations in printed plays. Her survey of annotated quartos from the period, supplemented by several excellent illustrations, represents a real contribution to textual studies. Some of these annotations were probably proof corrections, such as those in the Huntington copy of *The First Part of the Contention* (1600). Written in the outer forme of sheet B, these corrections were subsequently made in the type, and the corrected readings are found in other copies of the same edition. Other annotations were almost certainly made by later readers. Massai observes that these were often incorporated into subsequent editions: a manuscript correction in the Huntington copy of Q1 *Richard II*, for instance, crosses out an incorrect 'yorke' speech-prefix and inserts 'King', a change that is made in Q2. She argues that publishers who were committed 'to the perfection of dramatic copy' may have procured annotated and corrected copies of original editions to use as printer's copy for new reprints. (Perhaps Massai ought to have considered the possibility of reverse directionality as well. That is, might an early owner of a play quarto have borrowed a 'newly corrected' edition and marked any changes in his copy of the original? In such a scenario, the annotations would then derive from, rather than anticipate, the later print edition.)

In an extended analysis of the multiple editions of the history plays that Andrew Wise published between 1597 and 1602[5] – Q1 *Richard II* (1597), Q2 (1598), Q3 (1598); Q1 *Richard III* (1597), Q2 (1598), Q3 (1602); Q0 *1 Henry IV* (1598), Q1 (1598), Q2 (1599) – Massai finds substantive variants in speech-prefixes, stage directions and dialogue in the second and third quartos of these plays, indicating that they were seemingly corrected as they were repeatedly reprinted. Since these corrections 'imply some familiarity with the fictive world of the play', she provocatively suggests that the correct-ing annotator may have been Shakespeare himself. Such a speculation, she notes, might be encouraged by the title-page of Q2 *1 Henry IV*, which advertises the reprinted text as 'Newly corrected by W. Shakes-peare'. Elsewhere, Massai points to Heywood's longstanding collaboration with Nicholas and John Okes as evidence that Heywood may have prepared corrected copy for the reprints of his plays, and to Dryden's professional association with Henry Herringman to suggest that Dryden is at least a 'potential candidate' for the role of annotator of the printer's copy used for F4 *Coriolanus*.

In a book filled with fresh perspectives, the most important may be Massai's re-thinking of the motivation behind the infamously false dates on the Pavier quartos. Conventional wisdom (as in my entry on the subject in the *Oxford Companion to Shakespeare*) maintains that when the King's Men learned of Thomas Pavier's planned collection of ten Shakespeare plays in 1619, they obtained a letter from the Lord Chamberlain that was sent to the court of the Stationers' Company, whereupon it was ordered that in the future 'no plays that his majesty's players do play' should be printed without the consent of the King's Men. This standard account has assumed that presswork must have been already completed on several of Pavier's quartos (those that are correctly dated '1619'), and that the question was how to handle the plays yet to be printed. Greg suggested that since 'it was no longer safe to put the current date on the titles . . . it was decided that the dates on the titles should be those of the editions that were being reprinted, so that if necessary the reprints could be passed off as copies of the same'. Thus, Pavier's quartos of *King Lear* and *Henry V* were both fraudulently dated '1608', and *The Merchant of Venice* and *A Midsummer Night's Dream* were dated '1600'.

---

[5] Massai's assertion that Andrew Wise published 'five Shakespearian quartos' is surely a slip for 'plays' – Wise, in fact, published three quartos each of *1H4*, *R2* and *R3*, along with Q1 *Much Ado* and Q1 *2H4*. There are only a few other errors in the book: for 'two editions of *Everyman*' read 'four' (p. 41); for '1909' read '1908a' (twice on p. 112); for 'Hollan' read 'Holland' (p. 239); for 'Emry' read 'Emrys' (p. 240).

However, as Massai brilliantly observes, the fact that 'two of the plays whose rights Pavier *personally* owned bear the wrong date on their title pages' would seem to undermine Greg's narrative. She proposes that Pavier's 'highly unusual decision to pre-date some *but not all* of his quarto editions of 1619' may have been prompted by 'an attractive business proposal rather than by the Court order'. In Massai's view, it was Isaac Jaggard who, perhaps already looking forward to the publication of the First Folio and wanting to 'whet, rather than satisfy, readers' demand for a new collection', persuaded Pavier to issue his ten quartos – which were printed in the Jaggard shop – as a nonce collection, a volume gathering editions that are more recent and seemingly older. In support of this theory, Massai points to collections such as William Alexander's *The Monarchicke Tragedies*, which includes two new plays dated 1607 and two older plays bearing their 1604 issue dates. Pavier's false dates, she argues, were thus intended to deceive not the stationers or the King's Men but potential readers, who were led to believe that they were purchasing a nonce collection.

Massai's attractive narrative has already been endorsed by John Jowett. In *Shakespeare and Text*, Jowett concurs that Pavier's collection of new editions, along with books apparently taken from old stock, 'would have offered far more competition to the Folio if it had declared itself to be issued uniformly in 1619'. Like Massai, Jowett sees the form that the Pavier collection took as preparing the market for the First Folio: 'It revived the visibility of Shakespeare in the print medium at a time when it had faded away, while at the same time creating the very conditions in which the 1623 collection could claim to offer a superior and more authoritative text than those that had come before.'

Jowett's *Shakespeare and Text* in the Oxford Shakespeare Topics series is a predictably splendid introduction to textual studies, providing not only practical tools, such as a glossary of bibliographical terms, but also (unusually, for a book aimed at non-specialist readers) some insight into the political dimensions of the profession. Jowett acknowledges that there is often 'much tortuous

and impenetrable disagreement' in the field, particularly in authorship studies, and he highlights some unpleasant clashes, such as when a feminist critic challenged the findings of an analytical bibliographer 'by disparaging [his] gender, his specialism, and his reliance on an electron microscope'. But Jowett also shows the more serene side of the business of editing, one in which 'textual scholars spend many hours happily or unhappily collating copies of the edition, reading each copy letter by letter, usually against a photocopy of one copy that is used as a control text, on the lookout for unrecorded press variants'.

It is unusual for Jowett to make a factual error, but he slips when discussing the new plays added to the 1664 issue of the Shakespeare Third Folio and oddly implies that *The Two Noble Kinsmen* appeared 'in this volume, and in the later seventeenth- and eighteenth-century editions that followed it'. In fact, the play did not appear in F3, nor in F4, nor in any edition of Shakespeare until Knight included it in the 'Doubtful Plays' volume of his *Pictorial Shakespeare* in 1841; Dyce admitted it into the Shakespeare canon in his second edition in 1866.

Stephen Orgel's new essay that supplants Anthony Hecht's introduction in the updated edition of the New Cambridge *Sonnets* (in which G. Blakemore Evans's text remains unchanged) is an energetic tour of the 'emotional turmoil and non-vanilla sex' of the Sonnets. Although it's *de rigueur* for such introductions to mention Francis Meres's praise of Shakespeare's 'sugred sonnets among his private friends', Orgel is the first, so far as I know, to note the oddity of the adjective: 'it is difficult to imagine "sugred" applying to poems like "They that have pow'r to hurt and will do none" (94) or "Th'expense of spirit in a waste of shame" (129)'. Elsewhere in his essay, Orgel roundly condemns the Capell/Malone emendation of Sonnet 129's 'proud and very wo' to 'prov'd, a very woe', arguing that it manages 'both to falsify the text and abolish its history'. In Evans's text, however, the emendation 'prov'd' remains proudly undisturbed.

There are two or three glaring errors in Orgel's essay. He identifies the author of *Delia* and *The Complaint of Rosamond* as 'Drayton' rather than

Samuel Daniel. The assertion on page 5 that 'Thorpe's copies (of the Sonnets) certainly did not come from Shakespeare' would appear to contradict the claim on the next page that 'Shakespeare certainly might have given him a manuscript of sonnets to publish.' And, in an account of Shakespeare's best-selling plays, Orgel unaccountably ignores Shakespeare's best-selling play:

In his own time, Shakespeare was much better known to the reading public as a poet than as a playwright . . . *The Rape of Lucrece* . . . circulated far more widely than any of the plays, appearing in six editions during his life . . . The most popular of the plays for Elizabethan and Jacobean readers were *Richard III* and *Richard II*, each of which went through five editions before 1616.

This would be true only if the *six* quarto editions of *1 Henry IV* published before 1616 did not exist. In fact, it is *1H4* that appears to have been the most popular dramatic text for readers during Shakespeare's lifetime, and the extant editions suggest that this play circulated as widely as, if not more so than, *The Rape of Lucrece* during this period. (Q6 of *Lucrece* (1616) may have appeared after Shakespeare's death; given that it is the first edition of either of the narrative poems to feature Shakespeare's name on the title-page, Duncan-Jones and Woudhuysen speculate that 'his death may have encouraged publishers to exploit his celebrity and name him as the author'.)

As it happens, Jowett's *Shakespeare and Text* makes a similar error in asserting that 'by 1623 . . . *Richard III* had established itself as Shakespeare's

most popular play with readers, having run to six editions'. In fact, by 1623 (as Jowett correctly notes in an appendix listing 'Shakespeare in Early Editions and Manuscripts'), *1H4* had appeared in *seven* quarto editions. The confusion may be caused by the nomenclature: since the fragmentary first edition of *1H4* is often called 'Q0', it is easy to forget that 'Q1' is really the second edition, 'Q2' the third, and so forth. But, given the recent surge of interest in Shakespeare as a literary dramatist, we surely cannot allow this '0' without a figure to skew accounts of the early publication history of his plays.

WORKS REVIEWED

Jowett, John, *Shakespeare and Text*. Oxford Shakespeare Topics (Oxford, 2007).

Massai, Sonia, *Shakespeare and the Rise of the Editor* (Cambridge, 2007).

Shakespeare, William, *The First Quarto of Romeo and Juliet*, ed. Lukas Erne. The New Cambridge Shakespeare: The Early Quartos (Cambridge, 2007).

Shakespeare's Poems, ed. Katherine Duncan-Jones and H. R. Woudhuysen. The Arden Shakespeare Third Series (London, 2007).

The Sonnets, ed. G. Blakemore Evans, updated edition with a new introduction by Stephen Orgel. The New Cambridge Shakespeare (Cambridge, 2006).

The Winter's Tale, ed. Susan Snyder and Deborah T. Curren-Aquino. The New Cambridge Shakespeare (Cambridge, 2007).

The Winter's Tale, ed. Robert Kean Turner and Virginia Westling Haas, with Robert A. Jones, Andrew J. Sabol, and Patricia E. Tatspaugh. The New Variorum Shakespeare (New York, 2005).

3b. EDITIONS AND TEXTUAL STUDIES: THE RSC *COMPLETE WORKS*
reviewed by JOHN JOWETT

OVERVIEW

The RSC Shakespeare is the first freshly edited Complete Works since the Oxford Shakespeare of 1986.[1] It is in many ways a substantial achievement: the outcome of many years' work, a significantly different edition from its rivals, and a handsomely solid artifact. However, for reasons that will be explained, it has been edited according to

---

[1] William Shakespeare, *Complete Works*, ed. Jonathan Bate and Eric Rasmussen (Macmillan, 2007).

principles that, though beguiling at first glance, do not withstand scrutiny.

Questions of design and apparatus content have been carefully reconsidered at every level. The book, unusually for a Complete Works, presents most texts in a single column. The layout is therefore unusually spacious, and there is scope for stronger differentiation between verse and prose than is customary. The text is presented in an attractive and readable typeface. A distinct advantage over the Oxford Shakespeare in its current format is that the RSC edition supplies commentaries at the foot of the page. A panel of 'key facts' is printed after the introduction to each work. These usefully include a plot summary, a list of major parts with a statistical analysis of the length of each role, an analysis of the percentage of verse and prose, a discussion of date, a summary of sources, and a note on the text. Skeleton textual notes are printed after each text. There are black and white illustrations, mostly depicting scenes from RSC productions.

The editors make a strong and convincing team. Jonathan Bate is one of our finest Shakespeare critics and Eric Rasmussen amongst the most experienced and rigorous of Shakespearian textual scholars. Within the scope of their remit, they have done an excellent job. Rasmussen ensures that the text is reliable as regards both accuracy and consistency of presentation. The objections to the procedure I register below do not detract from the rigour and determination with which it has been implemented. The commentaries, supervised and partly written by Héloïse Sénéchal, offer apt and well-judged but unofficious help. Pre-publication publicity made much of the attention to sexual innuendo in the notes. For the most part this is in fact not overdone, though at *Romeo and Juliet* 2.3.106, where 'too much for a score' is glossed 'not worth having sex with', the note seems to impose a modern sense of 'score', and the information that Giulio Romano was 'infamous for erotic works', if true, seems determinedly beside the point.

In the general and individual introductions, Jonathan Bate writes with his customary engaging fluency. The pitch is slightly populist, aimed at the general reader as much as the academic community. New Historicism is pointedly left behind. Bate's General Introduction starts off with a section with a heading that recalls but vitally alters Jan Kott's early version of presentism, proclaiming 'Shakespeare our Perennial Contemporary'. The concerns of recent criticism are not neglected, but they are subordinated to a view of Shakespeare as accessible – edition permitting – and as worthy of access, to us, to all. As might be expected of Bate, in his introductions to individual plays he celebrates their reworking of classical tropes, and insists on their mythic and erotic textures, observing both the simplicity of the initial idea and the complex sophistication of Shakespeare's treatment of it. As might be expected too, and as is signalled when he invokes Shakespeare as universal genius, Bate often harks back to Romantic criticism to establish his bearings. And, while acknowledging that 'Shakespeare is the least autobiographical of great writers' (p. 1861), he is not put off from speculating about the pressure of life events such as the death of Shakespeare's son Hamnet on the imagination that formed the plays.

As compared with those in editions with introductions in many hands, such as the Riverside and Norton, the essays benefit from the consistency of perspective that allows differences of tone to respond to the complexion of each play. The introduction to *Twelfth Night* is a beguiling meditation on the eros of the divided self. The opening to the introduction to *Troilus and Cressida* hits the reader with a series of compact and well-aimed punches: 'It is highly intelligent, rich in rhetorical complexity and linguistic invention, mentally rigorous, morally sceptical, sexually charged, full of dangerous intellectual and political energy, markedly unpleasant.' Bate resorts to touches of sentimental character-based criticism such as will raise eyebrows in the academy: 'There are moments of exceptional tenderness between the Macbeths. Yet there is an emptiness at the core of their relationship.' The idiom itself – 'There are moments . . . there is something' – seems resolutely nostalgic. But Bate immediately lifts his game with a more arresting observation, 'The play is scarred by images of

sterility and harrowed by glimpses of dead babies.'
It is perhaps not so much the thought as Bate's
arresting language that make this a valuable point
of entry to the tragedy.

'WE HAVE EDITED A REAL BOOK'

There is, then, plenty to admire in the RSC edition. It will seem an excellent proposition to those
who do not search far into the nature of the editing
itself. My main critique of the edition is that it is
built on unsound foundations. This edition makes
high claims for itself; it is a 'fresh and definitive
edition for the twenty-first century', and in the
General Introduction Bate compares himself with
Samuel Johnson. If these claims are unjustified, the
main reason is that the RSC edition's absolute intellectual foundation on a nexus between the Folio as
an edition associated with the King's Men and itself
as an edition commissioned by the Royal Shakespeare Company is fatally misconceived in ways that
affect it systemically.

'Our claim to originality is that we have edited a
real book (the First Folio), not an imaginary construct ("the plays as they came from Shakespeare's
hand" . . . or "the plays as first performed" . . .)'
(56). This claim seems to be sustained in the
faux-facsimile title-page. Here the words 'William
Shakespeare' and 'Complete Works' appear in an
early modern typeface; the words are not reproduced from the Folio itself, where the expression
'Complete Works' is nowhere used. Bate's manifesto sounds persuasive, but the contrast it urges
between a 'real book' and an 'imaginary construct'
conflates two definitions of what it means to 'edit'.
The first sense is to follow a copy text, hence in
Bate's parlance to 'edit', or reproduce, 'a real book'.
The second sense is to depart from a copy text in
order to present something that differs from it, a
process that can be said to involve 'editing' as a
process of constituting the 'imaginary construct'. It
would seem that the first is clearly preferable, as the
second involves conjecture, falsification and editorial idealism. Yet to subject a 'real book' (by which
Bate presumably means not a specific object but an
edition) to scholarly editing is, absolutely inevitably,
to construct something different from the book (or
edition) itself – and nowhere more clearly so than
in the example under review. To edit is to recognize that the book is not, after all, best suited for
the purposes of a contemporary readership of the
text in the book.

It is in fact the text in the book, and not the
physical book itself, that is subject to the process
of editing. Excellent high-quality digital images of
the Folio are freely available online and meet most
of the needs of those who need to see the *book*.
Those who need to read the *text* of Shakespeare
turn to editions because they recognize the usefulness of editors not only reproducing the book
but also altering it. Editors definitively both follow
a copy text (which for a Shakespeare play may or
may not be best located in the Folio) and alter it
to construct something other than that copy text.
The RSC edition itself freely accepts quarto and
editorial readings where they are needed, as Bate
explains, to 'make sense'. 'Sense' is here seen as a
self-evident thing that needs no grounding in the
specifics of what makes sense to whom and when.
As we will see, this is by no means a merely abstract
or hypothetical consideration.

Bate's formulation therefore makes no acknowledgement that if one 'edits' a 'book' by changing its words, one inevitably creates a 'construct'.
The claim to have 'edited a real book' begs as
many questions as the Folio editors' own claim to
have 'Published according to the True Originall
Copies', a claim that, as again will be noted further below, lacks credibility. What the RSC edition
actually offers is very much a construct, an idealized
and modernized adaptation of the Folio, to which
is added all matter conservatively attributable to
Shakespeare but not in the Folio. In every respect
the adherence to the Folio is compromised. The
edition does not follow Folio punctuation and
spelling, because it is modernized – though it preserves a selection of Folio punctuation, much as the
Riverside edition preserves a selection of original
spellings. It does not follow Folio textual substance,
because it is committed to the emendation of
error – though it retains some readings that demonstrably are errors. It does not follow Folio lineation,

because it emends as occasion demands. It does not follow Folio stage directions, and although it straps on a second layer of stage directions in the margin and uses square brackets in the main run, it still alters some directions without record. Though it recognizes that Folio act–scene divisions do not for the majority of Shakespeare's plays reflect performance practice, it follows them, but compromises this system by adding on numbered 'running scenes', an arbitrarily defined and entirely modern system based on a filmic sense of action and respecting neither the act unit nor the scene unit of the original text. Most conspicuously, it does not follow Folio canon. Recognizing that an edition of Shakespeare simply cannot, after all, be an edition of the Folio, it includes the poems and the collaborative works that the Folio excluded.

THE FOLIO AS A REPRINT

The RSC edition's treatment of copy is well illustrated by considering examples predominantly taken from *Richard II*, which in F was mostly set in type from the Third Quarto of 1598. The quarto copy had been annotated with reference to a theatre manuscript, a typical procedure in the preparation of Folio plays. In this case the annotation was only about 50 per cent efficient, so that the Folio introduces what are potentially valuable readings from the manuscript whilst retaining what are usually errors introduced by the succession of quarto compositors.

The adherence to F where it introduces new readings for the first time can throw up interesting if questionable readings. In *Richard II* 5.5.31 Richard explains 'Thus play I in one prison many people'. This is not, of course, the familiar text, for where the RSC edition has 'prison', the usual reading is Q1's 'person'. 'Prison' makes completely good sense, and has what might be called the virtue of the unfamiliar. Nevertheless, I suspect that, however justified by the broader framework of the edition, F's reading is here wrong. Richard's point in the lines that follow and that elaborate the initial idea is the contrast between the one actor and the diversity of roles. That he might hypothetically play

in more than one prison but is confined to a single one seems irrelevant.

This is not to say that the edition's adherence to F is always rigorous to a fault. At *Hamlet* 3.4.72 Hamlet describes Claudius in the edition as 'Blasting his wholesome brother', as in Q2, where F has him 'blasting his wholsom breath'. It is the Q2 reading that is here familiar. Is F necessarily wrong? It could be glossed as 'blighting old Hamlet's wholesome life'. It could be defended, in much the same way as the edition defends 'prison', as 'a purposeful alteration, not a printer's error'. My own suspicion is that the editorial decision to emend the Folio is here justified, but the reading is no more suspect than 'prison'. It would be unreasonable, given the limited space available for textual explication, to expect the edition to establish a transparent self-consistency in treating such cases. However, the recurrence in F of readings that are possible but less plausible alternatives to more familiar quarto counterparts presents a particular challenge. This challenge is all the more tricky to handle because the later origination of Folio versions of plays leads us to expect that the deliberated changes will on the whole result in improvements, and because the edition's initial criteria for determining error are weakly defined.

With readings that F inherits from quarto copy it is clearer that it is in error. At *Richard II* 2.1.17–20 York laments that Bolingbrook's ear:

> is stopped with other flatt'ring sounds,
> As praises, of his state: then there are found
> Lascivious metres, to whose venom sound
> The open ear of youth doth always listen,

Thus the RSC edition, which follows F on the whole, whilst correcting 'sound' in the second line quoted to 'found'. F reads:

> is stopt with other flatt'ring sounds
> As praises of his state: then there are sound
> Lasciuious Meeters, to whose venom sound
> The open eare of youth doth alwayes listen.

The RSC reading is actually that of the Third Quarto, in which the text does not read 'of his state: then there are sound' but 'of his state: then there are found'. But this itself corrects the Second Quarto, which reads 'of whose state the wise are found', which itself corrects the First Quarto's 'of whose taste the wise are found'. Q1 is, for sure, clearly in need of emendation here. Most editors follow it as general copy, but here emend it to read 'of whose state the wise are fond'. Q3's alteration is mere guesswork. It is not even good guesswork, for, if the manuscript had read 'then there are found', the Q1 compositor is most unlikely to have read the manuscript as 'the wise are found'. So Q3 inherits an erroneous reading and miscorrects it, and this forms the basis for the text in the RSC edition. Unfortunately the documentation is not sufficiently refined to capture these nuances. The textual note simply reads '**found** = Q. F = sound'. If Q1 read 'then there are found', the status of F and the decision to emend it would be simple, but it does not. As it is, the foundation of the Folio reading for the whole phrase in larger error is left invisible.

The example is not isolated. In the same play at 3.4.55 the Gardener observes that the weeds of state 'Are pulled up root and all by Bullingbrook'. 'Pulled' is another printer's error in Q3 that is inherited in F. Q1 has the more unusual, and more physically disruptive and violent, 'pluckt'. There is every reason to suppose that Shakespeare used the verb to 'pluck', and that the Q3 compositor substituted the verb to 'pull' that finds its way into the RSC edition. At 3.4.74 the RSC edition reads 'To a dear friend of the Duke of York's', which is metrically defective because it follows the Folio, which itself follows Q3 in accidentally omitting the qualifier 'good' before 'Duke'. At 3.4.108 it is the turn of Q2 to be indirectly preferred over Q1 when the Gardener reports of the Queen, 'Here she did drop a tear'. Q1 has the verb as 'fall', perhaps a significant word in view of both the play's and the scene's echoes of the biblical Fall of Adam and Eve.

In truth, Rasmussen's task is unenviable, because the editorial task defies consistent regulation. In the cases considered so far, the Folio makes sense, but is almost certainly wrong. However, the editors are prepared to remove errors in quarto reprints in other instances where they make sense. At 4.1.113

the edition follows not F but Q1 in reading 'Of noble Richard! Then true noblesse would'. Q2 altered 'noblesse' to 'noblenesse', which is the Folio reading also.

Such inconsistencies are symptomatic of an underlying problem, which is how to define what the edited text actually represents, when it does not rigorously follow the Folio, but nevertheless knowingly accepts many Folio readings that depart from what Shakespeare wrote and from what would have been performed on stage. *Richard II* is particularly prone to display the difficulties, but they are widespread, for many Folio texts are set from quarto copy of one kind or another. Whether that copy has been modified or not, the procedure of following F without an inbuilt mechanism for fully acknowledging and dealing with its deficiencies will leave the text inaccurate.

REPOINTING THE FOLIO

Though the RSC edition is in modern spelling, a sprinkling of Folio-style punctuation is deferentially interspersed with modern features. Here is a passage from F and its representation in the RSC edition:

F—

> To haue no Schreene between this part he
>   plaid,
> And him he plaid it for, he needes will be
> Absolute *Millaine*, Me (poore man) my
>   Librarie
> Was Dukedome large enough: of temporall
>   roalties
> He thinks me now incapable. Confederates
> (so drie he was for Sway) with King of *Naples*

RSC—

> To have no screen between this part he played,
> And him he played it for, he needs will be
> Absolute Milan. Me – poor man – my library
> Was dukedom large enough: of temporal
>   royalties
> He thinks me now incapable. Confederates –
> So dry he was for sway – wi'th'King of
>   Naples . . .

This passage has been chosen because it demonstrates well the close relation between the Folio and RSC pointing. To discuss its detail is not to quibble about execution, but to address the basic principles of the RSC edition's declared aim to give 'more weight to Folio punctuation than many editors'. In the passage, the comma after 'played' is, as can be seen, true to the Folio, and so in accordance with this aim. It conflicts with normal modern usage that finds no place for a comma in the construction 'between A and B'. The risk is that this falsely intimates that a new clause begins at 'And'.

The two pairs of dashes in the passage follow the Folio's parentheses, whilst accepting the sound practice of finding a more modern equivalent. But they are stylistically ill at odds with the Folio colon after 'enough', which is preserved in letter as well as spirit. Setting aside this intermixing of Jacobean and modern pointing, the colon is certainly defensible on its own terms and in its own punctual context. It helps the reader to see that the repetition of 'me' may be for rhetorical emphasis: not only '[as for] me, . . . my library was dukedom large enough', but also '[as for] me, . . . of temporal royalties he thinks me now incapable'. At a level of reading beyond the primary establishment of syntax and sense, this second reading is valid, and demonstrates well the syntactical fluidity of the whole passage. Its validity is reinforced by the Folio's full-stop after 'incapable'.

However, this full-stop, and hence the entire construction of the passage in the RSC text, is seriously misleading to the modern reader. 'Confederates' is a verb, the crucial and necessary suspended construction being 'He . . . confederates'. To the modern reader unfamiliar with the passage, 'Confederates' will probably seem to be a noun: the punctuation implies it. Given the absence of a conjunction ('he thinks . . . [and] confederates'), a modern actor reading the passage would need to focus on clearly sustaining the flow of meaning from 'He' to 'confederates', not least because the verb governs no less than the following five lines. To this end, the putative 'Me . . . he thinks me' would probably have to be subordinated. The syntax of the passage is complex enough without imposing unnecessary hurdles and misplaced emphases based on a literalistic approach to F's punctuation. There is a particular reason to relinquish the literality of Folio punctuation in this play (and several others). The pointing of *The Tempest*, where it is distinctive, clearly derives from the belated manuscript of Ralph Crane, prepared for the specific purpose of giving the text a mid Jacobean 'literary' flavour that postdates the author's death, effaces the author's punctuation and shifts the text away from theatre culture.

It must therefore seriously be asked whether the RSC edition's adherence to the Folio, in the context of an edition modernized in spelling and punctuation, is more conducive to the reading of Shakespeare than the more thoroughly modern pointing of other editions:

To have no screen between this part he played
And him he played it for, he needs will be
Absolute Milan. Me, poor man, my library
Was dukedom large enough. Of temporal royalties
He thinks me now incapable; confederates,
So dry he was for sway, wi'th'King of Naples . . .

To have no screen between this part he played
And him he played it for, he needs will be
Absolute Milan. Me, poor man – my library
Was dukedom large enough – of temporal royalties
He thinks me now incapable; confederates,
So dry he was for sway, wi'th' King of Naples . . .

VERSE AND PROSE

The RSC edition notably rejects the usual convention of indenting the first lines of speeches where they make up the second part of a verse-line:

LEONTES   No, not these twenty years [full-stop
                        missing]
PERDITA   So long could I
    Stand by a looker-on.
PAULINA   Either forbear,

The convention of indenting was virtually unknown before the eighteenth century, and is abandoned because 'the Folio does not use it, and nor did actors' cues in the Shakespearian theatre'

(p. 58). However, the Folio also did not use any system of line numbering, and it might be considered over-insistent on the conventions of seventeenth-century typography to introduce a numbering that counts the above passage as four lines rather than two.

Especially in view of this typographical conservatism, it is disquieting to find that changes to lineation are nowhere recorded. This does not mean that changes are minimal or non-existent. The edition usually alters Folio lineation as occasion demands in accordance with standard editorial practice: necessarily so, as Folio compositors themselves demonstrably altered lineation. I noted one instance where the edition goes further, against the claim to have 'leaned towards the preservation of Folio layout' where there is 'ambiguity'. Where F unambiguously presents:

> The Statue is but newly fix'd; the Colour's
> Not dry.

– we here read:

> The statue is but newly fixed; the colour's
> not dry.

This shows a painfully indelicate disregard for the emotive effect of feminine endings in late Shakespeare.

AUGMENTING THE FOLIO THEATRICALLY

As mentioned above, the RSC edition adds a second tier of stage directions in the right margin. This tacitly recognizes that, for all its debt to theatre manuscripts, the Folio remains deficient for the purposes of studying Shakespeare's plays with performance in mind. The added stage directions are distinguished, as well as by position, by use of a smaller and variant font. They do not obviate the need for brackets in the main conventional run of stage directions. For an elaborate instance, in *Henry VIII* at 1.4.92 the stage direction based partly on F's '*Choose Ladies, King and An Bullen*' reads '[*The Masquers*] *choose Ladies* [*for the dance*]. [*The*] *King* [*chooses*] *Anne Bullen*'. A less familiar

intervention in the standard stage directions is the occasional downward arrow: '[↓*Exit Demetrius*↓]'. This means that Demetrius could exit either where the direction is placed or later on in the scene. The direction itself belongs to the first tier because an exit is necessary and fundamental, but the direction is not found in F and so its position is subject to uncertainty.

In contrast, the added tier in the right margin provides information that one would not inherently expect in the Folio even if it were more systematic than it is, but that is useful to readers and performers nonetheless. Typical examples, found on the same page opening as the exit for Demetrius, are '*He stands aside*', '*Shows the flower*' and '*Gives him some juice*'. Some indication of the layout may be given by reproducing neighbouring directions in closer proximity:

> [↓*Exit Demetrius*↓]
> *Exit*
> > *Shows the flower*
> > *Gives him some juice*

This makes effective use of the width afforded by the single-column format. The distinction between the activities of editing the original stage directions, in the sense of completing, correcting and clarifying them, and adding a species of information that is foreign to those directions strikes me as valid. More contentiously, it opens the door for a species of direction that permits different possibilities: '*Juliet could exit aloft and enter below*'. '*Kisses Juliet on forehead or hand or cheek*'. There are dangers of absurdity here, and one wonders whether the uncertainties might not have been presented with less programmatic display by making use of commentary notes.

The distinction between the two tiers is not always easy to maintain, and inconsistencies creep in. Opposite Autolycus's entry at *Winter's Tale* 4.4.233 is the second-tier far-right direction '*He wears a false beard and carries a pack*', which follows the procedure as I have described it of separating the basic from the directorial. But at *Midsummer Night's Dream* 5.1.210 the information '*with a lantern, thornbush and dog*' is added to main stage direction. The first-tier position is also accorded to '*Lion shakes Thisbe's mantle, and exits*' and Lance's '*leading his dog, Crab*'. Such directions bear no relation to what the Folio contains or might be expected to contain, and would more logically be placed in the right margin.

The use of brackets in tier-one stage directions suggests careful adherence to F where there are no brackets, as when '[*and*]' is added between names; and there is some highly specific detail in some textual notes, such as '**2.1.6 sh** FIRST LADY = Ed. F = *Lady*' (*Winter's Tale*), that points in the same direction. But we are not told that, in the stage direction at the opening of 2.1, F's '*Leontes, Antigonus, Lords*' has been removed from the text. There seems to be a consistent policy for unnoted removal of names from 'massed' stage directions in which all the speakers in a scene are listed at the beginning of the scene irrespective of where they enter. This silently effaces a conspicuous if inconveniently untheatrical feature found in several Folio texts. The effect is to simplify the relationship between F and the edition and so to heighten the edition's apparent claim for a close relationship with its copy.

INCOMPLETE WORKS

The strangest feature of this edition insofar as it purports to be based on the First Folio is that it includes most of the works ascribed to Shakespeare that do not appear in that book: the collaborative *Pericles* and *The Two Noble Kinsmen*, all of Shakespeare's poems, and 'A Scene for *Sir Thomas More*' (but not *Edward III*). The *Sir Thomas More* passage is presented in a transcript, followed by an edited text that follows the theatre annotator Hand C's alterations with the exception of his deletions. All of these non-Folio texts are printed in smaller type and presented in two columns. Paradoxically, the edition therefore restores a feature of the Folio, namely its two-column layout, at the very points where the Folio is not itself followed.

In its overall content, the RSC edition is distinct as an edition based on the Folio merely for its disadvantageous presentation of works that the Folio excludes. A publisher's re-run of the layout would cause the claim to disappear. The tension between a 'Complete' works and an edited 'real book' is most palpable here. For, even by the criterion of the Shakespeare canon as known to readers in the early seventeenth century, the Folio simply is not complete. The RSC edition stands awkwardly between a position of being stuck with the Folio editors' decisions and a reasonable wish to overrule them. The point about the Folio is that it defined Shakespeare exclusively as a dramatist, that it brushed issues of collaboration under the carpet, and that it organized Shakespeare's works in a specific and motivated sequence. For the modern Shakespeare reader, these are not congenial features. Whenever the RSC edition includes works not in the Folio, appends passages from Folio plays that were not printed in the Folio, or draws attention to issues of collaboration, it is defying the very spirit and informing logic of its acclaimed precursor.

TRUST

It is therefore hard to find coherence in the edition's variable practice of following or not following the Folio. The respects in which the RSC edition is not an edition of the book are sufficiently substantial for us to ask why the Folio was adopted in the first place. In his essay in defence of the RSC edition's procedures posted on the edition website, Bate praises Herbert Farjeon's Folio-based Nonesuch edition:

His superb yet rarely mentioned edition is the one that I would specify, beside a copy of the 1611 Authorized Version of the Bible, if I were ever invited onto Desert Island Discs.

Farjeon's text was originally published between 1929 and 1933 by Random House's Nonesuch Press, in a numbered limited edition of 1050 American and 500 British copies, but reprinted more accessibly in 1953 in four handsome yet conveniently compact volumes dedicated by permission to Queen Elizabeth II in honour of her coronation. This is that rare thing, an edition of Shakespeare that does exactly what it says on the title-page and that is rigorously true to its own principles: *The Complete Works of William Shakespeare: The text and order of*

JOHN JOWETT

the First Folio with Quarto variants and a choice of modern readings noted marginally: to which are added 'Pericles' and the first quartos of six of the plays with three plays of doubtful authorship: also the poems according to the original quartos and octavos.

Farjeon offers an old-spelling but modern-typography Folio text, with quarto variants and significant later editorial corrections and conjectures given in the margin.[2]

Farjeon's fine edition for collectors describes itself as 'designed by Francis Meynall, printed and made in England by Walter Lewis, M.A., printer to the University, at the Cambridge University Press, in Monotype Fournier with new capital letters made for this edition, and Bound in London by A. W. Bain'. Bate was so struck with it that he considered following the example of the 1953 Coronation reprint and reissuing it for the RSC edition. Unfortunately, 'the notion of an old-spelling edition in four volumes for some reason failed to excite the marketing team'. The RSC edition therefore emerged as a less exacting and less expensive compromise between Farjeon's typographically normalized reprint in old spelling and the standard modernized and emended edition of the current marketplace.

Plans for the edition therefore began with a search for established alternatives to standard practice; Farjeon's Folio-plus-add-ons was found to present a desirable model; this was then modified in the direction of a standard Complete Works. Bate worked in conjunction with the marketing team. His textual editor had yet to be appointed when these editorial foundations were laid. Rasmussen proceeded according to a plan in which the scope for the textual editor to act was prescribed and routinized. An effect of the remit to base the text on the Folio was to exclude any deep questions about the status and origin of the early printed texts insofar as they might affect the process of editing. Progress was further enabled by employing a team of assistants to provide first-run edited texts. These circumstances enabled Rasmussen to complete each play remarkably quickly, though it is perhaps a mixed blessing to be relieved of responsibility for both the founding

editorial principles and the burden of drudgery that Johnson embraced.

If indeed enough of the Folio's distinctive features remain in the RSC edition to justify its proclaimed editorial principles, the outcome lies not in reproducing the achievements of Farjeon but in establishing a nexus between the terms 'RSC' and 'Folio' embracing both ideology and commerce. The Folio is presented as what Bate describes as the edition of 'the original royal Shakespeare company – his own company, the King's Men' ('The Case', p. 42). The edition is thus both 'Royal' and 'Shakespeare' on account of its Folio grounding as well as its sponsorship.

This specific connection is fertilized by a more general sentiment in favour of the Folio found in some corners of the theatre world. Don Weingust's *Acting from Shakespeare's First Folio* (2006) has reviewed a tradition going back to Richard Flatter's 1948 study *Shakespeare's Producing Hand*, in which it is argued that the Folio contained subtle guidance to the actor as regards Shakespeare's intentions for the delivery of his plays on the stage. Flatter is fundamentally wrong on this question. It is clearly demonstrable that the Folio owes its characteristics of punctuation and the use of capitals primarily to compositors and scribes, not to the Bard. But his ideas have been given more recent currency in the work of Neil Freeman and Patrick Tucker, the latter the author of *First Folio Speeches for Men* and *First Folio Speeches for Women* (1997), and also in Doug Moston's introduction to his Applause facsimile of the Folio (1995). Tucker set up the Original Shakespeare Company to put these ideas into practice in productions at the Globe Theatre. These in turn influenced the Globe's former Artistic Director, Mark Rylance.

This brief history is the surface manifestation of a reverence for the Folio that reflects the emotional need for real authorial presence that textual scholars insist is simply not available to us. As it happens, the textualists were insisting with particular vigour in

---

[2] Jonathan Bate, 'The Case for the Folio', online at www.rscshakespeare.co.uk/pdfs/Case_for_Folio.pdf, 68–9.

the years leading to the mid 1990s when Freeman, Tucker, Moston and Rylance formed their views. John Heminge and Henry Condell, the actors who wrote the Folio's epistle 'To the great variety of readers', claimed that the plays in the book were printed from 'True Originall Copies'. On the contrary, however, the Folio texts are heavily mediated not only by theatre practice, but also by scribal transmission and print. They are far less authorial in their spelling and punctuation than their 'good' quarto counterparts.

Thus the RSC edition's association with the RSC has meant that a fallacy has contaminated editorial thinking. In his address to the reader, placed in the book in equivalent position to Heminge and Condell's epistle in the Folio, the RSC Artistic Director Michael Boyd advises that we 'trust the Folio-based text'. He is calling for faith in defiance of the facts. Editors are assumed to have assiduously corrupted the very texts that they were supposedly purging. The truth was always there, plain, monumental, unsullied, biblical; and that truth was the Folio. Such trust, such assurance of rescue, is unwarranted. In any construction of Heminge and Condell's words that readers today or in their own time could be expected to place on them, their statement is so misleading as to be a lie.

Though they have become implicated in it, Bate and Rasmussen are, of course, far from intellectually committed to any naive acceptance of the Folio of the kind I have documented. The more seriously deliberated justification for the Folio is, Bate explains, that it brings together the authority of the theatre and the book. Setting aside the not insignificant issues of canon and collaboration, the perspective has a certain attraction, at least in abstract. But it will always struggle to accommodate two key characteristics of the Folio: first, that it rarely if ever prints directly from a reliable theatre manuscript; second, that, as compared with the more reliable quartos, it almost invariably takes the reader not closer to Shakespeare's hand but further away from it.

The practice of the RSC edition is pragmatic, avoiding dogmatic adherence to the Folio. But the principle that the RSC edition advertises is to defer to the Folio editors, who knew better than their various successors with their 'deeply flawed' editions over the centuries since 'Rowe set editors off down the wrong path' in 1709 (p. 53). This viewpoint forgets what we have heard repeatedly over the past twenty years or more: that the volume was carefully planned with marketing considerations in mind. By criteria relevant to an edition of Shakespeare today, its editors' decisions were quite simply wrong: wrong as regards the content of the canon, wrong as regards the sequencing of texts, wrong as regards the grouping of texts within that sequence, and wrong as regards the treatment of copy-text. And the whole Folio project was founded on that tactical misinformation: that the Folio gives uniquely unmediated access to the mind of Shakespeare as singular author, and nothing else. We would be immeasurably poorer if it were not for the Folio. But our gratitude does not absolve us of responsibility to see it as a product of early modern textual culture. The Folio is itself deeply flawed by the editorial practices of its compilers, and offers no magical solution to the dilemmas presented to Shakespeare editors today.

INDEX

NOTE: Figures in italics denote illustrations.

INDEX

INDEX

INDEX

INDEX

INDEX